Psychological Disturbance in Adolescence

Psychological Disturbance in Adolescence

Second Edition

Irving B. Weiner
University of South Florida Psychiatry Center

A Wiley-Interscience Publication

John Wiley & Sons, Inc.

New York · Chichester · Brisbane · Toronto · Singapore

In recognition of the importance of preserving what has
been written, it is a policy of John Wiley & Sons, Inc., to
have books of enduring value published in the United
States printed on acid-free paper, and we exert our best
efforts to that end.

Copyright © 1992 by John Wiley & Sons, Inc.

This publication is designed to provide accurate and
authoritative information in regard to the subject
matter covered. It is sold with the understanding that
the publisher is not engaged in rendering legal, accounting,
or other professional service. If legal advice or other
expert assistance is required, the services of a competent
professional person should be sought. *From a Declaration
of Principles jointly adopted by a Committee of the
American Bar Association and a Committee of Publishers.*

Library of Congress Cataloging-in-Publication Data:

Weiner, Irving B.
    Psychological disturbance in adolescence / Irving B. Weiner. —
2nd ed.
      p. cm.—(Wiley series on personality processes)
      Includes bibliographical references and indexes.
      ISBN 0-471-82596-4 (alk. paper)
      1. Adolescent psychiatry. I. Title. II. Series.
RJ503.W4 1992
616.89'022—dc20   91-18344

Printed in the United States of America

10 9 8 7 6 5 4 3 2 1

Printed and bound by the Courier Companies, Inc.

To Fran, Jeremy, and Seth

Series Preface

This series of books is addressed to behavioral scientists interested in the nature of human personality. Its scope should prove pertinent to personality theorists and researchers, as well as to clinicians concerned with applying an understanding of personality processes to the amelioration of emotional difficulties in living. To this end, the series provides a scholarly integration of theoretical formulations, empirical data, and practical recommendations.

Six major aspects of studying and learning about human personality can be designated: personality theory, personality structure and dynamics, personality development, personality assessment, personality change, and personality adjustment. In exploring these aspects of personality, the books in the series discuss a number of distinct but related subject areas: the nature and implications of various theories of personality; personality characteristics that account for consistencies and variations in human behavior; the emergence of personality processes in children and adolescents; the use of interviewing and testing procedures to evaluate individual differences in personality; efforts to modify personality styles through psychotherapy, counseling, behavior therapy, and other methods of influence; and patterns of abnormal personality functioning that impair individual competence.

IRVING B. WEINER

University of South Florida
Tampa, Florida

Preface

Like its predecessor, the second edition of this book is addressed to clinicians, educators, and social scientists who are concerned with identifying and ameliorating psychological disturbance in adolescence. In the 22 years since the first edition appeared, new ideas and cumulative data have added considerably to what is known about the developmental psychopathology of adolescence and how to apply this knowledge in clinical practice. Accordingly, this second edition bears only passing resemblance to the first. All of the substantive topics covered in the 1970 edition appear again, but the text devoted to them is largely rewritten. In addition, there are newly written chapters on borderline disorders and substance abuse and new sections on bipolar disorder and obsessive-compulsive disorder. The extensive reference lists included with each chapter are also entirely new, except for various historically significant publications.

Psychological Disturbance in Adolescence begins with two introductory chapters concerned, respectively, with normality and abnormality in adolescence and with the classification of adolescent psychopathology. These chapters relate the subject matter of adolescent disturbance to broader issues in developmental psychology; they review guidelines for discriminating psychological disturbance from normative patterns of teenage behavior; and they place the differential diagnosis of adolescent psychopathology in the context of whether and how abnormal behavior can be categorized.

The topics for Chapters 3 through 10 are chosen from the perspective of the practicing clinician. Rather than attempting an encyclopedia coverage of psychopathology, these chapters consider in depth those relatively few patterns of psychological disturbance that account for the vast majority of presenting problems among troubled teenagers who come to professional attention.

Specifically, Chapters 3 through 6 discuss the adolescent manifestations of four major categories of diagnosable psychological disorder: schizophrenic disorders, affective disorders, borderline disorders, and neurotic disorders, with particular attention to obsessions, compulsions, and school phobia. These four chapters review clinical and experimental literature pertaining to the origins, symptoms, frequency, and cause of these disorders, and they delineate methods of intervention that are useful in treating them. Chapters 7 through 10 proceed in like fashion with respect to four major types of problem behavior: academic underachievement, delinquent behavior, suicidal behavior, and substance abuse.

The final chapter of the book (Chapter 11) presents and illustrates principles of conducting psychotherapy with disturbed adolescents. The discussion considers the goals of adolescent psychotherapy; aspects of initiating, building, and terminating the treatment relationship; and the role of work with parents.

Appreciation is expressed to the many colleagues, past and present, whose sensitivity to the psychological needs of adolescents and dedication to the well-being of young people have helped me formulate the conclusions and recommendations presented in this book.

IRVING B. WEINER

Tampa, Florida
November, 1991

Contents

Psychological Disturbance in Adolescence

CHAPTER 1

Normality and Abnormality in Adolescence

Problems of adolescence have concerned society since early in recorded history. Plato worried about the unreliability of young people and devoted Book III of *The Republic* to ways of educating youth for responsible adult citizenship. Aristotle worried about the fickle and unpredictable nature of youth, whom he described in his *Rhetoric* as impulsive, irascible, overly emotional, and incapable of delaying gratification or tolerating criticism. Socrates as well, despite his dedication to the teaching of young people, was alarmed by their behavior:

> Children now love luxury. They have bad manners, contempt for authority. They show disrespect for elders and love chatter in place of exercise. Children are now tyrants, not the servants of their households.

The formal literature of developmental and clinical psychology, of psychiatry, and of psychoanalysis also addresses adolescence, from the early beginnings of this literature. G. Stanley Hall published the first comprehensive psychology of adolescence in 1904, which was about the same time that developmental psychology in general was becoming established as a discipline. Hall himself, along with having pioneered adolescent psychology, is known as "the father of child psychology in the United States" (Dennis, 1949; Nance, 1970).

The first child guidance clinic in the United States appears to have been the Juvenile Psychopathic Institute, which was established by William Healy in 1909 to work with delinquent youth in Chicago and was the forerunner of what became the well-known Institute for Juvenile Research (Reisman, 1976, p. 78). Several years later, Healy (1915) published the first systematic study of psychological factors in juvenile delinquency. This focus on the needs of troubled adolescents followed soon after such other historical landmarks in clinical psychology and psychiatry as the opening of the first psychological clinic by Lightner Witmer in 1896, the development of the first useful test of intelligence by Binet and Simon in 1905 (1905/1916), and the publication in 1911 of Eugen Bleuler's monograph in which he coined the term s*chizophrenia* (1911/1950).

As for psychoanalytic theory, Sigmund Freud was interested in developmental events occurring primarily during the first 5 or 6 years of life, and he accordingly did not have much to say about adolescence. Nevertheless, he did include in one of his early works, the *Three Essays on the Theory of Sexuality*, published in 1905, a seminal discussion of changes in sexual aims and objects following puberty.

Despite these early beginnings, empirical data to help scholars understand problems of adolescence accumulated slowly, as did clinical formulations to help practitioners assess and treat such problems. As noted in the 1970 edition of the present book, this was especially the case with respect to ways of distinguishing meaningfully between normal and abnormal adolescent develoment. The relevant literature has grown enormously in the past 20 years, however; except for items having some historical significance, very few references cited in this second edition date from before 1970.

Although welcomed by clinicians and researchers, the expanded literature on adolescent disturbances has not yet resolved lingering uncertainties about the boundaries between normal and abnormal adolescent behavior. Faced with a confusing multitude of conceptual formulations, a plethora of diagnostic categorizations, and a sometimes bewildering array of data, many professionals have despaired of being able to establish clear and useful guidelines for identifying and classifying psychopathology during the adolescent years. This despair has drawn sustenance from persistent mythical notions of "normative adolescent turmoil," according to which the nature of adolescence precludes arriving at any such guidelines.

As background for considering specific kinds of psychological disturbance in adolescence, this introductory chapter reviews the myth of normative adolescent turmoil and indicates how it has interfered with adequate recognition and treatment of diagnosable disorder in young people. This notion is then corrected in light of research findings that point the way to reliable distinctions between normality and abnormality in adolescence.

THE MYTH OF NORMATIVE ADOLESCENT TURMOIL

In his pioneering textbook on the psychology of adolescence, Hall advanced an evolutionary theory of development based on a "law of recapitulation." According to this so-called law, individuals develop through predetermined stages from primitiveness to civilized behavior in a manner that re-creates the development of the human race (Hall, 1904, Vol. I, p. 2). Hall saw the adolescent era as analogous to the turbulent period in human history that heralded the beginning of modern civilization. Compared with childhood, he said, adolescent development "is less gradual and more saltatory, suggestive of some ancient period of storm and stress when old moorings were broken and a higher level attained" (Vol. I, p. xiii). As elaborated by Hall and by numerous influential clinicians who came to similar conclusions, this mythical notion of storm and stress blossomed into a vivid portrayal of typical adolescent development as a several-year period of discontinuity and disruption, of instability and emotional upset, of identity crisis, and of generational conflict.

Discontinuity and Disruption: G. Stanley Hall

Hall's evolutionary formulation construed adolescence as a sharply distinct developmental epoch with few connections either to the child behavior patterns preceding it or to the adult behavior following it. He argued that becoming an adolescent suddenly and precipitously severs a person's ties with the past:

> At dawning adolescence [the] old unity and harmony with nature is broken up; the child is driven from his paradise and must enter upon a long viaticum of ascent, must conquer a higher kingdom of man for himself, break out a new sphere and evolve a more modern story to his psycho-physical nature (1904, Vol. II, p. 71).

Hall considered it inevitable that, for several years following this disruption of "unity and harmony with nature," a young person's life would be marked by turmoil, uncertainty, and various kinds of troubling and troublesome behaviors. This period of unpleasantness and unpredictability must be endured until full adult status has been attained, he said, at which time the turmoil subsides and a new adult figure emerges, a civilized person bearing little resemblance to the unruly adolescent that has gone before: "Youth awakes to a new world . . . it is all a marvelous new birth" (1904, Vol. I, p. xv).

Instability and Emotional Upset: Anna Freud and Peter Blos

Hall was very explicit in his belief that the discontinuity and disruption that attend adolescent development produce an inevitable period of instability and upset, in which the major predictable feature of youthful behavior is its unpredictability:

> The "teens" are emotionally unstable and pathic. It is the age of natural inebriation without the need of intoxication, which made Plato define youth as spiritual drunkenness. It is a natural impulse to experience hot and perfervid psychic states, and it is characterized by emotionalism . . . .. We see here the instability and fluctuations now so characteristic. The emotions develop by contrast and reactions into the opposite (1904, Vol. 2, pp. 74-75)

Hall went on to list several antithetical traits that in his opinion characterized normal adolescence: alternations of eagerness, zest, enthusiasm, and intellectual curiosity with apathy, inertia, and cultivated indifference; oscillations between pleasure and pain, euphoria and melancholy; periods of both extreme egoism and abject humility; alternating selfishness and altruism, conservatism and radicalism, gregariousness and seclusiveness; changes from exquisite sensitiveness to imperturbability, hard-heartedness, and cruelty; vacillations between knowing and doing and between the ascendance of sense and intellect; and the juxtaposition of wisdom and folly (Vol. 2, pp. 75-88).

The first major psychoanalytic contribution to the understanding of adolescent dvelopment is generally regarded to be Anna Freud's *The Ego and the Mechanisms of Defence*, originally published in 1936. Her description of normal adolescence is strikingly similar to Hall's:

> Adolescents are excessively egoistic, regarding themselves as the center of the universe and the sole object of interest, and yet at no time in later life are they capable of so much self-sacrifice and devotion. They form the most passionate love-relations, only to break them off as abruptly as they began them. On the one hand they throw themselves enthusiastically into the life of the community and, on the other hand, they have an overpowering longing for solitude. They oscillate between blind submission to some self-chosen leader and defiant rebellion against any and every authority. They are selfish and materially-minded and at the same time full of lofty idealism. They are ascetic but will suddenly plunge into instinctual indulgence of the most primitive character. At times their behaviour to other people is rough and inconsiderate, yet they themselves are extremely touchy. Their moods veer between light-hearted optimism and the blackest pessimism. Sometimes they will work with indefatigable enthusiasm and at other times they are sluggish and apathetic. (A. Freud, 1936/1946, pp. 149-150)

In subsequent work, Anna Freud affirmed her belief that adolescence disrupts the continuity of personality development and produces stormy, unpredictable behavior:

> The upheavals in character and personality are often so sweeping that the picture of the former child becomes wholly submerged in the newly emerging image of the adolescent. . . . Adolescence constitutes by definition an interruption of peaceful growth which resembles in appearance a variety of other emotional upsets and structural upheavals. . . . The upholding of a steady equilibrium during the adolescent period is by itself abnormal. (A. Freud, 1958, pp. 267 & 275; 1969, p. 7)

Because of this "interruption of peaceful growth" Freud noted, adolescents will normally display maladaptive thoughts, feelings, and actions that would suggest psychopathology if they occurred in adults: "I take it that it is normal for an adolescent to behave for a considerable length of time in an inconsistent and unpredictable manner. . . . Such fluctuations would be deemed highly abnormal at any other time of life" (A. Freud, 1958, p. 267).

Anna Freud's theories and those of two other major psychoanalytic figures—Peter Blos and Erik Erikson—have influenced many of the ways in which adolescent development is viewed today by clinical practitioners and the general public as well. In his book *On Adolescence: A Psychoanalytic Interpretation*, published in 1962, Blos agreed with Anna Freud that the stresses and strains of adapting to adolescence produce a period of emotional turmoil in which "a relatively strong id confronts a relatively weak ego." He paid special notice to what he believed were inevitable upsets associated with the adolescent experience of learning to separate from one's parents and become an independent person:

> Adolescent individuation is accompanied by feelings of isolation, loneliness, and confusion. . . . The realization of the finality of the end of childhood, of the binding nature of commitments, of the definite limitation to individual existence itself—this realization creates a sense of urgency, fear, and panic. (Blos, 1962, p. 12)

Identity Crisis: Erik Erikson

The concept of *identity crisis* emerged from Erik Erikson's (1956, 1963) descriptions of the developmental tasks and jeopardies that people face during different periods of their lives. With respect to adolescence, Erikson, like Hall, regarded the advent of puberty as a time when "all sameness and continuity are more or less questioned again" (1963, p. 251). This requires young people to spend several years building bridges between the roles and skills they had cultivated as children and the roles and responsibilities they will have as adults.

Now widely known as *identity formation*, this developmental transition as described by Erikson is the process by which late adolescents and young adults arrive at some fairly clear and enduring sense of what kind of person they are, what they believe in, and what they want to do with their lives. Also widely known is Erikson's view that the process of identity formation typically involves episodes of *identity crisis*. The challenges of forming an identity cause young people to behave in erratic and maladaptive ways from time to time, says Erikson, so that turmoil and apparent psychopathology become normative features of adolescent development:

> In spite of the similarity of adolescent "symptoms" and episodes to neurotic and psychotic symptoms and episodes, adolescence is not an affliction but a *normative crisis*, i.e., a normal phase of increased conflict characterized by a seeming fluctuation in ego strength. . . .. What under prejudiced scrutiny may appear to be the onset of a neurosis is often but an aggravated crisis which might prove to be self-liquidating and, in fact, contributive to the process of identity formation . . . .. The same must be said of the adolescent's "fluidity of defenses," which so often causes raised eyebrows on the part of the worried

clinician. Much of this fluidity is anything but pathological, for adolescence is a crisis in which only fluid defenses can overcome a sense of victimization by inner and outer demands, and in which only trial and error can lead to the most felicitous avenues of action and self-expression. (Erikson, 1956, pp. 72 & 73)

Generational Conflict: Coleman, Keniston, and Mead

Over the years, three prominent social scientists contributed to the myth of normative adolescent turmoil by asserting that the nature of adolescent development, especially in modern industrialized environments, leads inevitably to conflicts between young people and their parents and between the adolescent and adult generations. James Coleman (1961) concluded in *The Adolescent Society* that, because contemporary adolescents must endure a marginal existence between childhood and adulthood, they become cut off from their parents' generation and enmeshed in a "youth culture" that is "alienated" from the adult world. Kenneth Keniston (1965) argued similarly in *The Uncommitted: Alienated Youth in American Society* that, because technologically advanced societies place so many obstacles in the path of achieving adult status and independence, their young people cannot avoid becoming alienated from adult value systems. The modernization of American society in particular has produced an adolescent "alienation syndrome," says Keniston, characterized by a futile quest for positive values, a pessimistic existentialist orientation, a distrust of commitment, and a disaffection for adulthood.

The widely quoted views of Coleman and Keniston have fostered an extensive literature on teenage alienation (see Weiner, 1972, 1976). The recurrent theme in these writings is that modern times are witnessing a breakdown of family organization and parental authority. Young people are being exposed to experiences their parents never had and cannot understand, say the authors of alientation, and they have grown scornful of an adult generation that has proved unable to eliminate war, injustice, poverty, and human degradation.

Margaret Mead (1970) carried this concern even further in *Culture and Commitment: A Study of the Generation Gap*, in which she warned that an ever-widening gap between the adult and adolescent generations was threatening to undermine the foundations of our society. Unless the older generation can find improved ways of communicating across this gap, she said, the younger generation will take over and tear down many of our basic institutions. Revising her book in 1978 to take account of events involving youth of the 1970s as well as the 1960s, Mead remained firmly convinced that our modern world is confronting a pervasive and potentially disruptive generation gap:

The young generation, however, the articulate young rebels all around the world who are lashing out against the controls to which they are subjected, are like the first generation born into a new country. . . . These are the two generations—pioneers in a new era and their elders who have as yet to find a way of communicating about the world in which they both live. (Mead, 1978, pp. 72, 83)

Themes of "adolescent alienation" and the "generation gap" have captured the imagination of authors writing for the general public, as well as those addressing professional audiences. Newspaper and magazine articles and movie and television scripts regularly portray today's youth as rebelling against their parents' wishes, rejecting traditional values, flouting authority, preferring fun and games to hard work and diligent planning, and plunging mindlessly into delinquency, drug abuse, and sexual promiscuity. At least partly as a result of such media influence, people in many different walks of life can be heard to complain about what young people are coming to these days (presumably all bad) and how "They don't make them like they used to" (presumably all good).

It is difficult to avoid noticing the resemblance between such language for the way youth used to be and the words of Socrates quoted at the outset of this chapter. Even then, 400 years B.C., Socrates was apparently not saying anything new. Lauer (1973) reports that a 4,000-year-old tablet discovered while excavating the biblical city of Ur carries the following inscription: "Our civilization is doomed if the unheard-of actions of our younger generation are allowed to continue" (p. 176).

Civilization did of course endure, but things seemed little better in Shakespeare's time:

> I would there were no age between ten and three-and-twenty, or that youth would sleep out the rest; for there is nothing in the between but getting wenches with child, wronging the ancientry, stealing, fighting. (*The Winter's Tale*, Act III, Scene iii)

As for G. Stanley Hall, with whom this discussion began, his 1904 view of what was happening to the youth of his time reads as follows: Modern life is hard, and in many respects, increasingly so, on youth. Home, school, church, fail to recognize its nature and needs and, perhaps most of all, its perils. . . . Never has youth been exposed to such dangers. . . . Increasing urban life with its temptations, prematurities . . . early emancipations and a lessening sense for both duty and discipline . . . the mad rush for sudden wealth (1904, Vol. I, pp. xiv-xvi).

These and many other similar expressions of concern that could be quoted from the pages of history raise some doubt about just how good the "good old days" actually were. In fact, as elaborated by Gillis (1974) and by Elder (1980), a careful reading of history suggests that the generational relations of contemporary youth are not much different from those of past times. Some mild degree of rebellion against their parents is an individuating aspect of adolescent development that seems to have characterized normative adolescence in all societies throughout recorded history. Likewise, episodes of youthful dismay about the structure of their society have come and gone over the years in response to cycles of war and peace, poverty and prosperity, freedom and repression, and intellectual enlightenment and stagnation.

Clinical Implications

Historical perspectives aside, the belief that the adolescent and adult generations are joined in destructive conflict has combined with presumptions about developmental discontinuity, emotional instability, and identity crisis during the teenage years to form the cornerstones of the mythical notion of normative adolescent turmoil. This notion has in turn led to the following three frequently expressed and widely endorsed opinions concerning problem behavior in adolescents:

1. Most adolescents show signs of apparent psychological disturbance that do not really constitute psychopathology.

    Although puberty may take many courses, we think predominantly of stormy and unpredictable behavior marked by mood swings between elation and melancholy. (Eissler, 1958, p. 224)

    During the ongoing struggle for identity, many more or less severe symptoms may arise. . . It is generally agreed that adolescence comes to an end after a painful struggle, of greater or less duration. (Deutsch, 1967, pp. 34, 37)

    One of the unique characteristics of adolescence . . . is the recurrent alternation of episodes of disturbed behavior with periods of quiescence. (Group for the Advancement of Psychiatry, 1968, p. 61)

    If there is anything that can be considered typical of the adolescent period, it is this quality of identity diffusion. (Giovacchini, 1978, p. 326)

2. It is difficult, if not impossible, to distinguish normal from abnormal adolescent development.

    The momentous biological and psychological changes are so great in this transition from childhood to young adulthood that the lines between normal and pathological are never more blurred or indistinct. (Redlich & Freedman, 1966, p. 693)

    Frequently these young people give us a distorted picture, puzzling to the clinician. At times, one can hardly differentiate between psychopathology and normal growth crises. (Ekstein, 1968, p. 347)

    Adolescence is a time of great internal psychological disturbance and, as a result, the assessment of normality or pathology is particulary difficult. (Settlage, 1970)

    In working with adolescents it is a most difficult task to tease out in the clinical picture what is a normal disturbance due to the developmental upheaval of the age and what constitutes a truly psychopathological condition. (Blos, 1983, p. l06)

3. Most instances of seemingly deviant behavior in adolescents are short-lived disturbances that will disappear of their own accord.

   My main therapeutic approach to the parents of adolescents . . . is the tried and true phrase of the men of the ancient church who, when beset by the unpredictable and seemingly uncontrollable, comforted themselves and one another with the words, "It will pass. It will pass." (Gardner, 1947, p. 540)

   The cure for adolescence belongs to the passage of time and the gradual maturation processes. (Winnicott, 1971, pp. 40–41)

Although these opinions have enjoyed considerable popularity, they are seriously flawed by the manner in which they were derived. They emerged not from systematic study of representative samples of adolescents, but from clinical impressions formed in the course of working with adolescent patients. There are many occasions in which clinical observations can generate rich hypotheses about human behavior that, when adequately validated, contribute to substantive knowledge. In the absence of adequate confirmation, however, generalizations about all adolescents based on the behavior of adolescents being evaluated or treated for adjustment difficulties are likely to produce errors—such as tarring normative adolescence with the brush of turmoil.

Large strides have been made over the years in avoiding unsystematic measurement and unrepresentative sampling in clinical studies of adolescents. Increasing numbers of studies have applied standardized assessment procedures to adolescents being treated for emotional or behavioral problems and also to representative groups of young people who would not otherwise have come to professional attention. The results of these studies have emphatically contradicted all three of the preceding opinions by demonstrating instead the following: (a) relatively few adolescents become developmentally disturbed; (b) normal and disturbed development can be clearly distinguished during adolescence; and (c) both normal and disturbed behavior patterns tend to remain stable from adolescence to adulthood. These findings can be summarized by providing three "correctives" to the mythical notion of normative adolescent turmoil.

CORRECTIVE I: NORMATIVE ADOLESCENCE IS ADAPTIVE

Contrary to widespread belief in teenage turbulence, empirical evidence demonstrates that adolescence is typically an adaptive phase of growth characterized by developmental continuity, emotional stability, identity formation without disabling crisis, and intergenerational harmony.

Personality Development Is Continuous

Hall's "new birth" view of adolescent development was questioned in the first major textbook of adolescent psychology that appeared after his, written by Leta Hollingworth in 1928. Hollingworth rejected the inevitability of teenage storm and stress and disagreed with Hall that entirely new character and personality traits begin to form at adolescence:

> The child grows by imperceptible degrees into the adolescent, and the adolescent turns by gradual degrees into the adult. . . . [The] widespread myth that every child is a changeling, who at puberty comes forth as a different personality, is doubtless a . . . folklore. (pp. 1, 17)

In support of Hollingworth's position, considerable longitudinal data have since demonstrated that development is in many respects continuous and transitional. This longitudinal work began with well-known studies undertaken in 1928 at the Institute of Human Development at the University of California at Berkeley and in 1929 at the Fels Research Institute. Over a period of 30 to 40 years, subjects in these studies were followed and evaluated in various ways as they developed from childhood to adolescence and matured into adulthood and midlife. Many adult characteristics of these subjects were found to be predictable from related behaviors they exhibited during childhood (including dependency, passivity, proneness to anger, and anxiety level) and from personality traits apparent during their adolescence (such as introspectiveness, assertiveness, likeability, overcontrol, talkativeness, and self-satisfaction (Eichorn, Mussen, Clausen, Haan, & Honzik, 1981; Kagan & Moss, 1962).

Two more recent research projects provide impressive evidence of continuity in personality development. In an ongoing study following children from birth through ages 10 to 11, Sroufe and Jacobvitz (1989) have found considerable continuity among 180 children in such characteristics as ego resiliency, self-confidence, competence, passivity, and dependency: "Our data lend evidence for continuity in individual adaptation, both from infancy to middle childhood and even more strongly from the preschool years to middle childhood" (p. 197).

With specific respect to adolescents, Bachman, O'Malley, and Johnston (1979) studied a representative national sample of 1628 boys from their entry into tenth grade until they reached age 23 years. Their data painted a picture primarily of stability, not change: "Contrary to what might have been expected by those who view adolescence as a period of great turbulence and stress, we found a good deal of consistency along dimensions of attitudes, aspirations, and self-concept" (p. 220).

These research findings do not mean that personality becomes fixed and immutable early in life. In the first place, what is consistent over time is not any specific set of behavior patterns, but rather dimensions of personality along which people tend to maintain their same relative position. For example, people tend to become increasingly capable of self-control as they mature, and most adults manifest more self-control than they did as adolescents. However, because this is a fairly consistent dimension of personality, individuals who have relatively poor self-control as teenagers are likely as adults to show less self-control than other people their age.

Recent reports in this vein demonstrate that boys and girls who at ages 4 and 5 years are less able than other children to delay receiving gratification show less stress tolerance than their peers at adolescence (Caspi, Elder, & Bem, 1987); that fourth-grade children of both sexes rated high or low in aggressiveness by their teachers are reasonably likely to be the same members of their class who are rated high or low in aggressiveness as tenthgraders (Cairns, Cairns, Neckerman, Ferguson, & Gariepy, 1989); and that 8- to 10-year-old boys and girls who are prone to temper tantrums become relatively ill-tempered adults 30 years later (Mischel, Shoda, & Peake, 1988).

Second, even for personality characteristics that have shown significantly greater than chance temporal stability in longitudinal studies, the obtained correlations have rarely been large enough to account for even as much as half of the variance in behavior (i.e., greater than .70; see Moss & Susman, 1980; Rutter, 1987). These greater-than-chance but still modest-sized correlations mean that ample opportunities exist for life experiences, as well as maturation, to change what people are like from adolescence to adulthood. A detailed review of the continuity issue led Rutter (1989) to a similar conclusion: "The process of development is concerned with change and it is not reasonable to suppose that the pattern will be set in early life . . ... However, continuities will occur because children carry with them the results of earlier learning and of earlier structural and functional change" (p. 26).

Third, some personality characteristics are more consistent than others over time, and people differ from each other in how consistently they behave from childhood to adulthood. As Block (1981) notes in commenting on the Berkeley data, "Some individuals [are] impressively predictable thirty to thirty-five years later from their character structures in early adolescence while other individuals are unrecognizable in later years from their junior high school descriptions" (p. 36).

What the available data document with respect to developmental continuity during adolescence, then, is not that people fail to change—which is definitely not the case—but only that what people are like as adolescents is not totally independent of or unrelated to what they were like as children and will be like as adults. People change over time, especially when they are young, and considerable variability in behavior is determined by factors other than persistent personality traits. Hence, adolescence is no more an unremarkable period completely continuous with childhood behavior patterns and predictive of adult personality than it is an inexplicable maelstrom unrelated to a calm latency that precedes it and a civilized adulthood that follows it.

Adolescents Are Emotionally Stable

Research of various kinds challenges the proposition that adolescence is or needs to be a period of emotional upset. In the first major normative study addressing this issue, Douvan and Adelson (1966) collected interview data from over 3000 boys and girls representative of junior and senior high school students in the United States. Very few of these young persons described their lives in terms of turmoil, conflict, and instability. Instead, the comments that Douvan and Adelson's interviewers most commonly heard from these subjects convinced them that it is only the adolescent at the extremes, not the typical young person, who "responds to the instinctual and psychosocial upheaval of puberty by disorder" (p. 351).

In another seminal research project, using an in-depth clinical approach rather than the survey research method of Douvan and Adelson, Daniel Offer and his collegues (Offer, 1969; Offer & Offer, 1975) conducted an 8-year study in which 73 typical middle-class midwestern boys were assessed in interviews, on psychological tests, and from parents' reports on several occasions from their freshman to their senior year of high school. Sixty-one of these young men were subsequently evaluated in the same way during 4 years of college. Only rarely did these subjects give evidence of personality disarray from ages 14 to 22 years. Instead, they were most likely to show a pattern of adaptive and reasonably unruffled progress from adolescence into young adulthood, and only one fifth of the group displayed any noteworthy inner unrest or overt behavior problems.

Offer and other researchers have obtained similar results over the past 20 years from extensive surveys, using a self-report instrument called the "Offer Self-Image Questionnaire" (Offer, Ostrov, & Howard, 1981a). This 130-item questionnaire has been administered to many thousands of adolescents in many different samples of male and female subjects living in diverse environments. The responses of these young persons strongly suggest that the vast majority of teenagers are nappy, self-confident, optimistic, and socially well-adjusted individuals free from any throes of adolescent turmoil:

> In essence, the teenagers we have surveyed portrayed themselves in ways that bear little resemblance to the stressed, stormy, and rebellious youths described originally by G. Stanley Hall (1904), Anna Freud (1946), and by later psychoanalytic theorists. As far as we know, almost every researcher who has studied a representative sample of normal teenagers has come to the conclusion that by and large good coping and a smooth transition into adulthood are much more typical than the opposite. Among middle-class high school students 80 percent can, in general, be described as normal, free of symptoms, and without turmoil. (Offer & Sabshin, 1984, pp. 100-101)

Many other studies have documented that turmoil is the exception rather than the rule among representative samples of nonpatient adolescents and that an interruption of peaceful growth is not necessary for normal adolescent development to occur. Contemporary research indicates that moving into adolescence does not entail widespread negative effects on psychological well-being and adaptation, nor does it produce any increase in daily emotional variability (Larson & Lampman-Petraitis, 1989; Nottelman, 1987; Simmons & Blyth, 1987). Reviews of this evidence leave little doubt that adolescent personality development is for the most part a relatively smooth process in which maturation occurs gradually and without tumult (Petersen, 1988; Powers, Hauser, & Kilner, 1989).

The marshalling of these research findings to correct misleading clinical impressions of adolescent development should not be taken as grounds for draping all clinicians in cloaks of ignorance. Despite the pervasive influence of the adolescent turmoil notion, there have always been perceptive clinicians who doubted its validity. Leo Kanner, for example, a distinguished pioneer in the field of child psychiatry who published the first English language textbook on child psychiatry in 1935, anticipated the best current research data some 50 years ago:

> A combination of innate soundness, wholesome childhood, and guidance from understanding elders helps most adolescents to feel their way safely through the groping and floundering which often precede maturation. The majority thread or fight their way through adolescence with reasonable efficiency and emerge with some kind of serviceable solution of their problems. They are helped by their ability to make use of their assets without being stumped by the obstacles. (Kanner, 1941, pp. 515, 525)

Having established that there is little basis for anticipating emotional instability and maladaptive behavior in normal adolescents, what can be said about the frequency with which adolescents do become psychologically disturbed? The first answer to this question was provided by James Masterson (1967), who assessed symptom patterns in i0l nonpatient 12- to 18-year-olds selected as a comparison group for a sample of adolescent patients being evaluated at the Payne Whitney Clinic. He found that 20% of these nonpatient subjects had psychological symptoms that were moderately or severely impairing their ability to function in school or in social relationships; 63% had occasional symptoms, mainly anxiety and depression, that from time to time caused mild impairments of their ability to function; and the remaining 17% were completely symptom free.

In another clinical study of nonpatients, Michael Rutter and his colleagues examined the education, health, and behavior of all children and adolescents on the Isle of Wight, a small island of 100,000 persons just off the southern coast of England and similar to it in social composition. Included in this study were detailed clinical evaluations conducted with 200 randomly selected 14- to 15-year-olds. About half of these adolescents reported feelings of anxiety or depression, but only 16.3% were considered to have significant psychological disorder (Rutter, Graham, Chadwick, & Yule, 1976).

These and other careful studies of the prevalence of psychological disorder in representative samples of adolescents generally concur that about 20% of teenagers experience clinically significant functioning impairments that constitute diagnosable psychopathology and warrant mental health treatment; another 60% have occasional episodes of anxiety or depression, but not to an extent that produces any major disruption in their daily lives; and the remaining 20% show few if any signs of psychological disorder (Esser, Schmidt, & Woerner, 1990; Kashani, Beck, Hoeper, Fallahi, Corcoran, McAllister, Rosenberg, & Reid, 1987; Offer, Ostrov, & Howard, 1987; Tuma, 1989).

Interestingly, these are about the same percentages that have been found in several large-scale normative studies of adult adjustment. At any point in time, between 16 and 25% of American adults have suffered, within the previous 6 months, from moderate to severe psychological problems that constitute a clinically diagnosable disorder; 51-58% currently have or have recently had mild or fleeting problems, and 18-19% have had few or no problems (Dohrenwend, Dohrenwend, Gould, Link, Neugebauer, & Wunsch-Hitzig, 1980; Myers, Weissman, Tischler, Holzer, Leaf, Orvaschel, Anthony, Boyd, Burke, Kramer, & Stoltzman, 1984). Thus, among adolescents and adults alike, about 60% of persons demonstrate mild forms of symptom formation, and the remaining 40% are about equally divided between symptom-free and moderately or severely impaired groups. Even if allowance is made for some minor error variation in these numbers, they would seem clearly to convey that (a) psychological disturbance is not broadly characteristic of adolescence and (b) adolescents are no more likely than adults to become psychologically disturbed.

Identity Formation Is Gradual

Research findings have confirmed many of Erikson's propositions concerning adolescent identity formation. Young people typically do spend several years trying on alternative roles and ideologies for size. They consider various job and career possibilities, they enter into friendship and dating relationships with different kinds of people, and they weigh the merits of divergent social, political, economic, and religious points of view. Because adolescents are actively examining alternatives before choosing among them, they often vacillate in what they like to do, with whom they want to associate, and what they prefer to believe. This means that young persons tend to be somewhat changeable and unpredictable, at least by adult standards, and they do have to struggle with some uncertainty while they are making up their minds about their future commitments (see Kimmel & Weiner, 1985, Chapter 8).

However, adolescents for the most part do not experience any maladaptive distress while they are working to achieve a sense of identity, nor does their vacillation ordinarily involve any pronounced emotional disequilibrium or disturbing concerns about who or what they presently are. Empirical studies have consistently found that disruptive crises accompanying the process of identity formation are the exception, not the rule (Coleman, Herzberg, & Morris, 1977; Larson, Czikszentmihalyi, & Graef, 1980; Waterman, 1982).

Moreover, the process of working on identity formation is associated with increasingly stable self-concepts rather than any disruption of an adolescent's self-image. Young people are vulnerable to an unstable self-image mainly during puberty, when they are coping with major changes in the size and appearance of their bodies. Following the pubescent growth spurt, teenagers' views of themselves are found to change only gradually and in the direction of progressively greater stability (Dusek & Flaherty, 1981; Protinsky & Farrier, 1980).

These findings bear out views expressed some years ago by Roy Grinker, another distinguised psychiatric clinician who, like Leo Kanner, questioned the notion of normative adolescent turmoil. On the basis of clinical interviews with male college students whom he considered "mentally healthy" and whom he described as "a type of young man I had not met before in my role as a psychiatrist," Grinker came to the following conclusion: "Biological and psychological growth or maturation is not naturally associated with crises . . . . Whatever changes took place in the worlds of our subjects were gradual and could be absorbed without too much strain" (Grinker, 1962, p. 449).

Generational Relationships Are Harmonious

Abundant research on relationships between the adolescent and adult generations indicates that very few young people are in rebellion against either their families or their society. To the contrary, most adolescents share their parents' sense of values and get along well with them. In previously mentioned studies by Douvan and Adelson (1966) and by Offer and his colleagues (Offer, 1969; Offer, Ostrov, & Howard, 1981a), for example, the majority of the thousands of adolescents surveyed reported that they respected their parents, wanted to be like them, and enjoyed harmonious relationships with them and with other adults as well. Most of the teenagers questioned in these studies expressed satisfaction with their homes and described their parents as knowledgeable, reliable, understanding, and sympathetic people. Although they reported disagreeing with their parents on such matters as curfews, use of the family car, and styles of dress and grooming, arguments over such relatively trivial issues seldom threatened the basic bonds of affection within their families: "Contrary to prevailing mythology, the normal adolescents we studied do not perceive any major problems between themselves and their parents" (Offer & Sabshin, 1984, p. 94).

Subsequent work involving large and socioculturally diverse groups of subjects has consistently yielded similar evidence of predominantly positive relationships between adolescents and their parents (Hill, 1987; Montemayor, 1983, 1986; Siddique & D'Arcy, 1984; Smetana, 1989; Steinberg, 1987). These studies, conducted at different times and in different settings, confirm that the typical pattern for relationships between the adolescent and adult generations involves harmony rather than strife, affection rather than alien-ation, and commitment to rather than rejection of family life. Even among young people who hold socially unconventional views, most are found to do so in agreement with their parents and not out of rebellion against them (Lerner & Knapp, 1975; Offer & Sabshin, 1984).

Taken together, these and other research findings have led numerous writers to conclude that, despite persistent popular notions to the contrary, "adolescent rebellion" and the "generation gap" are largely mythical con-cepts, at least with respect to the overwhelming majority of young people (Conger, 1981; Manning, 1983; Weiner, 1972, 1976).

CORRECTIVE II: ADOLESCENT TURMOIL REFLECTS DEVIANT ADJUSTMENT

In those infrequent instances in which adolescent turmoil does emerge, it is typically accompanied by signs and symptoms of psychological disturbance that distinguish reliably between normally and abnormally developing young persons. Contrary to expectations in some quarters that discontinuous person-ality development, emotional instability, identity crises, and disruptive fam-ily conflict ordinarily characterize normal adolescence, these features of adolescent turmoil are consistently found to reflect deviant, not normative adjustment.

With respect to emotional instability, for example, Offer et al. (1981a, Chapter 8) compared the Offer Self-Image Questionnaire responses of their normative adolescents with responses given by three diagnostically diverse samples of 13- to 18-year-olds receiving treatment in a psychiatric facility. These patients were much more likely than nonpatient adolescents to describe themselves as being emotionally upset, and they also reported less self-esteem than normative adolescents, a poorer image of their bodies, and more difficulty getting along with their peers. Numerous other studies have dem-onstrated relationships between these manifestations of emotional upset and other evidence of developing psychological disorder (Kashani et al., 1987; Offer, Ostrov, & Howard, 1986; Sroufe & Rutter, 1984; Tolan, Miller, & Thomas, 1988).

Regarding identity crises, empirical findings indicate that the more adoles-cents perceive themselves as changing and the more uncertain they are about their sex-role identity, the more likely they are to be having adjustment difficulties. Those relatively few young people who do experience an identity crisis are usually found to be sufficiently troubled to need professional help (Handel, 1980; Keyes & Coleman, 1983; Marcia, 1980).

As for relationships within the family, there is good evidence that adoles-cents who experience or report marked conflict with or alienation from their families are likely to be psychologically malajusted. In the Offer et al. (1981a) study the subjects receiving treatment were markedly more likely than normative adolescents to endorse negative attitudes toward their families (e.g., "I have been carrying a grudge against my parents for years"; "I try to stay away from home most of the time") and markedly less likely to endorse positive attitudes (e.g., "I can count on my parents most of the time"; "Most of the time my parents are satisfied with me"). In the Isle of Wight research, Rutter et al. (1976) found that a group of 156 14-year-olds with diagnosable psychological disorder were substantially more likely than a comparison group of 123 14-year-olds without disorder to display communication difficulty, altercations, and physical withdrawal in their relationships with their parents.

The work of many other investigators has confirmed that conflict, dissatisfaction, and poor communication among family members occur much more frequently in the homes of disturbed than of normative adolescents (Doane, 1978; Petersen, 1988; Schwarz & Getter, 1980). Family strife and generational conflict are associated with disturbed adolescent development, and dramatic rebellion against closeness within the family constitutes deviant behavior. Families that are seriously at odds with each other tend to have disturbed children in their midst, and disturbed young people are much more likely than their well-adjusted peers to come from families that are not functioning comfortably as a unit.

There is some question, however, concerning whether family tensions are a *cause* of adolescents becoming disturbed or are instead a *result* of the stressful impact that disturbed youngsters can have on their families. This important etiological issue is considered in later chapters in relation to specific kinds of psychological disturbance. The main point for the present discussion is that, regardless of whether disturbed adolescents have been the source of strained family relationships or have been made disturbed by them, family conflict occurs in association with abnormal adolescent development. Adolescents who are getting along poorly with their parents are not normally developing youngsters demonstrating problems common to their age group; instead, they are in all likelihood young people struggling with adjustment difficulties.

In addition to demonstrating that features of adolescent turmoil differentiate maladjusted from normal adolescents, clinical studies beginning with Masterson's (1967) work have identified some specific dimensions of symptom formation that help to sharpen this differentiation. Compared to the approximately 60% of adolescents who are developing normally but nevertheless show some symptom formation, disturbed adolescents who need professional care display a greater number of symptoms that last longer and are more likely to include cognitive and behavioral as well as emotional components (Hudgens, 1974; Weiner, 1990).

These findings provide three guidelines for differentiating normal from abnormal development in a symptomatic adolescent: (a) The more symptoms an adolescent displays, (b) the more these symptoms involve cognitive and behavioral problems instead of or in addition to emotional upsets, and (c) the longer any kinds of symptoms persist, the more likely the young person is to be psychologically disturbed.

CORRECTIVE III: SYMPTOM FORMATION IN ADOLESCENTS IS PSYCHOPATHOLOGICAL

Contrary to impressions that apparent symptom formation in adolescents is a normal, transient, and spontaneously remitting phenomenon, there is considerable evidence that symptoms of a psychological disturbance warrant concern and attention just as much in adolescents as in adults. To be sure, the likelihood and severity of a diagnosable disorder will vary with the number, kind, and persistence of symptoms a young person is manifesting, as noted in the previous section. On the other hand, clinical and research findings firmly contradict the belief that youthful symptom formation can largely be ignored in the expectation that it will be outgrown. Hence, any symptom formation in an adolescent should be regarded as at least potentially psychopathological.

This conclusion is supported by evidence from longitudinal studies of both nonpatient and disturbed subjects that a person's level of adjustment relative to his or her peers tends to remain fairly stable during adolescence and from adolescence to adulthood, for better or worse. Among normative populations, for example, Rutter et al. (1976) in the Isle of Wight research found considerable continuity of poor adjustment from early to middle adolescence. Children in this survey who showed emotional problems at ages 10 and 11 years were more than twice as likely as their agemates to have such problems at ages 14 and 15. In the Berkeley Growth Studies, good psychological health (PH) at age 40 years was found to be predictable from good adjustment in adolescence, for both males and females (Livson & Peskin, 1981).

Vaillant (1978) reported similar results from a 35-year study of 268 college sophomore males, 94 of whom were available to be interviewed at age 54 years. The adequacy of the high school adjustment of these men, as rated from the information they gave as college students, was significantly related to the adequacy of their psychological adjustment as adults. Good social adjustment in adolescence predicted good social adjustment at midlife for these men, and poor adjustment at midlife was typically preceded by poor adjustment in adolescence.

In another prospective study, Vaillant and Vaillant (1981) followed 456 inner-city males from 14 to 47 years of age. The effectiveness with which these subjects coped as adolescents with work-related activities at home, in school, and in part-time jobs significantly predicted their mental health and capacity for interpersonal relationships as adults. Other more recent studies of normative groups, both male and female, have confirmed the stability of individual differences in coping effectiveness from childhood through adolescence and into adulthood (Caspi et al., 1987; Lerner, Hertzog, Hooker, & Hassibi, 1988; Raphael, 1988; Rutter 1987).

Follow-up evaluations of disturbed adolescents have similarly identified consistency over time of a young person's level of adjustment relative to his or her peers. These studies indicate that, for the most part, adolescents who manifest obvious symptoms of diagnosable psychological disorder do not outgrow them. Those who *appear* disturbed are likely to *be* disturbed and to *remain* disturbed unless they receive adequate treatment. In Masterson's (1967) study, for example, a 5-year follow-up revealed that almost two thirds of his patient sample continued to have moderate or severe functioning impairments. Weiner and Del Gaudio (1976) obtained similar results in a long-term community study of 1334 12- to 18-year-olds who had visited a mental health facility or practitioner during a 2-year period. Over the next 10 years, 54.2% of these patients returned on one or more occasions for further professional care. This rate of persistent or recurring psychological difficulties far exceeds what would be expected if the initial disturbances had simply been maturational phenomena destined to pass with time.

As final testimony to the psychopathological significance of symptom formation, reports from numerous psychiatric hospitals indicate that adolescents who require inpatient treatment are at relatively high risk for poor adjustment in adulthood. Follow-up evaluations up to 10 years after hospital discharge have revealed that, although these disturbed youngsters improve in the majority of cases, they are subsequently much more likely than the general adult population to experience psychological difficulties that interfere with their lives. Consistently with other data on the temporal stability of relative adjustment level, the severity of the psychopathology exhibited by the disturbed adolescents in these studies is found to predict the degree of disturbance they show as adults (Gossett, Lewis, & Barnhart, 1983; Welner, Welner, & Fishman, 1979).

Because symptom formation in adolescents is psychopathological, as judged both by its deviation from normative expectation and its implications for subsequent maladjustment, it cannot and should not be ignored. Maladaptive behavior in young people needs to be identified, evaluated, and treated in order to minimize its incapacitating effects and negate its contribution to persistent psychopathology.

CONCLUSIONS

This chapter has delineated the mythical notion of normative adolescent turmoil and reviewed research findings that should serve to dispel it. Evidence has been marshaled to demonstrate in particular that normative adolescence is adaptive, that adolescent turmoil reflects deviant adjustment, and that symptom formation among adolescents is psychopathological. The following three conclusions can now be substituted for the mistaken opinions noted previously.

1. Psychological distress that results in symptoms other than fleeting episodes of anxiety or depression or that produces more than mild impairments of school and/or social functioning is not a normative feature of adolescent development.

2. Distinctions between normal and abnormal adolescent development can be readily and reliably made with adequate attention to the number, kind, and persistence of psychological symptoms an adolescent displays.

3. Apparent psychological disturbance in an adolescent is unlikely to disappear of its own accord; instead, in the absence of appropriate intervention, it tends to progress steadily into adult disturbance.

Is there anything new or dramatic about these conclusions, or are they already conventional wisdom? Was a detailed chapter really necessary to dispel the mythical notion of normative adolescent turmoil in these modern times? History confirms in this regard that contemporary clinical understanding of adolescent development and behavior is in many respects a rediscovery of the wheel. In 1905, when the notion of normative adolescent turmoil had just taken root in Hall's Adolescence, C. W. Burr wrote an article in the *Journal of the American Medical Association* that accurately reflects the best data available today:

> Any mental abnormality occurring during the developmental period is of importance, however trifling it may seem in itself, as indicating mental instability or a tendency toward deviation from the normal, which under proper education may be corrected, but which if left uncorrected will certainly lead to disaster in the future. (p. 36)

Once having flourished, however, myths can become exceedingly difficult to dispel. That is why Horrocks (1951), in writing a textbook on adolescent psychology half a century after Hall's work, had to say, "New thinking favors an approach which recognizes that the strains and stresses of adolescence are not inevitable. . . . This point of view, as is often the case of newer scientific insights, has not been fully heard or accepted by the public at large" (p. 5).

"Newer scientific insights" indeed. Burr's perceptive insights of 1905, conveyed in the most widely read medical journal, were repeated by Hollingworth in her 1928 adolescent psychology textbook and by Kanner in his 1941 observations on teenage normality (quoted previusly herein). Yet these clear statements of fact proved hardly sufficient to constrain the enthusiasm with which many clinicians subsequently embraced the notions of developmental discontinuity, emotional instability, identity crisis, and generational conflict as hallmarks of normative adolescent development.

Findings reported by Offer, Ostrov, and Howard (1981b) revealed that the myth of normative adolescent turmoil was still very much alive as the 1980s began. Offer et al. asked 62 mental health professionals, including psychiatrists, clinical psychologists, social workers, and psychiatric nurses, to fill out the Offer Self-Image Questionnaire as they thought a well-adjusted adolescent would. The responses of these professionals indicated that they thought of normal adolescents as experiencing many more problems than were actually endorsed on the same questionnaire by a sample of 407 nonpatient adolescents. In fact, the professionals attributed more self-perceived problems to well-adjusted adolescents than were expressed even by samples of emotionally disturbed and delinquent adolescents.

Hence, as this book is being written, the need remains to consider in detail the nature and origins of the "storm and stress" view of adolescence and to continue documenting its inaccuracy with research findings. Clinicians concerned with young people are urged to abandon misleading, outmoded perspectives on adolescent development that do not fit the facts and to encourage their colleagues to do likewise.

REFERENCES

Bachman, J. G., O'Malley, P. M., & Johnston, J. (1979). Adolescence to adulthood: Change and stability in the lives of young men. Ann Arbor, MI: Institute for Social Research.

Binet, A., & Simon, T. (1905/1916). New methods for the diagnosis of the intellectual level of subnormals. In A. Binet & T. Simon (Eds.), The development of intelligence in children. Baltimore: Williams & Wilkins.

Bleuler, E. (1911/1950). Dementia praecox or the group of schizophrenias. New York: International Universities Press.

Block, J. (1981). Some enduring and consequential structures of personality. In A. I. Rabin, J. Aronoff, A. M. Barclay, & R. A. Zucker (Eds.), Further explorations in personality (pp. 27-43). New York: Wiley.

Blos, P. (1962). On adolescence: A psychoanalytic interpretation. New York: Free Press of Glencoe.

Blos, P. (1983). The contribution of psychoanalysis to the psychotherapy of adolescents. In M. Sugar (Ed.), Adolescent psychiatry (Vol. 11, pp. 104-124). Chicago: University of Chicago Press.

Burr, C. W. (1905). Insanity at puberty. Journal of the American Medical Association, 45, 36-39.

Cairns, R. B., Cairns, B. D., Neckerman, H. J., Ferguson, L. L., & Gariepy, J. (1989). Growth and aggression: 1. Childhood to early adolescence. Developmental Psychology, 25, 320-330.

Caspi, A., Elder, G. H., & Bem, D. J. (1987). Moving against the world: Life-course patterns of explosive children. Developmental Psychology, 23, 308-313.

Coleman, J. S. (1961). The adolescent society. New York: Free Press of Glencoe.

Coleman, J., Herzberg, J., & Morris, M. (1977). Identity in adolescence: Present and future self-concepts. Journal of Youth and Adolescence, 6, 63-75.

Conger, J. J. (1981). Freedom and commitment: Families, youth, and social change. American Psychologist, 36, 1475-1484.

Dennis, W. (1949). Historical beginnings of child psychology. Psychological Bulletin, 46, 224-235.

Deutsch, H. (1967). Selected problems of adolescence. New York: International Universities Press.

Doane, J. A. (1978). Family interaction and communication deviance in disturbed and normal families: A review of research. *Family Process, 17*, 357–376.

Dohrenwend, B. P., Dohrenwend, B. S., Gould, M. S., Link, B., Neugebauer, R., & Wunsch-Hitzig, R. (1980). *Mental illness in the United States: Epidemiological estimates*. New York: Praeger.

Douvan, E., & Adelson, J. (1966). *The adolescent experience*. New York: Wiley.

Dusek, J. B., & Flaherty, J. F. (1981). The development of the self-concept during the adolescent years. *Monographs of the Society for Research in Child Development, 46* (Whole No. 4).

Eichorn, D. H., Mussen, P. H., Clausen, J. A., Haan, N., & Honzik, M. P. (1981). Overview. In D. H. Eichorn, J. A. Clausen, N. Haan, M. P. Honzik, & P. H. Mussen (Eds.), *Present and past in midlife* (pp. 411–434). New York: Academic Press.

Eissler, K. R. (1958). Notes on problems of technique in the psychoanalytic treatment of adolescents. *Psychoanalytic Study of the Child, 13*, 223–254.

Ekstein, R. (1968). Impulse—acting out—purpose: Psychotic adolescents and their quest for goals. *International Journal of Psycho-Analysis, 49*, 347–352.

Elder, G. H. (1980). Adolescence in historical perspective. In J. Adelson (Ed.), *Handbook of adolescent psychology* (pp. 3–46). New York: Wiley.

Erikson, E. H. (1956). The problem of ego identity. *Journal of the American Psychoanalytic Association, 4*, 56–121.

Erikson, E. H. (1963). *Childhood and society* (2nd ed.). New York: W. W. Norton.

Esser, G., Schmidt, M. H., & Woerner, W. (1990). Epidemiology and course of psychiatric disorders in school-age children: Results of a longitudinal study. *Journal of Child Psychology & Psychiatry, 31*, 243–263.

Freud, A. (1936/1946). *The ego and the mechanisms of defence*. New York: International Universities Press.

Freud, A. (1958). Adolescence. *Psychoanalytic Study of the Child, 13*, 255–278.

Freud, A. (1969). Adolescence as a developmental disturbance. In S. Lebovici & G. Caplan (Eds.), *Adolescence: Psychosocial perspectives* (pp. 5–11). New York: Basic Books.

Freud, S. (1905/1953). Three essays on the theory of sexuality. *Standard edition* (Vol. VII, pp. 125–243). London: Hogarth.

Gardner, G. E. (1947). The mental health of normal adolescents. *Mental Hygiene, 31*, 529–540.

Gillis, J. R. (1974). Youth and history. New York: Academic Press.

Giovacchini, P. L. (1978). The borderline aspects of adolescence and the borderline state. In S. C. Feinstein & P. L. Giovacchini (Eds.), *Adolescent psychiatry* (Vol. 6, pp. 320–338). Chicago: University of Chicago Press.

Gossett, J. T., Lewis, J. M., & Barnhart, F. D. (1983). *To find a way: The outcome of hospital treatment of disturbed adolescents*. New York: Burnner/Mazel.

Grinker, R. R. (1962). "Mentally healthy" young males (homoclites). *Archives of General Psychiatry, 6*, 405–453.

Group for the Advancement of Psychiatry (1968). *Normal adolescence: Its dynamics and impact*. New York: Scribners.

Hall, G. S. (1904). *Adolescence: Its psychology and its relations to physiology, anthropology, sociology, sex, crime, religion, and education* (Vols. 1, 2). New York: D. Appleton.

Handel, A. (1980). Perceived change of self among adolescents. *Journal of Youth and Adolescence, 9,* 507-519.

Healy, W. H. (1915). *The individual delinquent: A textbook of diagnosis and prognosis for all concerned in understanding offenders.* Boston: Little, Brown.

Hill, J. P. (1987). Research on adolescents and their families: Past and prospect. In C. E. Irwin (Ed.), *Adolescent social behavior and health* (pp. 13-31). San Francisco: Jossey-Bass.

Hill, J. P. (1985). Family relations in adolescence: Myths, realities, and new directions. *Genetic, Social & General Psychology Monographs, 111,* 233-248.

Hollingworth, L. S. (1928). *The psychology of the adolescent.* New York: D. Appleton.

Horrocks, J. E. (1951). *The psychology of adolescence.* Boston: Houghton Mifflin.

Hudgens, R. W. (1974). *Psychiatric disorders in adolescents.* Baltimore: Williams & Wilkins.

Kagan, J., & Moss, H. A. (1962). *Birth to maturity: A study in psychological development.* New York: Wiley.

Kanner, L. (1935). *Child psychiatry.* Oxford: Blackwell Scientific Publications.

Kanner, L. (1941). Mental disturbances in adolescents. *Medical Clinics of North America, 25,* 515-527.

Kashani, J. H., Beck, N. C., Hoeper, E. W., Fallahi, C., Corcoran, C. M., McAllister, J. A., Rosenberg, T. K., & Reid, J. C. (1987). Psychiatric disorders in a community sample of adolescents. *American Journal of Psychiatry, 144,* 584-589.

Keniston, K. (1965). *The uncommitted: Alienated youth in American society.* New York: Harcourt, Brace and World.

Keyes, S., & Coleman, J. (1983). Sex-role conflicts and personal adjustment: A study of British adolescents. *Journal of Youth and Adolescence, 12,* 443-460.

Kimmel, D. C., & Weiner, I. B. (1985). *Adolescence: A develomental transition.* Hillsdale, NJ: Erlbaum.

Larson, R., Czikszentmihalyi, M., & Graef, R. (1980). Mood variability and the psychosocial adjustment of adolescents. *Journal of Youth and Adolescence, 9,* 469-490.

Larson, R., & Lampman-Petraitis, C. (1989). Daily emotional states as reported by children and adolescents. *Child Development, 60,* 1250-1260.

Lauer, R. H. (1973). *Perspectives in social change.* Boston: Allyn & Bacon.

Lerner, J. V., Hertzog, C., Hooker, K. A., & Hassibi, M. (1988). A longitudinal study of emotional states and adjustment from early childhood through adolescence. *Child Development, 59,* 356-366.

Lerner, R. M., & Knapp, J. R. (1975). Actual and perceived intrafamilial attitudes of late adolescents and their parents. *Journal of Youth and Adolescence, 4,* 17-36.

Livson, N., & Peskin, H. (1981). Psychological health at age 40. In D. H. Eichorn, J. A. Clausen, N. Haan, M. P. Hoznik, & P. H. Mussen (Eds.), *Present and past in midlife* (pp. 183-194). New York: Academic Press.

Manning, M. L. (1983). Three myths concerning adolescence. *Adolescence, 18*, 823–829.

Marcia, J. E. (1980). Identity in adolescence. In J. Adelson (Ed.), *Handbook of adolescent psychology* (pp. 159–187). New York: Wiley.

Masterson, J. F. (1967). *The psychiatric dilemma of adolescence*. Boston: Little, Brown.

Mead, M. (1970). *Culture and commitment: A study of the generation gap*. New York: Doubleday.

Mead, M. (1978). *Culture and commitment: The new relationships between the generations in the 1970s* (rev. ed.). New York: Columbia University Press.

Mischel, W., Shoda, Y., & Peake, P. K. (1988). The nature of adolescent competencies predicted by preschool delay of gratification. *Journal of Personality & Social Psychology, 54*, 687–696.

Montemayor, R. (1983). Parents and adolescents in conflict: All families some of the time and some families most of the time. *Journal of Early Adolescence, 3*, 83–103.

Montemayor, R. (1986). Family variation in parent-adolescent storm and stress. *Journal of Adolescent Research, 1*, 15–32.

Moss, H. A., & Susman, E. J. (1980). Longitudinal study of personality development. In O. G. Brim & J. Kagan (Eds.), *Constancy and change in human development*. Cambridge, MA: Harvard University Press.

Myers, J. K., Weissman, M. M., Tischler, G. L., Holzer, C. E., Leaf, P. J., Orvaschel, H., Anthony, J. C., Boyd, J. H., Burke, J. D., Kramer, M., & Stoltzman, R. (1983). Six-month prevalence of psychiatric disorders in three communities. *Archives of General Psychiatry, 41*, 959–967.

Nance, R. D. (1970). G. Stanley Hall and John B. Watson as child psychologists. *Journal of the History of the Behavioral Sciences, 4*, 303–316.

Nottelman, E. D. (1987) Competence and self-esteem during transition from childhood to adolescence. *Developmental Psychology, 23*, 441–450.

Offer, D. (1969). *The psychological world of the teen-ager*. New York: Basic Books.

Offer, D., & Offer, J. B. (1975). *From teenage to young manhood: A psychological study*. New York: Basic Books.

Offer, D., Ostrov, E., & Howard, K. I. (1981a). *The adolescent: A psychological self-portrait*. New York: Basic Books.

Offer, D., Ostrov, E., & Howard, K. I. (1981b). The mental health professional's concept of the normal adolescent. *Archives of General Psychiatry, 38*, 149–152.

Offer, D., Ostrov, E., & Howard, K. I. (1986). Self-image, delinquency, and help-seeking behavior among normal adolescents. In S. Feinstein (Ed.), *Adolescent psychiatry* (Vol. 13, pp. 121–137). Chicago: University of Chicago Press.

Offer, D., Ostrov, E., & Howard, K. I. (1987). The epidemiology of mental health and mental illness among urban adolescents. In J. Call (Ed.), *Significant advances in child psychiatry* (pp. 82–88). New York: Basic Books.

Offer, D., & Sabshin, M. (1984). Adolescence: Empirical perspectives. In D. Offer & M. Sabshin (Eds.), *Normality and the life cycle* (pp. 76–107). New York: Basic Books.

Petersen, A. C. (1988). Adolescent development. *Annual Review of Psychology, 39*, 583–607.

Powers, S. I., Hauser, S. T., & Kilner, L. A. (1989). Adolescent mental health. *American Psychologist, 44*, 200–208.

Protinsky, H. O., & Farrier, S. (1980). Self-image changes in pre-adolescents and adolescents. *Adolescence, 15*, 887–893.

Raphael, D. (1988). High school conceptual level as an indicator of young adult adjustment. Jour*nal of Personality Assessment, 52*, 679–690.

Redlich, F. C., & Freedman, D. X. (1966). *The theory and practice of psychiatry.* New York: Basic Books.

Reisman, J. M. (1976). *A history of clinical psychology.* New York: Irvington.

Rutter, M. (1987). Continuities and discontinuities from infancy. In J. D. Osofsky (Ed.), *Handbook of infant development* (2nd ed.; pp. 1256–1296). New York: Wiley.

Rutter, M. (1989). Pathways from childhood to adult life. *Journal of Child Psychology and Psychiatry, 30*, 23–51.

Rutter, M., Graham, P., Chadwick, O. F. D, & Yule, W. (1976). Adolescent turmoil: Fact or fiction? *Journal of Child Psychology and Psychiatry, 17*, 35–56.

Schwartz, J. C., & Getter, H. (1980). Parental conflict and dominance in late adolescent maladjustment: A triple interaction model. *Journal of Abnormal Psychology, 89*, 573–580.

Settlage, C. F. (1970). Adolescence and social change. *Journal of the American Academy of Child Psychiatry, 9*, 203–215.

Siddique, C. M., & D'Arcy, C. (1984). Adolescence, stress, and psychological well-being. *Journal of Youth and Adolescence, 13*, 459–474.

Simmons, R. B., & Blyth, D. A. (1987). *Moving into adolescence: The impact of pubertal change and school context.* New York: Aldine de Gruyter.

Smetena, J. G. (1989). Adolescents' and parents' reasoning about actual family conflict. *Child Development, 60*, 1052–1067.

Sroufe, L. A., & Jacobvitz, D. (1989). Diverging pathways, developmental transformations, multiple etiologies and the problem of continuity in development. *Human Development, 32*, 196–203.

Sroufe, L. A., & Rutter, M. (1984). The domain of developmental psychopathology. *Child Development, 55*, 17029.

Steinberg, L. D. (1987). Family processes at adolescence: A developmental perspective. *Family Therapy, 14*, 78–86.

Tolan, P., Miller, L., & Thomas, P. (1988). Perception and experience of types of social stress and self-image among adolescents. *Journal of Youth and Adolescence, 17*, 147–164.

Tuma, J. M. (1989). Mental health services for children. *American Psychologist, 44*, 188–199.

Vaillant, G. E. (1978). Natural history of male psychological health: VI. Correlates of successful marriage and fatherhood. *American Journal of Psychiatry, 135*, 653–659.

Vaillant, G. E., & Vaillant, C. O. (1981). Natural history of male psychological health: X. Work as a predictor of positive mental health. *American Journal of Psychiatry, 138*, 1433–1440.

Waterman, A. S. (1982). Identity development from adolescence to adulthood: An extension of theory and a review of research. *Developmental Psychology, 18*, 341–358.

Weiner, I. B. (1972). Perspectives on the modern adolescent. *Psychiatry, 35*, 20–31.

Weiner, I. B. (1976). The adolescent and his society. In J. R. Gallaher, F. P. Heald, & D. C. Garell (Eds.), Medi*cal care of the adolescent* (3rd ed., pp. 1-10). New York: Appleton-Century-Crofts.

Weiner, I. B. (1990). Distinguishing healthy from disturbed adolescent development. *Journal of Developmental and Behavioral Pediatrics, 11*, 151–154.

Weiner, I. B., & Del Gaudio, A. C. (1976). Psychopathology in adolescence: An epidemiological study. *Archives of General Psychiatry, 33*, 187–193.

Welner, A., Welner, Z., & Fishman, R. (1979). Psychiatric adolescent inpatients: Eight- to ten-year follow-up. *Archives of General Psychiatry, 36*, 687–700.

Winnicott, D. W. (1971). Adolescence: Struggling through the doldrums. In S. C. Feinstein, P. L. Giovacchini, & A. A. Miller (Eds.), *Adolescent psychiatry* (Vol. I, pp. 40-50). New York: Basic Books.

CHAPTER 2

Classifying Adolescent Psychopathology

Classification of psychopathology serves important purposes in facilitating scientific inquiry, guiding clinical interventions, and promoting professional communication. Nevertheless, some social scientists and mental health professionals occasionally have questioned whether the diagnostic classification of psychological disturbance is an adequately conceived and empirically sound procedure. Others, while endorsing classification, have disagreed concerning how best to formulate diagnostic categories and apply them to disturbed adolescents. This chapter (a) reviews the purposes and some potential pitfalls of diagnostic classification, (b) describes various approaches to classifying behavior problems in young people, and (c) indicates how the topics were selected for the subsequent chapters of this book.

DIAGNOSTIC CLASSIFICATION: PURPOSES AND POTENTIAL PITFALLS

Scientific inquiry begins with the classification of objects and events. Researchers who wish to study plants or animals must first determine which objects in the world constitute *plants* and which constitute *animals*. Efforts to understand earthquakes or riotous behavior must proceed from criteria for deciding when an earthquake or a riot is taking place. Such discrimination of objects and events from each other is thus essential to systematic investigation of their distinctive characteristics.

Similarly, the diagnostic classification of psychological disorder facilitates research in psychopathology by designating appropriate subjects for study. To explore the characteristics that people may have, methods must be employed to identify people who have these characteristics. To study the nature of psychological disturbances, investigators need to be able to discriminate among individuals who are displaying various kinds of disturbances or no disturbances of any kind. Systems of classifying types of disorders make these discriminations possible, and the adequacy of available methods of classification calibrate the extent to which research in psychopathology can be conducted along scientific lines.

With respect to clinical practice, identifying the kinds of problems that people have provides a useful basis for determining what types of interventions are likely to benefit them. Mental health professionals generally concur with the 1973 statement of the Joint Commission on the Mental Health of Children in this regard: "Individual psychodiagnosis is seen as the necessary condition for prescribing one of the many forms of psychotherapeutic interventions" (p. 110). Klerman (1986) has more recently stated this contribution of classification as follows:

> Today, however, treatment decisions cannot be responsibly informed and implemented without a sound nosological basis. As effective treatments for mental disorders become diverse, the need for a highly differentiated diagnostic system becomes clearer. (p. 5)

More specifically, the classification of behavior disorders make it possible to determine whether a particular person's problems are similar to or different from problems that have previously proved amenable or refractory to specific kinds of intervention. Classification thus allows therapists to draw on cumulative knowledge concerning the best ways of treating people who show various previously observed characteristics. Without classificatory guidelines for identifying similarities among kinds of psychological disturbance, clinicians would have to formulate treatment plans from scratch every time they begin working with a new patient. Medin (1989) comments with particular cogency on this purpose of classification:

> Although one would expect treatment plans to be tailored to the needs of individuals, absolute uniqueness imposes the prohibitive cost of ignorance. Clinicians need some way to bring their knowledge and experience to bear on the problem under consideration, and that requires the appreciation of some similarity or relationship between the assessment situation and what has gone before. (p. 1469)

Because of the importance of adequate classification, both for fruitful scientific investigation and for effective clinical intervention, the subsequent chapters of this book emphasize careful diagnostic study as the foundation for understanding and helping disturbed adolescents. Numerous other authors in clinical psychology and psychiatry, representing diverse theoretical positions and concerning themselves with the problems of persons of all ages, similarly endorse the role of classification in psychopathology research and treatment planning (Cantwell, 1988a; Hersen & Last, 1989; Kazdin, 1983; Robins & Helzer, 1986).

As most of these writers also note, classification of psychological disorders has the additional value of promoting effective communication. Diagnostic categories help mental health professionals to exchange information economically. For example, disturbed people who can be described as meeting familiar criteria for "schizophrenia" or "major depressive disorder" can be discussed in supervisory sessions and treatment conferences with far fewer words than if basic features of schizophrenia or depressive disorder must be repeated in each instance. Having a common language serves further to assist the development and propagation of service programs intended to meet the needs of persons with specific kinds of identifiable problems.

While appreciating the facilitating role that diagnostic classification plays in research design, treatment planning, and communication, scholars and practitioners must also be cognizant of some potential pitfalls of designating individual persons as displaying various categories of disorder. Some of these pitfalls have led to conceptual concerns about the propriety of classifying behavior disorders, and others are reflected in empirical concerns about the reliability and validity of classification schemes.

The Propriety of Classifying Behavior Disorders

Some clinicians and social scientists have expressed concern that the diagnostic classification of psychopathology is a dehumanizing, stigmatizing procedure that does more harm than good and may even create disturbances that otherwise would not exist. With respect to dehumanization, the founding fathers of humanistic psychology argued that every person should be considered in his or her own uniqueness, as the sole member of his or her class. From this point of view, being assigned a classificatory label based on characteristics presumably shared by some group of people strips a person of his or her dignity and individuality (Bugental, 1978; Maslow, 1962; Rogers, 1961).

Clinicians need to heed this concern, to avoid the mistaken belief that a diagnostic category provides sufficient information for formulating a treatment plan. Classification summarizes salient features of a disturbed person's problems, but it does not necessarily specify how these problems originated or how they are being manifested in the particular person. Classification describes a disorder, but it says little about the life experiences and the adaptive characteristics of the person who has the disorder. Such individualized understanding of disturbed persons and their circumstances, which goes far beyond arriving at a diagnostic classification, is an essential ingredient of effective intervention planning.

With respect to possible stigmatizing effects of diagnostic classification, influential writers such as Goffman (1963), Hobbs (1975), and Rosenhan (1973) have voiced concern that being labeled "emotionally disturbed" can expose persons to devastating experiences of prejudice and rejection. Persons who are thought to be disturbed are at risk for being shunned by others, these writers contend, and they are likely to be denied access to schools they wish to attend, to careers they are qualified to pursue, and to neighborhoods where they want to live. These persons are often expected by others to behave in strange and destructive ways, even if they never have, and they are frequently perceived to be acting peculiarly even when they are not. As a result, conclude these writers and many others of similar persuasion, persons who have the misfortune to be labeled "disturbed" frequently fall victim to undeserved criticisms, unjust punishments, and unfair restrictions on what they are allowed to do.

The victimization of persons classified as having a psychological disorder has been the frequent subject of authors concerned with the impact of mental health practices on civil liberties (Halleck, 1971; Magaro, Gripp, & McDowell, 1978; Rothblum, Solomon, & Albee, 1986; Szasz, 1963, 1987). Diagnostic classification is at its harmful worst, these authors say, when it is used by institutions within a society to justify dealing with so-called undesirable persons by sending them to undesirable places—such as locking up disturbing adults in mental hospitals and relegating disruptive young persons to correctional facilities.

Like potential stigma and dehumanization, the possible victimization of persons with psychological disorders demands the vigilance of mental health professionals. Whatever the particular situation or hazard may be, ethical practice requires every reasonable effort to minimize possibly harmful effects of classifying psychological disorder.

Nevertheless, there are several reasons to think that the potential for harm through diagnostic classification is less than some concerned critics have suggested. In the first place, classification does not preclude or even restrict careful attention to individuality. An individual's uniqueness does not have to be ignored in order to identify some characteristics that he or she shares in common with other persons and that suggest some diagnostic classification. To the contrary, understanding individual behavior involves learning how a person resembles at least some other persons, as well as learning how he or she differs from most others. From a clinical perspective, the ways in which individuals resemble and differ from each other are complementary bits of information that can and should be used together in efforts to comprehend and alleviate psychological distress.

Second, with respect to probable exaggeration of the potential harm of diagnostic classification, the American public has, for many years, been growing increasingly knowledgeable about and tolerant of psychological disturbance, to the point where the average person's attitude toward disturbed individuals can more accurately be described as "accepting" than as "rejecting" (Aviram & Segal, 1973; Rabkin, 1974). Evidence of these changing attitudes includes the national establishment of Mental Illness Awareness Week, the growth of such organizations as the National Association for Mental Health and the National Alliance for the Mentally Ill, and the widespread emergence of self-help and support groups for patients and their families facing such mental health problems as substance abuse, schizophrenia, manic–depressive disorder, and autism. In the past, families often denied or concealed the presence of a disturbed member in their midst, even while surreptitiously seeking treatment for him or her. In the present families not only seek psychological treatment more openly than before, but also often welcome opportunities to share experiences with and learn from similarly troubled families.

As a third reason, there is evidence that prejudice and rejection directed toward disturbed persons is based more on how they are behaving than on how they are labeled (Fernald, Williams, & Droescher, 1985; Hemphill &

Siperstein, 1990). Fourth, negative attitudes and expectations created by labels have been found to diminish in response to becoming acquainted with someone who is so labeled, and becoming more knowledgeable about handicapping conditions generally results in attitudes toward persons labeled as handicapped becoming more positive and accepting (Fernald & Gettys, 1980; Handlers & Austin, 1980; Jones, Sowell, Jones, & Butler, 1981).

Turning from these research findings to clinical practice, it is important to recognize that instances of diagnostic classification resulting in individuals being stigmatized or disadvantaged usually involve a misuse or misinterpretation of diagnosis. There is nothing inherently prejudicial or depriving about being classified; adequate classification merely provides accurate information concerning the kind of problem an individual has and the type of professional help he or she may need. People who misjudge the meaning of a label are uninformed and should be educated. Professionals who know better but ignore or distort the implications of an accurate classification to serve some ulterior purpose are being unethical and should be sanctioned. Further, anyone who knowingly attaches an inaccurate classification to a person to justify taking some detrimental action against him or her is violating that person's rights and should be prosecuted.

The Labeling Theory of Deviance

An especially sweeping indictment of diagnostic classification has derived from a conviction held by some that distinctive kinds of psychopathology exist only in the eyes of the beholder and seldom constitute real characteristics of persons. From this perspective, diagnostic classification rarely represents a valid or justifiable response to demonstrable psychological disorder. Instead, it tends most often to occur as a pejorative judgment made when relatively influential members of a society, having found the attitudes or actions of certain less influential individuals objectionable, decide to label these individuals as "deviant."

Known as the "labeling theory of deviance," this presumed state of affairs is considered by its proponents to have two major implications: First, persons become labeled as deviant or as demonstrating some pattern of psychopathology, not because they are in fact psychologically impaired, but because their life-style is regarded as unfavorable by others who can wield authority over them. Second, the act of labeling and reacting to a person as if he or she were deviant contributes to the person's developing an identity as being deviant and starting to behave in deviant ways (Sarbin, 1969; Scheff, 1981, 1984; Schur, 1971).

From the labeling perspective, in other words, psychopathology does not exist until it is labeled, and most instances of truly deviant behavior would be transitory were it not for societal reactions, beginning with classification, that tend to reinforce and perpetuate deviance. According to Silverman (1983), for example, clearly definable types of psychopathology "are virtually nonexistent except in the minds and textbooks of professionals." Belief in their existence, he continues, is among a group of "ideologies that mask some program of intimidation and control by the socially powerful over the powerless" (pp. vii–viii).

Gibbs (1982, p. 15) similarly contends that "When mental health professionals engage in the labeling process, they assume a judgmental and moralistic stance toward the labeled person that emphasizes the superiority of the judge, the dependency of the labeled person, and that is contrary to a helping role." In the opinion of Rothblum et al. (1986, p. 182), "An overwhelming majority of the persons to whom we give psychiatric labels are not different in kind from the rest of us."

Like the concerns about potential dehumanizing and stigmatizing effects of diagnostic classification, the labeling theory of deviance raises issues that mental health professionals should not ignore. However, careful reviews of the literature seem clearly to indicate that (a) the vast majority of people who are diagnosed by clinicians as manifesting some form of psychopathology are in fact unable to function effectively, and (b) their demonstrable functioning impairments, and not pejorative social judgments, are the main reason for their being given some diagnostic label (Eron & Peterson, 1982; Gove, 1982; Robins, 1981; Strauss, 1979).

In addition, the experience of most clinicians would strongly suggest that the labeling process, when carefully implemented in the context of informed and responsible clinical practice, is more likely to initiate interventions that limit the severity and persistence of a psychological disorder than it is to foster reactions that intensify and prolong the disorder. Contrary to the central hypothesis of labeling theory, seriously disturbed adults who accept the label of being mentally ill are found subsequently to function better, not worse, than those who reject their diagnosis (Warner, Taylor, Powers, & Hyman, 1989). As for disturbed adolescents, diagnosis and hospitalization have not been demonstrated to perpetuate instances of abnormal behavior or to constitute an inevitably damaging influence on their self-concepts (Chassin, Young, Presson, & Light, 1981). The fact of the matter is that very little empirical support has even been generated for the argument that classification is harmful to individuals with psychological disorders (Cantwell, 1988a).

Because the potential benefits of diagnostic classification far outweigh its possible pitfalls, discussions in this book regarding the evaluation and treatment of psychological disturbances in adolescence involve identifying young persons as having one or another kind of disturbance. Nonetheless, clinicians should remain constantly alert to the alarms sounded by proponents of labeling theory. As clinicians do their own work and evaluate the work of others, care must be taken (a) to protect eccentric adults who offend mainstream sensitivities from consequently being called "schizophrenic" or "borderline" and being referred for hospitalization; (b) to prevent rambunctious children whose energy level overtaxes their teacher's tolerance from consequently being called "hyperactive" or "conduct disordered" and being excluded from regular classrooms; and (c) to ensure that unconventional adolescents who ruffle adult feathers are not consequently considered "antisocial" or "hypomanic" or given any other label that generates an inappropriate diagnosis or an unnecessary treatment recommendation.

Issues of Reliability and Validity

Numerous mental health professionals who are comfortable in principle with classifying psychopathology have nevertheless been concerned about the reliability and validity of efforts to do so. Research evidence summarized by Zubin in 1967 indicated that clinicians frequently disagreed in their diagnostic impressions, that diagnoses were not notably consistent over time, and that diagnostic labeling had not proved particularly helpful in identifying the origins of psychological disturbances or their likely course and response to treatment. Such empirical shortcomings led to some serious reservations about the scientific basis and clinical utility of traditional diagnostic categories and assessment methods. Behaviorally oriented psychologists, for example, tended during the 1970s to recommend replacing traditional diagnostic terms with less inferential and presumably more reliable descriptions of observable behavior patterns (Adams, Doster, & Calhoun, 1977; Costello, 1970; Goldfried & Kent, 1972).

Although these events spawned a period of discouragement about classification, a closer look at the data was in order. In the first place, classification has been approached in many different ways and with a multitude of alternative classification schemes. Some of these approaches have proved to be more reliable and valid than others, and alternative schemes reflecting the same general approach have also been found to differ in their reliability and validity (Achenbach, 1982; Sprock & Blashfield, 1983). Hence, any statement about the empirical justification for classifying psychopathology needs to be qualified with respect to the specific approach or classification scheme that is being discussed.

Second, the individual categories within a specific classification scheme are likely to vary in their empirical properties. For example, studies of broad diagnostic categories have consistently revealed that clinicians achieve better agreement in diagnosing organic and psychotic disorders than neurotic and personality disorders (Spitzer & Wilson, 1975). Thus the extent to which classification of psychopathology is reliable will depend not only on the approach and the particular diagnostic scheme being used, but also on the kind of psychopathology that is being identified.

Third, empirical shortcomings, like dehumanizing consequences, constitute a *potential* pitfall of classification, but not an inevitable impediment. Classification of psychopathology is not inherently unreliable or invalid, any more than it is inherently prejudicial or depriving. As noted earlier, the possible personal disadvantages of being classified can be minimized by the sensitivity of informed and responsible clinicians. In parallel fashion, the reliability and validity of classifying psychological disorder can be improved through careful attention by sophisticated researchers to ways of refining classification schemes and methods of assessment.

As a case in point, many of the early studies in which clinicians showed poor diagnostic agreement involved methodological flaws that stacked the deck against reliable judgments. These flaws included (a) asking clinicians to choose among diagnostic categories for which there were not clearly defined criteria or that share many overlapping characteristics; (b) providing few consistent guidelines as to the kinds of diagnostic data the clinicians should obtain and how they should evaluate these data; and (c) using as judges relatively inexperienced clinicians who lacked thorough training in how to elicit and interpret critical differential diagnostic data in a complex clinical case.

More recent research has demonstrated that diagnostic agreement improves substantially when various steps are taken to correct such methodological flaws. These include (a) developing clear and explicit criteria for deciding when a particular condition is present; (b) reducing as much as possible the overlap among criteria for identifying different conditions; (c) promulgating standardized ways for collecting diagnostic data, thereby ensuring both that clinical judges are working with the same kind and amount of information and that this information bears relevance to the criteria for the conditions to be differentiated; and (d) training clinical judges adequately in how to relate the information they obtain to the established criteria for the conditions they are attempting to diagnose. The more fully a research study meets these conditions, the more likely it is to provide an adequate assessment of the potential reliability of a classification scheme, and the more extensively clinicians are in fact found to agree in their diagnostic judgments (Grove, Andreasen, McDonald-Scott, Keller, & Shapiro, 1981).

These general considerations bore considerable fruit during the 1980s, which was an exciting decade for classification, marked by major advances in developing reliable diagnostic criteria and relating them in valid fashion to the origins, treatment, and course of psychological disorders.

APPROACHES TO CLASSIFYING BEHAVIOR PROBLEMS

To realize the benefits of classifying psychopathology, clinicians and researchers should be able to call on a clearly stated, conceptually sound, and internally consistent classification system that provides a valid basis for (a) understanding the nature and origins of distinctive conditions, (b) employing assessment methods that successfully identify and discriminate among these conditions, and (c) implementing effective means of treating or preventing them. Unfortunately, no such system exists. The task of classifying disturbed behavior has been approached in several different ways, each of which has contributed to realizing the purposes of classification but none of which has yet proved entirely satisfactory. The three most widely employed approaches to diagnostic classification reflect primarily *clinical, theoretical*, or *empirical* frames of reference.

Clinical Approaches

In clinical approaches to classifying psychopathology, practitioners first look for commonalities among the manifestations of disorders they observe in their patients and then describe apparently recurring patterns of symptoms as constituting a *syndrome*. The more frequently a particular symptom pattern is observed and the more clearly it seems associated with some distinctive antecedent and subsequent events, the more likely it is to become identified as a syndrome and to gain currency as a diagnostic label. Once they are identified clinically, syndromes may stimulate theoretical speculations and become the subject of systematic research studies. Initially, however, they derive neither from theory nor research, but from the observations and descriptions of practitioners who infer broad categories of disorder from the symptoms manifested by their patients.

As testimony to the importance of the individual practitioner in clinical approaches to classification, syndromes have frequently been named after the person who first observed and described them. Although this kind of identification has more often characterized physical than psychological disorders, developmental psychopathologists need to be familiar with such "named" conditions as Down's syndrome, Tourette's syndrome, and Briquet's syndrome.

Although no syndrome bears his name, Emil Kraepelin stands as the pioneering clinical classifier and systematizer of psychological disorders. His textbook of psychiatry, published in nine editions from 1883 to 1927, established the methods for using cumulative clinical observations of the onset and course of manifest symptomatology as a basis for differentiating discrete categories of psychological disorder. In recognition of his contribution, the clinical approach to classification, emphasizing symptom descriptions, is often referred to as the "Kraepelinian method."

Kraepelinian classification served practitioners and researchers well by bringing order out of the chaos that existed prior to its inception. Both historically and continuing to the present day, clinical approaches deserve much of the credit for fostering the contributions of classification to treatment planning, research design, and professional communication. Of special significance in this regard has been the close tie of clinically based classification to the everyday observation and interventions of practitioners working with disturbed persons. This connection has promoted diagnostic categorizations that clinicians find easy to use and easy to relate to the disturbances they are likely to need in their practices.

Unfortunately, however, traditional clinical classification is an open-ended system in which there are few constraints on the number and nature of syndromes that can be introduced into the nomenclature. As a result, this approach may fail to guard adequately against a proliferation of overlapping syndromes that may involve similar symptoms. The more such overlap there is in a classification scheme, with various different disorders including many features in common, the more difficult it becomes for clinicians to agree on which disorder is present and for the scheme to achieve respectable reliability.

In addition to this impediment to their reliability, clinical classification schemes have two other potential drawbacks that can limit their validity. First, a clinical–descriptive classification may not account adequately for the fact that one and the same condition may be manifest in different ways at different times. Some conditions produce changing symptoms as they run their course, and others are manifest in different ways at different ages. Sole reliance on presently manifest symptoms to classify psychopathology can consequently lead to diagnostic and conceptual errors.

Among young people, for example, the condition called "hyperactive child syndrome" (HACS) was at one time believed to be outgrown by adolescence, because its primary manifestation—hyperactivity—diminishes as children mature and pass puberty. Subsequent conceptualizations of HACS—first as minimal brain dysfunction (MBD), then as attention deficit disorder (ADD), and most recently as attention deficit-hyperactivity disorder (ADHD)— recognize that it is not "cured" by maturation. Instead, this condition persists in the absence of effective intervention in the form of changing symptoms over time. Thus, as adolescents, inadequately treated ADHD children are likely to show school learning problems and/or antisocial behavior (see Chapters 7 and 8).

Similarly, because children and early adolescents seldom display full-blown symptom patterns that characterize adult depression, it was asserted at one time that young people, especially before midadolescence, do not develop depressive disorders. More recent evidence documents that children and early adolescents can and do develop depressive disorders, but are inclined by virtue of their developmental status to manifest their depression differently from adults (see Chapter 4).

As a second drawback to their validity, diagnostic classifications based exclusively on manifest symptomatology can at times fail to predict treatment response and to identify effective interventions. This is especially likely to occur when an underlying disorder is producing symptoms that seem to reflect some other disorder. For example, adolescents who are depressed may in certain circumstances manifest their depression primarily through delinquent behavior. When such young people are treated for conduct problems, they show little progress, but when they are treated for their underlying depression, their general level of adjustment tends to improve and their delinquent behavior tends to disappear (see Chapters 4 and 9).

Like potential pitfalls of classification in general, such possible drawbacks of clinically based classification are not insurmountable. To the contrary, contemporary efforts to improve the reliability and validity of clinically derived classification schemes through systematic research have borne considerable fruit. Known as the neo-Kraepelinian movement, these efforts draw on empirical data to redefine traditional diagnostic categories in ways that will increase their interrater reliability and delineate distinctive nonoverlapping features of their etiology, course, and treatment response.

The neo-Kraepelinian movement in classification led to the now widely used third edition of the *Diagnostic and Statistical Manual*, published by the American Psychiatric Association in 1980 (*DSM-III*) and revised in 1987 (*DSM-III-R*). To a much greater extent than the previous two versions of this manual, the third edition provides detailed descriptions of disorders and fairly specific criteria for diagnosing and distinguishing among a broad range of conditions. These criteria have made it possible for adequately trained clinicians to achieve reasonably good diagnostic agreement. In two phases of field trials with *DSM-III* involving several hundred adults the kappa coefficient of agreement averaged around .70 for the major syndrome categories.

Consistent with experience of the past, however, the individual *DSM-III* categories have been found to vary in how reliably they can be identified. Organic, schizophrenic, and affective disorders have shown substantially higher rates of agreement among diagnosticians than anxiety, adjustment, and personality disorders. The criteria for many of the *DSM-III* disorders were modified in the 1987 revision, and subsequent research may demonstrate resulting improvements in reliability. Even so, some persistent difficulties in distinguishing among categories of personality disorder have already been identified. The *DSM-III-R* personality disorder categories appear to be internally consistent, but many of them have a sufficient number of overlapping characteristics to prevent clinicians from readily telling one from the other (Blashfield & Breen, 1989; Morey, 1988; Widiger, Frances, Spitzer, & Williams, 1988).

While recognizing the need for further improvements in reliability in *DSM-IV*, which is currently being developed, most nosologists believe that the advent of *DSM-III* injected at least a modicum of clinician agreement into diagnostic classification. In addition, *DSM-III* and *DSM-III-R* categories are gradually being tied to discriminating assessment procedures and differential treatment outcomes that help to validate them. With respect to assessment, several structured interview schedules have been designed to assist in identifying DSM categories in both adults and young people. Among the more carefully prepared and better known measures of this kind are the Structured Clinical Interview of *DSM-III-R* (SCID), the Schedule for Affective Disorders and Schizophrenia (SADS) and its "Kiddie" version for children (K-SADS), the Diagnostic Interview for Borderlines (DIB), and the Diagnostic Interview for Children and Adolescents (DICA). Overviews by Edelbrock and Costello (1990), McReynolds (1989), and Wiens (1990) provide further information on such measures.

With respect to treatment, the reliability of *DSM* for discriminating among the major types of disorder has facilitated studies of how these disorders differ in their natural course and in their response to alternative modes of intervention. This research has begun to bear fruit in the form of treatment manuals developed specifically to translate DSM diagnoses into differential treatment planning (Perry, Frances, & Clarkin, 1990; Reid, 1989).

Despite these positive developments, many clinicians remain concerned that *DSM-III* and *DSM-III-R* overemphasize criteria for classifying disorders at the expense of conceptual formulations for understanding disorders, and many researchers remain concerned that too many of these criteria still rest on clinical impressions rather than empirical findings (e.g., Epstein, 1987; Eysenck, 1986; Vaillant, 1984). Such concerns identify the need for further progress in validating DSM categories not only in relation to methods of assessment and treatment but also in terms of distinctive biopsychosocial origins. Enhanced utility of DSM-IV and its successors is generally regarded to hinge on expanded knowledge concerning the causes and premorbid indicators of the disorders that they classify (Cantwell, 1988b; Morphy, 1988; Quay, Routh, & Shapiro, 1987).

With specific respect to classifying disorders in young persons, D*SM-III* provided a substantial addition to its predecessors by adding several categories of "disorders usually first evident in infancy, childhood, or adolescence." As revised in *DSM-III-R*, these categories consist of developmental disorders (including mental retardation, pervasive developmental disorders, and specific developmental disorders); disruptive behavior disorders (including ADHD and conduct disorder); anxity disorders of childhood or adolescence; eating disorders; gender identity disorders; tic disorders; elimination disorders; speech disorders not elsewhere classified; and other disorders of infancy, childhood, or adolescence. Persons under age 18 may be assigned one or more of these age-specific categories or any of the adult syndrome diagnoses, as the nature of their disturbance appears to indicate.

The interrater agreements for these new child and adolescent categories were somewhat lower in the initial DSM-III field trials than were those achieved when evaluating adults, with kappa coefficients clustering around .60 for youths rather then the .70 for adults. Subsequently, however, perhaps as a result of clinicians becoming increasingly familiar with them, these new categories began to demonstrate reliabilities comparable to those found in diagnosis of adults (Quay, 1986; Rey, Plapp, & Stewart, 1989; Werry, Methven, Fitzpatrick, & Dixon, 1983). As in evaluations of adults, moreover, most categories of organic or psychotic disorder and such specific problems as conduct disorder, substance abuse, attention deficit disorder, and eating disorder have shown agreement coefficients above .70 among young people.

With respect to their validity, both the *DSM-III* child and adolescent categories and the adult categories appear to warrant guarded optimism. Considerable work remains to be done to tie these categories to discriminable ways of assessing and treating them and to distinctive biogenetic and psychosocial causes. As reviewed by Achenbach (1988), on the other hand, research already available supports the construct validity of many *DSM-III* syndromes in young people, including autism, conduct disorder, attention deficit disorder, and childhood depression.

Child clinicians, similarly to those concerned mainly with adults, have not been of one mind regarding the contribution of *DSM-III* and *DSM-III-R* to meeting the needs of their patients. Some have called *DSM-III* "a major advance" (Kazdin, 1983) and others "a step backward" (Rutter & Shaffer, 1980) with respect to classifying youthful disorder. Some emphasize the advantages of using *DSM-III* with young people, such as its definitional clarity and comprehensive coverage of developmental psychopathology (Hersen & Last, 1989; Mezzich & Mezzich, 1985), while others focus on the disadvantages of doing so, such as its inclusion of unreliable and as-yet-unvalidated diagnostic categories (Bemporad & Schwab, 1986; Tanguay, 1984).

Further research, particularly longitudinal studies on the emergence and course of psychological disorders, will have much to say about just how good *DSM-III-R* is or can be made. Information presently available would appear to indicate that *DSM-III-R* is (a) an imperfect system that will be shaped by additional data and new ideas into an improved *DSM-IV* and (b) a good system that constitutes a solid improvement over its predecessors and has achieved both reasonable scientific respectability and noteworthy clinical utility.

Theoretical Approaches

In theoretical approaches to classification, various disorders are identified not on the basis of their manifest symptoms, but instead according to inferred personality processes that are believed to give rise to particular disorders. As formulated primarily within the framework of psychodynamic conceptualizations of personality functioning, theoretically based classifications differentiate psychological disorders on the basis of such considerations as (a) the relative strengths and interrelationships of several inferred personality structures, most notably the id, the ego, and the superego; (b) the developmental status of these personality structures with respect to indications of immaturity, fixation points, and regression; (c) the specific kinds of internalized conflicts an individual appears to be experiencing; and (d) the kinds of psychological defenses with which the person is apparently trying to minimize anxiety flowing from these conflicts.

Classical examples in the psychoanalytic literature of this theoretical approach to classification include Freud's view of obsessional neurosis as constituting a fixation at the anal stage of psychosexual development and his distinction between neurosis and psychosis according to whether conflicts exist between the id and the ego (neurosis) or between the ego and the external world (psychosis) (Freud, 1913/1958, 1924/1961). A more contemporary example is Kernberg's (1977, 1978) delineation of borderline personality organization primarily in terms of inferences about identity diffusion and reliance on object-splitting as a defensive operation (see Chapter 5). Also noteworthy in this tradition have been the efforts of Vaillant (1977, 1986) to formulate differences among psychotic, characterological, and neurotic levels of psychopathology in terms of a developmental hierarchy of preferred ways of defending against anxiety.

Theoretical considerations were fairly prominent in the *DSM-II* that preceded *DSM-III* (American Psychiatric Association, 1968). For example, in *DSM-II*, phobic neurosis is defined in terms of "fears displaced to the phobic object or situation from some other object of which the patient is unaware" (p. 40). As a reflection of a shift in *DSM-III* from theoretical to neo-Kraepelinian classification, phobic neurosis is described without any reference to such defense mechanisms as displacement or to any unconscious aspects of the disorder (American Psychiatric Association, 1980, p. 225).

With specific respect to developmental psychopathology, theoretical approaches to classification had a staunch and extremely influential advocate in Anna Freud. She believed that traditional clinical–descriptive diagnostic categories are of little use in understanding and working with young persons and "increase rather than decrease the confusing aspects of the clinical picture" (Freud, 1965, p. 110). Freud urged clinicians to evaluate children and adolescents in terms of psychoanalytic conceptualizations of personality development, such as the normally expected progressions from primary to secondary thought processes and from the pleasure to the reality principle.

The only systematic effort to date to develop a theoretically based categorization of developmental psychopathology was reported in 1974 by the Group for the Advancement of Psychiatry (GAP). This GAP report distinguished among eight broad categories of disorders in children and adolescents: reactive disorders, developmental deviations, psychoneurotic disorders, personality disorders, psychotic disorders, psychophysiologic disorders, brain syndromes, and mental retardation. These categories are defined in psychodynamic terms that have much more in common with Anna Freud's approach than with the neo-Kraepelinian descriptions found in *DSM-III* and *DSM-III-R*. With respect to psychoneurotic disorders, for example, the GAP report states, "this category is reserved for those disorders based on unconscious conflicts over the handling of sexual and aggressive impulses which, though removed from awareness by the mechanism of repression, remain active and unresolved" (p. 57).

By focusing on personality functioning rather than on currently observable symptoms, theoretical approaches to classification can readily account for changing symptom patterns associated with a single condition, especially as these may occur during the developmental process. Similarly, by calling attention to underlying personality processes from which a disorder originates, theoretically based classification promotes treatment planning aimed at basic psychological problems rather than superficial manifestations of these problems. Clinicians operating with a sound theoretical approach to classifying psychopathology are thus unlikely to make such errors as treating a delinquent adolescent for a conduct disorder when his or her real problem consists of an underlying depressive disorder.

A price must be paid for these advantages of the theoretical approach, however. Whenever inference is added to observation, reliable classification becomes more difficult to achieve. The more levels of inference that are involved in arriving at a diagnosis, the more opportunities are created for diagnosticians to disagree. Likewise, the more that key differentiating criteria cannot be directly observed but must be supposed, as in the case of "object-splitting," the more difficult it becomes to formulate objective criteria for minimizing diagnostic disagreements. *DSM-II* and the GAP report both suffered from a lack of specific diagnostic criteria and specifiable assessment procedures. As a result, both systems demonstrated mediocre reliability, with coefficients for interrater agreement falling well below .70 for most categories of disorder (Beitchman, Dielman, Landis, Benson, & Kemp, 1978; Edelbrock & Costello, 1990).

Theoretically based classification may also generate treatment plans addressed exclusively to underlying personality processes at the expense of adequate attention to manifest behavioral difficulties. Suppose, for example, that an adolescent had become socially withdrawn as a consequence of underlying neurotic concerns about being exploited or rejected by other people. Psychotherapy focused on alleviating such unrealistic fears may prove insufficient to overcome this young person's withdrawal, especially if being isolated has become a habitual, self-reinforcing behavior pattern and if the adolescent lacks social skills for establishing good interpersonal relationships. To foster positive behavior change in such situations, therapy must go beyond resolving the underlying problems identified in a theoretical classification and must address such overt handicaps as habitually maladaptive behavior or inadequate social skills.

Despite the rich potential of theoretical approaches to classification for helping to explain and understand, as well as to describe, behavior, their psychometric shortcomings and inferential distance from observable phenomena seemed for many years to be the seeds of their undoing. No new major schemes or revisions came forward to improve or replace the GAP classification, and some current authors are beginning to refer to this approach only for its historical interest. At the same time, recent advances in personality assessment appear to be breathing new life into theoretically based classification by providing reliable psychological indices of previously unmeasured concepts.

Most notable in this regard has been the development of reliably scorable indices of Kernberg's object-splitting and other maladaptive interpersonal orientations that have proved successful in discriminating borderline personality disorder from other clinical conditions (Blatt & Lerner, 1983; Lerner & St. Peter, 1984; Stuart, Westen, Lohr, Benjamin, Becker, Vorus, & Silk, 1990). Additionally, Vaillant's notions of differentiating psychopathology according to preferred defenses has been operationalized in part in a Defense Mechanism Inventory that has been found to discriminate among adults and adolescents showing various patterns of symptom formation. For example, defenses that locate conflict outside the self, such as projection and displacement, are likely to be associated with such externalizing conditions as conduct disorder, whereas defenses that locate conflict within the self, such as introjections, are likely to be associated with such internalizing conditions as depressive disorder (Cramer, 1988; Noam & Recklitis, 1990).

These developments have so far been limited to specific theories and selected conditions, and they probably do not herald the emergence of comprehensive new classification schemes based on conceptual formulations. They are nevertheless heartening to psychodynamic theorists in demonstrating that carefully crafted and thoughtfully operationalized theoretical notions can contribute to empirically valid differentiations among, as well as enriched understanding of, psychopathological conditions.

Empirical Approaches

Whereas both clinical and theoretical approaches to classification originate with impressions, empirically derived classification of psychopathology begins with experimental procedures. Behavioral descriptions of disturbed persons rather than theories of personality functioning provide the starting point for empirical categorizations of disorder, and multivariate statistical techniques rather than clinical judgment are used to determine which of these behavioral descriptions cluster together and should be labeled as a type of disorder.

By avoiding clinicians' impressions of which symptom patterns cluster together and theorists' inferences about underlying processes, the multivariate statistical manipulation of descriptions of actual behavior has considerable potential for objectifying the diagnostic process and for generating categories of disorder that are relatively easy to agree on, validate, and communicate about. However, until fairly recently, some disadvantages of a strictly empirical approach have limited the realization of this potential.

With respect to reliability, empirical efforts to establish a consistent categorization of disorders were slowed by a plethora of measuring instruments and data sources to which this approach has been tied. Empirical classification has drawn on various combinations of case history information, behavioral observations, self-reports, and descriptions by peers, parents, teachers, and mental health professionals as the raw data to be cluster-analyzed. Because many different observational formats, checklists, rating scales, and questionnaires have been employed for this purpose, there was a time when the outcomes of empirically based efforts at classification fluctuated widely. Multivariate analyses of data from different sources yielded numerous categorizations of disorder that differed substantially among themselves in the number and nature of the categories they identified, and interrater reliabilities for even carefully developed categorizations of childhood disorder, while better than agreements for the GAP classification, lagged behind those achieved from *DSM-III* (Edelbrock & Achenbach, 1980; Morey, Skinner, & Blashfield, 1986; Quay, 1979).

As for validation, the content and predictive validity of empirically based classifications tend to be limited by the fact that nothing more can emerge from a multivariate analysis of behavioral descriptions than is covered adequately by the descriptions being analyzed. Hence, dramatic but infrequent conditions that would readily be identified and categorized in a clinical approach to classification may not emerge in a multivariate approach as a cluster of behaviors that should be labeled. For example, unless empirical studies are conducted in a specialized setting that includes a fair number of adolescents with schizophrenia or eating disorder, the behavioral dimensions that define these conditions will occur too infrequently to be identified as a distinct syndrome. As noted by Quay (1986), some noteworthy clinically derived disorders remain relatively unstudied by empiricists because of their low incidence in children (e.g., pervasive developmental disorder) or their very circumscribed nature (e.g., obsessive–compulsive disorder).

Regarding communication, multivariate classifiers have, in fact, traditionally focused on just a few broad dimensions of youthful behavior disorder, such as conduct disorder and anxiety–withdrawal disorder, in order to enhance diagnostic reliability and to establish validity in relation to differences in their origin, course, and treatment response. Practicing clinicians, however, are likely to require more than just a few categories in order to feel comfortable in diagnosing disturbed adolescents and formulating treatment plans for them.

Hence, the limited scope and specificity of most empirically derived classification schemes has prevented them from having much of an impact on the language with which mental health practitioners communicate. Largely because multivariate typologies have fallen short of denoting the range and variation of patterns of psychopathology seen in everyday work with disturbed adolescents, they have not yet entered very much into how clinicians think about and diagnose their patients (Skinner & Blashfield, 1982).

Accumulating data and modified perspectives have begun to change this situation by enhancing both the psychometric soundness and the clinical applicability of empirical classification. Despite their divergent sources, the findings from multivariate analyses are converging to identify at least seven clearly discriminable empirically derived syndromes in children and adolescents, which have different etiological and treatment response correlates: aggressive, anxious/depressed, attention problems, delinquent, schizoid, somatic complaints, and withdrawn (Achenbach, Conners, Quay, Verhulst, & Howell, 1989). At the same time, many influential empiricists who once were uncompromisingly critical of clinical approaches to classification are addressing similarities between multivariate and nosological syndromes, including counterparts of these empirical disorders in the *DSM-III-R* categories, respectively, of solitary aggressive conduct, dysthymia/overanxious, attention-deficit hyperactivity, group conduct, schizotypal personality, somatization, and avoidant disorders (Achenbach, 1988; Achenbach et al., 1989). These constructive efforts to build bridges between empirical and clinical approaches, in addition to reducing language barriers, are having salutary effects in both directions: Empirically derived categories of disorder are becoming more widely discussed and used by clinicians, and clinically derived categories are becoming increasingly refined by cluster-analytic methods.

Conclusion

With respect to reaping the potential benefits of classification, the clinical, theoretical, and empirical approaches each bring some advantages and some disadvantages to the process of formulating categories of disorder. None has as yet provided all of the answers. The most common theme in the history of efforts to improve the classification of psychological disorders has been a trade-off between precision and meaningfulness; typically, over the years, advances in one have been achieved at the expense of the other.

Nontheless, definite progress has been made, primarily as a result of the influence these divergent approaches have had on each other. Clinical classification as epitomized by *DSM-III-R* currently reflects a strong commitment to empirical demonstration of reliability and validity: Proponents of empirical classification are encouraging the formulation of typologies that clinicians can recognize and apply in their practices, and theoretical approaches have helped to inject into both clinical and empirical classification some recognition that there may be more to psychological disorder than immediately meets the eye.

Independently of one's preferred approach to classification, moreover, the soundness and utility of syndromes of psychological disorder are being enhanced by a shift from categorical to dimensional criteria for diagnosing them. When categorical criteria are used for making diagnoses, which has traditionally been the case, a person either meets the criteria for a diagnostic category, in which case he or she is given the diagnosis, or the person does not meet the criteria, in which case the diagnosis is not assigned. *DSM-III* was made somewhat flexible in this regard by the use of *polythetic* rather than *monothetic* criteria. This means that, instead of all of the criteria for a diagnosis having to be met before it is made, the presence of at least a certain number of a list of criteria is sufficient. For example, *DSM-III-R* lists 13 manifestations of conduct disorder, yet the presence of any 3 or more warrants diagnosing conduct disorder.

Being able to draw on selected symptoms of a disorder in diagnosing it, rather than having to document an entire list of symptoms, increases prospects for achieving reliable and valid classification. With respect to reliability, reducing the number of phenomena required to draw a conclusion reduces the number of opportunities there are for observers to disagree in drawing their conclusions. With respect to validity, being able to infer a disorder from various combinations of symptoms approximates the apparent reality that many conditions can present in various ways. Among depressed individuals, for example, some may be most notably dysphoric and anhedonic and others primarily pessimistic and self-critical.

Nevertheless, *DSM-III-R* remains a categorical classification scheme that cannot readily address real-world phenomena, which tend to be more or less similar to or different from each other, rather than completely so. As elaborated by numerous current nosologists, the next steps in enhancing diagnostic classification are likely to involve changes from categorical to dimensional statements. Instead of indicating whether a person does or does not have a specific condition, these dimensional statements will note the degree to which the person demonstrates the characteristics associated with various conditions. Criteria for a particular condition will then constitute a prototype, rather than a requirement, and patients will be assessed for the extent to which their difficulties resemble those associated with one or more prototypical conditions (Blashfield, Sprock, Haymaker, & Hodgin, 1989; Broughton, 1990; Cantor & Genero, 1986; McReynolds, 1989).

CATEGORIZING PSYCHOLOGICAL DISTURBANCE IN ADOLESCENCE

Beyond concerning themselves generally with the purposes and methods of classifying psychopathology, clinicians need to consider (a) whether specific disorders in adolescents are sufficiently stable and distinctive to be classified meaningfully and (b) whether traditional diagnostic categories, as embodied in *DSM-III-R*, are applicable to this age group. The first of these considerations would be moot were it not for the lingering mythical notion that adolescence is a turbulent, unpredictable time of life, in which transient developmental phenomena masquerade as psychological disturbances. If normative adolescent turmoil did in fact commonly produce symptoms of psychological disorder, then adolescent psychopathology might indeed be too fleeting and ill-defined to permit any systematic classification. However, compelling evidence to the contrary, as elaborated in Chapter 1, leaves little doubt that moderate or severe disturbances in adolescence are neither normative nor self-limiting and can and should be classified when they occur.

With respect to the application of diagnostic categories, the adolescent-turmoil notion has had the further unfortunate consequence of encouraging clinicians to avoid denotative terminology and to opt instead for such nonspecific diagnoses as transient situational disturbance. As specified in the 1968 *DSM-II*, transient situational disturbances constitute "an acute reaction to overwhelming environmental stress" occurring "in individuals without any apparent underlying mental disorders" and involving "symptoms that usually recede as the stress diminishes." These disturbances are divided into five age-related categories of "adjustment reaction" of infancy, childhood, adolescence, adult life, and later life.

As testimony to the popularity of assigning this kind of nonpathological diagnosis to adolescents prior to the advent of *DSM-III*, Weiner and Del Gaudio (1976) found in their community study mentioned in Chapter 1 that 27.1% of 1334 12- to 18-year-olds receiving psychiatric service were diagnosed as having a transient situational disorder. The frequency of such nonspecific diagnosis was even higher in a U.S. Department of Health and Human Services national survey of all persons under age 18 years, who were seen in psychiatric facilities in 1975. Among 160,036 10- to 14-year-old patients, 48.2% of those in outpatient facilities and 43.6% of those in inpatient units were classified as showing adjustment reaction of children and youth; among 149,033 15- to 17-year-olds, 37.6% of the outpatients and 25.4% of the inpatients were given this so-called diagnosis (Sowder, Burt, Rosenstein, & Milazzo-Sayre, 1981, pp. 50–51).

Follow-up studies have exposed the error of regarding such a large proportion of adolescents seen in mental health settings as being essentially without disorder and merely reacting transiently to acute environmental stress. When Weiner and Del Gaudio (1976) examined the frequency with which their patient population reappeared for psychiatric service in the 10 years following their initial evaluation, they found that those adolescents who had originally been diagnosed as having situational disorder were just as likely to seek further psychiatric care (51.9% of the group) as those who had initially been diagnosed as having a neurotic disorder (51.7% return rate) or a personality disorder (51.3% return rate). Moreover, those diagnosed as having a situational disorder averaged approximately the same number of subsequent psychiatric contacts during the follow-up period as those diagnosed as having a neurotic disorder or a personality disorder. Of the initial situational disorder group who received further care, 85% were subsequently given some diagnosis other than transient situational disturbances; 21.3% were even considered to have a schizophrenic disorder at some time in the 10 years following their initial evaluation.

These findings led Weiner and Del Gaudio (1976) to conclude that "situational disorder" was apparently being used to describe a substantial number of disturbed young persons who were in fact developing diagnosable psychpathology and qho were destined to suffer recurrent psychological distress. They accordingly cautioned clinicians to be wary of transient situational disturbance as a diagnosis for troubled adolescents, especially if paying homage in this way to the so-called normative turmoil notion of adolescence minimizes the seriousness of a young person's disorder and underestimates his or her need for treatment.

Data reported by Andreasen and Wasek (1980) bear further witness to the ill-advised use of the *DSM-II* category of transient situational disturbance to classify adolescents whose clinical history and course point to disorders that are more serious than acute, self-limiting reactions to environmental stress. These investigators reviewed the records of 199 adolescents seen in the psychiatric services of the University of Iowa Hospitals and given a *DSM-II* diagnosis of transient situational disturbance. Over 40% of these adolescents were admitted to the hospital following their initial evaluation, where two thirds of them remained for more than 2 weeks and almost one third remained for more than a month. Nearly 80% of the total group appeared to have been disturbed for more than 3 months at the time they were evaluated, and almost one half had apparently been having significant psychological problems for more than a year. Two thirds of these "situationally disordered" adolescents were taken into some form of treatment, and one quarter of those treated were given medication.

A randomly selected subset of these adolescents were reevaluated by

Andreasen and Hoenk (1982) 5 years after their initial diagnosis. Only 44% were considered to be psychiatrically well at that time, whereas 23% demonstrated diagnosable affective disorder, 19% were considered to have an antisocial personality disorder, and the rest gave evidence of a variety of other current or intervening disorders.

The import of these findings seems clear. Here was a group of psychologically disturbed adolescents, many of whom required hospitalization, many of whom had a long history of difficulties, most of whom needed treatment, and the majority of whom suffered disturbances in the subsequent 5 years. For many of these young persons, then, some disorder must have been present and classifiable other than the *DSM-II* category of transient situational disturbance, which was intended to identify an acute short-lived condition that remits in response to improved environmental circumstances.

Widespread dissatisfaction with transient situational disturbance as an available diagnosis led to its being eliminated from *DSM-III*, which retains a category of adjustment disorder but no longer specifies it in relation to different age groups. The *DSM-III* category of adjustment disorder is explicitly restricted to conditions that can be traced to an identifiable psychosocial stressor occurring no more than 3 months prior to onset, and it is to be used only when the person's disturbance does not meet criteria for any other condition. *DSM-III-R* specifies further that the presenting complaints must not have been in evidence for more than 6 months.

Although the DSM-III concept of adjustment disorder reduced problems of underdiagnosis associated with excessive use of the *DSM-II* category of transient situational disturbance, the last chapter of this story has not yet been written. In a study of the *DSM-III* diagnoses assigned in 100 randomly selected visits by adolescents (ages 13 to 17 years) to a general hospital psychiatric emergency service, Hillard, Slomowitz, and Levi (1987) found a 42% frequency of adjustment disorder. By contrast, 100 randomly chosen visits by adults to the same emergency service over the same period of time resulted in only a 13% frequency of adjustment disorder—this despite the facts that (a) just about as many of the adolescents (42%) as the adults (46%) making these emergency room visits were receiving some form of treatment at the time, and (b) the adolescent and adult patients in these samples were rated as having about equally urgent needs for intervention.

In another informative study, Mezzich and his colleagues examined the diagnoses given to more than 11,000 hospital and clinic patients seen over a 4-year period at the University of Pittsburgh Western Psychiatric Institute (Mezzich, Fabrega, Coffman, & Haley, 1989). Among those younger than age 18 years, 16.3% were diagnosed as having adjustment disorder, compared to 10.8% of those ages 18 to 59 years. There is no compelling reason to expect younger persons to be any more susceptible than older persons to an adjustment disorder. Hence, the age-group difference in these two contemporary studies, especially when the diagnosis of adjustment disorder is notably frequent in a group of adolescents who are currently receiving or judged to be urgently in need of treatment, suggest that underdiagnosis of young persons lingers on as an unfortunate legacy of the misbegotten notion of adolescent turmoil.

Turning to the general applicability of *DSM-III* categories to adolescent disturbances, positive findings were reported in a widely cited study by Strober, Green, and Carlson (1981). These investigators had two clinicians conduct independent evaluations of 95 12- to 17-year-old patients consecutively admitted to the UCLA Neuropsychiatric Institute. For only 5 of these adolescents did both clinicians find the presenting symptoms too vague or ambiguous to meet criteria for DSM-III diagnosis, in which case they classified them as "undiagnosed illness"; in 9 other instances, one of the clinicians came to this conclusion. Hence, 90 of the 95 adolescent patients in the study could be assigned a specific *DSM-III* diagnosis by at least one of the evaluators, and 81 were given a *DSM-III* diagnosis by both evaluators. The Strober et al. clinicians agreed in their diagnosis of 73 of the 95 patients, and their overall concordance yielded a kappa coefficient of .74. For most of the individual diagnostic categories the kappa coefficient was well above .70, and kappa fell below .60 only for anxiety disorders of childhood and adolescence and for "undiagnosed illness."

Other research has demonstrated adequate test–retest reliabilities for *DSM-III* diagnoses of adolescents. Edelbrock and his colleagues evaluated 85 14- to 18-year-old patients independently on two occasions, 2 to 3 weeks apart, using the Diagnostic Interview Schedule for Children (DISC). The DISC is a highly structured interview that covers a broad range of symptoms and behaviors and was designed specifically to diagnose youthful disorders according to *DSM-III* criteria. The DISC total symptom score showed a retest reliability of .81 among these adolescents. A cluster of behavior/conduct systems (including categories of anxiety, fears and phobias, obsessive-compulsive, schizoid/psychotic, and affective disorder) had a stability coefficient of .80 (Edelbrock, Costello, Dulcan, Kalas, & Conover, 1985).

Finally, with respect to the use of *DSM-III* in diagnosing adolescent disturbance, the Mezzich et al. (1989) data appear to confirm that clinicians can use these categories with young as well as older persons. Of the 1868 patients under age 18 years in their sample, 60.2% were diagnosed with one of the disorders usually first evident in infancy, childhood, or adolescence, which demonstrates the utility of having these categories available. For only 5.7% of the child and adolescent patient group was diagnosis deferred, and for just 2.1% was there no diagnosis made, compared to an 8.0% frequency of deferred diagnosis and a 2.9% frequency of no diagnosis in the adult patients. Hence, there was no age-related difference in the extent to which *DSM-III* lent itself to a diagnostic conclusion.

With respect to its development in general and in its applicability to young persons in particular, then, *DSM-III* appears to provide a reasonably precise and relevant basis for the diagnostic categorization of psychological disturbances in adolescence. On the other hand, most nosologists would agree that (a) no single approach to classifying developmental psychopathology has cornered the whole truth (see Achenbach, 1988; Cantwell, 1988a), and (b)

DSM-III-R still lacks specificity with respect to developmental issues of childhood and adolescence (see Schwab-Stone, 1989; Trad, 1989).

Accordingly, the chapters that follow are organized around a mix of traditional and behavioral categories. Chapters 3 through 6 concern categories of disorder that account for most of the psychopathological conditions observed in adolescents: schizophrenic disorders, affective disorders, borderline disorders, and anxiety disorders. Chapters 7 through 10 address problem behaviors that cut across these diagnostic categories and account for a large share of the reasons why adolescents are referred for psychological help: academic underachievement, delinquent behavior, suicidal behavior, and substance abuse. Chapter 11 concludes the book with a general discussion of guidelines for conducting psychotherapy with disturbed adolescents.

REFERENCES

Achenbach, T. M. (1982). Assessment and taxonomy of children's behavior disorders. In B. B. Lahey & A. E. Kazdin (Eds.), *Advances in clinical child psychology* (Vol. 5, pp. 1–38). New York: Plenum.

Achenbach, T. M. (1988). Integrating assessment and taxonomy. In M. Rutter, A. H. Tuma, & I. S. Lann (Eds.), *Assessment and diagnosis in child psychopathology* (pp. 300–343). New York: Guilford.

Achenbach, T. M., Conners, C. K., Quay, H. C., Verhulst, F. C., & Howell, C. T. (1989). Replication of empirically derived syndromes as a basis for taxonomy of child/adolescent psychopathology. *Journal of Abnormal Child Psychology, 17,* 299–323.

Adams, H. E., Doster, J. A., & Calhoun, K. S. (1977). A psychologically based system of response classification. In A. R. Ciminero, K. S. Calhoun, & H. E. Adams (Eds.), *Handbook of behavioral assessment* (pp. 47–78). New York: Wiley.

American Psychiatric Association (1968). *Diagnostic and statistical manual of mental disorders* (2nd ed.). Washington, DC: Author.

American Psychiatric Association (1980). *Diagnostic and statistical manual of mental disorders* (3rd ed.). Washington, DC: Author.

American Psychiatric Association (1987). *Diagnostic and statistical manual of mental disorders* (3rd ed., revised). Washington, DC: Author.

Andreasen, N. C., & Hoenk, P. R. (1982). The predictive value of adjustment disorders: A follow-up study. *American Journal of Psychiatry, 139,* 584–590.

Andreasen, N. C., & Wasek, P. (1980). Adjustment disorders in adolescents and adults. *Archives of General Psychiatry, 37,* 1166–1170.

Aviram, U., & Segal, S. P. (1973). Exclusion of the mentally ill. *Archives of General Psychiatry, 29,* 126–131.

Beitchman, J. H., Dielman, T. E., Landis, R., Benson, R. M., & Kemp, P. L. (1978). Reliability of the Group for the Advancement of Psychiatry diagnostic categories in child psychiatry. *Archives of General Psychiatry, 35,* 1461–1466.

Bemporad, J. R., & Schwab, M. E. (1986). The *DSM-III* and clinical child psychiatry.

In T. Millon & G. L. Klerman (Eds.), *Contemporary directions in psychopathology: Toward the* DSM-IV (pp. 135–150). New York: Guilford.

Blashfield, R. K., & Breen, M. J. (1989). Face validity of the *DSM-III-R* personality disorders. *American Journal of Psychiatry, 146,* 1575–1579.

Blashfield, R. K., Sprock, J., Haymaker, D., & Hodgin, J. (1989). The family resemblance hypothesis applied to psychiatric classification. *Journal of Nervous and Mental Disease, 177,* 492–497.

Blatt, S. J., & Lerner, H. D. (1983). The psychological assessment of object representation. *Journal of Personality Assessment, 47,* 7–28.

Broughton, R. (1990). The prototype concept in personality assessment. *Canadian Psychology, 31,* 26–37.

Bugental, J. F. T. (1978). *Psychotherapy and process: The fundamentals of an existentialist–humanistic approach.* New York: McGraw-Hill.

Cantor, N., & Genero, N. (1986). Psychiatric diagnosis and natural categorization. In T. Millon & G. L. Klerman (Eds.), *Contemporary directions in psychopathology: Toward the* DSM-IV (pp. 233–256). New York: Guilford.

Cantwell, D. P. (1988a). Classification of childhood and adolescent disorders. In C. J. Kestenbaum & D. T. Williams (Eds.), *Handbook of clinical assessment of children and adolescents* (pp. 3–30). New York: New York University Press.

Cantwell, D. P. (1988b). *DSM-III* studies. In M. Rutter, A. H. Tuma, & I. S. Lann (Eds.), *Assessment and diagnosis in child psychopathology* (pp. 3–36). New York: Guilford.

Chassin, L., Young, R. D., Presson, C. C., & Light, R. (1981). Self-concepts of institutionalized adolescents: A framework for conceptualizing labeling effects. *Journal of Abnormal Psychology, 90,* 143–151.

Costello, C. G. (1970). Classification and psychopathology. In C. G. Costello (Ed.), *Symptoms of psychopathology* (pp. 1–26). New York: Wiley.

Cramer, P. (1988). The Defense Mechanism Inventory: A review of research and discussion of the scales. *Journal of Personality Assessment, 52,* 142–164.

Edelbrock, C., & Achenbach, T. M. (1980). A typology of Child Behavior Profile patterns: Distribution and correlates for disturbed children aged 6–16. *Journal of Abnormal Child Psychology, 8,* 441–470.

Edelbrock, C., & Costello, A. J. (1990). Structured interviews for children and adolescents. In G. Goldstein & M. Hersen (Eds.), *Handbook of psychological assessment* (2nd ed., pp. 308–323). Elmsford, NY: Pergamon.

Edelbrock, C., Costello, A. J., Dulcan, M. K., Kalas, R., & Conover, N. C. (1985), Age differences in the reliability of the psychiatric interview of the child. *Child Development, 56,* 265–275.

Epstein, S. (1987). The relative value of theoretical and empirical approaches for establishing a psychological diagnostic system. *Journal of Personality Disorders, 1,* 100–109.

Eron, L. D., & Peterson, R. A. (1982). Abnormal behavior: Social approaches. *Annual Review of Psychology, 33,* 231–264.

Eysenck, H. J. (1986). A critique of contemporary classification and diagnosis. In T. Millon & G. L. Klerman (Eds.), *Contemporary direction in psychopathology: Toward the* DSM-IV (pp. 73–90). New York: Guilford.

Fernald, C. D., & Gettys, L. (1980). Diagnostic labels and perceptions of children's behavior. *Journal of Clinical Child Psychology, 9,* 229–233.

Fernald, C. D., Williams, R. A., & Droescher, S. D. (1985). Actions speak loud ... : Effects of diagnostic labels and child behavior on perceptions of children. *Professional Psychology, 16,* 648–660.

Freud, A. (1965). *Normality and pathology in childhood: Assessments of development.* New York: International Universities Press.

Freud, S. (1913/1958). The disposition to obsessional neurosis: A contribution to the problem of the choice of neurosis. *Standard edition* (Vol. 12, pp. 317–326). London: Hogarth.

Freud, S. (1924/1961). Neurosis and psychosis. *Standard edition* (Vol. 19, pp. 149–153). London: Hogarth.

Gibbs, M. S. (1982). Identification and classification of child psychopathology. In J. R. Lachenmeyer & M. S. Gibbs (Eds.), *Psychopathology in childhood* (pp. 5–29). New York: Gardner.

Goffman, E. (1963). *Stigma: Notes on the management of spoiled identity.* Englewood Cliffs, NJ: Prentice-Hall.

Goldfried, N. R., & Kent, R. N. (1972). Traditional vs. behavioral assessment: A comparison of methodological and theoretical assumptions. *Psychological Bulletin, 77,* 409–420.

Gove, W. R. (1982). The current status of the labelling theory of mental illness. In W. R. Gove (Ed.), *Deviance and mental illness* (pp. 273–300). Beverly Hills, CA: Sage.

Group for the Advancement of Psychiatry (1974). *Psychopathological disorders in childhood: Theoretical considerations and a proposed classification.* New York: Aronson.

Grove, W. M., Andreasen, N. C., McDonald-Scott, P., Keller, M. B., & Shapiro, R. W., (1981). Reliability studies of psychiatric diagnosis. *Archives of General Psychiatry, 38,* 408–413.

Halleck, S. L. (1971). *The politics of therapy.* New York: Science House.

Handlers, A., & Austin, K. (1980). Improving attitudes of high school students toward their handicapped peers. *Exceptional Children, 47,* 228–229.

Hemphill, L., & Siperstein, G. N. (1990). Conversational competence and peer response to mildly retarded children. *Journal of Educational Psychology, 82,* 128–134.

Hersen, M., & Last, C. G. (1989). Psychiatric diagnosis and behavioral assessment in children. In M. Last & C. G. Hersen (Eds.), *Handbook of child psychiatric diagnosis* (pp. 517–528). New York: Wiley.

Hillard, J. R., Slomowitz, M., & Levi, L. S. (1987). A retrospective study of adolescents' visits to a general hospital psychiatric emergency service. *American Journal of Psychiatry, 144,* 432–436.

Hobbs, N. (1975). *The futures of children: Categories, labels, and their consequences.* San Francisco: Jossey-Bass.

Joint Commission on the Mental Health of Children (1973). *Mental health: From infancy through adolescence.* New York: Harper & Row.

Jones, T. W., Sowell, V. M., Jones, J. K., & Butler, L. G. (1981). Changing children's perceptions of handicapped people. *Exceptional Children, 47,* 365-368.

Kazdin, A. E. (1983). Psychiatric diagnosis, dimensions of dysfunction, and child behavior therapy. *Behavior Therapy, 14,* 73-99.

Kernberg, O. (1977). The structural diagnosis of borderline personality organization. In P. Hartocollis (Ed.), *Borderline personality disorders* (pp. 87-122). New York: International Universities Press.

Kernberg, O. (1978). The diagnosis of borderline conditions in adolescence. In S. C. Feinstein & P. L. Giovacchini (Eds.), *Adolescent psychiatry* (Vol. 6, pp. 298-319). Chicago: University of Chicago Press.

Klerman, G. L. (1986). Historical perspectives on contemporary school of psychopathology. In T. Millon & G. L. Klerman (Eds.), *Contemporary directions in psychpathology: Toward the* DSM-IV (pp. 3-28). New York: Guilford.

Kraepelin, E. (1927). *Psychiatrie* (9th ed.). Leipzig, Germany: Barth.

Lerner, H. D., & St. Peter, S. (1984). Patterns of object relations in neurotic, borderline and schizophrenic patients. *Psychiatry, 47,* 77-92.

Magaro, P. A., Gripp, R., & McDowell, D. J. (1978). *The mental health industry.* New York: Wiley.

Maslow, A. H. (1962). *Toward a psychology of being.* Princeton, NJ: Van Nostrand Reinhold.

McReynolds, P. (1989). Diagnosis and clinical assessment: Current status and major issues. *Annual Review of Psychology, 40,* 83-108.

Medin, D. L. (1989). Concepts and conceptual structure. *American Psychologist, 44,* 1469-1481.

Mezzich, A. C., & Mezzich, J. E. (1985). Perceived suitability and usefulness of *DSM-III* vs. *DSM-II* in child psychopathology. *Journal of the American Academy of Child Psychiatry, 24,* 281- 285.

Mezzich, J. E., Fabrega, H., Coffman, G. A., & Haley, R. (1989). DSM-III disorders in a large sample of psychiatric patients: Frequency and specificity of diagnoses. *American Journal of Psychiatry, 146,* 212-219.

Morey, L. C. (1988). A psychometric analysis of the *DSM-III-R* personality disorder criteria. *Journal of Personality Disorders, 2,* 109-124.

Morey, L. C., Skinner, H. A., & Blashfield, R. K. (1986). Trends in the classification of abnormal behavior. In A. R. Ciminero, K. S. Calhoun, & H. E. Adams (Eds.), *Handbook of behavioral assessment* (2nd ed, pp. 47-75). New York: Wiley.

Morphy, M. A. (1988). DSM-III: An evaluation. In J. G. Howells (Ed.), *Modern perspectives in clinical psychiatry* (pp. 19-43). New York: Brunner/Mazel.

Noam, G. G., & Recklitis, C. J. (1990). The relationship between defenses and symptoms in adolescent psychopathology. *Journal of Personality Assessment, 54,* 311-327.

Perry, S., Frances, A., & Clarkin, J. F. (1990). *A DSM-III-R casebook of treatment selection.* New York: Brunner/Mazel.

Quay, H. C. (1979). Classification. In H. C. Quay & J. S. Werry (Eds.), *Psychopathological disorders of childhood* (2nd ed, pp. 1-42). New York: Wiley.

Quay, H. C. (1986). Classification. In H. C. Quay & J. S. Werry (Eds.), *Psychopathological disorders of childhood* (3rd ed.; pp. 1-34). New York: Wiley.

Quay, H. C., Routh, D. K., & Shapiro, S. K. (1987). Psychopathology of childhood: From description to validation. *Annual Review of Psychology, 38,* 491-532.

Rabkin, J. (1974). Public attitudes toward mental illness: A review of the literature. *Schizophrenia Bulletin, 10,* 9-33.

Reid, W. H. (1989). *The treatment of psychiatric disorders: Revised for the* DSM-III-R. New York: Brunner/Mazel.

Rey, J. M., Plapp, J. M., & Stewart, G. W. (1989). Reliability of psychiatric diagnosis in referred adolescents. *Journal of Child Psychology & Psychiatry, 30,* 879-888.

Robins, L. N. (1981). Critique of the labeling theory paradigm. In C. Eisdorfer, D. Cohen, A. Kleinman, & P. Maxim. (Eds.), *Models for clinical psychopathology* (pp. 43-52). New York: Spectrum.

Robins, L. N., & Helzer, J. E. (1986). Diagnosis and clinical assessment: The current state of psychiatric diagnosis. *Annual Review of Psychology, 37,* 409-432.

Rogers, C. R. (1961). *On becoming a person.* Boston: Houghton Mifflin.

Rosenhan, D. L. (1973). On being sane in insane places. *Science, 179,* 250-258.

Rothblum, E. D., Solomon, L. J., & Albee, G. W. (1986). A sociopolitical perspective of *DSM-III.* In T. Millon & G. L. Klerman (Eds.), *Contemporary directions in psychopathology: Toward the* DSM-IV (pp. 167-189). New York: Guilford.

Rutter, M., & Shaffer, D. (1980). *DSM-III.:*A step forward or back in terms of the classification of child psychiatric disorders? *Journal of the American Academy of Child Psychiatry, 19,* 371-394.

Sarbin, T. R., (1969). The scientific status of the mental illness metaphor. In S. Plog & R. Edgerton (Eds.), *Changing perspectives in mental illness.* New York: Holt, Rinehart and Winston.

Scheff, T. J. (1981). The labeling theory paradigm. In C. Eisdorfer, D. Cohen, A. Kleinman, & P. Maxim (Eds.), *Models for clinical psychopathology* (pp. 27-42). New York: Spectrum.

Scheff, T. J. (1984). *On being mentally ill: A sociological theory* (2nd ed.). Chicago: Aldine.

Schur, E. (1971). *Labeling deviant behavior.* New York: Harper.

Schwab-Stone, M. E. (1989). Diagnostic issues: *DSM-III* and *DSM-III-R.* In L. K. G. Hsu & M. Hersen (Eds.), *Recent developments in adolescent psychiatry* (pp. 31-49). New York: Wiley.

Silverman, I. (1983). *Pure types are rare: Myths and meanings of madness.* New York: Praeger.

Skinner, H. A., & Blashfield, R. K. (1982). Increasing the impact of cluster analysis research: The case of psychiatric classification. *Journal of Consulting and Clinical Psychology, 50,* 727-735.

Sowder, B., Burt, M., Rosenstein, M., & Milazzo-Sayre, L. (1981). *Use of psychiatric facilities by children and youth, United States, 1975.* Washington, DC: U.S. Department of Health and Human Services.

Spitzer, R. L., & Wilson, P. T. (1975). Nosology and the official psychiatric nomenclature. In A. M. Freedman, H. I. Kaplan, & B. J. Sadock (Eds.), *Comprehensive textbook of psychiatry* (2nd ed, pp. 826–845). Baltimore: Williams & Wilkins.

Sprock, J., & Blashfield, R. K. (1983). Classification and nosology. In M. Hersen, A. E. Kazdin, & A. S. Bellack (Eds.), *The clinical psychology handbook* (pp. 289–307). New York: Pergamon.

Strauss, J. S. (1979). Social and cultural influences on psychopathology. *Annual Review of Psychology, 30,* 397–415.

Strober, M., Green, J., & Carlson, G. (1981). Reliability of psychiatric diagnosis in hospitalized adolescents: Interrater reliability using DSM-III. *Archives of General Psychiatry, 38,* 141–145.

Stuart, J., Westen, D., Lohr, N., Benjamin, J., Becker, S., Vorus, N., & Silk, K. (1990). Object relations in borderlines, depressives, and normals: An examination of human responses on the Rorschach. *Journal of Personality Assessment, 55,* 296–318.

Szasz, T. S. (1963). *Law, liberty, and society.* New York: Macmillan.

Szasz, T. S. (1987). *Insanity: The idea and its consequences.* New York: Wiley.

Tanguay, P. E. (1984). Toward a new classification of serious psychopathology in children. *Journal of the American Academy of Child Psychiatry, 23,* 373–384.

Trad, P. V. (1989). A nosological approach to assessing childhood psychiatric disorders. In C. G. Last & M. Hersen (Eds.), *Handbook of child psychiatric diagnosis* (pp. 12–26). New York: Wiley.

Vaillant, G. E. (1977). *Adaptation to life.* Boston: Little, Brown.

Vaillant, G. E. (1984). A debate on *DSM-III*: The disadvantages of *DSM-III* outweigh its advantages. *American Journal of Psychiatry, 141,* 542–545.

Vaillant, G. E. (Ed.) (1986). *Empirical studies of ego mechanisms of defense.* Washington, DC: American Psychiatric Press.

Warner, R., Taylor, D., Powers, M., & Hyman, J. (1989). Acceptance of the mental illness label by psychotic patients: Effects on functioning. *American Journal of Orthopsychiatry, 59,* 398–409.

Weiner, I. B., & Del Gaudio, A. C. (1976). Psychopathology in adolescence: An epidemiological study. *Archives of General Psychiatry, 33,* 187–193.

Werry, J. S., Methven, R. J., Fitzpatrick, J., & Dixon, H. (1983). The interrater reliability of *DSM-III* in children. *Journal of Abnormal Child Psychology, 11,* 341–354.

Widiger, T. A., Frances, A., Spitzer, R. L., & Williams, J. (1988). The *DSM-III-R* personality disorders: An overview. *American Journal of Psychiatry, 145,* 786–795.

Wiens, A. N. (1990). Structured clinical interviews for adults. In G. Goldstein & M. Hersen (Eds.), *Handbook of psychological assessment* (2nd ed., pp. 324–341). Elmsford, NY: Pergamon.

Zubin, J. (1967). Classification of the behavior disorders. *Annual Review of Psychology, 18,* 373–406.

CHAPTER 3

Schizophrenic Disorders

Schizophrenia has traditionally been described as a disturbance beginning in the adolescent and early adult years. When Kraepelin (1896/1919) first applied the label *dementia praecox* to the variety of conditions that subsequently became designated as schizophrenic disorders, he observed that these disturbances typically first appear in adolescence or early adulthood. Bleuler (1911/1950), on introducing the term *schizophrenia* to the literature, noted that almost 40% of Kraepelin's large sample of dementia praecox patients had experienced onset of their disturbance before age 20 and more than 60% had done so before age 25, and he concluded that "the adolescent age period seems to offer a particular predisposition to this disease" (p. 340).

Clinical observations and research findings over the years have confirmed Bleuler's impression of greater vulnerability to schizophrenia in the early than in the later adult years (Lewis, 1989; Schulz & Koller, 1989). Subsequent data have also demonstrated an earlier onset in males than in females. Among 200 schizophrenic patients, Loranger (1984) found that 39% of the males, compared to 23% of the females, had experienced their first psychotic episode before age 20; a first episode before age 25 characterized 74% of the males and 49% of the females. Consistently with this difference, schizophrenic women tend to be older than schizophrenic men at the time of a first hospitalization for this disorder (Burack & Zigler, 1989), and other data indicate that women hospitalized with schizophrenia tend to have shorter hospital stays and fewer subsequent readmissions than men (Goldstein, 1988).

Whatever the origins of these sex differences, which have not yet been adequately explained, they do not derive from any greater vulnerability to schizophrenia among males than females. Schizophrenic disorders occur with equal frequency in both sexes (Helzer, 1986; Lewine, 1981).

Very few data have been published concerning the rate at which schizophrenia occurs in adolescents or is diagnosed among adolescent patients seen in mental health facilities. For the adult population age 18 or older, extensive community studies in the United States have established that schizophrenia has a 6-month prevalence of approximately 1% (Regier, Boyd, Burke, Rae, Myers, Kramer, Robins, George, Karno, & Locke, 1988). If the findings of Loranger and others are correct in suggesting that approximately one third of schizophrenic persons become disturbed before age 20, then schizophrenia may reasonably be expected to appear in 1 of every 300 adolescents. Lest a 0.33% rate seem negligible for clinical purposes, especially in comparison to the rate at which young persons become depressed or show conduct problems (see Chapters 4 and 8), it must be weighed against the fact that schizophrenia is a frequently chronic and potentially disabling disorder. The cost in wasted or diminished lives of persistent schizophrenic impairment, especially as a consequence of belated diagnosis or inadequate treatment, has established schizophrenia as a major public health problem.

Accordingly, mental health professionals must be alert to possible signs of schizophrenia in the young persons they evaluate, and most clinicians who work with adolescents are frequently engaged in evaluating or treating this disorder. The data in this regard are again much more extensive for adults than for adolescents. National mental information published in 1985 indicated that 38% of adult patients admitted to state and county mental hospitals are diagnosed as schizophrenic, as are 30% of those admitted to Veterans Administration inpatient psychiatric services, 25% of those admitted to psychiatric units of general hospitals, and 21% of patients entering private psychiatric hospitals (National Institute of Mental Health, 1985).

Although less comprehensive, available research reports on the frequency of schizophrenia among adolescent psychiatric patients are almost comparable, suggesting that schizophrenia is diagnosed in 25 to 30% of all adolescents admitted to public mental hospitals and in about 15% of those admitted to psychiatric units of general hospitals, and that about 15% of schizophrenic patients being treated in private psychiatric hospitals are under age 18 years (Rosenstein, Milazzo-Sayre, & Manderscheid, 1989; Strober, Green, & Carlson, 1981; Weiner & Del Gaudio, 1976). In addition to these instances of overt schizophrenia, many young persons who are destined to become schizophrenically disturbed as adults are likely to show prodromal signs of the disorder during their teenage years.

Although adolescents who are frankly schizophrenic usually pose little diagnostic difficulty, most young persons in the initial or mild stages of schizophrenic breakdown present a mixed clinical picture in which schizophrenic features are secondary, subtle, or submerged. Because accurate early diagnosis is necessary for effective early intervention, clinicians should be prepared to recognize indications of mild and incipient schizophrenia in young persons who do not present a definitive clinical picture of the disorder.

This chapter addresses the psychopathology, differential diagnosis, and treatment of schizophrenia in adolescence. The first three sections of this chapter review patterns of psychological impairment associated with adolescent schizophrenia, the origins and course of this disturbance, and predictors of its outcome; the next three sections address clinical aspects of diagnosing and treating schizophrenic adolescents.

PSYCHOLOGICAL IMPAIRMENT IN ADOLESCENT SCHIZOPHRENIA

Schizophrenia can be usefully conceptualized as a breakdown in certain cognitive, interpersonal, and integrative psychological functions. For example, normally functioning individuals are generally able to think coherently, logically, and at appropriate levels of abstraction; to perceive themselves and their experiences realistically; to establish and maintain rewarding relationships with other people; and to exert adaptive control over their thoughts, feelings, and impulses. In contrast, schizophrenic disturbance is characterized by *disordered thinking, inaccurate perception, interpersonal ineptness,* and *inadequate controls.* As elaborated in an extensive literature, the clinical phenomena of schizophrenia derive in large part from these four impairments of psychological functioning (see Arieti, 1974; Bellak, Hurvich, & Gediman, 1973; Neale & Oltmanns, 1980; Strauss & Carpenter, 1981; Weiner, 1966).

Although schizophrenic adolescents have been observed to display the full range of personality impairments that generally define schizophrenic disturbance, clinical and research findings demonstrate some distinctive profiles of impairment in adolescent schizophrenia. In addition, the developmental status of schizophrenic adolescents has distinctive implications for their presenting symptomatology and the likelihood of chronicity and paranoid features.

Profiles of Impairment

Because of differences related to maturation, some indices of schizophrenic impairment tend to occur more frequently in nonschizophrenic adolescents than in nonschizophrenic adults and must therefore be interpreted more conservatively for younger persons. Other pathological indicators are equally infrequent in nonschizophrenic adolescents and adults and hence are just as significant for schizophrenia in younger as in older persons. These differences vary, as follows, among the four main dimensions of schizophrenic impairment.

Disordered Thinking

The most prominent feature of schizophrenic disturbance is incoherent, illogical, or inappropriately abstract thinking. *Incoherent thinking* involves a cognitive disruption in which thoughts do not flow continuously from one to the next (*dissociation*), or the ideational process stops flowing entirely (*blocking* or *poverty of thought*). *Illogical thinking* consists of unreasonable conclusions drawn from minimal or circumstantial evidence and provides the basis for delusions and ideas of reference. *Inappropriately abstract thinking* is reflected either in an overly concrete, excessively literal manner of forming concepts and using words or in a preoccupation with numbers, shapes, philosophical ideas, and other complex concepts at the expense of adequate attention to mundane, practical aspects of experience (see Andreasen, 1979a; Chapman & Chapman, 1973; George & Neufeld, 1985; Harrow & Quinlan, 1985).

With respect to distinctive profiles of impairment, some important age-related differences in thinking derive from the fact that cognitive development is still taking place during adolescence. Most teenagers have not yet attained adult capacities for reasoning and concept formation, and they often deal with the uncertainty they feel in trying to understand and integrate many new kinds of experiences by latching on to premature or abstract conclusions (see Kimmel & Weiner, 1985, Chapter 3).

Because they frequently strain to feel sure about what is happening to and around them, even in the absence of solid support for their convictions and in the face of contradictory facts, adolescents are normatively more likely than adults to engage in circumstantial reasoning and to become overly involved with abstract concerns. The clearest evidence in this regard comes from research with the Rorschach test, which provides some well-defined and reliably scored indices of circumstantiality and abstract preoccupation. Noteworthy among large-scale Rorschach studies yielding data on normative patterns of adolescent thinking are assessments by Ames, Metraux, and Walker (1971), by Rychlak and O'Leary (1965), and by Exner and Weiner (1982). Also relevant are studies comparing schizophrenic adolescent patients, disturbed but nonschizophrenic adolescent patients, and nonpatient adolescents, conducted by Silverman, Lapkin, and Rosenbaum (1962) and by Weiner and Exner (1978).

The nonpatient adolescents in these studies gave a frequency of circumstantially reasoned and overly abstract Rorschach responses that would suggest disordered thinking if given by adults. Disturbed adolescents, especially those known to be schizophrenic, were even more likely to produce such responses than the nonpatient youngsters. Hence, circumstantial reasoning and preoccupation with abstractions help to identify schizophrenia in adolescents, but they must be more prominent than in adults to justify diagnosing the disorder.

These age-related differences in circumstantiality and abstract preoccupation diminish with maturation, however, and they usually disappear by late adolescence. Research with various psychodiagnostic instruments indicates that the normative elevations in indices of these aspects of thought disorder found in 12- to 16-year-olds are not displayed by older teenagers (Bilett, Jones, & Whitaker, 1982). Hence, the allowances that should be made in evaluating adolescents for disordered thinking should by limited to those under 17 years of age. In clinical work with young persons ages 17 years and older, adult standards should be applied in the assessment of all aspects of disordered thinking.

Likewise, adolescents of all ages ordinarily think as coherently as adults, and there is no convincing evidence that dissociation and blocking are any more likely to occur in nonschizophrenic adolescents than they are in nonschizophrenic adults. Whereas 12- to 16-year-old nonpatients in the Exner and Weiner study were 3 to 4 times more likely than adults to give responses indicating illogical reasoning, they were *less* likely than adults to give responses indicating dissociation. Thus incoherent thinking reflected in dissociation and blocking is equally suggestive of schizophrenia in adolescents and adults.

Inaccurate Perception

The perceptual distortions that characterize schizophrenic disturbance are reflected primarily in unusual sensory experiences and poor judgment. Persons with impaired capacity to assess themselves and external events realistically tend to develop strange views of the world, behave in peculiar ways, and harbor far-fetched ideas about themselves and the world around them. Being out of touch with reality makes it difficult for them to anticipate the consequences of their actions and to comprehend the actions of others. Impaired perceptual accuracy also provides the context in which hallucinations and distorted body imagery are likely to appear (see Assad & Shapiro, 1986; Cutting & Dunne, 1989).

Adolescents are as capable as adults of perceiving objects and events accurately. Although young people are often criticized by adults for showing "poor judgment," the basis for such criticism is typically to be found in adolescent inexperience or misinformation—or perhaps adult intolerance—rather than in any loss of contact with reality. Evidence from Rorschach research on reality-testing capacities is definitive in this regard. The previously mentioned studies reveal that adolescents at all ages demonstrate a high level of perceptual accuracy and an excellent capacity to recognize and endorse conventional modes of response. Young people give the same frequency of accurately perceived and conventional responses on the Rorschach as adults. Accordingly, indications of distorted perception, as manifest in unrealistic judgments and strange behavior, have as serious implications for schizophrenia in adolescents as they do in adults.

Interpersonal Ineptness

Good interpersonal relationships require certain social skills and some interest in approaching and being close to others. Schizophrenic persons frequently display both poor social skills and withdrawal from human interactions. With respect to social skills, schizophrenics' disordered thinking and inaccurate perception often prevent them from sending and receiving clear social messages and from dealing effectively with interpersonal problem situations. They are especially prone to misjudge the feelings, motives, and actions of others, which leads them to behave in ways that other persons find embarrassing, insensitive, inappropriate, presumptuous, tendentious, or in some other way objectionable. These manifestations of their poor social skills make it difficult for schizophrenic persons to make or keep friends even when they try, and schizophrenic persons are consistently found to interact with others less frequently and to have fewer close and confiding relationships than nonschizophrenics, including persons with other forms of psychological disorder (Erickson, Beiser, Iacono, Fleming, & Lin, 1989; Holzman, 1988; Wallace, 1984).

The withdrawal of schizophrenics may be either physical or emotional. Those who withdraw physically become loners, preferring solitary activity in both their work and recreation and avoiding situations that might bring them into close contact with others. Those who withdraw emotionally may actually seek out and enjoy crowds of people, particularly when they are all sharing some interest, as at a concert or baseball game. Such public events sometimes help schizophrenics preserve the fiction that they are meaningfully involved with other persons. In fact, however, withdrawn schizophrenics remain alone in the crowd, their isolation from others emotional rather than physical. Even when mingling with other persons, they hold themselves at a psychological distance by keeping their thoughts and feelings to themselves and interacting only on a formal, impersonal level (see Burnham, Gladstone, & Gibson, 1969).

Adolescents are still learning social skills and typically lack the interpersonal competence and self-assurance of mature adults. Nevertheless, research in developmental psychology documents that nothing about adolescence itself prevents young persons from maintaining close ties with their parents and siblings and from seeking and sustaining rewarding relationships with their peers (see Kimmel & Weiner, 1985, Chapters 5 & 6). In the normative Rorschach studies, moreover, young persons are rarely found to exclude human content or impressions of human activities from their responses, nor are they inclined to distort their impressions of human interactions. This indicates that the withdrawal from, disinterest in, and incapacity for social relationships suggested by such exclusions and distortions on the Rorschach are not generally characteristic of adolescent behavior.

Hence, evidence of physical or emotional withdrawal from others has the same implications for possible schizophrenia in adolescents as it does in adults. For some schizophrenic youngsters in whom a quiet, retiring, over-controlled behavioral style conceals difficulties they are having in thinking clearly and perceiving reality accurately, an inability to engage in meaningful relationships with parents and/or peers may even be the primary or sole manifest clue to their disturbance.

Inadequate Controls

Schizophrenic individuals are frequently unable to prevent anxiety-provoking and socially unacceptable ideas from occupying their minds. Uncontrollable aggressive and sexual fantasies and frightening anticipations of dreadful future events may make the schizophrenic's existence a waking nightmare. Consequently, schizophrenics at all ages are subject to severe bouts of anxiety and self-disgust, and they sometimes have difficulty distinguishing between their dreams and waking reality.

Schizophrenic persons also commonly have difficulty integrating their thoughts and feelings. Consequently, they are likely to experience and express affects that are inappropriate to their actual situation, and they may fall prey to such frequently observed symptoms of schizophrenia as emotional blunting and anhedonia. Additionally, schizophrenic persons may be unable to prevent their aggressive and sexual ideas from being directly expressed in their behaviors. They may then erupt into sudden outbursts of violence against themselves or others or into inappropriate or assaultive sexual advances (Tardiff & Sweillam, 1980).

Adolescents usually have the same capacity as adults to control their emotions and their actions. To be sure, adolescent immaturity sometimes produces fluctuating emotional states or impulsive decision making that obscure these basic capacities. Nevertheless, there is no evidence to indicate that nondisturbed adolescents are any more inclined than adults to lose control over aggressive and sexual impulses or to display clearly inappropriate emotional responses. For this reason, loss of self-control and inappropriate affective displays can have serious implications for possible schizophrenia in adolescents (Delga, Heinssen, Fritsch, Goodrich, & Yates, 1989; Inamdar, Lewis, & Siomopoulos, 1982). Likewise, adolescents who show flat emotions or who giggle or weep for no apparent reason are displaying unusual behavior with pathological implications.

On the other hand, many young persons have not yet attained mature control of their thinking. More so than adults, adolescents are prone to be-coming consciously aware of disturbing thoughts and images involving aggressive and sexual themes. The normative Rorschach data confirm that weakened ide-ational control may be less significant for schizophrenic impairment in ado-lescents than in adults. From 15 to 20% of the Rorschach re-sponses given by nonpatient adolescents involve such content themes as blood, guts, death, decay, destruction, and sex. Moreover, the average frequency of blatant sexual and aggressive content in Rorschach responses has been found not to differ among schizophrenic and nonschizophrenic adolescents.

To summarize, these similarities and differences involve the same types of impairment that define adult schizophrenia—disordered thinking, inaccurate perception, interpersonal ineptness, and inadequate controls. However, par-ticularly in its early or mild stages, schizophrenia tends to produce some distinctive patterns of impairment in the younger age group. On the one hand, dissociation, blocking, distorted perceptions, social withdrawal, strange or uncontrolled behavior, and inappropriate affective displays are equally sug-gestive of schizophrenic disturbance in adolescents and adults. On the other hand, circumstantial reasoning, preoccupation with abstractions, and con-scious awareness of blatant sexual and aggressive imagery have a somewhat broader range of normality in adolescents than in adults and must be more prominently in evidence in the younger than the older age group to identify schizophrenic disorder.

Clinicians also need to recognize that neither adult nor adolescent schizophrenics will necessarily manifest all of the defining characteristics of this disorder, nor is any of these functioning impairments unique to schizo-phrenia. Numerous clinical and research reports have confirmed the view of Mosher and Gunderson (1973) that "no one deficit characterizes *all* schizophrenics or is found *only* in schizophrenics" (p. 20). Indices of disor-dered thinking are not uncommon in patients with an affective disorder; poor reality testing characterizes many conditions in which people become psychotically incapacitated, including organic and drug-induced psychoses; social withdrawal occurs in shy, schizoid individuals; and poor self-control and inappropriate emotionality are seen, respectively, in instances of impul-sive or antisocial personality disorder and of depressive or histrionic disorder (see Andreasen, 1979b, 1988; Harrow, Grossman, Silverstein, & Meltzer, 1982; Millon, 1981; Oltmanns, Murphy, Berenbaum, & Dunlop, 1985).

Furthermore, each of the phenomena associated with schizophrenia can appear briefly in otherwise normal persons at times of stress, and no single characteristic of schizophrenia is by itself sufficient for conclusive identification of the disorder. However, when several of the kinds of functioning impairments described in this section occur together and persist for any length of time, especially when disordered thinking is prominent among them, the presence of schizophrenia is usually indicated.

Presenting Symptomatology

Adolescents are less likely than adults to have achieved a stable personality style, and they are more likely than adults to vary from one occasion to the next in how they react to situations and how they prefer to cope with problems (see Kimmel & Weiner, 1985, Chapter 8). For this reason, schizophrenic adolescents, especially in an early stage of the disorder, tend less frequently than adults to display an unequivocal symptom picture. Clinical studies of schizophrenic adolescents indicate that no more than 30 to 40% initially show clear indications of a schizophrenic disorder. The rest present a mixed symptom picture in which features of schizophrenia are secondary to or even obscured by other kinds of problems or complaints (Feinstein & Miller, 1979; Hudgens, 1974, Chapter 7; Masterson, 1967, Chapter 5).

Two kinds of mixed symptomatology are particularly likely to herald emerging schizophrenia in young persons. In one kind, the adolescent shows some signs of schizophrenia but presents primarily depressive complaints, including loss of interest in people, withdrawal from previously enjoyed activities, feelings of hopelessness, and thoughts about suicide. In the other kind, schizophrenic features are overshadowed by antisocial personality characteristics, such as alienation from the family, aggressive interactions with peers, and delinquent conduct. The clinician's alertness to schizophrenia may frequently be tested by apparently depressed adolescents who are apathetic and emotionally unresponsive and by apparently antisocial adolescents who manifest poor impulse control and shallow interpersonal relatedness. Differential diagnosis of schizophrenia in young people can also be challenging in cases of schizoid youngsters who are socially withdrawn and manic adolescents who display disordered thinking.

The diagnosis of schizophrenia in such cases must often be tentative and perhaps specified as "incipient" or "mild." Yet it is these incipient or mild stages of a developing schizophrenic disturbance that most call for expert clinical judgment. Inexperienced observers usually identify schizophrenia when it has become unequivocally full-blown, and by then the most opportune time for effective intervention will have passed. Hence, whatever their reluctance to rely on less than conclusive data, clinicians should attune themselves to early and subtle signs of schizophrenia in their adolescent patients and label these signs as such when they appear. To guide this effort, special note should be taken of the *persistence of the schizophrenic features*, the *extent of normative adolescent concerns*, and the *prominence of formal manifestations of disturbance.*

Persistence of the Schizophrenic Features

The longer the schizophrenic features in a mixed clinical picture persist, the more likely it becomes that the adolescent is experiencing a schizophrenic disorder. This likelihood increases when the schizophrenic features remain evident after other kinds of presenting complaints have become less noticeable, as in the case of a young person who is no longer depressed but is still not thinking clearly.

Persistence of the schizophrenic features has long been regarded as the most reliable guideline for differential diagnosis of this disorder in young persons (Masterson, 1967; Spotnitz, 1961). Unfortunately, however, the moment when persistent schizophrenic features become conclusive for the diagnosis varies considerably from one person to the next, and waiting for this moment to arrive can delay effective treatment planning. This is especially likely to be the case when adolescents with apparent manic disorder display signs of disordered thinking. Although features of thought disorder are more likely to persist and less likely to diminish over time in schizophrenia than in mania, this difference tends not to appear in young first-admission patients until they have recovered sufficiently to be discharged from the hospital (Grove & Andreasen, 1985; Harrow, Grossman, Silverstein, Meltzer, & Kettering, 1986; Harrow & Marengo, 1986). For differential diagnosis to assist in formulating initial therapeutic strategies in such cases, the symptom-persistence criterion must give way to the other two criteria, both of which invoke currently available information.

Extent of Normative Adolescent Concerns

The symptoms of troubled but nonschizophrenic adolescents are usually colored by such common adolescent concerns as adapting to bodily changes in early adolescence, attaining autonomy and gaining social skills in middle adolescence, and arriving at a sense of personal identity in late adolescence. Although the presence of such normative concerns cannot rule out the possibility of emerging schizophrenic disorder, their absence increases its likelihood.

Disturbed adolescents who are becoming schizophrenic are more likely than their peers to manifest an inability or reluctance to grapple with the developmental tasks of adolescence. Sometimes they remain strikingly immature in their attitudes, interests, and social relationships. In other cases they attempt to skirt the usual problems of adolescence by prematurely embracing adult perspectives and pursuits and thereby cloaking themselves in pseudomaturity.

Immature adolescents typically seek to maintain the kinds of chumship relationships that characterize the preadolescent years. As their peers become interested in broadening their circle of friends and beginning to date, they gravitate to younger playmates who have no such interests. This failure to keep pace in developing normal social relationships is usually accompanied by immature fantasies and a generally childish demeanor and life-style.

A 15-year-old boy, an urbanite who had never ridden a horse, indicated that his future plans were "to go to college and become a rodeo rider." A 15-year-old girl, asked what she liked to do after school, replied, "I go out and play." Both statements resemble what one would expect from an 8- or 9-year-old.

Pseudomature adolescents who are seeking to circumvent the developmental tasks of adolescence tend to present a facade of calm, serious, and mannerly behavior that makes a good impression on adults and seldom suggests psychological difficulties to untrained observers. Such pseudomature boys and girls are responsible and conscientious, discuss world events and the behavior of their peers from their parents' or teachers' point of view, and begin as early as age 12 or 13 years to identify themselves as adults.

A 15-year-old boy, an only child, attributed his being constantly teased by his classmates to "how unruly young people are today." He referred to his parents' social engagements as, "We had some of our friends over yesterday." Although his measured IQ was 90 and he had hardly ever engaged in any activity other than in the company of his parents, except for attending school, a number of people who had discussed his peer-group difficulties with him— principal, guidance counselor, minister—had consistently introduced their written record of the discussion with such statements as, "this bright, alert, clean-cut young man discussed the situation with me in a very open, sensible, and mature manner."

As in this example, the uneven psychosocial development of pseudomature adolescents is usually exposed by evidence of poor peer relationships. Their seemingly mature interests and comfortable interactions with adults exist at the expense of engagement in age-appropriate activities and friendships, and their adult frames of reference lead more often to their being excluded from than welcomed into teenage social groups.

Prominence of Formal Manifestations of Disturbance

Available data, derived largely from psychodiagnostic research, indicate a direct relationship between the prominence of formal manifestations of disturbance and the likelihood of schizophrenia in adolescent youngsters. *Formal* manifestations of disturbance refer to *how* a person is saying something that is peculiar or inappropriate; *content* manifestations refer to *what* the person is saying. As already noted, for example, schizophrenic and nonschizophrenic adolescents produce similar amounts of "unhealthy" content on the Rorschach but differ significantly in how frequently they display formal Rorschach indices of disordered thinking. Studies with various other clinical instruments, as well, have fostered a long and sound tradition emphasizing the diagnostic importance of distinguishing between formal and content aspects of psychological test data. Generally speaking, inferences based solely on the verbal content of adolescents' test protocols are likely to exaggerate the degree of psychopathology present, whereas the formal aspects of adolescents' thought processes support accurate estimates of their personality strengths and weaknesses.

The distinction between formal and content manifestations of disturbance applies to interview data, as well as to psychological test data. Adolescents who describe bizarre fantasies, strange dreams, or unusual preoccupations may be experiencing a schizophrenic disturbance; the likelihood of schizophrenia increases to the extent that such experiences are recounted in a blocked, dissociated, or circumstantial manner that demonstrates formal thought disorder.

For example, an adolescent who says, "I don't have time to do my homework because I'm busy figuring out when the world will come to an end" is exhibiting an unusual preoccupation that constitutes a content manifestation of disturbance; however, the content in this instance is expressed in a clear and comprehensible manner. By contrast, a 17-year-old boy who said, "I don't ever want to get married, because I don't have the physicalness for sexuality" was expressing himself in an odd and stilted manner, indicative of formal thinking disturbance. Although such content and formal manifestations of disturbance both help to identify schizophrenia, the probability of emerging schizophrenia in a disturbed adolescent increases in direct relation to the prominence of formal, as opposed to content, manifestations of the disorder.

Chronicity and Paranoid Status

Schizophrenic individuals differ considerably in the symptoms they manifest and in the course of their disorder. Indeed, one of the oldest and most consistent findings in clinical and research studies of schizophrenic patients has been how variable they are (Houlihan, 1977; Shakow, 1979; Strauss & Docherty, 1979). Much of this variability is accounted for by two broad dimensions of schizophrenic disorder—*chronicity* and *paranoid status*.

Chronicity

Traditions differ with respect to whether schizophrenia is considered basically a chronic or an acute condition. Bleuler (1911/1950) originally said that he had "never released a schizophrenic in whom I could not still see distinct signs of the disease" (p. 256), and this view has been captured in the clinical lore that "Once a schizophrenic, always a schizophrenic." As elaborated by Kety (1980), contemporary belief is widespread that schizophrenia is always a lifetime disturbance and that, even during periods of partial remission, when they may not be psychotically impaired, people who have had schizophrenic breakdowns remain schizophrenic.

In support of this belief, researchers have identified persistent features of schizophrenic impairment, especially disordered thinking, following apparent recovery from a disabling episode of disturbance (Exner, 1986; Grove & Andreasen, 1985; Marengo & Harrow, 1987). In the Marengo and Harrow study, young adult schizophrenics (average age 23 years) were assessed 2 and 4 years following their discharge after a hospitalization averaging 4 months' duration. Of these patients, 40% showed persistent thought-disorder symptoms at both reassessments, and another 37% demonstrated disordered thinking on either the first or the second follow-up evaluation. Speaking generally to psychological adjustment on the basis of a detailed review of long-term follow-up studies of schizophrenia, McGlashan (1988, p. 527) concludes, "Schizophrenia is a chronic disease, frequently disabling for a lifetime."

Adolf Meyer (1907/1948), on the other hand, disagreed with Bleuler by asserting that dementia praecox can occur as an acute reaction to environmental stress without having any necessarily chronic features. Each of these conflicting perspectives has been supported by clinical and research findings, which can be cited for either the Meyerian or the Bleulerian point of view. In fact, Bleuler's son Manfred concluded that 25% of all schizophrenics recover completely and remain recovered without relapse, after he followed 208 schizophrenic patients until their deaths or for at least 20 years after they initially had been hospitalized under his care (M. Bleuler, 1978, 1988). Consistent with this report, 23% of the patients studied by Marengo and Harrow were not thought disordered at either the 2-year or the 4-year follow-up. In all of the studies cited by McGlashan to demonstrate overall persistence of impaired functioning in schizophrenic patients, there are subgroups of 20 to 25% of schizophrenic individuals who do not show any such persistence and are considered recovered.

Zubin (1986) has even suggested in this regard that schizophrenia is always an acute disorder, at least initially. What persists in schizophrenia, he says, is not disorder but a vulnerability to episodic breakdown. With adequate treatment and some relief from environmental duress, according to Zubin, schizophrenic patients will recover and not experience relapse. Whereas the traditional model views schizophrenics as sick persons who are intermittently well, Zubin's "vulnerability" model views them as healthy persons who have intermittent episodes of disorder. When chronicity does appear, in the form of persistent or recurrent breakdown, it stems from inordinate stress or such factors as the labeling, hospitalization, and family criticism that schizophrenics must often endure. Some supporting evidence for this view indicates that chronically impaired social functioning and relapse in hospitalized psychiatric patients following discharge may indeed have less to do with the nature of their diagnosed condition than with their subsequent psychosocial experiences (Pogue-Geile & Harrow, 1987; Summers & Hersch, 1983). In one study of 88 adolescents discharged from a state mental hospital, for example, being able to remain out of the hospital over the next 6 months was related not so much to the type and severity of their disorder as to whether they had returned to school and were living with at least one biological parent (Bloom & Hopewell, 1982).

These different perspectives on the nature of schizophrenia pose questions that can be resolved only by further advances in theory and research. In the meantime, however, the acute–chronic distinction is important to pursue for clinical purposes, because the chronicity of a disorder has implications for its severity, its response to treatment, and its probable outcome. The more chronic the disorder is, the less favorably it will respond to efforts at intervention and the more likely it will be to eventuate in long-term disability; the less chronic it is, the better the prospects are for a positive treatment response and a good outcome. Because these differences between relatively chronic and relatively acute schizophrenia do not become apparent until some future time, they do not contribute to differential diagnosis and treatment planning in the present. However, three other characteristics associated with chronicity can be observed and utilized in a present status evaluation.

First, chronicity in schizophrenia can be assessed from the balance between positive and negative symptoms in the clinical picture. *Positive symptoms* involve the *presence* of behaviors or functions that do not ordinarily occur in normally functioning individuals; in schizophrenia, these consist of such dramatic and readily apparent manifestations of the disorder as markedly dissociated or illogical thinking, repetitively bizarre or disorganized actions, and prominent delusions or hallucinations. *Negative symptoms* involve the loss or *absence* of normal behaviors or functions, as reflected in such manifestations as impoverished thought, blunted affect, and social withdrawal. Positive and negative symptoms occur independently of each other, and most schizophrenics are likely to display both, in some proportion. With respect to clinical course, a predominance of negative symptoms correlates significantly with such features of chronicity as refractoriness to treatment and persistently serious incapacitation (Andreasen & Ohlsen, 1982; Docherty, Schnur, & Harvey, 1988; Guelfi, Faustman, & Csernansky, 1989; Lenzenweger, Dworkin, & Wethington, 1989; Walker, Harvey, & Perlman, 1988).

This distinction between positive and negative symptoms in schizophrenia can also help in differentiating schizophrenic from manic disorder. Emerging evidence indicates that schizophrenic patients display more prominent negative thought disorder than manic patients, whereas the disordered thinking seen in many manic patients tends to be limited to positive symptoms (Andreasen & Grove, 1986; Harrow & Marengo, 1986).

Second, with respect to chronicity, approximately 20-35% of diagnosed schizophrenics show evidence of brain abnormalities, including ventricular enlargement, cerebral atrophy, disturbed cerebral metabolism, visual–motor and visual–spatial deficits, and neurological "soft" signs. Most of these schizophrenics are likely also to show a predominance of negative symptoms, a minimal response to psychotherapy and pharmacotherapy, and a chronic course (Goetz & Van Kammen, 1986; Green & Walker, 1985; Levin, Yurgelun-Todd, & Craft, 1989; Meltzer, 1987).

Third, those schizophrenics who are destined to suffer relatively disabling and persistent disorder in the future, and who are relatively likely to manifest negative symptoms and indications of neuropathology in the present, are also likely to have a past history of interpersonal and school- or work-related adjustment difficulties (Keefe, Mohs, Losonczy, & Davidson, 1989). The present interpersonal life of schizophrenics with a preponderance of negative symptoms is also likely to be characterized by limited and dysfunctional social networks (Buchanan, Kirkpatrick, Heinrichs, & Carpenter, 1990; Hamilton, Ponzoha, Cutler, & Wiegel, 1989).

Accordingly, the current clinical evaluation of chronicity in schizophrenic individuals should address the nature and severity of their symptoms, their neurological status, and their premorbid history. The more psychologically incapacitated they are, the more prominently they manifest negative symptoms, the more evidence they give of brain dysfunction, and the poorer their premorbid history, the more chronically disturbed they are likely to be.

Tendencies toward chronicity are also likely to be reflected in patterns of insidious onset and symptom *tolerance*. Slow deterioration of a person's psychological functioning over a period of months or even years, in the absence of any clearly precipitating events, points toward the emergence of relatively chronic disorder, as do lack of concern about the schizophrenic features of one's behavior and minimal awareness that one's problems derive from such impairments.

By contrast, relatively acute schizophrenic disorder comprises mildly incapacitating and primarily positive symptoms occurring in the absence of neuropathological indicators and without a prior history of marked adjustment difficulties. Typically, the prior behavior of acutely schizophrenic individuals has been unremarkable, at least in the eyes of untrained observers, and their disturbance has emerged suddenly, to the surprise of their family and friends. The breakdown has typically followed on the heels of clearly precipitating events, and the person is usually aware of and worried about the unusual nature of his or her symptoms ("I don't know what's wrong with me; I just can't seem to think straight anymore and I end up doing all kinds of stupid things").

Paranoid Status

As described and documented in an extensive literature, paranoia consists of certain distinctive ways of looking at and thinking about one's world. *Paranoid* individuals tend to be alert and vigilant people who scan their surroundings carefully. However, because they are also inclined to be rigid, inflexible, and narrow minded, they typically find ways to fit whatever they sense or perceive into their previously held beliefs. Rare are the occasions when they consider changing their minds or altering their points of view. Paranoid persons see their environment as a hostile and dangerous place, and they consequently deal with people and events in a cautious and suspicious manner. They mistrust the motives of others and fear being exploited or victimized by circumstances. Consequently, they hold themselves aloof, shunning close involvement in group activities and keeping a formal distance in their social relationships. They would rather reflect on their experience than reveal themselves in words or deeds, and they prefer keeping their own counsel to sharing their thoughts and feelings with others. Because they constantly feel a need to protect their integrity and self-esteem, they tend to be pompous and self-righteous individuals who criticize others freely and blame external circumstances for their difficulties and shortfalls (see Akhtar, 1990; Magaro, 1980; Meissner, 1978; Millon, 1981, Chapter 13; Shapiro, 1965, Chapter 3).

The combination of these cognitive styles and attitudinal sets with schizophrenic impairments of thinking and reality testing produces such dramatic symptoms of paranoid schizophrenia as delusions of persecution ("I'm on a list to be killed"), delusions of grandeur ("I have superhuman eyesight and earsight"), and hallucinations with persecutory or grandiose overtones ("The voices keep saying terrible things will happen to me"; "I've been told I'll become a saint"). Such symptoms appearing in a schizophrenic person point to active presence of a paranoid form of the disorder. Schizophrenic individuals who display the attitudes and orientations associated with paranoia but are not currently manifesting obvious paranoid symptoms can reasonably be expected to develop such symptoms if their condition persists or worsens.

Although exceptions occur, paranoia is much more often a potential rather than an already established feature of schizophrenic episodes in adolescence. Paranoid forms of schizophrenia have a later onset than nonparanoid forms and rarely appear before age 20 (Lewine, 1980; Zigler & Levine, 1981). Developmental perspectives provide two plausible explanations for this age difference. First, the complexity and specificity of a paranoid orientation probably require a degree of cognitive maturation that most people do not achieve until adulthood. For example, the rigidity and inflexibility that are so central to the maintenance of a paranoid style seldom characterize young persons, who are much less likely than adults to have become set in their ways.

Second, the relatively late onset of paranoid forms of schizophrenia may relate to evidence that paranoid schizophrenics demonstrate greater social competence than nonparanoid schizophrenics prior to becoming disturbed and remain less functionally impaired during episodes of disorder (Burack & Zigler, 1989; Zigler & Glick, 1986). Having better coping resources, persons who are destined to develop paranoid schizophrenia may be less vulnerable to breakdown and more resilient in the face of stress than those who develop nonparanoid schizophrenia, and hence they may adapt for a longer period of time before becoming overtly disturbed. Nonparanoid schizophrenics, being less resilient and having fewer coping resources, are prone to earlier breakdown, which would account for the lower frequency of paranoid status among schizophrenics with adolescent as opposed to adult onset of disorder.

ORIGINS OF SCHIZOPHRENIA

Current knowledge strongly suggests that schizophrenia is caused by an interacting combination of genetic and experiential factors. According to the widely endorsed diathesis-stress theory of how schizophrenia originates, constitutional characteristics dispose certain individuals to develop this disorder, and stressful life experiences foster the emergence of the disorder in persons who are constitutionally vulnerable to it. Studies of how and when schizophrenic breakdown occurs have also identified some typical precursors of its initial appearance. Familiarity with these causative factors and prodromal patterns can help clinicians judge the future likelihood of schizophrenia in young persons who have not yet begun to manifest clear signs of the disorder.

Genetic Factors

Schizophrenia runs in families, which means that the more closely two persons are related, the more likely they are to be concordant for the disorder. Compared to its approximately 1% prevalence in the general population, the frequency of schizophrenia increases to approximately 10% in persons who have a schizophrenic sibling or nonidentical twin, to 10 to 15% in persons with a schizophrenic parent, to over 35% in persons born to two schizophrenic parents, and to over 50% among identical twins of schizophrenics (Eaves, 1988; Kendler & Robinette, 1983; McGue & Gottesman, 1989). In one illustrative study, Kendler, Gruenberg, and Tsuang (1985) found an 18-times-greater frequency of schizophrenia in 723 first-degree relatives of schizophrenic patients than in 1,056 first-degree relatives of matched surgical controls. On the basis of such data, the *heritability* of schizophrenia (i.e., the proportion of the variability in susceptibility that can be attributed to genetic factors) has been calculated as ranging from 0.68 to 0.76—which makes schizophrenia more heritable than such medical conditions as hypertension and coronary heart disease and almost as heritable as diabetes mellitus (Kendler, 1983; McGuffin, Farmer, Gottesman, Murray, & Reveley, 1984).

Some theorists have attributed the familial incidence of schizophrenia to the similar learning environment experienced by siblings and twins and to the likelihood that schizophrenic parents will rear their offspring in a detached and disorganized manner (e.g., Lidz & Fleck, 1985). However, research findings of several kinds cast doubt on any strictly environmental explanation.

In the first place, siblings often experience different environments, and the kinds of experiences that are particularly influential in shaping dimensions of personality tend not to be jointly experienced by family members. Moreover, the existing similarities among siblings result mainly from shared heredity rather than from a shared family environment (Daniel & Plomin, 1985; Goldsmith, 1983; Plomin, 1989). Second, identical twins are only slightly more likely than nonidentical twins to be treated similarly by their parents, which makes it difficult to account in environmental terms for their much greater concordance for schizophrenia (Ainslie, Olmstead, & O'Loughlin, 1987; Lytton, 1977). Third, identical twins who are reared apart in completely different environments are just as highly concordant for schizophrenia as identical twins reared in the same household (Farber, 1981, Chapter 6; Kessler, 1980).

Fourth, among children placed for adoption early in life, those whose biological mothers have a history of schizophrenia are much more likely to develop schizophrenia themselves than adopted-away children born to psychologically healthy parents. Correspondingly, adoptees who become schizophrenic are much more likely than nonschizophrenic adoptees to have schizophrenic persons among their biological relatives but not among their adoptive relatives (Kessler, 1980; Kety, 1988; Lowing, Mirsky, & Pereira, 1983).

Family studies point to a neurointegrative defect as the probable inherited characteristic that creates a constitutional vulnerability to becoming schizophrenic. Long before they become psychologically disturbed, children who are at risk for becoming schizophrenic by virtue of having a schizophrenic parent are more likely than their peers to show neuromotor abnormalities and delayed perceptual–motor development; deficits on tasks involving attention, perception, and information processing; and a heightened sensitivity to aversive stimulation, combined with generally low tolerance for stress (Asarnow, 1988; Nuechterlein, 1986). These indications of neurointegrative defect appear in only a small subgroup of high-risk children (Marcus, Hans, Mednick, Schulsinger, & Michelson, 1985), but this may well be an especially vulnerable group of young persons who become the 10 to 15% among offspring of a schizophrenic parent who develop the disorder.

Experiential Factors

The role of experiential as well as genetic factors in the development of schizophrenic disorder is apparent from the fact that about half of the identical twins of schizophrenics and more than 60% of children born to two schizophrenic parents do *not* become schizophrenic. This means that the life experiences of people with similar or identical genes have a bearing on which of them develop schizophrenia. Moreover, the incidence of serious psychopathology in adopted-away children born to schizophrenic mothers increases when there is psychological disturbance in their adoptive family as well. Accumulating evidence suggests that the highest rates of schizophrenia are associated with exposure to both genetic risk (i.e., a schizophrenic parent) and a disturbed child-rearing environment, whereas being reared in a psychologically healthy adoptive family appears to be a protective factor that reduces the likelihood of at-risk children becoming schizophrenic (Asarnow, 1988).

Life events contributing to susceptibility to schizophrenia have been theorized to include a variety of developmental experiences that interfere with forming a firm sense of reality, learning to think clearly, and becoming comfortable with close interpersonal relationships (see Goldstein, 1987a; Shapiro, 1981, Chapters 7–9). Research into these possibilities has identified two patterns of disturbed family communication that appear to contribute particularly to children's learning schizophrenic ways of adapting to their world: (a) deviant communication style and (b) negative affective style.

The first pattern involves a deviant communication style, in which parents express themselves in unclear and confusing language, often lose track of what they are saying, tend to avoid direct eye contact, and seldom seem truly engaged in an interpersonal exchange. Parents who communicate in this way leave their children feeling puzzled about what is being said to them, uncertain what to think, and unsure whether their parents are really listening to them. The more deviant the parental communication in a family, the more likely the children in that family are to develop a schizophrenic disorder (Doane, West, Goldstein, Rodnick, & Jones, 1981; Goldstein, 1987b; Sass, Gunderson, Singer, & Wynne, 1984).

The other pattern involves an affective style in which parents' messages to their children convey a negative emotional tone of hostility, criticism, intrusiveness (presuming to know what the adolescent is thinking or feeling), and guilt induction ("You're causing our family a lot of trouble"). Like deviant forms of communication, this kind of negative tone is relatively likely to have characterized the family experience of schizophrenic individuals while they were growing up, prior to their becoming seriously disturbed. Furthermore, the degree to which the families of schizophrenic individuals continue to communicate with them in these negative ways predicts more severe impairment, a relatively unfavorable response to treatment, and a greater likelihood of relapse following recovery from an initial schizophrenic episode (Asarnow, Goldstein, & Ben-Meir, 1988; Doane, Falloon, Goldstein, & Mintz, 1985; Leff & Vaughn, 1985; Lukoff, Snyder, Ventura, & Nuechterlein, 1984; Vaughn, 1989).

The Diathesis–Stress Theory

Research findings suggest that both a genetically transmitted neurointegrative defect and disturbed patterns of family communication contribute to schizophrenic disorder. Yet most people with a family history of schizophrenia do not develop the disorder, and the kinds of deviant family interaction that are associated with schizophrenia in some cases produce either no disorder or different disorders in other cases. These facts have led to the emergence of the *diathesis–stress theory*, according to which certain constitutional and experiential factors are both necessary for schizophrenia to emerge, but neither is sufficient by itself (see Asarnow & Goldstein, 1986; Mirsky & Duncan, 1986; Sameroff, Seifer, Zax, & Barocas, 1987; Walker, Downey, & Bergman, 1989).

This theory presumes an additive interaction between constitution and environment in determining whether a person will become schizophrenic. The stronger the genetic disposition to the disorder, the more likely it is to occur in the context of even minimal psychosocial stress. The milder the disposition, on the other hand, the more family disorganization and other environmental pressures the person can withstand without becoming schizophrenic (Gottesman & Bertelsen, 1989; Pogue-Geile & Harrow, 1987; Zubin & Spring, 1977).

Studies of schizophrenic patients reveal that stressful life events often cluster in a 3- to 4-week period preceding an overt schizophrenic episode (Dohrenwend & Egri, 1981; Lukoff et al., 1984; Ventura, Nuechterlein, Lukoff, & Hardesty, 1989). Often, these stressful events involve changed circumstances or surroundings that have removed the person from a familiar environment or set of expectations and placed him or her in a new location, among new people, or under new guidelines for what constitutes appropriate behavior.

Two such events often faced by late adolescents are going away to college and entering military service, both of which are commonly implicated in psychological breakdown. However, neither these particular events nor other stressful events of being in a new situation are specific to the precipitation of schizophrenia. Depending on their dispositions and coping skills, people differ in how they respond to the same kinds of life stresses. It is among those who are specifically vulnerable to schizophrenia, and whose vulnerability partly consists of low stress tolerance and limited coping capacity, that stressful events are likely to produce a schizophrenic breakdown.

Prodromal Patterns

Retrospective studies examining the life history of adult schizophrenics and longitudinal studies of children at risk for schizophrenia have confirmed the classic view of Arieti (1974, pp. 103-107) regarding two probable precursors of schizophrenia: a *schizoid* personality pattern marked by shy, sensitive, and seclusive behavior, and a *stormy* personality pattern marked by restless, aggressive, and antisocial behavior. This research has also revealed some interesting sex differences in these prodromal patterns.

The Schizoid Pattern

In a seminal study of preschizophrenic behavior, Bower, Shellhamer, and Daly (1960) reviewed the high school records and interviewed the teachers of 19- to 26-year-old hospitalized schizophrenic men and a comparison group of their classmates. They found a strong relationship between withdrawn behavior in adolescence and schizophrenia in early adulthood. More than half of the future schizophrenics in their sample, compared to fewer than 10% of the comparison group, were described as having shown little interest in social relations and group activities as high school students.

In a related study, designed to sample high school behavior without having to rely on teachers' recollections, Barthell and Holmes (1968) used the number of times that a graduating senior's pictures appeared in the high school yearbook as an index of his or her participation in peer-group activities. Adult schizophrenics were found to have had significantly fewer year-book pictures than a comparison group of their classmates. Other studies of this kind, together with direct evaluations of adolescent children of schizo-phrenic parents, consistently reveal a relatively high incidence of social isolation, weak friendship patterns, and underinvolvement in peer-group activities among preschizophrenic adolescents (Goldstein & Jones, 1977; Lewine, Watt, Prentky, & Fryer, 1980; Silberman & Tassone, 1985).

The Stormy Pattern

In a 30-year follow-up study of 524 child-guidance-clinic patients initially seen at a median age of 13 years, Robins (1966) found that more than half of those who became schizophrenic as adults had been prominently negativistic and antisocial as young people. Robins and others have found further that the predictive significance of antisocial behavior in stormy adolescents varies with the direction it takes. Antisocial children and adolescents who act selfishly and aggressively at home and toward their family and friends are relatively likely to become schizophrenic later on. Those who direct their aggression primarily toward strangers, authority figures, and community establishments, on the other hand, are more likely to become antisocial than schizophrenic as adults (Nameche, Waring, & Ricks, 1964; Watt & Lubensky, 1976).

Sex Differences

Evidence of schizoid behavior as a schizophrenic precursor in some studies and of stormy behavior in other studies reflects in part an apparent sex difference in developmental paths to schizophrenia. Life history research indicates that preschizophrenic girls tend to be quieter, more passive, less mature, and more socially introverted than other girls during their elementary school years. Later, in junior and senior high school, they become less passive but grow even more noticeably withdrawn. Preschizophrenic boys show few differences from other boys as children, but as adolescents they become noticeably unpleasant, disagreeable, and defiant (Glish, Erlenmeyer-Kimling, & Watt, 1982; John, Mednick, & Schulsinger, 1982; Kendler, Gruenberg, & Strauss, 1982; Wallace, 1984).

Hence, although either reclusiveness or aggressiveness during adolescence may herald schizophrenia, the former in females and the latter in males is especially likely to be predictive. On the other hand, no more than half of the schizophrenic subjects in these research studies showed either pattern as adolescents, which means that the possibility of subsequent schizophrenia cannot be ruled out just because neither kind of precursor has appeared.

PROGNOSIS IN ADOLESCENT SCHIZOPHRENIA

The earlier in life a serious psychological disorder begins, the more likely it is to persist. In general, then, schizophrenia appearing in adolescence has a less favorable outcome than adult-onset schizophrenia. Nevertheless, the circumstances and characteristics that predict outcome in schizophrenia are essentially the same at all ages.

General Outcome

Numerous follow-up studies of adolescents who have been hospitalized for schizophrenia indicate that approximately 25% recover, 25% improve but suffer lingering symptoms or occasional relapses, and the remaining 50% make little or no progress and require continuing residential care. Schizophrenic adults who enter a hospital are equally likely to recover, but more of them (about 50%) achieve at least partial remission and fewer (only 25%) remain permanently hospitalized or socially incapacitated (Shore, 1986; Weiner, 1980).

Although they document the seriousness of schizophrenic disorder, these outcome data are not entirely grim. They indicate that one half of the adolescent and three quarters of the adult schizophrenics who are admitted to a hospital can be expected to show improvement and be discharged. Reports from individual hospitals indicate that, in many cases, even long-term schizophrenic patients may recover sufficiently to resume their premorbid level of educational or occupational functioning (Helzer, Kendell, & Brockington, 1983; Huber, Gross, Schuttler, & Linz, 1980; McGlashan, 1984). Schizophrenic adolescents who can be treated on an outpatient basis, without having to be hospitalized, probably have better prospects for improvement and recovery than those who become inpatients. Unfortunately, there are no reliable data concerning the long-term course and future adaptation of nonhospitalized schizophrenic adolescents or adults. However, there is evidence to indicate that schizophrenic persons who have never been hospitalized are less likely to require inpatient treatment in the future than those who have already had at least one admission to a residential facility (Engelhardt, Rosen, Feldman, Engelhardt, & Cohen, 1982).

Specific Predictive Factors

The probable outcome of schizophrenia varies with certain aspects of (a) when the disturbance begins, (b) how it begins, (c) what the schizophrenic person's initial symptoms look like as well as the person's, (d) premorbid history, (e) family context, and (f) response to treatment. These specific predictive factors, as reviewed in detail by McGlashan (1988), are about equally applicable to schizophrenic adolescents and adults. Some additional considerations concerning young persons need also to be noted, however.

Age of Onset

Consistent with the general trend already noted, the older a person is when schizophrenic disturbance first appears, the better the prospects for his or her recovery. Conversely, the earlier in adolescence a young person becomes overtly schizophrenic, the more likely he or she is to suffer persistent or recurrent psychological impairment. In this vein, follow-up data indicate that schizophrenics who enter a hospital at age 15 to 19 years are twice as likely to become chronically hospitalized as those who are initially hospitalized at age 20 to 29 years, and both of these groups fare less well in later life than schizophrenics who are not initially hospitalized until after age 30 years (Kris, Schiff, & McLaughlin, 1971; Pollack, Levenstein, & Klein, 1968).

Nature of Onset

Generally speaking, better prospects for recovery may be expected for adolescents in whom schizophrenic breakdown occurs fairly suddenly, in response to identifiable precipitating events, than for those in whom onset occurs gradually in the absence of apparent stressful circumstances. This prognostic distinction between abrupt and insidious onset is consistent with the discussion earlier in this chapter regarding chronicity in schizophrenic disorder. In specific clinical terms, the shorter the time between the first signs of psychological difficulty and a full-blown schizophrenic breakdown, the shorter the duration of schizophrenic symptoms prior to a hospital admission, and the higher the level of life stresses prior to breakdown, the better are the young person's chances for recovery (Harder, Gift, Strauss, Ritzler, & Kokes, 1981; Helzer et al., 1983; Westermeyer & Harrow, 1984).

Initial Symptom Picture

Schizophrenic adolescents who present with confusion, distress, and exaggerated moods are generally more likely to improve or recover than those who appear unperturbed and display blunted affect. The significance of this difference in presenting symptoms is related to the symptom-tolerance criterion for identifying relatively chronic schizophrenic disorder, and it also reflects the fact that a predominance of negative over positive symptoms in the initial picture calls for a guarded prognosis. In addition, considerable evidence suggests that paranoid schizophrenia will have a more favorable outcome than nonparanoid forms of the disorder (Kendler, Gruenberg, & Tsuang, 1984; Zigler & Glick, 1984). The relatively favorable prognosis for paranoid schizophrenics is associated with their typical age at onset (older than in nonparanoid schizophrenics) and premorbid history (less disordered than among nonparanoid schizophrenics).

Some researchers have questioned whether affective symptoms in young, first-admission schizophrenic patients predict outcome (Westermeyer & Harrow, 1984); others report that only manic features in schizophrenic patients— not depressive features—are likely to predict an episodic rather than a chronic course (Clayton, 1982; Cloninger, Marton, Guze, & Clayton, 1985). Hence, the clinical use of exaggerated moods as a clue to favorable prognosis in schizophrenia should probably give greater weight to elevated than to depressed affect. This qualification notwithstanding, the prognostic significance of an affective component is supported by findings that patients who meet *DSM-III* criteria for schizoaffective disorder have a better outcome than *DSM-III* schizophrenics, but not as favorable a prognosis as patients with affective disorder (Harrow & Grossman, 1984; Samson, Simpson, & Tsuang, 1988).

Premorbid History

A premorbid history of good school and social adjustment improves a schizophrenic adolescent's prospects for recovery. A history of school failure and interpersonal difficulties prior to the onset of schizophrenia, on the other hand, increases the likelihood of persistent disorder (Roff & Knight, 1978; Shea, Hafner, Quast, & Hetler, 1978). Premorbid adjustment has been found to predict outcome among chronic as well as acutely disturbed schizophrenics, and, beginning in late adolescence, the person's ability to function on the job, as well as in school, becomes an important element of the history (Fenton & McGlashan, 1987; Kay & Lindenmayer, 1987).

In some circumstances, the premorbid history may provide better predictors of outcome in schizophrenia than a present status evaluation. That is to say, emotional and interpersonal features of schizophrenics' past behavior may contain more reliable clues to their probable future course than the current nature and severity of their symptoms. For the best possible prediction of outcome, then, clinicians should undertake a careful longitudinal assessment of a schizophrenic adolescent's symptoms, school performance, work history, and social functioning.

Family Context

Schizophrenic adolescents with schizophrenic relatives tend to have a less favorable prognosis than those whose family pathology, if any, is limited to nonschizophrenic disorders (Roff, 1974). This finding probably reflects some combination of the genetic loading for schizophrenia in families who manifest the disorder and the manner in which schizophrenic relatives often perpetuate the disorder in a young person by failing to provide an understanding and supportive environment. In clinical assessments of prognosis, special attention should be paid to the family support system. The same kinds of parental expression of negative attitudes and hostile affect that have been identified in the premorbid experience of youthful schizophrenics have been found to contribute to an unfavorable long-term course. Among schizophrenics discharged from hospital care, family environment is a better predictor of rehospitalization than the patient's clinical status, and the reception that schizophrenics receive from their family when they return home from the hospital may prove to be the best single predictor of whether they will suffer relapse (Spiegel & Wissler, 1986; Vaughn, Snyder, Jones, Freeman, & Falloon, 1984).

Response to Treatment

Schizophrenic adolescents who become meaningfully engaged with their therapist upon the inception of a treatment program and who show an early positive response are more likely to achieve long-term improvement than those who remain uninvolved and appear unaffected during the initial stage of treatment. This does not preclude an eventually successful treatment following an extended period of time needed to overcome a disturbed youngster's barriers to being touched psychologically; on the average, however, an initial lack of response calls for a guarded prognosis.

An early positive treatment response is an especially favorable indicator when there are no obstacles to sustaining the treatment program. Youthful schizophrenics who are able to complete a planned course of residential care have better long-term prospects for recovery than those who, for some reason, leave the hospital prematurely. Likewise, adequate arrangements for continuing outpatient care following discharge improve the outlook for maintaining and building on treatment gains among hospitalized adolescents (Blotcky, Dimpero, & Gossett, 1984; Gossett, Barnhart, Lewis, & Phillips, 1977).

Two other findings are important to note in concluding this section. First, no sex differences have been found in the long-term outcome of schizophrenic disorder (Loyd, Simpson, & Tsuang, 1985). It may be that the tendency of males to become schizophrenic at an earlier age than females (suggesting a better prognosis for females) and for males to develop paranoid forms of schizophrenia more frequently than females (suggesting a better prognosis for males) offset each other, thus canceling out any differences in recovery between them.

Second, the relative strength of predictive factors in the outcome of schizophrenia may vary over time. McGlashan (1986) examined 163 schizophrenic patients at three different intervals following their admission to a hospital: 0–9 years, 10–19 years, and 20 years or more. During the first decade following schizophrenic breakdown, aspects of premorbid functioning were found to be the best predictors of outcome. Family functioning emerged as the most reliable predictor of how these patients were doing during the second decade, and family genetics had the most bearing on their adjustment in the third decade and beyond.

CLINICAL CLUES TO ADOLESCENT SCHIZOPHRENIA

The nature of the functioning impairments and the presenting picture in adolescent schizophrenia identify to a large extent the clinical data necessary to evaluate its presence in the individual case. Certain specific aspects of the *clinical history, interview behavior,* and *psychological test performance* of young persons can provide additional helpful clues to schizophrenic impairments in thinking, reality testing, interpersonal relatedness, and self-control. Although none of the indicators discussed in this section is conclusive for or exclusively related to schizophrenia, each contributed to an accurate differential diagnosis in initially equivocal cases involving mixed symptomatology.

Clinical History

Clinicians concerned that a disturbed adolescent may have an underlying or incipient schizophrenic disorder should attend carefully in the clinical history to (a) evidence of deficient peer-group relationships, (b) indications of bizarre or peculiar actions and ideas, (c) any family history of schizophrenia, and (d) reports of previous behavior disturbances or developmental deviation.

Peer-Group Relationships

The importance of peer-group relationships in evaluating possible schizophrenia in a disturbed adolescent cannot be overemphasized. As noted earlier, there are some schizophrenic young persons whose disordered thinking and inaccurate perceptions remain concealed by virtue of the fact that they rarely communicate or interact with other people. Such youngsters may avoid doing anything "crazy" by avoiding doing anything at all, and clinicians must be alert in such cases to recognizing the absence of age-appropriate peer-group engagement as a potential index of underlying schizophrenia. Conversely, there are occasions when young persons with eccentric ways of thinking and behaving can be identified as not being schizophrenic on the basis of rewarding personal engagements with their peers.

Any evaluation of adolescent social relationships must distinguish between *real* and *apparent* peer engagements, however. In real engagements young persons take on group activities that they truly enjoy and in which they become actively involved. They are friendly with at least several different people whom they see regularly and with whom they share a variety of interests. These friendships are based on mutual respect, mutual decision making, mutual exchange of favors, and mutual investments in maintaining the relationship.

By contrast, some adolescents who appear engaged with their peers are only going through the motions of socially expected behaviors. Their group activities have been pressed on them by their parents or teachers, and they participate more as hangers-on and passive observers than as active enthusiasts. Their friendships are few, fleeting, and nonmutual. They have one friend at a time whom they see infrequently around a single shared interest, or they float among various "friends" with whom they have little in common and to whom they never become close, or they get involved in relationships in which they are exploited as the price of "friendship." In using the case history to evaluate the adequacy of an adolescent's peer-group engagements, clinicians should be careful not to take either the adolescent's report (e.g., "I've got lots of friends") or what their parents say (e.g., "She gets along well with other kids") as definitive evidence. Instead, they should form their own conclusions after having elicited specific and detailed information concerning (a) how many friends there are, (b) how often these friends are seen, (c) the number and variety of activities that are shared with these friends, and (d) the extent of mutuality that exists in these friendship relationships. The less favorable the findings in these respects, the more reason there is to be concerned about interpersonal withdrawal and inadequate social skills; the more favorable they are, the more justified it may be to rule out schizophrenia in a behaviorally disturbed young person.

Actions and Ideas

In the early and still equivocal phases of a schizophrenic disorder, prior to the appearance of markedly bizarre actions or peculiar ideas, careful attention to actions and ideas that seem only slightly unusual may identify diagnostically significant lapses in judgment and self-control. The following examples illustrate such initial suggestions of subsequently demonstrated schizophrenic disorder in adolescents who presented in an otherwise unremarkable fashion:

The parents of a 13-year-old boy, who were seeking guidance concerning his being emotionally immature, mentioned almost in passing that he was fascinated with timepieces and could spend hours absorbed in watching a clock tick. From their point of view, his preoccupation with watches and clocks was merely a nonproductive hobby. Clinically, it was identified as a maladaptive preoccupation with abstractions (an indication of disordered thinking) and as an index of interpersonal ineptness (because this preoccupation monopolized his time and contributed to social isolation from his peers).

A 17-year-old high school senior said he planned to enter college with a football scholarship the following fall. Asked about his high school football career, he reported that he had never played football, because he wanted to avoid the risk of injury and "save myself for the big time." The unreality of expecting to play college football on a scholarship without having had any prior experience with the sport reflects the kind of poor judgment that results from inaccurate perception.

A 16-year-old boy being evaluated in connection with a variety of obsessive-compulsive symptoms said he was hard at work writing a musical version of *The Hound of the Baskervilles*. Allowing for the wide range of serious stories that have successfully been set to music, his investment of energy seemed to reflect unrealistic judgment concerning the limits within which such creativity is possible.

When asked to indicate some things she wished for, a 13-year-old girl listed a motorcycle, an eagle, and a hawk. The uselessness of a motorcycle to a 13-year-old, who could not be licensed to drive it, spoke to the unusual quality of her first wish. Regarding the eagle and the hawk, she gave the following strange and unrealistic explanations: The eagle could be used to stop the school bus if she ever wanted to get someone off it, and the hawk could be used for delivering messages.

A 17-year-old boy took a hammer to his prized possession, a 10-speed bicycle, and smashed it to bits. Although aggressive outbursts are by no means specific to schizophrenic disorder, willful destruction of a person's own property is grounds for suspecting the kind of deficient self-control often associated with schizophrenia.

Such instances of apparently bizarre actions and peculiar ideas must always be considered carefully in light of normative adolescent behavior and the seriousness with which they are pursued. The more extremely they deviate from normative patterns and the less the adolescent is able to take some critical distance from them (as in such comments as "I guess I know that's really not a sensible expectation," "I'm just doing it for the fun of it, not to be taken seriously," or "That was really a dumb thing to do"), the more probable the presence of a schizophrenic disorder.

Family Background

The previously mentioned familial incidence data mean that the differential diagnosis of schizophrenia in an equivocal case can be sharpened by taking into account the family background. The greater the incidence of schizophrenia in a patient's family and the more closely any schizophrenic relatives are related, the more likely that he or she will develop a schizophrenic disorder. Although familial incidence therefore increases the likelihood of emerging schizophrenia in a disturbed adolescent, the absence of schizophrenic relatives does not reliably rule out this possibility. Of persons who become schizophrenic, over 60% do not have any family history of schizophrenia, and over 80% do not have a schizophrenic parent or sibling (Gottesman, McGuffin, & Farmer, 1987).

On the other hand, assistance in ruling out schizophrenia can sometimes come from the fact that affective disorder is rarely familially concordant with schizophrenia. This means that clinicians should be very cautious about diagnosing schizophrenia in young persons who have a close relative who is affectively disturbed, especially when there is a family history of bipolar affective disorder (see Gottesman et al., 1987; Kendler & Hays, 1983).

Developmental History

Adolescents who become incipiently schizophrenic have an underlying vulnerability to this disorder that has usually been manifest in some earlier form of disturbance or developmental deviation. The more chronic the schizophrenic disorder, the more prominent and long-standing these prior adjustment difficulties are likely to have been; conversely, the less dramatic any previous instances of behavioral disturbance and the more recently they have begun, the more acute the present schizophrenic condition is likely to be.

Thus, when the presenting schizophrenic picture is found to constitute only the result of a long and gradual development of disturbance, chronicity should be inferred. When the current schizophrenic symptoms have developed rapidly and recently, following an unremarkable childhood with few hints of identifying features of schizophrenia, an acute condition should be diagnosed. Additionally, because the absence of at least some early indications is so rare in adolescents who become schizophrenic, a premorbid history containing no suggestion whatsoever of vulnerability to severe psychopathology can provide critical evidence that an apparently seriously disturbed adolescent is experiencing some condition other than incipient schizophrenia.

Interview Behavior

In equivocal cases with mixed symptomatology, subtle peculiarities in an adolescent's interview behavior may tip the scales toward an impression of schizophrenic disorder. Of particular importance in this regard are (a) the young person's speech patterns, (b) style of relating, (c) appearance, and (d) quality of affect and judgment.

Speech Patterns

The manner in which people carry on a conversation frequently reveals any problems they are having in thinking coherently and at appropriate levels of abstraction. This is especially the case when incoherence due to dissociation results in a series of loosely related ideas that are difficult to follow. One dissociated adolescent, when asked "How are you?" replied, "I'm okay but my father never takes me fishing do you like to bait hooks?"

In early and mild stages of schizophrenia, dissociation may be subtle and fleeting, appearing sometimes only in the form of discontinuities between what the interviewer says and how the adolescent responds. Special attention should be paid to apparently irrelevant or tangential answers to questions, as in the preceding example and in the following question/answer sequences: "How are you?" / "I'm going on 16"; "How did you happen to come to the clinic?" / "My mother drove me", "It sounds like you feel sad most of the time" / "Is most of the time more than a lot of the time?" When interviewers are fairly certain that they are getting oblique answers to clear questions, and when they are convinced that the young person is not merely trying to be funny or provocative, they should suspect dissociated thinking. The following two exchanges with a 14-year-old boy are cases in point:

THERAPIST: What kinds of things do you like to do?
PATIENT: I like to play basketball; I'm a good aimer.
THERAPIST: You're a good shot?
PATIENT: Yes, last summer at camp we shot at targets with real bullets.

PATIENT: The kids at school tease me and call me all kinds of names.
THERAPIST: Like what?
PATIENT: Oh, like "stupid" and "mental" and "retarded" and like that.

THERAPIST: Do they call your brother those names (reference to patient's younger brother in the same school)?

PATIENT: No, no one calls me "brother."

The 13-year-old girl mentioned earlier, who wanted to have a motorcycle, an eagle, and a hawk, showed the following kind of subtle discontinuity at several points in her initial interview:

THERAPIST: What did you do the past weekend?

PATIENT: Our father took us to visit the museum on Sunday.

THERAPIST: Do you go out together like that very often?

PATIENT: No, my father is too busy, and usually on Sunday he's writing checks.

THERAPIST: What does your father do?

PATIENT: Oh, he took us to the museum and he stayed there with us to hear a man give a talk.

THERAPIST: I said what does he do.

PATIENT: Oh, you mean his business.

During an interview, when interviewees frequently seem to lose track of what they are saying and abruptly break off their train of speech or thought, the incoherence may be due to blocking or to poverty of thought, not to dissociation. Similarly suspect are repeated pauses during which they seem on the verge of saying something but not quite able to get it out. Especially when patients confirm such apparent difficulty in finding the right words or sustaining a train of thought by stating that they cannot recall what they were saying or meant to say, or that they have nothing to say, schizophrenic thought stoppage or impoverishment is very likely to be the source of the problem.

As a result of thinking at inappropriate levels of abstraction, schizophrenic persons often use or perceive words in an overly literal or concrete manner. This makes the meaning of puns and other comments that involve a play on words difficult for them to grasp. One adolescent told by the interviewer to "Stop pulling my leg" responded, "I'm not even touching your leg." Conversations of this kind, in which every word is taken at face value without allowance for alternative meanings or implied referents, often reflect schizophrenic concreteness, provided, of course, that a basic language disability or unfamiliarity with English is not responsible for the misperception.

Speech clues suggestive of thought disorder also include strange misuses of words that have similar sounds but different meanings (e.g., "I don't like the work we're doing in biography lab"; "Do you believe in the abdominal snowman?") and unusual variations in pitch, stress, and inflection. Young persons whose language is marred by peculiar or neologistic terminology, who talk in a monologue or a singsong way unrelated to the content of what they are saying, or whose pronunciation and inflection suggest that they are not speaking in their native tongue, when they are, are more likely to have thinking impairments than adolescents whose conversation is free from such speech peculiarities.

A research instrument developed by Andreasen (1979a, 1986)—the Scale for the Assessment of Thought, Language, and Communication—defines these and other conversational manifestations of disordered thinking in considerable detail. The examples she provides are recommended to the attention of clinicians as a further aid to detecting subtle indications of thought disorder during the interview process.

Style of Relating

The way in which adolescents relate to the clinician during an interview provides a representative sample of their capacity to engage in mutual relationships with other people. To utilize this sample diagnostically, clinicians need to examine how well they can engage in a direct conversation with an adolescent whom they suspect might be schizophrenic. Sometimes, apprehension or resentment diminishes a young person's involvement in the interview process, and sometimes, shyness or embarrassment prevents him or her from being open with the interviewer. With appropriate allowances made for such circumstances, the adolescent who seems not quite there, who avoids eye contact or stares vacantly at the interviewer with little evidence of interest or recognition, often lacks the basic capacity for interpersonal relatedness.

In some instances, adolescents who remain for the most part detached from the interviewer, with their gaze averted and their conversation minimal, nevertheless exhibit an occasional interested glance, appropriate smile, or argumentative retort. Such youngsters are less likely to be schizophrenically disturbed than those who cannot inject any such responsiveness into a general posture of withdrawal. For many seriously troubled but not schizophrenic adolescents who come for an initial interview frightened and mostly silent, such glimpses of personal contact may help point the way to a correctly made nonschizophrenic diagnosis.

Appearance

The way people look often provides clues to the adequacy of the psychological functioning. This is not a matter of style or taste, but a question of integration and age appropriateness. Adolescents from different places and backgrounds dress and groom themselves in many different fashions, and these fashions tend to change rapidly from one year to the next. Although some of the ways adolescents prefer to look may strike adults as outlandish or bizarre, such adult reactions do not constitute a reliable barometer of psychopathology. What does suggest psychopathology is an adolescent's looking different from any of the ways that at least some other young persons presently look, or not displaying any consistent pattern of dress and grooming. A totally idiosyncratic appearance often indicates peer-group estrangement, and a disorganized appearance often reflects inadequate attention to reality.

Accordingly, two questions should be considered with respect to an adolescent patient's appearance. First, does he or she look like an adolescent? "Looking like an adolescent" covers a lot of ground, but it does not include the teenager whose dress and grooming are reminiscent of either a much younger child or a middle-aged adult. The adolescent boy who looks like a Cub Scout and the adolescent girl who looks like a grandmother are probably not maintaining satisfactory social relationships with their peers.

Second, in whatever way the adolescent is trying to appear, does it all hang together in some coherent way? The more that bits and pieces of different fashions have been thrown together, apparently without regard for achieving a cohesive appearance, the more likely it is that the adolescent is having difficulty exercising realistic judgment. Needless to say, not every strange-looking youngster is likely to be schizophrenic. In the context of other evidence of schizophrenic impairments, however, failure to exhibit an organized or age-appropriate appearance may help to identify schizophrenic disorder.

Affect and Judgment

Even though adolescents are often reluctant to share their feelings in a diagnostic interview, the affects they do express should be appropriate to the content of what they are saying. When adolescents become childishly silly or inexplicably tearful during an interview, they are revealing inadequate control over their emotions. The same is true when they giggle, smirk, sigh, or become angry for no apparent reason, and when they respond to relatively innocuous statements with extreme reactions of shock, surprise, disbelief, or embarrassment—as in the case of a youngster who, when asked, "What's the name of the school you go to?" replied, "Why do you keep asking me all these awful questions?"

No matter how stressful the clinical situation is for a troubled adolescent, moreover, he or she should be able to share at least a few appropriate emotional exchanges with the interviewer—both smiling together over something that is amusing, for example, or the adolescent's showing some appropriate sadness or irritation when the interviewer has purposefully made a negatively toned or provocative comment in order to test out the young person's capacity for emotional responsiveness. When an adolescent's affective tone is so blunted that neither joking, sarcasm, sympathy, nor even browbeating elicits any emotional reaction, then a schizophrenic impairment of emotionality should be suspected. The presence of emotional blunting can be especially helpful in ruling out affective disorder among disturbed adolescents with mixed symptomatology.

Hints of poor judgment in dealing with the interview situation may also provide the initial clues to schizophrenic potential in a disturbed adolescent. The following excerpt from a clinician's report of an initial interview with a

13-year-old boy notes some unusual behavior that suggested difficulties in reality testing and in emotionality as well.

From the beginning of the interview and at several times during it, Jack's behavior left me concerned about the level of his judgment and the appropriateness of his affective responses. He initially exhibited none of the nervousness, guardedness, wariness, or obvious defenses against such feelings that might be normatively expected of a adolescent brought for his first visit with a psychologist. Rather, as I began to ask him what his understanding of coming to see me was, he broke in with a harangue about his father's always yelling at him, and he talked throughout the interview without hesitation and with no questions about why he was here or what we would be doing. At several points, he abruptly interrupted his own sentences with, "Is there anything else you want to ask me?" which was usually far removed from the context of our interaction. Similarly, his affect, though appropriate for the most part, sometimes involved a very unusual, singsong presentation of what he was saying and at times a demonstrative emotional style that in my view was neither appropriate to the content nor within the normal range for an adolescent boy in an interview situation.

Psychological Test Performance

The assessment of possible schizophrenic features in disturbed adolescents constitutes a substantial portion of many psychological examiners' consultative work. The frequency of this question among requests for psychodiagnostic testing reflects the difficulty of differentiating incipient schizophrenia from other diagnostic possibilities in disturbed adolescents on the basis of case history and interview data alone and also the sensitivity of psychodiagnostic tests to many of the personality impairments that define schizophrenic disturbance.

In particular, a carefully selected test battery permits relatively clear distinctions between the formal and the content aspects of disorder. On both structured and relatively unstructured assessment instruments, clinicians can usually clarify more readily than they can during an interview the extent to which any peculiar content in an adolescent's fantasy is accompanied by peculiarities in his or her thought processes. This is especially true for the kinds of combinations, condensations, and overgeneralizations that characterize illogical reasoning, most of which become more apparent in patients' responses to psychological tests than during typical diagnostic interviews.

Psychodiagnostic tests additionally provide some quantitative assessment of aspects of functioning capacity that facilitate the differential diagnosis of schizophrenia in equivocally disturbed adolescents. With respect to being in touch with reality, for example, the test battery yields numerical indices of the ability to perceive their environment accurately, to recognize conventional modes of response, and to comprehend social experiences at a level commensurate with their demonstrated intelligence. Such indices are helpful not only in assessing the presence of a schizophrenic disorder, but also in judging its severity and, through retesting, monitoring its course over time.

The pervasiveness of deviant test responses and the extent to which the person appears comfortable with them both reflect the extent to which a schizophrenic disorder has become chronic. For detailed information on the application of psychological test findings to the differential diagnosis of schizophrenia, the reader is referred to contributions by Archer (1987), by Exner and Weiner (1982, Chapter 7), by Johnston and Holzman (1979), and by Weiner (1966).

The following two cases illustrate common patterns of initially mild or mixed disturbance in adolescents whose clinical history, interview behavior, and psychological test performance subsequently pointed to schizophrenia. The first case involves a dramatic personality change with the sudden onset of aggressive, antisocial behavior; the other case features a gradual breakdown involving mainly depression and withdrawal.

Case 1.   Schizophrenia with Sudden Onset

Until 6 months before being admitted to the hospital, at age 16 years, Donald had been considered a bright and creative but quiet and retiring boy. He nevertheless had many friends, was well liked in school, and had never been in disciplinary difficulty. Shortly before beginning his sophomore year in high school, he was slightly injured in an unusual accident. While standing in his driveway, he was struck by a car driven by another teenager, who had veered off the road to scare him and misjudged his braking distance. Donald suffered only minor bruises and did not have any lingering physical discomfort as a result of the accident. Yet, in sharp contrast to his previously characteristic restraint and even-temperedness, he began shortly after this frightening experience to display frequent angry outbursts at home. He would yell and swear at his parents at the slightest provocation and would stamp around the house slamming doors whenever they disagreed with him.

On returning to school in the fall, Donald began to receive mainly Ds and Fs in his work instead of the above-average grades he had regularly earned in the past. He also became a school discipline problem for the first time, and, on one occasion, he was among a group of boys arrested while trying to break into the school building at night. In February of the school year, following 6 months of such problem behavior at home and in school, he responded to his principal's asking him to get a haircut by storming out of school and refusing to return. It was at this point that his parents sought professional help.

During an initial interview, Donald displayed flat affect and expressed little concern about his problem behavior and failing grades at school. There was no gross evidence of thought disorder. However, because of the extent of his loss of control, his refusal to return to school, and his strained relationship with his parents, it was decided to admit him to the hospital for further evaluation and treatment planning.

During a subsequent 1-month hospital stay, Donald proved refractory to efforts to help him control his aggressive, antisocial behavior; if anything, his hostility and recalcitrance increased. He regularly cursed out the staff, particularly his therapist ("You're a shitty doctor"), broke up furniture, threw his shoes and other handy objects at other patients, and twice ran away.

Midway during his hospitalization, his continued inability to control himself, his poor judgment, and some occasional displays of apparent dissociation and blocking suggested the possibility of a schizophrenic disorder, and psychological consultation was requested.

Donald's performance on psychological examination clearly identified features of schizophrenic disturbance. Particularly notable were poor reality testing and an impaired capacity for social judgments. Almost half of his Rorschach responses were perceptually unusual or inaccurate, and he failed to report most of the commonly seen and conventionally articulated percepts.

He responded to items of social comprehension on the Wechsler Adult Intelligence Scale in a spotty and inconsistent fashion, at times misinterpreting or suggesting impulsive reactions to fairly obvious and unambiguous situations and at other times offering sophisticated, carefully reasoned analyses of complex problems.

Donald's hospitalization at a university medical center ended after 30 days, with the expiration of his parents' insurance coverage. He was discharged with a diagnosis of acute undifferentiated schizophrenia, and continued care at a nearby state hospital was recommended. His family rejected this recommendation, and Donald returned home to continue his treatment on an outpatient basis. In light of his stormy hospital course and guarded prognosis at discharge, Donald did surprisingly well after leaving the hospital. It was almost as if the hospital regimen had somehow perpetuated his misbehavior and that only upon returning to his natural environment could he display gains he had made in therapy. A follow-up evaluation 2 years later indicated that, for the most part, he had resumed the quiet, controlled personality style that had characterized him before his sudden breakdown. He continued to show some strange behavior, but he had returned to school without incident, was performing well in his studies, and had avoided any further behavioral difficulty.

Donald's case illustrates the sudden and acute onset of personality decompensation during adolescence, with a mixture of schizophrenic and antisocial features. The psychological testing helped point the differential diagnosis toward schizophrenia, and his subsequent course, with continuing personality peculiarities but no further antisocial behavior, bore out this impression. His rapid and reasonably successful remission, together with the precipitous nature of his breakdown, demonstrates a relatively acute schizophrenic condition.

CASE 2. SCHIZOPHRENIA WITH GRADUAL ONSET

Karen was first seen at age 16 years at the request of her family doctor, to whom she had mentioned some thoughts about suicide. She complained during an initial psychiatric interview of having felt depressed for the past 2 to 3 years, following the death of two horses she had owned. Her apparently erroneous impression that she had in some way been responsible for these deaths had led her to give up riding, which had been her favorite pastime. She reported poor appetite, difficulty in sleeping, preoccupation with the meaning of life, and a generally bleak view of her future. She described herself as a "loner" who had little interest in being with people and no interest in dating. Although her mood was clearly depressed, she talked freely and without obvious incoherence or circumstantiality. Nevertheless, because of the possible suicidal risk, it was decided to arrange hospital admission.

During the first week of her hospital stay, Karen's behavior and some emerging details of her history began to suggest schizophrenic disturbance. She became markedly and strangely withdrawn. As if to shut out the world as much as possible, she would curl up in a corner of her room, with the blinds pulled and the lights out, wearing sunglasses. She frequently complained that "life is only pain and emptiness" and began to ask if she could remain in the hospital indefinitely. She said that she felt close to no one, particularly her parents—"I love them but I don't care about them." She also reported that at times, mainly when she was alone, she felt that eyes were watching her.

When asked about her disinterest in dating, Karen stated that, because all boys expect heavy petting on the first date and she did not want either to be touched or to have to "put men down," she had never accepted an invitation to go on a date. It was also learned, however, that between the ages of 13 and 14 years, she had often been embraced and kissed by an older brother when the two of them were alone in the house. Her stated reason for neither resisting her brother's advances nor complaining to her mother about them was, "I don't want to put anybody down."

Additional information from her parents indicated that Karen had always been a shy, introverted girl with little self-confidence. When asked about her shyness, Karen confirmed that she had never felt comfortable around people her own age and from age 7 or 8 years on had preferred associating with adults. The only two organized peer-group activities she had ever pursued were the 4-H Club and a horse club, both of which she had given up during the previous 2 years.

Karen's physical and emotional isolation from others, her unusual behavior, and her unrealistic ideas about dating and about being watched suggested schizophrenic impairments, and subsequent psychological examination demonstrated a schizophrenic extent of illogical reasoning and inaccurate perception. After a month in the hospital, during which she remained depressed and withdrawn but no longer appeared to be suicidal, she was discharged to office treatment. Three months later she was back in the hospital, complaining, "I'm not myself, they changed me in the hospital; I started out thinking someone was going to kill me, and now I think everyone wants to kill me." During her outpatient treatment, her condition had worsened, and, by her own report, she had done nothing but "sit around and lose all hope." Two weeks before her second admission, she had developed the specific delusion that a "tall man with a knife" was after her to kill her. On readmission, she appeared sullen and withdrawn, demonstrated flat affect and a tendency to stare blankly ahead of her, and she was preoccupied with her delusions of impending victimization.

Karen spent the next 8 months in the hospital, during which time her depression lifted somewhat and her paranoid ideation diminished. Once again, she was discharged to outpatient therapy, and several months later a second psychological evaluation was conducted to evaluate her progress. On this occasion the examination revealed considerably less anxiety and many fewer ruminations and fears about relationships with other people than had been apparent on her previous testing. However, her decreased interpersonal anxiety appeared to have been achieved at the cost of increased distance and withdrawal from other people. In addition, continued evidence of illogical reasoning and impaired reality testing marred her test performance.

These developments suggested that Karen was moving toward a relatively chronic schizophrenic adjustment. Although her withdrawal constituted a maladaptive concomitant of her schizophrenic disorder, it can also be seen as a means of reducing her anxiety level and allowing her to achieve a more stable course than in the past. Thus, her history illustrates the development of a relatively chronic schizophrenic disturbance, with gradual onset during adolescence and with prominent depressive features initially dominating the presenting symptomatology.

TREATMENT

The treatment of schizophrenic adolescents combines general procedures for treating schizophrenia with basic principles of conducting psychotherapy with young persons. Psychotherapy with adolescents is discussed in Chapter 11, and there is an extensive literature concerning the treatment of schizophrenic disturbance through individual psychotherapy (Arieti, 1974, Part 7; Mosher & Gunderson, 1979; Karon & Vandenbos, 1981; McGlashan, 1983; Stone, Albert. Forrest. & Arieti, 1983), through group and family therapy (Anderson, Reiss, & Hogarty, 1986; Goldstein; 1984, Morris, 1985; Mosher & Gunderson, 1979), through somatic therapies (Kane, 1987; Marder & May, 1986; Small, 1986), and through behavioral approaches (Moss & Rick, 1981; Salzinger, 1981; Wallace, Donahoe, & Boone, 1986). Without elaborating these broad topics, the following discussion addresses some focal guidelines in the *individual psychotherapy* of schizophrenic adolescents, some implications of adjunctive *drug therapy*, and some considerations in providing *residential care.*

Individual Psychotherapy

The distinguishing features of adolescent schizophrenia include two that are relatively accessible to psychological intervention: impaired capacity for interpersonal relatedness and diminished ability to perceive reality accurately. Accordingly, r*elationship building* and *reality testing* constitute the two Rs of conducting therapy with schizophrenic adolescents. The therapist needs first to create an engaged, trusting, and mutual relationship that gives the adolescent a positive experience of interpersonal relatedness.

This relationship can then be used to help schizophrenic young persons to recognize and revise their distorted impressions of themselves, their environment, and the consequences of their actions. Attention must also be paid to fostering family and community support systems that will facilitate and sustain a young person's improvement in therapy.

Relationship Building

Success in treating schizophrenic adolescents will typically hinge on how well the therapist can impress them as a warm, genuine, and understanding person who is interested in their welfare, can be relied on to nurture without exploiting them, and will bring special skills to bear on their behalf. Schizophrenic adolescents have often become physically or emotionally withdrawn, either because their disturbed cognitive functioning has prevented them from understanding other persons or because their poor social skills have undermined their capacity to cope with interpersonal problem solving. In both cases, their ineptness has typically resulted in numerous frustrations, humiliations, and rejections that have rendered them interpersonally aversive. It is therefore essential for the therapist to demonstrate that he or she is at least one person who can understand and be understood and who can be counted on not to ridicule, scold, or reject them.

This does not mean being uniformly accepting and agreeable in working with schizophrenic adolescents. Although a tolerant approach often fosters engagement when adolescents are frightened or depressed, it seldom has constructive impact when they are angry or rebellious. Angry and rebellious adolescents typically react negatively to permissive adults who remain pleasant in the face of abuse. Benign tolerance tends to be taken as evidence of being too disinterested to take the situation seriously, or too weak and cowardly to stand up for oneself and one's dignity, or too naíve or stupid to recognize when one is being insulted or manipulated, or too dishonest to admit feeling angry or upset. None of these impressions help to spark enthusiasm among hostile or resistive adolescents for an engaged treatment relationship.

What is required instead is an approach that actively challenges negative attitudes and sets strict limits on disruptive or destructive behavior. When criticism and firmness are properly employed without anger or punitiveness, they convey that the therapist cares enough and is strong enough to take a stand and to persist, even in the face of belligerence, with efforts to help the adolescent get along better in the world.

Whatever balance seems best to strike between tolerance and firmness in seeking to make contact with a schizophrenic adolescent, the therapist needs to anticipate that many of these young persons will enter therapy heavily insulated against forming any emotional ties. Fears of intimacy may lead them to fend off even the most carefully conceived and sensitively expressed personal overtures. It then may be necessary to pave the way for relationship-building by interpreting such fears and thereby diluting their impact. To be effective, these interpretations may need to be phrased with an ear for the frequently metaphorical quality of a schizophrenic adolescent's language. Thus to a young person who says, "I'm a machine," a useful response may be, "If you were a machine, you wouldn't have any feelings, and you wouldn't have to worry about anyone hurting you." The role of such metaphorical communications and other procedures in establishing a therapeutic relationship with schizophrenic adolescents has been elaborated in well-known books by Beulah Parker (*My Language Is Me*, 1962) and Hannah Green (*I Never Promised You a Rose Garden*, 1964).

Even skillful and dedicated psychotherapists working with techniques of proven effectiveness must be patient, however, in seeking to engage an interpersonally aversive schizophrenic adolescent in an emotionally positive treatment relationship. Research findings indicate that even if a few months pass without formation of an effective working alliance, the therapist should not become discouraged about the patient's eventually benefiting from psychotherapy, and that withdrawn schizophrenics who eventually improve may require as long as 6 months to enter into a comfortably collaborative relationship with their therapist (Frank & Gunderson, 1990; Karon, 1987).

Reality Testing

Therapists need to provide schizophrenic adolescents with continual and direct corrections of their distorted perceptions. Severely disturbed young persons who are having delusions or hallucinations must be helped to recognize that these impressions grow out of their fears and expectations and have no firm basis in reality. This involves neither pretending to accept delusions and hallucinations as real, which would be dishonest, nor disparaging them as not worth talking about, which would be rejecting. Instead, the therapist needs first to indicate that, although such experiences may seem real to the schizophrenic adolescent, they are not real to the therapist or to most other people. The next step is to help the patient identify from the content of such unreal experiences and from the circumstances in which they occur the nature of the underlying concerns they might reflect.

Gaining some understanding of why and when unreal experiences have probably been occurring tends to reduce the frequency with which they occur. Beginning to understand such experiences also helps a schizophrenic person to feel less anxious when they do occur and to prevent them from influencing what he or she says or does. It is generally the case that seriously disturbed persons become better able to exert self-control over behavioral manifestations of their disorder once they have come to recognize the maladaptive nature of these behaviors and the sequences of events that give rise to them (Breier & Strauss, 1983).

In less severely disturbed adolescents, impaired reality testing tends to be manifest primarily in poor social judgment. As indicated earlier, schizophrenics who are misperceiving the impact of their behavior on others and misinterpreting the significance of others' actions toward them are often awkward, inept, or even unintentionally offensive in interpersonal situations. This calls for the therapist to discuss unpleasant personal encounters an adolescent has experienced with an eye to improving his or her social skills. How could a particular situation have been seen more accurately? How could the impact of the actions taken have been anticipated more correctly? What alternative ways of responding might have led to a more desirable outcome?

This approach to sharpening the judgment of schizophrenic adolescents is elaborated in numerous books and papers on social skills training (Ladd, 1984; Mesibov, 1984). Future situations also provide opportunities to employ these strategies. For example, techniques of role-playing and role-rehearsal can often be used to good effect in helping schizophrenic adolescents prepare for and handle social interactions more effectively than they would otherwise. Like the elements of a positive relationship with the therapist, bits and pieces of improved reality testing achieved through such strategies elicit positive reinforcements from the environment, which in turn promote the generalization of more skillful social behavior to increasing numbers of situations. Once achieved, then, improved reality testing has good prospects for sustaining itself through the enhanced satisfaction it provides the schizophrenic person.

As in balancing tolerance and firmness to build a good treatment relationship with schizophrenic adolescents, efforts to sharpen reality testing must be undertaken judiciously. It is not easy to point out errors in how people view their world without seeming derogatory or hostile, and schizophrenic adolescents are quick to construe criticism as meaning, "I don't like you" or "I don't think much of you." Therapists cannot afford to be apostles of reality at the expense of undermining their relationship with a schizophrenic young person. This means that they must keep their efforts at improving reality testing within the limits of the young person's capacity to respond and his or her ability to interpret these efforts as well-intended help, rather than dislike or rejection.

Fostering Support Systems

The best planned and most sensitively delivered individual psychotherapy for schizophrenic adolescents may prove of little avail in the absence of adequate support systems in the young person's family and community. The contribution of hostile and rejecting family attitudes to perpetuating schizophrenic disorder has already been noted , and similar effects flow from peer, neighborhood, and school environments that make a disturbed adolescent feel demeaned and rejected. Therapists have limited capacity to create a caring and supportive environment for their patients outside of the treatment room. Nevertheless, they can take steps to foster such an environment through judicious involvement of a schizophrenic adolescent's family and community in the therapy.

For example, family therapy sessions often provide an opportunity for reducing deviant communication and promoting better understanding between schizophrenic adolescents and their parents. An interactive approach may not be feasible in the face of pronounced parent–child alienation, but this does not preclude family counseling aimed at helping parents recognize the nature of their child's disorder and play a positive role in his or her recovery. Parents who are included as important and respected participants in their child's treatment are likely to become effective therapeutic agents themselves, promoting and sustaining improvement. Parents who are excluded from the treatment program, who are given little help in dealing with their own problems in adjusting to their child's difficulties, and—even worse— who are made to feel as if they are pathogenic agents who should keep at a distance are likely to do just that—to the detriment of their child's recovery (see Bernheim, 1982; Costell & Reiss, 1982; Intagliata, Willer, & Egri, 1986; Jones, Pearson, & Dimpero, 1989; Morris, 1985; Rossman & Freedman, 1982).

The broader community may be more difficult for a therapist to reach than a schizophrenic adolescent's parents. Yet there are good data to indicate that supportive relationships outside the immediate family can help to buffer improved schizophrenics against relapse (Kettlewell, Jones, & Jones, 1985; Mirkin, Ricci, & Cohen, 1985; Mosher & Keith, 1980). For disturbed adolescents, the reception they receive in school and from adult leaders in various extracurricular activities can provide beneficial support. Hence, there are good reasons for the therapist to be in contact with key persons in the adolescent's life, other than his or her parents, as a means of fostering a supportive environment.

The idea of making such contacts may raise some questions about violating the adolescent's confidentiality, and some clinicians may be concerned that discussing a disturbed young person's special needs and problems with persons in the community exposes him or her to negative reactions associated with being a "mental case." Respect for confidentiality can be ensured by appropriate discussions with adolescent patients prior to conversations with persons in the community, including whatever efforts are necessary both to convince them that such contacts will be to their benefit and to obtain their permission.

As for negative reactions, two likely circumstances should be kept in mind. First, in the case of schizophrenic adolescents, information that they have a psychological disorder will usually not come as much of a surprise to a teacher, coach, pastor, or other adult who has been in a position to observe their behavior closely. Instead, this information can help to eliminate uncertainty concerning the reason for a young person's unusual behavior and may lead to a more accepting attitude (see Chapter 2). Second, carefully identified community members who are responsible individuals and who are personally or professionally involved in working with young persons deserve the benefit of the doubt; that is, therapists should expect that the community members will take information about an adolescent's disturbance not as a basis for rejecting or demeaning him or her, but as reason to make special efforts to be understanding and supportive.

Drug Therapy

Clinical and research findings have demonstrated the effectiveness of antipsychotic drugs in the treatment of schizophrenia. Especially among acutely disturbed schizophrenics who are anxious, agitated, and out of control, these drugs exert a calming effect that curtails psychotic symptoms, promotes socially acceptable behavior, and increases accessibility to psychotherapy. Chronicity of disorder tends to limit these beneficial aspects of medication, as does a preponderance of negative over positive symptoms in the clinical picture (Donaldson, Gelenberg, & Baldessarini, 1983, Gold & Hurt, 1990; Spohn & Strauss, 1989).

Accordingly, medication may play a role in treating schizophrenic adolescents, particularly in florid stages of the disorder. However, most clinical psychopharmacologists argue both for conservative use of drugs, especially with young persons, and for regarding them as an adjunctive modality used to facilitate progress in a multifaceted treatment program, rather than as the sole or primary agent for eliminating the disorder (Campbell, 1985; McDaniel, 1986; Werry, 1982). Work with seriously disturbed adolescents should strive not merely to eliminate psychotic behavior and restore a previous level of functioning, but also to promote continued personality growth. Drugs alone do not instill new interpersonal skills or teach more effective coping. Psychosocial interventions are necessary to improve social competence, and reliance on somatic therapy should not preclude adequate attention to psychological aspects of the treatment program.

As a second consideration, patients receiving medication tend to be passive participants in their treatment. They ingest what the physician prescribes, the drugs alter their body chemistry, and they do not have to do anything. Although passivity and not having to take responsibility may appeal to some adolescents, most are caught up in the developmental task of achieving a sense of self-determination and psychological independence from adults. They consequently take poorly to being controlled or manipulated by adults in ways they cannot understand. Before tranquillity is imposed on them through medication, then, therapists need to take special care to explain the nature of and need for the drugs and to elicit their participation in planning this and other aspects of the treatment program. Recognition of the importance of active patient participation in the treatment of schizophrenia has provided further basis for arguments that drug therapy should be limited as much as possible and applied within the context of a broad-based program of psychosocial intervention (Falloon & Liberman, 1983; Ryan & Puig-Antich, 1987).

Third, the psychological distress of acutely disturbed adolescents, no matter how painful, represents an active struggle to resolve their adjustment difficulties and provides motivation for entering and remaining involved in a treatment program. Assuaging this distress through tranquilizing medication may cost the therapist an important treatment ally—the patient's felt need to change. For these reasons, some clinicians have advocated reducing the amount of medication used, through such strategies as intermittent rather than continuous administration (Carpenter & Heinrichs, 1983; Schooler & Levine, 1983).

Residential Care

Of all psychological disturbances in adolescence, schizophrenia is the one for which hospitalization is most likely to be required. Moreover, the majority of schizophrenic persons entering treatment are admitted to an inpatient unit (Rosenstein et al., 1989). Hence, the treatment of this condition often involves some important issues in planning for and providing residential care. One of these is the decision concerning whether a disturbed adolescent should be hospitalized. There are good reasons both for attempting to work with adolescents on an outpatient basis, if at all possible, and for utilizing an inpatient setting for diagnostic and treatment purposes.

Hospitalization can be a very disruptive event in a young person's life. Adolescents belong at home with their family and in school with their peers. Removing them from these environments and from participation in their customary daily activities interrupts a host of interactions and pursuits that are vital to their continued personality development. In addition, being hospitalized because of their behavior conveys a frightening sense of inadequacy and helplessness to many young persons.

The risk of such consequences cautions against any routine or casual admission of adolescents to a residential facility. Concerns are currently being raised about recommendations for hospitalization of young persons based less on clinical necessity than on efforts to fill private hospital beds, and Schwartz (1989) cites evidence that large numbers of adolescents entering psychiatric hospitals could be treated as effectively with less intrusive interventions.

However this may be, the potential jeopardies of hospitalization also help to identify some guidelines for inpatient treatment programs: The hospitalization should be as brief as possible; parents should be involved to sustain the kinds of family interactions that help adolescents grow up; every effort should be made to keep adolescents current with their school work while they are in the hospital; and the damage done to their self-image by having been hospitalized needs to be addressed directly in the therapy. Adequate attention to these guidelines can minimize the discontinuity between hospital living and life outside the hospital. The more this discontinuity in minimized, the more easily a disturbed adolescent can enter into an inpatient treatment program and later make the transition back into his or her real life setting after discharge.

As for determining when adolescents should be admitted to an inpatient facility, three circumstances are generally regarded as calling for hospitalization to meet a disturbed adolescent's needs (see Hillard, Slomowitz, & Deddens, 1988; Mabe, Riley, & Sunde, 1989; Miller, 1980; Winsberg, Bialer, Kupietz, Botti, & Balka, 1980; Wurtele, Wilson, & Prentice-Dunn, 1983):

1. *When a more thorough evaluation seems indicated than can be accomplished on an outpatient basis.* Because of the frequently mixed symptomatology of adolescents who are becoming seriously disturbed, impending breakdown and destructive tendencies may not be immediately apparent. When such possibilities are suspected, continued observation in the relative protection of an inpatient setting, until such risks can be ruled out, is far preferable to exposing adolescents and those around them to a calamitous loss of control.

2. *When the adolescent is already out of control.* Young persons who have a history of destructive acts against themselves and others and who pose a present danger of such outbursts need the external controls imposed by a residential setting. In addition to protecting them and others from physical harm, these external controls can help to ease the painful psychological burden of feeling unable to control or predict their own behavior.

3. *When environmental stress has become intolerable.* The pressures of a disturbed or rejecting family setting, an overly demanding school situation, or an inhospitable peer group may counteract even the most carefully planned outpatient treatment program. In such circumstances, even young persons who are not seriously disturbed may need to be removed from their usual environment in order to benefit from therapy and to learn more effective ways of coping with their real life stress.

A second issue concerns whether disturbed adolescents who require hospitalization should be treated on an all-adolescent service or mixed adolescent-adult units. There are two distinct traditions in this regard. Some respected authorities on the inpatient treatment of adolescents have argued in favor of all-adolescent units on the basis that involvement with their peers, rather than with adults from whom they feel alienated, is more likely to provide the kind of supportive milieu that fosters accessibility to psychotherapeutic intervention (Beckett, 1965; Easson, 1969; Rinsley, 1980).

Other authorities have argued that all-adolescent units deprive young persons of living in a normal environment among persons of different ages, and thereby cause them to feel abandoned, deserted, and cut off from society. From this point of view, a mixed service has the advantage of maintaining communication between adolescents and adults, which is an aspect of adapting in the real world outside the hospital. In addition, the presence of adults has been viewed as a constructive restraint on misbehavior that sometimes occurs when groups of disturbed adolescents are isolated in a setting in which they can stimulate and encourage each other to act up (Bond & Auger, 1982; Garber, 1972; Hartmann, Glasser, Greenblatt, Solomon, & Levinson, 1968).

Informed opinion seems about equally divided on this matter, at least with respect to inpatient treatment in general (see Fineberg, Sowards, & Kettlewell, 1980). In more specific terms, however, two other considerations are important to note. First, there is some evidence that the more severely disturbed adolescents are, the better they respond to treatment on a mixed rather than all-adolescent service, and vice versa. Adolescents with neurotic or characterological difficulties appear relatively likely to benefit from a peer-group milieu, whereas schizophrenic adolescents appear to benefit more from the kinds of relationships and controls provided by an adult environment. Second, regardless of whether it is administered on an all-adolescent or a mixed service, a program especially tailored for hospitalized adolescents improves their prospects for recovery. This involves having in place a staff trained and committed to working with disturbed adolescents and a schedule of activities and procedures designed to meet the needs of this age group, from admission to discharge and beyond (Garber, 1972; Gossett, Lewis, & Barnhart, 1983; Steinberg, 1986).

In devising and implementing a specialized program for residential treatment of adolescents, care must be taken to keep the program from developing a life of its own, independent of the world outside the hospital and of the patient's needs and capacities. When enthusiasm clouds clinical judgment, psychotherapy programs can become overly intensive, to the neglect of practical psychosocial problems, and resocialization programs can become so intensive that they disrupt rather than stabilize patients' psychological functioning. Both kinds of imbalance have been found to yield poor results in the treatment of hospitalized schizophrenics (Ryan & Bell, 1983; Schooler & Spohn, 1982).

Finally, whatever the circumstances under which an adolescent is admitted to a residential facility, every effort should be made to involve him or her in a process of informed consent. Discussions of why hospitalization seemed indicated, what therapy will be like, and what can realistically be expected from the treatment program provide a basis for eliciting from an adolescent a statement of his or her willingness to participate. Combined with some early positive treatment experiences, informed consent procedures have been found by Bastien and Adelman (1984) to foster perceptions of having a choice about being in a residential facility, even among adolescents whose hospitalization was, in fact, mandated by court order. Among 55 hospitalized adolescents whose treatment Bastien and Adelman studied, perception of having a choice about placement was likely in turn to be associated with (a) recognition of needing help, (b) expectations that the program would be helpful, and (c) anticipations of remaining in the program long enough to get help—each of which is likely to contribute to a favorable outcome of residential care.

REFERENCES

Ainslie, R. C., Olmstead, K. M., & O'Loughlin, D. D. (1987). The early developmental context of twinship: Some limitations of the equal environment hypothesis. *American Journal of Orthopsychiatry, 57*, 120-124.

Akhtar, S. (1990). Paranoid personality disorder: A synthesis of developmental, dynamic and descriptive features. *American Journal of Psychotherapy, 44*, 5-25.

Ames, L. B., Metraux, R. W., & Walker, R. N. (1971). *Adolescent Rorschach responses* (rev. ed.). New York: Brunner/Mazel.

Anderson, C. M., Reiss, D. J., & Hogarty, G. E. (1986). *Schizophrenia and the family.* New York: Guilford.

Andreasen, N. C. (1979a). Thought, language, and communication disorders: I. Clinical assessment, definition of terms, and evaluation of their reliability. *Archives of General Psychiatry, 36*, 1315-1321.

Andreasen, N. C. (1979b). Thought, language, and communication disorders: II. Diagnostic significance. *Archives of General Psychiatry, 36*, 1325-1330.

Andreasen, N. C. (1986). Scale for the assessment of thought, language, and communication (TLC). *Schizophrenia Bulletin, 12*, 473-482.

Andreasen, N. C. (1988). Clinical phenomenology. *Schizophrenia Bulletin, 14*, 345-363.

Andreasen, N. C., & Grove, W. M. (1986). Thought, language, and communication in schizophrenia: Diagnosis and prognosis. *Schizophrenia Bulletin, 12*, 348-359.

Andreasen, N. C., & Ohlsen, S. (1982). Negative vs. positive schizophrenia. *Archives of General Psychiatry, 39*, 789-794.

Archer, R. P. (1987). *Using the MMPI with adolescents.* Hillsdale, NJ: Erlbaum.

Arieti, S. (1974). *Interpretation of schizophrenia* (2nd ed.). New York: Basic Books.

Asarnow, J. R. (1988). Children at risk for schizophrenia: Converging lines of evidence. *Schizophrenia Bulletin, 14,* 613-631.

Asarnow, J. R., & Goldstein, M. J. (1986). Schizophrenia during adolescence and early adulthood: A developmental perspective on risk research. *Clinical Psychology Review, 6,* 211-235.

Asarnow, J. R., Goldstein, M. J., & Ben-Meir, S. (1988). Parental communication deviance in childhood onset schizohrenia spectrum and depressive disorders. *Journal of Child Psychology and Psychiatry, 29,* 825-838.

Assad, G., & Shapiro, B. (1986). Hallucinations: Theoretical and clinical overview. *American Journal of Psychiatry, 143,* 1088-1097.

Barthell, C. N., & Holmes, D. S. (1968). High school yearbooks: A nonreactive measure of social isolation in graduates who later became schizophrenic. *Journal of Abnormal Psychology, 73,* 313-316. .

Bastien, R. T., & Adelman, H. S. (1984). Noncompulsory versus legally mandated placement, perceived choice, and response to treatment among adolescents. *Journal of Consulting and Clinical Psychology, 52,* 171-179.

Beckett, P. G. S. (1965). *Adolescents out of step: Their treatment in a psychiatric hospital.* Detroit: Wayne State University Press.

Bellak, L., Hurvich, M., & Gediman, H. (1973). *Ego functions in schizophrenics, neurotics, and normals.* New York: Wiley.

Bernheim, K. F. (1982). Supportive family counseling. *Schizophrenia Bulletin, 8,* 634-641.

Bilett, J. L., Jones, N. F., & Whitaker, L. C. (1982). Exploring schizophrenic thinking in older adolescents with the WAIS, Rorschach and WIST. *Journal of Clinical Psychology, 38,* 232-243.

Bleuler, E. (1911/1950). *Dementia praecox or the group of schizophrenias.* New York: International Universities Press.

Bleuler, M. E. (1978). The long-term course of schizophrenic psychoses. In L. C. Wynne, R. L. Cromwell, & S. Matthyse (Eds.), *The nature of schizophrenia* (pp. 631-636). New York: Wiley.

Bleuler, M. (1988). Prognosis of schizophrenic psychoses: A summary of personal research. In F. Flach (Ed.), *The schizophrenias* (pp. 1-10). New York: W. W. Norton.

Bloom, R. B., & Hopewell, L. R. (1982). Psychiatric hospitalization of adolescents and successful mainstream reentry. *Exceptional Children, 48,* 352-357.

Blotcky, M. J., Dimpero, T. L., & Gossett, J. T. (1984). Follow-up of children treated in psychiatric hospitals: A review of studies. *American Journal of Psychiatry, 141,* 1499-1507.

Bond, T. C., & Auger, N. (1982). Benefits of the generic milieu in adolescent hospital treatment. In S. C. Feinstein, J. G. Looney, A. Z. Schwartzberg, & A. D. Sorosky (Eds.), *Adolescent psychiatry* (Vol. 10, pp. 360-372). Chicago: University of Chicago Press.

Bower, E. M., Shellhamer, T. A., & Daly, J. M. (1960). School characteristics of male adolescents who later became schizophrenic. *American Journal of Orthopsychiatry, 30,* 712-729.

Breier, A., & Strauss, J. S. (1983). Self-control in psychotic disorders. *Archives of General Psychiatry, 40*, 1141–1145.

Buchanan, R. W., Kirkpatrick, B., Heinrichs, D., & Carpenter, W. T. (1990). Clinical correlates of the deficit syndrome of schizophrenia. *American Journal of Psychiatry, 147*, 290–294.

Burack, J. A., & Zigler, E. (1989). Age at first hospitalization and premorbid social competence in schizophrenia and affective disorder. *American Journal of Orthopsychiatry, 59*, 188–196.

Burnham, D. L., Gladstone, A. I., & Gibson, R. W. (1969). *Schizophrenia and the need–fear dilemma*. New York: International Universities Press.

Campbell, M. (1985). Schizophrenic disorders and pervasive developmental disorders/infantile autism. In J. M. Wiener (Ed.), *Diagnosis and psychopharmacology of childhood and adolescent disorders* (pp. 113–150). New York: Wiley.

Carpenter, W. T., & Heinrichs, D. W. (1983). Early intervention, time-limited, targeted pharmacotherapy of schizophrenia. *Schizophrenia Bulletin, 9*, 533–542.

Chapman, L. J., & Chapman, J. P. (1973). *Disordered thinking in schizophrenia*. New York: Appleton-Century-Crofts.

Clayton, P. J. (1982). Schizoaffective disorders. *Journal of Nervous and Mental Disease, 170*, 646–650.

Cloninger, C. R., Marton, R. L., Guze, S. B., & Clayton, P. J. (1985). Diagnosis and prognosis in schizophrenia. *Archives of General Psychiatry, 42*, 15–25.

Costell, R. M., & Reiss, D. (1982). The family meets the hospital. *Archives of General Psychiatry, 39*, 433–438.

Cutting, J., & Dunne, F. (1989). Subjective experience of schizophrenia. *Schizophrenia Bulletin, 15*, 217–231.

Daniel, D., & Plomin, R. (1985). Differential experience of siblings in the same family. *Developmental Psychology, 21*, 747–760.

Delga, I., Heinssen, R. K., Fritsch, R. C., Goodrich, W., & Yates, B. T. (1989). Psychosis, aggression, and self-destructive behavior in hospitalized adolescents. *American Journal of Psychiatry, 146*, 521–525.

Doane, J. A., Falloon, I. R. H., Goldstein, M. J., & Mintz, J. (1985). Parental affective style and the treatment of schizophrenia: Predicting course of illness and social functioning. *Archives of General Psychiatry, 42*, 34–42.

Doane, J. A., West, K. L., Goldstein, M. J., Rodnick, E. H., & Jones, J. E. (1981). Parental communication deviance and affective style: Predictors of subsequent schizophrenic disorders in vulnerable adolescents. *Archives of General Psychiatry, 38*, 679–685.

Docherty, N., Schnur, M., & Harvey, P. D. (1988). Reference performance and positive and negative thought disorder: A follow-up study of manics and schizophrenics. *Journal of Abnormal Psychology, 97*, 437–442.

Dohrenwend, B. P., & Egri, G. (1981). Recent stressful life events and episodes of schizophrenia. *Schizophrenia Bulletin, 7*, 10–23.

Donaldson, S. R., Gelenberg, A. J., & Baldessarini, R. J. (1983). The pharmacologic treatment of schizophrenia: A progress report. *Schizophrenia Bulletin, 9*, 504–527.

Easson, W. M. (1969). *The severely disturbed adolescent*. New York: International Universities Press.

Eaves, L. (1988). Genetics, immunology, and virology. *Schizophrenia Bulletin, 14,* 365–382.

Engelhardt, D. M., Rosen, B., Feldman, J., Engelhardt, J. Z., & Cohen, P. (1982). A 15-year followup of 646 schizophrenic outpatients. *Schizophrenia Bulletin, 8,* 493–503.

Erickson, D. H., Beiser, M., Iacono, W. G., Fleming, J. A., & Lin, T. (1989). The role of social relationships in the course of first-episode schizophrenia and affective psychosis. *American Journal of Psychiatry, 146,* 1456–1461.

Exner, J. E. (1986). Some Rorschach data comparing schizophrenics with borderline and schizotypal personality disorders. *Journal of Personality Assessment, 50,* 455–471.

Exner, J. E., & Weiner, I. B. (1982). *The Rorschach: A comprehensive system. Vol. 3. Assessment of children and adolescents*. New York: Wiley.

Falloon, I. R. H., & Liberman, R. P. (1983). Interactions between drug and psychosocial therapy in schizophrenia. *Schizophrenia Bulletin, 9,* 543–554.

Farber, S. L. (1981). *Identical twins reared apart*. New York: Basic Books.

Feinstein, S. C., & Miller, D. (1979). Psychoses of adolescence. In J. D. Noshpitz (Ed.), *Basic handbook of child psychiatry* (Vol. 2, pp. 708–722). New York: Basic Books.

Fenton, W. S., & McGlashan, T. H. (1987). Sustained remission in drug-free schizophrenic patients. *American Journal of Psychiatry, 144,* 1306–1309.

Fineberg, B. L., Sowards, S. K., & Kettlewell, P. W. (1980). Adolescent inpatient treatment: A literature review. *Adolescence, 15,* 913–925.

Frank, A. F., & Gunderson, J. G. (1990). The role of the therapeutic alliance in the treatment of schizophrenia. *Archives of General Psychiatry, 47,* 228–236.

Garber, B. (1972). *Follow-up study of hospitalized adolescents*. New York: Brunner/Mazel.

George, L., & Neufeld, R. W. J. (1985). Cognition and symptomatology in schizophrenia. *Schizophrenia Bulletin, 11,* 264–285.

Glish, M., Erlenmeyer-Kimling, L., & Watt, N. F. (1982). Parental assessment of the social and emotional adaptation of children at high risk for schizophrenia. In B. B. Lahey & A. E. Kazdin (Eds.), *Advances in child clinical psychology* (Vol. 5, pp. 181–218). New York: Plenum.

Goetz, K. L., & Van Kammen, D. P. (1986). Computerized axial tomography scans and subtypes of schizophrenia: A review of the literature. *Journal of Nervous and Mental Disease, 174,* 31–41.

Gold, J. M., & Hurt, S. W. (1990). The effects of haloperidol on thought disorder and IQ in schizophrenia. *Journal of Personality Assessment, 54,* 390–400.

Goldsmith, H. H. (1983). Genetic influences on personality from infancy to adulthood. *Child Development, 54,* 331–353.

Goldstein, J. M. (1988). Gender differences in the course of schizophrenia. *American Journal of Psychiatry, 145,* 684–689.

Goldstein, M. J. (1984). Schizophrenia: The interaction of family and neuroleptic therapy. In B. D. Beitman & G. L. Klerman (Eds.), *Combining psychotherapy and drug therapy in clinical practice* (pp. 167-186). New York: Spectrum.

Goldstein, M. J. (1987a). Psychosocial issues. *Schizophrenia Bulletin, 13*, 157-142.

Goldstein, M. J. (1987b). The UCLA high-risk project. *Schizophrenia Bulletin, 13*, 505-514.

Goldstein, M. J., & Jones, J. E. (1977). Adolescent and family precursors of borderline and schizophrenic conditions. In P. Hartocollis (Ed.), *Borderline personality disorders* (pp. 213-230). New York: International Universities Press.

Gossett, J. T., Barnhart, D., Lewis, J. M., & Phillips, V. (1977). A follow-up of adolescents treated in a psychiatric hospital: Precursors of outcome. *Archives of General Psychiatry, 34*, 1037-1042.

Gossett, J. T., Lewis, J. M., & Barnhart, F. D. (1983). *To find a way: The outcome of hospital treatment of disturbed adolescents*. New York: Brunner/Mazel.

Gottesman, I. I., & Bertelsen, A. (1989). Confirming unexpressed genotypes for schizophrenia. *Archives of General Psychiatry, 46*, 867-872.

Gottesman, I. I., McGuffin, P., & Farmer, A. E. (1987). Clinical genetics as clues to the "real" genetics of schizophrenia. *Schizophrenia Bulletin, 13*, 23-48.

Green, H. (1964). *I never promised you a rose Garden*. New York: Holt, Rinehart and Winston.

Green, M., & Walker, E. (1985). Neuropsychological performance and positive and negative symptoms in schizophrenia. *Journal of Abnormal Psychology, 94*, 460-469.

Grove, W. M., & Andreasen, N. C. (1985). Language and thinking in psychosis: Is there an input abnormality? *Archives of General Psychiatry, 42*, 26-32.

Guelfi, G. P., Faustman, W. O., & Csernansky, J. G. (1989). Independence of positive and negative symptoms in a population of schizophrenic patients. *Journal of Nervous and Mental Disease, 177*, 285-290.

Hamilton, N. G., Ponzoha, C. A., Cutler, D. L., & Weigel, R. M. (1989). Social networks and negative versus positive symptoms of schizophrenia. *Schizophrenia Bulletin, 15*, 625-634.

Harder, D. W., Gift, T. E., Strauss, J. S., Ritzler, B. A., & Kokes, R. F. (1981). Life events and two-year outcome in schizophrenia. *Journal of Consulting and Clinical Psychology, 49*, 619-626.

Harrow, M., & Grossman, L. S. (1984). Outcome in schizoaffective disorders: A critical review and reevaluation of the literature. *Schizophrenia Bulletin, 10*, 88-108.

Harrow, M., Grossman, L. S., Silverstein, M. L., & Meltzer, H. Y. (1982). Thought pathology in manic and schizophrenic patients. *Archives of General Psychiatry, 39*, 665-671.

Harrow, M., Grossman, L. S., Silverstein, M. L., Meltzer, H. Y., & Kettering, R. L. (1986). A longitudinal study of thought disorder in manic patients. *Archives of General Psychiatry, 43*, 781-785.

Harrow, M., & Marengo, J. T. (1986). Schizophrenic thought disorder at followup: Its persistence and prognostic significance. *Schizophrenia Bulletin, 12*, 373-393.

Harrow, M., & Quinlan, D. M. (1985). *Disordered thinking and schizophrenic psychopathology.* New York: Gardner Press.

Hartmann, E., Glasser, B. A., Greenblatt, M., Solomon, M. H., & Levinson, D. J. (1968). *Adolescents in a mental hospital.* New York: Grune & Stratton.

Helzer, J. E. (1986). Schizophrenia: Epidemiology. In J. E. Helzer & S. B. Guze (Eds.), *Psychoses, affective disorders, and dementia* (pp. 45-61). New York: Basic Books.

Helzer, J. E., Kendell, R. E., & Brockington, M. D. (1983). Contribution of the six-month criterion to the predictive validity of the *DSM-III* definition of schizophrenia. *Archives of General Psychiatry, 40,* 1277-1280.

Hillard, J. R., Slomowitz, M., & Deddens, J. (1988). Determinants of emergency psychiatric admission for adolescents and adults. *American Journal of Psychiatry, 145,* 1416-1419.

Holzman, P. S. (1988). Basic behavioral sciences. *Schizophrenia Bulletin, 14,* 413-426.

Houlihan, J. P. (1977). Heterogeneity among schizophrenic patients: Selective review of recent findings (1970-1975). *Schizophrenia Bulletin, 3,* 246-258.

Huber, G., Gross, G., Schuttler, R., & Linz, M. (1980). Longitudinal studies of schizophrenic patients. *Schizophrenia Bulletin, 6,* 592-605.

Hudgens, R. W. (1974). *Psychiatric disorders in adolescents.* Baltimore, MD: Willimas & Wilkins.

Inamdar, S. C., Lewis, D. O., & Siomopoulos, G. (1982). Violent and suicidal behavior in psychotic adolescents. *American Journal of Psychiatry, 139,* 932-935.

Intagliata, J., Willer, J., & Egri, G. (1986). Role of the family in case management of the mentally ill. *Schizophrenia Bulletin, 12,* 699-708.

John, R. S., Mednick, S. A., & Schulsinger, F. (1982). Teacher reports as a predictor of schizophrenia and borderline schizophrenia. *Journal of Abnormal Psychology, 91,* 399-413.

Johnston, M. H., & Holzman, P. S. (1979). *Assessing schizophrenic thinking.* San Francisco: Jossey-Bass.

Jones, J. M., Pearson, G. T., & Dimpero, R. (1989). Long-term treatment of the hospitalized adolescent and his family: An integrated systems-theory approach. In S. C. Feinstein (Ed.), *Adolescent psychiatry* (Vol. 16, pp. 449-472). Chicago: University of Chicago Press.

Kane, J. M. (1987). Treatment of schizophrenia. *Schizophrenia Bulletin, 13,* 133-156.

Karon, B. P. (1987). Current misconceptions about psychotherapy with schizophrenics. *Dynamic Psychotherapy, 5,* 3-15.

Karon, B. P., & Vandenbos, G. R. (1981). *Psychotherapy of schizophrenia.* New York: Aronson.

Kay, S. R., & Lindenmayer, J. (1987). Outcome predictors in acute schizophrenia: Prospective significance of background and clinical dimensions. *Journal of Nervous and Mental Disease, 175,* 152-160.

Keefe, R. S., Mohs, R. C., Losonczy, M. F., & Davidson, M. (1989). Premorbid sociosexual functioning and long-term outcome in schizophrenia. *American Journal of Psychiatry, 146,* 206-211.

Kendler, K. S. (1983). Overview: A current perspective on twin studies of schizophrenia. *American Journal of Psychiatry, 140,* 1413-1425.

Kendler, K. S., Gruenberg, A. M., & Strauss, J. S. (1982). An independent analysis of the Copenhagen sample of the Danish adoption study of schizophrenia. *Archives of General Psychiatry, 39,* 1257-1261.

Kendler, K. S., Gruenberg, A. M., & Tsuang, M. T. (1984). Outcome of schizophrenic subtypes defined by four diagnostic systems. *Archives of General Psychiatry, 41,* 149-154.

Kendler, K. S., Gruenberg, A. M., & Tsuang, M. T. (1985). Psychiatric illness in first-degree relatives of schizophrenic and surgical control patients. *Archives of General Psychiatry, 42,* 770-779.

Kendler, K. S., & Hays, M. B. (1983). Schizophrenia subdivided by the family history of affective disorder. *Archives of General Psychiatry, 40,* 951-955.

Kendler, K. S., & Robinette, C. D. (1983). Schizophrenia in the National Academy of Sciences-National Research Council twin registry: A 16-year update. *American Journal of Psychiatry, 140,* 1551-1563.

Kessler, S. (1980). The genetics of schizophrenia: A review. *Schizophrenia Bulletin, 6,* 404-416.

Kettlewell, P. W., Jones, J. K., & Jones, R. H. (1985). Adolescent partial hospitalization: Some preliminary outcome data. *Journal of Clinical Child Psychology, 14,* 139-144.

Kety, S. S. (1980). The syndrome of schizophrenia: Unresolved questions and opportunities for research. *British Journal of Psychiatry, 136,* 421-436.

Kety, S. S. (1988). Schizophrenic illness in the families of schizophrenic adoptees: Findings from the Danish national sample. *Schizophrenia Bulletin, 14,* 217-222.

Kimmel, D. C., & Weiner, I. B. (1985). *Adolescence: A developmental transition.* Hillsdale, NJ: Erlbaum.

Kraepelin, E. (1896/1919). *Dementia praecox and paraphrenia.* Chicago: Chicago Medical Book Company.

Kris, A., Schiff, L., & McLaughlin, R. (1971). Susceptibility to chronic hospitalization relative to age at first admission. *Archives of General Psychiatry, 24,* 346-352.

Ladd, G. W. (1984). Social skill training with children: Issues in research and practice. *Clinical Psychology Review, 4,* 317-337.

Leete, E. (1989). How I perceive and manage my illness. *Schizophrenia Bulletin, 15,* 197-200.

Leff, J., & Vaughn, C. (1985). *Expressed emotion in families: Its significance for mental illness.* New York: Guilford.

Lenzenweger, M. F., Dworkin, R. H., & Wethington, D. (1989). Models of positive and negative symptoms in schizophrenia: An empirical evaluation of latent structures. *Journal of Abnormal Psychology, 98,* 62-70.

Levin, S., Yurgelun-Todd, D., & Craft, S. (1989). Contributions of clinical neuropsychology to the study of schizophrenia. *Journal of Abnormal Psychology*, *98*, 341–356.

Lewine, R. (1980). Sex differences in age of symptom onset and first hospitalization in schizophrenia. *American Journal of Orthopsychiatry, 50*, 316–322.

Lewine, R. R. J. (1981). Sex differences in schizophrenia: Timing or subtypes? *Psychological Bulletin, 90*, 432–444.

Lewine, R. R., Watt, N. F., Prentky, R. A., & Fryer, J. H. (1980). Childhood social competence in functionally disordered psychiatric patients and in normals. *Journal of Abnormal Psychology, 89*, 132–138.

Lewis, M. S. (1989). Age incidence and schizophrenia: II. Beyond age incidence. *Schizophrenia Bulletin, 15*, 75–80.

Lidz, T., & Fleck, S. (1985). *Schizophrenia and the family* (2nd ed.). New York: International Universities Press.

Loranger, A. W. (1984). Sex difference in age at onset in schizophrenia. *Archives of General Psychiatry, 41*, 157–161.

Lowing, P. A., Mirsky, A. F., & Pereira, R. (1983). The inheritance of schizophrenia spectrum disorders: A reanalysis of the Danish adoptee study data. *American Journal of Psychiatry, 140*, 1167–1171.

Loyd, D. W., Simpson, J. C., & Tsuang, M. T. (1985). Are there sex differences in the long-term outcome of schizophrenia: Comparisons with mania, depression, and surgical controls. *Journal of Nervous and Mental Disease, 173*, 643–649.

Lukoff, D., Snyder, K., Ventura, J., & Nuechterlein, K. H. (1984). Life events, familial stress, and coping in the developmental course of schizophrenia. *Schizophrenia Bulletin, 10*, 258–292.

Lytton, H. (1977). Do parents create, or respond to, differences in twins? *Developmental Psychology, 13*, 456–459.

Mabe, A., Riley, W. T., & Sunde, E. R. (1989). Survey of admission policies for child and adolescent inpatient services: A national sample. *Child Psychiatry and Human Development, 20*, 99–111.

Magaro, P. A. (1980). *Cognition in schizophrenia and paranoia.* Hillsdale, NJ: Erlbaum.

Marcus, J., Hans, S. L., Mednick, S. A., Schulsinger, F., & Michelsen, N. (1985). Neurological dysfunctioning in offspring of schizophrenics in Israel and Denmark. *Archives of General Psychiatry, 42*, 753–761.

Marder, S. R., & May, P. R. (1986). Benefits and limitations of neuroleptics—and other forms of treatment—in schizophrenia. *American Journal of Psychotherapy, 40*, 357–369.

Marengo, J. T., & Harrow, M. (1987). Schizophrenic thought disorder at follow-up. *Archives of General Psychiatry, 44*, 651–659.

Masterson, J. F. (1967). *The psychiatric dilemma of adolescence.* Boston: Little, Brown.

McDaniel, K. D. (1986). Pharmacological treatment of psychiatric and neurodevelopmental disorders in children and adolescents (Parts 1, 2, and 3). *Clinical Pediatrics, 25*, 65–71, 143–146, 198–204.

McGlashan, T. H. (1983). Intensive individual psychotherapy of schizophrenia. *Archives of General Psychiatry, 40,* 909–920.

McGlashan, T. H. (1984). The Chestnut Lodge follow-up study: II. Long-term outcome of schizophrenia and the affective disorders. *Archives of General Psychiatry, 41,* 586–601.

McGlashan, T. H. (1986). Predictors of shorter-, medium-, and longer-term outcome in schizophrenia. *American Journal of Psychiatry, 143,* 50–55.

McGlashan, T. H. (1988). A selective review of recent North American long-term followup studies of schizophrenia. *Schizophrenia Bulletin, 14,* 515–542.

McGue, M., & Gottesman, I. I. (1989). Genetic linkage in schizophrenia: Perspectives from genetic epidemiology. *Schizophrenia Bulletin, 15,* 453–464.

McGuffin, P., Farmer, A. E., Gottesman, I. I., Murray, R. M., & Reveley, A. M. (1984). Twin concordance for operationally defined schizophrenia. *Archives of General Psychiatry, 41,* 541–545.

Meissner, W. W. (1978). *The paranoid process.* New York: Aronson.

Meltzer, H. Y. (1987). Biological studies in schizophrenia. *Schizophrenia Bulletin, 13,* 77–114.

Mesibov, G. (1984). Social skills training with verbal autistic adolescents and adults: A program model. *Journal of Autism and Developmental Disorders, 14,* 395–404.

Meyer, A. (1907/1948). Fundamental concepts of dementia praecox. In A. Lief (Ed.), *The commonsense psychiatry of Dr. Adolf Meyer* (pp. 184–192). New York: McGraw-Hill.

Miller, D. (1980). Treatment of the seriously disturbed adolescent. In S. C. Feinstein, P. L. Giovacchini, J. G. Looney, A. Z. Schwartzberg, and A. D. Sorosky (Eds.), *Adolescent psychiatry* (Vol. 8, pp. 469–481). Chicago: University of Chicago Press.

Millon, T. (1981). *Disorders of personality.* New York: Wiley.

Mirkin, M. P., Ricci, R. J., & Cohen, M. D. (1985). A family and community systems approach to the brief psychiatric hospitalization of adolescents. In M. P. Mirkin & S. L. Koman (Eds.), *Handbook of adolescents and family therapy,* (pp. 107–126). New York: Gardner Press.

Mirsky, A. F., & Duncan, C. C. (1986). Etiology and expression of schizophrenia: Neurobiological and psychosocial factors. *Annual Review of Psychology, 37,* 291–319.

Morris, J. (1985). The treatment of adolescent psychosis: An integrated perspective. In M. P. Mirkin & S. L. Koman (Eds.), *Handbook of adolescents and family therapy* (pp. 295–307). New York: Gardner Press.

Mosher, L. R., & Gunderson, J. G. (1973). Special report: Schizophrenia, 1972. *Schizophrenia Bulletin, 7,* 12–52.

Mosher, L. R., & Gunderson, J. G. (1979). Group, family, milieu, and community support systems treatment for schizophrenia. In L. Bellak (Ed.), *Disorders of the schizophrenic syndrome* (pp. 399–452). New York: Basic Books.

Mosher, L. R., & Keith, S. J. (1980). Psychosocial treatment: Individual, group, family, and community support approaches. *Schizophrenia Bulletin, 6,* 10–41.

Moss, G. R., & Rick, G. R. (1981). Overview: Applications of operant technology to behavioral disorders of adolescents. *American Journal of Psychiatry, 138*, 1161–1169.

Nameche, G. F., Waring, M., & Ricks, D. F. (1964). Early indicators of outcome in schizophrenia. *Journal of Nervous and Mental Disease, 139*, 232–240.

National Institute of Mental Health (1985). *Mental health, United States*. Washington, DC: U.S. Department of Health and Human Services.

Neale, J. M., & Oltmanns, T. F. (1980). *Schizophrenia*. New York: Wiley.

Nuechterlein, K. H. (1986). Childhood precursors of adult schizophrenia. *Journal of Child Psychology and Psychiatry, 27*, 133–144.

Oltmanns, T. F., Murphy, R., Berenbaum, H., & Dunlop, S. R. (1985). Rating verbal communication impairment in schizophrenia and affective disorders. *Schizophrenia Bulletin, 11*, 292–299.

Parker, B. (1962). *My language is me: Psychotherapy with a disturbed adolescent*. New York: Basic Books.

Plomin, R. (1989). Environment and genes: Determinants of behavior. *American Psychologist, 44*, 105–111.

Pogue-Geile, M. F., & Harrow, M. (1987). Schizophrenia: An evolving construct. In V. B. Van Hasselt & M. Hersen (Eds.), *Handbook of adolescent psychology* (pp. 351–380). New York: Pergamon.

Pollack, M., Levenstein, S., & Klein, D. F. (1968). A three-year posthospital follow-up of adolescent and adult schizophrenia. *American Journal of Orthopsychiatry, 38*, 94–109.

Regier, D. A., Boyd, J. H., Burke, J. D., Rae, D. S., Myers, J. K., Kramer, M., Robins, L. N., George, L. K., Karno, M., & Locke, B. Z. (1988). One-month prevalence of mental disorders in the United States. *Archives of General Psychiatry, 45*, 977–986.

Rinsley, D. B. (1980). *Treatment of the severely disturbed adolescent*. New York: Aronson.

Robins, L. N. (1966). *Deviant children grown up*. Baltimore: Williams & Wilkins.

Roff, J. D. (1974). Adolescent schizophrenia: Variables related to difference in long-term adult outcome. *Journal of Consulting and Clinical Psychology, 42*, 180–183.

Roff, J. D., & Knight, R. (1978). Young adult schizophrenics: Prediction of outcome and antecedent childhood factors. *Journal of Consulting and Clinical Psychology, 46*, 947–952.

Rosenstein, M. J., Milazzo-Sayre, L. J., & Manderscheid, R. W. (1989). Care of persons with schizophrenia: A statistical profile. *Schizophrenia Bulletin, 15*, 45–58.

Rossman, P. G., & Freedman, J. A. (1982). Hospital treatment for disturbed adolescents: The role of parent counseling groups. In S. C. Feinstein, J. G. Looney, A. Z. Schwartzberg, & A. D. Sorosky. (Eds.), *Adolescent psychiatry* (Vol. 10, pp. 391–406). Chicago: University of Chicago Press.

Ryan, E. R., & Bell, M. D. (1983). Follow-up of a psychoanalytically-oriented long-term treatment program for schizophrenic inpatients. *American Journal of Orthopsychiatry, 53*, 730–739.

Ryan, N. D., & Puig-Antich, J. (1987). Pharmacological treatment of adolescent psychiatric disorders. *Journal of Adolescent Health Care, 8*, 137–142.

Rychlak, J. F., & O'Leary, L. R. (1965). Unhealthy content in the Rorschach responses of children and adolescents. *Journal of Projective Techniques and Personality Assessment, 29*, 354–368.

Salzinger, K. (1981). Remedying schizophrenic behavior. In S. M. Turner, K. S. Calhoun, & H. E. Adams (Eds.), *Handbook of clinical behavior therapy* (pp. 162–190). New York: Wiley.

Sameroff, A., Seifer, R., Zax, M., & Barocas, R. (1987). Early indicators of developmental risk. *Schizophrenia Bulletin, 13*, 383–394.

Samson, J. A., Simpson, J. C., & Tsuang, M. T. (1988). Outcome studies of schizoaffective disorders. *Schizophrenia Bulletin, 14*, 543–554.

Sass, L. A., Gunderson, J. G., Singer, M. T., & Wynne, L. C. (1984). Parental communication deviance and forms of thinking in male schizophrenic offspring. *Journal of Nervous and Mental Disease, 172*, 513–520.

Schooler, C., & Spohn, H. E. (1982). Social dysfunction and treatment failure in schizophrenia. *Schizophrenia Bulletin, 8*, 85–98.

Schooler, N. R., & Levine, J. (1983). Strategies for enhancing drug therapy of schizophrenia. *American Journal of Psychotherapy, 37*, 521–532.

Schulz, S. C., Koller, M. M. (1989). Schizophrenia and schizophreniform disorder. In L. K. G. Hsu & M. Hersen (Eds.), *Recent developments in adolescent psychiatry* (pp. 289–308). New York: Wiley.

Schwartz, I. M. (1989). Hospitalization of adolescents for psychiatric and substance abuse treatment. *Journal of Adolescent Health Care, 10*, 473–478.

Shakow, D. (1979). *Adaptation in schizophrenia.* New York: Wiley.

Shapiro, D. (1965). *Neurotic styles.* New York: Basic Books.

Shapiro, S. A. (1981). *Contemporary theories of schizophrenia.* New York: McGraw-Hill.

Shea, M. J., Hafner, J., Quast, W., & Hetler, J. H. (1978). Outcome of adolescent psychiatric disorders: A long-term follow-up study. In E. J. Anthony, C. Koupernik, & C. Chiland (Eds.), *The child in his family: Vulnerable children* (Vol. 4, pp. 531–574). New York: Wiley.

Shore, D. (Ed.) (1986). *Schizophrenia: Questions and answers.* Washington, DC: U.S. Department of Health and Human Services.

Silberman, E. K., & Tassone, E. P. (1985). The Israeli high-risk study: Statistical overview and discussion. *Schizophrenia Bulletin, 11*, 138–145.

Silverman, L. N., Lapkin, B., & Rosenbaum, I. S. (1962). Manifestations of primary process thinking in schizophrenia. *Journal of Projective Techniques, 26*, 117–127.

Small, I. F. (1986). Electroconvulsive treatment—Indications, benefits, and limitations. *American Journal of Psychotherapy, 40*, 343–356.

Spiegel, D., & Wissler, T. (1986). Family environment as a predictor of psychiatric rehospitalization. *American Journal of Psychiatry, 143*, 56–60.

Spohn, H. E., & Strauss, M. G. (1989). Relation of neuroleptic and anticholinergic medication to cognitive functions in schizophrenia. *Journal of Abnormal Psychology, 98*, 367–380.

Spotnitz, H. (1961). Adolescence and schizophrenia: Problems in differentiation. In S. Lorand & H. I. Schneer (Eds.), *Adolescents* (pp. 217-237). New York: Hoeber.

Steinberg, D. (1986). *The adolescent unit*. Chichester, England: Wiley.

Stone, M. H., Albert, H. D., Forrest, D. V., & Arieti, S. (1983). *Treating schizophrenic patients*. New York: McGraw-Hill.

Strauss, J. S., & Carpenter, W. T. (1981). *Schizophrenia*. New York: Plenum.

Strauss, J. S., & Docherty, J. P. (1979). Subtypes of schizophrenia. *Schizophrenia Bulletin, 5*, 447-452.

Strober, M., Green, J., & Carlson, G. (1981). Reliability of psychiatric diagnosis in hospitalized adolescents. *Archives of General Psychiatry, 38*, 141-145.

Summers F., & Hersh, S. (1983). Psychiatric chronicity and diagnosis. *Schizophrenia Bulletin, 9*, 122-132.

Tardiff, K., & Sweillam, A. (1980). Assault, suicide and mental illness. *Archives of General Psychiatry, 37*, 164-169.

Vaughn, C. E. (1989). Expressed emotion in family relationships. *Journal of Child Psychology and Psychiatry, 30*, 13-22.

Vaughn, C. E., Snyder, K. S., Jones, S., Freeman, W. B., & Falloon, R. H. (1984). Family factors in schizophrenic relapse. *Archives of General Psychiatry, 41*, 1169-1177.

Ventura, J., Nuechterlein, K. H., Lukoff, D., & Hardesty, J. P. (1989). A prospective study of stressful life events and schizophrenic relapse. *Journal of Abnormal Psychology, 98*, 407-411.

Walker, E., Downey, G., & Bergman, A. (1989). The effects of parental psychopathology and maltreatment on child behavior: A test of the diathesis-stress model. *Child Development, 60*, 15-24.

Walker, E. F., Harvey, P. D., & Perlman, D. (1988). The positive/negative symptom distinction in psychoses: A replication and extension of previous findings. *Journal of Nervous and Mental Disease, 176*, 359-363.

Wallace, C. J. (1984). Community and interpersonal functioning in the course of schizophrenic disorder. *Schizophrenia Bulletin, 10*, 233-257.

Wallace, C. J., Donahoe, C. P., & Boone, S. E. (1986). Schizophrenia. In M. Hersen (Ed.), *Pharmacological and behavioral treatment: An integrative approach* (pp. 357-381). New York: Wiley.

Watt, N. F., & Lubensky, A. W. (1976). Childhood roots of schizophrenia. *Journal of Consulting and Clinical Psychology, 44*, 363-375.

Weiner, I. B. (1966). *Psychodiagnosis in schizophrenia*. New York: Wiley.

Weiner, I. B. (1980). Psychopathology in adolescence. In J. Adelson (Ed.), *Handbook of adolescent psychology* (pp. 447-471). New York: Wiley.

Weiner, I. B., & Del Gaudio, A. C. (1976). Psychopathology in adolescence: An epidemiological study. *Archives of General Psychiatry, 33*, 187-193.

Weiner, I. B., & Exner, J. E. (1978). Rorschach indices of disordered thinking in patient and nonpatient adolescents and adults. *Journal of Personality Assessment, 42*, 339-343.

Werry, J. S. (1982). Pharmacotherapy. In B. B. Lahey & A. E. Kazdin (Eds.), *Advances in clinical child psychology* (Vol. 5, pp. 283-322). New York: Plenum.

Westermeyer, J. F., & Harrow, M. (1984). Prognosis and outcome using broad (*DSM-II*) and narrow (*DSM-III*) concepts of schizophrenia. *Schizophrenia Bulletin, 10,* 624-637.

Winsberg, B. G., Bialer, I., Kupietz, S., Botti, E., & Balka, E. B. (1980). Home vs. hospital care of children with behavioral disorders. *Archives of General Psychiatry, 37,* 413-418.

Wurtele, S. K., Wilson, D. R., & Prentice-Dunn, S. (1983). Characteristics of children in residential treatment programs: Findings and clinical implications. *Journal of Clinical Child Psychology, 12,* 137-144.

Zigler, E., & Glick, M. (1986). A *developmental approach to adult psychopathology.* New York: Wiley.

Zigler, E., & Levine, J. (1981). Age on first hospitalization of schizophrenics: A developmental approach. *Journal of Abnormal Psychology, 90,* 458-467.

Zubin, J. (1986). Implications of the vulnerability model for *DSM-IV* with special reference to schizophrenia. In T. Millon & G. L. Klerman (Eds.), *Contemporary directions in psychopathology* (pp. 473-494). New York: Guilford.

Zubin, J., & Spring, B. (1977). Vulnerability: A view of schizophrenia. *Journal of Abnormal Psychology, 86,* 102-125.

CHAPTER 4

Affective Disorders

Conceptual advances and an expanded literature since the first edition of this book appeared have altered the manner in which a discussion of adolescent affective disorder should be introduced. It was once customary to begin by asserting that youthful depression and mania occur more frequently than is generally recognized and are probably underdiagnosed in clinical practice (see, for example, Cantwell, 1982; Carlson & Strober, 1979; Cytryn & McKnew, 1979; French & Berlin, 1979, Weiner, 1975). During the 1980s, however, clinical and research studies called considerable attention to affective disturbance in young persons. Of special note were such major integrative handbooks as Cantwell and Carlson's (1983) *Affective Disorders in Childhood and Adolescence* and Rutter, Izard, and Read's (1986) *Depression in Young People*. No longer are these conditions to be overlooked, nor is any purpose served by rehashing whether affective disorders emerge and can be identified in young persons.

Prior to 1980, psychopathologists also tended to see little connection between depressive disorder, which could involve a "neurotic" or "psychotic" degree of disturbance, and manic–depressive disorder, which was regarded as one of the "psychoses." Manic–depressive disorder was seldom diagnosed, and among adolescents, the possibility of affective psychosis was rarely even considered. In the previously mentioned epidemiological survey of 1334 12- to 18-year-old patients by Weiner and Del Gaudio (1976), only 1 of 1334 patients was diagnosed as having an "affective psychosis." Typical psychopathology texts, especially those dealing with young persons (and including the first edition of this book), had a chapter on depression but said little or nothing about mania.

This state of affairs was altered by the emergence of lithium carbonate treatment for manic symptomatology, by a developing research literature on the nature and origins of manic–depressive disorder, and by the advent of *DSM-III* criteria for classifying subtypes of affective disorder (see Belmaker & van Praag, 1980; Pokorny, 1987; Van Valkenburg & Akiskal, 1985). Depression and mania are now commonly regarded as variants of a general condition of affective disorder that may have either bipolar or unipolar manifestations; provision is made for diagnosing affective disorder across a wide range of severity, including even mild forms of bipolar disorder (cyclothymia); and manic–depressive disorder is not only more frequently diagnosed among adults than was formerly the case but has also become recognized clinically as a disorder of adolescence as well (see Strober, Hanna, & McCracken, 1989).

A third change from the past involves the once-popular view that depression is likely to be masked in young persons. The concept of "masked depression" was frequently applied to a wide range of behavior problems that were presumed to represent ways of coping with depressive affect and that could obscure the existence of a depressive disorder (Lesse, 1979; Toolan, 1974). Current conceptions have eliminated any need to speak of masked depression. Most developmental psychopathologists concur that affective disorders, like other disorders, typically comprise underlying impairments and a variety of ways in which these impairments may be manifest. These manifestations tend to differ from one person to the next and in relation to the age of the individual. Knowing how depression is likely to be manifested by adolescents allows clinicians to identify its presence, without having to refer to masking, and research studies indicate that alert clinicians, employing standard evaluation procedures, can successfully unmask depressive disorders in young people (Carlson & Cantwell, 1980).

Accordingly, the concept of masked depression, long a standard subject for review in discussions of adolescent affective disorder, does not receive further mention in this chapter. Good historical overviews of this and other issues in the conceptualization of youthful affective disorder are provided by Angold (1988), Carlson and Garber (1986), and Strober, McCracken, and Hanna (1989).

The chapter begins with a brief presentation of the epidemiology and symptom dimensions of affective disorder, following which attention is given to developmental variations in these conditions during the adolescent years. Subsequent sections discuss the causes of affective disorder, some considerations in its differential diagnosis, and its prognosis and treatment.

EPIDEMIOLOGY OF AFFECTIVE DISORDER

The conceptual advances and the expanded literature on adolescent affective disorders have not yet painted a clear picture of how frequently they occur. Numerous studies of the incidence and prevalence of these conditions have employed widely varying methods and have consequently yielded highly variable results (see Fleming & Offord, 1990; Strober, McCracken, & Hanna, 1989). With respect to depression, for example, some investigators have simply asked adolescents questions about their mood states. In the Isle of Wight studies, 47.7% of the females and 41.7% of the males in a nonpatient sample of 14- to 15-year-olds answered "Yes" when asked whether they "sometimes feel miserable and unhappy," and 23.0% of the girls and 20.8% of the boys agreed with the statement that they "often feel miserable or depressed" (Rutter, Graham, Chadwick, & Yule, 1976). In a survey by Kandel and Davies (1982) of 8206 14- to 18-year-old high school students,

19.7% reported being "much bothered" about "feeling sad or depressed in the past year."

Other investigators have gone beyond mood states by asking for self-reports or reports by peers, parents, or teachers of whether a young person was showing "depressive symptoms." Lefkowitz and Tesiny (1985) used the Peer Nomination Inventory of Depression in this way with 3020 elementary school children (average age 9.83 years) and concluded that 5.6% of the girls and 4.8% of the boys were manifesting severe depression. In a sample of 200 young persons referred to a child guidance clinic, Cass and Thomas (1979) found that 73% were considered by their parents to be showing symptoms of depression. In a study assessing 550 early adolescents with the Center for Epidemiological Studies Depression Scale on three occasions, in the seventh, eighth, and ninth grades, 8 to 10% received scores suggesting major depressive disorder each year—although there was considerable fluctuation in which young people gave these depressive self-reports on each occasion (Garrison, Jackson, Marsteller, McKeown, & Addy, 1990).

Still other investigators have conducted formal diagnostic assessments of patient and nonpatient adolescents using *DSM-III* criteria and such standardized techniques as the Beck Depression Inventory (BDI). Using the BDI, Kaplan, Hong, and Weinhold (1984) found a 13.5% frequency of mild depression and an additional 8.6% frequency of moderate or severe depression among 385 high school juniors and seniors. Reviewing the records of 302 ambulatory and hospitalized adolescent psychiatric patients, Mezzich and Mezzich (1979) concluded that 76% had a diagnosable depressive disorder, even though only 28% had previously received a depressive diagnosis from the clinical staff. In a similar study of 76 adolescents recently discharged from a psychiatric hospital, Friedman, Clarkin, Corn, Aronoff, Hurt, and Murphy (1982) concluded that 59% had suffered depressive disorders, whereas only 14% had been given a discharge diagnosis of depression.

Taken together, these and other similar studies mean very little, because of the differences among them in sample characteristics and assessment methods. For adults, systematic community studies conducted under the aegis of the National Institute of Mental Health (NIMH) now provide some fairly reliable epidemiological data. The lifetime prevalence of major depressive episodes and dysthymic disorder combined is 9.1%, their incidence over a 6-month period is 6.3%, and the frequency of cases within a 1-month period is 5.5% (Regier, Boyd, Burke, Rae, Myers, Kramer, Robins, George, Karno, & Locke, 1988).

The best available comparable data on adolescents, based on careful clinical assessments of nonreferred teenagers, comes from small community samples. In one group of 150 14- to 16-year-olds, Kashani and his colleagues found an 8.0% point prevalence of major depression or dysthymic disorder (Kashani, Carlson, Beck, Hoeper, Corcoran, McAllister, Fallahi, Rosenberg, & Reid, 1987). Among 356 secondary school students, Whitaker and her colleagues identified a lifetime prevalence of 8.9% for these disorders combined (Whitaker, Johnson, Shaffer, Rapoport, Kalikow, Walsh, Davies, Braiman, & Dolinsky, 1990).

Turning to mania, the lifetime prevalence of manic episodes among persons ages 18 years and above in the United States is 0.8%, and the percentage of adults who are likely to experience a manic episode within any one-month period is half that (0.4%) (Regier et al., 1988). Neither the prevalence nor the incidence of mania has yet been examined systematically in adolescents. However, the significance of bipolar affective disorder in the psychopathology of adolescence has been demonstrated by evidence that this condition frequently has its beginnings during the adolescent years.

The most extensive data in this regard come from the previously mentioned NIMH study, which is frequently referred to as the Environmental Catchment Area (ECA) program and involved use of the Diagnostic Interview Schedule with adult samples in five communities. Burke, Burke, Regier, and Rae (1990) conclude from the ECA data that bipolar disorder has a median age of onset of 19 years, which means that 50% of persons with this condition first become disturbed before they leave the teen years.

Although the median age of onset for depressive disorder occurs in the twenties rather than the teens, clinical and research findings indicate that puberty ushers in a substantial increase in the frequency with which young persons become diagnosably depressed. Estimates place the prepubertal incidence of depressive disorder at less than 3%, following which a growing susceptibility with each postpubertal year results in a threefold increase in this condition during adolescence (Fleming & Offord, 1990; Kashani et al., 1987). In one illustrative demonstration of this developmental change, Kashani, Rosenberg, and Reid (1989) found *DSM-III* depressive disorder in 1.4% of a community sample of 70 nonreferred 12-year-olds and a frequency of 5.4% in 70 nonreferred 17-year-olds in the same community.

Adolescence is also notable for the appearance of sex differences in the frequency of depressive disorders. Prior to puberty, boys and girls are equally likely to display both depressive phenomena and manic characteristics. During adolescence, the sex distribution of mania remains about even, but depression becomes much more common in females than in males. Among nonpatient high school students, girls are found to report significantly more numerous depressive symptoms than boys (Allgood-Merten, Lewinsohn, & Hops, 1990). Among adolescents who become affectively disturbed, unipolar but not bipolar disorder appears more frequently in girls than boys (Angold, 1988; Gillberg, Wahlstrom, Forsman, Hellgren, & Gillberg, 1986; Kandel & Davies, 1982).

This developmental change mirrors sex differences in affective disorder demonstrated in epidemiological studies of adults. Manic episodes occur slightly more often in women than in men, in a ratio of about 4 to 3, whereas women are twice as likely as men to develop dysthymia or a major depressive disorder (Regier et al., 1988). Among both adult and adolescent patients with an affective disorder, moreover, males show an approximately equal frequency of unipolar depression and bipolar disorder, whereas the ratio of unipolar depression to bipolar disorder in affectively disordered females is about 2 to 1 (Winokur & Crowe, 1983).

This demonstrably greater susceptibility of females than males to depressive disorder is as yet unexplained. Some researchers have hypothesized that it derives from elements of the traditional female role in our society, especially low social status, discrimination in achievement-related situations, and lack of choice in planning their lives (Chevron, Quinlan, & Blatt, 1978; Formanek & Gurian, 1987; Weissman & Klerman, 1979). Another possibility, suggested by Cramer and Carter (1978), is that in forming their sex-role identities, males begin during adolescence to show a preference for resolving conflict through external channels of expression ("acting out"), whereas females develop a preference for dealing with conflict internally ("acting in"). Studies of preferred defensive style confirm that, for adults and adolescents alike, males are more inclined than females to respond to interpersonal conflict by blaming or attacking someone else, whereas females are more inclined to respond by directing aggressive thoughts or actions toward themselves (Cramer, 1988).

Consistent with the Cramer and Carter hypothesis, there is some evidence that depression in adolescence is more likely to be associated with disobedience and misbehavior in males than in females, whereas females show higher correlations than males between their overall level of depression and such inward-focused manifestations as dysphoric mood and negative views of themselves (Gjerde, Block, & Block, 1988; Smucker, Craighead, Craighead, & Green, 1986). In a similar vein, Nolen-Hoeksema (1987) suggests that males who become depressed are more likely than females to seek distraction in behaviors that attenuate their mood state, thus decreasing the likelihood of their feeling or seeming to be depressed. Females, by contrast, are more likely to ruminate about a depressed state and ponder its cause, which amplifies their mood state and leads to a greater frequency of felt and diagnosed depression.

Confirmation of these hypotheses awaits further research. In the meantime, as is the case with many postulated sex-role differences in relation to psychopathology and personality functioning, question must be raised whether contemporary societal trends toward reduced sexism will correspondingly reduce these differences. One recent study of 498 adult patients with major depressive disorder, while finding the expected greater frequency of the condition in women than in men, did not demonstrate any differences between the sexes in how their depression was being manifest, with the exception of more frequent weight gain in the women (Young, Scheftner, Fawcett, & Klerman, 1990).

DIMENSIONS OF AFFECTIVE DISORDER

For purposes of clinical evaluation and treatment planning, affective disorder can usefully be conceived as consisting of maladaptive changes in a person's *mood, attitudes, energy level,* and *physical status.* Such maladaptive changes constitute the basic dimensions of both depression and mania, and the extent to which a person's behavior fluctuates toward one or both poles of these dimensions provides a yardstick for assessing the presence and nature of an affective disorder.

Mood

Whereas schizophrenia is primarily a disorder of thinking (see Chapter 3), affective disorders are primarily disorders of mood, running from profound misery in the depths of depression to sheer ecstasy at the peak of mania. Pathologically depressed moods typically involve persistent feelings of sadness, spells of tearfulness and crying, loss of interest in people and previously enjoyed pursuits, and diminished ability to experience pleasure. Pathologically elevated moods, by contrast, are reflected in unrelieved joyfulness, constant smiling and laughing, infectious good humor, enthusiasm spreading in all directions, and pleasure experienced at every turn.

Depressed people tend to withdraw into themselves emotionally, are difficult if not impossible to cheer up, and usually have an unpleasant dampening effect on those around them. Manic individuals, by contrast, actively reach out to other people and enliven social gatherings. However, because their bubbling gaiety persists even when the needs of others call for more subdued behavior, they can also make themselves socially disagreeable. In addition, both depressed and manic persons are likely to experience episodes of anger and irritability that make it difficult for them and those around them to enjoy each other's company (see Coyne, Kessler, Tal, Turnbull, Wortman, & Greden, 1987; Post, Rubinow, Uhde, Roy-Byrne, Linnoila, Rosoff, & Cowdry, 1989; Riley, Treiber, & Woods, 1989; Youngren & Lewinsohn, 1980).

Attitudes

Affective disorder frequently involves very negative or very positive attitudes toward oneself, the world, and the future. Persons who are depressed tend to think poorly of themselves and feel helpless to control their destiny or improve their circumstances. They view themselves as inadequate, unattractive, and unlovable, and they often harbor a sense of guilt for having behaved improperly or sinfully. The low self-esteem and self-depreciation of depressed individuals lead to a degree of pessimism and hopelessness that often discourages them from even trying to escape their unhappiness. Instead, they persist in looking on the dark side of things, comparing themselves unfavorably to other persons and experiencing painful discrepancies between their goals and their expectations (see Ahrens, 1987; Kanfer & Zeiss, 1983; Kovacs & Beck, 1978; Prosen, Clark, Harrow, & Fawcett, 1983).

At the opposite pole of this dimension, mania is characterized by inflated self-esteem, unrealistically high expectations, and an uncritical sense of optimism. No task is too difficult to achieve, no obstacle too great to surmount, and no shortcoming too serious to be overcome. Manic people expect to be loved and admired by all and to succeed in everything they attempt. Should they recognize failure when it occurs, they attribute it to the inadequacy or interference of others rather than to their own limitations. Whereas depressive attitudes discourage activity, the grandiosity that accompanies mania and the rose-colored glasses through which manic individuals view the world generate ambitious plans and an enormous investment in carrying them out (see Carpenter & Stephens, 1980; Lerner, 1980).

Each of these extreme attitudes distorts reality in some way. For this reason, both depression and mania can assume psychotic proportions should the person's present perceptions and future expectations deviate markedly from what reality holds in store. Then, like schizophrenics, affectively disordered individuals may develop strange ideas about who they are and what they can or cannot do, and they may exercise poor judgment in conducting their daily lives. As a case in point, approximately three quarters of patients with bipolar affective disorder are likely to become delusional during manic episodes, and many of the beliefs they form at these times involve unwarranted convictions of grandiosity (Neale, 1988). The more seriously depressed or manic people become, the more likely they are to suffer such a psychotic loss of touch with reality or to demonstrate disordered thinking (Harder, Strauss, Kokes, & Ritzler, 1984).

Energy Level

Depression often consists partly of diminution in mental and physical energy that becomes manifest in lethargy and difficulty concentrating. Like a windup toy that is running down, depressed individuals move slowly, talk slowly, and think slowly, giving rise to the phenomenon of psychomotor retardation. Because of how difficult it is for them to get their bodies to move and their minds to focus, people who are depressed typically accomplish less than their capabilities would otherwise make possible. At times, the deficits that depressed persons are likely to show in processing information, solving learning and reasoning problems, and coordinating their attention and memory functions are regarded as constituting a thinking disorder. However, these deficits can be understood more parsimoniously as resulting from the depleted mental energy available to depressed persons for performing cognitive tasks (see Cohen, Weingartner, Smallberg, Pickar, & Murphy, 1982; Cornell, Suarez, & Berent, 1984; Silberman, Weingartner, & Post, 1983).

In mania, the tide flows in the other direction. Vast stores of energy appear to be at the person's disposal, frequently in greater amounts than they can harness effectively. This accounts for a characteristic pressure of speech observed in manic persons, whose words often stumble over each other faster than they can be pronounced clearly. Thoughts similarly flow in quick succession, producing flights of ideas and causing the person to lose track of the point he or she was trying to make. The actions of manic persons likewise proceed in many directions at once, making them appear driven and disorganized and causing them to waste more effort than they use constructively.

Physical Status

The onset of an affective disorder often brings with it changes in physical status. Known as the "biological" or "vegetative" features of these conditions, such physical changes most commonly consist of disturbed patterns of sleeping and eating. Persons who are depressed tend to fall asleep slowly, sleep poorly, and wake easily. When they are successful in avoiding insomnia, fitfulness, and early morning awakening, they are still likely to get up from long hours of sleep feeling fatigued and unrefreshed. A person's appetite during episodes of depression often becomes either much smaller or much larger than usual. Depressed persons consequently tend to lose or gain a great deal of weight and may even show alternating periods of what appear to be anorexia or bulimia. These changes in physical status do not inevitably accompany depression; they tend to be associated with severe rather than mild depression and therefore provide a barometer of how deeply depressed the person has become (Casper, Redmond, Katz, Schaffer, David, & Koslow, 1985).

Even mild depression is additionally likely to be reflected in a general sense of physical malaise and an exaggerated concern with health and bodily functions. As an aspect of such hypochondriasis, depressed persons frequently regard themselves as being in poorer condition than they used to be, and they are in fact likely to experience an unusual number of aches, pains, and other somatic complaints that add to their worries about deteriorating health.

Manic individuals, by contrast, typically present a picture of robust health. They sleep soundly and require less sleep than usual to feel rested. They eat heartily, describe themselves as being "in the pink of condition," and rarely complain of any physical symptoms. In mania, this sense of well-being persists even in the face of actual physical ailments that should be causing the person concern. Manic individuals are consequently likely to deny conditions that require medical treatment and to overlook symptoms that herald the onset of illness.

Dimensions of Affective Disorder in Adolescents

Although these various manifestations of affective disorder have been identified primarily in studies of adult patients, each of the four dimensions of depression and mania has been demonstrated to characterize young persons as well. In one illustrative study, symptom formation was examined in 92 adolescent patients with major depressive disorder (Ryan, Puig-Antich, Ambrosini, Rabinovich, Robinson, Nelson, Iyengar, & Twomey, 1987). With respect to mood, 95% of these adolescents displayed depressed mood, 86% demonstrated anhedonia, and 82% were notably angry or irritable. With respect to their attitudes, 73% of these young persons had a negative self-image, 65% complained of hopelessness and helplessness, and 49% expressed guilt feelings. As for their energy level, 86% of the group had impaired concentration, 80% complained of fatigue, and 68% showed psychomotor retardation. Regarding their physical status, 71% were insomniac and 63% had somatic complaints.

Numerous other reports indicate that the disturbances in mood, attitudes, energy level, and physical status traditionally associated with affective disorder in adults can be readily identified and reliably measured in adolescents (Hughes, 1984; Kaslow, Rehm, & Siegel, 1984; Kovacs, 1989; McCauley, Mitchell, Burke, & Moss, 1988). Clinicians and researchers have accordingly come to agree that only minor modifications of the criteria used with adults are necessary to identify these conditions in young persons (see Kendall, Cantwell, & Kazdin, 1989; Ryan, 1989; Strober, McCracken, & Hanna, 1989).

DEVELOPMENTAL VARIATIONS IN AFFECTIVE DISORDER

Although the same basic dimensions of disturbance characterize affective disorder at all ages, the most prominent manifestations of these disorders vary somewhat with the age of the person. A broad consensus argues for viewing affective disorders among children, adolescents, and adults within a developmental perspective that recognizes age-related influences on symptom manifestations while also emphasizing similarities and continuity throughout the life cycle in the basic phenomenology of these conditions (Carlson & Kashani, 1988; Kazdin, 1990; Kendall et al., 1989; Strober, McCracken, & Hanna, 1989).

Most notably with respect to adolescence, the cognitive immaturity and egocentrism of young persons make them more likely than adults to externalize the focus of any depressive concerns they have. Whereas depressed adults usually become preoccupied with their own view of themselves and perceive themselves as failures in their own eyes, depressed adolescents tend to become preoccupied with how others view them and to perceive themselves as failures in the eyes of others (Stehouwer, Bultsma, & Blackford, 1985). This and other adolescent variations in affective disorder are most marked during early and middle adolescence and gradually diminish by late adolescence.

Early and Middle Adolescence

The developmental tasks that young persons face from puberty until age 16 or 17 years—including adjusting to rapid changes in their bodies, becoming more autonomous in relation to their parents, widening and deepening their friendships, and learning to deal with dating and sexuality—pose serious challenges to their self-esteem. They must regularly confront new and unfamiliar situations in which coping effectively and "looking good" call for behaviors with which they have little prior experience. Because they often have to rely on untried and uncertain strategies, young persons live constantly with the threat of failure and humiliation. To help themselves keep working on developmental tasks despite such risks, adolescents often resort to a form of denial. They refuse to admit to themselves or anyone else that they harbor self-critical attitudes or concerns about being a competent person. They avoid even thinking about being unable to cope, because such thoughts make them feel childish or dependent.

As one consequence of this developmental phenomenon, younger adolescents are somewhat unlikely to experience or display the gloom, self-depreciation, and feelings of helplessness and hopelessness that commonly characterize depression in older adolescents and adults. As a result, younger adolescents with an affective disorder are more likely to manifest easily recognizable signs of mania than of depression. When they do become depressed, they often express their disorder in efforts to ward off depression through *restlessness*, a *flight to or from people*, and *problem behavior*.

Restlessness

Common lore says correctly that keeping busy is a good way to "keep your mind off things" and avoid feeling depressed. Because young adolescents are usually intent on avoiding depressive feelings, they sometimes become more rather than less active in the face of depressing circumstances. This increased energy seldom results in any sustained accomplishments, however. Instead, it makes depressed youngsters restless, easily bored, and constantly in need of stimulation and excitement. They take up new pursuits with great enthusiasm, only to lose interest and drop them as soon as familiarity sets in. Routine of any kind becomes difficult for them to tolerate, quiet contemplation and low-key activities cannot be endured, and cravings for novelty and adventure become their marching orders.

Flight to or from People

In their relationships with people, younger adolescents with an affective disorder may exhibit an urgent need for companionship and a continuous search for new and "more interesting" friends. Like restlessness, such a flight toward people helps to keep the person stimulated and occupied, one step ahead of being overtaken by depressive thoughts or feelings.

Sometimes, however, when being around others evokes fears of being criticized or rejected, depressed youngsters may flee from instead of toward people. Because they may still feel a need to ward off depression through activity, these avoidant adolescents may then become intensely involved in solitary pursuits or turn their attention to pets, toward which they can feel and show affection with little risk of rejection. In the previously mentioned Ryan et al. (1987) sample, 71% of the depressed adolescents gave evidence of being socially withdrawn. Other research findings confirm that seventh- and eighth-grade students who are struggling with depressing thoughts and feelings are more likely than their nondepressed peers to prefer being by themselves and to avoid public places (Larson, Raffaelli, Richards, Ham, & Jewell, 1990).

Problem Behavior

In some cases, younger adolescents express depression primarily through temper tantrums, running away, stealing, truancy, and other defiant, rebellious, or antisocial acts. To the extent that such problem behavior is novel and exciting, it meets the needs of these youngsters for stimulation and helps them avoid dwelling on what may be troubling them. Public displays of resisting authority or outwitting the establishment may also result in some notoriety that at least fleetingly lifts their self-esteem. Perhaps of even greater significance, problem behavior compels the attention of important persons in the adolescent's life and thereby provides an indirect way of letting them know that he or she is struggling with depressing concerns that cannot be directly expressed (see Bemporad & Lee, 1988; Bodiford, Eisenstadt, Johnson, & Bradlyn, 1988; Koenig, 1988; Ney, Colbert, Newman & Young, 1986). The ways in which depression can contribute to delinquent behavior are discussed further in Chapter 8.

CASE 3.   DEPRESSION IN EARLY ADOLESCENCE

Wilma was an academically average, plain-looking eighth-grade student, age 13 years, who lived in the shadows of her family and peer-group life. Her father owned a small business that monopolized his time, and her mother— a youthful, attractive, and fashionable woman whose appearance contrasted markedly with Wilma's usual drabness—was actively engaged in a business career of her own. During their limited moments at home, both parents concentrated their attention on Wilma's two younger brothers. Although the parents recognized that Wilma felt less favored than her brothers, in their opinion, she was being adequately cared for and had no grounds for what was her typical sullenness and constant complaining. From Wilma's perspective, however, she was the least able, least attractive, least loved, and least important member of her family.

Among her peers, Wilma tagged along with many different groups, but more often as a tolerated hanger-on than as a valued member. "If I disappeared tomorrow," she said, "my friends wouldn't miss me or even notice I wasn't there." Wilma's parents took a dim view of many of these friends and frequently criticized them for their sloppy dress and undisciplined behavior. Yet they never established any rules about Wilma's choice of companions or about how she should dress and act. In most respects, in fact, they gave little indication of caring what she did or what happened to her.

One day at school, Wilma overheard some classmates talking about a recent bomb scare at a nearby school, which they described as a "neat" prank. Later that same day, she went to a telephone booth and called her principal's office to report that a bomb was about to go off in the school building. Within a few minutes an alarm was sounded, the building was evacuated, and the police arrived to search the premises.

Wilma subsequently confided to several classmates that she had been the anonymous caller. Word of her guilt spread quickly, and before the day was out, school officials had summoned her parents and notified the police, who subsequently sent the family to juvenile court. Said Wilma, "It was the first time in months I was in a room with both of my parents at the same time." The court proceedings required many hours of her parents' time, and they were ordered by the judge to keep a close watch on her behavior. Everybody in her school now knew who she was and what she had done. At whatever the price she eventually had to pay, this lonely, discouraged, ignored girl's actions pulled her from the shadows into the limelight momentarily.

Late Adolescence

As adolescents mature, they become more capable than before of thinking about themselves and of sharing self-doubts with others. Compared to early and middle adolescents, late adolescents accordingly resemble adults more closely in both their manic and their depressive symptoms, should they develop an affective disorder. Nevertheless, some older adolescents may still express depression indirectly, through maladaptive behavior. The most common behavioral indices of depression in late adolescents are *drug abuse*, *sexual promiscuity*, *alienation*, and *suicidal behavior*. Each of these problem behaviors may have other causes, and none of them points only or even necessarily to depression. Yet they can and do arise as secondary reactions to depression, which means that clinicians are well-advised to evaluate and treat them with an eye to possible depressive concerns in their origin.

Drug Abuse

The popular media often suggest that regular drug use has become a widespread and normal feature of contemporary teenage behavior. The facts run quite to the contrary: Drug abuse characterizes only a small minority of adolescents and reflects serious maladjustment when it occurs. The more frequently high school students use drugs, for example, the more likely they are to do poorly in school, to be uninvolved in either academic or extracurricular school activities, to have interpersonal problems, and to lack any serious commitment to social, occupational, or recreational pursuits (Kovach & Glickman, 1986; Mills & Noyes, 1984; Sutker, 1982).

The disengagement and low energy level found among adolescent drug abusers speak in part to possible depressive underpinnings of their problem. In addition, persistent regular drug use may emerge as an effort to ward off depressive feelings. The intoxicating effects of drugs can offer escape from depressing concerns, the process of illegally obtaining and using drugs can satisfy needs for excitement and stimulation, and sharing a drug experience with other young persons can establish a sense of companionship and provide a hedge against loneliness. For such reasons, substance abuse is found in about one fourth of depressed adolescents, and adolescents with depressive disorder are more than four times more likely than their nonpatient peers to abuse alcohol and more than three times more likely to use other potentially addictive substances (Fleming & Offord, 1990; Ryan, 1989). These and other aspects of adolescent drug abuse are elaborated in Chapter 10.

Sexual Promiscuity

Sexual promiscuity, like abuse of drugs, is sometimes regarded as a common characteristic of today's teenagers. Contrary to popular belief, however, abundant research demonstrates that there has been no sexual revolution in the United States since the 1920s. Young persons are more open and sophisticated about sexual matters than in the past and more inclined to become physically intimate in the context of a close, trusting, and relatively enduring relationship. However, they are no more likely than in previous years to approve of or engage in promiscuous sexuality, which consists of physical intimacy without personal intimacy and a rapid succession of multiple sex partners. Casual, indiscriminate sexuality is rare among young persons, especially females, and it is typically associated with psychological maladjustment when it occurs (Antonovsky, Shoham, Kavenaki, Lancet, & Modan, 1980; Brooks-Gunn & Furstenberg, 1989; Chilman, 1983; Miller & Simon, 1980).

Although adolescent girls are less active sexually than boys, they are more likely to use promiscuity to ward off depression. This sex difference occurs because sexual encounters ordinarily place more demands on the male than on the female to be knowledgeable and to perform well. Teenage boys are relatively inexperienced and uncertain of their ability to perform, which makes sexual activity a risky way for them to attempt to bolster flagging feelings of adequacy. The strong possibility of embarrassment or failure means that they could end up feeling worse instead of better about themselves. For girls, on the other hand, being promiscuous requires only willingness, not performance. Hence they can more safely turn to sexuality to compensate for negative self-attitudes. In this regard, the promiscuity of a depressed adolescent girl is seldom sexual, in the sense of providing erotic gratification. Instead, it serves primarily as an avenue for intimate physical contact with other persons. The attention she receives from boys and young men seeking her favors, the experience of feeling needed and wanted, and the sensations of being held and caressed all may help a depressed girl combat feelings of being unattractive, alone, and unloved.

Alienation

References to alienated youth become popular from time to time as a way of describing the manner in which young persons relate to their society. In fact, however, alienation is no more typical of adolescence than drug abuse or sexual promiscuity. Most adolescents are keenly interested in what is going on in their community and share with their parents and other adults the basic values of their society. As noted in Chapter 1, those young persons who lack close ties with their families and broader community are likely to be maladjusted rather than developing normally.

Especially when depression clouds their lives, late adolescents may become prone to a pattern of alienation in which they retreat from seeking a place for themselves in the world. Concerned about their adequacy, they avoid efforts that could end in failure and aspirations that could lead to disappointment. Such restricted horizons not infrequently result in pervasive underachievement or inactivity that is justified by a cynical, what's-the-use-of-it-all view of the world.

Adolescents who are coping in this way with underlying depression sometimes join together to form groups of young persons who become visible for their unconventional, antiestablishment ideas. Although some members of such groups may hold deep convictions, many are less concerned with the group's avowed purposes than with being able to use the group to escape from depressing feelings of being alone, unimportant, or ineffective (see Bemporad & Lee, 1988; Cambor, 1973).

Suicidal Behavior

Depression, more than any other psychological disorder, poses a risk of suicidal behavior. Abundant evidence confirms that the more depressed persons become, especially when they form increasingly negative attitudes toward themselves and their future, the more likely they are to consider taking their own lives (Husain & Vandiver, 1984, Chapter 12; Pfeffer, 1986, Chapter 5; Robbins & Alessi, 1985; Sheras, 1983).

This is not to say that suicidal individuals are always depressed. To the contrary, clinically manifest depression is found in just 30–40% of adolescents who commit or attempt suicide, which means that the majority are not noticeably depressed (Schneer, Perlstein, & Brozovsky, 1975; Shaffer, 1974, 1986). On the other hand, suicidal ideation was reported by 58% of the depressed adolescents in the Ryan et al. (1987) study, and the likelihood of suicide attempts by these young persons was directly correlated with how long their depression had lasted. Clinicians must accordingly be especially alert to possible suicidal behavior among adolescents who are depressed. Such behavior by depressed adolescents is typically a desperate, last-ditch effort to get other people to recognize and help them with pressing problems for which they have been unable to find a solution. These and other aspect of youthful suicidal behavior are discussed more fully in Chapter 9.

Case 4. Depression in Late Adolescence

Dwight was 16 when he made a suicide attempt with 20 aspirin tablets. The previous several years of his life had been marked by family instability. His mother had been hospitalized recurrently with a chronic schizophrenic condition, and while at home she had been too disorganized to function adequately as a parent and homemaker. To spare him the distress of their home life, Dwight's father had sent him to live with his grandparents in another city while he was in junior high school, and he had gotten along reasonably well. On returning home to begin his freshman year in high school, however, Dwight was dismayed at discovering that his father had been having an affair with their neighbor, a divorced woman whose children were his schoolmates.

At this point, Dwight began increasingly to withdraw from activities and to isolate himself from his former friends, whom he felt embarrassed to face. He started going to bars, where he used fake identification to be served, and he took to late hours, delinquent companions, and neglect of his studies. This period of withdrawal culminated in his running away to a distant city, where he spent 2 weeks hanging around bars, living in rooming houses, and developing increasing feelings of isolation.

He then returned home, only to learn that in his absence, his father had gone to Mexico for a divorce and had married the neighbor. Thus in 2 short weeks, his home as he had known it had ceased to exist. He refused to move in with his father and new stepmother and instead rented a room by himself. In this setting, his previous efforts to ward off depression through flight gave way to full-blown depressive changes in his mood, attitudes, and energy level. In his own subsequent words, his life at this point "seemed a big pointless nothing; nothing was good for me in the past, and I'll probably end up in a mental hospital or as a bum." After 4 days of progressive gloom, lethargy, and despair, he swallowed the aspirins and then called his father to ask for help.

Dwight was admitted to an inpatient psychiatric unit, where his history of social withdrawal and his mother's known schizophrenic disturbance initially suggested that he might be developing schizophrenia himself. However, he did not manifest any behavioral peculiarities, and he quickly developed appropriate and positive relationships with the hospital staff. Psychological testing helped further to rule out the presence of any impairments of his thinking, reality testing, or basic ability to establish meaningful social relationships. Dwight responded well to an individual and family therapy program aimed at easing his depressive concerns and reestablishing his relationship with his father, and he was discharged to outpatient care after a brief hospitalization. During a subsequent 5-year period in which follow-up was available, he did not require further professional attention.

CASE 5.   BIPOLAR DISORDER

During the summer before she was to begin junior high school, about which she was extremely apprehensive, 12-year-old Janet became uncharacteristically nervous, hyperactive, and insomniac. In September, she turned despondent, and her mother, having heard her say, "It's too much for me; I want to kill myself," brought her to an outpatient clinic. The interviewer described her as coherent, tense, depressed, and imminently psychotic and recorded a diagnosis of adolescent adjustment reaction. She was seen for the next several months in group therapy, during which time her depression lifted and her initial shyness and withdrawal in the group setting abated.

The following September, she was back at the clinic, in relation to entering a new parochial school on which her parents had decided. She complained of vivid and frightening nightmares, and her parents described a recent history of disabling lethargy and psychomotor retardation. The interviewer felt she was overtly psychotic and paranoid and arranged admission to an inpatient unit. In the hospital, she initially seemed confused, demonstrated apparently disconnected speech and thought blockage, and expressed delusional beliefs that other patients were saying bad things about her. She was diagnosed as schizophrenic and placed on phenothiazine medication.

Sometime later, in talking about this episode of breakdown, Janet described it as a time when her thoughts were so slow and her concentration so poor that she could not fully comprehend what others were saying or respond promptly and effectively. Her apparent paranoia was closely tied to her own heavily guilt-laden self-recriminations (such as being unworthy of sacrifices her mother had made on her behalf). Interestingly, in light of these reasons to question the diagnosis of schizophrenia, the phenothiazines were ineffective.

Janet's psychotic symptoms gradually remitted during the first 6 months of her hospital stay. However, she remained persistently dysphoric, withdrawn, and lethargic and had little appetite. These depressive symptoms lifted over the next 6 months, and, now age 14, she was discharged to a day school for emotionally disturbed children.

For the next year and a half, she functioned relatively well at home and in this day school, but she then began to experience a sense of "having to do things fast." Her parents observed her becoming overactive, sleepless, talkative, and emotionally labile, as she had been prior to her first breakdown almost 3 years earlier. Her teachers felt she was becoming increasingly uncontrollable and unpredictable, and, after 3 months of escalating symptoms, she was diagnosed as manic–depressive and hospitalized for a course of lithium treatment.

In the hospital, Janet was initially described as intrusive, hyperactive, hypersexual, labile, and euphoric. These manic symptoms diminished considerably after 2 weeks of the lithium medication, but she was continued in inpatient care for several months. Following discharge, she was maintained on lithium and seen in weekly outpatient psychotherapy. No further breakdown requiring hospitalization occurred during a subsequent 2-year period for which follow-up data were available.

Janet's history of cyclical depressive and manic symptoms and her propensity for psychotic breakdown painted in retrospect a clear picture of bipolar affective disorder emerging in adolescence. Her history as a patient also demonstrates some of the misdirections in which clinicians may be led during the developmental stages of this disorder: seeing the first breakdown as an adjustment reaction instead of recognizing the onset of diagnosable psychopathology; then focusing on her depressive symptoms without attending adequately to their being preceded by periods of hypomania; and misinterpreting the cognitive consequences of her psychomotor retardation and concentration difficulty as schizophrenic thought disorder and prescribing neuroleptics, to no effect. Stabilization was achieved, at least over 2 years, only when bipolar disorder was diagnosed and lithium added to the treatment plan.

CAUSES OF AFFECTIVE DISORDER

Affective disorder, like schizophrenia, appears to result from a pathological interaction between genetic dispositions (*diathesis*) and unpleasant life experiences (*stress*). Available evidence indicates in particular that affective disorders run in families, that this familiar incidence derives at least in part from genetic factors, and that life events also influence individual susceptibility to affective disorder and precipitate its expression in depressive and manic episodes.

Genetic Factors

In affective disorder as in schizophrenia, the more closely two people are related, the more likely they are to share the condition. With respect to twins, various studies demonstrate that approximately 65% of the identical twins of patients with bipolar disorder or major depressive disorder develop an affective disorder themselves, whereas the concordance for affective disorder among nonidentical twins is approximately 14% (Kazdin, 1990). Among nonpatient subjects without diagnosable disorder, identical twins are significantly more likely than nonidentical twins to resemble each other in the extent of their tendencies toward depressive moods and affective lability (Wierzbicki, 1986).

Such differences cannot be attributed to any greater commonality of experience among identical as opposed to nonidentical twins. Identical twins who have been reared apart from an early age still show a high concordance for affective disorder and emotional lability (Farber, 1981, Chapters 6 & 8). Moreover, many of the kinds of environmental events that participate in the etiology of affective disorder are often found not to have been shared by both members of a twin pair (Kendler, Heath, Martin, & Eaves, 1986).

It is additionally of note that the 14% concordance for affective disorder among nonidentical twins closely matches the findings for other first-degree relatives (siblings, parents, and offspring), who resemble them in genetic relatedness but usually have much less experience in common. Compared to the approximate 7% lifetime risk for bipolar or major depressive disorder in the general population, the risk among parents, children, and siblings of persons with an affective disorder also falls in the 10–20% range in various studies (Klein, Depue, & Slater, 1985; Plomin, 1989; Ryan, 1989; Strober, 1984).

Cross-fostering research has also helped to substantiate genetic factors in the etiology of affective disorder. Cadoret (1978), studying adults who had been placed for adoption soon after their birth, found that 3 of 8 biological children of mothers with affective disorder had become affectively disordered themselves (37.5%), compared to only 8 of 118 of adopted-away children of nondisturbed mothers (7%, close to the general population average). Other studies indicate that the biological parents of individuals who develop bipolar affective disorder are significantly more likely to be affectively disordered themselves than either the biological or adoptive parents of normal children; this increased risk for morbidity holds equally whether the disordered offspring are reared by their biological parents or in an adoptive home (Mendlewicz & Rainer, 1977; Wender, Kety, Rosenthal, Schulsinger, Ortmann, & Lunde, 1986).

Familial studies of affective disorder have consistently demonstrated greater concordance for bipolar disorder than for unipolar depression. Relatives of patients with bipolar disorder are more likely than the general population to develop either bipolar or unipolar disorder, whereas relatives of patients with unipolar disorder have an elevated rate of unipolar disorder but no greater risk than people in general of developing a bipolar disorder. Similarly, patients with a bipolar disorder are more likely than patients with a unipolar disorder to have a family history of affective disturbance (Andreasen, Rice, Endicott, Coryell, Grove, & Reich, 1987; Baron, Klotz, Mendlewicz, & Rainer, 1981; Winokur, Tsuang, & Crowe, 1982).

Familial incidence also relates to the age at which affective disorders first appear and whether they recur. Among patients with depressive disorders, those with depressed parents show an earlier onset of their condition than those whose parents have no history of depression. Among depressed offspring of depressed parents, moreover, those whose parents had their first depressive episode before age 20 years are eight times more likely to have become depressed as adolescents themselves than those whose parents had an adult onset of the condition (Rutter, Macdonald, Le Couteur, Harrington, Bolton, & Bailey, 1990; Weissman, Gammon, John, Merikangas, Warner, Prusoff, & Sholomskas, 1987). As for bipolar disorders, the risk of having this condition themselves is four times greater among the parents and siblings of bipolar adolescents than among the first-degree relatives of persons who first become bipolar as adults (Strober, Hanna, & McCracken, 1989). Hence, there is reason to believe that a greater genetic liability may be necessary for affective disorder to appear during the developmental years than in adulthood.

Research findings indicate further that the genetic influences in affective disorder operate independently from genetic factors in schizophrenia. The relatives of schizophrenic persons do not show an elevated frequency of affective disorder, and the relatives of people with affective disorder are not more likely than the general population to become schizophrenic (Kendler, Gruenberg, & Tsuang, 1985; Strober, McCracken, & Hanna, 1989; Strober, Morrell, Burroughs, Lampert, Danforth, & Freeman, 1988).

On the other hand, the children of parents with an affective disorder are at elevated risk for developing a variety of nonschizophrenic emotional and behavioral problems other than depression and mania, including anxiety disorders, conduct disorders, and substance abuse disorders. Available data indicate that as many as 40–50% of young persons with affectively disturbed parents are likely to become diagnosably symptomatic, primarily but not exclusively with mood disorders (Downey & Coyne, 1990; Keller, Beardslee, Dorer, Lavori, Samuelson, & Klerman, 1986; Orvaschel, Walsh-Allis, & Ye, 1988). Even when they manage to avoid diagnosable disorder, the offspring of affectively disordered parents tend to have more academic and social problems in school than their classmates and to be regarded by their teachers as more deviant and less competent (Beardslee, 1986; Weintraub, Winters, & Neale, 1986; Weissman et al., 1987). Clinicians working with adult patients who have had manic or depressive episodes should accordingly be alert to indications of psychological impairment in their children that call for evaluation and preventive intervention.

Although the evidence for genetic contributions in the etiology of affective disorders has grown to compelling proportions, little is yet known about the mode of genetic transmission by which parents pass to their offspring a disposition to these disorders. The most promising theories in this regard attribute the primary manifestations of affective disorder to biological irregularities that could originate in constitutional factors transmitted from one generation to the next. Thus far, however, research findings have identified only a heterogeneous array of biochemical and neurophysiological irregularities in samples of depressed patients, without pointing to any single or comprehensive biological factor to which causation could be attributed (Faraone, Kremen, & Tsuang, 1990; McNeal & Cimbolic, 1986; Puig-Antich, 1986).

As important as genetic factors may be in the etiology of affective disorder, moreover, they clearly do not account for all instances of this condition or for the extent of its familial incidence. In the first place, family studies commonly reveal a negative milieu and nonnurturant parental practices in the households of affectively disordered parents that mediate the influences they have on their children (Billings & Moos, 1983; Orvaschel et al., 1988). Second, the contribution of inept parenting to youthful affective disorder appears related more to the presence and severity of psychopathology in the parents than to what kind of disorder they have (Goodman & Brumley, 1990; Lee & Gotlib, 1989). Third, the familial incidence data themselves show that some 35% of the identical twins of persons with affective disorder and over 80% of the nonidentical twins and other first-degree relatives of depressive and bipolar patients avoid becoming affectively disturbed.

Hence, there is good reason to believe that life experiences as well as heredity are involved in susceptibility to affective disorder. Rutter et al. (1990) suggest further that, whereas genetic factors are likely to predominate in bipolar disorders and perhaps also in unipolar disorder severe enough to require inpatient care, milder depressive disorder treatable on an outpatient basis derives primarily from environmental influences.

Experiential Factors

Depressive disorders emerge primarily in response to some experience of loss. Depression in response to loss is most apparent when a loved one dies, moves away, or rejects a person's affections, leaving him or her to mourn the lost relationship. Other experiences that often precipitate depression include damage to objects one holds dear, failure to achieve some desired goal, and loss of bodily integrity related to illness, physical handicap, disfigurement, or even normal biological changes. This way of conceptualizing the cause of depression was originally formulated by Freud (1917/1957) and later elaborated from a psychoanalytic perspective by Bibring (1953). Contemporary psychodynamic formulations call special attention to the origins of depressive disorder in an eroded sense of well-being occasioned by events that undermine self-esteem and disrupt interpersonal relatedness (Bemporad & Lee, 1988; Gabbard, 1990, Chapter 8).

The sense of loss that contributes to persons becoming depressed can often be identified as either *real* or *fantasied*. A real loss is an actual event that deprives persons of something important to them. Among adolescents, for example, rejection by a boyfriend, finishing last in a race, or having to wear braces can deprive a young person, respectively, of a valued personal relationship, a highly desired success, or a gratifying sense of bodily integrity. A fantasied loss is an unrealistic concern that causes persons to feel deprived in the absence of any apparent reason. Feelings of being rejected, having failed, or becoming unattractive, arising without solid basis in fact, are among the common fantasied losses that contribute to depression.

The distinction between real and fantasied loss in the origin of depression provides some grounds for differentiating between reactive and endogenous forms of the disorder. *Reactive depressions* have typically been precipitated by real losses, involving readily identifiable environmental changes that constitute depressing circumstances. Like normal grief, reactive depression tends to be a self-remitting condition that heals with the passage of time and the gradual replacement of lost objects and goals with new ones. *Endogenous depression*, on the other hand, often involves fantasied rather than real losses.

Instead of being reactive, it tends to be an autonomous condition in which the origins of the person's distress are not apparent. Endogenous depression is additionally likely to be a chronic and lingering condition that produces recurrent episodes of disorder in the absence of environmental change (Zimmerman, Coryell, & Pfohl, 1986).

With respect to environmental change, research findings confirm that young persons and adults who become depressed are much more likely than nondepressed individuals to have experienced disruptive life events signifying personal, interpersonal, or achievement-related losses (Barnett & Gotlib, 1988; Hammen & Goodman-Brown, 1990; Shrout, Link, Dohrenwend, Skodol, Stueve, & Mirotznik, 1989). In addition, persons differ in the types of loss experiences that are likely to cause them to become depressed. Hammen, Ellicott, Gitlin, and Jamison (1989), examining symptom patterns and life events in patients with affective disorder, found personality-related differences among unipolar depressives in the kinds of negative events that were associated with onset or exacerbation of their symptoms over a 6-month period.

Specifically, the symptoms of those who were primarily socially oriented in their personality style were more likely to be influenced by interpersonal losses or disappointments than by negative achievement events. By contrast, the symptoms of those whose motivations were centered more around achievement than affiliation were affected more by unsuccessful striving than by interpersonal difficulties. Interestingly, however, this interaction between personality orientation and types of events influencing symptom formation was not found by Hammen et al. (1989) in patients with bipolar disorder. Hence, although loss experiences precipitated episodes of disorder in bipolar as well as unipolar patients, the particular nature of these losses seems less important among bipolar individuals. If confirmed in further research, this difference may relate to the generally more important role of genetic than experiential factors in the disposition to bipolar disorder.

Whatever the content of a loss may be, people also differ in the extent of loss they can sustain without becoming disturbed. What seem to be equivalent losses may cause one person to experience an overwhelming sense of deprivation and become deeply depressed, while another person takes the loss in stride without any adverse reaction. Such individual differences in sensitivity to extent of loss and capacity to cope with loss experiences appear determined in large part by developmental experiences. Especially important with respect to susceptibility to depression are experiences of *parental deprivation* and the emergence of a *negative attributional personality style*. Susceptibility to mania is likewise heightened by such negative circumstances in persons who become excessively defensive in trying to ward off or deny the distress that they cause.

Parental Deprivation

Numerous studies suggest that the disposition to becoming depressed in the face of loss stems from childhood experiences of parental deprivation that sensitize a person to such losses. The data are uncertain concerning whether such experienced deprivation necessarily involves actual parental loss, however. Some researchers report that depressed patients are especially likely to have experienced parental death or separation before age 6 years or between ages 10 and 15 years and furthermore that this relationship is specific to depression and not characteristic of serious psychopathology in general (Barnes & Prosen, 1985; Brown, Harris, & Bifulco, 1986; Pfohl, Stangl, & Tsuang, 1983). Other investigators have failed to find either an increased incidence of childhood parental loss among depressed patients or any specific association of early parental death with depression as opposed to other forms of psychopathology (Ragan & McGlashan, 1986; Sines, 1987).

There is reason to believe that this uncertainty may be resolved by closer attention to what causes a young person to lose a parent and to the impact of this loss on family climate in the home. Other things being equal, death of a parent (which from the child's perspective would have been difficult to avoid and should not be taken personally) is much less likely to be associated with developmental psychopathology than separation (which is avoidable and frequently conveys parental dislike and desertion to the child). Other things are rarely equal in these circumstances, however, and the consequences of both parental death and parental separation depend on the kinds of nurturance, support, and guidance the remaining parent can provide (see Breier, Kelsoe, Kirwin, Beller, Wolkowitz, & Pickar, 1988; Roy, 1988; Tennant, 1988).

Although parental loss has attracted considerable research attention, it is much less important clinically than the broader concept of parental deprivation. No more than 15% of depressed adults are found in any studies to have experienced permanent separation from a parent before age 18 years (Ragan & McGlashan, 1986; Roy, 1985). Hence, most persons who become depressed will not have had such an experience. On the other hand, parental deprivation often arises independently of whether both parents are physically present in the home. Children who are reared by one loving and devoted parent are likely to experience less psychological deprivation than children who live with two parents, both of whom dislike or ignore them. Growing up deprived of the kinds of praise and encouragement that help young persons learn to feel good about themselves and the world in which they live is the unfavorable childhood event that fosters susceptibility to depression, not merely the absence of a parent because of death, divorce, separation, or illegitimacy. In this same regard, other factors implicated in the etiology of depression include rejection by parents (whether actual or perceived) and even parental disharmony, which almost always diminishes the attention children receive from their parents and tends to lower their self-esteem (Lefkowitz & Tesiny, 1984; Long, 1986; Parker, 1983).

Negative Attributional Personality Style

A negative attributional personality style consists of a disposition to attribute bad experiences to causes that are internal, stable, and global. When persons who are disposed to view their experiences in this way encounter stressful life events, they conclude that their difficulties derive from relatively permanent and pervasive shortcomings within themselves. The more inclined the persons are to this kind of self-blaming negative attributional style, the more prone they are to becoming depressed in the face of frustrating or disappointing circumstances. This cognitive view of the origins of depression has been elaborated by Seligman in his reformulated learned-helplessness model (Peterson & Seligman, 1984; Seligman & Peterson, 1986), and other cognitive approaches to formulating depressive disorder similarly identify its causes in the way that persons think about themselves and their experiences (see Hammen, 1990).

Some question has been raised, however, concerning whether a negative attributional style is truly a disposing influence in depression or is instead just one of the attitudinal manifestations of becoming depressed. Although dysfunctional negative attitudes are consistently found to characterize depressed persons of all ages, they are also typically found to abate as a depression lifts. Children, adolescents, and adults who have been depressed and displayed negative attitudes are found, upon recovery from their depressive episodes, no longer to differ from nondepressed people in dysfunctional attributions (Asarnow & Bates, 1988; Dohr, Rush, & Bernstein, 1989; McCauley, Mitchell, Burke, & Moss, 1988; Schrader, Gibbs, & Harcourt, 1986.) These findings strongly suggest that depressive cognitions are consequences of depression, not antecedent or causative factors.

There is, nevertheless, reason to consider the possibility that negative attributions have both *trait* (depressing) and *state* (depressive) features. Regarding oneself as blameworthy and inadequate when confronted with stressful events may sensitize persons to becoming depressed and may contribute to episodes of the disorder, while such negative cognitions are also exacerbated by the onset of depression and show a state-related course of intensification and abatement that parallels the course of the depressive episode. Miranda and Persons (1988) suggest, in this regard, that it is primarily during a depressive episode, in response to their mood state, that depressed persons have access to and are likely to report persistent dysfunctional attitudes that constitute a trait vulnerability to becoming depressed.

A negative attributional style that may place persons at risk for becoming depressed stems largely from developmental experiences that foster a sense of incompetence and unworthiness. Especially important in this regard are parental childrearing practices that combine limited or inconsistent expressions of affection and low rates of reward with authoritarian control, power-assertive discipline, and inducement of guilt. Such practices are found to hinder normal development of self-esteem, to increase a young person's vulnerability to feelings of helplessness and failure, and to generate a disposition toward depressive mood (Cole & Rehm, 1986; Kandel & Davies, 1982; McCranie & Bass, 1984). Other research has demonstrated that depressed children and adolescents are more likely than control subjects to be immersed in strained family relationships and to perceive a lack of support from parents, siblings, and peers (Beck & Rosenberg, 1986; Compas, Slavin, Wagner, & Vannatta, 1986).

The Dynamics of Mania

Experiental factors that produce a disposition to bipolar affective disorder and precipitate episodes of mania have not yet been studied as extensively as those associated with unipolar depression. Nevertheless, there is good reason to believe that stressful experiences of loss precipitate manic as well as depressive reactions and that parental deprivation and a negative attributional style are disposing factors in both bipolar and unipolar forms of affective disorder. Mania can be usefully conceptualized as arising in part as an effort to ward off depression subsequent to loss, and patients with mania can be expected to slide into depression at times when they are unable to muster or sustain manic behavior patterns (see Davenport & Adland, 1988; Post et al., 1989).

In support of this formulation, there are clinical reports of manic attacks precipitated by object loss (Aleksandrowitz, 1980) and of manic patients who have suffered childhood experiences of loss similar to those that increase susceptibility to depressive episodes (Carpenter & Stephens, 1980). Follow-up studies have shown that only 10–20% of persons with a major depressive disorder also develop episodes of mania (Strober & Carlson, 1982; Winokur et al., 1982), whereas manic individuals almost always have a prior history of periodic depressive episodes as well (Abrams & Taylor, 1974; Mendelwicz, 1980).

In research with manic and depressed patients following remission of their episode of disorder, Winters and Neale (1985) found that the remitted manics reported higher self-esteem than the remitted depressives on a self-report measure. However, on a more subtle pragmatic inference task, the manics were more likely than normal controls and just as likely as depressives to attribute negative events to internal causes—that is, to display a negative attributional style. This finding strongly implies that typical manic displays of inflated self-esteem constitute defensive clinging to a positive self-image created to deny or at least suppress basically negative self-attitudes.

With respect to experiences of loss, Neale (1988) reports further that stressful events may be less apparent in the lives of manic than of depressed persons in the weeks or months preceding onset of their episode. However, mania occurring in the absence of stressful behavioral events will often turn out to have been precipitated by stressful cognitive events, particularly a loss of self-esteem related to anticipating future failures or recalling past inadequacies.

Finally, of note is an examination by Dunner, Patrick, and Fieve (1979) of stressful life events recalled by manic–depressive patients as having occurred in the 3 months prior to the onset of their bipolar disorder in either a manic or a depressive episode. Approximately half of the patients remembered such an event, and there was very little difference between the kinds of precipitating events recalled by those with a manic onset and those who had had a depressive onset. For both groups, these comprised mainly difficulties at work, marital problems, and interpersonal conflicts. The chief exceptions to this similarity occurred among female patients and involved becoming pregnant, which was exclusively associated with initial mania, and then giving birth, which was followed only by depression among those patients in whom it precipitated an affective disorder.

DIFFERENTIAL DIAGNOSIS

As in the case of schizophrenia and other forms of psychopathology as well, the differential diagnosis of affective disorder proceeds from familiarity with the manifestations and origins of the condition to the informed utilization of historical, observational, and test data. What is the nature of the person's symptoms of psychological disturbance, and how did they develop? What are the salient characteristics of the person's developmental history and his or her family background? How does the person appear, talk, and relate during an interview? What patterns of personality functioning can be inferred from standardized assessment techniques?

With specific respect to affective disorder in adolescents, the clinician's pursuit of answers to these questions should focus (a) on the young person's mood states, attitudes, energy level, and somatic functioning; (b) on restlessness, interpersonal avoidance or stimulation seeking, and various kinds of problem behavior, especially suicidal tendencies; (c) on the family history for affective disorder; and (d) on indications of real or fantasied loss experiences, past and present. The more that clinical inquiry identifies patterns similar to those associated with affective disorder, the greater the likelihood that an adolescent is suffering from such a disorder.

A wide variety of structured interview, rating scale, and psychological test methods have been developed to assist clinicians in assessing affective disorder in young persons, particularly in assessing depression (Exner & Weiner, 1982, Chapter 6; Finch, Casat, & Carey, 1990; Kendall et al., 1989; Kolko, 1987; Kovacs, 1986). In addition, neuroendocrinological correlates observed in some depressed patients have suggested a possible biological marker of depression, the dexamethasone suppression test (DST), in which the critical finding is the failure of dexamethasone administration to suppress plasma cortisol concentrations.

Although potentially useful in differential diagnosis, the DST has not yet proven as efficient in clinical practice as in carefully controlled research settings. DST abnormalities appear in only 50% of depressed patients and are commonly found in other conditions as well, including obsessive–compulsive disorder, eating disorder, and schizophrenia (Kaplan & Sadock, 1988). In addition to identifying this high rate of false-negative diagnoses and lack of specificity to depression, research findings suggest that the DST is less sensitive to depression in adolescents than in adults and is less sensitive to mood and attitudinal changes than to vegetative features of depression (Ha,

Kaplan, & Foley, 1984; Miller & Nelson, 1987; Shapiro & Lehman, 1983). On the other hand, the DST is unlikely to be positive in the absence of psychological disorder with depressive features, and nonsuppression appears to hold some promise for distinguishing endogenous from reactive depression and severe from mild depression (Whiteford, Peabody, Csernansky, & Berger, 1986; Zimmerman, Coryell, & Pfohl, 1986).

Along with assessing the presence of an affective disorder, differential diagnosis requires determining whether the disorder is unipolar or bipolar. Drawing on information presented previously in this chapter, the unipolar–bipolar distinction can usually be made on the basis of the following three considerations:

1. The more prominent the indications of mania are in a presenting clinical picture—including elevated mood, unrealistically positive attitudes, heightened energy level, and a false sense of bodily well-being—the more likely it is that the patient has a bipolar disorder in which episodes of depression will occur in the future. Among specific symptoms that may be manifest, the presence of grandiose delusions in an affectively disordered young person is especially likely to indicate a bipolar condition (Neale, 1988; Strober, Hanna, & McCracken, 1989).

2. Among patients presenting with exclusively depressive manifestations of disorder, a history of apparently manic episodes or hypomanic tendencies suggests bipolar disorder, whereas the absence of any such history points to unipolar disorder. Not uncommonly, previous manic episodes in bipolar patients will have involved bizarre, assaultive, and destructive behavior of a kind rarely seen in patients with unipolar depression, and depressed adolescents with bipolar disorder will frequently have come to attention previously for conduct problems. At the same time, bipolar disorder should not be ruled out too quickly in the absence of conduct problems. In some bipolar young persons, initial breakdown may be preceded by mild mood elevations and an expansive, energetic life-style that has been channeled in constructive directions and not perceived by others as abnormal (see Davenport & Adland, 1988; O'Connell, 1988).

3. Affectively disordered patients who have a first-degree relative with diagnosed bipolar disorder or a history of manic episodes are relatively likely to have a bipolar disorder themselves, whereas a negative family history of mania and/or a positive history of unipolar disorder increase the likelihood of unipolar disorder. Especially when an adolescent's presenting symptoms and/ or clinical history are equivocal with respect to distinguishing between unipolar and bipolar affective disorder, family history can provide useful clues to the young person's probable clinical course and treatment needs.

The differential diagnosis of affective disorder also frequently calls for consideration of possible schizophrenia or antisocial personality disorder, both of which share some symptoms in common with these conditions.

Schizophrenia

The manner in which affectively disordered adolescents form attitudes, channel their energies, approach social situations, and modulate their emotions may result in maladaptive behavior patterns that need to be differentiated from manifestations of schizophrenia. Regarding attitudes, as noted earlier, the exaggerated views that characterize affective disorder can result in strange or delusional ideas and instances of poor judgment or unrealistic expectation that resemble schizophrenic consequences of disordered thinking and inaccurate perception. Especially during manic episodes, in which the person's typical talkativeness and high activity level provide ample opportunity for cognitive peculiarities to be expressed, evidence of impaired thinking and reality testing may be prominent. As an aid to differential diagnosis, the thinking and perceptual deficits associated with affective disorder have been observed to differ in three respects from those that characterize schizophrenia:

1. Thinking and perceptual deficits tend to be less severe in affective disorder than in schizophrenia (Asarnow & MacCrimmon, 1981; Oltmanns, Murphy, Berenbaum, & Dunlop, 1985).

2. After an acute episode has subsided, cognitive impairments, particularly when manifest in negative rather than positive symptoms (see page 67), are less likely to persist in affective disorder than in schizophrenia (Docherty, Schnur, & Harvey, 1988; Earle-Boyer, Levinson, Grant, & Harvey, 1986; Grossman, Harrow, & Sands, 1986; Grove & Andreasen, 1985; Pogue-Geile & Harrow, 1985).

3. Manic and schizophrenic patients are likely to display thought disorder in qualitatively different ways (Holzman, Shenton, and Solovay, 1986; Solovay, Shenton, & Holzman, 1987). There is a playful, breezy quality to the communications of manic individuals, and they seem to be enjoying themselves as they make plays on words and bounce from one subject to another. The interviewer, even when struggling to follow the patient's stream of consciousness, seldom experiences the interview as a tense situation for him or her or for the patient. By contrast, disordered schizophrenic communications tend to be delivered with earnest concern, rather than with any exuberance or frivolity. Incoherent and illogical statements seem to clank rather than flow along, and the patient is much more intent on straightening out his or her own confusion and being understood than in having fun or showing off.

Thus, the more serious and persistent a patient's cognitive impairments are and the more they interfere with clear and comfortable interpersonal communication, the more likely he or she is to have a schizophrenic disorder; the milder and more fully remitting such deficits are and the less communication difficulty they cause, the more likely it is that a patient who, in other respects, is demonstrating features of depression or mania has an affective disorder.

Turning to energy level, the psychomotor retardation that appears in depression can easily be confused with the apathy that constitutes one of the negative symptoms of schizophrenic disorder. The clinician can minimize such confusion by probing how a lethargic patient views his or her own inactivity. Apathetic persons are doing little or nothing because they do not care about anything, one way or another; as far as they are concerned, nothing is worthwhile and nothing matters. Depressed persons, on the other hand, care very much but simply cannot get their bodies and minds moving. This is not to overlook the fact that depressed persons frequently feel discouraged and helpless. When asked why they don't get moving, they may say "What's the use?" However, this kind of response should not be taken for apathy. When apathetic patients are asked, "Would you like to feel better?" or "Do you want to be able to leave the hospital?" or "Are you interested in getting back to school and catching up on your studies?" they are likely to give such replies as "I don't know," and "What for?" and "It makes no difference."

When asked these same questions, psychomotorically retarded depressed patients tend to respond more to the tune of "Sure," "I only wish I could," and "Yes, but it's too much to expect." As a further example of this diagnostic clue, a low-energy depressed patient who is asked, "How would you like things to be different for you?" will usually have something poignant to say; an apathetic schizophrenic asked the same question will seldom go beyond a shrug of the shoulders.

At the other pole of the energy dimension, the pressure of speech that appears in mania tends to result in rambling streams of consciousness that can easily be mistaken for dissociated thinking. To avoid this mistake, the interviewer needs to listen closely for evidence of connectedness in the patient's flow of ideas. The basic problem with manic communications is their pace. If the patient could slow down or the interviewer process information more rapidly, the relationships among successive ideas would become clarified. No such change of pace would be sufficient to eliminate the incoherence in schizophrenic communications; strange use of words, idiosyncratic referents, interpenetration of themes, and unrelatedness of successive thoughts to each other persist, no matter how slowly and carefully dissociated speech is delivered.

As observed by Hoffman, Stopek, and Andreasen (1986) in this regard, the apparent incoherence of manic speech involves abrupt shifts from one coherent discourse to another, whereas schizophrenics show deficiencies in being able to construct even isolated discourses in a coherent fashion. Accordingly, the easier it is to follow a rapidly talking patient's ideas, the more likely he or she is to be manifesting a manic pressure of speech, as a reflection of heightened energy level, and not a schizophrenic dissociation due to disordered thinking.

As for social situations, the manner in which depressed adolescents sometimes seek to avoid depressing experiences by keeping away from people can produce the same kind of disengagement seen in schizophrenics who are interpersonally averse. In such instances, the patient's history of interpersonal relatedness provides the critical diagnostic information. Interpersonal aversion is a basic feature of schizophrenic disorder, and withdrawn schizophrenics will typically show a long premorbid history of limited and strained interpersonal relationships. In depression, by contrast, social withdrawal and loss of interest in people tend to have a relatively recent onset, concurrent with or subsequent to the emergence of overt depressive disorder. Thus, the more recently a pattern of withdrawal has appeared, especially when it contrasts with previously adaptive interpersonal contacts in a young person with basically adequate social skills, the more likely it is to identify depressive rather than schizophrenic disorder.

Finally, with respect to emotionality, the dramatic or cyclical moods that accompany affective disorder may superficially resemble the inappropriate and inadequately controlled affective expression that characterizes schizophrenia. Most important in this regard is the distinction between dejection and emotional blunting. Both depressed and schizophrenic patients may at times appear emotionally unresponsive. Careful clinical investigation will reveal that depressed individuals are unresponsive because of painful negative affects that prevent them from experiencing pleasure, whereas blunted schizophrenics are unresponsive because they are experiencing no affects at all, either positive or negative.

As a further diagnostic clue, the mood disturbances of affectively disordered patients involve exaggeration, in that the person is more intensely and persistently dejected than a sad situation justifies or more intensely and persistently happy than pleasant circumstances justify. The inappropriate affect of schizophrenics, by contrast, involves being notably happy or sad in the absence of any apparent justifying circumstances, or even in response to circumstances that would have been expected to elicit just the opposite affective tone.

In the face of equivocal symptomatology, the distinctive genetic loadings in schizophrenia and affective disorder can also be utilized in differentiating between them should there be a positive family history on which to draw. Those patients who have a first-degree relative with schizophrenia should be considered likely to have a schizophrenic disorder, whereas those with a family history of affective disorder are in all probability experiencing an affective disorder (Guze, Cloninger, Martin, & Clayton, 1983; Kendler & Hays, 1983). The utility of this diagnostic guideline will vary with the kind of affective disorder that is being considered; however, the familial incidence data presented earlier indicate that diagnosing affective disorder on the basis of a positive family history or ruling it out on the basis of a family history of schizophrenia is more likely to be accurate with respect to endogenous depression and bipolar disorder than to reactive unipolar depression.

The case of Dwight (see pp. 126–127), who was diagnosed as having a depressive disorder despite his mother's schizophrenic history, illustrates this distinction. The relatively acute onset of his disorder in response to obviously stressful events, his rapid and lasting recovery, and the absence of hypomanic tendencies identified his depression as reactive and unipolar. His case also exemplifies some of the other characteristics mentioned in this section as helping to differentiate affective disorder from schizophrenia: the absence of serious or persisting thinking difficulties; recent onset, rather than a long history of social withdrawal, and the absence of impaired capacities for interpersonal relatedness; painful negative affective displays rather than emotional blunting; and a general tone of discouragement and despair rather than apathy.

Antisocial Personality Disorder

The problem behaviors through which adolescents sometimes express depression may resemble the disruptive, disturbing, inconsiderate, and delinquent conduct manifested by young persons who are developing an antisocial personality disorder and a psychopathic orientation to life. The differentiation between misconduct as a symptomatic expression of depression and misconduct as a reflection of emerging psychopathy requires a careful examination of the adolescent's developmental history and basic personality style. The more a young person's problem behavior contrasts with his or her prior modes of adaptation, as revealed by the history, and with his or her preferred coping style, as inferred from interview or psychological test data, the greater is the likelihood that the behavior is symptomatic rather than characterological in nature.

Adolescents with an emerging antisocial personality disorder have typically been aggressive, demanding, self-centered children with minimal frustration tolerance and little inclination to subordinate their gratification to the needs of others. With little or no prompting, persons who have known them will offer such comments as, "I knew all along she was headed for trouble," or "He's just the kind of boy I expected would turn out this way."

In young persons who begin at adolescence to misbehave symptomatically as an expression of depression, the reports from parents and teachers paint quite a different picture. These adolescents have often been quiet and retiring as children, obedient and restrained, kind and gentle with siblings and pets, and well behaved in school. Observers say that the recent appearance of their rebellious or delinquent behavior took them by surprise. Such a sharp difference between adolescent problem behavior and previously commendable conduct usually identifies symptomatic rather than characterological deviance.

Regarding coping style, the antisocial behavior manifested by some young persons seems clearly consistent with their personality orientation. Psychopathy as the basis of problem behavior becomes increasingly likely the more an adolescent's interview behavior and performance on psychological examination suggest that he or she is an unreflective and emotionally labile individual who (a) relates to others in a shallow and superficial manner,

(b) seldom exercises self-restraint or an analytic approach to experiences, (c) prefers doing things to either talking or thinking about things, and (d) operates in terms of what is concrete and immediate rather than abstract and conceptual (see Quay, 1987; Weiner, 1985).

For other young persons, their getting into behavioral difficulties stands in marked contrast to a basically ideational approach to dealing with experience. Rebellious, poorly conceived antisocial conduct in adolescents whose demeanor and test protocols suggest that by nature they are thoughtful and introspective individuals who are disinclined to act on or to express their feelings spontaneously probably represents a symptomatic rather than a characterological propensity for misconduct. Particularly when indices of dysphoria or self-depreciation are also in evidence, a depressive rather than a psychopathic interpretation of the problem behavior is indicated. The following case illustrated a pattern of misconduct that arose in response to an essentially depressive disturbance.

Karol was 16 years old when she was admitted to an inpatient psychiatric unit as a result of her parents' progressive inability to control her behavior and their fears that she would carry out threats of suicide, with which she had been blatantly manipulating them. Over the previous 6 months, she had become increasingly rebellious at home, refusing to obey any parental orders, using the family car without permission, and on occasion staying out all night. It was learned that several months prior to the onset of her problem behavior, in the setting of being assigned major supervisory responsibilities for her younger siblings while the family was vacationing at their summer home, Karol had come to the conclusion that her parents did not love her. At this same time, a boyfriend broke off their dating relationship, and her younger brother developed a serious kidney infection that temporarily threatened his life.

Clinical exploration of these real and fantasied losses suggested that Karol was experiencing a basically depressive disorder for which her misbehavior was serving to divert her attention from her feelings of loss and powerlessness.

Subsequent psychological examination supported this impression. On tests, Karol revealed many unresolved concerns about the extent to which she wished to be independent of her parents, with urges for independence competing with ungratified needs for nurturance and support. Yet she gave no indications of poor impulse control, nor did she display any particular tendencies toward labile or spontaneous emotional expression. Rather, she seemed oriented toward imaginative ideational activity. These test findings helped to identify her problem behavior as a symptomatic reflection of an underlying depression rather than as a characterological commitment to acting in this way.

PROGNOSIS AND TREATMENT

Although most persons recover from individual bouts of depression and mania, affective disorder often occurs as a lifetime susceptibility to recurring episodes of disorder. Among adults who become diagnosably depressed, approximately 50% are likely to recover within 1 year after the initial onset of their symptoms and another 30% within the second year, which leaves about 20% who show an unremitting course 2 years after onset. Of adults experiencing a first episode of depression, 45% can be expected to have a second episode, and one third of those who have a second episode are likely to have a third episode as well (Keller, Friedman, & Lavori, 1988; Lewinsohn, Zeiss, & Duncan, 1989). The outlook in mania is a little less favorable, with 35% of adults discharged from hospital care following a manic episode showing poor outcome over the next 2 years (Harrow, Goldberg, Grossman, & Meltzer, 1990).

Young persons who develop an affective disorder are especially prone to recurrent difficulties. Most adolescents will recover from an initial episode of depression for which they are referred for treatment, but two thirds can be expected to become depressed again while they are still in their teens, and 20% are likely to give evidence of bipolar disorder before they reach adulthood (Kovacs, 1989).

In a particularly significant follow-up study, Harrington and his colleagues reported on long-term reevaluations (after an average of 18 years) of 80 persons who had become markedly depressed as children or adolescents. As adults, these persons were no more likely than a comparison group of disturbed but not depressed youthful patients to demonstrate nonaffective disorders, but 58% of them, compared to 25% of the comparison group, became affectively disturbed adults (Harrington, Fudge, Rutter, Pickles, & Hill, 1990). Within nonpatient adolescents as well, tendencies to experience maladaptive mood states show considerable continuity from adolescence to adulthood; high school students who report depressive symptoms, for example, are more likely than the general population to do so in their mid-20s as well (Kandel & Davies, 1986).

Even so, the outlook in affective disorder is more favorable than in schizophrenia. In one long-term follow-up study of several hundred adults admitted to a psychiatric inpatient unit, 50% of the manic and 61% of the depressed patients subsequently achieved a good level of psychological functioning, compared to only 20% of the schizophrenics; at the other end of the scale, subsequently poor overall adjustment was found in 54% of the schizophrenics but only in 21% of the manics and in 30% of the depressives (Tsuang, Woolson, & Fleming, 1979).

As in schizophrenia, however, the prognosis for affective disorder becomes more guarded when it begins early and is so incapacitating as to require hospital care. Available evidence indicates that only about one third of adolescents hospitalized with a unipolar depressive disorder recover completely, without further recurrences, and almost all young persons who develop severe bipolar disorder are likely to suffer continuing susceptibility to further episodes. Generally speaking, the younger they are when they develop a first episode of affective disorder, the more disturbed they are likely to be, the more difficult they are to treat successfully, and the greater their likelihood of relapse following recovery (Cohen, Khan, & Cox, 1989; Gonzales, Lewinsohn, & Clarke, 1985; Kovacs, Feinberg, Crouse-Novak, Paulauskas, & Finkelstein, 1984; McGlashan, 1988).

Although the implications of early breakdown for unfavorable outcome have not yet been fully explained, one likely possibility is an inverse relationship, on the average, between age of onset and strength of the disposition to affective disorder. The stronger the diathesis, according to this hypothesis, the sooner the disorder appears, the less environmental stress is necessary to precipitate it, the more serious and persistent it is, and the more likely it is to recur. Conversely, with life stress assumed equal, the older the age people reach before developing an affective disorder, the less strongly they were probably disposed to it.

Consistent with this formulation, the data indicate that the older an adolescent patient is at the time of an initial manic or depressive episode and the less incapacitating the disorder, the better the young person's prospects are for recovery and subsequently good adjustment, without relapse. When there have been previous episodes of disorder, the present prognosis is improved if these episodes have been (a) few rather than many in number, (b) brief rather than long in duration, (c) widely spaced rather than back-to-back, and (d) mild rather than severe. Future prospects for avoiding or minimizing the severity of relapses are also improved when the young person has no family history of affective disorder and has the benefit of a close and supportive family environment (Belsher & Costello, 1988: Coryell, Lavori, Endicott, Keller, VanEerdewegh, 1984; Moos, 1990; Teri & Lewinsohn, 1986).

Even when the outlook in affective disorder is favorable, appropriate intervention can still help to shorten episodes of depression and mania and to minimize vulnerability to relapse. An extensive literature demonstrates the effectiveness of many different types of psychotherapy in treating affective disorder, including psychodynamic, behavioral, cognitive, and interpersonal approaches (Beckham, 1990; Jarrett & Rush, 1986; Karasu, 1990; Robinson, Berman, & Neimeyer, 1990). Depending on the individual case, the treatment should include some combination of *psychotherapy*, *environmental manipulation*, and, especially in mania, appropriate *medication*.

Psychotherapy

As discussed earlier, depressed adolescents are responding to past and present experiences of loss that have caused them to feel deficient or deprived. Manic adolescents are likely to be actively engaged in warding off the depressing impact of similar loss experiences that have sensitized them to and precipitated their disorder. Hence, the key element in successful psychotherapy of affective disorder is *relieving the* disturbed person's *sense of loss*. In addition, recovery from an affective disorder can be facilitated by psychotherapeutic strategies aimed at *minimizing* the patient's *manifest symptomatology* and *dealing with* any intercurrent episodes of *mania*.

Relieving the Sense of Loss

The origin of affective disorder partly in experienced loss has two implications for treating it psychologically. First, by entering the lives of affectively disordered adolescents as someone genuinely concerned, interested, and wanting to be of help, the therapist can usually begin to relieve the person's sense of loss beginning with the very first treatment session. The therapist becomes a new object for the adolescent and thereby increases by one the number of dependable relationships he or she has with other people. This new relationship reduces the patient's underlying feelings of being cut off from other people. Unlike psychotherapy with schizophrenic adolescents, in which an extended period of incremental and delicate relationship building may precede any visible movement in the treatment, an explicit commitment to a treatment relationship by a warm and caring therapist often produces some lifting of depression or toning down of mania after an initial interview, especially among young persons who are mildly enough disturbed to be treated on an outpatient basis.

Second, recovery from affective disorder can be hastened by helping affectively disordered adolescents effectively come to grips with the particular circumstances that are causing them to experience a sense of loss. When loss has been experienced in relation to a real event, such as a broken friendship or a failure in school, a resulting depression often responds to relatively superficial discussions that help a patient (a) see the loss as less tragic and less permanent than he or she had thought and (b) identify ways of going about recouping the loss through making new friends or finding new avenues to success in school. If the sense of loss stems from fantasied or unrealistic concerns, especially when the young person is not fully aware of them, then a more intensive exploration may be necessary to identify and arrive at a less troubling perspective on the problem. The more remote the loss experiences and the more difficult they are to identify (i.e., the more endogenous the depression has become), the more extensive the therapy will need to be, and the greater are the obstacles to rapid, total, and lasting recovery.

These efforts to help depressed adolescents overcome their sense of loss share much in common with the strategies recommended by Klerman and his colleagues (1984) in their Interpersonal Psychotherapy (IPT) for depression (see also Klerman & Weissman, 1986) and by Nezu (1986) and his colleagues in their Problem-Solving Therapy (PST) for depression (see also Nezu, Nezu, & Perri, 1989). These are short-term treatments that facilitate recovery from acute depression by alleviating depressive symptoms and helping the patient understand and deal more effectively with social and interpersonal problems.

Minimizing Manifest Symptomatology

Although tracing and resolving a sense of loss undergirds the psychological treatment of affective disorder, a young person's presenting symptoms cannot be ignored in the process. Over time, these symptoms can become so habitual that they persist even after the depressive concerns that prompted them have been dispelled. Hence, these symptoms require direct treatment concurrently with the therapist's efforts to provide a meaningful relationship and help affectively disordered adolescents work through their sense of loss.

With respect to dejected mood, for example, most sensitive observers recognize that depressed people cannot easily be cheered up; if they could, the efforts of well-meaning friends and relatives would suffice to relieve depressive disorder, without help from a professional. The treatment relationship provides a context in which it is usually possible to raise the spirits of a depressed adolescent by ignoring his or her dejection and ferreting out whatever opportunities there may be to talk about positive emotional experiences he or she is still having. Because of the self-remitting nature of depressed moods, they tend to diminish in time if the person can avoid dwelling on them. The more time and attention that is devoted to thinking and talking about pleasant emotional experiences, both in and outside of the therapy, the less time and attention will be left for brooding about the unpleasant ones, and the sooner their impact will fade. Although seemingly simplistic, this reinforcement approach reflects the theoretical formulations underlying a variety of behavior-shaping techniques that have proved effective in the treatment of depression (see Kolko, 1987; Reynolds & Coats, 1986).

Similarly, with respect to negative attitudes, therapists can draw on various treatment techniques, derived from cognitive conceptualizations of depression, to facilitate progress toward less gloomy and more realistic perspectives (see Beck, 1979; Emery, Bedrosian, & Garber, 1983; Zeiss, Lewinsohn, & Munoz, 1979). As in efforts to improve the reality testing of schizophrenic adolescents, this involves discussing specific events and circumstances for the purpose of identifying and resolving discrepancies between what actually is or was the case and whatever depressing impressions the young person has formed. These techniques help depressed adolescents to recognize that they are feeling badly as a result of what they are thinking and saying to themselves, not because of insurmountable obstacles to their happiness in the real world.

As a further step in combating the negative self-attitudes of depressed adolescents and their depleted energy level as well, therapists need to find ways of getting these young persons moving again. This involves learning where their talents lie, what situations they have enjoyed or succeeded in previously, and what remaining embers of aspiration might still be stirred into some blaze of enthusiasm. Any progress they can be encouraged to make in one or more of these directions creates an opportunity for pleasurable experience and drives a wedge into their symptomatic pattern of lethargy and self-depreciation. Each step a depressed adolescent takes toward engagement in rewarding pursuits promises to replace discouragement with hopefulness and alienation with activity. Even becoming involved in a community service project or a regular exercise program has been found to minimize feelings of alienation and depression (Calabrese & Schumer, 1986; McCann & Holmes, 1984).

In the treatment, attention must also be paid to maladaptive ways in which adolescents have been attempting to ward off feeling depressed or to avoid potentially depressing situations. Social withdrawal is especially important in this regard, because being removed from interpersonal interactions deprives young persons of experiences that could assuage their sense of loss, reinforce their engagement in productive pursuits, and bolster their self-esteem. For this reason, social skills training can be a valuable aspect of the treatment, to the extent that it helps overcome a flight from people based on historically negative experiences and expectations in interpersonal situations (see Becker, Heimberg, & Bellack, 1987; Brady, 1984; Kolko, 1987; Ladd & Asher, 1985).

Similarly, adolescents who have turned to problem behavior to escape feeling depressed need encouragement to give up these maladaptive efforts at avoiding psychological pain. Behavior change can rarely be legislated simply by the therapist or anyone else telling young persons what they should not do, however. Instead, therapists need to find ways of demonstrating that such symptomatic behavior is self-defeating, that it costs a personal price too great to justify any pleasure it gives, and that acting otherwise would be in these youngsters' own best interests. Such intrinsic motivation to change, once instilled, proves far more powerful than pleas, promises, or threats in getting young persons to give up problem behavior. Treatment strategies for curbing problem behavior are discussed further in Chapter 9.

Dealing with Mania

Relieving a sense of loss and promoting more realistic attitudes are important for the effective treatment of manic as well as depressive episodes. With respect to some of the manifestations of affective disorder, however, the treatment of manic and depressed patients calls for different objectives. Whereas depression calls for guidance, encouragement, and reinforcement aimed at helping the person become more active and engaged, mania is best treated by using these techniques to help the person slow down and back off.

The pursuit of this objective, including attempts to tone down the elevated mood and inflated self-esteem of the manic patient, requires utmost caution, however. The therapist must constantly keep in mind that manic symptoms serve defensive purposes and are embedded in the context of a bipolar disorder. Therapists who move too quickly to disabuse manic patients of their expansiveness and grandiosity will rarely see them achieve a normal affective tone. Instead, having undermined the coping style of such patients and crippled their defenses against underlying depression, they are likely to witness the rapid emergence of dysphoria and despair. The exuberance and inflated self-esteem of manic individuals must be deflated slowly and gently; a sudden puncture puts the person at considerable risk for depression and also for suicidal behavior.

Environmental Manipulation

Therapists working with affectively disordered adolescents should look for constructive opportunities to influence how they are being treated at home, in school, and in their community. Bringing about changes that diminish the frustration or disappointment that patients are experiencing can help to relieve their distress, and changes that increase the frequency of gratifying experiences in patients' lives can enhance their self-esteem and promote increased activity.

Attention to stressful environmental impact is by no means exclusive to the treatment of affective disorder, and few if any patterns of developmental psychopathology can be treated effectively without the enlightened engagement of parents and teachers. However, in most other conditions, environmental manipulation is employed primarily to minimize stress and thereby reduce factors contributing to the origin and persistence of the disorder; this can be termed *lessening the negatives* in the situation. Because affective disorder is so critically tied to experiences of loss and deprivation, environmental manipulation can accomplish much more than just a lessening of the negatives. Expanded environmental support, by diminishing disappointment and increasing gratification through activity, directly addresses primary features of the disorder. This constitutes *accentuating the positives* in the situation, and it means that wisely implemented changes in the environment not only reduce pathogenic elements but also provide a directly active therapeutic ingredient in the treatment.

Constructive environmental manipulation on behalf of affectively disordered adolescents proceeds mainly through discussions with their parents. Parents of depressed and manic young persons are often perplexed by the way their children have been acting and are unable to decide whether their children are really disturbed or are just making an unnecessary fuss. Frequently, they will have been alternating between worrying about their children's condition and feeling angry and resentful about it ("Why are you making things so difficult for us?" "What you need is a good swift kick in the pants"). Helping parents understand how and why their adolescents are manifesting an affective disorder can ease the parents' anxieties, and convincing them of their children's needs for increased attention, affection, and reassurance can foster parental provision of a supportive home environment. The more progress parents can make toward becoming less anxious and more supportive, the more their changed behavior is likely to hasten their children's recovery from a depressive or a manic episode and insulate them against relapse.

Parent counseling along these lines can have a particularly beneficial impact in relation to the role of a negative attributional style in depressive disorder. The findings of Seligman and Peterson (1986) suggest that young persons develop a negative attributional style not only in response to how their parents rear them, but also through identification with parents who are themselves inclined to pessimism and self-blame. Accordingly, there may be instances in which helping an entire family alter a negative attributional style that has characterized its way of looking at the world will contribute substantially to ameliorating the symptoms of an adolescent in the family who has become clinically depressed. Various other strategies for treating adolescent depression through restructuring patterns of family interaction are elaborated by Oster and Caro (1990, Chapter 10).

Discussions with teachers and other adults in the community who figure prominently in a young person's life may also serve usefully to help them recognize ways in which they can present fewer frustrations and provide more rewards. There are, of course, limits to environmental manipulation in clinical practice, especially beyond a patient's immediate family. The world cannot be reshaped to meet a disturbed adolescent's needs, and therapists have neither the right nor the authority to dictate how other persons should conduct their lives. Nevertheless, when new information and appropriate suggestions from the therapist can promote some compromise and accommodation by key persons in an adolescent's environment, both recovery from the present episode and avoidance of further episodes will be facilitated.

These recommendations concerning environmental manipulation relate closely to widely endorsed treatment strategies for mobilizing social support on the behalf of persons with psychological disorder. Research with affectively disordered patients in particular documents that strong social support systems help both to alleviate current symptoms and to buffer the person against relapse (Anashensel & Stone, 1982; Belsher & Costello, 1988; Flaherty, Gavaria, Black, Altman, & Mitchell, 1983; Moos, 1990; Phifer & Murrell, 1986).

Medication

Various antidepressant medications have been found beneficial in the treatment of adults with depressive disorder. Approximately 70% of depressed patients improve in response to medication, and depressed patients treated solely with appropriate drugs show the same kinds of improvements in their mood and attitudes as patients treated with various forms of psychotherapy (Baldessarini, 1988; Garbutt, 1988; Robinson et al., 1990; Simons, Garfield, & Murphy, 1984). On the other hand, outcome studies indicate that psychotherapy alone is an effective treatment for depression and suggest further that behavioral therapy, cognitive therapy, interpersonal therapy, social learning therapy, and marital therapy all produce greater treatment effects in adults with unipolar depression than does drug therapy (Free & Oei, 1989; Nietzel, Russell, Hemmings, & Gretter, 1987; Steinbrueck, Maxwell, & Howard, 1983).

These findings notwithstanding, most clinicians and researchers are currently less concerned with arguing the relative merits of psychotherapy and pharmacotherapy in the treatment of depression than they are with establishing guidelines for their effective use in combination. This effort is reflected in research studies that have yielded three clinically relevant findings. First, although both psychotherapy alone and drug therapy alone are demonstrably effective in treating depressed adults, their combined use does not produce substantially better short-term results than either used alone; with respect to symptom improvement, in other words, little additive effect derives from combining drug therapy and psychotherapy in the treatment of adult depressives (Beck, Hollon, Young, Bedrosian, & Budenz, 1985; Conte, Plutchik, Wild, & Karasu, 1986; Rush, 1984).

Second, however, when the focus shifts from short-term gains to maintenance of symptomatic improvement and avoidance of relapse, treatment approaches that combine psychotherapeutic and pharmacologic modalities have been observed to achieve better results than either used alone. This finding holds regardless of which modality was considered primary and which adjunctive in the treatment (Hollon, Spoden, & Chastek, 1986; Kupfer & Frank, 1987; Simons, Murphy, Levine, & Wetzel, 1986).

Third, with respect to both short-term and longer-term results, the most efficacious treatment is likely to vary in the individual case in relation to the nature and severity of the disorder. The less seriously disabling and more clearly reactive a depressive disorder is, the more likely it is that psychosocial intervention alone will be sufficient to provide as much benefit as is possible to achieve, with nothing to be gained from medication. Conversely, the more debilitating and endogenous the depression—especially when the patient manifests depleted energy or a psychotic degree of cognitive impairment and requires hospitalization—the more likely it is that medication will be necessary to achieve improvement and psychotherapy will make little contribution to progress (Nelson, Charney, & Quinlan, 1981; Rush, 1984).

The extent to which these findings can be generalized to young persons is uncertain, primarily because the data regarding drug therapy for depressed adolescents is much less extensive than the findings with adults. With specific respect to tricyclic antidepressants, the evidence available so far does not demonstrate effectiveness of these medications in treating adolescent depression (Koplewicz & Williams, 1988; Ryan & Puig-Antich, 1987). When antidepressant medication is nevertheless used in an effort to alleviate depressive symptoms, psychotherapy should be included in the treatment plan to promote adequate social readjustment following any symptom reduction achieved by the drugs. With this consideration in mind, Hodgman (1985) cautions that a favorable symptomatic response to medication in a depressed adolescent may have the counterproductive effect of lessening the young person's investment in the psychotherapy that will still be needed to achieve and sustain recovery.

Antidepressant medications have also been found to cause some undesirable side effects in young persons when they are used in sufficiently large doses to reduce depressive symptomatology. These include sedative effects, gastrointestinal distress, cardiovascular toxicity, extrapyramidal effects (including possible tardive dyskinesia), and seizure potential (Hodgman, 1985; Law, Petti, & Kazdin, 1981; Puig-Antich, Ryan, & Rabinovich, 1985). Moreover, bipolar adolescents who present with depression may be precipitated into manic episodes by antidepressant medication (O'Connell, 1988; Wehr & Goodwin, 1987). As a result of the uncertain benefits and the potential hazards of using antidepressant medication with young persons, some authorities urge restraint if not total avoidance of this treatment modality until its value and safety have been more adequately demonstrated (Digdon & Gotlib, 1985; Werry, 1982). Others argue that the potential seriousness and persistence of depressive disorder appearing in young persons warrant pharmacotherapy despite its attendant risks and possible disadvantages (Rancurello, 1986).

When affective disorder is manifest in episodes of mania, medication with lithium carbonate has consistently been found helpful. For adolescents as well as adults, lithium can be expected to curb manic behavior without producing untoward side effects (Puig-Antich et al., 1985; Strober, Hanna, & McCracken, 1989). However, this potentially beneficial effect of lithium needs to be construed as a symptomatic improvement rather than as a specific cure of bipolar affective disorder. As in the case of depression, alleviated symptomatology in response to medication may not prove sufficient to achieve improved social adjustment, unless coordinated with psychotherapy and environmental manipulation, and drug effects are likely to provide little buffer against relapse in the absence of psychosocial intervention (see Kestenbaum & Kron, 1987; Prien, Kupfer, Mansky, Small, Tuason, Voss, & Johnson, 1984). Especially in the absence of adequate psychological intervention, manic adolescents treated with initial success with lithium are highly likely to relapse when their medication is discontinued (Strober, Morrell, Lampert, & Burroughs, 1990).

REFERENCES

Abrams, R., & Taylor, M. A. (1974). Unipolar mania. *Archives of General Psychiatry, 30*, 441–443.

Ahrens, A. H. (1987). Theories of depression: The role of goals and the self-evaluation process. *Cognitive Therapy and Research, 11*, 665–680.

Aleksandrowicz, D. R. (1980). Psychoanalytic studies of mania. In R. H. Belmaker & H. M. van Praag (Eds.), *Mania: An evolving concept* (pp. 309–322). New York: Spectrum.

Allgood-Merten, B., Lewinsohn, P. M., & Hops, H. (1990). Sex differences and adolescent depression. *Journal of Abnormal Psychology, 99*, 55–63.

Anashensel, C. S., & Stone, J. D. (1982). Stress and depression: A test of the buffering model of social support. *Archives of General Psychiatry, 39,* 1392-1396.

Andreasen, N. C., Rice, J., Endicott, J., Coryell, W., Grove, W. M., & Reich, T. (1987). Familial rates of affective disorder. *Archives of General Psychiatry, 44,* 461-469.

Angold, A. (1988). Childhood and adolescent depression: II. Research in clinical populations. *British Journal of Psychiatry, 153,* 476-492.

Antonovsky, H. F., Shoham, I., Kavenaki, S., Lancet, M., & Modan, M. (1980). Gender differences in patterns of adolescent sexual behavior. *Journal of Youth and Adolescence, 9,* 127-141.

Asarnow, J. R., & Bates, S. (1988). Depression in child psychiatric inpatients: Cognitive and attributional patterns. *Journal of Abnormal Child Psychology, 15,* 601-615.

Asarnow, R. F., & MacCrimmon, D. J. (1981). Span of apprehension deficits during the postpsychotic stages of schizophrenia. *Archives of General Psychiatry, 38,* 1006-1011.

Baldessarini, R. J. (1988). Update on recent advances in antidepressant pharmacology and pharmacotherapy. In F. Flach (Ed.), *Psychobiology and psychopharmacology* (pp. 90-108). New York: W. W. Norton.

Barnes, G. E., & Prosen, H. (1985). Parental death and depression. *Journal of Abnormal Psychology, 94,* 64-69.

Barnett, P. A., & Gotlib, I. H. (1988). Psychosocial functioning and depression: Distinguishing among antecedents, concomitants, and consequences. *Psychological Bulletin, 104,* 97-126.

Baron, M., Klotz, J., Mendlewicz, J., & Rainer, J. (1981). Multiple-threshold transmission of affective disorders. *Archives of General Psychiatry, 38,* 79-84.

Beardslee, W. R. (1986). The need for the study of adaptation in the children of parents with affective disorders. In M. Rutter, C. E. Izard, & P. B. Read (Eds.), *Depression in young people* (pp. 189-204). New York: Guilford.

Beck, A. T. (1979). *Cognitive therapy of depression.* New York: Guilford.

Beck, A. T., Hollon, S. D., Young, J. E., Bedrosian, R. C., & Budenz, D. (1985). Treatment of depression with cognitive therapy and amitriptyline. *Archives of General Psychiatry, 42,* 142-148.

Beck, S., & Rosenberg, R. (1986). Frequency, quality, and impact of life events in self-rated depressed, behavioral-problem, and normal children. *Journal of Consulting and Clinical Psychology, 54,* 863-864.

Becker, R. E., Heimberg, R. G., & Bellack, A. S. (1987). *Social skills training treatment for depression.* New York: Pergamon.

Beckham, E. E. (1990). Psychotherapy of depression research at a crossroads: Directions for the 1990s. *Clinical Psychology Review, 10,* 207-228.

Belmaker, R. H., & van Praag, H. M. (Eds.). (1980). *Mania: An evolving concept.* New York: Spectrum.

Belsher, G., & Costello, C. G. (1988). Relapse after recovery from unipolar depression: A critical review. *Psychological Bulletin, 104,* 84-96.

Bemporad, J. R., & Lee, K. W. (1988). Affective disorders. In C. J. Kestenbaum & D. T. Williams (Eds.), *Handbook of clinical assessment of children and adolescents* (pp. 626–649). New York: New York University Press.

Bibring, E. (1953). The mechanisms of depression. In P. Greenacre (Ed.), *Affective disorders* (pp. 13–48). New York: International Universities Press.

Billings, A. G., & Moos, R. H. (1983). Comparisons of children of depressed and nondepressed parents. *Journal of Abnormal Child Psychology, 11*, 463–486.

Bodiford, C. A., Eisenstadt, T. H., Johnson, J. H., & Bradlyn, A. S. (1988). Comparison of learned helpless cognitions and behavior in children with high and low scores on the Children's Depression Inventory. *Journal of Clinical Child Psychology, 17*, 152–158.

Brady, J. P. (1984). Social skills training for psychiatric patients: II. Clinical outcome studies. *American Journal of Psychiatry, 141*, 491–498.

Breier, A., Kelsoe, J. R., Kirwin, P. D., Beller, S. A., Wolkowitz, O. M., & Pickar, D. (1988). Early parental loss and development of adult psychopathology. *Archives of General Psychiatry, 45*, 987–993.

Brooks-Gunn, J., & Fursternberg, F. F. (1989). Adolescent sexual behavior. *American Psychologist, 44*, 249–257.

Brown, G. E., Harris, T. O., & Bifulco, A. (1986). Long-term effects of early loss of parent. In M. Rutter, C. E. Izard, & P. B. Read (Eds.), *Depression in young people* (pp. 251–296). New York: Guilford.

Burke, K. C., Burke, J. D., Regier, D. A., & Rae, D. S. (1990). Age at onset of selected mental disorders in five community populations. *Archives of General Psychiatry, 47*, 511–518.

Cadoret, R. J. (1978). Evidence for genetic inheritance of primary affective disorder in adoptees. *American Journal of Psychiatry, 35*, 463–466.

Calabrese, R. L., & Schumer, H. (1986). The effects of service activities on adolescent alienation. *Adolescence, 21*, 675–687.

Cambor, C. G. (1973). Adolescent alienation syndrome. In J. C. Schoolar (Ed.), *Current issues in adolescent psychiatry* (pp. 101–117). New York: Brunner/ Mazel.

Cantwell, D. P. (1982). Childhood depression: A review of current research. In B. B. Lahey & A. E. Kazdin (Eds.), *Advances in child clinical psychology* (Vol. 5, pp. 39–93). New York: Plenum.

Cantwell, D. P., & Carlson, G. A. (Eds.). (1983). *Affective disorders in childhood and adolescence*. New York: Spectrum.

Carlson, G. A., & Cantwell, D. P. (1980). Unmasking masked depression in children and adolescents. *American Journal of Psychiatry, 137*, 445–449.

Carlson, G. A., & Garber, J. (1986). Developmental issues in the classification of depression in children. In M. Rutter, C. E. Izard, & P. B. Read (Eds.), *Depression in young people* (pp. 399–434). New York: Guilford.

Carlson, G. A., & Kashani, J. H. (1988). Phenomenology of major depression from childhood through adulthood: Analysis of three studies. *American Journal of Psychiatry, 145*, 1222–1225.

Carlson, G. A., & Strober, M. (1979). Affective disorders in adolescence. *Psychiatric Clinics of North America, 2*, 511-526.

Carpenter, W. T., & Stephens, J. H. (1980). The diagnosis of mania. In R. H. Belmaker & H. M. van Praag (Eds.), *Mania: An evolving concept* (pp. 7-24). New York: Spectrum.

Casper, R. C., Redmond, E., Katz, M. M., Schaffer, C. B., David, J. M., & Koslow, S. H. (1985). Somatic symptoms in primary affective disorder. *Archives of General Psychiatry, 42*, 1098-1104.

Cass, L. K., & Thomas, C. B. (1979). *Childhood pathology and later adjustment.* New York: Wiley.

Chevron, E. S., Quinlan, D. M., & Blatt, S. J. (1978). Sex roles and gender differences in the experience of depression. *Journal of Abnormal Psychology, 87*, 680-683.

Chilman, C. S. (1983). *Adolescent sexuality in a changing American society* (2nd ed.). New York: Wiley.

Cohen, R. M., Weingartner, H., Smallberg, S. A., Pickar, D., & Murphy, D. L. (1982). Effort and cognition in depression. *Archives of General Psychiatry, 39*, 593-597.

Cohen, S., Khan, A., & Cox, G. (1989). Demographic and clinical features predictive of recovery in mania. *Journal of Nervous and Mental Disease, 177*, 638-642.

Cole, D. A., & Rehm, L. P. (1986). Family interaction patterns and childhood depression. *Journal of Abnormal Child Psychology, 14*, 297-314.

Compas, B. E., Slavin, L. A., Wagner, B. M., & Vannatta, K. (1986). Relationship of life events and social support with psychological dysfunction among adolescents. *Journal of Youth and Adolescence, 15*, 205-222.

Conte, H. R., Plutchik, R., Wild, K. V., & Karasu, T. B. (1986). Combined psychotherapy and pharmacotherapy for depression. *Archives of General Psychiatry, 43*, 471-479.

Cornell, D. G., Suarez, R., & Berent, S. (1984). Psychomotor retardation in melancholic and nonmelancholic depression: Cognitive and motor components. *Journal of Abnormal Psychology, 93*, 150-157.

Coryell, W., Lavori, P., Endicott, J., Keller, M., & VanEerdewegh, M. (1984). Outcome in schizoaffective, psychotic, and nonpsychotic depression. *Archives of General Psychiatry, 41*, 787-791.

Coyne, J. C., Kessler, R. C., Tal, M., Turnbull, J., Wortman, C. B., & Greden, J. F. (1987). Living with a depressed person. *Journal of Consulting and Clinical Psychology, 55*, 347-352.

Cramer, P. (1988). The Defense Mechanism Inventory: A review of research and discussion of the scales. *Journal of Personality Assessment, 52*, 142-164.

Cramer, P. & Carter, T. (1978). The relationship between sexual identification and the use of defense mechanisms. *Journal of Personality Assessment, 42*, 63-73.

Cytryn, L., & McKnew, D. H. (1979). Affective disorders. In J. D. Noshpitz (Ed.), *Basic handbook of child psychiatry* (Vol. 2, pp. 321-340). New York: Basic Books.

Davenport, Y. B., & Adland, M. L. (1988). Management of manic episodes. In J. F. Clarkin, G. L. Haas, & I. D. Glick (Eds.), *Affective disorders and the family* (pp. 173-195). New York: Guilford.

Digdon, N., & Gotlib, H. (1985). Developmental considerations in the study of childhood depression. *Developmental Review, 5,* 162–199.

Docherty, N., Schnur, M., & Harvey, P. D. (1988). Reference performance and positive and negative thought disorder: A follow-up study of manics and schizophrenics. *Journal of Abnormal Psychology, 97,* 437–442.

Dohr, K. B., Rush, A. J., & Bernstein, I. H. (1989). Cognitive biases and depression. *Journal of Abnormal Psychology, 98,* 263–267.

Downey, G., & Coyne, J. C. (1990). Children of depressed parents: An integrative review. *Psychological Bulletin, 108,* 50–76.

Dunner, D. L., Patrick, V., & Fieve, R. R. (1979). Life events at the onset of bipolar affective illness. *American Journal of Psychiatry, 136,* 508–511.

Earle-Boyer, E. A., Levinson, J. C., Grant, R., & Harvey, P. D. (1986). The consistency of thought disorder in mania and schizophrenia: II. An assessment of consecutive admissions. *Journal of Nervous and Mental Disease, 174,* 443–447.

Emery, G., Bedrosian, R., & Garber, J. (1983). Cognitive therapy with depressed children and adolescents. In D. Cantwell & G. Carlson (Eds.), *Affective disorders in childhood and adolescence* (pp. 445–472). New York: Spectrum.

Exner, J. E., & Weiner, I. B. (1982). *The Rorschach: A comprehensive system: Vol. 3. Assessment of children and adolescents.* New York: Wiley.

Faraone, S. V., Kremen, W. S., & Tsuang, M. T. (1990). Genetic transmission of major affective disorders: Quantitative models and linkage analyses. *Psychological Bulletin, 108,* 109–127.

Farber, S. L. (1981). *Identical twins reared apart.* New York: Basic Books.

Finch, A. J., Casat, C. D., & Carey, M. P. (1990). Depression in children and adolescents. In S. B. Morgan & T. M. Okwumabua (Eds.), *Child and adolescent disorders* (pp. 135–172). Hillsdale, NJ: Erlbaum.

Flaherty, J. A., Gavaria, F. M., Black, E. M., Altman, E., & Mitchell, T. (1983). The role of social support in the functioning of patients with unipolar depression. *American Journal of Psychiatry, 140,* 473–476.

Fleming, J. E., & Offord, D. R. (1990). Epidemiology of childhood depressive disorders: A critical review. *Journal of the American Academy of Child and Adolescent Psychiatry, 29,* 571–580.

Formanek, R., & Gurian A. (Eds.). (1987). *Women and depression: A lifespan perspective.* New York: Springer.

Free, M. L., & Oei, T. P. S. (1989). Biological and psychological processes in the treatment and maintenance of depression. *Clinical Psychology Review, 9,* 653–688.

French, A., & Berlin, I. (Eds.). (1979). *Depression in children and adolescents.* New York: Human Sciences Press.

Freud, S. (1957). Mourning and melancholia. In *Standard edition* (Vol. 14, pp. 243–258). London: Hogarth. (original work published 1917).

Friedman, R. C., Clarkin, J. F., Corn, R., Aronoff, M. S., Hurt, S. W., & Murphy, M. C. (1982). *DSM-III* and affective pathology in hospitalized adolescents. *Journal of Nervous and Mental Disease, 170,* 511–521.

Gabbard, G. O. (1990). *Psychodynamic psychiatry in clinical practice.* Washington, DC: American Psychiatric Press.

Garbutt, J. C. (1988). L-Triiodothyronine and lithium in the treatment of tricyclic antidepressant nonresponders. In F. Flach (Ed.), *Psychobiology and psychopharmacology* (pp. 109-120). New York: W. W. Norton.

Garrison, C. Z., Jackson, K. L., Marsteller, F., McKeown, R., & Addy, C. (1990). A longitudinal study of depressive symptomatology in young adolescents. *Journal of the American Academy of Child and Adolescent Psychiatry, 29*, 581-585.

Gillberg, C., Wahlstrom, J., Forsman, A., Hellgren, L., & Gillberg, I. C. (1986). Teenage psychoses: Epidemiology, classification and reduced optimality in the pre-, peri-, and neonatal periods. *Journal of Child Psychology and Psychiatry, 27*, 87-98.

Gjerde, P. F., Block, J., & Block, J. H. (1988). Depressive symptoms and personality during late adolescence: Gender differences in the externalization-internalization of symptom expression. *Journal of Abnormal Psychology, 97*, 475-486.

Gonzales, L. R., Lewinsohn, P. M., & Clarke, G. N. (1985). Longitudinal follow-up of unipolar depressives: An investigation of predictors of relapse. *Journal of Consulting and Clinical Psychology, 53*, 461-469.

Goodman, S. H., & Brumley, H. E. (1990). Schizophrenic and depressed mothers: Relational deficits in parenting. *Developmental Psychology, 26*, 31-39.

Grossman, L. S., Harrow, M., & Sands, J. R. (1986). Features associated with thought disorder in manic patients at 2-4-year follow-up. *American Journal of Psychiatry, 143*, 306-311.

Grove, W. M., & Andreasen, N. C. (1985). Language and thinking in psychosis. *Archives of General Psychiatry, 42*, 26-32.

Guze, S. B., Cloninger, C. R., Martin, R. L., & Clayton, P. J. (1983). A follow-up and family study of schizophrenia. *Archives of General Psychiatry, 40*, 1273-1276.

Ha, H., Kaplan, S., & Foley, C. (1984). The dexamethasone suppression test in adolescent psychiatric patients. *American Journal of Psychiatry, 141*, 421-423.

Hammen, C. (1990). Cognitive approaches to depression in children. In B. B. Lahey & A. E. Kazdin (Eds.), *Advances in clinical child psychology* (Vol. 13, pp. 139-173). New York: Plenum.

Hammen, C., Ellicott, A., Gitlin, M., & Jamison, K. R. (1989). Sociotropy/autonomy and vulnerability to specific life events in patients with unipolar depression and bipolar disorders. *Journal of Abnormal Psychology, 98*, 154-160.

Hammen, C., & Goodman-Brown, T. (1990). Self-schemas and vulnerability to specific life stress in children at risk for depression. *Cognitive Therapy and Research, 14*, 215-227.

Harder, D. W., Strauss, J. S., Kokes, R. F., & Ritzler, B. A. (1984). Self-derogation and psychopathology. *Genetic Psychology Monographs, 109*, 223-250.

Harrington, R., Fudge, H., Rutter, M., Pickles, A., & Hill, J. (1990). Adult outcomes of childhood and adolescent depression. *Archives of General Psychiatry, 47*, 465-473.

Harrow, M., Goldberg, J. F., Grossman, L. S., & Meltzer, H. Y. (1990). Outcome in manic disorders: A naturalistic follow-up study. *Archives of General Psychiatry, 47*, 665-671.

Hodgman, C. H. (1985). Recent findings in adolescent depression and suicide. *Journal of Developmental and Behavioral Pediatrics, 6*, 162-170.

Hoffman, R. E., Stopek, S., & Andreasen, N. C. (1986). A comparative study of manic vs schizophrenic speech disorganization. *Archives of General Psychiatry, 43*, 831–838.

Hollon, S. D., Spoden, F., & Chastek, J. (1986). Unipolar depression. In M. Hersen (Ed.), *Pharmacological and behavioral treatment: An integrative approach* (pp. 199–239). New York: Wiley.

Holzman, P. S., Shenton, M. E., & Solovay, M. R. (1986). Quality of thought disorder in differential diagnosis. *Schizophrenia Bulletin, 12*, 360–371.

Hughes, M. C. (1984). Recurrent abdominal pain and childhood depression: Clinical observations of 23 children and their families. *American Journal of Orthopsychiatry 54*, 146–155.

Husain, S. A., & Vandiver, T. (1984). *Suicide in children and adolescents.* New York: Spectrum.

Jarrett, R. B., & Rush, A. J. (1986). Psychotherapeutic approaches for depression. In J. E. Helzer & S. B. Guze (Eds.), *Psychoses, affective disorders, and dementia* (pp. 209–243). New York: Basic Books.

Kandel, D. B., & Davies, M. (1982). Epidemiology of depressive mood in adolescents. *Archives of General Psychiatry, 39*, 1205–1212.

Kandel, D. B., & Davies, M. (1986). Adult sequelae of adolescent depressive symptoms. *Archives of General Psychiatry, 43*, 255–262.

Kanfer, R., & Zeiss, A. M. (1983). Depression, interpersonal standard setting, and judgments of self-efficacy. *Journal of Abnormal Psychology, 92*, 319–329.

Kaplan, H. I., & Sadock, B. J. (1988). *Synopsis of psychiatry* (5th ed.). Baltimore: Williams & Wilkins.

Kaplan, S. L., Hong, G. K., & Weinhold, C. (1984). Epidemiology of depressive symptomatology in adolescents. *Journal of the American Academy of Child Psychiatry, 23*, 91–98.

Karasu, T. B. (1990). *Psychotherapy for depression.* Northvale, NJ: Aronson.

Kashani, J. H., Carlson, G. A., Beck, N. C., Hoeper, E. W., Corcoran, C. M., McAllister, J. A., Fallahi, C., Rosenberg, T. K., & Reid, J. C. (1987). Depression, depressive symptoms, and depressed mood among a community sample of adolescents. *American Journal of Psychiatry, 144*, 931–934.

Kashani, J. H., Rosenberg, T. K., & Reid, J. C. (1989). Developmental perspectives in child and adolescent depressive symptoms in a community sample. *American Journal of Psychiatry, 146*, 871–875.

Kaslow, N. J., Rehm, L. P., & Siegel, A. W. (1984). Social-cognitive and cognitive correlates of depression in children. *Journal of Abnormal Child Psychology, 12*, 605–620.

Kazdin, A. E. (1990). Child depression. *Journal of Child Psychology and Psychiatry, 31*, 121–160.

Keller, M. B., Beardslee, W. R., Dorer, D. J., Lavori, P. W., Samuelson, H., & Klerman, G. L. (1986). Impact of severity and chronicity of parental affective illness on adaptive functioning and psychopathology in children. *Archives of General Psychiatry, 43*, 930–937.

Keller, M. B., Friedman, B., & Lavori, P. W. (1988). The nature of recovery and relapse in depressive disorders. In F. Flach (Ed.), *Affective disorders* (pp. 38-51). New York: W. W. Norton.

Kendall, P. C., Cantwell, D. P., & Kazdin, A. E. (1989). Depression in children and adolescents: Assessment issues and recommendations. *Cognitive Therapy and Research, 13,* 109-146.

Kendler, K. S., Gruenberg, A. M., & Tsuang, M. T. (1985). Psychiatric illness in first-degree relatives of schizophrenic and surgical control patients. *Archives of General Psychitary, 42,* 770-779.

Kendler, K. S., & Hays, P. (1983). Schizophrenia subdivided by the family history of affective disorder. *Archives of General Psychiatry, 40,* 951-955.

Kendler, K. S., Heath, A., Martin, N. G., & Eaves, L. J., (1986). Symptoms of anxiety and depression in a volunteer twin population. *Archives of General Psychiatry, 43,* 213-221.

Kestenbaum, C. J., & Kron, L. (1987). Psychoanalytic intervention with children and adolescents with affective disorders: A combined treatment approach. *Journal of the American Academy of Psychoanalysis, 15,* 153-174.

Klein, D. N., Depue, R. A., & Slater, J. F. (1985). Cyclothymia in the adolescent offspring of parents with bipolar affective disorder. *Journal of Abnormal Psychology, 94,* 115-127.

Klerman, G. L., & Weissman, M. M. (1986). The interpersonal approach in understanding depression. In T. Millon & G. L. Klerman (Eds.), *Contemporary directions in psychopathology* (pp. 429-456). New York: Guilford.

Klerman, G. L., Weissman, M. M., Rounsaville, B. J., & Chevron, E. S. (1984). *Interpersonal psychotherapy of depression.* New York: Basic Books.

Koenig, L. J. (1988). Self-image of emotionally disturbed adolescents. *Journal of Abnormal Child Psychology, 16,* 111-126.

Kolko, D. J. (1987). Depression. In M. Hersen & V. B. Van Hasselt (Eds.), *Behavior therapy with children and adolescents* (pp. 137-183). New York: Wiley.

Koplewicz, H. S., & Williams, D. T. (1988). Psychopharmacological treatment. In C. J. Kestenbaum & D. T. Williams (Eds.), *Handbook of clinical assessment of children and adolescents* (pp. 1084-1110). New York: New York University Press.

Kovach, J. A., & Glickman, N. T. (1986). Levels and psychosocial correlates of adolescent drug use. *Journal of Youth and Adolescence, 15,* 61-78.

Kovacs, M. (1986). A developmental perspective on methods and measures in the assessment of depressive disorders: The clinical interview. In M. Rutter, C. E. Izard, & P. B. Read (Eds.), *Depression in young people* (pp. 435-465). New York: Guilford.

Kovacs, M. (1989). Affective disorders in children and adolescents. *American Psychologist, 44,* 209-215.

Kovacs, M., & Beck, A. T. (1978). Maladaptive cognitive structures in depression. *American Journal of Psychiatry, 135,* 525-533.

Kovacs, M., Feinberg, T. L., Crouse-Novak, M. A., Paulauskas, S. L., & Finkelstein, R. (1984). Depressive disorders in childhood: I. A longitudinal prospective study of characteristics and recovery. *Archives of General Psychiatry, 41,* 229-237.

Kupfer, D. J., & Frank, E. (1987). Relapse in recurrent unipolar depression. *American Journal of Psychiatry, 144,* 86–88.

Ladd, G. W., & Asher, S. R. (1985). Social skill training and children's peer relations. In L. L'Abate & M. A. Milan (Eds.), *Handbook of social skills training and research* (pp. 219–244). New York: Wiley.

Larson, R. W., Raffaelli, M., Richards, M. H., Ham, M., & Jewell, L. (1990). Ecology of depression in late childhood and early adolescence: A profile of daily states and activities. *Journal of Abnormal Psychology, 99,* 92–102.

Law, W., Petti, T. A., & Kazdin, A. E. (1981). Withdrawal symptoms after graduated cessation of imipramine in children. *American Journal of Psychiatry, 138,* 647–650.

Lee, C. M., & Gotlib, I. H. (1989). Maternal depression and child adjustment: A longitudinal analysis. *Journal of Abnormal Psychology, 98,* 78–85.

Lefkowitz, M. M., & Tesiny, E. P. (1984). Rejection and depression: Prospective and contemporaneous analyses. *Developmental Psychology, 20,* 776–785.

Lefkowitz, M. M., & Tesiny, E. P. (1985). Depression in children: Prevalence and correlates. *Journal of Consulting and Clinical Psychology, 53,* 647–656.

Lerner, Y. (1980). The subjective experience of mania. In R. H. Belmaker & H. M. van Praag (Eds.), *Mania: An evolving concept* (pp. 77–88). New York: Spectrum.

Lesse, S. (1979). Behavioral problems masking severe depression—Cultural and clinical survey. *American Journal of Psychotherapy, 33,* 41–53.

Lewinsohn, P. M., Zeiss, A. M., & Duncan, E. M. (1989). Probability of relapse after recovery from an episode of depression. *Journal of Abnormal Psychology, 98,* 107–116.

Long, B. H. (1986). Parental discord vs. family structure: Effects of divorce on the self-esteem of daughters. *Journal of Youth and Adolescence, 15,* 19–28.

McCann, I. L., & Holmes, D. S. (1984). Influences of aerobic exercises on depression. *Journal of Personality and Social Psychology, 46,* 1142–1147.

McCauley, E., Mitchell, J. R., Burke, P., & Moss, S. (1988). Cognitive attributes of depression in children and adolescents. *Journal of Consulting and Clinical Psychology, 56,* 903–908.

McCranie, E. W., & Bass, J. D. (1984). Childhood family antecedents of dependency and self-criticism: Implications for depression. *Journal of Abnormal Psychology, 93,* 3–8.

McGlashan, T. H. (1988). Adolescent versus adult onset of mania. *American Journal of Psychiatry, 145,* 221–223.

McNeal, E. T., & Cimbolic, P. (1986). Antidepressants and biochemical theories of depression. *Psychological Bulletin, 99,* 361–374.

Mendlewicz, J. (1980). X-linkage of bipolar illness and the question of schizoaffective illness. In R. H. Belmaker & H. M. van Praag (Eds.), *Mania: An evolving concept* (pp. 89–96). New York: Spectrum.

Mendlewicz, J., & Rainer, J. D. (1977). Adoption study supporting genetic transmission in manic-depressive illness. *Nature, 268,* 327–329.

Mezzich, A. C., & Mezzich, J. E. (1979). Symptomatology of depression in adolescents. *Journal of Personality Assessment, 43,* 267–275.

Miller, K. B., & Nelson, J. C. (1987). Does the dexamethasone suppression test relate to subtypes, factors, symptoms, or severity? *Archives of General Psychiatry, 44,* 769-774.

Miller, P. Y., & Simon, W. (1980). The development of sexuality in adolescence. In J. Adelson (Ed.), *Handbook of adolescent psychology* (pp. 383-407). New York: Wiley.

Mills, C. J., & Noyes, H. L. (1984). Patterns and correlates of initial and subsequent drug use among adolescents. *Journal of Consulting and Clinical Psychology, 52,* 231-243.

Miranda, J., & Persons, J. R. (1988). Dysfunctional attitudes are mood-state dependent. *Journal of Abnormal Psychology, 97,* 76-79.

Moos, R. H. (1990). Depressed outpatients' life contexts, amount of treatment, and treatment outcome. *Journal of Nervous and Mental Disease, 178,* 105-112.

Neale, J. M. (1988). Defensive functions of manic episodes. In T. F. Oltmanns & B. A. Maher (Eds.), *Delusional beliefs* (pp. 138-156). New York: Wiley.

Nelson, J. C., Charney, D. S., & Quinlan, D. M. (1981). Evaluation of the *DSM-III* criteria for melancholia. *Archives of General Psychiatry, 38,* 555-559.

Ney, P., Colbert, P., Newman, B., & Young, J. (1986). Aggressive behavior and learning difficulties as symptoms of depression in children. *Child Psychiatry and Human Development, 17,* 3-14.

Nezu, A. M. (1986). Efficacy of a social problem-solving therapy approach for unipolar depression. *Journal of Consulting and Clinical Psychology, 54,* 196-202.

Nezu, A. M., Nezu, C. M., & Perri, M. G. (1989). *Problem-solving therapy for depression.* New York: Wiley.

Nietzel, M. D., Russell, R. L., Hemmings, K. A., & Gretter, M. L. (1987). Clinical significance of psychotherapy for unipolar depression: A meta-analytic approach to social comparison. *Journal of Consulting and Clinical Psychology, 55,* 156-161.

Nolen-Hoeksema, S. (1987). Sex differences in unipolar depression: Evidence and theory. *Psychological Bulletin, 101,* 259-282.

O'Connell, R. A. (1988). Depression. Bipolar or unipolar? In F. Flach (Ed.), *Affective disorders* (pp. 29-37). New York: W. W. Norton.

Oltmanns, T. F., Murphy, R., Berenbaum, H., & Dunlop, S. R. (1985). Rating verbal communication impairment in schizophrenia and affective disorders. *Schizophrenia Bulletin, 11,* 292-299.

Orvaschel, H., Walsh-Allis, G., & Ye, W. (1988). Psychopathology in children of parents with recurrent depression. *Journal of Abnormal Child Psychology, 16,* 17-28.

Oster, G. D., & Caro, J. E. (1990). *Understanding and treating depressed adolescents and their families.* New York: Wiley.

Parker, G. (1983). Parental "affectionless" control as an antecedent to adult depression. *Archives of General Psychiatry, 40,* 956-960.

Peterson, C., & Seligman, M. E. (1984). Causal explanation as a risk factor for depression: Theory and evidence. *Psychological Review, 91,* 347-374.

Pfeffer, C. R. (1986). *The suicidal child.* New York: Guilford.

Pfohl, B., Stangl, D., & Tsuang, M. T. (1983). The association between parental loss and diagnosis in the Iowa 500. *Archives of General Psychiatry, 40,* 965–967.

Phifer, J. F., & Murrell, S. A. (1986). Etiologic factors in the onset of depressive symptoms in older adults. *Journal of Abnormal Psychology, 95,* 282–291.

Plomin, R. (1989). Environment and genes. *American Psychologist, 44,* 105–111.

Pogue-Geile, M. F., & Harrow, M. (1985). Negative and positive symptoms in schizophrenia and depression: A followup. *Schizophrenia Bulletin, 11,* 371–387.

Pokorny, A. D. (1987). *DSM-III* and affective disorders. In F. Flach (Ed.), *Diagnostics and psychopathology* (pp. 72–82). New York: Norton.

Post, R. M., Rubinow, D. R., Uhde, T. W., Roy-Byrne, P. P., Linnoila, M., Rosoff, A., & Cowdry, R. (1989). Dysphoric mania. *Archives of General Psychiaatry, 46,* 353–358.

Prien, R. F., Kupfer, D. J., Mansky, P. A., Small, J. G., Tuason, V. B., Voss, C. B., & Johnson, E. W. (1984). Drug therapy in the prevention of recurrences in unipolar and bipolar affective disorder. *Archives of General Psychiatry, 41,* 1096–1104.

Prosen, M., Clark, D. C., Harrow, M., & Fawcett, J. (1983). Guilt and conscience in major depressive disorders. *American Journal of Psychiatry, 140,* 839–844.

Puig-Antich, J. (1986). Psychobiological markers: Effects of age and puberty. In M. Rutter, C. E. Izard, & P. B. Read (Eds.), *Depression in young people* (pp. 341–381). New York: Guilford.

Puig-Antich, J., Ryan, N. D., & Rabinovich, R. (1985). Affective disorders in childhood and adolescence. In J. M. Wiener (Ed.), *Diagnosis and psychopharmacology of childhood and adolescent disorders* (pp. 151–178). New York: Wiley.

Quay, H. C. (1987). Patterns of delinquent behavior. In H. C. Quay (Ed.), *Handbook of juvenile delinquency* (pp. 118–138). New York: Wiley.

Ragan, P. V., & McGlashan, T. H. (1986). Childhood parental death and adult psychopathology. *American Journal of Psychiatry, 143,* 153–157.

Rancurello, M. (1986). Antidepressants in children: Indications, benefits, and limitations. *American Journal of Psychotherapy, 40,* 377–392.

Regier, D. A., Boyd, J. H., Burke, J. D., Rae, D. S., Myers, J. K., Kramer, M., Robins, L. N., George, L. K., Karno, M., & Locke, B. Z. (1988). One-month prevalence of mental disorders in the United States. *Archives of General Psychiatry, 45,* 977–986.

Reynolds, W. M., & Coats, K. I. (1986). A comparison of cognitive–behavioral therapy and relaxation training for the treatment of depression in adolescents. *Journal of Consulting and Clinical Psychology, 54,* 653–660.

Riley, W. T., Treiber, F. A., & Woods, M. G. (1989). Anger and hostility in depression. *Journal of Nervous and Mental Disease, 177,* 668–674.

Robbins, D. R., & Alessi, N. E. (1985). Depressive symptoms and suicidal behavior in adolescents. *American Journal of Psychiatry, 142,* 588–592.

Robinson, L. A., Berman, J. S., & Niemeyer, R. A. (1990). Psychotherapy for the treatment of depression: A comprehensive review of controlled outcome research. *Psychological Bulletin, 108,* 30–49.

Roy, A. (1985). Early parental separation and adult depression. *Archives of General Psychiatry, 42,* 987–991.

Roy, A. (1988). Early parental loss and depression. In F. Flach (Ed.), *Affective disorders* (pp. 19-28). New York: W. W. Norton.

Rush, A. J. (1984). Cognitive therapy in combination with antidepressant medication. In B. D. Beitman & G. L. Klerman (Eds.), *Combining psychotherapy and drug therapy in clinical practice* (pp. 121-148). New York: Spectrum.

Rutter, M., Graham, P., Chadwick, O. F. D., & Yule, W. (1976). Adolescent turmoil: Fact or fiction? *Journal of Child Psychology and Psychiatry, 17*, 35-56.

Rutter, M., Izard, C. E., & Read, P. B. (Eds.). (1986). *Depression in young people.* New York: Guilford.

Rutter, M., Macdonald, H., Le Couteur, A., Harrington, R., Bolton, P. & Bailey, A. (1990). Genetic factors in child psychiatric disorders: II. Empirical findings. *Journal of Child Psychology and Psychiatry, 31*, 39-83.

Ryan, N. D. (1989). Major depression. In C. G. Last & M. Hersen (Eds.), *Handbook of child psychiatric diagnosis* (pp. 317-329). New York: Wiley.

Ryan, N. D., & Puig-Antich, J. (1987). Pharmacological treatment of adolescent psychiatric disorders. *Journal of Adolescent Health Care, 8*, 137-142.

Ryan, N. D., Puig-Antich, J., Ambrosini, P., Rabinovich, H., Robinson, D., Nelson, B., Iyengar, S., & Twomey, J. (1987). The clinical picture of major depression in children and adolescents. *Archives of General Psychiatry, 44*, 854-861.

Schneer, H. I., Perlstein, A., & Brozovsky, M. (1975). Hospitalized suicidal adolescents. *Journal of the American Academy of Child Psychiatry, 14*, 268-280.

Schrader, G., Gibbs, A., & Harcourt, R. (1986). Dysfunctional attitudes in former psychiatric patients. *Journal of Nervous and Mental Disease, 174*, 660-663.

Seligman, M. E. P., & Peterson, C. (1986). A learned helplessness perspective on childhood depression: Theory and research. In M. Rutter, C. E. Izard, & P. B. Read (Eds.), *Depression in young people* (pp. 223-250). New York: Guilford.

Shaffer, D. (1974). Suicide in childhood and early adolescence. *Journal of Child Psychology and Psychiatry, 15*, 275-291.

Shaffer, D. (1986). Developmental factors in child and adolescent suicide. In M. Rutter, C. E. Izard, & P. B. Read (Eds.), *Depression in young people* (pp. 383-396). New York: Guilford.

Shapiro, M. F., & Lehman, A. F. (1983). The diagnosis of depression in different clinical settings: An analysis of the literature on the dexamethasone suppression test. *Journal of Nervous and Mental Disease, 171*, 714-720.

Sheras, P. L. (1983). Suicide in adolescence. In C. E. Walker & M. C. Roberts (Ed.), *Handbook of clinical child psychology* (pp. 759-784). New York: Wiley.

Shrout, P. E., Link, B. G., Dohrenwend, B. P., Skodol, A. E., Stueve, A., & Mirotznik, J. (1989). Characterizing life events as risk factors for depression: The role of fateful loss events. *Journal of Abnormal Psychology, 98*, 460-467.

Silberman, E. K., Weingartner, H., & Post, R. M. (1983). Thinking disorders in depression. *Archives of General Psychiatry, 40*, 775-780.

Simons, A. D., Garfield, S. L., & Murphy, G. E. (1984). The process of change in cognitive therapy and pharmacotherapy for depression. *Archives of General Psychiatry, 41*, 45-51.

Simons, A. D., Murphy, G. E., Levine, J. L., & Wetzel, R. D. (1986). Cognitive therapy and pharmacotherapy for depression. *Archives of General Psychiatry, 43,* 43–48.

Sines, J. O. (1987). Influence of the home and family environment on childhood dysfunction. In B. B. Lahey & A. E. Kazdin (Eds.), *Advances in clinical child psychology* (Vol. 10, pp. 1–54). New York: Plenum.

Smucker, M. R., Craighead, W. E., Craighead, L. W., & Green, B. J. (1986). Normative and reliability data for the Children's Depressive Inventory. *Journal of Abnormal Child Psychology, 14,* 25–40.

Solovay, M. R., Shenton, M. E., & Holzman, P. S. (1987). Comparative studies of thought disorders: I. Mania and schizophrenia. *Archives of General Psychiatry, 44,* 13–20.

Stehouwer, R. S., Bultsma, C. A., & Blackford, I. T. (1985). Developmental differences in depression: Cognitive–perceptual distortion in adolescent versus adult female depression. *Adolescence, 20,* 291–299.

Steinbrueck, S. M., Maxwell, S. E., & Howard, G. S. (1983). A meta-analysis of psychotherapy and drug therapy in the treatment of unipolar depression with adults. *Journal of Consulting and Clinical Psychology, 51,* 856–863.

Strober, M. (1984). Familial aspects of depressive disorder in early adolescence. In E. B. Weller & R. A. Weller (Eds.), *Major depressive disorders in children* (pp. 38–48). Washington, DC: American Psychiatric Press.

Strober, M., & Carlson, G. (1982). Bipolar illness in adolescents with major depression. *Archives of General Psychiatry, 39,* 549–555.

Strober, M., Hanna, G., & McCracken, J. (1989). Bipolar disorder. In C. G. Last & M. Hersen (Eds.), *Handbook of child psychiatric diagnosis* (pp. 299–316). New York: Wiley.

Strober, M., McCracken, J., & Hanna G. (1989). Affective disorders. In L. K. G. Hsu & M. Hersen (Eds.), *Recent developments in adolescent psychiatry* (pp. 201–203). New York: Wiley.

Strober, M., Morrell, W., Burroughs, J., Lampert, C., Danforth, H., & Freeman, R. (1988). A family study of bipolar I disorder in adolescence: Early onset of symptoms linked to increased familial loading and lithium resistance. *Journal of Affective Disorders, 15,* 255–268.

Strober, M., Morrell, W., Lampert, C., & Burroughs, J1. (1990). Relapse following discontinuation of lithium maintenance therapy in adolescents with bipolar I illness: A naturalistic study. *American Journal of Psychiatry, 147,* 457–461.

Sutker, P. B., (1982). Adolescent drug and alcohol behaviors. In T. M. Field, A. Huston, H. C. Quay, L. Troll, & G. E. Finley (Eds.), *Review of human development* (pp. 356–380). New York: Wiley.

Tennant, C. (1988). Parental loss in childhood. *Archives of General Psychiatry, 45,* 1045–1050.

Teri, L., & Lewinsohn, P. M. (1986). Individual and group treatment of unipolar depression: Comparison of treatment outcome and identification of predictors of successful treatment outcome. *Behavior Therapy, 17,* 215–228.

Toolan, J. M. (1974). Masked depression in children and adolescents. In S. Lesse (Ed.), *Masked depression* (pp. 141–164). New York: Aronson.

Tsuang, M. T., Woolson, R. F., & Fleming, J. A. (1979). Long-term outcome of major psychoses. *Archives of General Psychiatry, 36,* 1295-1301.

Van Valkenburg, C., & Akiskal, H. S. (1985). Affective disorders. In M. Hersen & S. M. Turner (Eds.), *Diagnostic interviewing* (pp. 79-110). New York: Plenum.

Wehr, T. A., & Goodwin, F. K. (1987). Can antidepressants cause mania and worsen the course of affective illness? *American Journal of Psychiatry, 144,* 1403-1411.

Weiner, I. B. (1975). Depression in adolescence. In F. F. Flach & S. C. Draghi (Eds.), *The nature and treatment of depression* (pp. 99-117). New York: Wiley.

Weiner, I. B. (1985). Assessing children and adolescents with the Rorschach. In H. M. Knoff (Ed.), *The assessment of child and adolescent personality* (pp. 141-171). New York: Guilford.

Weiner, I. B., & Del Gaudio, A. C. (1976). Psychopathology in adolescence: An epidemiological study. *Archives of General Psychiatry, 33,* 187-193.

Weintraub, S., Winters, K. C., & Neale, J. M. (1986). Competence and vulnerability in children with an affectively disordered parent. In M. Rutter, C. E. Izard, & P. B. Read (Eds.), *Depression in young people* (pp. 205-220). New York: Guilford.

Weissman, M. M., Gammon D., John, K., Merikangas, K. R., Warner, V., Prusoff, B. A., & Sholomskas, D. (1987). Children of depressed parents. *Archives of General Psychiatry, 44,* 847-853.

Weissman, M. M., & Klerman, G. L. (1979). Sex differences and the epidemiology of depression. In E. S. Gomberg & V. Franks (Ed.), *Gender and disordered behavior* (pp. 381-425). New York: Brunner/Mazel.

Wender, P. H., Kety, S. S., Rosenthal, D., Schulsinger, F., Ortmann, J., & Lunde, I. (1986). Psychiatric disorders in the biological and adoptive families of adopted individuals with affective disorders. *Archives of General Psychiatry, 43,* 923-929.

Werry, J. S. (1982). Pharmacotherapy. In B. B. Lahey & A. E. Kazdin (Eds.), *Advances in clinical child psychology* (Vol. 5, pp. 283-322). New York: Plenum.

Whitaker, A., Johnson, J., Shaffer, D., Rapoport, J. L., Kalikow, K., Walsh, B. T., Davies, M., Braiman, S., & Dolinsky, A. (1990). Uncommon troubles in young people. *Archives of General Psychiatry, 47,* 487-496.

Whiteford, H. A., Peabody, C. A., Csernansky, J. G., & Berger, P. A. (1986). The severity of depression and nonsuppression on the DST. *American Journal of Psychiatry, 143,* 1634-1635.

Wierzbicki, M. (1986). Similarity of monozygotic and dizygotic twins in level and lability of subclinical depressed mood. *Journal of Clinical Psychology, 42,* 577-585.

Winokur, G., & Crowe, R. R. (1983). Bipolar illness. *Archives of General Psychiatry, 40,* 57-58.

Winokur, G., Tsuang, M. T., & Crowe, R. R. (1982). The Iowa 500: Affective disorder in relatives of manic and depressed patients. *American Journal of Psychiatry, 139,* 209-212.

Winters, K. C., & Neale, J. M. (1985). Mania and low self-esteem. *Journal of Abnormal Psychology, 94,* 282-290.

Young, M. A., Scheftner, W. A., Fawcett, J., & Klerman, G. L. (1990). Gender differences in the clinical features of unipolar major depressive disorder. *Journal of Nervous and Mental Disease, 178,* 200–203.

Youngren, M. A., & Lewinsohn, P. M. (1980). The functional relation between depression and problematic interpersonal behavior. *Journal of Abnormal Psychology, 89,* 333–341.

Zeiss, A. M., Lewinsohn, P. M., & Munoz, R. F. (1979). Nonspecific improvement effects in depression using interpersonal skills training, pleasant activity schedules, or cognitive training. *Journal of Consulting and Clinical Psychology, 47,* 427–439.

Zimmerman, M., Coryell, W., & Pfohl, B. (1986). The validity of the dexamethasone suppression test as a marker for endogenous depression. *Archives of General Psychiatry, 43,* 347–355.

CHAPTER 5

Borderline Disorders

In some clinical settings, any patient who manifests marked psychological disturbance without being clearly schizophrenic or affectively disordered is likely to be diagnosed "borderline." In other settings, "borderline disorder" is dismissed as a mythical condition, created without substance by object relations theorists and the architects of *DSM-III*, and is rarely diagnosed. Reality, as judged from the currently available clinical and research literature, is probably somewhere in between—borderline disorders are likely to be present neither in most nor in very few patients presenting for psychological help, but rather in some modest but noteworthy percentage.

Some borderline patients display prominent features of schizophrenia, and others display prominent features of affective disorder. This has led some psychopathologists to infer that borderline disorder is a variant of schizophrenia and others to infer that it is a variant of affective disorder. In all likelihood, it is neither. Schizophrenia and affective disorder are essentially symptomatic disorders, in that the underlying impairments of personality functioning by which they are defined produce symptoms that wax and wane. Schizophrenic patients have their good days and bad days. They alternate between lucidity and incoherence and between being relatively realistic and relatively inappropriate, and at any point in time they can be described as being more or less overtly schizophrenic. The successful treatment of schizophrenia is measured by a gradual remission of symptoms and an increasing excess of good days over bad. Affectively disordered patients are similarly suffering from a cyclical disorder marked in its natural course by episodes of remission and relapse and dramatic alternations in prevailing mood state.

Borderline disorders, by contrast, are defined not so much by symptoms that come and go as by persistent ways of viewing and coping with experience. To be sure, the hallmarks of borderline disorder discussed in this chapter include emotional instability and a vulnerability to brief psychotic episodes. However, these are stable and enduring characteristics of a borderline disorder, not indices of its severity. Having a temper tantrum or a psychotic episode does not make the person more seriously borderline than before, nor does the passing of the anger or the psychosis signal recovery from the borderline condition. Borderline disorders can accordingly be more reasonably viewed as characterological than as symptomatic conditions, and they merit consideration as distinct disorders in their own right rather than as variants of schizophrenia or affective disorder.

Psychopathologists with different points of view have delineated a great many patterns of borderline disturbance, and this profusion of possibilities has caused some mental health professionals to suspect that borderline disorder is an unreliable concept without clinical utility. Despite the heterogeneity of patients with borderline disorder, however, they share several distinct characteristics in common. These core features of borderline psychopathology can be reliably assessed with structured interviews and psychological tests; they validly differentiate borderline individuals from persons with schizophrenia, affective disorder, and other characterological disorders; and they have important implications for differential diagnosis and treatment planning.

Like other characterological disorders, borderline conditions originate early in life and produce prodromal manifestations during childhood. However, it is in middle and especially late adolescence, when individual personality style begins to crystallize, that borderline disorders tend to become fully established and clearly diagnosable. In addition to being more recognizable than before, when personality style was less settled, borderline disorder in adolescence is more treatable than it will be later on, when personality style has become more firmly entrenched. This chapter addresses the core characteristics and categories of borderline psychopathology, the origin and development of borderline disorders, considerations in the differential diagnosis of these disorders, and strategies in conducting psychotherapy with borderline adolescents.

CATEGORIES OF BORDERLINE DISORDER

For purposes of clinical diagnosis and treatment planning, borderline disorder can be usefully conceptualized as a cluster of personality impairments that define a *borderline core*. These impairments include certain disruptions in cognitive, affective, and interpersonal functioning that characterize all persons with borderline disorder. Variations in which of these impairments are most prominent and how they are manifest help to specify two categories of borderline disorder. Those borderline persons whose persistent dysfunctions are primarily cognitive in nature and who display interpersonal isolation can be said to have a *schizotypal personality disorder*. Those whose characterological difficulties are primarily affective in nature and who display interpersonal overinvolvement can be said to have a *borderline personality disorder.*

This particular approach to categorizing borderline disorders was suggested by Spitzer and his colleagues (Spitzer & Endicott, 1979; Spitzer, Endicott, & Gibbon, 1979), whose work provided the basis for listing schizotypal and borderline personality disorders as separate diagnostic categories in *DSM-III*. The notion of a borderline core linking these two conditions has been elaborated by Meissner (1984) in terms of a "borderline spectrum" of disorders. Both of these formulations are consistent with research evidence indicating that borderline disorders can be reliably distinguished from other forms of psychopathology; that most patients with borderline disorder will show a clearly differentiable emphasis on either cognitive or affective manifestations; and that the remaining patients will show a mixture of these features and function at some intermediate point on the borderline spectrum at which schizotypal and borderline personality disorder overlap.

The Borderline Core

Over the years, numerous clinical scholars have described psychopathological conditions that bear some kinship to present-day concepts of borderline disorder. These efforts produced a rich lode of diagnostic guidelines and treatment recommendations, but they also left a legacy of jumbled terminology and conflicting theoretical conviction. These earlier contributions are discussed in detail elsewhere and are not reviewed here (see Goldstein, 1983; Kroll, 1988, Chapter l; Millon, 1981, Chapters 12 & 14; Stone, 1980, Chapter l). Suffice it to say that borderline disorder has had ascribed to it a very broad range of possible manifestations in dysfunctional thoughts, feelings, and actions. Covering all bases, Grinker (1977, p. 162) noted early on that borderline disorder can be described as a form of psychopathology that combines features of psychotic, neurotic, and characterological disturbance with elements of normality as well.

Despite the range and complexity of borderline phenomena, six common elements have traditionally been considered to constitute core characteristics of this condition (see Dahl, 1990; Gunderson & Singer, 1975; Gunderson & Kolb, 1978; Perry & Klerman, 1980). These core characteristics, as described below, continue to provide a reliable basis for diagnosing borderline disorder in clinical practice.

1. *Intense Emotions.* Borderline individuals are subject to episodes of intense anger, anxiety, and depression. Because they often seem so bristling with rage or racked with worry and despair, their emotional intensity tends to make other people feel uncomfortable. Although the pent-up fury of the borderline patient is sometimes discharged in outbursts of temper and violence, it more often seeps out in the form of irritability, impatience, petulance, argumentativeness, sarcasm, and devaluation of other people and what they are doing. The depressive experiences associated with borderline disorder typically involve a sense of emptiness or loneliness and the feeling that life is not worth living.

Along with their prevailing affects of anger, anxiety, and depression, borderline persons may also cycle at times through periods of self-satisfaction and elation. The quality of their affect is always less distinctive than its quantity, however. Borderline persons will, at various points in time, become very anxious, very mad, very happy, or very sad, but they will rarely, if ever, display any of these affects in mild or muted form. Flat affect and emotional blandness are in fact so uncharacteristic of borderline disorder that their presence usually points to some other form of psychopathology.

2. *Poor Self-Control.* The actions of borderline people are frequently poorly planned and poorly controlled. Characteristic impulsivity and intolerance for frustration place the borderline at high risk for both antisocial and self-destructive behavior. Many borderline patients will have brushed with the law as a result of their poor self-control, and in young persons, the likelihood of truancy, running away, and other delinquent conduct is increased by the presence of borderline disorder.

As for self-destructive behavior, persons with a borderline condition are more likely than people in general to abuse alcohol and other drugs, to become sexually promiscuous, to engage in acts of self-mutilation, and to make suicide attempts. The suicidal behavior of borderline individuals is often blatantly manipulative, with threats or some minor but very dramatic self-injury being used in an obvious effort to influence the attitudes or actions of other people.

3. *Illusory Social Adaptation.* Persons with borderline disturbance often appear to be functioning adequately, provided that they can confine themselves to situations in which their coping capacities are not taxed. They may show a conventional face to the world, appear appropriately engaged with other people, and present a seemingly good record of effort and accomplishment in school and on the job. However, closer scrutiny reveals that this apparently good adaptation has been maintained within the boundaries of undemanding social, academic, and work environments in which the person's abilities were far more than adequate to guarantee success.

Borderline individuals cannot cope effectively with challenge and uncertainty, nor can they easily tolerate stress or ambiguity. When unsure what is expected of them or faced with changing demands that strain their capacities, they are likely to perform poorly until they can get themselves back into a comfortable, predictable, and easily manageable situation. Hence, borderline patients will usually show either a history of apparently successful adaptation that in fact represents marked underachievement in relation to their abilities, or they will have a spotty record, in which periods of accomplishment have alternated with social and school or occupational failure.

4. *Strained Interpersonal Relationships.* Although borderline individuals can ordinarily handle superficial relationships with other people, they cannot deal effectively with close or intimate relationships. They tend to opt either for social isolation, in which case they rebuff overtures of friendliness and concern, or for overinvolvement, in which case no amount of interest and attention on the part of others satisfies them for very long.

When borderline persons are functioning in social isolation, they typically suspect the motives of others and fear being exploited or rejected. Such fears prevent them from reaching out for intimacy, no matter how lonely they feel. The social isolation of some borderline individuals is compounded by a tendency to misperceive or ignore various characteristics of other people and to form whatever inaccurate or incomplete image fits their needs at the moment. This tendency contributes to the very outcome they fear—they court exploitation and rejection by treating other people without realistic regard for what they are like and without sensitivity to their needs and expectations.

When, instead of being isolated, borderline individuals are overinvolved with others, they tend to form intense, clinging, dependent relationships. Like social isolation, such overinvolvement is governed by self-serving rather than altruistic motives. Borderline individuals are interpersonal takers, not givers, and their cup is virtually impossible to fill. Their egocentric demandingness places a heavy burden on those who befriend or attempt to love them. They are likely to greet the slightest suggestion of flagging devotion with torrents of unwarranted rage and revilement. The relationships of the overinvolved borderline are consequently as unstable as they are intense. Today's most wonderful friend can be discarded tomorrow for his or her callousness or treachery and replaced with a new most wonderful friend.

5. *Vulnerability to Brief Psychotic Episodes.* Although borderline individuals are not overtly psychotic, they are highly vulnerable to psychotic breakdown, particularly in unstructured situations that give few clues to what is required of them. These psychotic episodes may involve dissociation, paranoid ideation, delusions and hallucinations, a loss of reality sense, or incapacitation by depression or mania. Psychological breakdown associated with borderline disorder tends to be short-lived, stress-related, and readily reversible. Episodes appear suddenly, with little advance warning, usually in the context of an obviously anxiety-provoking experience, and they remit with equal suddenness, shortly after the person is placed in a supportive and predictable environment that minimizes or eliminates the precipitating stress. The possible precipitants of breakdown in borderline patients include immersion in insight-oriented psychotherapy that is not geared to their intolerance for ambiguity. This result was first identified by Knight (1953), in a rich description of patients in psychoanalysis who "fall apart on the couch." Borderline patients who are treated with insufficient regard for their need to have structure are at high risk for becoming too anxious and disorganized to participate effectively in the treatment, and they will very quickly develop a destructively intense transference relationship.

This particular feature of borderline psychopathology has obvious implications not only for treatment planning but for psychodiagnostic evaluation as well. Research with psychological tests has consistently documented the vulnerability of borderline persons to breaking down in unstructured situations. Borderline individuals respond in a relatively coherent, logical, and realistic manner to test procedures that specify precisely what should be said and done. On tasks that provide few such guidelines, by contrast, they tend to manifest loose associations, arbitrary reasoning, and strange ideas. Hence, a borderline patient is likely to perform relatively well on such structured tests as the Wechsler Adult Intelligence Scale (WAIS) while giving substantial evidence of disordered thinking and impaired reality testing on such unstructured tests as the Rorschach (Carr, Schwartz, & Fishler, 1989; Edell, 1987b; Gartner, Hurt, & Gartner, 1989). The data in this regard support an assertion by Singer (1977) that relatively intact performance on the Wechsler contrasting with a clearly deviant performance on the Rorschach is almost axiomatic for a diagnosis of borderline disorder.

6. *Persistence of Disorder.* As already noted, the dysfunctions that define borderline disorder constitute characteristic ways of dealing with experience, and borderline disorder is a persistent rather than an episodic pattern of psychopathology. Like other characterological disorders, it originates in early life experiences, is gradually shaped by formative experiences during the developmental years, and, once consolidated, is unlikely to change except in response to extraordinary life events or therapeutic intervention.

Yet there is a paradox in the behavior of borderline individuals, because their affective, social, and interpersonal lives are so dramatically marked by shifting sands. How they think, feel, and act one day may bear little relationship to how they will be or behave the next day. What is most predictable in the lives of borderline individuals is their unpredictability. Grinker (1977) captured this fact by identifying "stable instability" as the overriding characteristic of borderline disorder. What persists in borderline disorder, in other words, is a chronic, characterological disposition to dramatic variations in affective tone, self-control, social adaptation, personal relatedness, and cognitive functioning.

The chronic, characterological nature of borderline disorder is manifest in considerable tolerance for one's psychopathology. Unlike patients with symptomatic disorders, who regard their psychopathology as ego-alien, borderline individuals typically maintain an ego-syntonic stance; that is, they view the core features of their disorder as perfectly natural and comfortable ways they happen to be. Depressed borderlines may feel emotional pain and wish to escape their despair, but they will not see anything unusual in the emotional intensity and lability that make them vulnerable to episodes of depression. Angry borderlines will rail against a friend or therapist they feel has let them down, but they will not regard their anger as unjustified or the intense interpersonal need that led to it as inappropriate. On psychological tests, borderline individuals, in common with other chronically disturbed patients, frequently display this ego-syntonic stance by giving deviant and distorted responses without showing any discomfort or recognizing that they are responding strangely.

Various features of these six core characteristics of borderline disorder have been translated by Gunderson (1981) into a useful assessment tool, the Diagnostic Interview for Borderlines (DIB). The DIB provides an interviewing guide for collecting 132 items of information from which to score 29 statements about a patient's social adaptation, impulse–action patterns, affects, psychotic experiences, and interpersonal relations. Research to date indicates that the DIB is a useful instrument that reliably differentiates borderline patients from schizophrenic and depressed patients, both in hospital and in outpatient settings, and from patients with other types of personality disorder as well (Hurt, Clarkin, Koenigsberg, Frances, & Nurnberg, 1986; McManus, Lerner, Robbins, & Barbour, 1984; Soloff & Ulrich, 1981). Moreover, work with the DIB and other diagnostic criteria has fairly convincingly demonstrated that the various characteristics of borderline disorder can be as readily identified and differentiated from other disturbances in adolescents as in adults (Esman, 1989; Ludolph, Westen, Misle, Jackson, Wixom, & Wiss, 1990; Salwen, Reznikoff, & Schwartz, 1989).

Research by Barrash, Kroll, Carey, and Sines (1983) indicated further that patients who meet DIB criteria for borderline disorder are likely to manifest two distinct clusters of symptoms. Some of their borderline subjects showed DIB indications mainly of cognitive and perceptual disturbances, including a past history of (a) delusions, hallucinations, and apparent psychotic episodes; (b) social isolation; and (c) emotional guardedness. Others were notable more for a history (a) of antisocial rather than psychoticlike behavior; (b) unstable intense interpersonal relationships and seeking company rather than shunning it; and (c) exhibiting dramatic affects rather than keeping them contained.

These findings lend weight to the previously mentioned suggestions by Spitzer and Meissner concerning the discrimination between *schizotypal personality disorder* and *borderline personality disorder*, as variants of core borderline disturbance. This distinction was reasserted in *DSM-III-R* (see Meissner, 1984; Widiger, Frances, Spitzer, & Williams, 1988), and it has been elaborated in numerous clinical formulations and research studies.

Schizotypal Personality Disorder

Schizotypal personality disorder is a form of borderline psychopathology that, in addition to core borderline characteristics, is marked by features of schizophrenic disorder. These include (a) such indices of disordered thinking as peculiar language usage, odd speech patterns, ideas of reference, and persecutory delusions; (b) such signs of impaired reality testing as harboring far-fetched ideas, misperceiving aspects of one's experiences, misjudging the consequences of one's actions, and misinterpreting the actions of others; (c) such evidence of interpersonal ineptness as a high level of anxiety and suspiciousness in social situations and withdrawal from human contact; and (d) such indices of poor self-control as a long history of self-defeating and self-destructive behavior (see Gunderson, Siever, & Spaulding, 1983; Jacobsberg, Hymowitz, Barasch, & Frances, 1986; McGlashan, 1983b, 1986b; Widiger, Frances, & Trull, 1987).

Because of these schizophrenic features, the condition that is currently most widely known as schizotypal personality disorder has also been designated by such labels as "borderline schizophrenia" (Kety, Rosenthal, Wender, & Schulsinger, 1968), "masked schizophrenia" (Strahl, 1980), and "pseudoschizophrenia" (Meissner, 1984, Chapter 7). However, the schizophrenic elements of schizotypal disorder differ from their counterparts in schizophrenia in two respects. First, suggestions of schizophrenic impairments are neither as severe nor as apparent in schizotypal disorder as they are in schizophrenia. Except in the event of a transient psychotic episode, schizotypal difficulties in thinking clearly and logically and in perceiving experience accurately are usually less serious than would warrant a diagnosis of schizophrenia. Second, the relatively mild cognitive dysfunctions of schizotypal individuals tend to be obscured in structured situations, either by the illusory social adaptation of borderline patients or by multiple and some-times dramatic neurotic symptom formations. Schizotypal individuals are especially likely to manifest obsessive–compulsive features, and some are also inclined toward somatization or pervasive free-floating anxiety (Gunderson, et al., 1983; McGlashan, 1986b; Meissner, 1984, Chapter 7). For this reason, schizotypal disorder has also been referred to in the past as "pseudoneurotic schizophrenia" (Hoch & Polatin, 1949).

Rorschach test findings reported by Exner (1986) help to specify these distinctive features of schizotypal personality disorder in relation to schizo-phrenic and normal functioning. He compared the records of 76 schizotypal patients, as diagnosed by *DSM-III* criteria, with those of 80 first-admission schizophrenic patients examined shortly after entering an inpatient setting, and with those of 600 nonpatient volunteer subjects. The schizotypal patients were substantially more likely than the nonpatients to present Rorschach evidence of impaired reality testing, disordered thinking, and distorted inter-personal perceptions, but in each of these respects, they were noticeably less deviant from normative expectation than the schizophrenic patients.

The Exner data also confirm the preference of schizotypal individuals for an ideational rather than an expressive coping style. Compared to approxi-mately 40% of the nonpatient reference group who demonstrated a contem-plative and emotionally reserved approach to dealing with their experience, almost 70% of the schizotypals clearly preferred an ideational style, and fewer than 3% opted for a more trial-and-error, emotive, action-oriented approach. As a related finding, most of the schizotypals gave evidence of being fairly well-insulated against losing control of themselves or of being overwhelmed by their own impulses or affects. This result does not negate the fact that the ideational mechanisms used by schizotypal patients to maintain self-control frequently involve cognitive dysfunctions, nor does it contravene the persistent vulnerability of these individuals to transient psychotic break-down at times of stress. It simply indicates that, when they are functioning in their usual manner, patients with schizotypal personality disorder are rela-tively unlikely to act impulsively or to become carried away by their feelings.

Borderline Personality Disorder

Borderline personality disorder is a form of borderline psychopathology that is marked by extraordinary instability in behavior, mood, interpersonal rela-tionships, and self-image. The instability that typifies this condition led Spitzer et al. (1979) initially to suggest calling it "unstable personality disorder," and it has also been referred to as "psychotic character" by Meissner (1984, Chapter 7) and others. Compared to patients with the schizotypal form of borderline disorder, however, persons with borderline personality disorder are less vulnerable to psychotic breakdown and less likely to manifest schizophreniclike impairments of thinking and reality testing (Evans, Ruff, Braff, & Ainsworth, 1984; McGlashan, 1987; Pope, Jonas, Hudson, Cohen, & Tohen, 1985; Schulz, Cornelius, Schulz, & Soloff, 1988).

The specific hallmarks of borderline personality disorder include marked impulsivity, intense emotionality, excessive involvement with others, and identity diffusion (Kernberg, 1978; McGlashan, 1986a; Nurnberg, Hurt, Feldman, & Suh, 1988; Ochoa & Morey, 1990). Persons with this disorder tolerate frustration poorly and can be precipitated with little provocation into episodes of ill-conceived, offensive, and self-destructive behavior. They are likely to be viewed by those around them as touchy, excitable, and unpredictable persons who must be handled with care. When they are angry, they are more inclined to vent their spleen than to hold their feelings in check, and their experiences of depression or elation promptly result in dramatic emotional displays.

Individuals with this condition pursue interpersonal attachments with a vengeance, alternating frequently between feelings of love and hate toward their close associates, regularly changing their minds about whom they consider their friends and whom their enemies, and making enormous demands on their friends and lovers of the moment for unswerving loyalty and unwavering affection. They have great difficulty achieving and maintaining a cohesive sense of their personal identity, and they consequently tend to vacillate in their impressions of what kind of person they are, what they believe in, what they want to do with their lives, and how they value themselves in comparison to other persons.

Like schizotypal disorder, borderline personality disorder is clearly distinguishable from schizophrenia. Long-term follow-up studies indicate that schizophrenic impairments of personality functioning are neither characteristic of the formative stages of borderline personality disorder nor likely to appear during its course (Fenton & McGlashan, 1989; McGlashan, 1983b; Pope, Jonas, Hudson, Cohen, & Gunderson, 1983). The strong affective coloring of borderline personality disorder has at times suggested that it might be a variant of affective disorder. However, most investigators have concluded that, despite some symptomatic similarities between them and the possibility of their co-occurring in the same person, borderline personality disorder and affective disorder are separate conditions, especially with respect to the interpersonal attachment difficulties that are distinctively borderline phenomena (Bell, Billington, Cicchetti, & Gibbons, 1988; Gunderson & Elliott, 1985; McGlashan, 1983b; Pope et al., 1983).

Borderline personality disorder is additionally distinguished by extensive use of "splitting" as a defense. As delineated by Kernberg (1977, 1978), Mahler (1974), and Masterson (1975), *splitting* refers to an immature way of viewing the world, in which other people are seen as "all good" or "all bad," and life experiences are regarded as either fully gratifying or totally frustrating. This process involves splitting in the sense that persons and events are not recognized in their entirety, which in reality involves having some good points and some bad and at times being mildly gratifying or frustrating. Instead, attention focuses entirely on a split-off part that includes only what is perfect and gratifying or what is flawed and frustrating, without allowance for any qualities that are indefinite or in-between.

This kind of splitting serves as a defense against anxiety by keeping potentially contradictory attitudes out of mind, thus protecting the individual against painful or unsettling experiences of ambivalence and uncertainty. Unfortunately, this kind of insulation against anxiety is achieved at considerable psychological cost. By seeing other persons as all good or all bad, rather than as combining some mix of good and bad qualities in the way that most persons in fact do, individuals who split are led to idealize some people and depreciate others, both to an extreme, and to shift from one extreme view to the other in their attitudes toward the same person. Other persons become caricatures rather than truly human figures in their eyes, which results in the kinds of intense and unstable interpersonal relationships that characterize individuals with borderline personality disorder.

In similar fashion, the mutually exclusive categorization of life experiences as totally positive or totally negative cripples the person's capacities for effective decision making. Choices are made with undue haste, between options viewed either as unquestionably perfect or undoubtedly undesirable. Such ill-considered judgments set the stage for yesterday's perfect choice to become today's intolerable option, and for today's marvelous opportunity to become tomorrow's crushing disappointment. Splitting also contributes to the uncertain self-image of persons with borderline personality disorder, because their tendency to view themselves, as well as others, as being all good or all bad makes them susceptible to dramatic shifts in their self-esteem. Finally, the way in which splitting promotes extreme, all-or-none attitudes can also be seen as contributing to the tendency of borderline individuals to experience and display intense rather than mild affects (see Akhtar & Byrne, 1983).

Several of these distinguishing features of borderline personality disorder appeared in Exner's Rorschach study, which included 84 patients who had received this diagnosis according to *DSM-III* criteria. His findings document the following differences between patients with borderline personality disorder and those with schizotypal disorder:

1. With respect to indices of impaired reality testing, disordered thinking, and distorted interpersonal perception, individuals with borderline personality disorder deviate from normative expectations, but not as much as do schizotypal individuals, and not nearly as much as do schizophrenics.

2. Borderline personality disorder is much more likely to be associated with an expressive style of coping with experience, and much less

likely to be associated with an ideational coping style, than is schizotypal personality disorder.

3. Individuals with borderline personality disorder are more likely than those with schizotypal personality disorder to feel overwhelmed by their own impulses or affects and consequently to be at risk for being propelled into impulsive actions and loss of self-control.

Other work with frequently used psychodiagnostic tests has helped to confirm further the distinctive features of borderline personality disorder and its differences from schizotypal personality disorder. Edell (1987a), using the Minnesota Multiphasic Personality Inventory (MMPI) found significantly higher elevations among schizotypal than among borderline patients on scales indicative of obsessive tendencies, disordered thinking, and unrealistic perceptions. The borderline patients, in turn, scored significantly higher on these scales than a nonpathological comparison group.

Rorschach studies indicate that individuals with borderline personality disorder are significantly more likely than depressed and nonpatient comparison groups to become preoccupied with complex concerns about the motives of other persons and to attribute potentially malevolent characteristics to human interactions (Stuart, Westen, Lohr, Benjamin, Becker, Vorus, & Silk, 1990). Research with the Thematic Apperception Test (TAT) demonstrates that among adolescents in particular, those with borderline personality disorder are more inclined than normal young persons and those with other types of psychological disorders to attribute motivations to others in an oversimplified, illogical manner and to have trouble getting involved with people, except in ways intended to gratify their needs (Westen, Ludolph, Lerner, Ruffins, & Wiss, 1990).

Overlapping Conditions

Schizotypal and borderline personality disorder define subtypes of borderline disorder with distinctive combinations of features, and the evidence to date indicates that these distinctions can be reliably drawn among young persons, as well as adults (Petti & Vela, 1990; Rosenberger & Miller, 1989; Wenning, 1990). However, among people in general there are many significant correlations among the features that define these subtypes of disorder. Consequently, although most borderline individuals manifest either a clearly schizotypal or a clearly borderline personality disorder, some will have an overlapping condition in which distinctive features of both conditions are present. Clinical studies indicate specifically that 60–65% of persons with a borderline condition will demonstrate either schizotypal or borderline personality disorder alone, while the remaining 30–35% who meet *DSM-III* criteria for one of these conditions will also meet criteria for the other (Gunderson et al., 1983; Widiger, Frances, Warner, & Bluhm, 1986).

Three identifying characteristics mark the presence of an overlapping borderline condition. First, impairments in thinking and reality testing are likely to be less marked than in schizotypal disorder but more prominent than is typical of borderline personality disorder. Second, instead of evincing a clear preference for either ideational or expressive modes of coping with experience, patients with an overlapping condition tend to fluctuate in their coping style, without showing any definite preference. Third, those individuals who are intermediate on the borderline spectrum are likely to display neither the consistent interpersonal isolation found in schizotypal personality disorder nor the interpersonal overinvolvement that typifies borderline personality disorder. Instead, as a reflection of their overlapping condition, they are likely to have a history of vacillation between these two social orientations.

Overlapping conditions of borderline psychopathology are made possible by the fact that adequacy of cognitive functioning, preferred coping style, and interpersonal orientation are independent dimensions of personality functioning. Patients who share the core characteristics of borderline disorder may accordingly display varying combinations of typically schizotypal or borderline personality features. One borderline individual may show considerable cognitive impairment, combined with an expressive coping style and interpersonal overinvolvement; another may combine mild cognitive impairment with an ideational style and interpersonal isolation; and so on. These possible combinations account for the finding that about one third of persons with borderline disorder occupy an intermediate position on the borderline spectrum and display a mixture of features.

ORIGIN AND DEVELOPMENT OF BORDERLINE DISORDERS

There is little certain knowledge about what causes borderline disorders and how they develop. Theory and conjecture on the subject abound, but reliable empirical data are few. Only since the mid-1980s, stimulated by the promulgation of *DSM-III* and *DSM-III-R* criteria and the availability of such research instruments as the DIB, have well-designed studies of the origin and course of borderline disorders begun to appear. Although much work remains to be done, some preliminary sense of how borderline disorders originate and develop can be gained from considering (a) the status of borderline disorders as a form of personality disorder and (b) emerging evidence of familial factors in the susceptibility to these disorders.

Borderline Disorders as Personality Disorders

As noted at the beginning of this chapter, borderline disorders are basically neither symptomatic nor cyclical conditions but instead comprise persistent ways of viewing and coping with experience. Researchers generally concur that these disorders can best be understood as characterological variants of psychopathology that become manifest as generalized ways of adapting to experience rather than as specific or transient reactions to stressful situations (Perry, 1988; Widiger, 1989). Borderline conditions accordingly share three essential features with other conditions that are regarded as personality disorders:

1. These conditions begin early in life and are shaped by dispositions and experiences that start shortly after birth to influence how people characteristically think, feel, and relate to others.

2. They gradually become identifiable during the developmental years, as young persons mature and take on increasingly stable personality characteristics, and they become more or less crystallized during late adolescence and early adulthood, when adult identities and orientations typically become established.

3. They are ego-syntonic, inasmuch as their identifying characteristics are viewed by the disordered individuals as how they naturally happen to be, and not as aberrations or alterations in personality functioning that are bothersome, unwelcome, or in need of modification.

Millon (1981, p. 327) has provided the following apt description of these features of borderline and other personality disorder:

All patterns of pathological personality . . . are deeply etched and pervasive characteristics of functioning that unfold as a product of the interplay of constitutional and experiential influences. The behaviors, self-descriptions, intrapsychic mechanisms, and interpersonal coping styles that evolve out of these transactions are embedded so firmly within the individual that they become the very fabric of his or her make-up, operating automatically and insidiously as the individual's way of life.

Because of these features of characterological pathology, children who are destined to manifest full-blown borderline disorders by the time they pass from adolescence into adulthood can be expected to display forerunners of this condition long before it becomes fully established. Even though borderline disorders probably originate in events of infancy and early childhood, however, prodromal symptoms are unlikely to emerge during the preschool years. Basic personality structures are normally still too amorphous to differ appreciably among children at this early age.

During the elementary school years, children become capable of focusing their thoughts and harnessing their feelings much more effectively than before, and they also begin to take on consistently distinctive ways of managing social interactions. Such maturation makes it increasingly possible to distinguish normal development from the kinds of cognitive, affective, and interpersonal incapacities that characterize borderline disorders. With this in mind, most developmental psychopathologists concur that the elementary school age is the time when an emerging borderline disorder begins to become identifiable (see Pine, 1983). Although the possible childhood fore-runners of borderline disorders are many and varied, borderline children are widely agreed to display some combinations of the following six behavior patterns (see Vela, Gottlieb, & Gottlieb, 1983):

1. Disturbed interpersonal relationships, marked by extremely ambiva-lent feelings toward other people and either persistent or alternating periods of excessive clinging and demandingness or withdrawal and social isolation

2. A disturbed sense of reality, marked by extreme withdrawal into grandiose fantasies, difficulty distinguishing pretend play from real life, paranoid ideation, and magical thinking

3. Severe anxiety, marked by panic states, fears of impending disaster or bodily disintegration, inability to tolerate separation, perception of the world as a dangerous place, difficulty concentrating, and inability to relax both while awake and when trying to sleep

4. Excessive impulsivity and emotionality, marked by unmanageable aggressive behavior and recurrent outbursts of uncontrolled temper and rage

5. Neurotic symptom formation, including ritualistic or obsessive behav-ior, multiple phobias, and somatization

6. Early developmental deviation, such as irregular eating and sleeping patterns, head-banging, and delayed acquisition of language or motor skills

Kernberg (1988) notes in addition that borderline children, because of their defensive use of splitting, may show some particular peculiarities in how they relate to their parents. These include a tendency to idealize or devalue either parent in unreasonable ways and an inability to accept and deal with them as a couple who, along with their individual relationship with their child, have shared roles as parents and an interpersonal relationship of their own.

The appropriate diagnosis for school-age children who display some criti-cal number of these symptom patterns is a matter of debate. Can they properly be regarded as having a personality disorder when they have not reached the level of maturity at which personality is sufficiently formed to be considered disordered? Some clinicians prefer to call these youngsters "borderline chil-dren" and to formulate assessment and treatment strategies for working with them as if they have a discrete and specific condition (Chethik, 1986; Kernberg, 1983b; Leichtman & Nathan, 1983; Nagy & Szatmari, 1986). Others question whether any discrete borderline syndrome exists in children and worry about this label being overused, without providing any real as-sistance in treatment planning, for children whose problems are difficult to understand (Greenman, Gunderson, Cane, & Saltzman, 1986; Gualtieri, Koriath, & Van Bourgondien, 1983; Shapiro, 1983).

However this issue may be resolved, the fact remains, as previously noted, that symptom patterns closely resembling characteristic manifestations of schizotypal and borderline personality disorder are consistently observed to cluster together in some disturbed children. This does not mean that all or even most such children will eventually become borderline adolescents or adults. Persons with similar symptomatology early in life can have different clinical outcomes, and the "borderline children" pattern of disturbance can be a way station on the road to a variety of adolescent and adult disorders. In a 10- to 25-year follow-up of seven patients who had been diagnosed border-line as children, for example, Kestenbaum (1983) found seven different adult diagnoses—one case each of schizophrenia, bipolar disorder, schizoaffective disorder, schizotypal personality disorder, borderline personality disorder, schizoid personality disorder, and anxiety neurosis.

What the likely prodromal significance of these childhood patterns does mean is that older persons who manifest borderline disorders can be expected to have displayed forerunners of their disorder as school-age children. Although this longitudinal relationship has not yet been documented by case history research data, it draws considerable support from what is generally known about childhood manifestations of developing personality disorder. Clinicians should, in fact, hesitate to diagnose borderline disorders in adolescents or adults in whom there is no clear developmental history of the symptom patterns associated with the childhood borderline syndrome.

During the adolescent years, when personality patterns become increasingly stable, borderline disorders also start to become fully established. The subsequent continuity in personality development between adolescence and adulthood mentioned in Chapter 1 also applies to this form of disordered personality functioning. As Kernberg (1983a, p. 102) notes, "Borderline adults represent chronologically older borderline adolescents." For this reason, most authors who write about borderline disorders in both adolescents and adults have traditionally described them in the same way (see Kernberg, 1978; Masterson, 1980). This is not to ignore that, as in all forms of psychopathology, the content of borderline disorders will vary with the age of the individual. Thus, the interpersonal difficulties of borderline patients are likely to focus on friendship and dating relationships while they are adolescents but on love and marital relationships when they become adults. However, the basic nature of their cognitive, affective, and interpersonal incapacities does not change when borderline adolescents become borderline adults.

With respect to the longer-term course of borderline disorders, McGlashan (1983a, 1986b) reports some interesting follow-up data on the 15-year status of patients with schizophrenia, schizotypal personality disorder, and border-line personality disorder. Those who had initially been diagnosed as schizophrenic showed the least favorable outcome and the most persisting or recurring adjustment difficulty. Those with borderline personality disorder had the best long-term course among the three groups, and those with schizotypal personality disorder occupied an intermediate position. The schizophrenics were especially likely to suffer from long-term incapacity to form meaningful and rewarding interpersonal relationships. Over the long term, the schizotypal patients were more capable than the schizophrenics of forming viable relationships with others, but they tended to opt for detached relationships and rarely had close friends or lovers. The patients with borderline personality disorder, although socially unpredictable, were able to form both friendship and love relationships over the course of this follow-up period. An additional group who were considered to have overlapping schizotypal and borderline personality disorder were able to make friends but were unlikely to become involved in love relationships.

Familial Factors

Like schizophrenia and affective disorder, borderline disorders run in families. The first-degree relatives of persons with schizotypal personality disorder are significantly more likely to develop schizotypal personality disorder than the relatives of people in general; likewise, first-degree relatives of persons with borderline personality disorder are at significantly greater risk for this disorder than normally would be expected, with 15–18% for the parents and siblings of people with borderline personality disorder meeting criteria for this condition (Baron, Gruen, Asnis, & Lord, 1985; Links, Steiner, & Huxley, 1988; Zanarini, Gunderson, Marino, Schwartz, & Frankenburg, 1988). Both genetic and experiential influences contribute to these familial patterns, but schizotypal and borderline personality probably differ in this regard: genetic influences appear more prominent in the origin of schizotypal personality disorder, and experiential influences seem to have more to do with the onset of borderline personality disorder.

With respect to schizotypal personality disorder, studies of families, twins, and adopted children of the type described in Chapters 3 and 4 point to some genetic similarities between this condition and schizophrenia. Although relatives of persons with a schizotypal personality disorder do not show any elevated risk of becoming schizophrenic, relatives of schizophrenic patients are more likely than people in general to manifest a schizotypal personality disorder (Baron, Gruen, Rainer, Cohen, Asnis, & Lord, 1985; Mednick, Parnas, & Schulsinger, 1987; Siever & Kendler, 1986; Torgersen, 1985). This suggests that schizotypal personality disorder stems in part from a similar but less pathological diathesis than is involved in schizophrenia; that is, the schizotypal diathesis is not so incapacitating as to result in schizophrenia, but the schizophrenic diathesis, if minimal, may contribute to schizotypal disorder.

Three specific findings increase the likelihood that this familial relationship between schizotypal disorder and schizophrenia derives from genetic rather than experiential influences. First, adopted children who have biological relatives with schizophrenia are at elevated risk for schizotypal disorder, whereas those with adoptive relatives who are schizophrenic do not show any such elevated risk (Kendler, Gruenberg, & Strauss, 1981). Second, children with one schizophrenic parent are more likely than most people to develop schizotypal personality disorder, and children of two schizophrenic parents are even more likely than those with one schizophrenic parent to develop a schizotypal condition (Baron, Gruen, Asnis, & Kane, 1983). Third, identical twins of persons with schizotypal personality disorder are several times more likely than nonidentical twins to manifest this disorder (Torgersen, 1984).

Patients with borderline personality disorder, by contrast, do not show any genetic linkage with schizophrenia; the prevalence of schizophrenia in first-degree relatives of borderline personality disorder patients without schizotypal features is essentially zero (Schulz, Soloff, Kelly, Morgenstern, Di Franco, & Schulz, 1989; Zanarini et al., 1988). Moreover, identical and nonidentical twins of persons with borderline personality disorder do not differ in their susceptibility to this condition (Torgersen, 1984). What does appear to play an important role in the emergence of borderline personality disorder are certain early life experiences, especially in relation to mothering figures.

The most widely endorsed hypothesis in this regard is that borderline personality disorder derives from an early developmental arrest in which inadequate mothering leads to impaired capacities for interpersonal relatedness. During the second year of life, children begin to separate themselves from their mothers or other primary caregivers and become individuals in their own right. This individuation process helps young children learn to recognize and deal with people as they really are, as whole objects who are sometimes rewarding and sometimes frustrating, sometimes good and sometimes bad.

Some mothers or other primary caregivers may be unable to meet their children's needs for separation and individuation, perhaps because of psychological difficulties they have in encouraging or tolerating their children's having an identity distinct from their own. Others may simply be unavailable for one reason or another to promote the kinds of learning and psychological growth that make individuation possible. In either case, the result is likely to be a persistent, infantile pattern of viewing people as part objects—as always gratifying or rejecting, or as all good or all bad. As described in the previous section, this orientation toward interpersonal relatedness defines the splitting that characterizes borderline personality disorder and fosters the extreme and fluctuating attitudes associated with this condition.

Although this object relations hypothesis has become prominent in the clinical literature on the etiology of borderline disorder (see Grotstein, Solomon, & Lang, 1987; Mahler & Kaplan, 1977; Masterson, 1981), empirical data to validate it are still meager. With good reason, Millon (1988), among others, has warned clinical scholars against taking speculative notions about the experiential origins of borderline personality disorder as confirmed fact, when they are still only hypotheses awaiting empirical evaluation.

On the other hand, findings consistent with relationships between problematic interpersonal relatedness during the developmental years and the emergence of borderline personality disorder have begun to appear. Adolescent and young adult borderline patients, compared to nonborderline patient comparison groups, are more likely to perceive their parents as having been uncaring and to have clinical histories indicative of parental neglect, family disruption, and physical and sexual abuse (Ludolph et al., 1990; Paris & Frank, 1989).

A Rorschach study by Coonerty (1986) suggests further that adequately designed research can generate data supportive of object relations concepts of borderline personality disorder. She developed a brief scale for identifying separation–individuation themes in the Rorschach that takes particular note of responses in which (a) human or animal figures are merging with or engulfing each other; (b) responses suggesting narcissistic preoccupations, such as looking at oneself in a mirror or feelings of omnipotence or insignificance; (c) responses in which figures are coming together or separating in the context of some struggle or indecision; and (d) responses in which the form or affect attributed to a figure changes while the response is being given. Significantly, more frequent themes of separation–individuation were found.

FURTHER GUIDELINES IN DIFFERENTIAL DIAGNOSIS

Differential diagnosis of borderline disorders can ordinarily be based on what is known about the nature, origins, and development of these conditions. Certain aspects of a disturbed adolescent's previous history, interview behavior, and psychological test performance provide some further guidelines for the assessment.

Previous History

Because borderline disorders are disorders of personality functioning that begin early in life, careful attention should be paid to the adolescent's previous psychological adjustment. As already noted, persons who are in fact manifesting or developing a borderline disorder can be expected to have shown many of the kinds of emotional and behavioral problems observed in borderline children. The absence of a prior history of such adjustment difficulties—including poor emotional control, disturbed social interactions, problems in relating to reality, and neurotic symptom formation—makes it unlikely that a currently disturbed adolescent has a borderline condition. In this same vein, the more recent and acute the onset of the present difficulties has been, and the more different from, rather than continuous with, past behavior patterns they are, the more likely it is that these present difficulties reflect some disturbance other than borderline disorder.

Clinicians should also be alert to any prior history of apparently psychotic episodes of brief duration. One of the truly distinctive manifestations of borderline disorder is the sudden onset and equally sudden remission of serious psychological breakdown involving disorientation and other flagrant indications of cognitive incapacitation. Particularly when they have occurred in the absence of any known toxicity, these episodes have usually left a trail of puzzled observers in their wake: How could anyone who was so disorganized, delusional, and out of control just the other day now appear so completely free of obvious psychopathology?

The answer to this question is unlikely to be found in psychotic episodes associated with schizophrenia, which typically last more than a few days even when they eventually remit. Instead, the answer will usually lie with borderline disorder, as a manifestation of the susceptibility of persons with this condition to brief psychotic episodes. This is not to say that most persons with borderline disorders will have had brief psychotic episodes or that the absence of such episodes is reason for calling the diagnosis into question. However, any historical data suggesting transient psychotic reactions should raise the possibility of borderline disorder even when other clinical findings have not yet begun to suggest it.

The circumstances in which a brief psychotic episode has occurred help further in differentiating between schizotypal and borderline personality disorder. As noted earlier, schizotypal individuals are generally more vulnerable to psychotic breakdown than those with borderline personality disorder. Various kinds of psychological stresses in daily living may be sufficient to disrupt the adaptation of persons with a schizotypal disorder, whereas persons with a borderline personality disorder seldom decompensate, except in the context of an intense interpersonal relationship, particularly in the course of psychotherapy. The patient who meets Knight's description of "falling apart on the couch" may have either a schizotypal or borderline personality disorder. The patient whose history indicates a propensity to fall apart in other stressful situations as well is probably suffering from a schizotypal but not a borderline personality disorder.

A patient's family history can also help to identify schizotypal and borderline personality disorder and to distinguish between them. In both types of borderline condition, one can expect to find individual psychopathology or family turmoil that has prevented parents from effectively separating themselves from their children. In addition, the genetic evidence indicates that when a borderline adolescent's family includes relatives with schizophrenia, he or she is more likely to have a schizotypal than a borderline personality disorder.

Interview Behavior

The interview situation allows clinicians to experience firsthand the emotional intensity, cognitive peculiarities, and disturbed interpersonal relatedness that characterize borderline disorder. With respect to emotionality, clinicians can often use themselves as barometers—the nonpsychotic patient who fills the room with so much palpable rage or devastating despair as to make even an experienced professional feel uncomfortable should be considered likely to have a borderline condition. With respect to cognitive functioning, it is essential to listen closely for the kinds of deviant communication described in Chapter 3 as indications of impaired capacity to think clearly and logically and to perceive experience realistically. Such communication difficulties, in the absence of demonstrable schizophrenia, increase considerably the likelihood of a borderline disorder.

The relative prominence of cognitive and affective indications of disorder assist in differentiating what kind of borderline condition is present. When cognitive disruption is more prominent than affective disturbance, the borderline patient probably has a schizotypal disorder; when affective disturbance is more prominent, borderline personality disorder is the more appropriate inference; and when both kinds of disturbance are about equally in evidence, the presence of an overlapping condition is indicated.

However, the distinction between cognitive and affective manifestations of disorder needs always to be taken as a relative rather than an absolute basis for differentiating between schizotypal and borderline personality disorder. Intense emotionality is not uncommon in patients who are clearly schizotypal, and patients with borderline personality disorder often display strange and unrealistic cognitions (O'Connell, Cooper, Perry, & Hoke, 1989; Rosenberger & Miller, 1989; Silk, Lohr, Westen, & Goodrich, 1989; Zanarini, Gunderson, Frankenburg, & Chauncey, 1989).

With an eye to the relative prominence of cognitive and affective manifestations of disorder, in fact, clinicians will have less difficulty discriminating schizotypal and borderline personality disorders from each other than from certain other conditions. As elaborated by Morey (1988), schizotypal is frequently difficult to distinguish from schizoid personality disorder, because of the interpersonal ineptness and avoidance common to both. The peculiar thinking and poor reality testing of schizotypal patients provides the best clue to this often uncertain distinction. Borderline is frequently difficult to distinguish from histrionic and narcissistic personality disorder as defined in *DSM-III-R*, because of the dramatic emotionality and interpersonal involvements common to both. The ambivalent object relatedness of borderline patients often helps to clarify this often uncertain distinction.

The borderline person's limited tolerance for ambiguity and uncertainty has some further specific implications for using the diagnostic interview to detect cognitive and affective disturbances. The more structured the interview is, the more easily the borderline person can maintain his or her illusory social adaptation and avoid manifesting indications of psychopathology. Conversely, the less guidance the interviewer provides, the fewer barriers there are to the expression of markedly deviant communications and excessively intense affects.

An interviewer who actively directs the conversation and asks only for specific bits of information may observe nothing unusual in a borderline patient's behavior and may miss a diagnosis that should have been made. On the other hand, relatively silent interviewers who limit themselves to enigmatic observations and open-ended questions are likely to engender considerable confusion and loss of control in borderline patients, beyond what would have sufficed to identify serious psychological disorder. Although the tactics of structure and silence may both serve constructive purposes during psychotherapy with borderline patients, neither tactic is by itself suitable for a diagnostic interview. In conducting an evaluation, clinicians need to provide sufficient ambiguity for clues to borderline disorder to emerge, but also sufficient structure to spare the patient from any more distress than is necessary to obtain critical diagnostic information.

The following example is instructive in this regard. A 17-year-old boy who returned home within a few weeks of having gone away to college because of feeling confused and uncertain about what he wanted to do with his life presented a fluent and psychologically sensitive account of various conflicting choices he was facing. This was taken as evidence of an acutely sensed but realistically recognized and expressed identity moratorium; in retrospect, it could also have been seen as a freer sharing of deeply personal information than is customary among adolescents during an initial interview.

The patient began the second session by reporting a dream that was manifestly concerned with whether he would be able to keep this appointment with the therapist. This was taken as indicating some ambivalence about becoming involved in psychotherapy; attention could also have been paid to how unusual it is for a dream of any kind, especially one involving the therapist, to be reported as early as a second session—except in persons who are extremely transference-prone.

Because this adolescent was saying so much in these first two sessions, the interviewer said little. In the third session, the patient fell silent and asked the interviewer to put questions to him. When the interviewer declined to do so, he became agitated and insistent. This was taken as an indication of resistance, and he was given instructions about the patient's responsibility in psychotherapy for continuing to talk as he had during the first two sessions; it could also have been seen as revealing an inability to tolerate ambiguity and an already intensely ambivalent relationship with the interviewer. Lending weight to these latter alternatives, the third session ended with the patient's complaining bitterly that he had not been given the full amount of time he was paying for, when in fact he had.

Early the next morning, following this third session, the therapist received a call from the patient's mother. During the night she had seen a light on in his bedroom and had gone to investigate. She had found him sitting up in bed with a blanket wrapped around him mumbling to himself. She was initially unable to engage him in conversation. As best she could make out, he was saying over and over, "I'm not going to talk anymore, Dr. _____ has to talk now." When she finally was able to get his attention, he pleaded to be taken to the interviewer's home immediately. She prevailed on him to wait until morning, when her telephone call at last enabled the therapist to get the message: This was a boy with a borderline disorder who had been precipitated into a psychotic episode by unstructured diagnostic interviewing.

Although such inadvertent stress interviewing needs to be avoided, there may be occasions when possible intolerance for ambiguity can be tested intentionally for diagnostic purposes. If a patient does have a borderline disorder, the interviewer should be able to influence his or her responses dramatically by varying the amount of structure that is provided. The borderline person can be expected to become increasingly upset and disorganized if the clinician begins to say less and to give fewer indications of what is expected. Conversely, borderline patients who have become upset and disorganized during an unstructured interview can be expected to pull themselves together rapidly if the clinician begins to say more and specify what they should talk about. By shifting their approach with this in mind, interviewers may be able to identify sudden changes in adaptation level that will signal borderline disorder. On the other hand, the less affected patients are by changes in the amount of structure the clinician is providing, the less likely they are to have a borderline condition.

Turning to interpersonal relatedness, the manner in which borderline patients respond to the interviewer facilities the differentiation between schizotypal and borderline personality disorder. Some patients will be cautious and keep their distance, physically and psychologically. These are patients who push back their chair, lean their bodies away, avoid direct eye contact, and express little interest in who the interviewer is or in having a closer relationship with him or her. Others will open up and reach out interpersonally from the moment they enter the room for a first interview. These are patients who pull their chair up close, lean forward, look intently into the interviewer's eyes, ask for or demand personal information, and insist on or plead for an unqualified expression of the interviewer's interest in them. Such differing patterns help the interviewer identify the characteristic social isolation of the schizotypal individual on the one hand and the clinging, dependent engulfing interpersonal style that characterizes borderline personality disorder on the other.

To summarize these differential diagnostic guidelines one further time, the borderline patient who displays cognitive difficulties more prominently than affective symptomatology and who is inclined toward interpersonal isolation rather than interpersonal overinvolvement is likely to have a schizotypal personality disorder. The borderline patient whose disturbance is more prominently affective than cognitive in nature and who seeks intense social relationships is likely to have a borderline personality disorder.

Finally, with respect to interviewing patients with possible borderline disorder, numerous semistructured interview schedules are available to assist clinicians in sorting through the various criteria that distinguish borderline and schizotypal personality disorders from each other and from other conditions. The effectiveness of such measures is reviewed by Widiger and Frances (1987). The original DIB has also been revised to sharpen its ability to differentiate borderline conditions from such other personality disorders as schizoid, histrionic, and narcissistic (Zanarini, Gunderson, Frankenburg, & Chauncey, 1989).

Psychological Test Performance

The sensitivity of persons with borderline disorder to variations in structure make psychological testing especially useful in the differential diagnosis of these conditions. Although the clinical interview provides opportunities to vary structure for diagnostic purposes, as just noted, the need to collect certain kinds of information may preclude open-ended interviewing in initial session. This is especially so when circumstances require ruling out suicidal risk or other potential emergencies. The clinician may also wish to spare a borderline patient the distress of an unstructured interview and to avoid a tense interaction that could complicate any subsequent treatment relationship. A psychological test battery that includes both relatively structured and relatively unstructured measures can assess ambiguity tolerance without delaying information-gathering or intruding on the patient–interviewer relationship.

The significance of dramatically different levels of performance on these two kinds of measures in identifying borderline disorder has already been noted. Four additional aspects of this diagnostic clue are helpful to keep in mind. First, the relatively good performance of borderline individuals on structured tests does not mean that they will look normal on these tests. To the contrary, the Wechsler responses of borderline patients are likely to be scattered and inconsistent and to contain indication of disordered thinking and impaired reality testing (Berg, 1983; Carr et al., 1989).

Such evidence of cognitive dysfunction is less marked than in schizophrenic patients but is nevertheless sufficient to separate the Wechsler protocols of borderline patients, especially those with schizotypal disorders, from those of nonpatients. On the MMPI, borderline individuals similarly show scale elevations that distinguish their profiles from those of normal subjects (Edell, 1987a; Evans, Ruff, Braff, & Ainsworth, 1984; Resnick, Goldberg, Schulz, & Schulz, 1988). Among adolescents in particular, there is evidence that MMPI profiles can distinguish borderline patients from patients with affective disorder, conduct disorder, and other personality disorders (Archer, Ball, & Hunter, 1985).

Second, the relatively poor performance of borderline individuals on unstructured tests does not mean that their protocols cannot be distinguished from those of schizophrenic patients. Despite their prominent difficulties in thinking clearly and logically, persons with schizotypal personality disorder display significantly less cognitive slippage on the Rorschach than schizophrenics (Exner, 1986). In addition to manifesting even less thought pathology than schizotypal patients, persons with borderline personality disorder display, on both the Rorschach and the Thematic Apperception Test, indications of object relations difficulties, especially those related to defensive use of splitting, that are not characteristic of schizophrenia (Stuart et al., 1990; Westen et al., 1990).

Of even more significance is the contrast between indications of disturbance in the unstructured test protocols of borderline patients and their performance on more structured tests. In the typical examination of a borderline patient, examiners can expect to find themselves surprised that an individual who produces only fleeting indications of cognitive dysfunction on the Wechsler has given so many deviant responses on the Rorschach.

The MMPI in this regard, interestingly, is more akin to the Rorschach than to the Wechsler. Although the MMPI has a relatively structured format and calls for specific answers, its requests for self-reports refer in the main not to matters of fact, such as what is the capital of Italy, but to subjective judgments and personal experiences (e.g., "I don't feel as good as I used to"). This explains why patients with borderline disorders who perform relatively effectively in structured situations are nevertheless found to earn clinically significant and sometimes surprisingly high scale elevations on the MMPI.

Third, the performance of borderline persons on unstructured tests such as the Rorschach often features a characteristic drift that seldom occurs except in persons who have limited tolerance for ambiguity. *Drift* refers to a tendency to become progressively more disorganized, illogical, and unrealistic during the course of responding to an ambiguous situation. A group of borderline subjects examined by Singer and Larson (1981) showed such drift by consistently declining in the quality of the responses they gave to each of the Rorschach cards. This kind of deteriorating within-card performance was not found among comparison groups of normal, neurotic, acute schizophrenic, and chronic schizophrenic subjects. In contrast to the borderline subjects' tendency to drift to a lesser quality of responses as they proceeded with each card, the acute schizophrenics, whose Rorschach protocols were most similar to those of the borderlines, tended to give a better-quality response subsequent to giving a poor one.

Fourth, because borderline disorders are chronic conditions in which the person has developed considerable tolerance for manifestations of his or her disturbance, borderline individuals typically feel comfortable with their psychological test responses. They may be anxious or angry about being examined, but they rarely express any concern about how they are responding. Unlike persons with an acute disorder, who frequently recognize and disavow their deviant verbalizations ("That's not very good, is it?"; "I don't know where I get such strange ideas from"; "Let me take that back and give a better answer"), those with chronic conditions tend to deliver even the most bizarre responses with bland self-assurance. Although chronic schizophrenics share this ego-syntonic stance, patients with a relatively acute schizophrenic disturbance, from whom the differentiation of borderline patients is more likely to present a diagnostic challenge, do not.

CASE 6.   SCHIZOTYPAL PERSONALITY DISORDER

Susan was 20 when she first underwent a detailed psychological evaluation. Her history indicated many of the features that can be expected to character- ize the developmental history of young persons with an emerging schizotypal personality disorder.

Susan's father was a newspaper reporter whose career commitments and frequent bouts with alcoholism left him little time or enthusiasm for family involvement. Her parents had been divorced when she was very young, and her mother had subsequently remarried—interestingly, to another newspaper reporter who also had a drinking problem. She grew up living with her mother and stepfather but never felt she had an important place in the home. Two stepsiblings from her stepfather's previous marriage and two younger half- siblings born to her mother and stepfather "ruled the roost," in her words, and her needs and activities attracted little attention.

Susan went through elementary and high school with good grades but without forming close friendships and without becoming involved in dating or extra- curricular activities. She could accurately be described as having been an unnoticed if not invisible member of her graduating class. At age 17, she went away to college, where she did well academically but did not enjoy herself. She quit after her first year and went home, but not to live with her parents. Instead, she got a small apartment by herself and took a job as a grocery clerk. At this point, her mother, concerned about her lack of direction, prevailed on her to see a psychiatrist. After several sessions over a 3-month period, she concluded that it was not doing her any good and dropped out of treatment.

A while later, she was laid off from her grocery store job and joined a small group of young persons who were hiring themselves out as house painters. She worked on house-painting jobs and continued to live alone for some months, during which time she felt she was getting along very well. Then she was persuaded by another young woman in the house-painting group to join her in visiting a commune. This was an all-female farming commune, located in a remote rural area, that stressed a rigorous way of life. A brief visitation period was allowed, after which visitors were required either to make a firm commitment to stay or to leave. Susan's friend decided to stay, but Susan, feeling uncomfortable with the "cultish atmosphere there," chose to leave.

Upon returning to her apartment and her work painting houses, she found herself feeling confused and unsettled. One day, while walking to a job for her group, painting a church, she noticed a van in the church parking lot. It reminded her of a van belonging to the commune she had visited, and she concluded that the women from the commune had put it there as a message that she should come back. She climbed in, found the keys in the ignition, and drove off. She was 25 miles down the highway in the direction of the commune when the police caught up with her.

The officers who stopped her later described her as having been incoherent and disorganized. After arresting her, they took her to a psychiatric facility. There, she continued to appear disoriented and out of touch with reality. She talked about the snow and cold outside, even though it was a warm spring day. No history of drug use was obtained, and the initial diagnosis was probable schizophrenia or reactive psychosis.

After 3 days in the hospital, Susan's psychotic symptoms cleared completely. She was fully aware of who and where she was and of what she had done. She could offer no explanation for having driven off in the van—"I don't know what came over me; it was a stupid thing to do." She insisted that she now felt perfectly fine, although "I have been a little depressed recently," and she wanted only to be able to return to her apartment and her work.

On psychological examination, she displayed above-average intelligence and especially good capacities for exercising realistic social judgment in structured situations. When she took the Rorschach, however, almost one fourth of her responses involved grossly distorted perception, and almost one half contained evidence of disordered thinking. Consistent with her acknowledging little that was unusual about herself outside of her psychotic episode, she gave no indication of recognizing or being concerned about her frequently illogical and unrealistic manner of responding to the Rorschach. The test data indicated further that Susan was primarily an ideational rather than an expressive kind of person who was inclined to misinterpret the implications of interpersonal events and to avoid emotional exchange with other people.

The most salient clue to borderline disorder in Susan's case was the documented history of her brief psychotic episode. Against this backdrop, other features of her past and current life-style can be seen as consistent with the emergence of such disorder: (a) her limited social relatedness, as reflected in her distance from her family, her lack of close friends, and her preference for living by herself; (b) her underachievement, as reflected in the gap between her college-level abilities and her work as a grocery clerk and house painter and in her efforts to minimize her social involvements and obligations, which, taken together with her underachievement, identify a pattern of illusory adaptation; and (c) the dramatic difference between her functioning capacity on the relatively structured and unstructured portions of the psychological examination. In addition, the extent of her deviant responses in the Rorschach, her avoidant rather than overinvolved relationships with people, and the primarily cognitive rather than affective focus of her disturbance pointed specifically to schizotypal personality disorder.

CASE 7.   BORDERLINE PERSONALITY DISORDER

Joseph was 17 and already a sophomore in college when he sought help in the mental health service for problems in his social relationships. He complained of being unable to relax in the presence of other persons, primarily because "I always have to be on my guard, so that people won't perceive how much hostility I have within myself."

Joseph was the youngest of three sons born to parents who had little to give their children psychologically. His father was a bitter man, outwardly successful but frustrated by his perceived failures in life, who rarely expressed himself at home and avoided social contacts outside of it; Joseph described him as overcontrolled, unemotional, and "of no importance in my life." His mother, by contrast, was a highly emotional and self-centered woman who sought the attention of others and frequently intruded on her sons' lives in a demanding and possessive way. The only thing his parents had in common, Joseph said, was that neither of them had ever been able to love him or his brothers.

As an elementary school student, Joseph brought enormous feelings of inadequacy into peer-group situations, where they were reinforced by his often being considered stupid and clumsy and being excluded from games and other activities. At age 9 years, he suffered a particularly distressing experience of peer rejection and withdrew completely from social interactions. For the next 2 years, he left home only to attend school. He had no friends and ate constantly, becoming very fat. During this period, he was plagued by fears of dying and by nightmares in which he was victimized by witches, gorillas, and other threatening nonhuman figures.

At age 11, he made a friend with whom he had a reasonably normal chumship relationship for the next 2 years. When this friend then dropped him for a new best friend, he had a recurrent period of nightmares. Throughout high school, his only extracurricular activity was membership in a chess club. Because he was highly intelligent and used absorption in school work as a replacement for social relatedness, he was able to graduate from high school at age 16 and enter college. During the summer before going away to college, he decided, in his words, to "turn over a new leaf." He took off his excess weight and became determined to end his social isolation. In his freshman year, he did extremely well academically and, although awkward and unsure of himself in social situations, did in fact become friendly with some other students who shared his intellectual interests.

Charting these new waters of social relatedness became problematic for him in his sophomore year, primarily because his interpersonal repertoire made little provision for casual relationships or mild feelings of attachment. Once he emerged from his isolation, he became an unswervingly faithful and obliging friend, and he expected anyone he selected as a companion to reciprocate such total commitment. If he became attracted to a girl, he would fall swiftly and deeply in love and demand unflagging devotion in return. When friends or a girl he was dating disappointed him by not matching his passion for their relationship, he would become furious and could think of little else except how much he hated the person. These emotional storms would blow over quickly, without leading to anything more than harsh words, and he would soon put the person out of his mind and turn his attentions elsewhere. However, as he became more active socially, his emotional volatility and the intensity of the anger he was likely to turn on other people began to earn him an undesirable reputation on the campus—as a very demanding, touchy, irritable, and ill-tempered person who could make your life miserable if you got involved with him.

Joseph was sufficiently sensitive to recognize that this state of affairs was standing between him and the rewarding social life he now craved—hence, his opening statement about needing to keep others from perceiving his hostility. Significantly, however, he did not express any concern about being so intensely emotional, nor did he seem open to any suggestion that his anger when it arose was not fully justified. Rather than seeking to change or to understand himself better as a person, he was looking for guidance in how to manage interpersonal relationships more effectively, in order to be better liked and better able to secure commitments from other people.

Joseph's intense affect, especially his anger, was as apparent from his initial interview behavior as in the clinical history he gave. He fastened a piercing gaze on the interviewer and rarely looked away when talking about painful childhood experiences. When he spoke of hatreds past and present toward people who had misused him, his eyes would flash, he would clench his jaw and grind his teeth, and the muscles of his face would begin to twitch. Although he communicated clearly and was open and spontaneous in providing information, the heavily charged atmosphere he created left the interviewer feeling he had worked very hard during the session.

On subsequent psychological examination, Joseph's Rorschach responses conformed reasonably well to reality and involved only minimal perceptual distortion. However, he frequently lost distance from the test stimuli and wove his percepts into complex personalized fantasies and symbolic associations. Of further note, the content of his responses featured recurrent images of aggressive interactions and numerous instances in which figures were engaged in some aspect of coming together or pulling apart from each other.

Joseph's unstable, intense affective style, his equally intense and unpredictable social relatedness, and the tense and urgent climate he created beginning in the first interview suggested borderline disorder early in the evaluation process. This impression was subsequently supported by the emerging indications that his distant father and possessive mother probably made it difficult for him to individuate in early childhood and that he had experienced prominent anxiety and phobic symptoms in middle childhood. In retrospect, there was good reason to believe he would have been diagnosed as a borderline child if he had been evaluated at that time. Presently, his description of his distaste for casual relationships painted a clear picture of object splitting—Either you loved Joseph without reservation, in which case he would love you in return, or you offered something less than a total commitment, in which case he despised you and wanted nothing to do with you. Finally confirming the diagnosis was the psychological examination, in which his circumstantial and overly abstract thinking on the Rorschach contrasted with his excellent cognitive functioning on more structured tests and in the classroom, and in which his fantasy identified preoccupation with themes of aggression and separation.

Joseph's reasonably intact reality testing and the prominence of affective over cognitive difficulties suggest borderline rather than schizotypal personality disorder. On the other hand, his currently intense involvement with other people had been preceded by long developmental stretches in which he was socially withdrawn and isolated. Furthermore, his heavy investment in fantasy and his frequently ruminative style identify ideational channels for coping with experience. These indications of interpersonal avoidance and ideational orientation raise the possibility of some overlapping schizotypal features.

STRATEGIES IN PSYCHOTHERAPY

Because borderline disorders are so diverse, their treatment embraces many of the strategies discussed in other chapters of this book. In some cases, the most prominent presenting problems will call for attention to modifying strange ways of thinking; in other cases, the indicated treatment focus, at least initially, will be on alleviating depressive and anxiety-producing affects; in still other instances, the first priority may be behavioral control to minimize suicide risk or other impulsive propensities to antisocial or self-harmful acts. As an illustration of this treatment diversity, psychopharmacologists who address borderline disorders typically recommend a broad range of antipsychotic, antidepressant, and antianxiety medications, with selection among them to be made on the basis of the individual patient's most pressing difficulties (Buysse, Nathan, & Soloff, 1990; Cowdry & Gardner, 1988; Schulz, Schulz, & Wilson, 1988).

As an alternative to dealing broadly with aspects of intervention in borderline disorders, the following discussion is more specifically concerned with strategies of psychotherapy. Psychotherapy with borderline adolescents can be an extraordinarily difficult undertaking. Because borderline disorders are characterological disorders, first of all, they change slowly in response even to energetic intervention. Like other personality traits, the borderline individual's dispositions to view and cope with experience in some distinctive ways cannot readily be exchanged for other traits. As is generally the case in efforts to modify disorders of personality functioning, then, effective psychotherapy in cases of borderline disorder is almost inevitably an extended process in which considerable effort is necessary to achieve only modest goals. Brief supportive intervention focused on specific incidents or problems may relieve situational anxiety or depression in borderline individuals. However, there is widespread agreement that definitive change in the reaction patterns or coping styles of persons with a borderline disorder requires long-term intensive treatment (see Meissner, 1984, Chapter 7; Stone, 1985).

As a second obstacle to rapid or sweeping improvements, the nature of borderline disorder limits the utility of the treatment relationship as an agent of change. In most psychopathological conditions, the empathy and warmth of the therapist contribute substantially to an effective working alliance. In some conditions, especially depression, the interest and attention of the therapist, by compensating for object loss, may alone be sufficient to produce positive change (see Chapter 4). The borderline individual's penchant for either interpersonal avoidance and suspiciousness or interpersonal overinvolvement and demandingness makes it difficult to draw on such relationship variables to initiate or sustain progress in the treatment. Instead, the therapist must guard against manifold ways in which the treatment relationship formed or sought by borderline patients can undermine an effective alliance.

Third, in addition to their interpersonal demands, the emotional intensity, instability, and impulsivity of borderline patients can challenge even the most heroic and steadfast therapists to keep an even keel and maintain their commitment to the treatment. Borderline patients have been observed to elicit negative reactions and inappropriate responses not only from individual therapists but also from entire treatment teams responsible for their care in an inpatient setting (McCready, 1987; Miller, 1989). Shay (1987, p. 712) puts the problem well with respect to borderline adolescents: "When they are not making our lives difficult *in* the treatment, they are making us feel worse by refusing to have anything to do *with* the treatment."

Finally, in attempting to overcome chronicity, volatility, and strained interpersonal relatedness, therapists working with borderline patients labor under twin risks that are likely to escalate in relation to how hard they try to make an impact. One of these risks is the susceptibility of the borderline person to psychological breakdown when pushed beyond the boundaries of what is comfortable and familiar; the other is the tendency of borderline individuals to defend themselves by object-splitting, which can result in their viewing a challenging therapist as an all-bad person and showering him or her with ill will.

On the other hand, the youthfulness of adolescents means that their personality traits, including borderline disorder, are not yet as entrenched as they are destined to become. To take advantage of this fact and circumvent obstacles to change, the therapist needs to provide a carefully controlled and structured treatment atmosphere in which ambiguity is kept at a minimum and the patient–therapist relationship is clearly defined and limited. Over a sufficiently long period of time, a well-planned and implemented treatment program can modify borderline traits in young persons while minimizing the likelihood of breakdown and reducing reliance on object-splitting. Two key tactics for implementing this strategy comprise (a) techniques of confrontation and of coping-skill training and (b) methods of managing the treatment relationship.

Confrontation and Coping-Skill Training

Psychotherapy with borderline adolescents needs to be intensive, not in the sense of uncovering underlying thoughts and feelings, but rather with respect to actively confronting them with how they are currently misperceiving the implications of their experiences or overreacting emotionally to certain people or events. Experienced clinicians generally concur that the majority of patients with borderline disorders respond most favorably to a treatment approach that strikes some balance between exploratory and supportive strategies and focuses on everyday issues in the person's life rather than on dynamic reconstruction of past events (Aronson, 1989; Kroll, 1988, Chapter 4; Pollack, 1990; Stone, Hurt, & Stone, 1987). Focusing directly on present events in which maladaptive behavior patterns are clearly in evidence achieves two purposes: (a) uncertainty and speculation of the kind that make borderline individuals anxious and defensive are minimized, and (b) the stage is set for examples of realistic perception and appropriate emotionality, from which the patient can learn more adaptive patterns.

Confrontation and coping-skill training complement each other in such efforts to promote behavior change. Take, for example, an overemotional, overinvolved borderline adolescent describing an interpersonal falling-out in which "I got so mad I called him some bad names and said I never wanted to see him again, and he had it coming, but now I'm afraid I'll miss having him to be close to." Confrontation in this instance would begin with the therapist's exploring exactly what happened prior to the patient's outburst and would end, if appropriate, with the therapist's saying "It doesn't seem to me that what he did was enough reason for you to get so angry."

When the patient is able to accept such a confrontation, as by granting that the therapist may be right and the anger disproportionate to any offense, the time for coping-skill training has arrived: How could the patient have responded differently in this situation, in order to have it end on a more positive note? Drawing less hasty conclusions, considering alternative explanations, and expressing anger less abusively are examples of coping skills that would have been helpful and that therapists can promote by such commonly used techniques as description and explanation, modeling, and role rehearsal. The objective in such sequences of confrontation and coping-skill training is to expand the patient's repertoire of capabilities for coping effectively with everyday life experiences (see Curran & Monti, 1982; Liberman, Mueser, Wallace, Jacobs, Eckman, & Massel, 1986; Linehan & Wasson, 1990).

Sequences of confrontation and coping-skill training rarely proceed smoothly in the treatment of borderline adolescents, especially early on. Even confrontations that are confirmed without doubt by the obvious facts of a situation are likely initially to be viewed by the patient as hostile and unwarranted criticism. Only over time, as confrontations of the same kind are repeatedly justified by recurrent events and as the patient gradually develops a sense of trust in the therapist, can observations be acknowledged as accurate and accepted as grounds for considering alternative ways of behaving.

The focus of confrontation and coping-skill training should be determined in relation to whether the patient's disorder involves primarily schizotypal or borderline personality features. Schizotypal disorder calls mainly for attention to cognitive distortions, including unrealistic perceptions or expectations, unreasonable or unjustified conclusions, and peculiar use of language or communication. Borderline personality disorder requires attention mostly to affective dysfunction, including (as in the preceding example) excessive emotional reactions and inadequately modulated affective expression.

For all varieties of borderline disorder, the confrontation and coping-skill training process must eventually address defensive object-splitting. Because this phenomenon lies so close to the core of borderline disorder and is so critical to borderline patients' maintaining what little equilibrium they have, it can rarely be touched until considerable progress has already been made in identifying and modifying cognitive and affective dysfunctions. A premature lunge at object-splitting threatens to knock the pins out from under the borderline individual and is more likely to precipitate decompensation or premature termination than to foster progress.

Like other aspects of impaired interpersonal relatedness, object-splitting often becomes most apparent and accessible for discussion in the context of the patient–therapist relationship. Before turning to relationship issues, a final caution is helpful to keep in mind in pursuing confrontation and coping-skill training. Not infrequently, borderline patients will object to an active confrontational approach as being superficial. "This is all obvious stuff," they will say or imply, "Things I can figure out for myself; I'm not coming in here just to talk about what I did yesterday, but to find out the reasons why I got to be like I am." The patient may then clamor for "a deeper approach" that will be "more meaningful" and "really get us somewhere."

Therapists must avoid being misled by such complaints into deserting active confrontation for a more uncovering approach in which they will be saying less and commenting more speculatively. In the first place, a borderline patient's objections to active confrontation need to be recognized for what they typically are, which is resistance. Unlike persons with symptomatic disorders, who usually find it easier to talk about the nature of their currently maladaptive behavior than to explore its origins, persons with personality disorders do not take easily to concrete illustrations of how their own characterological style is causing their present difficulties. Hence, they may seek to probe and speculate about past events that touch only peripherally on their daily lives as a way of avoiding present realities that would be painful to face.

Second, any shift by the therapist to less activity and more speculation exposes borderline patients to the kind of unstructured situation they tolerate poorly. Whatever appreciation a borderline patient may initially show for a therapist's agreeing to a "deeper" approach will soon give way to mounting anxiety and intense transference reactions. Unless this therapist error is recognized and reversed, progress in the treatment is likely to be seriously disrupted by the patient's inability to cope.

Managing the Treatment Relationship

Borderline patients find it very difficult to develop a comfortable and constructive relationship with a therapist. As a function of their disorder, they misperceive the characteristics and intentions of the therapist; they hope for love and nurturance while fearing rejection and abandonment; and they form unrealistic expectations of how the therapy will proceed and what it will accomplish. Overcoming such relationship difficulties is not merely a prelude to behavior change, as it is in most other disorders, but is by itself a significant therapeutic accomplishment. Adler (1985) has noted in this regard that "At the point that the patient is capable of a solid therapeutic alliance, that patient no longer has a borderline or narcissistic personality disorder; in fact, he is well within the neurotic spectrum and approaching the end of therapy" (p. 115). Progress toward this point can be facilitated by managing the treatment relationship in ways that *minimize transference reactions, avoid giving and taking,* and *moderate object-splitting* (see Waldinger, 1987).

Minimizing Transference Reactions

Because transference-related misperceptions can so irreparably undermine the treatment relationship with borderline adolescents, every effort should be made to minimize the intensity and impact of their transference reactions. To take preventive action in this regard, therapists should present themselves as much as possible as real objects with clearly defined characteristics and views. The less ambiguous the therapist is as a stimulus, the less latitude there is for the patient to ponder what he or she is like or to become caught up in erroneous attributions. This does not eliminate the need for limits on therapist disclosure, however, especially with adolescents who press the theme, "If I only knew more about you, I'd be able to trust you and tell you more about the things that are really bothering me." For example, the question, "Where did you go to college?" can and should be answered, whereas the question, "How often do you have sex?" calls for pointing out that this is private matter, and asking about it is an example of not using good social judgment.

When transference reactions do occur, they should be diluted by interpreting them promptly and in general terms. Indications of transference are usually ignored in dynamic psychotherapy until they have begun to occupy center stage in the course of the treatment and can consequently lend themselves to weighty interpretations (see Weiner, 1975, Chapter 10). For patients with borderline disorders, allowing transference reactions to build in this way is contraindicated, because of the damage they can do to the patient's peace of mind and to the treatment relationship. The purposes of the treatment are better served when even subtle and fleeting manifestations of transference, whether in thoughts, feelings, or actions, are pointed out as soon as they appear.

Once identified, a borderline patient's transference reactions should be explained away by describing them as how people generally respond in psychotherapy. The impact of transference interpretations is heightened when the therapist conveys that the behavior being interpreted is an unusual, surprising, and highly personal event understandable only in terms of the individual patient's needs and coping style. This is precisely what should be avoided in working with a borderline person. Instead, what should be conveyed is that transference reactions, although worth mentioning, are in no way special or uniquely meaningful (e.g., "Everyone who's involved in the kind of therapy we're doing gets angry when they're told about something they didn't handle well, so I expect you to feel this way now and then"). Messages of this kind strip transference reactions of their otherwise considerable potency for occupying a patient's attention and influencing his or her behavior. The importance of energetic transference interpretations within the context of confrontational therapy with borderline patients, especially adolescents, has been elaborated by Kernberg (1984, Chapter 9) and by Masterson (1981, Chapter 9).

Avoiding Giving and Taking

Therapists working with borderline patients need to take special care to avoid any giving or taking that goes beyond the ordinary limits of the treatment contract. With respect to giving, borderline individuals, especially those with borderline personality disorder, can be expected to press the therapist to become involved in their lives. They may insist that having some relationship outside of the therapy is necessary for them to learn what the therapist is "really like." They may ask for more frequent sessions, or for the therapist to extend the time of a session in progress, or even for the therapist to stop seeing other patients in order to concentrate on their needs. Borderline patients not infrequently become upset when, in their coming and going, they see another patient in the waiting room, because this confirms that they are sharing the therapist rather than having him or her all to themselves.

Borderline patients may ask for mementos from the therapist's office, they may yearn to be held or touched, and they may try in various ways to maneuver the therapist into taking over their lives. The borderline patient can become a seemingly constant presence in the therapist's life—literally following the therapist around, sending letters and leaving messages, and calling on the telephone with dramatic requests for advice on how to deal with daily problems ("You've simply got to tell me whether I should go out on this date tonight, or I'm going to go out of my mind").

As these few illustrations indicate, borderline patients' requests for therapist giving may range from the almost reasonable to the clearly outrageous.

The more closely they approach being reasonable, the more tempted the therapist may be to give extra amounts of time, support, and reassurance. To resist such temptation, therapists need to remind themselves that the demands of these patients stem from their pathological interpersonal relatedness and reflect unrealistic perceptions and expectations. Should they give more than they have in the past, thus allowing themselves to be manipulated and depended on, the patient may for a time feel better. With borderline patients, however, the more that is given, the more that is expected, and escalating commitments become necessary for them to continue feeling reassured. Each nurturant response from the therapist is thus likely to engender greater dependence, more intense needs for nurturance, and increasingly inappropriate demands on the part of the patient.

When finally the therapist who has established a pattern of giving draws the line and stops acceding to the patient's demands, the resulting disappointment and frustration can fuel a towering rage that seriously disrupts the progress of the treatment. Unwarranted angry feelings cannot be avoided in the treatment of borderline patients, who will inevitably receive less personal gratification from the therapist than they want or believe is their just due. From the beginning of the treatment, the intensity of these angry feelings can be curtailed by taking care not to stimulate any false hopes and expectations concerning how much giving there will be.

With respect to taking, borderline patients often seek to cement a bond of closeness with the therapist by pressing gifts or favors on him or her. As with giving, the taking of such gifts and favors may be difficult for a caring and empathic therapist to resist. The patient may ask, "How can you be such a Scrooge as not to take this little Christmas decoration I made for you that only cost a few lousy cents and that it would make me feel so good just to have in your office?" The content of this question carries the seeds of the answer. Gifts from borderline individuals, in light of their difficulties with reality testing and interpersonal relatedness, will have problematic surplus meaning. Taking one small gift means that the therapist will be agreeable to taking more and larger gifts; each gift accepted means that something once belonging to the patient, an extension of him or her, is now part of the therapist's life; further, having had the benefit of receiving so much from the patient means that the therapist is obliged and can be expected to reciprocate with as much affection and nurturance as the patient wants.

Hence, taking, like giving, nourishes false hopes and sets the stage for bitter recriminations when these hopes are not realized. The farther the therapist has proceeded along the primrose path of accepting grander gifts or bigger favors, the more intense the negative reactions are likely to be when he or she calls a halt. The easiest and best place to draw the line is at the very beginning, which means not taking anything from the patient other than what he or she has to say in the therapy.

For both giving and taking, the therapeutic alternative to inappropriate involvement consists of identifying for borderline adolescents the kinds of interpersonal needs that are prompting their request. Like other confrontations, such explanations rarely find a responsive ear, at least not the first time around. The therapist's refusal to give or receive may elicit dismay or disgust that produces a very sticky situation. Yet "stickiness" aptly depicts most aspects of the treatment relationship with borderline patients, and the situation is more easily manageable when the therapist has been firm from the beginning than when he or she is refusing a big favor after having accepted many smaller ones along the way. In addition, a consistently firm stance on giving and taking contributes to the therapist's placing clear limits on the nature of the treatment relationship. No matter how distressing such limits may be to some borderline patients, they foster progress in therapy by providing the protection of a structured, unambiguous, and predictable situation.

Moderating Object-Splitting

The treatment relationship can be used with good effect to help borderline patients recognize and moderate their defensive reliance on object-splitting. These patients ordinarily alternate between wanting the therapist to love and nurture them and being angry at him or her for not doing so, and their tendency toward object splitting frequently leads them to view the therapist in extreme ways—as extremely kind or sadistically cruel, as enormously attractive or terribly ugly, as highly skilled or tremendously inept, and so on. When such extreme views are expressed, the therapist should focus on helping patients recognize that they are seeing the therapist as they want to see him or her, not as he or she really is; that they are forming black-or-white opinions without allowing for the possibility of shades of gray (e.g., that the therapist is *sometimes* unkind or *moderately* attractive) and that they are focusing only on certain isolated characteristics or actions of the therapist and not giving balanced attention to the totality of his or her nature or behavior.

Once tendencies toward distorted interpersonal perception have been brought into bold relief in the context of the treatment relationship, the therapist will be well-positioned to show the patient how he or she has been object-splitting in other relationships as well. Like maladaptive cognitions, and like affects in general, these defensive interpersonal distortions, once recognized by the patient for what they are, become accessible for modification through further confrontation and coping-skill training.

Mention finally needs to be made of countertransference issues that typically arise in the treatment of borderline patients. Much has already been said about the difficulties that borderline patients are likely to cause their therapists by virtue of the chronicity of their condition, the intensity of their affects, the precariousness of their interpersonal relatedness, and the limits of their tolerance for ambiguity. Therapists treating borderline individuals must constantly make delicate strategic decisions during sessions and on-the-spot judgments about crisis situations that crop up between sessions. Rarely can they relax their vigil.

To make matters worse, borderline patients who impose this heavy burden are rarely satisfied with the therapist's best efforts to shoulder it. Instead, as a function of their psychopathology, they expect more than is reasonable, ask for more than should be given, and hold the therapist responsible for depriving them of what they believe they are entitled to receive. This induces them to subject their therapists to frequent angry attacks in which they assail their inhumanity, disparage their professional competence, and ridicule their personal style. Giovacchini (1985) suggests, in this regard, that, having been treated as transitional objects by their parents, borderline adolescents tend to treat their therapists in the same way—denying their existence as a person and using them as objects to control, manipulate, and abuse psychologically without regard for their feelings.

As elaborated in rich detail by Adler (1985, Chapter 10), such devaluation can be painful for therapists to endure. Even while recognizing that the patient's pathology is doing the talking, and not the voice of fair and realistic appraisal, the therapist will be hard put to avoid feeling helpless ("This patient is untreatable"), inadequate ("The patient is treatable but I'm not capable"), guilty ("The patient is treatable and I'm capable, but I haven't been doing my best work"), or angry ("I'm doing good work, and the patient has no call to talk to me this way").

In a similar vein, Kroll (1988, Chapter 8) elaborates how countertransference engendered by borderline patients can cause therapists to experience potentially conflicting motivations that must be recognized and prevented from resulting in inappropriate therapist behaviors. These include, for example, needs to (a) guard against being too passive while also guarding against being too controlling in the face of patient manipulativeness; (b) protect oneself against criticism from the patient while also avoiding the temptation to court patient flattery and approval; and (c) avoid being mistaken while also avoiding insistence on always being correct.

Being prepared to experience such feelings while treating a borderline patient can help therapists avoid nonproductive countertransference manifestations. Therapists who fail to keep a proper perspective in this regard may respond to a borderline patient's angry attacks by (a) losing interest in or terminating the therapy; (b) setting out to prove with greater vigor and increased doses of nurturance that they really do care; or (c) retaliating with a stirring defense of their conduct of the therapy and a denunciation of the patient's anger. All such therapist actions, when provoked by the therapist's personal needs rather than by considered judgment concerning how best to meet the patient's needs, tend to have negative consequences and should be avoided.

REFERENCES

Adler, G. (1985). *Borderline psychopathology and its treatment.* New York: Aronson.

Akhtar, S., & Byrne, J. P. (1983). The concept of splitting and its clinical relevance. *American Journal of Psychiatry, 140,* 1013–1016.

Archer, R. P., Ball, J. D., & Hunter, J. A. (1985). MMPI characteristics of borderline psychopathology in adolescent inpatients. *Journal of Personality Assessment, 49,* 47–55.

Aronson, T. A. (1989). A critical review of psychotherapeutic treatments of the borderline personality: Historical trends and future directions. *Journal of Nervous and Mental Disease, 177,* 511–528.

Baron, M., Gruen, R., Asnis, L., & Kane, J. M. (1983). Familial relatedness of schizophrenic and schizotypal states. *American Journal of Psychiatry, 140,* 1437–1442.

Baron, M., Gruen, R., Asnis, L., & Lord, S. (1985). Familial transmission of schizotypal and boderline personality disorders. *American Journal of Psychiatry, 142,* 927–934.

Baron, M., Gruen, R., Ranier, J. D., Kane, J., Asnis, L. & Lord, S. (1985). A family study of schizophrenic and normal control probands: Implications for the spectrum concept of schizophrenia. *American Journal of Psychiatry, 142,* 447–455.

Barrash, J., Kroll, J., Carey, K., & Sines, L. (1983). Discriminating borderline disorder from other personality disorders. *Archives of General Psychiatry, 40,* 1297–1302.

Bell, M., Billington, R., Chicchetti, D., & Gibbons, J. (1988). Do object relations deficits distinguish BPD from other diagnostic groups? *Journal of Clinical Psychology, 44,* 511–516.

Berg, M. (1983). Borderline psychopathology as displayed on psychological tests. *Journal of Personality Assessment, 47,* 120–133.

Buysse, D. J., Nathan, R. S., & Soloff, P. H. (1990). Borderline personality disorder: Pharmacotherapy. In A. S. Bellack & M. Hersen (Eds.), *Handbook of comparative treatments for adult disorders* (pp. 436–458). New York: Wiley.

Carr, A. C., Schwartz, F., & Fishler, P. (1989). The diagnosis of schizotypal personality disorder by use of psychological tests. *Journal of Personality Disorders, 3,* 36–44.

Chethik, M. (1986). Levels of borderline functioning in children: Etiological and treatment considerations. *American Journal of Orthopsychiatry, 56,* 109–119.

Coonerty, S. (1986). An exploration of separation–individuation themes in the borderline personality disorder. *Journal of Personality Assessment, 50,* 501–511.

Cowdry, R. W., & Gardner, D. L. (1988). Pharmacotherapy of borderline personality disorder. *Archives of General Psychiatry, 45,* 111–119.

Curran, J. P., & Monti, P. M. (Eds.). (1982). *Social skills training.* New York: Guilford.

Dahl, A. A. (1990). Empirical evidence for a core borderline syndrome. *Journal of Personality Disorders, 4,* 192–202.

Edell, W. S. (1987a). Relationship of borderline syndrome disorders to early schizophrenia on the MMPI. *Journal of Clinical Psychology, 43,* 163–176.

Edell, W. S. (1987b). Role of structure in disordered thinking in borderline and schizophrenic disorders. *Journal of Personality Assessment, 51,* 23–41.

Esman, A. H. (1989). Borderline personality disorder in adolescents: Current concepts. In S. C. Feinstein (Ed.), *Adolescent psychiatry* (Vol. 16, pp. 319–336). Chicago: University of Chicago Press.

Evans, R. W., Ruff, R. M., Braff, D. L., & Ainsworth, T. L. (1984). MMPI characteristics of borderline personality inpatients. *Journal of Nervous and Mental Disease, 172*, 742-748.

Exner, J. E. (1986). Some Rorschach data comparing schizophrenics with borderline and schizotypal personality disorders. *Journal of Personality Assessment, 50*, 455-471.

Fenton, W. S., & McGlashan, T. H. (1989). Risk of schizophrenia in character disordered patients. *American Journal of Psychiatry, 146*, 1280-1284.

Gartner, J., Hurt, S. W., & Gartner, A. (1989). Psychological test signs of borderline personality disorder: A review of the empirical literature. *Journal of Personality Assessment, 53*, 423-441.

Giovacchini, P. L. (1985). The borderline adolescent as a transitional object: A common variation. In S. C. Feinstein, M. Sugar, A. H. Esman, J. G. Looney, A. Z. Schwartzberg, & A. D. Sorosky (Eds.), *Adolescent psychiatry* (Vol. 12, pp. 233-250). Chicago: University of Chicago Press.

Goldstein, W. N. (1983). DSM-III and the diagnosis of borderline. *American Journal of Psychotherapy, 37*, 312-327.

Greenman, D. A., Gunderson, J. G., Cane, M., & Saltzman, P. R. (1986). An examination of the borderline diagnosis in children. *American Journal of Psychiatry, 143*, 998-1003.

Grinker, R. R. (1977). The borderline syndrome: A phenomenological view. In P. Hartocollis (Ed.), *Borderline personality disorders* (pp. 159-172). New York: International Universities Press.

Grotstein, J. S., Solomon, M. F., & Lang, J. A. (Eds.) (1987). *The borderline patient.* Hillsdale, NJ: Analytic Press.

Gualtieri, C. T., Koriath, U., & Van Bourgondien, M. E. (1983). "Borderline" children. *Journal of Autism and Developmental Disorders, 13*, 67-71.

Gunderson, J. G. (1981). Diagnostic interview for borderline patients. *American Journal of Psychiatry, 138*, 896-903.

Gunderson, J. G., & Elliott, G. R. (1985). The interface between borderline personality disorder and affective disorder. *American Journal of Psychiatry, 142*, 277-288.

Gunderson, J. G., & Kolb, J. E. (1978). Discriminating features of borderline patients. *American Journal of Psychiatry, 135*, 792-796.

Gunderson, J. G., Siever, L. J., & Spaulding, E. (1983). The search for a schizotype: Crossing the border again. *Archives of General Psychiatry, 40*, 15-22.

Gunderson, J. G., & Singer, M. T. (1975). Defining borderline patients: An overview. *American Journal of Psychiatry, 132*, 1-10.

Hoch, P. H., & Polatin, P. (1949). Pseudoneurotic forms of schizophrenia. *Psychiatric Quarterly, 23*, 248-276.

Hurt, S. W., Clarkin, J. F., Koenigsberg, H. W., Frances, A., & Nurnberg, H. G. (1986). Diagnostic interview for borderlines: Psychometric properties and validity. *Journal of Consulting and Clinical Psychology, 54*, 256-260.

Jacobsberg, L. B., Hymowitz, P., Barasch, A., & Frances, A. J. (1986). Symptoms of schizotypal personality disorder. *American Journal of Psychiatry, 143*, 1222-1227.

Kendler, K. S. (1984). Diagnostic approaches in schizotypal disorder: A historical perspective. *Schizophrenia Bulletin, 11*, 538-553.

Kendler, K. S., Gruenberg, A. M., & Strauss, J. S. (1981). An independent analysis of the Copenhagen sample of the Danish adoption study of schizophrenia. *Archives of General Psychiatry, 38*, 982-987.

Kernberg, O. (1977). The structural diagnosis of borderline personality organization. In P. Hartocollis (Ed.), *Borderline personality disorder* (pp. 87-121). New York: International Universities Press.

Kernberg, O. (1978). The diagnosis of borderline conditions in adolescence. In S. C. Feinstein & P. L. Giovacchini (Eds.), *Adolescent psychiatry* (Vol. 6, pp. 298-320). Chicago: University of Chicago Press.

Kernberg, O. (1984). *Severe personality disorders: Psychotherapeutic strategies.* New Haven, CT: Yale University Press.

Kernberg, P. F. (1983a). Borderline conditions: Childhood and adolescent aspects. In K. S. Robson (Ed.), *The borderline child* (pp. 101-119). New York: McGraw-Hill.

Kernberg, P. F. (1983b). Issues in the psychotherapy of borderline conditions in children. In K. S. Robson (Ed.), *The borderline child* (pp. 224-234). New York: McGraw-Hill.

Kernberg, P. F. (1988). Children with borderline personality organization. In C. J. Kestenbaum & D. T. Williams (Eds.), *Handbook of clinical assessment of children and adolescents* (pp. 604-625). New York: New York University Press.

Kestenbaum, C. J. (1983). The borderline child at risk for major psychiatric disorder in adult life: Seven case reports with follow-up. In K. S. Robson (Ed.), *The borderline child* (pp. 49-81). New York: McGraw-Hill.

Kety, S. S., Rosenthal, D., Wender, P. H., & Schulsinger, F. (1968). The types and prevalence of mental illness in the biological and adoptive families of adopted schizophrenics. In D. Rosenthal & S. S. Kety (Eds.), *The transmission of schizophrenia* (pp. 345-362). New York: Pergamon.

Knight, R. P. (1953). Borderline states. *Bulletin of the Menninger Clinic, 17*, 1-12.

Kroll, J. (1988). *The challenge of the borderline patient.* New York: W. W. Norton.

Leichtman, M., & Nathan, S. (1983). A clinical approach to the psychological testing of borderline children. In K. S. Robson (Ed.), *The borderline child* (pp. 121-170). New York: McGraw-Hill.

Liberman, R. P., Mueser, K. T., Wallace, C. J., Jacobs, H. E., Eckman, T., & Massel, H. K. (1986). Training skills in the psychiatrically disabled: Learning coping and competence. *Schizophrenia Bulletin, 12*, 631-647.

Linehan, M. M., & Wasson, E. J. (1990). Borderline personality disorder: Behavior therapy. In A. S. Bellack & M. Hersen (Eds.), *Handbook of comparative treatments for adult disorders* (pp. 420-435). New York: Wiley.

Links, P. S., Steiner, M., & Huxley, G. (1988). The occurrence of borderline personality disorder in the families of borderline patients. *Journal of Personality Disorders, 2*, 14-20.

Ludolph, P. S., Westen, D., Misle, B., Jackson, A., Wixom, J., & Wiss, C. A. (1990). The borderline diagnosis in adolescents: Symptoms and developmental history. *American Journal of Psychiatry, 147*, 470-476.

Mahler, M. S. (1974). Symbiosis and individuation: The psychological birth of the human infant. *Psychoanalytic Study of the Child, 29*, 89–106.

Mahler, M. S., & Kaplan, L. (1977). Developmental aspects in the assessment of narcissistic and so-called borderline personalities. In P. Hartocollis (Ed.), *Borderline personality disorders* (pp. 71–86). New York: International Universities Press.

Masterson, J. F. (1975). The splitting defense mechanism of the borderline adolescent: Developmental and clinical aspects. In J. E. Mack (Ed.), *Borderline states in psychiatry* (pp. 93–101). New York: Grune & Stratton.

Masterson, J. (1980). *From borderline adolescent to functioning adult.* New York: Brunner/Mazel.

Masterson, J. F. (1981). *The narcissistic and borderline disorders.* New York: Brunner/Mazel.

McCready, K. F. (1987). Milieu countertransference in treatment of borderline patients. *Psychotherapy, 24*, 720–728.

McGlashan, T. H. (1983a). The borderline syndrome: I. Testing three diagnostic systems. *Archives of General Psychiatry, 40*, 1311–1318.

McGlashan, T. H. (1983b). The borderline syndrome: II. Is it a variant of schizophrenia or affective disorder? *Archives of General Psychiatry, 40*, 1319–1323.

McGlashan, T. H. (1986a). The Chestnut Lodge follow-up study. III. Long-term outcome of borderline personalities. *Archives of General Psychiatry, 43*, 20–30.

McGlashan, T. H. (1986b). Schizotypal personality disorder. Chestnut Lodge follow-up study: VI. Long-term follow-up perspectives. *Archives of General Psychiatry, 43*, 329–334.

McGlashan, T. H. (1987). Testing DSM-III symptom criteria for schizotypal and borderline personality disorders. *Archives of General Psychiatry, 44*, 143–148.

McManus, M., Lerner, H., Robbins, D., & Barbour, C. (1984). Assessment of borderline symptomatology in hospitalized adolescents. *Journal of the American Academy of Child Psychiatry, 23*, 685–694.

Mednick, S. A., Parnas, J., & Schulsinger, F. (1987). The Cophenhagen high-risk project, 1962–86. *Schizophrenia Bulletin, 13*, 485–496.

Meissner, W. W. (1984). *The borderline spectrum.* New York: Aronson.

Miller, L. J. (1989). Inpatient management of borderline personality disorder: A review and update. *Journal of Personality Disorders, 3*, 122–134.

Millon, T. (1981). *Disorders of personality.* New York: Wiley.

Millon, T. (1988). Falling short of the border line. *Contemporary Psychology, 33*, 902–903.

Morey, L. C. (1988). A psychometric analysis of the DSM-III-R personality disorder criteria. *Journal of Personality Disorders, 2*, 109–124.

Nagy, J., & Szatmari, P. (1986). A chart review of schizotypal personality disorders in children. *Journal of Autism and Developmental Disorders, 16*, 351–368.

Nurnberg, H. G., Hurt, S. W., Feldman, A., & Suh, R. (1988). Evaluation of diagnostic criteria for borderline personality disorder. *American Journal of Psychiatry, 145*, 1280–1284.

O'Connell, M., Cooper, S. H., Perry, J. C., & Hoke, L. (1989). The relationship between thought disorder and psychotic symptoms in borderline personality disorder. *Journal of Nervous and Mental Disease, 177,* 273-278.

Ochoa, E. S., & Morey, L. C. (1990). Clinical diagnosis of borderline personality: Examination of professional differences. *Professional Psychology, 21,* 54-59.

Paris, J., & Frank, H. (1989). Perceptions of parental bonding in borderline patients. *American Journal of Psychiatry, 146,* 1498-1499.

Perry, J. C. (1988). A prospective study of life stress, defenses, psychotic symptoms, and depression in borderline and antisocial personality disorders and Type II affective disorder. *Journal of Personality Disorders, 2,* 49-59.

Perry, J. C., & Klerman, G. L. (1980). Clinical features of the borderline personality. *American Journal of Psychiatry, 137,* 165-173.

Petti, T. A., & Vela, R. M. (1990). Borderline disorders of childhood: An overview. *Journal of the American Academy of Child and Adolescent Psychiatry, 29,* 327-337.

Pine, F. (1983). Borderline syndromes in childhood: A working nosology and its therapeutic implications. In K. S. Robson (Ed.), *The borderline child* (pp. 83-100). New York: McGraw-Hill.

Pollack, W. S. (1990). Borderline personality disorder: Psychotherapy. In A. S. Bellack & M. Hersen (Eds.), *Handbook of comparative treatments for adult disorders* (pp. 393-419). New York: Wiley.

Pope, H. G., Jonas, J. M., Hudson, J. L., Cohen, B. M., & Gunderson, J. G. (1983). The validity of *DSM-III* borderline personality disorder. *Archives of General Psychiatry, 40,* 23-30.

Pope, H. G., Jonas, J. M., Hudson, J. I., Cohen, B. M., & Tohen, M. (1985). An empirical study of psychosis in borderline personality disorder. *American Journal of Psychiatry, 142,* 1285-1290.

Resnick, R. J., Goldberg, S. C., Schulz, S. C., & Schulz, P. M. (1988). Borderline personality disorder: Replication of MMPI profiles. *Journal of Clinical Psychology, 44,* 354-360.

Rosenberger, P. H., & Miller, G. A. (1989). Comparing borderline definitions: *DSM-III* borderline and schizotypal personality disorders. *Journal of Abnormal Psychology, 98,* 161-169.

Salwen, R. S., Reznikoff, M., & Schwartz, F. (1989). Identity integration and ego pathology in disturbed adolescents. *Journal of Clinical Psychology, 45,* 138-149.

Schulz, P. M., Soloff, P. H., Kelly, T., Morgenstern, M., Di Franco, R., & Schulz, S. C. (1989). A family history study of borderline subtypes. *Journal of Personality Disorders, 3,* 217-229.

Schulz, S. C., Cornelius, J., Schulz, P. M., & Soloff, P. H. (1988). The amphetamine challenge test in patients with borderline disorder. *American Journal of Psychiatry, 145,* 809-814.

Schulz, S. C., Schulz, P. M., & Wilson, W. H. (1988). Medication treatment of schizotypal disorder. *Journal of Personality Disorders, 2,* 1-13.

Shapiro, T. (1983). The borderline syndrome in children: A critique. In K. S. Robson (Ed.), *The borderline child* (pp. 11-29). New York: McGraw-Hill.

Shay, J. J. (1987). The wish to do psychotherapy with borderline adolescents—And other common errors. *Psychotherapy, 24,* 712-729.

Siever, L. J., & Kendler, K. S. (1986). Schizoid/schizotypal/paranoid personality disorder. In A. M. Cooper, A. J. Frances, & M. H. Sacks (Eds.), *The personality disorders and neuroses* (pp. 191-201). New York: Basic Books.

Silk, K. R., Lohr, N. E., Westen, D., & Goodrich, S. (1989). Psychosis in borderline patients with depression. *Journal of Personality Disorders, 3,* 92-100.

Singer, M. T. (1977). The borderline diagnosis and psychological tests: Review and research. In P. Hartocollis (Ed.), *Borderline personality disorders* (pp. 193-212). New York: International Universities Press.

Singer, M. T., & Larson, D. G. (1981). Borderline personality and the Rorschach test. *Archives of General Psychiatry, 38,* 693-698.

Soloff, P. H., & Ulrich, R. F. (1981). Diagnostic interview for borderline patients. *Archives of General Psychiatry, 38,* 696-692.

Spitzer, R. L., & Endicott, J. (1979). Justification for separating schizotypal and borderline personality disorders. *Schizophrenia Bulletin, 5,* 95-104.

Spitzer, R. L., Endicott, J., & Gibbon, M. (1979). Crossing the border into borderline personality and borderline schizophrenia. *Archives of General Psychiatry, 36,* 1979.

Stone, M. H. (1980). *The borderline syndromes.* New York: McGraw-Hill.

Stone, M. (1985). Schizotypal personality: Psychotherapeutic aspects. *Schizophrenia Bulletin, 11,* 576-589.

Stone, M. H. (1986). Borderline personality disorder. In A. M. Cooper, A. J. Frances, & M. H. Sacks (Ed.), *The personality disorders and neuroses* (pp. 203-217). New York: Basic Books.

Stone, M. H., Hurt, S. W., & Stone, D. K. (1987). The PI 500: Long-term follow-up of borderline inpatients meeting *DSM-III* criteria: I. Global outcome. *Journal of Personality Disorders, 1,* 291-298.

Strahl, M. O. (1980). *Masked schizophrenia.* New York: Springer.

Stuart, J., Westen, D., Lohr, N., Benjamin, J., Becker, S., Vorus, N., & Silk, K. (1990). Object relations in borderlines, depressives, and normals: An examination of human responses on the Rorschach. *Journal of Personality Assessment, 55,* 296-318.

Torgersen, S. (1984). Genetic and nosological aspects of schizotypal and borderline personality disorders. *Archives of General Psychiatry, 41,* 546-554.

Torgersen, S. (1985). Relationship of schizotypal personality disorder to schizophrenia. *Schizophrenia Bulletin, 11,* 554-563.

Vela, R. M., Gottlieb, E. H., & Gottlieb, H. P. (1983). Borderline syndromes in childhood: A critical review. In K. S. Robson (Ed.), *The borderline child* (pp. 32-48). New York: McGraw-Hill.

Waldinger, R. J. (1987). Intensive psychodynamic therapy with borderline patients: An overview. *American Journal of Psychiatry, 144,* 267-274.

Weiner, I. B. (1975). *Principles of psychotherapy.* New York: Wiley.

Wenning, K. (1990). Borderline children: A closer look at diagnosis and treatment. *American Journal of Orthopsychiatry, 60,* 225-232.

Westen, D., Ludolph, P., Lerner, H., Ruffins, S., & Wiss, F. C. (1990). Object relations in borderline adolescents. *Journal of the American Academy of Child and Adolescent Psychiatry, 29,* 338–348.

Widiger, T. A., & Frances, A. (1987). Interviews and inventories for the measurement of personality disorders. *Clinical Psychology Review, 7,* 49–75.

Widiger, T. A., Frances, A., Spitzer, R. L., & Williams, J. B. (1988). The *DSM-III-R* personality disorders: An overview. *American Journal of Psychiatry, 145,* 786–795.

Widiger, T. A., Frances, A., & Trull, T. J. (1987). A psychometric analysis of the social–interpersonal and cognitive–perceptual items for the schizotypal personality disorder. *Archives of General Psychiatry, 44,* 741–745.

Widiger, T. A., Frances, A., Warner, L., & Bluhm, C. (1986). Diagnostic criteria for the borderline and schizotypal personality disorders. *Journal of Abnormal Psychology, 95,* 43–51.

Zanarini, M. C., Gunderson, J. G., Frankenburg, F. R., & Chauncey, D. L. (1989). The revised diagnostic interview for borderlines: Discriminating BPD from other Axis II disorders. *Journal of Personality Disorders, 3,* 10–18.

Zanarini, M. C., Gunderson, J. G., Marino, M. F., Schwartz, E. O., & Frankenburg, F. R. (1988). *DSM-III* disorders in the families of borderline patients. *Journal of Personality Disorders, 2,* 292–302.

CHAPTER 6

Anxiety Disorders: Obsessions, Compulsions, and School Phobia

Like depression, anxiety is a universal emotional reaction. Everyone experiences moments of uncertainty and concern that elicit familiar manifestations of being anxious: such motor reactions as shaking, trembling, twitching, tension, weakness, and inability to relax; such physiological reactions as sweating, dry mouth, difficulty breathing, palpitations, butterflies in the stomach, and diarrhea; and such cognitive reactions as apprehension, worry, rumination, and impaired concentration. The more frequently such reactions occur, the longer they persist, the less justified they are by identifiable life stresses, and the more they interfere with a person's capacity to function socially and in school or on the job, the more likely they are to constitute a pathological anxiety disorder.

Anxiety disorders occur in two varieties, one in which the anxiety is for the most part experienced and one in which it is largely bound. When excessive anxiety is *experienced*, the individual suffers in one of two ways: (a) more or less continuously from various motor, physiological, and cognitive manifestations of anxiety (the condition commonly referred to as "free-floating anxiety" or "generalized anxiety disorder"); or (b) episodically from acute attacks of these symptoms (the condition usually called "panic disorder"). When excessive anxiety is *bound*, the person engages in some persistent, repetitive, maladaptive patterns of thinking and acting that spare him or her from experiencing overt anxiety.

Generalized anxiety disorder may occur in adolescents, as can panic attacks consisting of sometimes inexplicable episodes of intense distress. However, these types of anxiety disorder are not particularly frequent among adolescents, nor do they have any special significance for adolescent development. By contrast, obsessive–compulsive disorder and phobic disorder, the two most common anxiety disorders in which anxiety is bound by maladaptive behavior, have special significance for adolescent development. Obsessive–compulsive disorder frequently has its initial onset during the teenage years, and, although most varieties of phobic disorder are not associated with any distinctive adolescent onset or characteristics, social phobia related to school attendance is a noteworthy teenage problem. This chapter on anxiety disorders accordingly addresses the characteristics, origins, and treatment of *obsessive–compulsive disorder* and of *school phobia*.

OBSESSIVE–COMPULSIVE DISORDER: CHARACTERISTICS

Until fairly recently, obsessive–compulsive disorder was considered to occur infrequently, especially among young persons, and neither research concerning its nature nor recommendations concerning its clinical management were plentiful in the literature. However, much as in the case of bipolar disorder, advances in diagnostic classification and epidemiological methods demonstrated that the condition was more prevalent than had previously been believed, while advances in treatment methods, especially involving behavioral and pharmacological approaches, fostered increased attention to this disorder (see Jenike, Baer, & Minichiello, 1986).

Extensive community survey data indicate that approximately 2.5% of adults in the United States will develop a diagnosable obsessive–compulsive condition at some time during their lifetime. Approximately 1.5% demonstrate this disorder during every 6-month period, and it is equally common among men and women (Henderson & Pollard, 1988; Karno, Golding, Sorenson, & Burnam, 1988). Large-scale evaluations of high school students have identified a 1.9% lifetime prevalence of obsessive–compulsive symptoms sufficiently severe to interfere substantially with their daily activities (Whitaker, Johnson, Shaffer, Rapoport, Kalikow, Walsh, Davies, Braiman, & Dolinsky, 1990).

Aside from its incidence in young persons, which is less than affective disorder but greater than schizophrenia, obsessive–compulsive disorder is developmentally significant because, like these other conditions, it often has its first beginnings during adolescence. Many obsessive–compulsive adults experience the onset of their disorder during their late teens, and at least one third suffer their first episode by age 15 years (Burke, Burke, Regier, & Rae, 1990; Flament, Whitaker, Rapoport, Davies, Berg, & Shaffer, 1989). A full-blown obsessive–compulsive disorder sometimes appears suddenly in young persons on the heels of stressful experiences involving loss of self-control, victimization by circumstances, or a friend or relative's becoming seriously ill or injured. In these instances, the disorder clearly constitutes their attempt to protect themselves against danger by adopting a cautious, circumspect, and constrained approach to dealing with experience. More commonly, however, the disorder takes shape gradually and less obviously. Initially, mild and fleeting symptomatic episodes give way to progressively more persistent and incapacitating obsessions and compulsions that mount, over time, to the extent of diagnosable psychopathology (see Mavassakalian, 1986; Rapoport, 1986; Shear & Frosch, 1986).

Obsessive–compulsive disorder can take the form either of symptomatic manifestations that the individual experiences as undesirable and ego-alien or of a personality style that, no matter how maladaptive in fact, the person perceives ego-syntonically as his or her customary and appropriate way of being. As formulated in *DSM-III-R*, obsessive–compulsive symptoms define the presence of an anxiety disorder or *symptom* neurosis (which falls on Axis

I), whereas a maladaptive obsessive–compulsive personality style identifies a *personality* disorder or *character* neurosis (which falls on Axis II). Obsessive–compulsive personality disorder is therefore not an anxiety disorder, and it does not necessarily undergird obsessive–compulsive neurosis. Nevertheless, appreciation for the nature of obsessive–compulsive character traits can facilitate the understanding and treatment of patients with a symptomatic obsessive–compulsive disorder.

Obsessive–Compulsive Symptoms

Obsessions consist of recurrent ideas, fears, or doubts that intrude on conscious awareness despite a person's finding them unpleasant and not wanting to think about them. These cognitions rarely serve any constructive purpose, and they engender a degree of rumination that often paralyzes the obsessional person's capacity to come to definite conclusions or take decisive action. At least six common types of obsessional thought can be identified:

1. *Worries* about becoming contaminated or infected through direct contact with people or objects: These worries extend well beyond taking conventional care to avoid persons with communicable diseases, to make sure that food is stored and prepared in a sanitary manner, and to minimize one's exposure to pollutants in the environment. Obsessive dread of contamination causes constant concern that the world is potentially the source of illness-producing germs and must be kept at a distance—as by never shaking hands with anyone, insisting that family members always wear gloves in the kitchen, or refusing to leave the house whenever the predicted air quality reported in the morning newspaper is anything but excellent.

2. *Urges* to carry out foolish, socially disruptive, or even assaultive actions: One high school boy was obsessed with the notion of standing up in the middle of class and singing the national anthem; another boy, while riding the bus, thought constantly about reaching out and touching the breasts of young women sitting or standing next to him. In obsessive–compulsive disorder, such acts are only contemplated, never carried out. The actual occurrence of totally inappropriate or blatantly aggressive actions points more to a schizophrenic breakdown in judgment and self-control (see Chapter 3) or an antisocial disregard for the rights of others (see Chapter 8) than to an anxiety disorder.

3. *Anticipations* of losing self-control and behaving in an inappropriate or embarrassing manner: A 17-year-old girl was concerned that she would be unable to prevent herself from blurting out details of her sexual intimacies with her boyfriend to casual acquaintances or even total strangers on the street. This symptom is sometimes referred to as a "compulsion to confess"; so long as it is not acted on, however, but mainly anticipated and worried about, it is strictly speaking an obsession and not a compulsion.

4. *Doubts* about whether certain actions have been carried out in the past ("Did I set the alarm clock?") or should be carried out in the future ("Would it be better to take the bus or to walk to school tomorrow?"): The trivial nature of many of these ruminations is a hallmark of obsessive–compulsive disorder. Most persons become preoccupied from time to time with reflections on whom they love, what they believe in, and how they are going to choose among alternative directions affecting their education, careers, and social relatedness. When considerable cognitive effort is devoted to conclusions and choices that make very little difference in the person's life, however, a symptomatic anxiety disorder is probably present.

5. *Dreads* concerning bad or terrible things that may happen in the future: Some people tend to be more pessimistic than others, especially when they become depressed, and hold little hope that personal or world events will turn out favorably. Some are more fearful than others of being victimized by accidents or natural disasters, including otherwise symptom-free individuals who do everything possible to avoid flying on airplanes. When such negativism and aversions assume the proportions of morbid preoccupations with impending calamity and constant brooding about the inevitability of unfortunate outcomes, they constitute obsessive symptoms.

6. *Images* that flash before the mind's eye and keep the person constantly reminded of a distressing event, whether real or imagined: Philip Roth (1967) provides a superb example of obsessional imagery in his novel *Portnoy's Complaint*. Portnoy, portrayed as a classic obsessive–compulsive, has an unrelieved penchant for translating much of his daily behavior into blaring newspaper headlines that he anticipates will appear the next day and announce his foibles and misdeeds to the whole world.

Compulsions are repetitive, nonproductive acts that persons feel required to carry out, even against their better judgment. Failure or inability to perform self-prescribed rituals fills compulsive individuals with an unbearable sense of dread and impending catastrophe. Compulsive rituals typically appear in the context of such everyday tasks as eating, getting dressed, using the bathroom, handling money, and going back and forth to school or a job. Most frequently, these rituals take the form of handwashing or other cleaning behavior, avoidance or repetition of certain actions or movements, and various types of counting, checking, and touching behaviors.

Some of these compulsive acts arise as a way of yielding to or expressing an obsessive concern. This occurs, for example, when persons who are fearful of contamination begin to wash their hands every hour on the hour, or persons who doubt their alarm-setting behavior check the clock five separate times before falling asleep. Other compulsive acts serve to deflect attention away from obsessive concerns and provide some magical assurance of being able to keep them under control. Thus, the boy in the previous example might think to himself, if you keep eight coins in your pocket, no more or less, and touch both sides of the door as you get on the bus, you will be able to keep control of yourself and not grab a girl's breast. The shortcoming of this approach to self-control is, of course, that the compulsive ritual now controls the person rather than being under his or her control.

Clinical studies with obsessive-compulsive adolescents indicate that most are likely to present with multiple combinations of these various symptoms, including both obsessions and compulsions. With respect to individual symptoms, those that are most commonly observed, occurring in 50% or more of these patients, are obsessions involving contamination and compulsions involving repetitive washing, ordering, arranging, checking, and other ritualistic actions. In contrast to age-related differences in symptomatology that characterize most other types of psychological disorder, these symptom patterns as observed in obsessive-compulsive adolescents are virtually identical to those seen in younger children and in adults with this condition (Riddle, Scahill, King, Hardin, Towbin, Ort, Leckman, & Cohen, 1990; Swedo & Rapoport, 1989).

Taken together, these symptom patterns identify the essential nature of obsessive-compulsive disorder as a feeling of being driven to take certain actions or think certain thoughts, regardless of how ridiculous or repugnant they are and how desperately the person wants to act or think otherwise. Obsessive-compulsive patients accordingly complain mainly of constant worrying over which they have no control or of rituals they must carry out in order to prevent something terrible from happening to themselves or their family. Panic lingers constantly on the threshold of their experience, whether directly from their worries and self-doubts or indirectly in relation to the disastrous consequences they anticipate should they fail to complete their rituals.

Because the manifestations of obsessive-compulsive disorder can be fairly clearly delineated, clinicians working with structured interview schedules and various specially designed assessment inventories have been able to achieve a respectable level of agreement in diagnosing this condition and differentiating it from phobic, panic, and generalized anxiety disorders (Berg, 1989; Di Nardo, O'Brien, Barlow, Waddell, & Blanchard, 1983). The diagnostic challenge in working with obsessive-compulsive patients is thus less likely to involve distinguishing this disorder from other conditions than determining when obsessive or compulsive behavior patterns are sufficiently pronounced to warrant a diagnosis of obsessive-compulsive disorder.

This determination should be made in light of the fact that some degree of ritualistic, magical behavior is normal at all ages. Many of the games that children play have a routinized or repetitive quality in which certain things are to be done in precisely specified ways or a particular number of times, and most children walking along a street will sooner or later be sure to touch all of the pickets in a fence or avoid stepping on the cracks in the sidewalk. With maturity, young persons outgrow children's games, but they also approach an adult world in which a certain amount of routine and orderliness is expected, and there is no shortage of persons who knock on wood, avoid walking under ladders, and feel uneasy on Friday the 13th.

Moreover, normative rituals and pathological compulsions provide similar kinds of protection against experiencing anxiety. Both can be seen as ways of imposing control on an unpredictable and potentially dangerous world and thereby making it safer and less threatening. Both are also means of imposing control on oneself and thereby minimizing the risk of impulsive or ill-advised actions that would later be regretted. In the same way, normal childhood fears and pathological obsessive concerns both constitute alertness to potential sources of harm against which one may need to mount self-protective measures.

In obsessive–compulsive disorder, as in other forms of psychopathology, then, the mechanisms underlying symptom formation also determine behavioral variation within the normal range. However, this genotypic continuity between normal and abnormal behavior does not mean that childhood rituals and adult superstitions are phenotypically similar to obsessive–compulsive disorder, nor are obsessive–compulsive symptoms merely exaggerations of developmentally normative phenomena.

The most extensive data in this regard have emerged from studies by Rapoport (1986, 1989) and her colleagues at the National Institute of Mental Health, who evaluated more than 100 children and adolescents with obsessive–compulsive disorder. According to reports from parents, these young persons had shown significantly more ritualistic behavior early in life than a comparison group of normal children and adolescents. However, the kinds of nonpathological rituals that occur normatively in children differ in kind from manifestations of obsessive–compulsive disorder and are in particular unlikely to include the repetitive washing and checking behaviors seen in obsessive–compulsive patients. Furthermore, normative developmental rituals are neither distressing to a young person nor detrimental to his or her social development. By contrast, obsessive–compulsive rituals are typically upsetting to the person compelled to carry them out and constitute maladaptive behaviors that can become personally and socially incapacitating (Leonard, 1989a; Leonard, Goldberger, Rapoport, Cheslow, & Swedo, 1990).

Interestingly, however, the likelihood that orderly and ritualistic behaviors identify diagnosable psychopathology cannot necessarily be determined by how frequent or pervasive they are. Rapoport (1986) describes a group of high school students, estimated to comprise 0.3% of their peer population, who report numerous obsessive–compulsive behavior patterns but do not see their functioning as impaired by them in any way. Having interviewed many such adolescents, Rapoport suggests that they could be called "supernormals." She found them to be highly ambitious and energetic young persons who far surpassed their classmates in their level of academic and extracurricular activity and in the number of responsibilities they had undertaken. Although immersed in heavily scheduled lives that left them little flexibility, they described enjoying themselves and achieving considerable success in a broad array of pursuits—classes, teams, jobs, exercise, community volunteer work, and so on.

Such supernormal accomplishments do not necessarily rule out obsessive–

compulsive disorder, but they do help to highlight the questions that need to be raised in drawing the line between obsessive–compulsive features and an obsessive–compulsive anxiety disorder. Does the young person feel comfortable with what he or she is like and how he or she is conducting his or her life? Does the person feel able to exert sufficient control over his or her thoughts and actions? Has his or her school and social adjustment remained adequate despite the presence of any ritualized patterns of thinking and acting? The more clearly these questions can be answered in the affirmative, the less basis there is for diagnosing obsessive–compulsive disorder. Conversely, evidence of discomfort, limited mastery, and adjustment difficulties tip the scale toward diagnosable disorder in the evaluation of adolescents with obsessive–compulsive symptoms.

Obsessive–Compulsive Personality Style

The emergence of pathological obsessions or compulsions does not always imply the presence of an obsessive–compulsive personality style, and many individuals with obsessive–compulsive traits never develop ego-alien obsessive–compulsive symptoms. The precise frequency with which obsessive–compulsive traits precede or co-occur with obsessive–compulsive disorder is presently uncertain. Until recently, it was generally believed that the majority of patients with an obsessive–compulsive anxiety disorder have an obsessional personality style and that this personality style is much more likely than any other characterological orientation to be found in association with pathological obsessions and compulsions (Goodwin & Guze, 1984, Chapter 5; Shear & Frosch, 1986). Research reported by Black (1974) and by Rasmussen and Tsuang (1986) seemed sufficient to warrant these beliefs.

However, Black and his colleagues subsequently expressed concern that previous studies of this relationship had not employed reliable assessment procedures and appropriate comparison groups (Black, Yates, Noyes, Pfohl, & Kelley, 1989). Newer and more systematically collected data have begun to suggest only modest links between obsessive–compulsive disorder and obsessive–compulsive personality style, especially in young persons, and it seems increasingly reasonable to expect patients with obsessive–compulsive symptoms to display a heterogeneous range of personality styles (Black et al., 1989; Keller, 1989; Swedo, Rapoport, Leonard, Lenane, & Cheslow, 1989).

Whatever is learned from further research about the co-occurrence of obsessive–compulsive symptoms and styles, familiarity with obsessive–compulsive personality disorder is likely to continue proving helpful to clinicians working with symptomatic obsessive–compulsive adolescents. Obsessive–compulsive personality style revolves around the "three Ps" of *parsimony*, *pedantry*, and *petulance*. Derived from Freud's (1908/1959; 1913/1958) observations on the obsessional, these three Ps refer to the tendency of obsessive–compulsive people to be cautious and frugal, neat and orderly, and rigid and stubborn. Subsequent formulations have translated these characteristics into typically obsessive–compulsive patterns of *ideation*, *affect*, *social relationships*, and *behavior* (see Adams, 1973, Chapter 3; Millon, 1981, Chapter 8; Salzman, 1968; Shapiro, 1965, Chapter 2).

Ideation

Obsessive-compulsive persons have strong needs to be absolutely sure of themselves and to ponder all aspects of a situation before coming to any conclusion about it. Theirs is a thorough, cautious, conservative, reflective approach to forming judgments and making decisions, and chronic uncertainty and indecisiveness often become their cross to bear. For a boy with an obsessive-compulsive style, choosing between the blue shirt and the yellow shirt may go on for half an hour and may remain unsettled in his mind long after an impatient parent has decided for him which he should wear.

The pedantic ideational style of obsessive-compulsive adolescents can make conversing with them trying. These young people are rarely satisfied with an explanation and repeatedly question whether every fact and alternative possibility has been considered. They fuss excessively about the precise meaning of what other persons are saying, frequently interrupting to ask for clarifications of how particular words are being used, and they may with annoying regularity begin their response to a question or declarative statement with a criticism of how it has been framed: "It's not clear what you mean." "Could you be more specific?" "I'm not sure what you're referring to."

The needs of obsessive-compulsive personalities for a point of reference can result, at times, in their sounding snotty or silly when neither is their intent. Asked "How are you feeling today?", for example, the person may respond, "Compared to what?" Because of their cautious ideational style, obsessive-compulsive persons are also likely to use many more words than are necessary to say something and to clutter their speech with superfluous qualifications and elaborations. While trying to be precise and avoid being misunderstood, they frequently end up being long-winded, rambling, digressive, and very, very boring.

Affect

"Still waters run deep" captures the affective style of obsessive-compulsive personalities—strong undercurrents but nary a ripple on the surface. Despite feeling hate, love, and other emotions very deeply, obsessive-compulsives typically show an unemotional face to the world. Their affective style is shaped by defensive reliance on isolation, through which they strip their thoughts of the emotions that would ordinarily accompany them. The result is a somewhat colorless and offhand manner of expressing highly charged attitudes. Whereas another kind of young person might say, "I hate my mother," for example, an obsessive-compulsive adolescent may say, "Sometimes I think I don't like my mother very much."

In this fashion, the verbal communications of individuals with an obsessive-compulsive style typically qualify ("sometimes"), intellectualize ("I think"), and minimize ("not very much") emotions. Like their words, their bodily expressions of emotion are typically constrained and unspontaneous. They rarely show joy and exuberance, nor do they laugh or cry easily. Occasionally, obsessive-compulsive adolescents will be commended by their parents or teachers for their "maturity." In these instances, the adults are usually reacting to what they regard as grown-up emotional control; what they are in fact seeing is more likely to be an abnormal degree of reserve in a drab, overcontrolled youngster who is having difficulty learning to experience affect and enjoy life.

Social Relationships

In keeping with their emotional restraint, obsessive-compulsive adolescents do not mix well socially. They tend to be formal and reserved in how they relate to others, which often contributes to their getting along better with adults than with their peers. With persons of any age, however, they have difficulty expressing their feelings and achieving any kind of easy intimacy. They make friends slowly, if at all, and the relatively few friendships they do form tend to become more intense and to last longer than is common at their age. What is sorely lacking in these young persons as they attempt to relate to others is the capacity to be casual.

Behavior

Caution, restraint, and rigidity pervade the observable behavior of young persons with obsessive-compulsive styles. Activities, like interpersonal relationships, are never taken casually. Plans are made carefully in advance, leaving little to chance, and nothing is done on the spur of the moment. These adolescents tolerate risk poorly, they avoid situations that have an uncertain outcome, and they make a production of everything they do. They pursue their interests doggedly, but rarely with enthusiasm, and they seem constantly to act out of a sense of what should or ought to be done, rather than what would be fun to do.

By virtue of their conservative nature, obsessive-compulsive adolescents often please their parents by their conformity, conventionality, and dependability in such matters as coming home on time, holding on to their money, and taking good care of their belongings. Above all else, in fact, obsessive-compulsive adolescents impose orderliness on their lives. They are neat, clean, and well organized. Everything is kept in its proper place, from the hairs on their head to the books on their desk. Their meticulousness, like several other features of their affective and behavioral style, often makes a favorable impression on adults. After all, points are awarded, not taken off, for neatness.

Obsessive-compulsive youngsters go beyond a reasonable degree of punctuality, thrift, and neatness, however. Such carefulness is not an elective way of life for them, to be pursued when it brings pleasure or rewards and to be exchanged for laxity and sloppiness when they feel like it. Instead, caution and constraint are necessities, obligations that must be met to avoid feeling remiss, even when they result in punishment or ridicule. For example, a boy submits a school assignment late, because he took time to recopy it, and gets a lower grade than he would have received by turning in the original messy copy on time. A girl dresses carefully in a skirt and sweater and appears at a beach cookout looking out of place and is greeted with snickers rather than the compliments that were expected.

Finally, the rigidity of obsessive–compulsive adolescents may extend to their motor behavior. Often, the way they hold themselves seems stiff and uncomfortable, as if they find it as difficult to relax their bodies as their thoughts and feelings. Their movements may look awkward and unnatural, even if they happen to be well-coordinated and athletic. When they use facial expressions or gestures, which is less often than most people, these too strike others as forced or restrained. One observer described an especially constricted, obsessive–compulsive person by saying, "When he smiles, it looks as if his face is going to crack."

OBSESSIVE–COMPULSIVE DISORDER: ORIGINS

The causes of obsessive–compulsive disorder are largely unknown. Because this condition has only recently begun to attract attention from clinical investigators, relatively few reliable data are available concerning its origins. Nevertheless, the literature does provide some suggestions concerning probable *genetic* and *experiential factors* that interact to cause it.

Genetic Factors

A modest body of research indicates that anxiety disorders, like so many other features of behavior, normal and abnormal, run in families. Turner, Beidel, and Costello (1987) report that a group of 7- to 12-year-old children of parents with a diagnosed anxiety disorder were generally more anxious and fearful than two comparison groups of children of normal parents and more than seven times as likely to meet criteria for an anxiety-disorder. The parents and siblings of anxiety-disorder patients are also found to be much more likely than persons in general to develop an anxiety disorder (Rutter, Macdonald, Le Couteur, Harrington, Bolton, & Bailey, 1990). Torgersen (1983) found twice as much concordance for anxiety disorders in 32 identical twin pairs than in 53 nonidentical twin pairs. Barlow (1988) concludes from the available data that "some aspects of anxiety . . . are almost certainly heritable" (p. 176).

Turning specifically to obsessive–compulsive disorder, the results of various studies indicate that approximately 25–30% of obsessive–compulsive children and adolescents have at least one first-degree relative with this same disorder, and up to 70% of the parents of such young persons are likely to show some obsessive–compulsive traits (Lenane, Swedo, Leonard, Pauls, Sceery, & Rapoport, 1990; Riddle et al., 1990; Swedo, 1989). In several twin studies summarized by Inouye (1972), concordance for obsessive-compulsive disorder was found in 27 of 35 identical pairs but not in any of 7 nonidentical pairs.

Because these figures far exceed the general population frequencies for anxiety disorders in general and for obsessive-compulsive disorder in particular, they suggest at least a genetically influenced vulnerability to these disorders. However, family members sharing anxiety disorders often display different symptom patterns, and no specific mode of genetic transmission has yet been identified for these conditions. On this basis, Barlow (1988, Chapter 5) has concluded that the determining factors of any specific anxiety disorder are to be found more in experiential factors than in genetic influences.

Experiential Factors

Numerous theories have been advanced concerning the evolution of obsessive-compulsive disorder from youthful experiences (see Adams, 1973, Chapter 5; Salzman & Thaler, 1981; Sturgis & Meyer, 1981). Common to most of these theories is the previously mentioned postulate that obsessive-compulsive symptoms arise as a way of dealing with or defending against anxiety; specifically, obsessions and compulsions are viewed as helping persons to avoid behaving in ways that they consider unacceptable or fear will get them in difficulty. Most theorists additionally assign an important role to underlying anger in their explanation of obsessive-compulsive symptom formation. The focus on control that characterizes this disorder can easily be seen as reflecting a need to keep aggressive impulses from getting out of hand or even being expressed at all.

However sensible these formulations may be, they do more to describe obsessive-compulsive disorder than to account for its origins. They share with other teleological explanations the shortcoming of attributing the origin of a behavior to consequences of the behavior that do not occur until after the behavior has been expressed. Hence, these explanations say nothing about why the behavior occurred in the first place. Even if obsessions and compulsions do in fact prevent persons from becoming upset, why do individuals choose these particular symptoms instead of phobias, antisocial behavior, or some nonpathological way of coping with anxiety? As for underlying anger, why do some adolescents struggling with underlying anger develop obsessive-compulsive symptoms while other equally hostile adolescents show other forms of psychopathology or none at all?

There are currently no good answers to these questions, but there are some indications that obsessive-compulsive symptoms are most likely to appear in persons who have an obsessive-compulsive personality and that these traits emerge in response to some specific ways in which parents treat their children and set examples for them to follow. Such childrearing influences were first proposed in Freud's (1908/1959; 1913/1958) early papers, in which he attributed an obsessive-compulsive personality style to stressful toilet training. Referring to this personality style as "anal character," he related its primary characteristics to excessive parental zeal in training bowel control. Lavish reward for learning to retain stools leads to frugality, he suggested; high praise for controlling excretion contributes to orderliness; and demandingness against which children rebel produces obstinacy.

Research findings have confirmed that the traits Freud ascribed to the anal character do in fact occur together consistently in some people. There is also some evidence that the degree of a person's "anality" is directly related to the intensity of "anal" attitudes expressed by his or her mother. On the other hand, Freud's description of the anal character has stood the test of time better than his explanations of how it originates. Whereas obsessive–compulsive personality style as he described it is a reliably occurring and identifiable phenomenon, no relationship has been demonstrated between how children are toilet trained and whether they will become frugal, orderly, and obstinate (Fisher & Greenberg, 1977, Chapter 3; Pollack, 1979).

It could be suggested that how children *experience* their toilet training, rather than how it looks to others, determines whether they develop an obsessive–compulsive personality style. However, this type of hypothesis involves circular reasoning that, like teleology, should be avoided in attempting to account for the origins of personality characteristics or psychological disorder. The hypothesis assumes that obsessive–compulsive persons have experienced their toilet training as harsh and traumatic; yet, because of the limited capacity of young children to conceptualize, verbalize, and recollect their experience, the only evidence of their having been stressfully toilet trained is the emergence of obsessive–compulsive traits.

Clinical reasoning tends toward such circularity whenever the quality of a person's experience is not or cannot be assessed independently of the outcome that this experience is postulated to cause. Hypotheses involving this type of reasoning cannot be disproved: If the outcome fails to appear, you simply conclude that the experience did not occur.

Although sometimes stimulating as articles of faith, hypotheses involving circular reasoning contribute little to the advancement of knowledge. To provide powerful explanations of how experiential factors shape obsessive–compulsive traits and other personality characteristics, developmental theories should be derived from current observations of how children are actually being reared. Although toilet training has not been singled out in this regard, observational data do indicate that parents promote obsessive–compulsive personality development by the rewards and punishments they mete out and by the models they set. By specifically encouraging the ideational, affective, interpersonal, and behavioral features of this style while specifically discouraging other patterns, and by conducting their own lives in an obsessive–compulsive fashion, parents shape their children's coping style along obsessive–compulsive lines. The more demanding and perfectionistic they are and the more their children identify with them, the more likely this result becomes (Clark & Bolton, 1985; Hoover & Insel, 1984).

There is good reason to expect that future findings concerning the origins of obsessive–compulsive disorder will implicate both genetic and experiential factors, particularly with respect to personality style. Experiential sources of variation in personality style involve many events that are not shared by family members. This means (a) that shared experience is not especially important in producing personality similarities among persons and (b) that an unequivocal genetic contribution to the familial incidence of obsessive-compulsive and other personality characteristics is likely to be documented (see Goldsmith, 1983). At the same time, because genetic vulnerabilities to psychological disorder undoubtedly interact with family processes in influencing the onset and persistence of any disorder, an unequivocal role for experiential factors in obsessive–compulsive disorder and the same kind of diathesis-stress model introduced in Chapter 3 will prove necessary to account for emerging data on the origins of obsessive–compulsive disorder (see Scarr & McCartney, 1983; Turner, Beidel, & Nathan, 1985).

CASE 8.   OBSESSIVE–COMPULSIVE DISORDER

Gerald was an only child in a middle-class family with no history of psychological disturbance. He had no serious adjustment problems as a child, but at age 11, he was seen by a psychologist in relation to parental concerns about his doing poorly in school and being socially withdrawn. A diagnostic evaluation at that time indicated that he was a shy, somewhat isolated boy who appeared to be developing an obsessive–compulsive personality style but was not manifesting any significant psychopathology. He and his parents were counseled briefly, and although he did not make much progress in forming friendships, the next 4 years passed without significant psychological difficulty.

When he was 15, his grandfather, with whom he had a very close relationship, died after a brief illness. Gerald had visited his bedside daily during the terminal illness. A few weeks following the funeral, he began to develop compulsive rituals. He had to wash his face for 15 minutes in the morning; school assignments had to be read four times and written work copied four times; his school locker had to be checked four times whenever he locked it; and every object he handled had to be placed in a certain way. His waking life became dominated by such rituals, and he was plagued by fears that if he failed to carry them out to the letter, something terrible would happen to his parents or "I'll be drafted into the army and sent to Vietnam and killed" (the year was 1965).

Gerald told his parents about this problem, and they arranged for him to enter therapy. He responded well to a behavioral focus on gaining control of his rituals and became essentially symptom-free over the next 2 months. Some of the specific treatment methods used are described in the next section of this chapter.

During the course of working behaviorally on curbing his rituals, Gerald reported some persistent fantasies that cast some light on his underlying concerns. The number "4," which figured prominently in his rituals, reminded him of the 1940s, which in turn reminded him of World War II. He enjoyed reading war stories and often imagined himself being transported by a time machine back to that war, where he could fight, kill people, and take prisoners without having to risk being harmed himself.

Gerald also revealed that he was a physical fitness enthusiast who kept to an arduous routine of daily calisthenics, was studying judo and karate, and liked to think about "cleaning up on anyone who messes with me." In fact, however, he had never been in a physical fight and had always avoided rough-and-tumble games and sports, because "someone could get hurt." For someone so obviously concerned about being either the agent or the victim of aggression in real life, while so inclined to dwell on both in his fantasies, the sudden death of his grandfather can be seen as an impetus for extreme ritualistic control, intended to minimize the likelihood of any harmful or life-threatening behavior being perpetrated either by or on him.

OBSESSIVE–COMPULSIVE DISORDER: TREATMENT

Obsessive-compulsive disorder can be treated effectively with behavioral methods designed to reduce the frequency of maladaptive responses and increase self-control. Obsessive thoughts are less responsive to behavioral interventions than compulsions, but drug therapy has shown some promise for alleviating excessive rumination. Both behavioral and pharmacological therapies are maximally successful when they are administered in the context of a positive working alliance; accordingly, although psychotherapy is rarely sufficient by itself to eliminate obsessive-compulsive disorder, certain principles of conducting psychotherapy with obsessive-compulsive individuals contribute to rapid and sustained progress in implementing other techniques.

Behavioral Methods

Behavioral therapy of obsessive-compulsive symptoms consists of graduated exercises in exposure and response prevention. As a starting point, therapists need to immerse their patients in the kinds of situations that typically elicit or exacerbate their maladaptive reactions. Such exposure, when planned in concert with reassurance, anticipatory rehearsals, relaxation strategies, and other desensitization techniques designed to minimize discomfort in the situation, lessens the person's needs for anxiety-reducing symptom formation. Most behavior therapists concur, however, that such exposure should be paired with guided practice in preventing maladaptive obsessive-compulsive responses from occurring, in order to provide the individual with the anxiety-provoking situation (see Foa & Rowan, 1990; Kozak, Foa, & Steketee, 1988; Reid, 1983, Chapter 8; Shear & Frosch, 1986).

Exposure and response prevention techniques in the treatment of anxiety disorders, as first formulated by Wolpe (1958), were originally administered in fantasy. The patient, sitting in the therapist's office, was asked to imagine anxiety-provoking situations and was helped to rehearse ways of feeling more comfortable in these situations and responding in a nonsymptomatic manner. Such exposure and rehearsal in fantasy has largely been replaced over the years by more potent confrontation in real life. Real-life confrontation with an anxiety-provoking situation and actual practice in preventing obsessive-compulsive symptoms from occurring have generally proven more effective in helping persons to master these symptoms than merely imagining situations and how they might be managed (Barlow, 1988, Chapter 16; Marks, 1981, Chapter 3).

The emergence of live-exposure methods paved the way for discovering the efficacy of homework assignments in the treatment of obsessive-compulsive disorder. These assignments call for patients to confront problematic situations on their own, armed by the therapist with a repertoire of alternative responses for moderating their distress and minimizing their obsessive-compulsive tendencies.

In addition to whatever immediate symptom reduction is achieved through such practice in exposure and response prevention, considerable benefit derives from the fact that homework assignments are carried out by the patient, in the therapist's absence. Such self-directed assertion of mastery is enormously reinforcing. It signals to obsessive-compulsive patients that they have the ability to suppress maladaptive behaviors that have seemed beyond their control. Discovering that they can harness—even if only temporarily—the forces that have been driving them to distraction creates some optimism about overcoming their condition. Such emerging self-confidence generates positive expectations that increase the likelihood of further success in efforts to hold their symptoms in check. The therapist's task is to engender an ameliorative cycle in which a beginning glimmer of progress spurs some hope and effort, which results in greater progress and even more hope and effort, and so on.

Three other considerations should be kept in mind in crafting homework assignments for obsessive-compulsive patients. First, these assignments should be presented in ways that are congruent with and capitalize on any obsessive-compulsive features in the patient's personality style. Vagueness and generalities should be avoided. Instead, by presenting a precise and detailed plan that appears to leave nothing to chance, the therapist can harmonize with needs the person may have to maximize orderliness and minimize ambiguity. Telling these patients exactly what they should do helps them to feel both comfortable with the treatment plan and able to carry it out.

Second, the therapist should anticipate the possibility of failure, or at least incomplete success, in order to avert premature discouragement. Patients need to be told that their initial efforts at response prevention are akin to trying to start a large boulder rolling downhill. The first efforts to budge such a formidable object may dislodge it only slightly, if at all. Initial difficulties are to be expected and do not mean that the task cannot be accomplished.

Continuing to put a shoulder to the obstacle will eventually get it moving, and, once its inertia is overcome, it will begin to roll along with increasing speed. Arming patients with this kind of message helps them persevere with homework assignments, especially early in the treatment before they have benefited from the reinforcing effects of initial success in exerting control over their symptoms.

Third, successful implementation of homework assignments with adolescent patients may require active involvement of family members. The lives of parents and siblings are often affected by an adolescents' obsessive-compulsive symptoms, as when a girl's cleanliness checks regularly delay mealtimes, and family members sometimes become direct participants in a patient's symptoms, as when a boy can go comfortably to bed at night only after being allowed to kiss everybody on both cheeks and say a prayer over them. If homework assignments are to succeed, others in the household may have to join in as willing reinforcement agents. This is especially the case when ritualistic behavior is being treated by efforts to replace it with different or less extreme rituals.

A first step in getting the kissing and praying boy under control, for example, may consist of getting him to skip the prayer, and the next step may be getting him to feel satisfied with kissing on just one cheek instead of two. The therapeutic task for family members in this plan would be to refrain from criticizing the adolescent for still becoming frantic without one kiss from everybody and instead to praise his progress in first doing without the prayer and then cutting back from two kisses to one. As this example illustrates, the therapist working with obsessive-compulsive adolescents needs to enlist family collaboration in response prevention and also to guide family members in responding supportively to the pace of progress in the treatment.

Available evidence indicates that most obsessive-compulsive patients improve in response to a systematically orchestrated behavioral intervention. Although few are totally and permanently relieved of their symptoms, considerable reduction in the intensity and pervasiveness of symptoms can be expected. Symptoms removed or reduced by this approach are ordinarily not replaced by new and different symptoms. To the contrary, successful behavioral intervention in these cases is typically followed not by symptom substitution but by general functioning improvement in a broad range of situations and activities that were not even discussed in the therapy. A favorable outcome is more likely in adolescents than in adults, particularly when the episode of disorder being treated is the first to have occurred, has been of short duration, and emerged suddenly in the presence of apparent precipitating factors. Conversely, treatment becomes more difficult and success less assured when an obsessive-compulsive adolescent has an earlier history of symptomatic episodes unrelated to obvious precipitants (see Marks, 1981, Chapter 4; Marks, 1987, Chapter 15; Steinberg, 1983, Chapter 10).

Various methods in the behavioral treatment of obsessive-compulsive disorder are described in detail by Berg, Rapoport, and Wolf (1989); Foa and Tillmanns (1980); Lichstein (1988); Rachman and Hodgson (1980); and

Sturgis and Meyer (1981), among others. These methods can be illustrated further by returning briefly to the case of Gerald, whose treatment was elaborated in an earlier publication (Weiner, 1967).

The central strategy in working with Gerald was to replace his pervasive rituals with delimited and less maladaptive rituals. Implicit in this plan were companion efforts to utilize rather than to challenge his obsessive-compulsive style and to promote his sense of self-determination. These goals were pursued by establishing some positive purpose for each of a series of target rituals and then constructing a substitute ritual that would achieve the same purpose more quickly and efficiently.

The first target, identified by asking him to choose where the treatment should begin, was his compulsive checking of his school locker four times whenever he locked it. Asked why he checked the lock, he responded, "Because if I don't I'm afraid I'll end up in Viet Nam." He was then told that this was a negative reason, indicating what was *bad* about *not* checking his lock, and that he was being asked what was *good* about checking it. After some reflection, he replied that checking the lock was a worthwhile precaution against having things stolen. The therapist praised this concern with safeguarding his belongings as a sound *positive* reason for making sure that his locker was locked, following which he asked him to specify exactly what actions were reasonably necessary to guarantee such protection. Gerald concluded that locking the lock carefully and then checking it once should be sufficient to ensure the safety of his belongings.

Gerald was then told that for the next week, every time he closed his locker he was to lock the lock carefully, check it once, and then take one step back, put his hands in his pockets, and say to himself the following: "I have checked the lock; I can now be certain it is locked, and everything in the locker is safe and protected; there is absolutely no positive reason for me to check it again; I am now going to walk away from my locker and go to class." He was further instructed that he might not always be able to succeed in this assignment, and that, should he feel unable to resist rechecking the lock, he should go ahead and do so. However, he was not to fret about such lapses and was by all means to try the prescribed formula the next time and every subsequent time he used his locker.

Similar procedures were applied to a long list of rituals that Gerald selected as treatment targets. For each, he was helped to identify some positive value in the behaviors (most of the values he specified involved neatness, cleanliness, or thoroughness); he was asked to decide what steps should be sufficient to ensure the positive value (in each instance, he expressed confidence in actions far less repetitive than his current rituals); and he was rehearsed in some alternate, relatively economical ritual based on his specifications and a series of justifying statements to repeat to himself as he executed the modified behavior. He was also repeatedly instructed that some failures were inevitable, should not concern him, and did not mean that he was losing the battle against his disturbance.

Gerald carried out his instructions faithfully, and, in the course of six weekly sessions, he achieved marked behavior change. In each case, the newly prescribed rituals either replaced or greatly diminished his former rituals. For example, instead of washing his face for 15 minutes in the morning, he was now using his watch to terminate his face-washing precisely after 3 minutes, a time period he had specified as sufficient to ensure cleanliness. As he succeeded in attenuating his rituals, his feelings of being dominated by unrealistic, uncontrollable urges and his general anxiety level abated dramatically. Over an ensuing 7-month follow-up period, he remained essentially free of seriously maladaptive symptoms and even began spontaneously to give up most of the substitute rituals that had been established in the therapy.

Drug Therapy

Clinical reports indicate that behavioral methods are more effective in treating compulsive rituals than obsessive thoughts. Whereas the combination of live exposure and response prevention can be expected to yield positive results in about 75% of patients with prominent compulsions and rituals, only 40–45% of obsessional patients without rituals improve in response to these techniques (Christensen, Hadzi-Pavlovic, Andrews, & Mattick, 1987; Mavassakalian, 1986).

Two likely reasons for this differential effect can be suggested. First, with respect to exposure, the situations that elicit compulsive rituals, such as starting to get dressed, are more specific and easier to identify than situations that provoke obsessive ruminations. Hence, assignments designed to provide live exposure can be devised more readily and with more assurance of evoking symptomatic behavior in treating rituals than in working with ruminations. Second, with respect to response prevention, it is more within the realm of possibility for people to stop themselves from executing some motor movement, no matter how difficult this may be, than for them to stop themselves from thinking certain thoughts.

Pharmacological developments in the 1980s demonstrate that clomipramine hydrochloride, a tricyclic antidepressant marketed as Anafranil, can be useful in the treatment of obsessive–compulsive disorder, especially with respect to obsessional thinking. About 50% of both adult and child patients in various clinical trials have shown marked reduction in both obsessive and compulsive symptoms within a few weeks of beginning clomipramine therapy (Christensen et al., 1987; Jaffe & Magnuson, 1985; Jenike, Baer, Summergrad, & Weilburg, 1989; Leonard, 1989b). These positive effects have been noted in patients who had previously been unresponsive to other tricyclic medication, and both observed and self-reported improvements while on clomipramine appear independent of any of its antidepressant effects. Accordingly, although the nature of the clomipramine effect is not yet known, there is some reason for regarding it as having specific antiobsessional properties (Flament, Rapoport, Berg, Sceery, Kilts, Mellstrom, & Linnoila, 1985; Reid, 1983, Chapter 8).

On the other hand, even among those obsessive–compulsive patients who respond favorably to clomipramine therapy, their symptoms become less intense but rarely disappear. Furthermore, the benefits of the drug persist for only as long as it is being taken. When medication has been the only therapy, its cessation is likely to be followed by a relapse in which the obsessive–compulsive symptoms return in full force (Flament et al., 1985; Mavassakalian, 1983, 1986; Pato, Zohar-Kadouch, Zohar, & Murphy, 1988).

These findings identify the importance of combining whatever drug therapy may seem indicated with psychological interventions designed to promote self-directions and sustained improvement that is not drug dependent. This is especially true for adolescents, concerned as they usually are about being in control of their own fate and avoiding imperfections of mind and body. Requiring them to ingest substances that control them and to submit to daily routines that signify being flawed (such as having to take medication) can interfere with their feeling good about themselves and moving rapidly to overcome their difficulties. Drug therapy that seems necessary and appropriate typically works best with adolescents when it is implemented not as the central focus of the therapy, but instead in the context of an ongoing therapist-patient relationship and as part of a broadly focused, multimodal treatment plan (Ryan & Puig-Antich, 1987).

Even the most advantageous combinations of behavioral and pharmacological treatment often fail to prevent obsessive–compulsive disorder from running a chronic course, however, even when there is an initially positive response to the therapy. On the positive side, research studies indicate that, among obsessive–compulsive patients treated with exposure and response prevention, approximately one half become either symptom-free or much improved by the end of their therapy, and another 40% show moderate improvement (Barlow, 1988, Chapter 16). Obsessive-compulsive patients treated with appropriate medication show a 30-60% reduction in their symptoms, which is typically experienced by them as a very significant improvement in their capacity to function effectively and avoid feeling anxious (White & Cole, 1990).

On the other hand, the majority of persons who develop obsessive–compulsive disorder, despite benefiting from treatment, remain symptomatic to some extent. This persistence of disorder obtains for adolescents as well as for adults. Of the obsessive–compulsive disorder patients studied by the Rapoport research group, 25 who were first seen between age 10 and age 18 years were reevaluated 2-7 years following their treatment. Seventeen of these patients demonstrated diagnosable obsessive–compulsive disorder on this follow-up (Flament, Koby, Rapoport, & Berg, 1990).

Psychotherapy

Clinicians of many different theoretical persuasions generally concur that traditional psychotherapy is relatively ineffective in ameliorating obsessive-compulsive disorder and rarely succeeds as the sole mode of intervention (see Jenike, 1990; Rapoport, 1986; Reid, 1983; Sturgis & Meyer, 1981; Salzman & Thaler, 1981). The main shortcoming of insight-oriented therapy in overcoming this disorder derives from the poor fit between free-associative techniques and the communication style that obsessive-compulsives typically bring to the patient-therapist interaction. Spontaneity is anathema to these individuals, and selecting from among their vast array of mental contents those that are most pertinent to the purposes of the therapy is foreign to their nature.

Consequently, when given the traditional injunction of dynamic psychotherapy to talk as freely as they can about their thoughts, feelings, and experiences, obsessive-compulsives are likely to proceed in one of several sterile directions: (a) They may find it so difficult to talk in the absence of guidance concerning what they should talk about that they say little or nothing; (b) they may curb their anxiety in the face of uncertainty by carefully rehearsing or even writing down in advance what they will say in each session; or (c) they may simply avoid making choices by reporting everything they can recall or that pops into their minds, thereby going into excruciatingly irrelevant detail and rambling, unfocused digressions. The therapist who hews strictly to a free-association approach will have a patient who produces either too little material to support the construction of useful interpretations or too much material to allow opportunities for incisive interventions—that is, the therapist has trouble getting a word in edgewise.

At the same time, the development and implementation of behavioral strategies cannot proceed effectively in the context of a mechanical, impersonal interaction. Patient and therapist need to have a working alliance in which they can talk together about the symptoms to be addressed, about the kinds of anxieties these symptoms are serving to allay, and about the successes and failures the patient experiences in trying to overcome them. As elaborated by Salzman (1968, Chapter 9), these conversations should be directed by the therapist in an active, energetic fashion, from the beginning to the end of the treatment. Especially important in this regard is therapist dedication to intruding on the obsessive-compulsive patient's inclinations either to digress or to avoid spontaneity.

Digression and irrelevant detail can be minimized by the therapist's pointing out when they occur and explicitly directing the patient back to the mainstream of the topic under discussion. In addition to keeping a therapy session moving, these intrusions, when presented in a manner that helps the patient take them as well-intended observations and not as hostile criticism, foster patient progress toward being able to recognize and curb such rambling without therapist intervention.

Spontaneity is promoted whenever the therapist finds an appropriate occasion either for disallowing discussion of some well-rehearsed topic or insisting on discussion of some thought, feeling, or experience that has just arisen without the patient having had time to cogitate on what to say about it. The obsessive-compulsive patient who brings in a written statement ("I wanted to be sure to explain this in just the right way, so I've put down the words that really say it best") should be required, however much he or she protests, to talk about what is on the piece of paper rather than to read it or hand it over to the therapist. The patient who stumbles onto a new idea or recollection during a session and proposes to go into it further next time, after being able to go home and give it "proper and full" consideration, should be told that the time is now. Like incursions against digression, such insistence on spontaneity, delivered in a supportive and encouraging fashion, serve a dual purpose: It enriches the content of therapy sessions, and it helps obsessive-compulsive patients recognize aspects of their behavior that they should and can modify to good effect.

SCHOOL PHOBIA: CHARACTERISTICS

Phobias are unrealistic, disruptive fears of relatively harmless objects or events. Unlike rational fears of dangerous situations, phobic dread serves no obvious protective purpose. It persists out of proportion to any actual danger present and typically cannot be relieved by explanations or reassurances that there is nothing to fear.

Three categories of phobic disorder can be reliably discriminated: *agoraphobia*, an irrational dread of being among crowds of people; *simple phobia*, an unreasoning fear of such phenomena as snakes, storms, and the dark; and *social phobia*, an unwarranted anticipation of humiliation and embarrassment in the presence of others (see Di Nardo et al., 1983; Taylor & Arnow, 1988, Chapters 8-10). Epidemiological studies indicate that phobic disorders have a median age of onset of just 13 and are more likely to begin between the ages of 5 and 9 than during any other 5-year age period (Burke, Burke, Regier, & Rae, 1990). Neither agoraphobia nor simple phobia has any special relevance to adolescent development, but social phobia touches on some common developmental concerns of young people and is particularly likely to begin following puberty (Barbaree & Marshall, 1985; Fyer & Klein, 1986; Marks, 1987, Chapter 11).

Adolescence is normatively a period of heightened self-consciousness and worrying about "looking good" and saying and doing the right thing. Bodily changes cause concerns about growing to a desirable size and shape in the right places. Increasing autonomy and involvement in dating and sexuality cause concerns about how best to respond in a host of previously unfamiliar situations. Adolescents must frequently fly by the seat of their pants, trying to appear competent and self-assured while engaging in many behaviors for the first time, and they anticipate correctly that others will be measuring their adequacy and attractiveness by how quickly they can master a new repertoire of social and interpersonal skills.

Given the myriad possibilities for steering the wrong course in such uncharted waters, early and middle adolescence becomes, for most young persons, a succession of gingerly taken steps dogged by ever-present risk of blundering into scorn and disapproval. The normative self-consciousness generates a keen sensitivity to being observed and judged, especially by persons whose opinion and esteem are valued. Even when no one is really paying much attention to them, adolescents typically conduct their affairs while wondering who might be watching and what impressions they are likely to form. This not-uncommon preoccupation with being observed by persons who are passing judgment, even when no one else is around, is captured in Elkind's concept of the "imaginary audience" (Elkind & Bowen, 1979; Lechner & Rosenthal, 1984).

Among adolescents who develop anxiety disorders, this normatively el-evated self-consciousness and sensitivity to being observed and evaluated provides a disposition to social phobia that is not found in children and that rarely emerges for the first time in adulthood (Strauss & Lahey, 1987; Turner & Beidel, 1989). Among possible settings likely to provoke social phobias in young persons, the school merits most attention: Adolescents ordinarily spend much of their time at school or in school-related activities; being in school creates considerable exposure to being observed; and, as a peer-group environment, the school subjects adolescents to the scrutiny of those whose judgments are particularly crucial to their self-esteem.

For these reasons, phobic dread of attending school emerges as a notewor-thy and distinctive pattern of anxiety disorder among adolescents, especially during the junior high school and early high school years. The actual fre-quency of this disorder is uncertain, however, partly because it has never been employed as a standard diagnostic category and partly because it often goes unrecognized or unreported. In one study, for example, one third of a group of adults who gave a clear history of school phobia had never been referred for professional help (Tyrer & Tyrer, 1974). Best estimates are that this condition occurs in 0.5 to 1.0% of the school population each year; that it is present in 3 to 8% of young persons who are seen clinically; and that it peaks as a reason for referral to a mental health professional between 13 and 15 years of age (Ferrari, 1986; Hersov, 1990; Last & Strauss, 1990).

Two other basic facts about school phobia have emerged from clinical surveys. First, it occurs about equally in males and females. Among several hundred cases of school phobia included in 17 different studies reviewed by Gordon and Young (1976), 260 were boys and 267 were girls. Subsequent assessments concur that both school phobia and its expression in school refusal occur with similar frequency in males and females (Hersov, 1990; Turner & Beidel, 1989).

Second, school-phobic young persons do not differ from their classmates in intelligence or achievement level. Both IQ scores and levels of attainment are distributed similarly in school-phobic youngsters and in the general school population (Hampe, Miller, Barrett, & Noble, 1973).

School phobia is manifested clinically in certain patterns of symptom formation that help to establish its differential diagnosis. In addition, school phobia occurs in both acute and chronic forms, the difference between which has important implications for treatment planning.

Symptom Patterns

School phobia consists of a reluctance or refusal to go to school because of intense anxiety experienced in the school setting. School-phobic adolescents typically express their reluctance to attend school through physical complaints that convince their parents to keep them home, such as a headache, stomachache, nausea, or a sore throat. Although they may exaggerate such complaints, school-phobic youngsters usually suffer real physical distress at the prospect of being in the classroom, including pain, diarrhea, vomiting, and even fever. Occasionally, they anticipate rather than suffer such problems, in which case they warn their parents that they are certain to become ill if they are sent to school. In other instances, either in addition to or instead of physical ailments, school-phobic adolescents offer various criticisms of the school situation as their reason for not wanting to attend: The teachers are unfair, the work is boring, the bus ride is too long, the other students are unfriendly, and so forth.

Whether expressed as physical complaints or as criticisms of the school, school-phobic apprehensions cannot be ignored or suppressed. If these young persons are forced to go to school, they often become so ill or upset that they have to be sent home. Nevertheless, neither their physical discomfort nor their other complaints can be taken at face value.

The bodily symptoms of school-phobic adolescents tend to appear in the morning when they wake up and to disappear shortly after it has been decided that they can stay home. Should it later be suggested that, because they are feeling better, they should go to school after lunch, their symptoms quickly reappear. If they are then given permission to remain at home for the rest of the day, their symptoms abate once more and do not return until the next morning. Should their parents then decide to forget about school for the rest of the week, they are likely to stay in good health and spirits until the following Monday, when the aches and pains resume in full force. Weekends are an especially good time for school-phobic adolescents, because they can be active and enjoy themselves without risking any pressures to go to school. For concerned parents, school phobia is similarly a roller-coaster experience. A symptom-free afternoon or weekend lulls them into believing that the problem is over, but the dawn of the next day or the arrival of Monday morning puts a sick child back on their hands.

As for criticisms of the school raised by school-phobic adolescents, these invariably turn out to be rationalizations rather than their real reasons for wanting to avoid the school setting. Attempts to respond constructively to their complaints, as by arranging for different teachers, putting them into alternative classes, driving them to school, or even sending them to a different school, bring only temporary relief. At first, the adolescent expresses pleasure and appreciation and approaches the changed school situation with enthusiasm. A few days or weeks later, however, he or she is back home again, feeling ill or complaining about some aspect of the new situation. Beginning with a 1941 article by Johnson, Falstein, Szurek, and Svendsen that introduced the term *school phobia* into the literature, clinical reports over the years have consistently demonstrated that this condition originates not in the stated complaints, but in unstated and sometimes unconscious concerns about being in school (see Eisenberg, 1958; Kahn & Nursten, 1962; Radin, 1967; Waldfogel, Coolidge, & Hahn, 1957).

These and other features of school phobia distinguish it from realistic fears about school and from truancy. A boy who is being intimidated by a bully or who expects to fail an examination may be realistically apprehensive about going to school. Should he learn that the bully has been expelled or the examination canceled, his fears will evaporate. Phobic anxiety, because it derives from exaggerated concerns that go beyond what is immediately apparent, rarely disappears following such obvious or superficial changes in the environment.

With respect to truancy, it is interesting to note that one of the first clinical descriptions of school phobia appeared in a paper by Broadwin (1932) addressed to "the study of truancy." Broadwin reviewed his experience with young persons who were consistently absent from school for extended periods of time during which they remained at home with their parents' knowledge. These absentees could offer no comprehensible reason for their school refusal, other than that they were fearful and unable to function there. While at home, on the other hand, they remained happy, content, and otherwise symptom-free.

Subsequent clinical and research reports have established that such a pattern of difficulty attending school has little in common with typical truancy. Truant adolescents usually dislike school, are doing poorly in their studies, and are busy seeking ways to amuse themselves away from home without their parents' knowledge or consent. By contrast, most school-phobic youngsters linger at home with their parents' consent if not their approval. At school, they tend to be earning at least average grades, and they typically want to do well in their studies and are worried about falling behind. When asked, they say they enjoy school and wish they could find a way to return (see Barth, 1986, Chapter 7; Galloway, 1985; Hersov & Berg, 1980; Sommer, 1985).

School phobia also should be differentiated from separation anxiety. Refusal to attend school shows two distinct peaks of incidence, one between ages 5 and 7 years and the other from ages 11 to 14 years (Blyth & Simmons, 1983; Hersov, 1990; Rutter, Tizard, Yule, Graham, & Whitmore, 1976). These two peak periods of onset correspond to times of major transition in a young person's life, the early years of elementary school and entrance into junior and senior high school.

When school refusal appears in the first few grades of elementary school, its symptoms typically have less to do with concerns about being in school than with anxieties about being separated from one's parents. School-age children with separation anxiety usually fear that being away from home or their parents opens the door to some calamity. These apprehensions are often evoked or exacerbated by such events as a parent becoming ill or entering the hospital for an operation, a fire or burglary occurring at home while no one was there, or hearing parents talk about getting a divorce or going away on a vacation. Children in whom such events precipitate inordinate separation anxiety seem to feel a responsibility to be at home to "make sure" that nothing bad happens there (see Atkinson, Quarrington, & Cyr, 1985; Estes, Haylett, & Johnson, 1956; Nader, Bullock, & Caldwell, 1975).

By contrast, true school phobia consists not of school refusal related to anxieties about being away from home, but of apprehensions and trepidations about distressing aspects of the school situation. Developmental anxieties about being separated from their parents and home may and often do dispose young persons to school-phobic reactions. However, separation anxieties more commonly occur prior to than during adolescence, and they do not produce a phobic aversion to the school setting in the absence of embarrassments and humiliations associated specifically with being in school. Because of the enhanced propensity to social discomfort that accompanies becoming an adolescent, the 11- to 14-year-old incidence peak for school refusal derives mainly from school phobia, as precisely defined, whereas the 5- to 7-year-old peak occurs chiefly as a reflection of separation anxiety.

These and other differences between the separation-anxiety disorders of younger children and the school-phobic disorders of adolescents have been carefully examined by Last and her colleagues (Last, Francis, Hersen, Kazdin, & Strauss, 1987; Last & Strauss, 1990). Their findings confirm that school-phobic disorder has a later age of onset and leads to more refusal to attend school than separation-anxiety disorder. On the other hand, 92% of the separation-anxiety subjects they studied, compared to 63% of their school-phobic subjects, had some other diagnosable condition as well, most often an affective disorder or some other anxiety disorder. Their two groups differed sharply in whether their fears were primarily of being in school (the school-phobic group) or of being away from home (the separation-anxiety group). As they note, their data seem sufficient to validate distinguishing between these two kinds of disorders, either of which can result in school phobia but for different reasons.

Acute and Chronic School Phobia

School-phobic reactions first appear as an acute disorder. The symptoms emerge suddenly in a young person without previous school attendance or other behavioral problems, and they can easily be traced to recent anxiety-provoking school events. Although acute episodes of school phobia may recur, they do not interfere with activities outside of school. Acute school phobics typically keep busy and feel content so long as they are allowed to stay at home. They maintain their friendships, enjoy social activities, and, if their schoolwork is sent home, pursue their studies without complaint.

Although acute school phobia can occur at any age and has even been reported in college students (Hodgman & Braiman, 1965), it is much more likely to occur early rather than later in adolescence. As time passes, the prevailing pattern of school phobia shifts from episodic reactions to chronic and persistent disorder. Chronic school phobia develops gradually, in the absence of obvious stressors, in adolescents who have a history of behavior problems, including acute school phobia. Consistent with this distinction, acute school phobia has traditionally been described as "neurotic crisis" and chronic school phobia as a "way of life" (Coolidge, Hahn, & Peck, 1957; Miller, Barrett, & Hampe, 1974; Paccione-Dyszlewski & Contessa-Kislus, 1987).

Unlike acute school phobia, chronic school phobia involves adjustment difficulties beyond refusal to attend school. Chronically school-phobic adolescents tend to withdraw not just from the classroom but from other previously enjoyed activities as well. They mope around the house without accomplishing very much and show little inclination to work at their studies or to pursue hobbies. They become uncomfortable in interpersonal or unfamiliar situations outside of school as well as in it, and they cling to their home and parents at the expense of social contact with their peers. In one study of 26 chronically school-phobic adolescents, 18 met *DSM-III* criteria for depressive disorder, 16 met criteria for anxiety disorder, and 13 had both other conditions (Bernstein & Garfinkel, 1986). The longer that school-phobic reactions last and the more frequently they recur, the more likely it becomes that such widespread adjustment problems will also be present.

SCHOOL PHOBIA: ORIGINS

The etiology of phobic disorders is largely unknown. Various theories have attributed phobias to fears generalized from traumatic learning experiences, to the modeling by young persons of fears they observe in their parents, and to the displacement of feelings and attitudes from their real source to previously neutral objects or situations. Regarding the first of these theories, the generalization of conditioned responses is known to shape many aspects of human behavior, but most phobias actually develop in the absence of specific frightening experiences. As for modeling, even though excessive fears can undoubtedly be fostered by parental behavior, many kinds of phobias, including school phobia, develop without young persons having observed their parents showing similar aversive reactions. Also, displacement, like many psychoanalytic concepts of neurotic symptom formation, provides a useful description of the process that is taking place but does not adequately account for why this particular process rather than some other process is occurring.

In contrast to these uncertainties, research findings clearly demonstrate that phobic disorder is a familial condition. First-degree relatives of patients with phobias are more likely than people in general to develop phobic reactions; there is greater concordance for phobic disorder among identical than nonidentical twins; and children with agoraphobic mothers show an elevated likelihood of becoming school phobic (Harris, Noyes, Crowe, & Chaudry, 1983; Kendler, Heath, Martin, & Eaves, 1986; Noyes, Crowe, Harris, Hamra, McChesney, & Chaudry, 1986; Rutter et al., 1990).

As is generally the case for anxiety disorders, however, critical data regarding the heritability of phobic disorder are sparse. The available information points to a lesser role for biogenetic factors in phobias than in schizophrenia and affective disorders. There is little basis for suggesting any genetic transmission beyond a probable constitutional vulnerability to these conditions in general, and current data are inadequate to support either a psychosocial formulation of how phobias originate or a biogenetic theory of what causes them (see Delprato, 1980; Fyer & Klein, 1986; Turner & Beidel, 1989).

In the absence of definitive etiological studies, the origins of phobias in general and of school phobia in particular can still be conceptualized effectively according to an interaction hypothesis embracing vulnerability to disorder and negative life events. Accordingly, the probability that a young person will become unreasonably fearful of being in school can be estimated from a particular set of disposing and precipitating factors that are typically found in association with school-phobic disorder.

Disposing Factors

Clinical experience and numerous case findings strongly suggest that the disposition to school phobia emerges from a pattern of family interaction that promotes excessive dependency. Mother, father, and child are each active participants in this interaction.

The Mother's Role

The mothers of school-phobic youngsters tend to be dependent women who resent having had to sacrifice their own needs to the nurturant requirements of their children and who doubt their own capacity to provide their children with adequate mothering. Having such thoughts and feelings typically induces these mothers to overprotect their children from early in life. Every possible effort is made to satisfy their children's wants, to shield them from deprivation and frustration, and to court their children's love and affection. Being solicitous and dedicated to their children often helps these mothers to deny their resentment of parental responsibilities and to suppress their feelings of being an incompetent parent: "Look at what a good job I am doing," their actions say, "and how much my child loves me" (see Berg & McGuire, 1974; Clyne, 1966; Waldron, Shrier, Stone, & Tobin, 1975).

Yet even the most solicitous of parents encounter demands that try their patience and sense of propriety. The mothers of school-phobic children often sow the seeds for school refusal by failing to deal calmly and firmly with such demands. Because of their dependent nature, these women retreat from angry confrontations; because of their need to keep in their children's good graces, they give in to requests they consider unreasonable or excessive. This capitulation has unfortunate consequences for both mother and child. The mother, already burdened by her limited sense of competence, feels overwhelmed and exploited by her child and becomes increasingly resentful of having to bear a parent's burden. The child, having discovered that insistence can triumph over adult authority, power, and good sense, gravitates toward further manipulative tactics and unrealistic expectations: "I can get my own way if I make enough fuss."

Typically, then, these are mothers who foster dependency in their children: They go to great lengths to cushion them from discomfort; they discipline their children through bribes, appeals to reason, and pleas for consideration; and they prefer to keep their children close physically as well as psychologically. When school phobia first threatens, they usually respond in ways that compound the problem. Should their youngster grumble about a situation in school, they are quick to commiserate and agree or even suggest that a few days away from school might be in order. Hearing complaints of headache or stomach pain, they seldom doubt the advisability of remaining at home.

These mothers are transparently ambivalent toward a school-phobic pattern once it has become established and toward the efforts of any therapist whose counsel they seek. While paying lip service to a prompt return to school, they covertly communicate to their nonattending children that they enjoy having them at home and are not contemplating drastic action to abort their school refusal: "You're supposed to go back to school today, but it looks like rain, and I don't want you catching cold, so let's wait until the weather clears." While appealing for the therapist's help in altering their children's nonattendance and their overdependence as well, they convey that what they really want is for little to be changed.

The mixed feeling these mothers have concerning treatment for their school-phobic youngsters are often apparent from the first interview. The therapist may find the mother huddled close to her child in the waiting room, as if preparing him or her for the worst. She may promptly advise the therapist that the youngster will have difficulty leaving her side, even as she clutches the child firmly or by the tone of her voice reveals that she does not want to surrender him or her to another's care. In the older adolescent, where such blatant infantilizing is rare, at least in public, it is still common for the mother to intrude on the interviewer's initial efforts to relate to the patient, as if to ensure that any diagnostic or therapeutic transactions will proceed only through her. These mothers customarily expect and prefer to be interviewed first and to have their youngster interviewed in their presence.

Should the adolescent respond eagerly to the therapist's overtures, these mothers often exhibit disappointment and hurt. If the therapist then takes the adolescent alone into the office, the mother may hover just outside the door, ever-ready to rush in and soothe the anguish she anticipates or hopes her child will experience when thus separated from her. In a joint interview, these mothers usually dominate the conversation to such an extent that the therapist has little opportunity to engage the youngster or begin to kindle a positive treatment relationship.

The Father's Contribution

The fathers of school-phobic youngsters typically intensify the problematic mother–child relationship in the family by failing to provide any counteractive balance to their wives' overprotection. Most often, these fathers are passive, dependent men who share with their wives a need to protect and cater to their children as a way of keeping them close and ensuring their love. These fathers tend to be more concerned with maintaining peace in the home, at whatever price, than with providing rules or administering discipline. Like their wives, they accordingly retreat from any hint of impending unpleasantness and yield to their children's demands at the first sign of tears or tantrums. This leaves the child confronting not one but two parents whose approach to childrearing fosters the dependency, inflated self-confidence, and manipulative proclivities that are associated with susceptibility to school phobia (see Chotiner & Forrest, 1974; Malmquist, 1965; Skynner, 1974).

These fathers also share their wives' ambivalence toward school phobia and its treatment. They exhort their youngster to return to school, and they express to the therapist their unqualified support for whatever measures may be necessary to resolve the attendance difficulty. Yet these men show a striking inclination to seize on reasons for delay ("Maybe we should wait until the beginning of next week rather than tomorrow to take him back, sort of give him the weekend to enjoy himself"); to capitulate to blatant manipulation ("But, Doctor, she says she'll stop eating if we make her go back as we agreed on, and we shouldn't risk letting her get sick, should we?"); and directly to dilute or sabotage the treatment ("I know he's supposed to see you today, but I've got this important meeting that came up, and my wife doesn't like to drive in afternoon traffic, and there's no other way to get him there, so maybe we could let it go for this week").

In some instances, fathers foster the disposition to school phobia indirectly, not by being overprotective themselves but by encouraging their wives to be. These tend to be men who are detached from their families and too absorbed in their own activities to pay much attention to what goes on at home. A close mother–child relationship suits the purposes of the disinterested father well, because it spares him from being bothered with parental responsibilities. Not unusually, this type of father of a school-phobic remains unaware that his youngster is missing school until the nonattendance comes by chance to his attention—he calls home during the day and his child answers, for example, or the school principal contacts him to discuss a prolonged absence.

Such obliviousness often reflects not only paternal detachment but also a pact between mother and child to keep the attendance problem as their "secret." These pacts usually develop from the mother's attempts to cultivate her child's tractability at home by bribing him or her with the promise not to tell the father of the school refusal. The youngster in turn capitalizes on this opportunity to trade good behavior at home for the pledge that the father, who can be expected to be unsympathetic and less manipulable than the mother, will not be informed. When this type of father finally learns of the school-phobic situation, he usually becomes furious and blames the problem on his wife. Should the school-phobic reaction persist, he tends to vacillate between berating his wife for her inept motherhood and "washing his hands" of the whole business; in either case, his behavior serves only to intensify the previously existing difficulties.

The School Phobic's Orientation

In response to the childrearing practices of their parents, young persons who are disposed to school phobia usually develop three characteristic orientations to their experience. First, having been overprotected, they tend to grow through childhood and into adolescence as highly dependent and clinging individuals. Their poor preparation for autonomy and self-reliance exposes them to considerable anxiety whenever they are expected or required to act on their own. Their first inclination in such situations is to withdraw to the safe and undemanding dependency they have known at home under their parents' wing.

Second, because of the way in which their parents have catered to them and even encouraged them to impose their needs on the family, these children frequently become demanding and manipulative. They want what they want when they want it. They whine, plead, cry, yell, stamp their feet, hold their breath, make all sorts of promises and threats—whatever they think may be effective in bending a situation to their will. When they cannot get their own way, they take their marbles and go home, which is a metaphor that aptly captures what happens when they refuse to stay in school because something there is not exactly the way they want it to be.

Third, as a result of their parents' reluctance to discipline or frustrate them, school-phobic youngsters usually develop an exaggerated sense of mastery. Often they have been able to govern not only their own affairs, but even such household matters as when meals will be served and when their parents will go out or have company in, through demands, tantrums, threats, and physical complaints. While becoming expert at getting their parents to capitulate, however, school-phobic youngsters have usually had little opportunity for a realistic appraisal of how much mastery they can assert outside of their home. Typically, then, they approach the school situation with unwarranted faith in their own powers and little self-assurance to fall back on when they learn painfully that the world does not fall at their feet the way their parents do (see Bernstein, Svingen, & Garfinkel, 1990; de Aldaz, Feldman, Vivas, & Gelfand, 1987; Jackson, 1964; Leventhal & Sills, 1964).

These patterns of family interaction are neither unique to school phobia nor always predictive of it. Some school-phobic adolescents and their parents may not fit the preceding description in every way; likewise, a family constellation of an overprotective mother, an equally overprotective or detached father, and a clinging, manipulative, overconfident youngster may be associated with a variety of pathological states or with no psychopathology at all. Furthermore, the onset of an overt school-phobic reaction requires the interaction of predisposing family patterns, with precipitating events that generate concerns about being in school, as discussed next. With full allowance for these considerations, the family patterns that have been outlined in this section will nevertheless be found to characterize most instances of school phobia.

Precipitating Factors

Episodes of school phobia occur in response to experiences that make adolescents intensely anxious about being in school. These precipitating events are especially obvious in acute school-phobic reactions and tend to be less apparent as school phobia becomes a more chronic way of life. Even gradually developing, long-standing inability to attend school begins somewhere, however, and a thorough history will usually reveal distressing experiences that, although now remote, set the chronic school-phobic adolescent's nonattendance in motion.

The most common precipitating factors in school phobia involve changes or embarrassments that young persons who are disposed to this condition cannot handle. Change is difficult for overly dependent, overconfident adolescents whenever it puts them in new situations that call for them to act more independently than they have before. Moves to a new neighborhood and school are especially likely to be involved in the onset of a school phobia, because they require starting fresh in establishing relationships with new teachers and classmates.

The rigors of coping with change help to explain why school phobia so commonly begins following entrance to junior high school. Young persons must now give up their previously familiar primary classroom relationship with one main teacher. They change classes and teachers several times a day, under minimal supervision, and they are given increasing responsibility for budgeting their time, organizing their studying, and even choosing their subjects. Adolescents who are poorly prepared for such independence may become acutely anxious when they move from a relatively structured elementary school program to such ambiguous junior high school settings, and one result may be a reluctance to attend school. Typically, adolescents would much rather look ahead to what they will become than backward to what they have been. By contrast with this normative developmental preference, seventh- and eight-grade school-phobics not uncommonly talk about how great things were in the sixth grade and how they miss their former school and teacher.

As for embarrassments, school phobia in adolescence is often brought on by unpleasant and demeaning experiences that lead overdependent, falsely secure youngsters to prefer remaining at home, safe from further assaults on their dignity and self-regard. Often, these experiences will not be included among the reasons young persons initially give their parents for not wanting to go to school because they are too painful to talk or even think about. Particularly common in this regard among early adolescents are embarrassments related to developmental concerns about the growth and adequacy of their bodies. An athletically inept boy who is humiliated in his gym class may develop headaches or bouts of nausea that, significantly, appear only on the days when he has gym. A physically advanced 12- or 13-year-old girl who is self-conscious about her breast development may become so upset about her classmates staring at her, whether they are in fact paying any special attention to her physical appearance, that she begins to find reasons for staying home—which appeared to happen in the case of Beverly, considered next. Even without some specific distressing event, young persons who are worried about how they look, whether for good or imagined reasons, may find school generally intolerable just because it puts them under constant scrutiny by teachers and peers.

By high school, the peak of normal bodily concern among adolescents has passed, and young persons are increasingly caught up in developmental tasks involving social relationships, dating, and sexuality. School phobia is then likely to be precipitated by experiences of failure or rejection that make adolescents feel incapable of participating successfully in the social world of their peer group. For those who develop such feelings, going to school becomes a trying daily reminder of their social inadequacy and the school a venue for constant reexposure to being mocked, rebuffed, or simply ignored. In such circumstances, adolescents who are already disposed to deal with stress by clinging to the bosom of their family can easily be precipitated into a school-phobic reaction.

CASE 9. ACUTE SCHOOL PHOBIA

Beverly, a 12-year-old sixth-grade student, announced to her parents on a Monday morning that she would no longer attend school. When pressed for her reasons, she referred only to having been laughed at by several boys in her class the previous Friday when she was unable to answer a question. After failing for a week to get Beverly to change her mind, her parents sought professional help. They reported that, although her school refusal had arisen suddenly, she had been increasingly irritable, short-tempered, and insistent on having her own way since she had begun to menstruate several months earlier. Beverly was a large, well-developed girl who looked older than her

12 years. When interviewed, she was pleasant and agreeable and expressed regret over the worry she was causing her parents. She denied having any problems or concerns and stated that she missed being with her friends and was ready to return to school. The therapist supported these positive statements (perhaps being manipulated by them), and her return to school was planned for the next day.

The following evening, the therapist received a telephone call from Beverly's father, during which she could be heard screaming in the background. She had talked her mother into allowing her to remain at home that morning ("Let me have just one more day to feel up to it"). When her father had come home from work in the evening and expressed displeasure at this turn of events, she had responded by breaking dishes until he stopped scolding her. He was able, however, to muster sufficient resolve to call the therapist over her objections.

When the family was seen for their second interview the next day, their information left little doubt that Beverly kept her parents constantly on the defensive with insistent demands, rapid changes of mind, and well-timed tantrums. She was a very perceptive girl who had become adept at exploiting her parents' pressing needs to placate her and their companion fears about doing the wrong thing as parents.

In interviews and telephone calls over the subsequent week, the therapist concentrated on encouraging Beverly's parents to deal with her firmly and to insist that she make good on her daily promises to return to school. Gradually, with the therapist's urging and regular reassurance that they were behaving properly, they became better able to ignore Beverly's tantrums, avoid getting into arguments with her, and stand fast in requiring her to attend school. They later reported having felt guilty while they were treating her "so cruelly." However, not only did Beverly return to school without further complaint once her parents stopped backing down, but, to their pleasant surprise, she also became much better tempered and less demanding as they succeeded in resisting being pushed around.

The onset of Beverly's school refusal immediately following the apparent precipitating event of being laughed at in class suggested an acute school-phobic reaction. Consistent with this impression were the absence of other adjustment difficulties or peer-group withdrawal and her rapid recovery in response to brief intervention. Because of her prompt return to school, the basic sources of her anxiety were not explored further. It seems reasonable to speculate that her distress stemmed from more than just being unable to answer a question, however. As a physically well-developed sixth-grader who had to stand to recite in her classroom, she may well have become upset about her physical attributes being on display—especially in light of her report that it was some boys in particular who had laughed (perhaps giggled?) at her. Also noteworthy in this case was the ability and willingness of the parents to modify their behavior, considering that the school-phobic reaction stopped as soon as they stopped accepting it as a way of dealing with whatever problems their daughter was having in school.

CASE 10. CHRONIC SCHOOL PHOBIA

Mary, age 16, became nervous and upset on the first day of classes as she began her junior year in high school. She attributed her nervousness to "just being around" her classmates and to a lack of confidence that she could perform adequately in her subjects—which was striking since she had always been a B+ student. She came home at midday, and her parents did not insist that she return. During the next 2 weeks, she did not leave the house or make any attempt to contact her friends, some of whom had called to find out where she was. She seemed sad and lethargic at home, spoke very little, and limited her activities to reading and watching television.

Her withdrawal and apparent depression, more than her refusal to go to school, eventually led Mary's parents to ask their family doctor for referral to a psychologist. When Mary was interviewed, she was so anxious about being in a classroom that even talking about school caused her to become tearful and to wring her hands in dismay. She was able to say that she had no idea why school had become unpleasant for her, and no specific precipitants of her phobic reaction could be identified. From her mother, however, it was learned that in the fourth grade, Mary's convalescence from a mild midwinter illness had extended to the end of the school year. The parents had not encouraged her to return to school ("You can't rush these things") and had arranged instead for a medical exemption and home tutoring. Mary's mother added that she was a former nurse and had always enjoyed having Mary at home under her care.

The close mother–daughter relationship that existed in this family rarely involved Mary's father. He was a self-employed man who spent long hours at his business. He failed to join his wife and daughter for the initial consultation, which he had agreed to do, and during the subsequent therapy, he remained unavailable. At no point did he express interest in his daughter's progress, and he was never mentioned by Mary unless the therapist asked about him. The parents in this case, then, were an uninterested, uninvolved father and a nurturant mother who communicated to her daughter that her presence at home was welcome. Mary, in turn, had apparently grown up disposed to withdrawing to her home whenever she felt threatened. The past history in this case, together with the absence of precipitating events and accompanying problems of withdrawal and depression, identified a chronic school-phobic pattern.

The evaluation indicated that Mary was unlikely to be able to function in school in the immediate future and would require ongoing psychotherapy for both her school aversion and her depressive disorder. Regular therapy sessions and home tutoring were therefore arranged. During the first 6 months of treatment, she kept up with her studies and began discussing with the therapist many concerns she had about her social adequacy and whether she could handle the dating relationships in which her friends were getting involved. In midwinter, as the first outward sign of progress in the treatment, she started getting out of the house and becoming reinvested in peer-group activities, first going on shopping trips with her mother, then beginning to see her girlfriends again, and finally even going to school parties and out on dates. In the spring, she decided she was ready to return to school. "I'm around people all the time and doing everything else with them, so I might as well be in class with them." She returned to finish out the last 2 months of the school year without further complaint, and the therapy was terminated at the end of June.

In this case, the school-attendance problem involved long-standing feelings of social inadequacy that had been waiting in the wings for many years and an accompanying depressive disorder. Hence, Mary's return to school was accomplished first by helping her to come to grips with her underlying concerns, and then by supporting her own initiatives in going back to the classroom.

SCHOOL PHOBIA: TREATMENT

Persistent school phobia that goes unrecognized and untreated has serious implication for subsequent maladjustment. Because school phobia takes young persons out of the school and social arenas in which many significant learning experiences occur, it can seriously interfere with their academic progress and their social development. Adolescent school phobia often predicts poor further adaptation in situations that require independence and self-reliance, and about one third of young persons with an anxiety-based reluctance or refusal to attend school are likely to have persistent emotional problems, social impairments, and difficulty coping with the demands of subsequent college and work-related activities (Berg, Butler, & Hall, 1976; Kandel, Raveis, & Kandel, 1984; Steinberg, 1983, Chapter 10).

In light of the far-reaching consequences of prolonged school absence, the treatment of this disorder should ordinarily aim at getting the adolescent back to school as soon as possible. Historically, however, clinicians writing about school phobia have disagreed concerning what constitutes "soon." Some have recommended employing psychotherapy to help school-phobic adolescents understand and resolve their anxieties before they attempt to return to the classroom. In this approach, returning to school 6 to 12 months after beginning treatment has been considered a successful outcome (Coolidge, Brodie, & Feeney, 1964; Greenbaum, 1964; Hersov, 1960). Others have argued that keeping a youngster out of school for psychotherapy reinforces the symptom of nonattendance and delays recovery. From this perspective, school phobia calls for crisis intervention in which reestablishing attendance is the first priority, and exploring the origins of the problem can come later (Leventhal, Weinberger, Stander, & Stearns, 1967; Millar, 1961; Paccione-Dyszlewski & Contessa-Kislus, 1987).

Although sharp debates on this subject may sometimes still be heard, practitioners have gradually come to recognize that such differences of opinion can usually be resolved by selecting the treatment approach that best meets the needs of the individual adolescent. In cases of school phobia, this treatment decision should be guided by the differential diagnosis between acute and chronic forms of the disorder (see McDonald & Sheperd, 1976; Shapiro & Jegede, 1973; Sperling, 1967). When school phobia is acute, as in the case of Beverly, adolescents are likely to benefit most from vigorous efforts to get them back to school before they become accustomed to staying at home. If the school phobia has become chronic, on the other hand, some period of psychotherapy must usually precede attempts to return, as in the case of Mary, in order to avoid an intolerable level of anxiety that will defeat the purposes of the treatment. These two approaches can be labeled "early return" and "deferred return."

Early Return

A variety of behavioral and family-oriented treatment methods have proven effective in getting acutely school-phobic adolescents back into the classroom in short order. As in treating other anxiety disorders, behavioral methods work best when they combine live exposure and response prevention (see Marks, 1981, Chapter 3; Marks, 1987, Chapter 14; Strauss, 1987). This means that, in addition to being reintroduced to the school situation, school-phobic adolescents need to be helped to achieve sufficient relief from their school-related anxieties to avert recurrences of their phobic withdrawal.

Accordingly, anxiety-reducing techniques such as desensitization, relaxation training, and situation rehearsal play a central role in the therapy, both before the initial return to school occurs and during the time when the adolescent has resumed attendance but is still feeling uneasy about it. The proper dosage of anxiety is a key determinant of success in this early return approach. If anxiety is avoided or minimized by not pressing the topic of school or by limiting exposure to fantasy without live experiences, the treatment, especially of an acute school-phobic, will progress less rapidly than might have been possible and is likely to result in an unnecessarily deferred return. On the other hand, live exposure that generates more anxiety than the adolescent has been prepared to handle can undermine response prevention. Feeling overwhelmed, the young person flees from school once more, which reinforces the symptom, fosters discouragement about the treatment and lack of confidence in the therapist, and usually ensures having to opt for a deferred return.

Proper dosage may require combining anxiety-reducing exercises in the therapist's office with a gradual reintroduction to school. Instead of being forced to choose between staying home or going to school, the school-phobic adolescent may benefit from the option of returning at first for just mornings or just afternoons, or on some days but not others, or perhaps only for some classes but not others. Discussing such alternatives often eases the return to school and serves two other treatment purposes as well. Identifying which times or classes the adolescent prefers to tackle first and which to continue avoiding can help to elucidate his or her underlying concerns, and becoming actively involved in this aspect of planning the treatment can sustain his or her sense of self-determination.

A strategy of partial return requires the school to cooperate in accepting a special schedule. However, the school should be dissuaded from regarding this as anything other than a temporary arrangement. Any permanent dispensations or reduced requirements that may be contemplated, no matter how well-intended, reward the school-phobic's characteristic manipulativeness and pose obstacles to his or her complete recovery. A plan for partial return must similarly be understood between patient and therapist as a first step in problem-solving, not a solution; the adolescent should be fully prepared that, as soon as the reduced schedule seems to be manageable, ways of expanding it will become the next treatment target.

In some cases, a school-phobic youngster's anxiety about school may have generalized to a point where attending even one class, or even going into the school building, generates more anxiety than can be tolerated. Then, in order to avoid deferring live exposure, the therapist may need to construct a less ambitious set of graduated experiences: for example, walking or riding in a car up to within 1 mile from the school, going all the way to the school but standing across the street, going across the street and walking around on the school grounds, and eventually going into the building. As in homework assignments used in treating obsessive–compulsive disorder, such exercises should be planned carefully in the therapist's office with the active involvement of the adolescent; they should include various reassurances and anxiety-reducing prescriptions provided by the therapist concerning what patients are to do and say to themselves while approaching the feared situation; and they can often be carried out best with the help and involvement of others, especially parents, whom the therapist also instructs in the nature and purpose of the exercise. Numerous special circumstances may call for therapists using these behavioral techniques to use some further ingenuity in designing live experiences that will help school-phobic adolescents to overcome their aversion to being in the classroom (see Barth, 1986, Chapter 7; Jones & Kazdin, 1981; Ollendick & Mayer, 1984; Taylor & Adelman, 1990; Taylor & Arnow, 1988, Chapter 9).

When working with the families of school-phobic adolescents, the therapist also needs to educate them in avoiding the kinds of overprotective behaviors that encourage nonattendance at school. Although such reeducation may be a longer-term project than can be accommodated within an early return strategy, ample opportunities are usually present to help these parents reestablish their authority in the family. These parents need support and encouragement to stand up to their son or daughter who is calling the shots at home, and they need reassurance that, by taking charge and challenging the school refusal, they will be doing what is best for their child; and they may need guidance to resolve differences between them in how to handle their daughter or son (see Hsia, 1984; Yule, 1989). Then, as in the case of Beverly, the therapist may succeed in enlisting the parents as allies in the treatment; without parental determination to curtail their overprotectiveness, to resist being manipulated, and to follow the therapist's instructions, the possibilities for early return in school phobia are severely limited.

The success of early return strategies is maximized by implementing them with a crisis approach. The family needs to be seen promptly after calling or being referred for help, and they need to be spoken with in person or on the telephone daily during the initial stages of formulating the treatment plan. As soon as a diagnosis of acute school phobia has been established, the therapist needs to impress on the parents that their youngster's interests are not being served by nonattendance. Acutely school-phobic adolescents should be told that their problems will not be solved by remaining at home, that return to school is obligatory, and that the therapist's role will be to help them get back into school and to assist them in dealing with any distress they experience in returning. Then, guided by the particular characteristics of the individual case, the therapist can lay out a schedule for when and how a return to school will be attempted, for sessions with the adolescent to work on anxiety reduction, and for meetings with the parents to provide them guidance and support.

Active treatment programs that combine helping adolescents manage school-related anxieties with keeping them in the classroom can be expected to return most acutely school-phobic adolescents to school with reasonable comfort in anywhere from a few days to a few months (Blagg & Yule, 1984; Kennedy, 1965; Rodriguez, Rodriguez, & Eisenberg, 1959). At times, two other treatment adjuncts can improve these treatment prospects even further. On occasion, a very specific disturbing aspect of the school situation can be modified on the school-phobic adolescent's behalf without compromising ordinary academic requirements. A highly critical teacher who appears to delight in exposing students' ignorance may be prevailed on to ease up a bit, for example; or, as in Beverly's case, being allowed to recite while sitting at her desk rather than having to stand and have her body observed, may go a long way in reducing reluctance to be in the classroom (see Cretekos, 1977).

In other instances, especially when school-phobic reaction borders on panic and experienced anxiety is especially intense, a variety of medications have been reported to facilitate progress in the treatment. Best results in these situations have been achieved with small doses of imipramine (Tofranil), a tricyclic antidepressant (Bernstein, Garfinkel, & Borchardt, 1990; Klein, Ross, & Cohen, 1987; McDaniel, 1986). Generally speaking, however, psychopharmacologists recommend reserving pharmacotherapy for school phobia to cases in which the young person is unresponsive to psychosocial interventions (Jaffe & Magnuson, 1985; Marks, 1987, Chapter 15).

Deferred Return

The younger school-phobic adolescents are, the shorter the time they have been out of school, and the more their difficulties are limited to the school-attendance problem, the better the prospects for success in implementing an early return strategy in which the parents are involved as therapeutic agents, and work with the young person needs to be only as intensive as is necessary to effect his or her comfortable return to school. For older adolescents in whom school phobia has already become chronic, with repeated absences of long duration and social withdrawal or other psychological difficulties extending beyond anxiety about attending school, the opportune time for effective crisis intervention may have passed. These more chronic cases are likely to require ongoing psychotherapy, focused more on the individual patient than on patterns of family interaction, and return to school may have to be viewed as one of the outcomes of successful treatment rather than an essential prerequisite for progress.

Psychotherapy with chronic school-phobics, as in the intensive treatment of other neurotic disorders, should focus on helping patients to express and evaluate the underlying concerns that have led to their symptoms. The more freely they can be encouraged to talk about their unpleasant experiences in school, the more opportunity there will be for them to assess the reality of their concerns and to consider alternative, more adaptive ways of feeling and acting. At the same time, however, because chronic school phobia has so often become embedded in a more pervasive pattern of social phobia, the therapist needs to be prepared to allow concerns about school to remain in the background while other issues of interacting with peers or functioning in a competitive interpersonal environment are addressed. Sometimes, as in the case of Mary, anxieties about being in school will dissipate as a result of overcoming more general social anxieties, without the school situation ever having become a major topic of discussion.

When deferred return seems indicated by the necessity of preceding even a gradual return to the classroom with substantial progress in psychotherapy, tutoring at home should be included in the treatment plan. Whereas home tutoring is to be avoided in treating acute school phobia, because it runs counter to the principles of an early return strategy, in chronic school phobia, it facilitates the eventual return to the classroom. If, after many months of psychotherapy, a chronically school-phobic adolescent feels sufficiently in control of his or her social anxieties to consider returning to school but then must face concerns about having fallen behind in the classroom material, progress can come to a sudden halt. Return to school after an extended absence can be difficult enough without having to experience the strangeness and potential embarrassment of not knowing what the other students have learned in the interim or what topics they are currently considering. A well-orchestrated plan for having assignments sent home and for completing required papers and examinations smoothes the transition back into the classroom when an adolescent feels socially ready for it.

Chronic school phobia requiring extended treatment before return to school has a less favorable outcome than acute school-phobic conditions that can be treated with crisis intervention and early return. Nevertheless, even among a group of school-refusing adolescents who required inpatient treatment, Berg and Jackson (1985) found in a follow-up study that one half were free from serious adjustment problems as adults in their twenties. The recovery rate was even more favorable among those who had been treated before age 14 and who showed a good initial response to therapy.

REFERENCES

Adams, P. L. (1973). *Obsessive children*. New York: Brunner/Mazel.

Atkinson, L., Quarrington, B., & Cyr, J. J. (1985). School refusal: The heterogeneity of a concept. *American Journal of Orthopsychiatry, 55*, 83-101.

Barbaree, H. E., & Marshall, W. L. (1985). Anxiety-based disorders. In M. Hersen & S. M. Turner (Eds.), *Diagnostic interviewing* (pp. 55-77). New York: Plenum.

Barlow, D. H. (1988). *Anxiety disorders*. New York: Guilford.

Barth, R. P. (1986). *Social and cognitive treatment of children and adolescents*. San Francisco: Jossey-Bass.

Berg, C. Z. (1989). Behavioral assessment techniques for childhood obsessive-compulsive disorder. In J. L. Rapoport (Ed.), *Obsessive–compulsive disorder in children and adolescents* (pp. 41-72). Washington, DC: American Psychiatric Press.

Berg, C. Z., Rapoport, J. L., & Wolff, R. P. (1989). Behavioral treatment for obsessive-compulsive disorder in childhood. In J. L. Rapoport (Ed.), *Obsessive-compulsive disorder in children and adolescents* (pp. 169-185). Washington, DC: American Psychiatric Press.

Berg, I., Butler, A., & Hall, G. (1976). The outcome of adolescent school phobia. *British Journal of Psychiatry, 128*, 80-85.

Berg, I., & Jackson, A. (1985). Teenage school refusers grow up: A follow-up study of 168 subjects, ten years on average after inpatient treatment. *British Journal of Psychiatry, 147*, 366-370.

Berg, I., & McGuire, R. (1974). Are mothers of school-phobic adolescents overprotective? *British Journal of Psychiatry, 124*, 10-13.

Bernstein, G. A, & Garfinkel, B. D. (1986). School phobia: The overlap of affective and anxiety disorders. *Journal of the American Academy of Child Psychiatry, 25*, 235-241.

Bernstein, G. A., Garkinkel, B. D., & Borchardt, C. M. (1990). Comparative studies of pharmacotherapy for school refusal. *Journal of the American Academy of Child and Adolescent Psychiatry, 29*, 773-781.

Bernstein, G. A., Svingen, P. H., & Garfinkel, B. D. (1990). School phobia: Patterns of family functioning. *Journal of the American Academy of Child and Adolescent Psychiatry, 29*, 24–30.

Black, A. (1974). The natural history of obsessional neurosis. In H. R. Beech (Ed.), *Obsessional states*. New York: Methuen.

Black, D. W., Yates, W. R., Noyes, R., Pfohl, B., & Kelley, M. (1989). *DSM-III* personality disorder in obsessive–compulsive study volunteers: A controlled study. *Journal of Personality Disorders, 3*, 58–62.

Blagg, N. R., & Yule, W. (1984). The behavioural treatment of school refusal: A comparative study. *Behavior Research and Therapy, 22*, 119–127.

Blyth, D. A., & Simmons, R. G. (1983). The adjustment of early adolescents to school transitions. *Journal of Early Adolescence, 3*, 105–120.

Broadwin, I. T. (1932). A contribution to the study of truancy. *American Journal of Orthopsychiatry, 2*, 253–259.

Burke, K. C., Burke, J. D., Regier, D. A., & Rae, D. S. (1990). Age at onset of selected mental disorders in five community populations. *Archives of General Psychiatry, 47*, 511–518.

Chotiner, M. M., & Forrest, D. U. (1974). Adolescent school phobia: Six controlled cases studied retrospectively. *Adolescence, 9*, 467–480.

Christensen, H., Hadzi-Pavlovic, D., Andrews, G., & Mattick, R. (1987). Behavior therapy and tricyclic medication in the treatment of obsessive–compulsive disorder: A quantitative review. *Journal of Consulting and Clinical Psychology, 55*, 701–711.

Clark, D. A., & Bolton, D. (1985). Obsessive–compulsive adolescents and their parents: A psychometric study. *Journal of Child Psychology and Psychiatry, 26*, 267–276.

Clyne, M. B. (1966). *Absent: School refusal as an expression of disturbed family relationships*. London: Tavistock.

Coolidge, J. C., Brodie, R. D., & Feeney, B. A ten-year follow-up study of sixty-six school-phobic children. *American Journal of Orthopsychiatry, 34*, 675–684.

Coolidge, J. C., Hahn, P. B., & Peck, A. L. (1957). School phobia: Neurotic crisis or way of life? *American Journal of Orthopsychiatry, 27*, 296–306.

Cretekos, C. J. G. (1977). Some techniques in rehabilitating the school phobic adolescent. *Adolescence, 12*, 237–246,

de Aldaz, E. G., Feldman, L., Vivas, E., & Gelfand, D. (1987). Characteristics of Venezuelan school refusers: Toward the development of a high-risk profile. *Journal of Nervous and Mental Disease, 175*, 402–407.

Delprato, D. J. (1980). Hereditary determinants of fears and phobia: A critical review. *Behavior Therapy, 11*, 79–103.

DiNardo, P. A., O'Brien, G. T., Barlow, D. H., Waddell, M. T., & Blanchard, E. B. (1983). Reliability of *DSM-III* anxiety disorder categories using a new structured interview. *Archives of General Psychiatry, 40*, 1070–1074.

Eisenberg, L. (1958). School phobia: A study in the communication of anxiety. *American Journal of Psychiatry, 114*, 712–718.

Elkind, D., & Bowen, R. (1979). Imaginary audience behavior in children and adolescents. *Developmental Psychology, 15,* 38-44.

Estes, H. R., Haylett, C. H., & Johnson, A. M. (1956). Separation anxiety. *American Journal of Psychotherapy, 10,* 682-695.

Ferrari, M. (1986). Fears and phobias in childhood: Some clinical and developmental considerations. *Child Psychiatry and Human Development, 17,* 75-87.

Fisher, S., & Greenberg, R. P. (1977). *The scientific credibility of Freud's theories and therapy.* New York: Basic Books.

Flament, M. F., Koby, E., Rapoport, J. L., & Berg, C. J. (1990). Childhood obsessive-compulsive disorder: A prospective follow-up study. *Journal of Child Psychology and Psychiatry, 31,* 363-380.

Flament, M. F., Rapoport, J. L., Berg, C. J., Sceery, W., Kilts, C., Mellstrom, B., & Linnoila, M. (1985). Clomipramine treatment of childhood obsessive-compulsive disorder. *Archives of General Psychiatry, 42,* 977-983.

Flament, M., Whitaker, A., Rapoport, J. L., Davies, M., Berg, C. Z., & Shaffer, D. (1989). An epidemiological study of obsessive-compulsive disorder in adolescence. In J. L. Rapoport (Ed.), *Obsessive-complusive disorder in children and adolescents* (pp. 253-267). Washington, DC: American Psychiatric Press.

Foa, E. B., & Rowan V. (1990). Obsessive-compulsive disorder: Behavior therapy. In A. S. Bellack & M. Hersen (Eds.), *Handbook of comparative treatments for adult disorders* (pp. 256-265). New York: Wiley.

Foa, E. B., & Tillmanns, A. (1980). The treatment of obsessive-compulsive neurosis. In A. Goldstein & E. B. Foa (Eds.), *Handbook of behavioral interventions* (pp. 416-500). New York: Wiley.

Freud, S. (1959). Character and anal eroticism. In *Standard edition* (Vol. 9, pp. 169-175). London: Hogarth. (original work published 1908)

Freud, S. (1958). The disposition to obsessional neurosis. In *Standard edition* (Vol. 12, pp. 317-326). London: Hogarth. (original work published 1913)

Fyer, A. J., & Klein, D. J. (1986). Agoraphobia, social phobia, and simple phobia. In A. M. Cooper, A. J. Frances, & M. H. Sacks (Eds.), *The personality disorders and neuroses* (pp. 339-352). New York: Basic Books.

Galloway, D. (1985). *Schools and persistent absentees.* New York: Pergamon.

Goldsmith, H. H. (1983). Genetic influences on personality from infancy to adulthood. *Child Development, 54,* 331-353.

Goodwin, D. W., & Guze, S. B. (1984). Psychiatric diagnosis (3rd ed.). New York: Oxford.

Gordon, D. A., & Young, R. D. (1976). School phobia: A discussion of etiology, treatment, and evaluation. *Psychological Reports, 39,* 783-804.

Greenbaum, R. S. (1964). Treatment of school phobias—theory and practice. *American Journal of Psychotherapy, 18,* 616-634.

Hampe, E., Miller, L. C., Barrett, C. L., & Noble, H. (1973). Intelligence and school phobia. *Journal of School Psychology, 11,* 66-70.

Harris, E. L., Noyes, R., Crowe, R. R., & Chaudry, D. R. (1983). Family study of agoraphobia. *Archives of General Psychiatry, 40,* 1061-1064.

Henderson, J. G., & Pollard, C. A. (1988). Three types of obsessive-compulsive disorder in a community sample. *Journal of Clinical Psychology, 44,* 747-752.

Hersov, L. (1990). School refusal: An overview. In C. Chiland & J. G. Young (Eds.), *Why children reject school* (pp. 16-44). New Haven, CT: Yale University Press.

Hersov, L. A. Refusal to go to school. *Journal of Child Psychology and Psychiatry, 1,* 137-145.

Hersov, L. A., & Berg, I. (Eds.). (1980). *Out of school: Modern perspectives in truancy and school refusal.* Chichester, England: Wiley.

Hodgman, C. H., & Braiman, A. (1965). "College phobia": School refusal in university students. *American Journal of Psychiatry, 121,* 801-805.

Hoover, C. F., & Insel, T. R. (1984). Families of origin in obsessive-compulsive disorder. *Journal of Nervous and Mental Disease, 172,* 207-215.

Hsia, H. (1984). Structural and strategic approach to school phobia/school refusal. *Psychology in the Schools, 21,* 360-367.

Inouye, E. (1972). Genetic aspects of neurosis: A review. *International Journal of Mental Health, 1,* 176-189.

Jackson, L. (1964). Anxiety in adolescents in relation to school refusal. *Journal of Child Psychology and Psychiatry, 5,* 59-73.

Jaffe, S. L., & Magnuson, V. (1985). Anxiety disorders. In J. M. Wiener (Ed.), *Diagnosis and psychopharmacology of childhood and adolescent disorders* (pp. 199-214). New York: Wiley.

Jenike, M. A. (1990). Obsessive-compulsive disorder: Psychotherapy. In A. S. Bellack & M. Hersen (Eds.), *Handbook of comparative treatments for adult disorders* (pp. 245-255). New York: Wiley.

Jenike, M. A., Baer, L., & Minichiello, W. E. (Eds.). (1986). *Obsessive-compulsive disorders: Theory and management.* Littleton, MA: PSG Publishing.

Jenike, M. A., Baer, L., Summergrad, P., & Weilburg, J. B. (1989). Obsessive-compulsive disorder: A double-blind, placebo-controlled trial of clomipramine in 27 patients. *American Journal of Psychiatry, 146,* 1328-1330.

Johnson, A. M., Falstein, E. I., Szurek, S. A., & Svendsen, M. (1941). School phobia. *American Journal of Orthopsychiatry, 11,* 702-711.

Jones, R. T., & Kazdin, A. E. (1981). Childhood behavior problems in the school. In S. M. Turner, K. S. Calhoun, & H. E. Adams (Eds.), *Handbook of clinical behavior therapy* (pp. 568-606). New York: Wiley.

Kahn, J. H., & Nursten, J. P. (1962). School refusal: A comprehensive view of school phobia and other failures of school attendance. *American Journal of Orthopsychiatry, 22,* 707-718.

Kandel, D. B., Raveis, V. H., & Kandel, P. I. (1984). Continuity in discontinuities: Adjustment in young adulthood of former school absentees. *Youth and Society, 15,* 325-352.

Karno, M., Golding, J. M., Sorenson, S. B., & Burnam, A. (1988). The epidemiology of obsessive-compulsive disorder in five US communities. *Archives of General Psychiatry, 45,* 1094-1099.

Keller, B. B. (1989). Cognitive assessment of obsessive compulsive children. In J. L.

Rapoport (Ed.), *Obsessive–compulsive disorder in children and adolescents* (pp. 33–39). Washington, DC: American Psychiatric Press.

Kendler, K. S., Heath, A., Martin, N. G., & Eaves, L. J. (1986). Symptoms of anxiety and depression in a volunteer twin population. *Archives of General Psychiatry, 43,* 213–221.

Kennedy, W. A. (1965). School phobia: Rapid treatment of fifty cases. *Journal of Abnormal Psychology, 70,* 285–289.

Klein, D. F., Ross, D. C., & Cohen, P. (1987). Panic and avoidance in agoraphobia. *Archives of General Psychiatry, 44,* 377–385.

Kozak, J. M., Foa, E. B., & Steketee, G. (1988). Process and outcome of exposure treatment with obsessive–compulsives: Psychophysiological indicators of emotional processing. *Behavior Therapy, 19,* 157–169.

Last, C. G., Francis, G., Hersen, M., Kazdin, A. E., & Strauss, C. C. (1987). Separation anxiety and school phobia: A comparison using *DSM-III* criteria. *American Journal of Psychiatry, 144,* 653–657.

Last, C. G., & Strauss, C. C. (1990). School refusal in anxiety-disordered children and adolescents. *Journal of the American Academy of Child and Adolescent Psychiatry, 29,* 31–35.

Lechner, C., & Rosenthal, D. (1984). Adolescent self-consciousness and the imaginary audience. *Genetic Psychology Monographs, 110,* 289–305.

Lenane, M. C., Swedo, S., Leonard, H., Pauls, D. L., Sceery, W., & Rapoport, J. L. (1990). Psychiatric disorders in first degree relatives of children and adolescents with obsessive compulsive disorder. *Journal of the American Academy of Child and Adolescent Psychiatry, 29,* 407–412.

Leonard, H. L. (1989a). Childhood rituals and superstitions: Developmental and cultural perspective. In J. L. Rapoport (Ed.), *Obsessive–compulsive disorder in children and adolescents* (pp. 289–309). Washington, DC: American Psychiatric Press.

Leonard, H. L. (1989b). Drug treatment of obsessive–compulsive disorder. In J. L. Rapoport (Ed.), *Obsessive–compulsive disorder in children and adolescents* (pp. 217–236). Washington, DC: American Psychiatric Press.

Leonard, H. L., Goldberger, E. L., Rapoport, J. L., Cheslow, D. L., & Swedo, S. E. (1990). Childhood rituals: Normal development or obsessive–compulsive symptoms? *Journal of the American Academy of Child and Adolescent Psychiatry, 29,* 17–23.

Leventhal, T., & Sills, M. (1964). Self-image in school phobia. *American Journal of Orthopsychiatry, 37,* 64–70.

Leventhal, T., Weinberger, G., Stander, R. J., & Stearns, R. P. (1967). Therapeutic strategies with school phobia. *American Journal of Orthopsychiatry, 37,* 64–70.

Lichstein, K. L. (1988). *Clinical relaxation strategies.* New York: Wiley.

Malmquist, C. P. (1965). School phobia: A problem in family neurosis. *Journal of the American Academy of Child Psychiatry, 4,* 293–319.

Marks, I. (1981). *Cure and care of neuroses.* New York: Wiley.

Marks, I. (1987). *Fears, phobias, and rituals.* New York: Oxford University Press.

Mavassakalian, M. (1983). Antidepressants in the treatment of agoraphobia and obsessive-compulsive disorder. *Comprehensive Psychiatry, 24,* 278-284.

Mavassakalian, M. (1986). Obsessive compulsive disorder. In M. Hersen (Ed.), *Pharmacological and behavioral treatment* (pp. 240-259). New York: Wiley.

McDaniel, K. D. (1986). Pharmacologic treatment of psychiatric and neuro-developmental disorders in children and adolescents. *Clinical Pediatrics, 25,* 65-71.

McDonald, J. E. & Sheperd, G. (1976). School phobia: An overview. *Journal of School Psychology, 14,* 291-308.

Millar, T. P. (1961). The child who refuses to attend school. *American Journal of Psychiatry, 118,* 398-404.

Miller, L. C., Barrett, C. L., & Hampe, E. (1974). Phobias of childhood in a prescientific era. In A. Davids (Ed.), *Child personality and psychopathology: Current topics* (pp. 89-134). New York: Wiley.

Millon, T. (1981). *Disorders of personality.* New York: Wiley.

Nader, P. R., Bullock, D., & Caldwell, B. (1975). School phobia. *Pediatric Clinics of North America, 22,* 605-617.

Noyes, R., Crowe, R. R., Hamra, B. J., McChesney, C. M., & Chaudry, D. R. (1986). Relationship between panic disorders and agoraphobia: A family study. *Archives of General Psychiatry, 43,* 227-232.

Ollendick, T. H., & Mayer, J. A. (1984). School phobia. In S. M. Turner (Ed.), *Behavioral theories and treatment of anxiety* (pp. 367-411). New York: Plenum.

Paccione-Dyszlewski, M. R., & Contessa-Kislus, M. A. (1987). School phobia: Identification of subtypes as a prerequisite to treatment intervention. *Adolescence, 22,* 377-384.

Pato, M. T., Zohar-Kadouch, R., Zohar, J., & Murphy, D. L. (1988). Return of symptoms after discontinuation of clomipramine in patients with obsessive-compulsive disorder. *American Journal of Psychiatry, 145,* 1521-1525.

Pollack, J. M. (1979). Obsessive-compulsive personality: A review. *Psychological Bulletin, 86,* 225-241.

Rachman, S. J., & Hodgson, R. J. (1980). *Obsessions and compulsions.* Englewood Cliffs, NJ: Prentice-Hall.

Radin, S. (1967). Psychodynamic aspects of school phobia. *Comprehensive Psychiatry, 8,* 119-128.

Rapoport, J. L. (1986). Childhood obsessive-compulsive disorder. *Journal of Child Psychology and Psychiatry, 27,* 289-295.

Rapoport, J. L. (Ed.). (1989). *Obsessive compulsive disorder in children and adolescents.* Washington, DC: American Psychiatric Press.

Rasmussen, S., & Tsuang, M. (1986). Clinical characteristics and family history in DSM-III OCD. *American Journal of Psychiatry, 143,* 317-322.

Reid, W. H. (1983). *Treatment of the DSM-III psychiatric disorders.* New York: Brunner/Mazel.

Riddle, M. A., Scahill, L., King, R., Hardin, M. T., Towbin, K. E., Ort, S. I., Leckman, J. F., & Cohen, D. J. (1990). Obsessive compulsive disorder in children and adolescents: Phenomenology and family history. *Journal of the American Academy of Child and Adolescent Psychiatry, 29*, 766-772.

Rodriguez, A., Rodriguez, M., & Eisenberg, L. The outcome of school phobia: A follow-up study based on 41 cases. *American Journal of Psychiatry, 116*, 540-544.

Roth, P. (1967). *Portnoy's complaint*. New York: Random House.

Rutter, M., Macdonald, H., Le Couteur, A., Harrington, R., Bolton, P., & Bailey, A. (1990). Genetic factors in child psychiatric disorders: II. Empirical findings. *Journal of Child Psychology and Psychiatry, 31*, 39-83.

Rutter, M., Tizard, J., Yule, W., Graham, P., & Whitmore, K. (1976). Isle of Wight studies, 1964-1974. *Psychological Medicine, 6*, 313-332.

Ryan, N. D., & Puig-Antich, J. (1987). Pharmacological treatment of adolescent psychiatric disorders. *Journal of Adolescent Health Care, 8*, 137-142.

Salzman, L. (1968). *The obsessive personality*. New York: Science House.

Salzman, L., & Thaler, F. H. (1981). Obsessive-compulsive disorders: A review of the literature. *American Journal of Psychiatry, 138*, 286-291.

Scarr, S., & McCartney, K. (1983). How people make their own environments: A theory of genotype-environment effects. *Child Development, 54*, 424-435.

Shapiro, D. (1965). *Neurotic styles*. New York: Basic Books.

Shapiro, T., & Jegede, R. O. (1973). School phobia: A babel of tongues. *Journal of Autism and Childhood Schizophrenia, 3*, 168-186.

Shear, M. K., & Frosch, W. A. (1986). Obsessive-compulsive disorder. In A. M. Cooper, A. J. Frances, & M. H. Sacks (Eds.), *Psychiatry* (Vol. 1, pp. 353-362). New York: Basic Books.

Skynner, A. C. (1974). School phobia: A reappraisal. *British Journal of Medical Psychology, 47*, 1-16.

Sommer, B. (1985). What's different about truants: A comparison study of eighth-graders. *Journal of Youth and Adolescence, 14*, 411-422.

Sperling, M. (1967). School phobias: Classification, dynamics, and treatment. *Psychoanalytic Study of the Child, 22*, 375-401.

Steinberg, D. (1983). *The clinical psychiatry of adolescence*. Chichester, England: Wiley.

Strauss, C. C. (1987). Anxiety. In M. Hersen & V. B. Van Hasselt (Eds.), *Behavior therapy with children and adolescents* (pp. 109-136). New York: Wiley.

Strauss, C. C., & Lahey, B. B. (1987). Anxiety. In V. B. Van Hasselt & M. Hersen (Eds.), *Handbook of adolescent psychology* (pp. 332-350). New York: Pergamon.

Sturgis, E. T., & Meyer, V. (1981). Obsessive-compulsive disorders. In S. M. Turner, K. S. Calhoun, & H. E. Adams (Eds.), *Handbook of clinical behavior therapy* (pp. 68-102). New York: Wiley.

Swedo, S. E., & Rapoport, J. L. (1989). Phenomenology and differential diagnosis of obsessive-compulsive disorder in children and adolescents. In J. L. Rapoport (Ed.), *Obsessive-compulsive disorder in children and adolescents* (pp. 13-32). Washington, DC: American Psychiatric Press.

Swedo, S. E., Rapoport, J. L., Leonard, H., Lenane, M., & Cheslow, D. (1989).

Obsessive-compulsive disorder in children and adolescents. *Archives of General Psychiatry, 46,* 335-341.

Taylor, C. B., & Arnow, B. (1988). *The nature and treatment of anxiety disorders.* New York: Free Press.

Taylor, L., & Adelman, H. S. (1990). School avoidance behavior: Motivational bases and implications for intervention. *Child Psychiatry and Human Development, 20,* 219-233.

Torgersen, S. (1983). Genetic factors in anxiety disorders. *Archives of General Psychiatry, 40,* 1085-1089.

Turner, S. M., & Beidel, D. C. (1989). Social phobia: Clinical syndrome, diagnosis, and comorbidity. *Clinical Psychology Review, 9,* 3-18.

Turner, S. M., Beidel, D. C., & Costello, A. (1987). Psychopathology in the offspring of anxiety disorder patients. *Journal of Consulting and Clinical Psychology, 55,* 229-235.

Turner, S. M., Beidel, D. C., & Nathan, S. (1985). Biological factors in obsessive-compulsive disorders. *Psychological Bulletin, 97,* 430-450.

Tyrer, P., & Tyrer, S. (1974). School refusal, truancy, and adult neurotic illness. *Psychological Medicine, 4,* 416-421.

Waldfogel, S., Coolidge, J. C., & Hahn, P. B. (1957). The development, meaning, and management of school phobia. *American Journal of Orthopsychiatry, 27,* 754-780.

Waldron, S., Shrier, D., Stone, B., & Tobin, F. (1975). School phobia and other childhood neuroses: A systematic study of the children and their families. *American Journal of Psychiatry, 132,* 802-808.

Weiner, I. B. (1967). Behavior therapy in obsessive-compulsive neurosis: Treatment of an adolescent boy. *Psychotherapy: Theory, Research and Practice, 4,* 27-29.

Whitaker, A., Johnson, J., Shaffer, D., Rapoport, J. L., Kalikow, K., Walsh, B. T., Davies, M., Braiman, S., & Dolinsky, A. (1990). Uncommon troubles in young people. *Archives of General Psychiatry, 47,* 487-496.

White, K., & Cole, J. O. (1990). Obsessive-compulsive disorder: Pharmacotherapy. In A. S. Bellack & M. Hersen (Eds.), *Handbook of comparative treatments for adult disorders* (pp. 266-284). New York: Wiley.

Wolpe, J. (1958). *Psychotherapy by reciprocal inhibition.* Stanford, CA: Stanford University Press.

Yule, W. (1989). Parent involvement in the treatment of the school phobic child. In C. E. Schaefer & J. M. Breismeister (Eds.), *Handbook of parent training* (pp. 223-244). New York: Wiley.

CHAPTER 7

Academic Underachievement

Academic underachievement is a disparity between capacity and performance that is reflected in students receiving lower grades than they are intellectually capable of earning. Underachievement does not include poor grades attributable to limited intelligence. Clinicians evaluating low-achieving students should routinely utilize intelligence test data to identify instances in which poor grades are consistent with deficient intellectual ability. Unlike slow learners, underachievers are students of average or better intelligence who are showing unexpectedly poor performance in their school work.

School learning problems and academic underachievement are among the most frequent reasons why adolescents are referred to mental health professionals (Cass & Thomas, 1979; Sugar, 1987). Being unable or unwilling to utilize their intellectual potential, these young people are typically squandering educational and occupational opportunities that would otherwise be within their grasp. Longitudinal studies have indicated a substantial positive correlation between intellectual involvement and academic achievement during the teenage years, on the one hand, and achievement behavior and occupational level in adulthood on the other (Vaillant & Vaillant, 1981). As an important case in point, approximately 15% of young people in the United States are presently dropping out of school without completing a high school education, and these dropouts are more than twice as likely as high school graduates to be unemployed in their mid-20s. Those who do find work are only one third as likely as graduates to have white-collar jobs, and even highly intelligent young people without a high school diploma are at risk for ending up in the ranks of the unskilled and unemployed (Bachman, O'Malley, & Johnston, 1979; Blau, 1981; Wetzel, 1987).

Although adolescent underachievement may develop suddenly in junior or senior high school, underachieving patterns often begin earlier. A seminal study by Shaw and McCuen (1960) traced the elementary school performance of equally bright achieving and underachieving high school students who had been classmates since the first grade. The underachieving boys in their sample had tended to receive lower grades than the achieving boys beginning in the first grade. These underachievers had dropped to a significantly lower performance level by the third grade and had shown increasingly poorer achievement in each succeeding year up to the tenth grade. A similar but later developing pattern was found for the underachieving girls, who began to receive lower grades than the achieving girls in the sixth grade and declined to a significantly lower performance level by the ninth grade.

Other research with students doing poorly in or dropping out of high school confirms a characteristically long history of poor academic performance and increasingly negative attitudes toward school (Cairns, Cairns, & Neckerman, 1989; Chapman, 1988). Once underway, poor school performance tends to generate cumulative detrimental effects. Students who are underachieving find themselves inadequately prepared in subject matter they have failed. They lose confidence in their ability to learn, form depreciated concepts of themselves as students, and lower their expectations of ever doing well. Lacking positive reinforcement, they derive little pleasure from the learning process. Such experiences contribute to progressively larger gaps between capacity and performance as underachievement persists from one year to the next. Frequent absences from school and a variety of behavioral and emotional problems in the classroom have also been observed as the legacy of persistent underachievement (see Berndt & Miller, 1990; Jamieson, Lydon, Stewart, & Zanna, 1987; Skinner, Wellborn, & Connell, 1990; Zarb, 1984).

Academic underachievement results from one or a combination of several possible motivational, educational, developmental, and family-interaction determinants. Whereas the presence and extent of academic underachievement can be readily assessed by comparing a student's measured intelligence with his or her scholastic attainment, the complex and multiple etiology of this problem calls for careful differentiation of its origins in the individual case. This chapter discusses the various determinants of academic underachievement and their implications for the treatment of underachieving adolescents.

MOTIVATIONAL AND EDUCATIONAL DETERMINANTS

For students to realize their academic potential, they must apply themselves to their studies. Research findings over many years have consistently indicated that young people who do well in school tend to be interested in learning. They feel good about receiving high marks, and they see a clear relationship between achieving in high school and fulfilling a wish to attend college or qualify for a particular occupation. By contrast, young persons who have no commitment to intellectual values or academic goals lack motivation to work hard in school. They may take pains to avoid the inconvenience of outright failure, but they see little reason to extend themselves more than is necessary to get by. Typically, they dislike school and do not expect to derive either inner satisfaction or external rewards from doing well academically. Unmotivated underachievers are especially unlikely to perceive their schoolwork as related to what they will be doing in the future or as helping them to reach any long-term objectives (Gottfried, 1985; Pintrich & de Groot, 1990).

For purposes of differential diagnosis, the hallmark of low motivation as a determinant of academic underachievement is its ready acknowledgment. The adolescent will openly indicate that he or she dislikes school, does not attach much importance to getting an education, and may even prefer to receive mediocre grades. To plan a helpful response in this circumstance, the clinician needs to explore the possible origins of noneducational values and goals in family, peer-group, sex-role, and school influences.

Family Influences

Young people customarily identify with their parents' attitudes toward education. As a result, parents who value the educational process usually foster positive feelings about school learning, whereas parents who doubt the usefulness of formal education as a way of getting ahead in life often instill negative feelings. Lack of enthusiasm for learning and a distaste for school can be heightened by parents who belittle teachers, mock the content of the curriculum, and show little personal interest in reading, broadening their knowledge, or engaging in intellectual discussions. Such parents largely ignore how their children are doing in school and seldom base their demonstrations of approval on whether they are doing their homework and receiving decent grades. Reared in this way, adolescents are unlikely to develop much motivation to achieve academically.

Research comparing achieving and underachieving high school students of comparable intelligence confirms that the parents of achievers are generally more encouraging with respect to performance in the classroom; that the families of achievers more actively promote intellectual interests in their children and foster a positive attitude toward teachers and the school; and that achievers are less inclined than underachievers to express negative attitudes about school or to view their teachers as unreasonable or unsupportive (Butler-Por, 1987, Chapter 2; Gesten, Scher, & Cowen, 1978; Wood, Chapin, & Hannah, 1988). Empirical data also demonstrate the academic impact of parental involvement in teenagers' lives. The more parents of adolescents are keeping track of where they are and what they are doing, are engaged with them in planning for their future, and are monitoring their performance in school, the more time adolescents spend on their homework and the better grades they receive (Fehrmann, Keith, & Reimers, 1987; Keith, Reimers, Fehrmann, Pottebaum, & Aubey, 1986).

Experienced clinicians are familiar with how frequently parents of underachieving adolescents complain, "She just doesn't take any interest in her studies" or "We can't find a way to get him motivated." In some of these instances, the young person's poor school performance may turn out to reflect some personal problem that he or she is struggling to resolve. With respect to shared value systems, however, this particular complaint often reveals that the parents, even while giving lip service to the contrary, harbor a disdain for education that is being reflected by their youngster in the form of low academic motivation.

Typical in this regard is the self-made man who, having succeeded in the business world despite limited schooling or a poor academic record, scolds an underachieving son for his low grades and "bad attitude" but nevertheless considers him "a chip off the old block." Such tacit approval of academic underachievement seldom fails to find expression in subtle but unmistakable parental messages that reinforce the adolescent's scholastic torpor. There is, in fact, good evidence that the less schooling parents have had themselves, the less likely they are to become involved in their children's school activities and the more likely their children are to receive low grades and become dropouts (Fehrmann et al., 1987; Stevenson & Baker, 1987; Wetzel, 1987). Conversely, the more education parents have had themselves, the better grades their children are likely to earn, the higher their educational aspirations are likely to be, and the more likely they are to care about being perceived by their parents as academically oriented (De Santis, Ketterlinus, & Youniss, 1990; Kurdek & Sinclair, 1988; Miller & Sneesby, 1988).

There has been an unfortunate tendency to ascribe differences in family support for educational attainment to parental socioeconomic status. Middle- and upper-status parents were described as well-educated and likely to regard schooling as a way of preparing for life, socially and psychologically, as well as vocationally. Hence, they were expected to speak well of what schooling has to offer and to follow their children's school activities closely. They were also expected typically to appreciate and discuss with their children the significance of what they were learning in school and to reward their academic accomplishments. Lower-status parents, in comparison, were described as more likely to be minimally educated, to regard the school as an alien and unsympathetic institution, and to view their children's attendance merely as a legal requirement or perhaps a way of getting a better job. Hence, they were expected to be relatively unlikely to discuss school activities with their children, to understand and help them with their studies, and to praise their classroom achievements (see Katz, 1967).

In the present days of cultural diversity and expanded access to educational opportunities, especially through financial aid at the college level, such generalizations regarding disadvantaged families no longer hold—if they ever did. In the first place, there is no sociocultural or socioeconomic group within which all adolescents share the same educational and occupational orientation. In one study of tenth-grade students from a lower-middle status neighborhood, for example, Zarb (1981) found that some had developed good study habits and a realistic perception of themselves as academically successful and were doing well in their studies, whereas others had poor study habits and a low academic self-concept and were underachieving.

Second, families within any subcultural group may hold widely differing attitudes and bring different influences to bear on their children. In studies comparing low-income black students who were doing well in school with similar groups who were doing poorly, the parents of the achieving students were found to be more interested in their children's education, more knowledgeable about the school system, and more likely to encourage self-motivated academic achievement. The parents of the nonachieving students, on the other hand, offered little in the way of intellectual stimulation (such as having books in the home or providing adequate study space) and conveyed few aspirations for educational attainment or vocational enhancement (Clark, 1983; Scheinfeld, 1983).

Delgado-Gaitan (1986b) reports interviews with parents of Chicano high school students, most of whom had not completed high school and were in blue-collar jobs, who believed that schooling was the key to their family's future economic success and were determined to do everything possible to ensure their children's graduation from high school. Asian-Americans, although highly achieving as a group, are a heterogeneous minority in the United States who, despite a common cultural heritage, include many who are substantially undereducated and unsuccessful (Sue & Okazaki, 1990).

Finally, ethnic background and economic status exert independent effects on academic achievement. Black and Hispanic adolescents are more likely to drop out of high school than white teenagers, for example, but only in relation to the income level of their families. Students from poor families are three to four times more likely to drop out than those from more affluent families, regardless of race, and young people of comparable economic status from all ethnic backgrounds are comparably likely to remain in and complete high school (Wetzel, 1987).

Taken together, these findings demonstrate that parents influence the academic attitudes and achievements of their children through the environment they create at home independently of their socioeconomic status (SES) or ethnic background. Further, compelling evidence to this effect is presented by White (1982) in an integrative review of 101 published studies of the relationships among academic achievement, socioeconomic background factors, and atmosphere in the home, as measured by (a) parents' attitudes toward education, (b) parents' aspirations for their children, (c) family participation in cultural and intellectual activities, and (d) availability of reading materials in the home. On the average, the measures of home atmosphere correlated substantially more strongly with academic achievement in these studies than parents' educational level, occupational level, income, and all combinations of these socioeconomic indices. This leaves little doubt that many lower-SES parents successfully create a home environment that fosters learning, whereas many socially and economically advantaged parents may not.

Peer-Group and Sex-Role Influences

Negative peer-group influences can induce adolescents to neglect their studies even in the face of strong family commitment to intellectual pursuits. Adolescents who are striving for acceptance within a social group that endorses nonintellectual values and belittles academic achievement may be tempted to turn their back on academic interests. In some pioneering research on such peer-group influence, Coleman (1961) found that in high schools in which the student body generally endorsed academic accomplishment, the most intelligent youngsters were getting the highest grades, as would be expected. In schools where their peer group devalued scholarship, on the other hand, the most able students were not the highest achievers, apparently because many of them were forsaking good grades to avoid being unpopular.

Consistently with normal development trends in conformity behavior, avoiding academic accomplishment to preserve popularity is more likely to occur in early than in middle or late adolescence. Pressures to conform to group standards ordinarily mount during the elementary school years, reach their peak at ages 11 to 13 years, and then diminish as a function of the increasing importance to young people of asserting their independence and uniqueness (Berndt, 1979; Coleman, 1980; Delgado-Gaitan, 1986a). In a study addressed specifically to classroom performance, Ishiyama and Chabassol (1985) compared early adolescent girls and boys (grades 7-9) with middle adolescents (grades 10-12) on a measure of concern about potential negative social consequences of academic success, such as peer rejection and criticism. The older adolescents of both sexes were significantly less worried than the younger subjects about getting high grades. These findings are consistent with the expectation that, with maturation, early adolescent uneasiness about being different or standing out from one's peers will give way during middle adolescence to individual aspirations for achievement and the forging of one's own independent academic and occupational identity.

Because low motivation stemming from peer-group influences is most likely to contribute to underachievement in early adolescence, clinicians evaluating poor school performance in an older adolescent should usually look elsewhere for its cause. When concerns about peer approval do surface in older adolescents with academic difficulties, the origins of the learning problem probably extend beyond normative peer conformity and involve elements of immaturity or maladaptive family interaction, which are among the psychological determinants of underachievement to considered in subsequent sections of this chapter.

With respect to sex-role influences, prevailing group attitudes toward what constitutes appropriate male and female behavior can also exert a powerful influence on motivation to achieve in school. In groups in which academic effort and attainment are viewed as essentially feminine, boys who are conscientious and successful in their studies risk being regarded as something other than a "regular guy" or a "cool dude." In groups that consider scholastic excellence and career-mindedness masculine characteristics, girls who value their studies above their social life and have serious career objective may find their femininity called into question by family and friends. Especially problematic in this regard are parents who reserve their enthusiasm for the intellectual achievements of their sons and take little interest or pleasure in their daughters' educational plans and accomplishments. Such a double standard can extinguish academic motivation in able girls and lead to underachievement, just as being called a "sissy" may dissuade a bright boy from putting full effort into his studies.

A good description of how these sets of attitudes can operate was reported some years ago by Crandall (1972), in a study of academically motivated families. The parents in these families were more likely to communicate the importance of learning to their daughters than to their sons, but they set higher standards for their sons' than for their daughters' achievements. Crandall attributed these sex differences to commonly held sex-role stereotypes: Boys should not get too wrapped up in their studies at the expense of more "masculine" activities, whereas for girls, schoolwork is a natural and appropriate activity that they should feel free to enjoy; at the same time, doing well in school is more important for boys than for girls in the long run, because it is primarily the boys who will have to qualify for jobs and earn a living. From these stereotypes came the apparently inconsistent finding that these parents were providing more support for their daughters' viewing school as important but expressing more concern with the actual school performance of their sons.

Modern movements away from these traditional sex-role definitions have gradually reduced their influence on academic motivation. The premium that is placed in contemporary society on maximum educational advancement for all talented people has done much to replace the socially acceptable "gentleman's C" of earlier days and the restriction of career-minded girls to teaching, nursing, and social work. Such views have largely been replaced by more egalitarian attitudes toward what constitute appropriate roles for men and women, together with increased masculine goal-directedness and reduced feminine conflict between intellectual and interpersonal needs. Differences in intellectual abilities that once were reported between males and females are no longer evident in contemporary research. Frittering away opportunities to learn and failing to prepare for a career no longer passes muster as "being one of the boys," and students of both sexes are much less inclined than before to devalue competence, resourcefulness, and intelligence in their female classmates (see Deaux, 1985; Jacklin, 1989; Kaufman & Richardson, 1982, Chapter 2; Tittle, 1986).

Old stereotypes die hard, however, and the potential for sex-role attitudes to attenuate academic motivation and performance has continued to surface in various lines of research. Reports from the 1980s indicate that, as early as the first grade, children are likely to state occupational preferences that embody such traditional sex-role stereotypes as boys becoming doctors and girls becoming nurses (Huston, 1985; Spare & Dahmen, 1984). Other evidence of persistent sex-role attitudes that can be expected to have a negative influence on adolescent girls' motivation to achieve in school appears in studies in which many high school seniors were found to prefer a marriage in which the wife works part-time or not at all (Herzog, Bachman, & Johnston, 1983); junior and senior high school teachers were found to interact more frequently with the boys than the girls in their classes (Tittle, 1986); and fathers were found more likely to expect their sons than their daughters to complete college (Mandel & Marcus, 1988, Chapter 7).

Finally, data collected by Gorell and Shaw (1988) from junior and senior high school students suggest that, while they report seeing very little difference between males and females in general in the jobs they can do, many young people cling to traditional gender-typed beliefs when it comes to the kinds of jobs they think they personally could learn to do.

School Influences

Able adolescents who are adequately motivated to achieve in school may be prevented from realizing their goals by educational circumstances that limit their opportunities to study and learn. The most widely publicized of these circumstances is the failure of elementary education to prepare young people adequately for high school and college work. This problem is most acute in inner-city and depressed rural areas, where educational resources are likely to be in shortest supply. Students who attend underequipped and understaffed schools where they sit in crowded classrooms listening to bored or inept teachers may not acquire the basic academic skills and study habits they will need later on. Children who begin high school without having learned to multiply, read fluently, or take examinations, for example, and adolescents who enter college without even having had to write a composition or to conduct a laboratory experiment are ill-prepared to meet the educational demands that await them.

A considerable body of research has documented that the way in which elementary and secondary schools deliver their curriculum makes a difference in the education their students receive. The more conscientiously schools attend to their educational task, emphasize academic objectives, and convey respect for their students, the better their students perform in the classroom. The instructional styles and strategies employed by individual teachers also affect their students' performances. Adapting curricular materials to student characteristics, pacing the coverage of this material briskly but in small steps, modeling correct examples, providing ample opportunity for class participation, and rewarding effort as well as accomplishment are among strategies that have been demonstrated to facilitate learning (see Barth, 1986, Chapter 8; Brophy, 1986; Good & Weinstein, 1986; Hallinan, 1987; Pokay & Blumenfeld, 1990).

Aspects of the climate in a school that can influence individual achievement also include the overall intellectual level of the student body. Generally speaking, students of equal ability tend to form lower academic self-concepts in high-ability schools than in low-ability schools. Because students' conceptions of how well they can expect to do influence the grades they actually earn, equally able students tend to perform less well in academically strong than in academically weak schools (Marsh, 1987).

The educational impact of a school's climate is also likely to vary with its size. Schools that are large and impersonal may not engage their students adequately. Overcrowded inner-city schools serving disadvantaged youngsters are particularly prone to this shortcoming, but it is by no means theirs alone. Large suburban junior and senior high schools furnished with abundant resources and attended by affluent students often provide their strongest programs at the top and bottom of the intellectual range. In the gaps between their opportunities for gifted students to pursue accelerated programs and their special educational services for slow learners, many of their average students may get lost in the shuffle.

Outside of the classroom as well, a large school's athletic teams, performing groups, and even its clubs and service societies are often available to only a small percentage of the student body who are especially talented and determined. Research studies confirm that students in smaller schools enjoy more opportunities for participation and experience more emotional support in their community of students and teachers than students in larger schools (Gump, 1980). Lacking such participation and support, adolescents may lag in developing the kinds of involvement that make the school experience an important part of their lives and motivate them to do well in the classroom.

Young people who have had the benefit of attending good schools may still lack preparation to achieve academically if illness or changing circumstances have disrupted the continuity of their learning. For example, transferring in midyear from one elementary school where the class is about to begin studying fractions in arithmetic to another school where the class has just finished fractions and is starting decimals can leave a student temporarily behind or perhaps chronically deficient in his or her understanding of fractions. In a bright youngster, such a deficiency might pass unnoticed until he or she runs into unanticipated difficulty with algebra a few years later. The assessment of school learning problems should routinely include sufficient inquiry into an adolescent's educational history to identify any such events that could have left him or her inadequately prepared for the courses in which he or she is currently doing poorly.

Academic underachievement can also result from extracurricular circumstances that detract from adolescents' attention to their studies. Having to work long hours at a job or take on burdensome responsibilities can interfere with schoolwork, even among young persons who are able and committed to doing well. Available evidence indicates that working more than 15 to 20 hours per week results in high school students spending less time on their homework than they should, and the more hours they work, the more likely they are to perceive their jobs as interfering with their education and the lower the grades they receive (Greenberger & Steinberg, 1986; Wirtz, Rohrbeck, Charner, & Fraser, 1988).

DEVELOPMENTAL DETERMINANTS

The motivational and educational factors that contribute to academic underachievement involve circumstances that are, for the most part, external to the individual. Underachievement can also derive from internal psychological states that exert their impact independently of an adolescent's academic motivation or educational opportunities. For example, any generalized anxiety reaction that disorganizes or distracts young people can impair their performance in school. Many specific psychological disorders, especially schizophrenia, depression, and school phobia, are also likely to result in underachievement. Young persons who cannot think clearly, maintain a normal energy level, or tolerate being in the classroom face an uphill struggle to maintain grades commensurate with their intellectual ability.

In other cases, psychological states may have specific implications for the learning process and may contribute directly to underachievement. In particular, clinicians need to evaluate whether unexpectedly low grades are resulting from immaturity, specific learning disabilities, or aversions to the learning process.

Immaturity

Several aspects of immaturity can interfere with an adolescent's maintaining an expected level of performance in school. Most notable among these is the extent to which cognitive immaturity sometimes retards academic progress in relation to a student's capacity for abstract thinking. As first described by Piaget (Inhelder & Piaget, 1958, Chapter 18), during adolescence, young people begin to advance from primarily concrete operations, which characterize the thinking of children, toward formal operational thinking, which typifies mature cognition. They become better able than before to manipulate ideas verbally, in the absence of tangible referents; to formulate and grasp notions of how things might be, as well as how they are, and thus to deal with possibilities, hypotheses, and even contrary-to-fact ideas, and to pass judgment on the logicality of their own ideas, as well as the ideas of others.

Because adolescents grow more capable of thinking in the abstract, their classroom requirements become increasingly geared to their assuming abstract attitudes. With each advancing grade, teachers are more likely to present material and to prepare examinations in ways that call for their students to exercise formal operational thinking. Otherwise normal adolescents who are lagging behind their peers in cognitive maturation may be handicapped in their studies by an inability to abstract at grade level.

For example, an eighth-grade student whose science teacher begins by saying, "Imagine that the earth is flat" cannot follow the discussion if he or she can think only about having been taught previously that the earth is unquestionably round. Similarly, whereas 10-year-olds are likely to define time specifically in terms of the clock—that is, in hours, minutes, and seconds—15-year-olds can usually conceive of time as an interval between two points of measurement. This means that 15-year-olds whose class comments and test answers reflect such relatively concrete orientations as "time is what the clock tells" may well be destined for lower grades than equally intelligent peers whose more typical rate of cognitive development allows them to think abstractly of time as an interval of measurement.

Research findings confirm that most young persons show developmental changes in abstract thinking from childhood to adolescence and do eventually become capable of formal operational thought (see McLaughlin & Pea, 1987). Hence, before drawing any conclusions about disorder, clinicians need to recognize instances in which school performance has fallen off temporarily in adolescents who are developmentally delayed but not permanently incapacitated with respect to operating in the abstract. Patience and support at home and in school until such young persons catch up, perhaps including specific training in abstract thinking, will then be a more appropriate recommendation than any clinical intervention.

Immaturity can also contribute to underachievement by deterring young persons from formulating their future plans. The normative late adolescent process of achieving a sense of personal identity involves pointing oneself in certain educational and career directions. When young people lag behind in this regard, they may remain undecided, or they may not even be engaged in thinking about their future.

Basic research on vocational immaturity has long demonstrated that not having appropriate long-range occupational goals can generate indifference to working hard and thereby foster academic underachievement. Among both high school and college students, achievers are more likely than underachievers to have decided on a specific vocational goal, and vocationally undecided students show less work involvement, earn lower grades, and more frequently drop out of school than those who have a goal in mind (Holland & Holland, 1977; Lunneborg, 1975). At the same time, there are numerous instances in which young persons who have shown little interest or accomplishment in the classroom blossom into superior and industrious students on discovering a field of study or a career direction that excites them.

Finally, some attention in the evaluation of underachieving adolescents should be given to possible emotional immaturity. Generally speaking, emotional immaturity contributes to school learning problems in the same way as cognitive immaturity. That is, the gap between classroom requirements and teacher expectations geared to a modal level of maturity makes it difficult for emotionally immature adolescents to earn grades commensurate with their ability.

Academically talented adolescents who have been accelerated are at particular risk for this pattern of academic difficulty. Sound personality and social development is fostered by being in classes with students of one's own age, with whom one shares similar needs and interests and comparable levels of physical, cognitive, and emotional development. For this reason, prevailing practice keeps bright young people with their agemates, even while enriching their learning with advanced placement courses and specially tailored assignments.

Sometimes, however, gifted students may be sent off to college before they have reached late adolescence. In a study of markedly accelerated students who began college before age 16, Janos, Sanfilippo, and Robinson (1986) found that most of them did well during and after their college years.

Some, however, became lackluster students, primarily because their continuing struggles with a variety of juvenile concerns prevented from applying their intellect effectively. These underachieving adolescent collegians had not necessarily been immature for 14- or 15-year-olds when they arrived on campus, but their relative immaturity in the college environment had proved their academic undoing. Any such placement in which the learning environment calls for more emotional maturity than an adolescent can muster may pave the way to underachievement.

Specific Learning Disabilities

Specific learning disabilities consist of deficits in essential learning processes that cause young people to achieve below expectation in their schoolwork in the absence of any general intellectual handicap, primary emotional disorder, or inadequate opportunity to learn. These disabilities are widely believed to result from dysfunctions in the central nervous system that impair spatial perception, visual–motor coordination, memory, capacity for abstraction, and ability to understand or use written or spoken language. In the classroom, such impairments take their toll primarily on the acquisition and utilization of skills in listening, speaking, reading, writing, reasoning, and mathematics (see Hammill, Leigh, McNutt, & Larsen, 1987; Obrzut & Hynd, 1983; Ysseldyke & Stevens, 1986).

Perceptual cognitive deficits causing learning difficulties often occur in conjunction with the condition that has been known over the years as "hyperactive child syndrome" (HACS), "minimal brain dysfunction" (MBD), and "attention deficit disorder" (ADD) and has most recently been labeled "attention-deficit hyperactivity disorder" (ADHD). There is currently widespread agreement that ADHD begins in early childhood and is characterized primarily by an age-inappropriate extent of inattentiveness, impulsivity, and hyperactivity (American Psychiatric Association, 1987; Cantwell, 1986a; Hunt, 1988; Loney, 1987). An estimated 50–80% of children with ADHD also have specific learning disabilities. The rest do not, however. Despite considerable overlap between the two conditions, 20–50% of ADHD children do not manifest specific learning disabilities. Likewise, many children with specific learning disabilities do not have the ADHD syndrome (Lambert & Sandoval, 1980; Routh, 1986; Rutter, 1983).

The primary characteristics of ADHD typically produce dramatic behavioral and learning problems from the time children enter elementary school. Because ADHD children are restless and distractible, they have difficulty focusing attention on their teachers and assignments. They absorb less than other students from group discussions, they benefit less from individual study, they are slow to complete their homework and test papers, and they often fail to remember and follow directions. Because they are impulsive and excitable, ADHD children frequently make themselves unpopular. Their aggressive and disruptive ways lead classmates and teachers to dislike and reject them. Frustrating experiences of academic ineptness and social isolation contribute to their forming low opinions of themselves and being drawn into various kinds of antisocial behavior (Grenell, Glass, & Katz, 1987; Ross & Ross, 1982, Chapter 8; Whalen & Henker, 1985). Even in the absence of an ADHD syndrome, school failures caused by specific learning disabilities are found to lead to contentious interpersonal relationships, a deflated self-image, and an inclination to misbehave (Bender & Smith, 1990; McConaughy & Ritter, 1986; Miller, 1984; Stone & La Greca, 1990).

Perceptual–cognitive deficits and the learning disabilities they spawn run a different developmental course from the primary behavioral manifestations of ADHD. Youngsters with ADHD are likely to remain more restless, distractible, and impulsive than other children, but they gain increased self-control as they mature and become less different from their classmates in these respects. In contrast to this diminution of ADHD behaviors during adolescence, perceptual–cognitive deficits tend to persist, and learning difficulties tend to become worse in the absence of adequate intervention (Brown & Borden, 1986; Cantwell, 1986b; Lambert, 1988; Wallander & Hubert, 1985; Weiss & Hechtman, 1986, Chapter 4).

The cumulative nature of learning difficulties is important to note in this regard. As subject matter becomes more difficult during high school and builds on previous learning, students with deficient skills and spotty prior learning find it increasingly hard to keep up. Mildly learning-disabled children who have managed to struggle through junior high school science and mathematics, for example, may fall by the wayside in algebra and chemistry, and those who read well enough to cope with seventh- and eighth-grade assignments may not be able to maintain the reading pace required in high school English and social science courses.

Maladaptive secondary reactions to school learning difficulties are also likely to outlast the primary manifestations of ADHD and worsen over time if allowed to run their natural course. Repeated experiences of failure and rejection during middle childhood frequently propel ADHD and learning-disabled youngsters toward increasing unhappiness, withdrawal, and self-depreciation as adolescents. Episodes of feeling sad, discouraged, incompetent, and apathetic mar their lives. Socially, they tend either to have few friends or to seek the company of younger children, who pose less threat to their fragile sense of adequacy than other adolescents do (Dollinger, Horn, & Boarini, 1988; Pihl & McLarnon, 1984; Waddell, 1984).

In a similar way, the mounting frustrations and needs for attention that cause some ADHD children to engage in antisocial behavior often lead to increasingly serious conduct problems during adolescence. Sometimes, delinquent behavior obscures all of the other difficulties these youngsters have as teenagers, and, in some cases, adolescents with learning problems that have never been detected come to professional attention for the first time because of fighting, stealing, vandalism, and other kinds of blatant disregard for authority and the law. Various follow-up studies indicate that as many as 60% of ADHD children are likely to display diagnosable conduct disorder or oppositional defiant disorder as adolescents, and 25–35% engage in antisocial acts that frequently lead to contact with the police (Barkley, Fischer, Edelbrock, & Smallish, 1990; Larson, 1988; Satterfield, Hoppe, & Schell, 1982; Weiss & Hechtman, 1986, Chapter 4).

These features of ADHD and specific learning disabilities point to some special considerations in the evaluation of adolescents who are underachieving in school. First, although ADHD can be at the root of unexpectedly poor academic performance in a junior or senior high school student, it seldom raises a new diagnostic question at this age. ADHD is a disorder that emerges in childhood, not adolescence, and there is widespread professional and general public awareness of its manifestations. The sensitivity of school personnel to age-inappropriate inattentiveness, impulsivity, and hyperactivity, supported by sophisticated methods available for the neuropsychological assessment of children, make it unlikely for instances of ADHD to pass unnoticed during the elementary school years (see Franzen & Berg, 1989; Goldstein & Goldstein, 1990; Hynd, Snow, & Becker, 1986; Taylor, Fletcher & Satz, 1984).

Second, in contrast to the relative ease with which they can usually identify long-standing ADHD, clinicians working with underachieving adolescents must be alert to the possibility of specific learning disabilities that have either previously gone undetected or have only recently become manifest in underachievement. There are distinctive and discriminable behavior patterns among (a) learning-disabled elementary school children who do not have ADHD, (b) ADHD children who are not learning disabled, and (c) children with both ADHD and specific learning disabilities (Ackerman, Oglesby, & Dykman, 1981; Tarnowski, Prinz, & Nay, 1986). Whereas all three groups may be underachieving as adolescents, it is the learning-disabled youngsters without ADHD whose basic problem is most likely to have escaped notice. Typically, they will have displayed age-appropriate behavior developmentally, without restlessness, distractibility, or impulsivity; they will not begin to show any untoward social or emotional reactions unless or until they have suffered repeated school failures; and, especially if they are highly intelligent or have developed good compensatory skills, they may have underachieved without failing or may even have received good grades prior to the current academic problems that have led to their referral.

Learning-disabled adolescents who have only recently begun to receive unexpectedly low grades often have a difficult time coming to grips with their situation. The less aware they are of having a learning disability, the more troubled and perplexed they are by finding themselves suddenly unable to maintain their customary academic standing. Being correctly diagnosed and told they have a perceptual–cognitive handicap is not welcome news for adolescents either, given their normative developmental concerns about having a well-functioning mind and body. On the other hand, receiving such information, especially when it is accompanied by an educational plan for reducing or circumventing their skill deficits, has the beneficial impact of sparing learning-disabled adolescents from simply feeling stupid, inept, or, worse yet, at the mercy of some unidentifiable or irremediable aberration that is undermining their ability to perform in school.

As a further hazard for adolescents with learning disabilities who have only recently begun to underachieve, their previously normal adjustment and adequate school performance may lead other people to assume that their currently declining grades are due to slacking off or some psychological conflict, rather than to basic deficits in conceptual, language, or mathematical skills. This can lead to unpleasant interactions with parents and teachers who believe that increased diligence on the adolescent's part will solve the problem and are harshly critical of him or her when the problem persists. Misdiagnosis can also lead to superfluous psychotherapy, should mental health professionals read into these situations some acute crisis or neurotic reaction where none exists. Although learning-disabled adolescents who have begun to underachieve in junior or senior high school may need help in dealing with maladaptive emotional reactions to their faltering academic performance, the key to their improvement is educational remediation, not psychotherapy.

In recent years, clinicians and educators have begun to recognize this type of late-onset learning problem, even among students starting college. It may seem reasonable to assume that high school graduates who have done well enough in the classroom and on aptitude tests to qualify for admission to college cannot be learning disabled. As reported by Cohen (1983), however, an estimated 6% of college freshmen in the United States are learning disabled. They have made it into college in most cases by dint of hard work, good general intelligence, and a high school situation that allowed them to excel in areas of strength while avoiding areas of weakness. In college, no longer able to avoid areas of weakness and often lacking special assistance, these students may have difficulty keeping up in courses that emphasize reading, writing, mathematical processes, and the learning of foreign or computer languages.

Aversions to the Learning Process

In *The Psychopathology of Everyday Life,* Freud (1901/1960) suggested that certain types of forgetting, erroneous acts, and mistakes in speaking, reading, and writing are due to unconscious influences, specifically, the disguised expression of repressed impulses. Mistakes that represent the return of the repressed can detract from students' academic performance when, for example, a college freshman, upset by the bisexuality of men in ancient Greece and needing to disparage its leading figures, writes a philosophy paper in which he refers to the work of "Pluto"; or when a high school social science student who resents authority and has not outgrown childish preoccupations with the functions of elimination refers to Sir Stafford Cripps, a distinguished British statesman from the World War II era, as "Stifford Craps."

Going beyond such specific slips, some psychoanalytic theorists attempted to trace generalized learning difficulties in normally intelligent, otherwise well-adjusted young persons to the effects of unconscious needs or motives. In this earlier literature, certain aggressive or sexual aspects of the learning process were seen as causing "emotional blocks" in underachievers. For example, the taking in of information, as in looking at a page in a book, can be interpreted both as an active encounter with the environment and as an expression of curiosity. Aversions to the learning process can develop if this kind of activity makes students feel that they are being too aggressive or if being curious is associated in their minds with sexual curiosity that might lead them to ask too many embarrassing questions or see things they are not supposed to see (see Harris, 1965).

The specific content of course material may also be a potential source of aversions to learning in young persons with pressing sexual or aggressive concerns. Adolescents who are struggling with inhibited or unsatisfied childhood curiosity about bodily and sexual functions may have difficulty concentrating on such subjects as biology. Similarly, students troubled by aggressive fantasies may be uncomfortable with violence-filled novels assigned for English, the study of wars and other catastrophes in history, and dissections required in biology. Cohen (1983), for example, describes a student who reported, "I keep failing science, I get so nervous with all the blood and stuff" (p. 181).

Although such specific aversions may be involved in learning difficulties, they do not provide a particularly powerful explanation of these problems. Evidence of their validity is limited to case illustrations of the kind mentioned and has not yet emerged from any systematic empirical research. Moreover, clinical experience and research findings suggest that the vast majority of achievement problems involving psychological conflicts can be adequately understood in terms of maladaptive patterns of family interaction, as discussed next, without hypothesizing unconscious implications of the learning process itself.

FAMILY-INTERACTION DETERMINANTS

When psychological conflicts are leading to primary problems in school learning, they typically involve maladaptive patterns of family interaction comprising (a) considerable anger that young persons feel toward their parents but cannot express directly; (b) concerns about rivalry that generate marked fears of failure or of success; and (c) a preference for passive-aggressive modes of coping with stressful situations. None of these patterns is unique to psychologically conflicted academic underachievers. However, they so frequently contribute to a reluctance or refusal to achieve, especially in families that value education, that underachievement can often be predicted for students in whom all are present. Learning difficulties determined by unresolved hostile impulses toward family members, fears of competing with parents and siblings, and a passive-aggressive behavioral style constitute a fairly specific form of psychological disturbance that can, for convenience, be referred to as *passive–aggressive underachievement.*

Anger Toward Parents

Psychological test findings, interview data, ratings by teachers, and parents' reports have consistently indicated that underachieving adolescents are basically angrier people than equally intelligent students who are getting adequate grades. However, they are less likely to display their anger in overtly hostile behavior than through such covert channels as snide remarks, hypercritical attitudes, and smoldering resentments (Mandel & Marcus, 1988).

Other studies of underachieving students have traced their anger specifically to resentment of parental authority that they perceive as restrictive and unjust. Low-achieving high school and college students are more likely than their equally capable but academically successful peers to describe their parents as too strict and overcontrolling. Parents of low achievers, compared to parents whose children are doing well in schools, are in turn more likely to be either overly permissive or excessively authoritarian in their parenting style (Dornbusch, Ritter, Leiderman, & Roberts, 1987; Steinberg, Elman, & Mounts, 1989).

Permissiveness can lead to underachievement by signifying to an adolescent the kinds of disinterest and uninvolvement discussed earlier as parental determinants of low motivation to achieve. *Authoritarianism*, which consists of insisting that adolescents comply with parental demands and giving them little opportunity to participate in decisions about what would be best for them, can lead to underachievement by breeding resentment. Feeling unwilling or unable to express this resentment directly, and perceiving its source in their parents' undemocratic stance, passive–aggressive underachievers are drawn to poor academic performance as an indirect way of venting their anger and retaliating for being deprived of their autonomy.

For such retaliation to succeed—that is, for poor grades to function as an aggressive act—an adolescent's parents must care enough about his or her school performance to become visibly upset when it falls off. Typically, then, passive–aggressive underachievement occurs in families in which the parents have considerable stake in their children's academic success and take the children's flagging performance very much to heart. What these parents fail to recognize is the extent to which their authoritarian expectations, riding roughshod over the underachieving adolescent's own choices and preferences, have fueled the resentments that initiated the problem.

Common in this regard are pressures from upward-striving parents to do well and the imposition of academic or career goals that their children do not share. For example, the child of a lawyer or physician may be encouraged to follow in his or her footsteps, despite being uncertain of what he or she would like to do or perhaps wanting instead to become an artist or a biologist. Or a student who is the only, the oldest, or the brightest child in a family may be selected to become its standard-bearer as a successful professional person, when he or she would rather pursue a nonprofessional career or perhaps not even attend college. Young persons who cannot find ways to challenge or resist such parental pressures openly may utilize underachievement to solve the problem. Their solution is to avoid a career or course of study in which they have little interest by failing to qualify for it, while they get back at their parents by frustrating the aspirations they have for them.

Paul was a 14-year-old boy from a socially prominent family who was about to be dismissed from boarding school because of his poor academic record. His father had attended the same school and had gone on from there to an elite preparatory school and then to a distinguished university. He had planned for his son to do likewise. Discussion with Paul and his father revealed that the father was an emotionally cold, domineering person who demanded outstanding accomplishment and absolute obedience from his son. Paul had long rankled under his father's constant prodding and criticism and lack of overt affection. However, the prospect of ever disagreeing with his father or showing any anger was out of the question—"I'd just get clobbered," he said. When it was suggested to Paul that his school failure was one area in which he could exert some control over his father, he smiled broadly and responded, "You said it; there's not a darn thing he can do about it; when he got the call from the headmaster he hit the ceiling, but he can't do a thing about it!"

Karen was a 15-year-old sophomore whose grades had dropped from a B average in junior high school to just a shade above failing. Her clearly stated ambition was to attend vocational school after graduation from high school and be trained as a legal secretary, a career her mother had happily pursued for many years. Her father, however, had other plans for her. He was determined that she be a top student and attend a "first-rate" liberal arts college. Karen was enrolled in a college preparatory program at her father's insistence, despite her different wishes and the school's recommendation that she transfer to a less demanding curriculum consistent with her interests. Test scores indicated that Karen was bright enough to earn good grades in the precollege program if she wished to. However, deep resentment of her father's imposition of his values on her clearly seemed to be causing her declining performance, which represented an indirect aggressive action against him.

Although the origins of the anger inhibition that figures so prominently in such instances of passive–aggressive underachievement has not been studied empirically, some generally shared clinical impressions proved helpful in understanding this feature of the disorder. Inability or reluctance to express anger directly appears to derive from developmental experiences in which people come to believe that such expressions would be dangerous, fruitless, or immoral. Individuals who worry that expressing anger directly is *dan-*

gerous fear that other people will retaliate or will reject them. Such fears typically emerge in the context of harsh, punitive parenting. Individuals who regard actively asserting themselves as *fruitless* tend to have been reared in ways that minimize self-esteem and maximize feelings of helplessness; from this, they have concluded that their best prospects for influencing events to their advantage will be found in indirect avenues not obvious to others. Individuals who consider anger *immoral* view competitive striving as an aggressive act that improperly deprives others of their chance for success; usually they have grown up averse to anger in a family atmosphere in which humility and self-sacrifice are guiding moral principles (see Burns & Epstein, 1983; Stricker, 1983).

Neither punitive, depreciatory, nor self-abnegating parenting is specific to passive–aggressive underachievement. Young persons reared in these ways may display a variety of psychological disorders or none at all, and individuals who are anxious about or averse to expressing anger may have become so without having had such early experiences. Nevertheless, in exploring the origins of underachievement and seeking to undo or counteract their effects, clinicians should keep in mind the likelihood that the anger inhibition central to this disorder has its roots in these kinds of parental influence.

Concerns about Rivalry

Concerns about rivalry frequently lead people to avoid the competitive pursuit of excellence. Through inaction or by a variety of self-defeating maneuvers, they refrain from their best possible effort and never accomplish as much as they could. With specific regard to the classroom, passive–aggressive underachievers typically suffer from fears of failing or fears of succeeding that inhibit their academic efforts.

Fear of Failure

Persons who fear failure doubt their own abilities and seek at all times to buffer themselves against the experience of having failed. Most notably, they set high goals for themselves and then work only half-heartedly to attain them. This maneuver allows underachievers to deny having any limitations and to dismiss any suggestion that they have been unable to do well. When they fall short of their stated goals, which they inevitably do, they shrug off embarrassment by pointing out how ambitious these goals were to begin with—"I didn't do as well as I had hoped, but look at how much I was aiming for." When they do poorly, they call attention to their lackadaisical effort: "I didn't put much time into it, you know; if I had cared about it and really tried, I could have done a lot better." Were failure-fearing persons to set goals realistically within their grasp and work diligently toward then, they would then risk coming up short without having such ready-made excuses with which to cushion the resulting blow to their self-esteem. Students who fear failure rarely take such risks. They seldom chance doing or saying anything that might be wrong, they consistently deny having worked hard even when they have, and they pride themselves on how much they have accomplished without much effort—"I think I did pretty well, considering that I hardly cracked a book the whole term." These students know full well that failure signifies lack of ability only when a sincere effort has been made. As the insightful father of one underachieving boy put it, "I think he's afraid to work hard, because if he tried hard and still wasn't doing well, he would really have to feel terrible."

This particular pattern of underachievement often emerges at educational transition points that confront students with more difficult subject matter than they have previously been assigned. Being promoted from elementary school to junior high school and from junior to senior high school can cause young persons who are worried about lacking ability to become increasingly concerned about failure and begin backing away from their studies. Likewise, fear-of-failure students who transfer schools and perceive their classmates as brighter, more industrious, or better prepared than their former ones may at this point retreat from competitive effort and begin to underachieve. Among late adolescents, the transition from high school to college, which involves both more difficult assignments and more capable classmates, can also be the challenge that elicits this pattern of difficulty.

Another feature of the potentially discouraging impact of starting college was elaborated insightfully by McArthur (1971), who described the dilemma of students whose family and friends expect them to maintain the same relative excellence they displayed in high school, despite the fact that they are now competing with students who also did well in high school. Such young persons often suffer "big league shock" when they realize the nature of their competition. Should they despair of ever being able to hold their own in the collegiate academic environment, they may choose not to make the effort and thereby ensure the onset of underachievement.

Competitive concerns within the family also commonly mark the lives of underachieving adolescents whose self-defeating approach to their studies reflects fear of failure. Most students who fear failure have suffered from unfavorable comparisons with a successful parent or sibling whose abilities they cannot match. Directly stated or implied disappointment that they are not living up to family standards may then contribute to their shirking the work that would earn them grades commensurate with their ability—"What's the use of trying? I could never do as well as my brother did anyway."

CASE 11.   ACADEMIC UNDERACHIEVEMENT INVOLVING FEAR OF FAILURE

After having spent 2 years in the sixth grade, 13-year-old John was on the verge of being asked to repeat his seventh-grade courses when his parents first sought psychological help for him. His low achievement had begun in the third grade and had been attributed by his teachers primarily to his being inattentive in class and neglecting his daily assignments. He had never presented any behavior problems in school, and current psychological testing indicated high average intelligence with no suggestion of specific learning disabilities.

John's father, a teacher in the same school system where John was a pupil, willingly explored his role in his son's difficulties. He volunteered that he was known as an authoritarian, bossy person who yelled a lot and was unpleasant to work with, and he added that perhaps he was too intolerant and punitive when his son did not behave exactly as he wanted him to. Although John did not overtly complain about how his father treated him, he did appear to resent many of his parents' attitudes. Yet he could never bring himself to any direct expression of anger or resentment. To the contrary, he consistently retreated from any situation that involved verbal or physical aggression (he had dropped out of the Boy Scouts because "they do too much roughhousing"), and he was known among his peers as someone who could be counted on not to defend himself. His teachers' observations rounded out the picture of a shy, quiet, unassertive boy with little self-confidence who was often picked on by his classmates.

John's parents reported that he characteristically set perfectionistic standards for himself, became extremely upset over minor setbacks, and avoided any situation in which he had ever been a loser. Recently, during a game of catch with his father and some other boys and their fathers, he had become so humiliated at dropping the ball, even though it had been badly thrown to him, that he left the game and would not return. John himself could describe clearly how his limited self-confidence and fear of failure interfered with his performance in school. His teachers were wrong in considering him inattentive in class, he said; in truth, he was just reluctant to volunteer or answer questions for fear he would say something wrong and give his classmates an excuse for laughing at him.

John also faced major problems in competing with his 1-year-younger brother who was also in the seventh grade. The brother was an outgoing, academically successful boy who at times joined in the teasing that John received at school. The scholastic attainments of his brother and teacher-father had intensified John's fears that he could never meet his family's standards and discouraged him even further from utilizing what academic ability he possessed.

Fear of Success

People who fear success are concerned that doing well will bring them more unhappiness than failing to achieve. This seemingly paradoxical disadvantage of success was first elaborated clinically in descriptions by Freud (1916/ 1957) of patients "wrecked by success." These patients had become troubled just when they had attained a valued goal for which they had worked long and hard. Such aversion to being successful derives from the expectation that one's achievements will be envied or resented by one's parents and siblings.

For success-fearing persons the fruits of victory in competitive situations leave a bad aftertaste that prevents them from enjoying what they have achieved and leads them to abandon their aspirations and undo their accomplishments.

To avoid the disapproval or rejection they anticipate in the wake of achievement, people who are made anxious by success approach achievement-related situations much differently from people who are concerned with failure. As just mentioned, fear-of-failure students tend to set very high goals and then expend little energy to reach them. In this way, they escape the anxiety of a near miss and can say that their attainments only partially reflect their true ability. By contrast, students who are leery of success make light of their own abilities, even when they are considerable ("I'm not very good in math"); they set limited, unrealistically low goals that are easily within their grasp ("I'll be happy to get a C average; that's all I'm working for"), and they exert themselves just enough to reach these minimal goals, after which they desist from any additional effort and disavow any further aspirations ("I was lucky to do as well as I did, and you couldn't expect me to do better"). By such attitudes toward their schoolwork, fear-of-success students avoid any accomplishments or even appearances that might threaten their loved ones or diminish the affection and support they receive from them.

This underachieving pattern has been demonstrated in the laboratory, as well as in the consulting room. When success-fearing persons perform well on a task or are led to believe that they have performed well, they tend to become anxious and to experience difficulty in concentrating; on subsequent trials, their performance level goes down. When they are doing poorly on a series of laboratory tasks, their performance gradually improves with practice—until such time they are told or conclude that they are doing well, at which point they become uncomfortable and slack off. In this same vein, when success-fearing persons happen to be successful, they attribute their accomplishments to external factors, such as luck. When they fail, they attribute the outcome to internal factors, such as their own limited ability.

A further diagnostically helpful difference between failure-fearing and success-fearing underachievers involves the actual or perceived accomplishments of their parents and sibling. As previously noted, persons who fear failure are troubled by rivalry with successful individuals. The more impressive the accomplishments of their parents and siblings, the more they worry about falling short of expectations and the more seriously they are likely to underachieve as a consequence of avoiding competitive effort. Students who fear success, on the other hand, welcome being surrounded by talented people, for then the risk of incurring their envy or resentment is minimized. Their school-learning problems are intensified instead by having unsuccessful parents and siblings. The more that success-fearing persons regard other members of their family as less able than they are, the more they anticipate negative reactions to what they themselves may accomplish.

As happened to Freud's patients "wrecked by success," passive–aggressive underachievers who fear doing well are most likely to falter when they reach the threshold of some noteworthy academic accomplishment. Such thresholds can be especially disconcerting if they signify surpassing what their parents and siblings have been able to achieve. An important case in point is first-generation college students; children of high-school-educated parents may have mixed feelings about going to college, especially if their family has waxed enthusiastic about high education while subtly communicating a quite different message. For example, the parents may say to their college-bound adolescent, "Now you'll have opportunities we never had and be able to do all the things we never could." Although such a message may imply pride, pleasure, and encouragement, it can also convey underlying feelings of disappointment, envy, rejection, and even anger, as if to say, "We've had a good life without a college education, and now you're going to go away, and it will cost us a lot of money, and you'll get all kinds of new ideas, and it will never be the same between us again."

Faced with these circumstances, capable young persons who fear success not infrequently manage, by neglect of their studies, either to do poorly in college after a strong high school performance or to begin doing poorly in their final years of high school. The former kind of academic swoon can get success-fearing students dismissed from college, whereas the latter kind, which has aptly been called "senior neurosis" (Hogenson, 1974), reduces their chances of getting accepted into college in the first place. These and other fear-of-success patterns, like fears of failure, can disrupt striving in any kind of competitive pursuit. Should talented but success-fearing young persons begin to become better athletes or musicians than their parents, for example, their performance may suddenly and without apparent reason fall victim to diminished dedication and slackened effort.

For precision in the evaluation and treatment of academic underachievement, fears of success rooted in intrafamily concerns about rivalry need to be differentiated from a reluctance to perform well determined by peer-group or sex-role influence. As noted earlier, peer-group conformity is a transient developmental phenomenon that influences youthful behavior primarily from late childhood to midadolescence. While it is holding sway, young persons are fully cognizant of how and why they are being influenced by it—they are avoiding being a good student to avoid peer disapproval. Although sex-role influences may involve family as well as peer attitudes toward appropriate feminine and masculine roles, these influences too are consciously recognized and tied to a developmental task, the formation of one's sex-role identity.

Unlike peer-group and sex-role influences on underachievement, the fear-of-success experiences of some passive–aggressive underachievers are long-term, exclusively family-related, and largely unconscious. They emerge out of early life experiences and, unless modified by subsequent events, persist as an attitudinal set independently of whether they are causing underachievement at a particular moment in time. They revolve around concerns about being loved and accepted by one's parents and siblings, and, unless some negative peer-group influences also happen to be operating, passive–aggressive underachievers do not care what their classmates think of their school performance. Finally, and of most significance in planning intervention strategies, fear of success exerts its influence without the underachieving students even being aware that their low grades and their typically benign attitude toward mediocre performance stem from concerns about becoming a threat to members of their family.

Passive-Aggressive Behavioral Style

Underachievers concerned with problems of anger and rivalry typically earn low or declining grades by taking a passive-aggressive approach to their studies. Whether limited to the academic situation or employed as a pervasive personality style, passive-aggressive modes of coping with experience consist of purposeful inactivity intended to express underlying hostility that cannot be expressed directly (see Esman, 1986; Millon, 1981, Chapter 9; Stricker, 1983). Passive-aggressive adolescents are angry young persons who keep their true feelings to themselves and channel their resentments into orchestrated inaction. They exert a telling impact on those who care about them, not by committing dastardly or disobedient acts, but merely by not doing what is expected of them or what would please others. They frustrate and provoke the important persons in their lives by just sitting there—a stubborn, disinterested, unmotivated lump under whom their parents and teachers would like to build a fire.

In school, passive-aggressive underachievers tend to study less than their achieving peers, they procrastinate in completing their assignments, and they reserve their enthusiasm for extracurricular activities. The energy they expend in sports, hobbies, and part-time jobs may contrast sharply with their academic lassitude. They may even read widely and keep themselves well informed, while making sure not to read material assigned in their courses and taking care not to become informed about matters that will come up in class discussions or on examinations.

Passive-aggressive underachievers usually go to great lengths in other ways, as well, to steer clear of getting good grades. They "forget" to write down assignments; they study the wrong material in preparation for examinations; they turn in test papers in which they have "overlooked" a section or an entire page; and they sit silently through class discussions when they have something to contribute. Through such carelessness and inactivity, students with this pattern of difficulty effectively undermine whatever chances they would have had of receiving grades commensurate with their abilities.

The academic orientation of passive-aggressive underachievers is often reflected in two distinctive features of their performance on psychological tests. On measures of intellectual functioning such as the Wechsler, they are likely to receive lower scores on tasks that require previous school learning and concentrated effort than on tasks that can be handled with a relatively effortless application of general social knowledge or specific abilities unrelated to school learning. On projective tests such as the Rorschach, their responses typically contain little evidence of overt hostility but considerable evidence of underlying resentments, a disposition to stubborn and oppositional behavior, and a preference for coping with problems through inactivity (Exner & Weiner, 1982, Chapter 8). Although by no means unique to passive–aggressive underachievers, such test patterns are typically found in adolescents with this particular problem and are often associated with failure to achieve up to their potential in school.

Like the ways in which adolescents who fear failure or success protect themselves, the academic blundering of the passive–aggressive underachiever, though purposeful, is not consciously intentional. These adolescents differ from low achievers who directly make it known that they are disinterested in receiving an education and openly resist the efforts of the school to give them one. Instead, passive–aggressive underachievers are young persons who otherwise would embrace and pursue academic goals but whose struggle with underlying conflicts about anger and rivalry, set in the context of maladaptive patterns of family interaction, is producing a psychological handicap. Their passive–aggressive maneuvers are indirect, neurotic efforts to resolve their conflicts, and they are unlikely to recognize either how their coping style is crippling their academic performance or how it is serving as an aggressive act against their parents. Increasing these two areas of awareness accordingly becomes a focal point in treating the passive–aggressive underachiever.

CASE 12.   PASSIVE–AGGRESSIVE STYLE IN ACADEMIC UNDERACHIEVEMENT

Bob, an 18-year-old high school junior, had managed to get by in school with C grades through the ninth grade. At that point, his parents, concerned that continuing mediocre performance would prevent him from getting into a good college, had sent him, against his wishes, to a private boarding school. They hoped he would improve his academic credentials at this school. Instead, he managed to fail every one of his courses and was asked not to return. Back home the next year, he had repeated the tenth grade, with barely passing grades, and was doing very poorly in the eleventh grade.

Bob stated flatly that he received low grades because he disliked studying and consistently avoided doing his schoolwork. Contrary to his parents' educational aspirations for him, he was undecided about attending college, especially a demanding school where he would have to work hard to stay in. Yet he was convinced he could be an excellent student if he wanted to apply himself. He reported that, during the evening hours designated by his parents as "study time," he regularly read books, newspapers, and magazines but seldom studied his school assignments or absorbed any information related to his courses.

Further discussion with Bob indicated that he was not a generally lazy person, nor was he untalented or averse to success. He pursued several nonintellectual activities with industry and enthusiasm. He liked to hunt, fish, and camp and was an accomplished outdoorsman. He was a skilled carpenter and had completed several ambitious woodworking projects around his home. He enjoyed painting, drawing, and ceramics, and during the previous summer, he had done very well in a special art course. Where it counted for his parents, however—getting good grades in a demanding school—he was successfully resisting their wishes by not working to capacity and was punishing them in the process.

Bob's performance on the Wechsler revealed generally superior intellectual abilities, with a Full-Scale IQ of 125. Yet, consistently with expectation in underachievers, he fell down markedly on tasks related to specific school learning and persistent intellectual effort. His two lowest subtests were Information and Digit Symbol, whereas he did best, at very superior levels of performance, on measures of social intelligence (Comprehension) and perceptual organization (Block Design).

TREATMENT

Treatment strategies in working with underachieving adolescents must be as diverse as the circumstances that lead to this problem. Intervention must be preceded by careful attention to which of the possible motivational, educational, developmental, and family interaction determinants of underachievement are in evidence. This differential assessment of the origins of unexpectedly low academic performance will guide the therapist in implementing as many of the following four interventions as are necessary to ameliorate a student's learning difficulties: (a) strengthening deficient reward systems; (b) filling instructional gaps; (c) alleviating cognitive and emotional handicaps; and (d) modifying passive–aggressive propensities.

Strengthening Deficient Reward Systems

Young persons who are minimally invested in school as a result of sociocultural influences that have lowered their motivation to learn can be difficult to treat. When they are conforming to parental or peer-group values that denigrate school learning, underachievers typically do not regard themselves as having a problem. Unlike learning-disabled or passive–aggressive underachievers, who usually endorse the value of good grades, whatever their defensive protestations to the contrary, unmotivated underachievers see little to gain and perhaps something to lose by improving their scholarship. They rarely come to professional attention except under duress, and, although they may be pleasant and superficially cooperative when interviewed, they seldom show much interest in considering new ways of thinking or acting in relation to school.

The therapist's task in these circumstances is to find ways of building a reward system that will support concerted effort in the classroom. In individual psychotherapy, this involves impressing on unmotivated students the advantages of becoming as well educated as they can. To make such an impression, therapists need first to overcome the unmotivated underachiever's indifference to being treated. This requires conversations about his or her current experiences that foster a sense of confidence, trust, and respect in the treatment relationship. Once established, this relationship can be used as a basis for influencing the young person toward broader perspectives on the potential rewards of becoming generally knowledgeable and occupationally well-qualified.

Parent counseling offers an additional and sometimes vital resource for building academic rewards into the lives of unmotivated underachievers. Parents who have been dispensing few such rewards but would sincerely like to see their children succeed in school, or who are at least willing to cooperate with a treatment program, can be encouraged to provide a more academically supportive home environment. This includes speaking positively about education, showing interest in what their adolescent is doing in school, endorsing participation in school activities, and praising their child's accomplishments. These kinds of increased parental involvement have a demonstrably positive impact on the academic performance of previously unmotivated students (see Adelman & Taylor, 1983; Barth, 1986, Chapter 8; Fehrmann et al., 1987; Rodick & Henggeler, 1980).

Often, the school can also be enlisted as a fruitful collaborator in generating academic motivation. Therapists working with underachieving adolescents should familiarize themselves with the resources available in their schools and discuss their special needs with school personnel. Efforts to promote more engagement in classroom and extracurricular activities and strategies for delivering the experience of success produce school-based rewards that help counteract academic disincentives in the lives of unmotivated underachievers (see Berkovitz, 1985; Green, 1985; Tolmach, 1985). The poor school performance of unmotivated adolescents can also be improved at times through training in academic skills. Special instructional programs in language, reading, and mathematics, even in the absence of specific learning disabilities, have been found to enhance the performance and personal satisfaction of underachieving students to good effect, especially among adolescents from disadvantaged backgrounds (Becker & Carnine, 1980; Coie & Krehbiel, 1984).

Filling Educational Gaps

When poor preparation or limited opportunities to learn are preventing otherwise able and motivated adolescents from working to their academic potential, there may be little that mental health professionals can do, except in their role as public citizens. The negative effects of crowded schools, inferior instruction, and long hours of after-school work are social problems that extend beyond the capacity of psychotherapists to resolve.

Nevertheless, in a counseling role to the family or as a consultant to the school, the individual practitioner may be able to offer useful educational advice. Perhaps an adolescent whose academic self-concept has been deflated in his or her particular learning environment should be transferred to a less-demanding school, class, or course of study. Perhaps special tutoring should be instituted in some area in which an underachieving student has missed out on previous opportunities to acquire basic skills and knowledge. Moving to more sensitive matters, perhaps the school should consider in-service training programs for some of its teachers, to help them conduct their classes more effectively and with greater sensitivity to the impact that their attitudes and behavior can have on their students, and perhaps families can be counseled to find economic alternatives that will reduce an underachieving adolescent's income-producing responsibilities. Each of these kinds of interventions has been demonstrated to improve the performance of educationally handicapped students (Butler-Por, 1987, Chapter 3; Maher & Zins, 1987; Shapiro, 1987).

When young persons are underachieving as a secondary consequence of generalized anxiety, schizophrenic or depressive disorder, or school phobia, improved schoolwork usually follows successful treatment of the primary disturbance. When underachievement reflects cognitive or emotional immaturity, patience rather than professional intervention is usually the proper prescription. As long as slowly developing young persons do not develop excessive concerns about being less mature than their peers, and as long as their parents and teachers do not jump to premature conclusions that they are academically inept, they will in time outgrow the concrete thinking, childishness, and lack of future orientation that can temporarily handicap their academic performance.

When excessive concerns arise or patience wears thin, counseling may be indicated for these young persons and for their parents and teachers as well. Sometimes, this counseling needs to focus on explaining how an academic difficulty has arisen from a developmental lag rather than from more serious or lasting handicaps. Sometimes, the focus must fall on candid discussions with all concerned of how to rectify the errors of placing an intellectually precocious adolescent in circumstances calling for emotional maturity far beyond his or her current capacity. At other times, especially among late adolescents, the resolution of underachievement may depend on vocational counseling that helps a young person make a commitment to future educational and occupational goals he or she finds attractive.

While looking to maturation to make the difference in these cases, the clinician must also remain alert to major anxiety and depressive reactions that may have emerged secondarily to the underachievement problem. Any such psychopathological reaction will have to be treated in its own right as part of the intervention plan. Psychotherapy for upsetting emotional reactions to specific learning disabilities may also play a role in the treatment of psychologically determined underachievement. Individual psychotherapy is frequently indicated to help learning-disabled adolescents deal with distress stemming from their cognitive shortcomings and academic setbacks. A supportive relationship with an understanding adult who can help them put their limitations and future prospects in clear perspective can bolster these underachievers' self-image and can spur them to fuller utilization of their abilities.

More germane than individual counseling in the treatment of learning-disabled adolescents, however, is a comprehensive psychoeducational approach comprising a variety of remedial education and behavioral strategies. Most of these students can benefit from special classes or individual tutoring in reading, mathematics, or other subject areas in which they have become deficient as a consequence of their cognitive disabilities (see Deshler, Schumaker, Lenz, & Ellis, 1984a; Lane & Campbell, 1986; Levin, Zigmond, & Birch, 1985; Montague & Bos, 1986). In addition, other aspects of their curriculum may be tailored to take maximum advantage of their strengths and minimize the impact of their deficiencies. For example, in working with underachieving adolescents who have good verbal skills but limited ability to grasp abstract concepts, the therapist may recommend that the school assign them to advanced English and social studies classes but to a relatively undemanding general science course rather than chemistry or physics. Such planning can curtail the kinds of failure experience that typically undermine a learning-disabled adolescent's confidence and discourage him or her from studying.

With respect to behavioral strategies, intervention on behalf of learning-disabled adolescents can beneficially include (a) encouraging their teachers to provide a more positive and rewarding climate for these students in the classroom and (b) employing social-skills training with the adolescents themselves, to improve the frequency and quality of their peer interactions (see La Greca & Mesibov, 1981; Siperstein & Goding, 1985; Zigmond, Levin, & Laurie, 1985). Academic effort in the classroom can also be promoted by such methods as token economies, contingency contracting, modeling verbal feedback, and orchestrated group support (see Deshler, Schumaker, & Lenz, 1984b; Shapiro, 1987).

The parents of learning-disabled adolescents should be counseled to help them deal with their feelings about the problem and to guide them in responding in ways that will support their children's efforts to overcome it. The families of these underachievers often have formed inflated impressions of their children's potential, based on observing flashes of accomplishment in areas not affected by the young person's specific disability, and frequently they hold either poor parenting on their own part or willful bumbling on their children's part responsible for their children's poor school performance. Blaming themselves makes them feel guilty, and blaming their children makes them feel angry. Neither reaction is justified, and both suffuse the underachievement problem with an emotional overlay that makes it worse.

Parental disappointment and finger-pointing are particularly likely to occur when adolescents are disabled in areas that have special significance for the family. Thus, it may be difficult for parents who are accountants or engineers to accept the fact that their child cannot grasp arithmetic and to feel for him or her the same parental warmth they might feel for a child endowed more in their image. The therapist's task in such instances is to engage the parents in frank discussion of their reaction and to help them achieve a realistic and constructive sense of their child's problems and prospects.

When learning disability has coexisted with ADHD, underachieving adolescents who remain noticeably hyperactive and distractible may benefit from appropriate medication. There is an extensive literature concerning the potential efficacy of stimulant drugs, in particular, in curbing the disruptive behaviors associated with ADHD (see Abikoff & Gittelman, 1985; Donnelly & Rapoport, 1985; Dulcan, 1986). However, with respect to specific learning disabilities occurring in the absence of hyperactivity, there is little evidence to indicate that medication facilitates academic achievement or even enhances the beneficial effects of educational and behavioral interventions (Gadow, 1985).

Modifying Passive–Aggressive Propensities

Although more likely to involve psychological disturbance than poor performance attributable to motivational, educational, and cognitive determinants, passive–aggressive underachievement is relatively responsive to psychotherapy. The therapist should focus on helping adolescents with this problem recognize and express their anger toward their parents, work through their concerns about failure or success, and appreciate the manner in which they have been using passivity to ensure poor grades in school and to make their parents unhappy. Definitive psychotherapy to eliminate the symptom of underachievement in such cases by thus unraveling its motivations is not necessarily long term. For many underachieving adolescents, merely being helped to acknowledge and ventilate underlying resentments toward their parents is sufficient to begin reversing their underachievement. Oppositional young persons who are given safe and supportive opportunities to deal openly with their hostilities no longer need to seek covert means of rebelling against parental demands, and passive–aggressive underachievers whose parental resentments can be elicited and related to their academic efforts may within a few months of treatment demonstrate a markedly improved school performance.

Despite this generally favorable outlook in psychotherapy with passive-aggressive underachievers, some other considerations may temper the success that can be expected. First, the less accessible an underachieving adolescent's underlying feelings toward his or her parents are and the more his or her learning difficulties are complicated by concerns about failure and success, the more likely it becomes that extended psychotherapy will be necessary to produce significant improvement. Second, the more an underachiever's passive–aggressive propensities have blossomed into a long-standing and pervasive coping style, as opposed to an academically delimited defensive maneuver of recent origin, the more likely they are to resist modification and to provide an obstacle in the treatment.

Therapists need to be prepared that underachievers in whom chronic and generalized passive-aggressive proclivities indicate the need for extended psychotherapy are rarely motivated to undertake it. They are instead likely to deny that they have any difficulties that call for professional attention and to doubt that talking about themselves will serve any meaningful purpose. If they refrain from overt refusal to attend sessions, they then typically combine a facade of treatment compliance with subtle forms of resistance that are difficult to detect and dispel.

The likelihood of a good treatment outcome with passive-aggressive underachievers is much better for those who come willingly rather than reluctantly to psychotherapy, and any progress at all for those who come unwillingly will depend on the therapist's success in getting them to acknowledge that they are having difficulties for which they need help. Repeated confrontation may be necessary in such cases, to foster candid self-observation. Capitalizing on the school failures and family discord that usually accompany entrenched passive-aggressive underachievement, therapists should strive by repeated reference to these undesirable circumstances to establish that things are not going as well as the adolescent would like. Once such well-intended badgering succeeds in convincing these young persons at least to give therapy a try, the conversations that ensue will ordinarily furnish numerous occasions for the therapist to point out elements of their disorder and to whet their interest in finding a better way to lead their lives.

Because passive-aggressive underachievement emerges in the context of maladaptive family interaction, its treatment can be facilitated by focused parent counseling. Parents should be given accurate information about their underachieving youngster's potential, which they may not have perceived correctly; they should be reassured that their son's or daughter's declining grades do not signify inevitable academic or occupational failure; and, above all, they should be encouraged to relax whatever pressures they are placing on their child for superior performance or noteworthy attainments.

Accurate information and persuasive guidance can prevent parents from expecting too much or expressing invidious comparisons. When parents become less insistently demanding, their passive-aggressive children become less resentful of them. When these adolescents hear fewer such comments as "You don't seem to have what it takes," or "With your ability, you should be putting us all to shame," they become less concerned about rivalry. When parents can be counseled to refrain from expressing inordinate concern or becoming visibly upset about a passive-aggressive underachiever's low grades, poor school performance no longer serves as an effective way for an adolescent to act aggressively toward them.

There are times when parents of passive-aggressive underachievers seek to have their children diagnosed as having a specific learning disability, in order to avoid having to confront aspects of family interaction that are causing the school difficulties and to escape the necessity of their becoming personally involved in an intervention program. Clinicians need to be alert to such instances of parental resistance, in which case they need to emphasize that the problem cannot be resolved by educational remediation alone but instead will give way only to psychotherapeutic strategies involving the parents, as well as their underachieving adolescent.

Along with lessening the impetus to passive–aggressive underachievement by inducing more understanding and tolerant parental behavior, therapists may gain some leverage in modifying passive–aggressive propensities in these cases by showing these adolescents that their underachievement is a self-defeating maneuver that will prevent them from realizing educational and career goals of their own. This strategy involves helping adolescents to recognize their abilities and interests, clarify their personal value systems and preferred goals, and pursue their studies to serve their own purposes rather than to meet or frustrate the needs of others.

What underachievers learn when this approach is successful is that their method of making an impact on their parents is damaging their own prospects to achieve an education and a career commensurate with their abilities—They are cutting off their noses to spite their faces. If passive–aggressive underachievers can gain this recognition and be encouraged to look out more sensibly for their own best interests, their motivation to do well in school (in order to make themselves happy) may be increased sufficiently to inhibit their motivation to do poorly (in order to make their parents unhappy).

REFERENCES

Abikoff, H., & Gittelman, R. (1985). The normalizing effects of methylphenidate on the classroom behavior of ADDH children. *Journal of Abnormal Child Psychology, 33*, 313–44.

Ackerman, P. T., Oglesby, D. M., & Dykman, R. A. (1981). A contrast of hyperactive, learning disabled, and hyperactive-learning disabled boys. *Journal of Clinical Child Psychology, 10*, 168–173.

Adelman, H. S., & Taylor, L. (1983). Enhancing motivation for overcoming learning and behavior problems. *Journal of Learning Disabilities, 16*, 384–392.

American Psychiatric Association (1987). *Diagnostic and statistical manual of mental disorders* (3rd ed., rev.). Washington, DC: American Psychiatric Press.

Bachman, J. G., O'Malley, P. M., & Johnston, J. (1979). *Adolescence to adulthood: Change and stability in the lives of young men.* Ann Arbor, MI: Institute for Social Research.

Barkley, R. A., Fischer, M., Edelbrock, C. S., & Smallish, L. (1990). The adolescent outcome of hyperactive children diagnosed by research criteria: I. An 8-year prospective follow-up study. *Journal of the American Academy of Child and Adolescent Psychiatry, 29*, 546–557.

Barth, R. P. (1986). *Social and cognitive treatment of children and adolescents.* San Francisco: Jossey-Bass.

Becker, W. C., & Carnine, D. W. (1980). Direct instruction: An effective approach to educational intervention with the disadvantaged and low performers. In B. B. Lahey & A. E. Kazdin (Eds.), *Advances in clinical child psychology* (Vol. 3, pp. 429–473). New York: Plenum.

Bender, W. N., & Smith, J. K. (1990). Classroom behavior of children and adolescents with learning disabilities: A meta-analysis. *Journal of Learning Disabilities, 23,* 298-305.

Berkovitz, I. H. (1985). The adolescent, schools, and schooling. In S. C. Feinstein (Ed.), *Adolescent psychiatry* (Vol. 12, pp. 162-176). Chicago: University of Chicago Press.

Berndt, T. J. (1979). Developmental changes in conformity to peers and parents. *Developmental Psychology, 15,* 608-616.

Berndt, T. J., & Miller, K. E. (1990). Expectancies, values, and achievement in junior high school. *Journal of Educational Psychology, 82,* 319-326.

Blau, Z. S. (1981). *Black children /white children: Competence, socialization, and social structures.* New York: Free Press.

Brophy, J. (1986). Teacher influences on student achievement. *American Psychologist, 41,* 1069-1077.

Brown, R. T., & Borden, K. A. (1986). Hyperactivity at adolescence: Some misconceptions and new directions. *Journal of Clinical Child Psychology, 15,* 194-209.

Burns, D. D., & Epstein, N. (1983). Passive-aggressiveness: A cognitive-behavioral approach. In R. D. Parsons & R. J. Wicks (Eds.), *Passive–aggressiveness* (pp. 72-97). New York: Brunner/Mazel.

Butler-Por, N. (1987). *Underachievement in school.* New York: Wiley.

Cairns, R. B., Cairns, B. D., & Neckerman, H. J. (1989). Early school dropout: Configurations and determinants. *Child Development, 60,* 1437-1452.

Cantwell, D. P. (1986a). Attention deficit and associated childhood disorders. In T. Millon & G. L. Klerman (Eds.), *Contemporary directions in psychopathology* (pp. 403-427). New York: Guilford.

Cantwell, D. P. (1986b). Attention deficit disorder in adolescents. *Clinical Psychology Review, 6,* 237-247.

Cass, L. K., & Thomas, C. B. (1979). *Childhood pathology and later adjustment.* New York: Wiley.

Chapman, J. W. (1988). Cognitive-motivational characteristics and academic achievement of learning disabled children: A longitudinal study. *Journal of Educational Psychology, 80,* 357-365.

Clark, R. M. (1983). *Family life and school achievement: Why poor black children succeed or fail.* Chicago: University of Chicago Press.

Cohen, J. (1983). Learning disabilities and the college student: Identification and diagnosis. In M. Sugar (Ed.), *Adolescent psychiatry* (Vol. XI, pp. 177-198). Chicago: University of Chicago Press.

Coie, J. D., & Krehbiel, G. (1984). Effects of academic tutoring on the social status of low-achieving, socially rejected children. *Child Development, 55,* 1465-1478.

Coleman, J. C. (1980). Friendship and the peer group in adolescence. In J. Adelson (Ed.), *Handbook of adolescent psychology* (pp. 408-431). New York: Wiley.

Coleman, J. S. (1961). *The adolescent society.* New York: Free Press of Glencoe.

Crandall, V. C. (1982). The Fels study: Some contributions to personality development and achievement in childhood and adulthood. *Seminars in Psychiatry, 4,* 383-397.

Deaux, K. (1985). Sex and gender. *Annual Review of Psychology, 36,* 49–81.

Delgado-Gaitan, C. (1986a). Adolescent peer influences and differential school performance. *Journal of Adolescent Research, 1,* 449–462.

Delgado-Gaitan, C. (1986b). Teacher attitudes on diversity affecting student socio-academic responses: An ethnographic view. *Journal of Adolescent Research, 1,* 103–114.

De Santis, J. P., Ketterlinus, R. D., & Youniss, J. (1990). Black adolescents' concerns that they are academically able. *Merrill-Palmer Quarterly, 36,* 287–299.

Deshler, D. D., Schumaker, J. B., & Lenz, B. K. (1984a). Academic and cognitive interventions for LD adolescents: I. *Journal of Learning Disabilities, 17,* 108–117.

Deshler, D. D., Schumaker, J. B., Lenz, B. K., & Ellis, E. (1984b). Academic and cognitive intervention for LD adolescents: II. *Journal of Learning Disabilities, 17,* 170–179.

Dollinger, S. J., Horn, J. L., & Boarini, D. (1988). Disturbed sleep and worries among learning disabled adolescents. *American Journal of Orthopsychiatry, 58,* 428–434.

Donnelly, M., & Rapoport, J. L. (1985). Attention deficit disorders. In J. M. Wiener (Ed.), *Diagnosis and psychopharmacology of childhood and adolescent disorders* (pp. 179–197). New York: Wiley.

Dornbusch, S. M., Ritter, P. L., Leiderman, P. H., & Roberts, D. F. (1987). The relation of parenting style to adolescent school performance. *Child Development, 58,* 1244–1257.

Dulcan, M. K. (1986). Comprehensive treatment of children and adolescents with attention deficit disorders: The state of the art. *Clinical Psychology Review, 6,* 539–569.

Esman, A. H., 1986. Dependent and passive-aggressive personality disorders. In A. M. Cooper, A. J. Frances, & M. H. Sacks (Eds.), *The personality disorders and neuroses* (pp. 281–289). New York: Basic Books.

Exner, J. E., & Weiner, I. B. (1982). *The Rorschach: A comprehensive system: Vol. 3. Assessment of children and adolescents.* New York: Wiley.

Fehrmann, P. G., Keith, T. Z., & Reimers, T. M. (1987). Home influence on school learning: Direct and indirect effects of parental involvement on high school grades. *Journal of Educational Research, 80,* 3230–337.

Franzen, M., & Berg, R. (1989). *Screening children for brain impairment.* New York: Springer.

Freud, S. (1901/1960). *The psychopathology of everyday life. Standard Edition* (Vol. VI, pp. 1–289). London: Hogarth.

Freud, S. (1916/1957). Some character-types met with in psychoanalytic work. *Standard Edition* (Vol. XIV, pp. 311–333). London: Hogarth.

Gadow, K. D. (1985). Relative efficacy of pharmacological, behavioral, and combination treatments for enhancing academic performance. *Clinical Psychology Review, 5,* 513–533.

Gesten, E. L., Scher, K., & Cowen, E. L. (1978). Judged school problems and competencies of referred children with varying family background characteristics. *Journal of Abnormal Child Psychology, 6,* 247–255.

Goldstein, S., & Goldstein, M. (1990). *Managing attention disorders in children.* New York: Wiley.

Good, T. L., & Weinstein, R. S. (1986). Schools make a difference: Evidence, criticisms, and new directions. *American Psychologist, 41,* 1090-1097.

Gorell, J., & Shaw, E. L. (1988). Upper elementary and high school students' attitudes toward gender-typed occupations. *Journal of Adolescent Research, 3,* 189-199.

Gottfried, A. E. (1985). Academic intrinsic motivation in elementary and junior high school students. *Journal of Educational Psychology, 77,* 631-645.

Green, B. J. (1985). System intervention in the schools. In M. P. Mirkin & S. L. Koman (Eds.), *Handbook of adolescents and family therapy* (pp. 193-206). New York: Gardner Press.

Greenberger, E., & Steinberg, L. (1986). *When teenagers work: The psychological and social costs of adolescent employment.* New York: Basic Books.

Grenell, M. M., Glass, C. R., & Katz, K. S. (1987). Hyperactive children and peer interaction: Knowledge and performance. *Journal of Abnormal Child Psychology, 15,* 1-13.

Gump, P. V. (1980). The school as a social situation. *Annual Review of Psychology, 31,* 553-582.

Hallinan, M. (Ed.) (1987). *Social organization of schools: New conceptualizations of the learning process.* New York: Plenum.

Hammill, D. D., Leigh, J. E., McNutt, G., & Larsen, S. C. (1987). A new definition of learning disabilities. *Journal of Learning Disabilities, 20,* 109-113.

Harris, I. D. (1965). *Emotional blocks to learning.* New York: Free Press.

Herzog, A. R., Bachman, J. G., & Johnston, L.D. (1983) Paid work, child care, and housework: A national survey of high school seniors' preferences for sharing responsibilities between husband and wife. *Sex Roles, 9,* 109-135.

Hogenson, D. L. (1974). Senior neurosis: Cause-effect or derivative? *School Psychologist, 28,* 12-13.

Holland, J. L., & Holland, J. E. (1977). Vocational indecision: More evidence and speculation. *Journal of Counseling Psychology, 24,* 404-414.

Hunt, E. (1988). Attention deficit disorder and hyperactivity. In C. J. Kestenbaum & D. T. Williams (Eds.), *Handbook of clinical assessment of children and adolescents* (pp. 519-561). New York: New York University Press.

Huston, A. C. (1985). The development of sex typing: Themes from recent research. *Developmental Review, 5,* 1-17.

Hynd, G. W., Snow, J., & Becker, M. G. (1986). Neuropsychological assessment in clinical child psychology. In B. B. Lahey & A. E. Kazdin (Eds.), *Advances in clinical child psychology* (Vol. 9, pp. 35-86). New York: Plenum.

Inhelder, B., & Piaget, J. (1958). *The growth of logical thinking from childhood to adolescence.* New York: Basic Books.

Ishiyama, F. I., & Chabassol, D. J. (1985). Adolescents' fear of social consequences of academic success as a function of age and sex. *Journal of Youth and Adolescence, 14,* 37-46.

Jacklin, C. N. (1989). Female and male: Issues of gender. *American Psychologist, 44,* 127-133.

Jamieson, D. W., Lydon, J. E., Stewart, G., & Zanna, M. P. (1987). Pygmalion revisited: New evidence for student expectancy effects in the classroom. *Journal of Educational Psychology, 79,* 461–466.

Janos, P. M., Sanfilippo, S. M., & Robinson, N. M. (1986). "Underachievement" among markedly accelerated college students. *Journal of Youth and Adolescence, 15,* 303–313.

Katz, I. (1967). The socialization of academic motivation in minority group children. *Nebraska Symposium on Motivation, 15,* 133–191.

Kaufman, D. R., & Richardson, B. L. (1982). *Achievement and women: Challenging the assumptions.* New York: Free Press.

Keith, T. Z., Reimers, T. M., Fehrmann, P. G., Pottebaum, S. M., & Aubey, L. W. (1986). Parental involvement, homework, and TV time: Direct and indirect effects on high school achievement. *Journal of Educational Psychology, 78,* 373–380.

Kurdek, L. A., & Sinclair, R. J. (1988). Relation of eighth graders' family structure, gender, and family environment with academic performance and school behavior. *Journal of Educational Psychology, 80,* 90–94.

La Greca, A. M., & Mesibov, G. B. (1981). Facilitating interpersonal functioning with peers in learning disabled children. *Journal of Learning Disabilities, 14,* 197–199.

Lambert, N. M. (1988). Adolescent outcomes for hyperactive children. *American Psychologist, 43,* 786–799.

Lambert, N. M., & Sandoval, J. (1980). The prevalence of learning difficulties in a sample of children considered hyperactive. *American Journal of Orthopsychiatry, 8,* 33–50.

Lane, D. S., & Campbell, N. J. (1986). Performance of adolescents following instruction in conditional reasoning: A six-month follow-up. *Journal of Adolescent Research, 1,* 417–430.

Larson, K. A. (1988). A research review and alternative hypothesis explaining the link between learning disability and delinquency. *Journal of Learning Disabilities, 21,* 357–363.

Levin, E. K., Zigmond, N., & Birch, J. W. (1985). A follow-up study of 52 learning disabled adolescents. *Journal of Learning Disabilities, 18,* 2–7.

Loney, J. (1987). Hyperactivity and aggression in the diagnosis of attention deficit disorder. In B. B. Lahey & A. E. Kazdin (Eds.), *Advances in child clinical psychology* (Vol. 10, pp. 99–135). New York: Plenum.

Lunneborg, P. W. (1975). Interest differentiation in high school and vocational indecision in college. *Journal of Vocational Behavior, 7,* 297–303.

Maher, C. A., & Zins, J. E. (1987). *Psychoeducational interventions in the schools.* New York: Pergamon.

Mandel, H. P., & Marcus, S. I. (1988). *The psychology of underachievement.* New York: Wiley.

Marsh, H. W. (1987). The big-fish-little-pond effect on academic self-concept. *Journal of Educational Psychology, 79,* 280–295.

McArthur, C. C. (1971). Distinguishing patterns of student neuroses. In G. R. Blaine & C. C. McArthur (Eds.), *Emotional problems of the student* (2nd ed., pp. 52–72). New York: Appleton-Century-Crofts.

McConaughy, S. H., & Ritter, D. R. (1986). Social competence and behavioral problems of learning disabled boys aged 6–11. *Journal of Learning Disabilities, 19,* 39–45.

McLaughlin, J. A., & Pea, R. D. (1987). The likelihood of correlational thinking in adults: A comparative study and methodological critique. *Genetic, Social, & General Psychology Monographs, 113,* 461–485.

Miller, B. C., & Sneesby, K. R. (1988). Educational correlates of adolescents' sexual attitudes and behavior. *Journal of Youth and Adolescence, 17,* 521–530.

Miller, M. (1984). Social acceptability characteristics of learning disabled students. *Journal of Learning Disabilities, 17,* 619–621.

Millon, T. (1981). *Disorders of personality.* New York: Wiley.

Montague, M., & Bos, C. S. (1986). The effect of cognitive strategy training on verbal math problem solving performances of learning disabled adolescents. *Journal of Learning Disabilities, 19,* 26–33.

Obrzut, J. E., & Hynd, G. W. (1983). The neurobiological and neuropsychological foundations of learning disabilities. *Journal of Learning Disabilities, 16,* 515–520.

Pihl, R. O., & McLarnon, L. D. (1984). Learning disabled children as adolescents. *Journal of Learning Disabilities, 17,* 96–100.

Pintrich, P. R., & de Groot, E. V. (1990). Motivational and self-regulated learning components of classroom academic performance. *Journal of Educational Psychology, 82,* 33–40.

Pokay, P., & Blumenfeld, P. C. (1990). Predicting achievement early and late in the semester: The role of motivation and use of learning strategies. *Journal of Educational Psychology, 82,* 41–50.

Rodick, J. D., & Henggeler, S. W. (1980). The short-term and long-term amelioration of academic and motivational deficiencies among low-achieving inner-city adolescents. *Child Development, 52,* 1126–1132.

Ross, D. M., & Ross, S. A. (1982). *Hyperactivity* (2nd ed.). New York: Wiley.

Routh, D. K. (1986). Attention deficit disorder. In R. T. Brown & C. R. Reynolds (Eds.), *Psychological perspectives on childhood exceptionality* (pp. 467–507). New York: Wiley.

Rutter, M. (1983). Behavioral studies: Questions and findings on the concept of a distinctive syndrome. In M. Rutter (Ed.), *Developmental neuropsychiatry* (pp. 259–279). New York: Guilford.

Satterfield, J. H., Hoppe, C. M., & Schell, A. M. (1982). A prospective study of delinquency in 110 adolescent boys with attention deficit disorder and 88 normal adolescent boys. *American Journal of Psychiatry, 139,* 795–798.

Scheinfeld, D. R. (1983). Family relationships and school achievement among boys of lower-i1ncome urban black families. *American Journal of Orthopsychiatry, 53,* 127–143.

Shapiro, E. S. (1987). Academic problems. In M. Hersen & V. B. Van Hasselt (Eds.), *Behavior therapy with children and adolescents* (pp. 362–384). New York: Wiley.

Shaw, M. C., & McCuen, J. T. (1960). The onset of academic underachievement in bright children. *Journal of Educational Psychology, 51,* 103–108.

Siperstein, G. N., & Goding, M. J. (1985). Teachers' behavior toward LD and non-LD children: A strategy for change. *Journal of Learning Disabilities, 18,* 139–144.

Skinner, E. A., Wellborn, J. G., & Connell, J. P. (1990). What it takes to do well in school and whether I've got it: A process model of perceived control and children's engagement and achievement in school. *Journal of Educational Psychology, 82,* 22–32.

Spare, K. W., & Dahmen, L. A. (1984). Vocational sex-stereotyping in elementary schoolchildren. *Journal of Genetic Psychology, 144,* 297–298.

Steinberg, L., Elman, J. D., & Mounts, N. S. (1989). Authoritative parenting, psychosocial maturity, and academic success among adolescents. *Child Development, 60,* 1424–1436.

Stevenson, D. L., & Baker, D. P. (1987). The family–school relation and the child's school performance. *Child Development, 58,* 1348–1357.

Stone, W. L., & La Greca, A. M. (1990). The social status of children with learning disabilities: A reexamination. *Journal of Learning Disabilities, 23,* 32–37.

Stricker, G. (1983). Passive-aggressiveness: A condition especially suited to the psychodynamic approach. In R. D. Parsons & R. J. Wicks (Eds.), *Passive-aggressiveness* (pp. 5–24). New York: Brunner/Mazel.

Sue, S., & Okazaki, S. (1990). Asian-American educational achievements. *American Psychologist, 45,* 913–920.

Sugar, M. (1987). Diagnostic aspects of underachievement in adolescents. In S. C. Feinstein (Ed.), *Adolescent psychiatry* (Vol. 14, pp. 427–440). Chicago: University of Chicago Press.

Tarnowski, K. J., Prinz, R. J., & Nay, S. M. (1986). Comparative analysis of attentional deficits in hyperactive and learning-disabled children. *Journal of Abnormal Psychology, 95,* 341–345.

Taylor, H. G., Fletcher, J. M., & Satz, P. (1984). Neuropsychological assessment of children. In G. Goldstein & M. Hersen (Eds.), *Handbook of psychological assessment* (pp. 211–234). Elmsford, NY: Pergamon.

Tittle, C. K. (1986). Gender research and education. *American Psychologist, 41,* 1161–1168.

Tolmach, J. (1985). "There ain't nobody on my side": A new day treatment program for black urban youth. *Journal of Clinical Child Psychology, 14,* 214–219.

Vaillant, G. E., & Vaillant, C. O. (1981). Natural history of male psychological health: X. Work as a predictor of positive mental health. *American Journal of Psychiatry, 138,* 1433–1440.

Waddell, K. J. (1984). The self-concept and social adaptation of hyperactive children in adolescence. *Journal of Clinical Child Psychology, 13,* 50–55.

Wallander, J. L., & Hubert, N. C. (1985). Long-term prognosis for children with attention deficit disorder with hyperactivity. In B. B. Lahey & A. E. Kazdin (Eds.), *Advances in child clinical psychology,* (Vol. 8, pp. 113–147). New York: Plenum.

Weiss, G., & Hechtman, L. K. (1986). *Hyperactive children grown up.* New York: Guilford.

Wetzel, J. R. (1987). *American youth: A statistical snapshot.* Washington, DC: William T. Grant Foundation.

Whalen, C. K., & Henker, B. (1985). The social worlds of hyperactive (ADDH) children. *Clinical Psychology Review, 5,* 447–478.

White, K. R. (1982). The relation between socioeconomic status and academic achievement. *Psychological Bulletin, 91,* 461–481.

Wirtz, P. W., Rohrbeck, C. A., Charner, I., & Fraser, B. S. (1988). Employment of adolescents while in high school: Employment intensity, interference with schoolwork, and normative approval. *Journal of Adolescent Research, 3,* 97–105.

Wood, J., Chapin, K., & Hannah, M. E. (1988). Family environment and its relationship to underachievement. *Adolescence, 23,* 283–290.

Ysseldyke, J. E., & Stevens, L. J. (1986). Specific learning deficits: The learning disabled. In R. T. Brown & C. R. Reynolds (Eds.), *Psychological perspectives on childhood exceptionality* (pp. 391–422). New York: Wiley.

Zarb, J. M. (1981). Non-academic predictors of successful academic achievement in a normal adolescent sample. *Adolescence, 16,* 981–900.

Zarb, J. M. (1984). A comparison of remedial, failure, and successful secondary school students across self-perception and past and present school performance variables. *Adolescence, 19,* 335–348.

Zigmond, N., Levin, E., & Laurie, T. E. (1985). Managing the mainstream: An analysis of teacher attitudes and student performance in mainstream high school programs. *Journal of Learning Disabilities, 18,* 535–541.

CHAPTER 8

Delinquent Behavior

Delinquent behavior is difficult to define and measure. Law-breaking may involve a single delinquent act, a single episode of multiple delinquent acts, occasional but repetitive delinquent acts, or a continually delinquent way of life. Delinquent acts can range in severity from *major crimes* against people or property (assault, theft) to relatively *minor offenses* (disorderly conduct, vandalism), and they also include *status offenses*, which are illegal only by virtue of the youthfulness of the person committing them (curfew violations, running away). Of young people who commit illegal acts, only some are caught; of those who are caught, only some are arrested; of those arrested, only some come to trial; and of those tried, only some are adjudicated as delinquents (see Empey, 1982; Farrington, 1987).

For these reasons, there is no simple way to determine how much delinquency there is, who should be called a "delinquent," or which kinds of young people should be studied to learn more about delinquent behavior. Statements about the frequency, cause, treatment, or prevention of delinquency that ignore these complexities should not be given serious consideration. Research findings have thus far failed to demonstrate systematic relationships between any unitary concept of delinquency and various aspects of delinquent behavior (Arbuthnot, Gordon, & Jurkovic, 1987; Quay, 1987a).

Global references to "juvenile delinquents," as if they constitute a homogeneous group of young people, should similarly be considered suspect. *Delinquency* can be uniformly defined according to the acts it comprises, regardless of who commits them or why; *delinquents*, on the other hand, are a markedly heterogeneous collection of individuals with respect to their background and motivations.

Clinical and research studies suggest a four-fold classification of youthful law-breakers: (a) *socialized* delinquents, who show little psychological disturbance but engage in antisocial acts as members in good standing of a delinquent subculture; (b) *characterological* delinquents, in whom antisocial conduct derives from a chronically self-centered, exploitative, and inconsiderate personality style; (c) *neurotic* delinquents, who misbehave as a symptomatic expression of underlying needs and concerns; and (d) *psychotic* or *neuropsychological* delinquents, whose law-breaking results from substantial impairments of judgment, impulse control, and other integrative functions of the personality.

Delinquent acts, taken together with antisocial behaviors that may not break any laws but nevertheless violate the rights of others, regularly confront clinicians who work with young people. More children and adolescents are referred to mental health professionals for misconduct than for any other reason, and between one third and one half of all young people seen in outpatient clinics have been in difficulty because of antisocial behavior (Gardner, 1988; Kazdin, 1987; Quay, 1986; Tolan, Ryan, & Jaffe, 1988).

This chapter first discusses the frequency of delinquent behavior and some implications of the available data concerning its prevalence and incidence. Subsequent sections then elaborate the nature and origins of socialized, characterological, neurotic, and psychotic and neuropsychological delinquency, and a final section considers methods of intervention.

FREQUENCY OF DELINQUENT BEHAVIOR

The two primary sources of information about the frequency of delinquency are official delinquency statistics and actual delinquency estimates. The *official statistics* consist of government reports on the arrest and disposition of law-breakers under age 18 years. Although limited to young people who have been arrested and adjudicated, these reports provide systematic annual information on the total national population of juveniles entering the criminal justice system, including such demographic data as age, sex, social class, and place of residence.

The *actual estimates* derive from surveys of selected samples of young persons whose involvement in illegal activities is examined. Such surveys have the benefit of investigating delinquent behavior independently of whether it has come to police attention, and they also monitor more characteristics of delinquent youths than are usually included in official statistical reports. Unlike official statistics, however, these estimates may or may not approximate true population figures, depending on how representative the sampling has been, and they are rarely repeated on an annual basis to identify trends over time. Although each has its shortcomings, these two kinds of data combine to provide a detailed picture of the frequency of youthful law-breaking.

Official Delinquency Statistics

Statistical reports from the U.S. Department of Justice indicate that approximately 4% of 10- to 17-year-olds in this country appear in juvenile court each year for offenses other than traffic violations. During the 1980s, young people under age 18 accounted for a smaller percentage of arrests nationwide than had been the case during the 1970s: 16.8% in 1986, compared to 24.3% in 1977. This decrease is attributable in part to adolescents constituting a smaller proportion of the population than previously, but it also appears to identify a gradual diminution that began during the late 1970s, in the rate of detected law-breaking among young people. On the other hand, adolescents are still disproportionately likely to enter the criminal justice system. In 1986, young people ages 13 to 18 years constituted 9.0% of the United States population but accounted for 19.9% of all arrests (Flanagan & Jamieson, 1988).

With respect to demographics, the most dramatic difference among arrested adolescents is their sex: males outnumber females by a ratio of 3.5 to 1. Theorists have attributed this sex difference to such factors as biologically determined male–female differences in aggressiveness, differential socialization of males toward externalizing and females toward internalizing coping styles, and sex-differentiated patterns of identity formation and role expectations (Eme, 1984; Farrington, 1987; Widom, 1984).

Interestingly, the extent of male prevalence among arrested adolescents decreased somewhat during the 1980s, from what had been a 3.9 to 1 ratio in 1979. This change could reflect contemporary societal trends toward less sex-distinctive childrearing practices and more similar role-identity training for males and females. Although attractive to some theorists, this hypothesis has been tempered by failure to find differences between delinquent and nondelinquent girls in their sex-role identity (Campbell, 1988) and by evidence that changing views on women's roles, whatever their other impact, have not had any systematic effect on female crime (Gora, 1982).

In the absence of any solid cause-and-effect data, moreover, the changing male–female ratio in arrests of young people could, with equal plausibility, be attributed to attitudes among law enforcement officials. Perhaps contemporary sex-role expectations are contributing not to more female crime but to more females being arrested. Who gets arrested is known to be influenced by prevailing community attitudes and police department policies, and minor temporal variations or group differences in arrest data may consequently be more apparent than real.

Teenage boys are more likely to be arrested than girls who have committed the same offense, for example, and lower socioeconomic-class young people living in poor neighborhoods are more likely to be arrested than middle-class adolescents from advantaged neighborhoods (Binder, 1988; Gold, 1987; Rutter & Giller, 1984, Chapter 4). Hence, official statistics may at times say as much about the orientation of criminal justice officials as about youthful crime, and inferences about social class and neighborhood differences in the frequency of delinquency must accordingly be drawn with caution.

Similarly calling for caution in the interpretation of official delinquency statistics are additional indications that community responses to behavior problem adolescents are influenced by their sex and their ethnicity. Adolescents entering the juvenile justice system are found to differ from young people entering the mental health system less in the types of personality and psychopathology they present than in whether they are male or they come from an ethnic minority group (Cohen, Parmelee, Irwin, Weisz, Howard, Purcell, & Best, 1990; Westendorp, Brink, Roberson, & Ortiz, 1986). Court actions point to a general tendency to regard violent behavior in boys as deliberate acts of psychologically stable youngsters who should be sent to a correctional facility, while equally violent acts committed by girls are more likely to be regarded as psychological aberrations requiring mental health care. Research similarly shows that violent adolescent males from comparable socioeconomic backgrounds and with comparable degrees of psychological difficulty are more likely to be incarcerated if they are black and more likely to be hospitalized if they are white (Lewis, Shanok, Cohen, Kligfeld, & Frisone, 1980).

Official statistics on the nature of the offenses committed by young persons also merit mention. Despite widespread community concerns about teenage violence, adolescents are less likely than adults to commit crimes against people. In 1986, youngsters under age 18, constituting 27.7% of the population in the United States, accounted for 33.3% of arrests for serious crimes against property (burglary, larceny–theft, motor-vehicle theft, arson) but just 15.4% of violent crimes. Among adolescents arrested that year, only 4.1% were charged with violent crimes (Flanagan & Jamieson, 1988). Although this extent of youthful criminality remains unacceptable by any standard of community safety and decency, it is still less marked than is widely believed or suggested by the media.

In further contrast to popular opinion, violent crime by young people has not recently been on the rise. In 1977, youths under age 18 accounted for 20.8% of arrests for violent crimes, compared to the 15.4% in 1986, and 3.8% of youthful arrests were for offenses against people, about the same as the 4.1% in 1986 (Flanagan, Hindelang, & Gottfredson, 1980).

When, as sometimes happens, newspaper and magazine articles based on official statistics appear to document substantial increases in youthful violence and other criminal activity, they will typically be found to cite absolute numbers of arrests rather than percentage data. These arrest numbers can be misleading, because the U.S. Department of Justice reports vary from year to year in the number of agencies from which data have been obtained. Hence, to be reliable, inferences about trends over time should be drawn from changes in percentages, not from changes in numbers of arrests.

For example, the official statistics for 1979 show 2.1 million arrests of young people under age 18, including 87,000 for violent crimes, and are based on reports from 11,758 agencies (Flanagan, Van Alstyne, & Gottfredson, 1982). The official statistics for 1986 show 1.6 million arrests of under-18s, 66,000 of them for violent crimes, and are based on reports from only 8,494 agencies (Flanagan & Jamieson, 1988). Taken out of context, these arrest numbers would appear to identify a 25% reduction in youthful criminality and violence. Much more likely than any such reduction is poor comparability of these absolute numbers because of differences in the size of the reporting base. When percentages are calculated, to provide a more reliable trend indicator, the 1979 report indicates that young people accounted for 20.1% of all arrests for violent crimes and that 4.1% of youthful arrests were for violent crimes—which closely match the previously noted percentage findings for 1977 and 1986.

The distress caused by serious juvenile crime and the publicity surrounding it can also contribute to exaggerated impressions of how many young criminals there are. Only 6% of young people who break the law can be considered chronic offenders, and this small fraction of youthful law-breakers accounts for approximately one half of all adolescent arrests and convictions (Farrington, 1983; Wolfgang, Figlio, & Sellin, 1972). It is further significant that 63.4% of the total arrests of juveniles are for various kinds of misdemeanors rather than for more serious crimes. Three status offenses—curfew violations, running away, and liquor-law violations—account for 20% of juvenile arrests; vandalism, disorderly conduct, drunkenness, and minor violations of drug laws account for another 15% (Flanagan & Jamieson, 1988). As elaborated in the following discussion of actual delinquency estimates, adolescents who persist in criminal activities come largely from the small percentage of juvenile law-breakers who commit serious or repetitive offenses, whereas the infrequent and trivial offenses in which most official delinquents are involved do not predict subsequent criminal behavior.

Actual Delinquency Estimates

Large-scale surveys of self-reported delinquent behavior have fairly consistently indicated that about 80% of adolescents in the United States commit one or more delinquent acts for which, if detected, they could be arrested and brought into court. As in the case of official delinquency, however, most of these offenses are minor, most of the perpetrators are infrequent offenders, and a small number of repetitive offenders is responsible for the majority of delinquent acts reported. Undetected delinquents commit similar offenses as official delinquents, and for the same reasons, and most of what has been learned from studies of identified delinquents is generally considered applicable to undetected delinquents as well (Farrington, 1987; Feldman, Caplinger, & Wodarski, 1983; Hindelang, Hirschi, & Weis, 1981).

Demographic Findings

Paralleling the sex difference among official delinquents, three to four times as many males as females admit to having committed acts for which they could have been arrested. As a further similarity, neither self-reported nor official delinquency shows any relationship to socioeconomic status; that is, social class is unrelated to how many youthful law-breakers there are. On the other hand, socioeconomic status is negatively related to how much youthful crime is committed, and lower social-class adolescents admit to more frequent delinquent behavior than middle-class youth (Elliot & Huizinga, 1983; Farrington, 1987; Hindelang et al., 1981; Thornberry & Farnworth, 1982).

Black and white adolescents differ neither in the *prevalence* (number committing crimes) nor the *incidence* (number of crimes they commit) of delinquency they self-report (Farrington, 1986; Williams & Gold, 1972). However, this ethnic similarity in self-reported delinquency stands in sharp contrast to indications that black young people are much more likely than white youths to become official delinquents (Hindelang et al., 1981). Hence there remains reason to believe that any apparent overrepresentation of lower-SES or minority youth in official delinquency statistics may be more a function of who gets arrested than who gets caught breaking the law.

Longitudinal Findings

Actual delinquency estimates combine with official statistics to demonstrate dramatic age differences in delinquent behavior among adolescents. The frequency of actual delinquent behavior increases sharply during adolescence, with 18-year-olds of both sexes admitting to almost five times as many nontrivial delinquent acts during the previous 3 years as 11-year-old girls and boys (Gold & Petronio, 1980). The peak incidence for law-breaking varies with the nature of the offense, however. Arrest rates for theft and burglary peak at ages 15 to 17 years and decline thereafter; the rate of violent crimes, on the other hand, increases steadily throughout the adolescent years and into adulthood.

For the vast majority of adolescents who break the law, especially status and trivial offenders, delinquency begins and ends with adolescence. Very few youthful law-breakers are found to be persistently antisocial people who start behaving badly prior to adolescence and continue doing so as adults (Farrington, 1987; Loeber, 1982, 1990; Murray, 1983). At the same time, law-breaking tendencies do show considerable developmental continuity. Young people retain their relative standing in their peer group, on the average, and those who are most delinquent at one age tend to be the ones who are most delinquent at another age (Olweus, 1979; Rutter & Giller, 1984, Chapter 2).

This continuity is especially marked when misconduct begins in childhood. Research findings indicate that prepubertal antisocial behavior substantially increases the likelihood of a young person becoming seriously and repetitively delinquent by late adolescence (Hanson, Henggeler, Haefele, & Rodick, 1984; Loeber & Dishion, 1983; Patterson, DeBaryshe, & Ramsey, 1989; Tolan, 1987). Generally speaking, adolescent onset of delinquent behavior is likely to be associated with transient and trivial types of misconduct, whereas childhood onset tends to be associated with serious and chronic delinquency that persists into adulthood (Loeber, 1982, 1990; Olweus, 1979).

Developmental continuity also characterized the types of serious crimes young people commit. Children who steal tend to become adolescents who commit crimes against property; children who are overly aggressive tend to become adolescents who commit crimes against people; and those who are both larcenous and assaultive are likely to end up committing both property and violent crimes (Loeber & Schmaling, 1985a, 1985b). Also noteworthy is evidence that adolescents convicted for either larceny or assault alone receive only half as many criminal convictions in adulthood as those who are both larcenous and assaultive (McCord, 1980).

Repetitive delinquency involving nontrivial offenses against people and property foreshadows not only adult criminality but numerous other adjustment difficulties as well. The best evidence in this regard comes from a 30-year follow-up study of 524 young people initially evaluated at a median age of 13 in the St. Louis Municipal Psychiatric Clinic, of whom 406 had been referred for antisocial behavior. As reported by Robins (1966, 1978), the primarily neurotic patients in this sample were found as adults to resemble closely a control group of 100 nonpatients similar in age, sex, race, intelligence, and place of residence. The primarily antisocial youngsters, on the other hand, were notable as adults for their high frequency of arrests, alcoholism, divorce, work failure, child neglect, dependency on social agencies, and psychiatric hospitalization.

These and similar findings by other investigators leave little doubt that antisocial behavior during the developmental years increases the likelihood both of subsequent antisocial personality disorder and of adult antisocial behavior that cuts across diagnostic lines (Huesmann, Eron, Lefkowitz, & Walder, 1984; Roff & Wirt, 1984; Stattin & Magnusson, 1989). Most adolescents who break the law do not become adult criminals, as already noted. On the other hand, criminality does not arise de novo in adulthood. Antisocial adults come from the ranks of misbehaving children and adolescents who have not had the benefit of salutary life circumstances or helpful professional interventions.

SOCIALIZED DELINQUENCY

Socialized delinquency consists of illegal behavior associated with membership in a subculture that endorses antisocial standard of conduct. The members of delinquent subcultures collaborate in law-breaking activities that are a regular—and for them unremarkable—part of their daily lives. This pattern of behavior is also commonly referred to as "subculturally deviant" or "group type" delinquency (American Psychiatric Association, 1987; Quay, 1987b).

As this definition indicates, socialized delinquency is characterized by adaptive rather than maladaptive behavior and by social rather than solitary acts. The *adaptive* nature of socialized delinquency was first described by Jenkins (1955), who did some of the early research on differentiating delinquents according to their personality style. As Jenkins and other writers have elaborated, socialized delinquents engage in planned, easily understandable behavior that breaks the law as an expression of their group's needs and attitudes. Socialized delinquents have not been found to differ behaviorally from nondelinquents in any major ways, aside from their law-breaking. They do, however, account for an estimated one third of young people incarcerated by the criminal justice system (Quay, 1987b).

Subcultures that foster group delinquency respect the successful law-breakers in their midst and reject those who decline to participate in antisocial activities. In such circumstances, delinquent youths experience a sense of belongingness and well-being, whereas nondelinquents feel outcast and unworthy. Socialized delinquents identify with and feel close to their peers; they are well-integrated members of a social group that they value and to which they feel loyal; and they are no more likely than adolescents in general to demonstrate adjustment difficulties (see Arbuthnot et al., 1987; Quay, Routh, & Shapiro, 1987).

The *social* nature of this form of delinquency refers to the fact that it typically involves group rather than individual behavior. Socialized delinquents rarely commit crimes by themselves, except perhaps to impress their friends or as required by the group, and they are unlikely to keep any solitary criminal acts a secret from their peers. By contrast, a preference for solitary delinquent behavior usually indicates a psychological problem related to individual disturbance rather than a manifestation of group influence. This does not rule out the possibility that some members of a delinquent gang may be psychologically disturbed. Typically, in such instances, the group itself recognizes which of its members are relatively unstable and unreliable (and hence not to be put in positions of trust or leadership), and which members lack realistic regard for their own safety or the concerns of others (and hence can be called on for particularly dangerous or foolhardy assignments).

Origins of Socialized Delinquency

As would be expected from their adequate psychological adjustment and positive peer-group attachments, socialized delinquents have usually enjoyed good family relationships early in life. Attentive parents and siblings have helped them develop adequate basic capacities for judgment, self-control, and interpersonal relatedness during their infancy and preschool years. Later, however, in middle childhood and adolescence, they have typically lacked adequate parental supervision and been influenced less by their family than by antisocial models in their neighborhood. More often than not, then, socialized delinquency is found in association with unsupervised development in a disorganized home located in a deteriorated, high-delinquency neighborhood (Brown, Clasen, & Eicher, 1986; Elliott, Huizinga, & Ageton, 1985; Farnworth, 1984).

These risk factors for socialized delinquency are typically observed to exert their influence interactively. Parents in conflict-ridden homes who get along poorly with each other and with their children tend to lack interest in monitoring their delinquent youngsters' whereabouts and requiring them to comply with family rules and regulations (Borduin, Pruitt, & Henggeler, 1986; Farrington, 1986; Masten & Garmezy, 1985). Adolescents who lack firm and dedicated parental supervision tend to be relatively susceptible to peer influence toward misconduct. Antisocial peer models are relatively numerous in disadvantaged or deteriorated neighborhoods, and such neighborhoods, because of their usual dense population and clutter of buildings, complicate the parental task of keeping track of where their children are and what they are doing (Quinton, 1988; Snyder & Patterson, 1987; Steinberg, 1986, 1987).

Yet socialized delinquency is by no means a unique product of economic disadvantage or inner-city neighborhoods. In the first place, economic hardship has not been shown to bear any relationship to delinquency independently of inconsistent parental discipline (Lempers, Clark-Lempers, & Simons, 1989). Second, neither inadequate parental supervision nor lack of community cohesion is limited to disadvantaged neighborhoods. Affluent suburbs, often populated with some number of transient families on the move and parents preoccupied with their own goals and interests, can also fail to provide young people with a sense of direction and belonging. Rich and poor parents alike can be guilty of paying insufficient attention to how or with whom their adolescent children are spending their time.

Third, even though delinquent groups are found more often in lower socioeconomic class neighborhoods, neither delinquency nor the formation of trouble-making gangs is foreign to middle-class life. In Robins's (1966) previously mentioned study of child-guidance-clinic patients, participation in group delinquent acts was found in 53% of the boys from slum areas but also in 26% of the boys from better neighborhoods. There is, in fact, an extensive literature on the existence and nature of middle-class delinquency (Lowney, 1984; Richards, Berk, & Forster, 1979; Shoemaker, 1984, Chapter 11). Also of interest is evidence that rural adolescents as well as urban youth, and girls as well as boys can and do become involved in group delinquency and delinquent gangs (Bowker & Klein, 1983; Erickson & Jensen, 1977; Thompson & Lozes, 1976). In light of available evidence, then, the circumstances that eventuate in socialized delinquency do not appear restricted to any demographically distinct groups.

Sociocultural Theories of Delinquency

Efforts to provide a theoretical framework for the origins of delinquent behavior have tended to emphasize either sociocultural, psychological, or biological determinants of behavior (see Gibbons, 1980; Rutter & Giller, 1984, Chapter 8; Shaw, 1983; Shoemaker, 1984). Some of these theoretical formulations have attempted to embrace all delinquent behavior within a single perspective, which, considering the already noted multifaceted nature of juvenile law-breaking, has proved neither conceptually nor empirically sound. As noted by Rutter and Giller (1984), "Delinquent activities are too varied and too widespread in society for it to be sensible even to contemplate a single explanation" (p. 266).

Nevertheless, the nature of socialized delinquency has prompted numerous attempts to account for all juvenile law-breaking from a sociocultural perspective. These sociocultural theories revolve around the notions of adaptation and frustration. According to some theorists, for example, group delinquency is a fairly common lower socioeconomic class behavior that represents a consistent, adaptive adherence to values and mores at variance with middle-class standards (Kvaraceus & Miller, 1959; Miller, 1958).

Contrary to this view, however, most people recognize that group delinquency is just as disturbing and unacceptable to law-abiding adults and young people in economically disadvantaged neighborhoods as in middle-class neighborhoods. Delinquent subcultures are, in fact, considered deviant by the majority of people within all socioeconomic classes and do not really serve any adaptive function beyond providing group membership. The wages of crime, including as they do disapproval from most members of society and the constant risk of arrest and imprisonment, call into question how adaptive such acts are, even when they are committed by psychologically stable group delinquents.

Data from Robins's (1966, p.199) long-term follow-up of her subjects cast further doubt on the adaptive value of antisocial behavior among lower socioeconomic class youngsters. The relationships she found between youthful antisocial conduct and adult behavior problems were as strong among lower-SES as middle-class youngsters. Hence the "adaptive" nature of socialized delinquency must be understood in a relative sense. Group delinquents are less likely to be disturbed than solitary delinquents and are more likely to be misbehaving in response to social influences than to personal problems. Nevertheless, considering its maladaptive future implications and its likelihood of leading to arrest and incarceration, even socialized delinquency should probably not be considered a normal way of life.

As for frustration, the major sociocultural analysis of gang and subcultural delinquency stresses the role of common frustrations in the genesis of socialized delinquent acts. This emphasis is particularly clear in the "reaction formation" theories introduced by Cohen (1955) and Cloward and Ohlin (1960). Cohen interpreted subcultural delinquency as frustrated efforts to attain middle-class status and prerogatives eventuating in a reactive endorsement of antisocial values. Cloward and Ohlin argued that "pressures toward the formation of delinquent subcultures originate in marked discrepancies between culturally induced aspirations among lower class youth and the possibilities of achieving them by legitimate means" (p. 78).

Similarly invoking a prominent element of frustration are the "cultural transmission" theories of delinquency originated by Shaw and McKay (1942). Based on their studies of deteriorated, high-crime neighborhoods, these researchers described delinquency as a group tradition transmitted from older adolescents to younger ones in neighborhoods where parental authority is ineffective. They attributed lack of parental influence in the neighborhoods they studied to frustrated efforts of first-generation American young people to identify comfortably with the standard of their immigrant parents. Although the Shaw and McKay studies were conducted half a century ago, their conclusions may have timely implications for youthful conduct among the present-day wave of immigrant families coming to the United States.

Whether emphasizing adaptation or frustration, sociocultural approaches have been limited by their focus on studying and interpreting delinquent behavior primarily as a lower-socioeconomic-class phenomenon. The pioneering and perhaps still best-known research on delinquency was done by Sheldon and Eleanor Glueck (1950, 1952), who compared 500 reform-school boys from disadvantaged neighborhoods with a group of nondelinquent boys from similar neighborhoods. Their findings, like those of other studies based on such restricted sampling, said more about lower-class life than about the origins of delinquency. For example, Glueck and Glueck (1950, p. 109) reported that delinquency is significantly associated with "lack of cultural refinement in the home"; cultural refinement was indeed found lacking in the homes of 92% of their lower-SES delinquents, but it was also lacking for 82% of their lower-SES nondelinquent subjects.

Although sociocultural theories help to explain why some disadvantaged young people commit crimes, they do not provide an adequate basis for distinguishing between lower-SES and middle-class delinquency or for explaining delinquent behavior in general. Most adolescents living in lower-socioeconomic-class circumstances do not become delinquent, despite lacking middle-class opportunities, and there is nothing to prevent lower-class youths from becoming antisocial because of psychological disturbance rather than subcultural influence. Nor can these theories account for the delinquent acts of advantaged youngsters who have broad social, cultural, and economic horizons in front of them.

Yet it would be just as overdrawn to neglect sociocultural determinants of delinquent behavior in favor of exclusively psychological or biological hypotheses. To the extent that shared frustrations of lower-social-class membership can generate cooperative delinquency, psychobiological approaches are no more adequate than sociocultural formulations to explain all delinquent behavior. Both group–sociocultural and individual–psychobiological perspectives are necessary for an adequate understanding of delinquent behavior. Despite possible overlaps between adaptive-social and maladaptive-solitary categories of delinquency, these labels refer to a meaningful distinction between the apparently primary influence of sociocultural determinants in generating some delinquency and of psychobiological determinants in producing other delinquent behavior.

CHARACTEROLOGICAL DELINQUENCY

Characterological delinquency comprises illegal acts that reflect a primarily asocial personality orientation. Unlike socialized delinquents, characterological delinquents are usually loners who have no group membership or loyalties. They break the law either by themselves or in temporary alliance with one or to other delinquents, whom they seldom regard as friends. They trust no one and are loyal only to themselves. They may pretend trust and loyalty when it serves their purpose to do so, but the collaboration of characterological delinquents in criminal activity fits the adage, "There is no honor among thieves." Whatever honor may exist among thieves occurs in socialized delinquents committed to the well-being of their companions, not in characterological delinquents.

The offenses of characterological delinquents occur as a consequence of their disregard for the rights and feelings of others and their inability or unwillingness to refrain from doing them harm. They promptly translate aggressive, acquisitive, and pleasure-seeking impulses into action, with few second thoughts and scant concern for how others may suffer in the process. They break the law not in response to group influence or needs for peer acceptance, but merely in the course of expressing anger, satisfying a whim, or obtaining something they want.

For these reasons, characterological delinquency is frequently classified as "undersocialized" or "solitary type" delinquency (American Psychiatric Association, 1987; Quay, 1987b). The interpersonal orientation and behavioral pattern of characterological delinquents constitute in budding form the adult condition diagnosed as *psychopathic* or *antisocial personality disorder.*

Implications for Psychopathic Personality Disorder

Although personality disorders originate in early life experiences, they take shape gradually and rarely become fully established until late adolescence or early adulthood, when personality styles in general become fairly crystallized. Personality disorders are widely agreed to consist of chronically maladaptive ways of thinking, feeling, and acting that interfere with social relationships and impair daily functioning at home, in school, and on the job (Millon, 1981; Soloff, 1985). In clinical practice, however, the diagnosis of these disorders is complicated by an uncertain boundary between personality *style* and personality *disorder.* Commonly, the difference between them is defined by subjective external criteria: An individual's personality style becomes a personality disorder when other people regard his or her behavior as incompetent, offensive, self-defeating, or antisocial.

Such external criteria for personality disorders characterize those who have them, as well as their observers. Individuals who have personality disorders typically feel comfortable with their maladaptive behavior patterns and regard them in ego-syntonic fashion as part of their nature. Unlike people with neurotic disorders, who view their symptoms as ego-alien and wonder, "What's the matter with me?" personality-disordered individuals wonder what the matter is with everyone else or the world at large.

Psychopathic personality disorder rests on two cornerstones: an underdeveloped conscience and a disinclination to identify with other people. Lacking conscience, psychopaths are guiltless individuals who rarely regret trampling on the rights and feelings of others. Lacking identification, they are loveless individuals who shun interpersonal intimacy and seldom form deep or enduring relationships with others. Instead, psychopaths keep interpersonally distant, neither giving nor expecting to receive sympathy, support, or trust. For them, other people exist to be used and manipulated, not to be cared about or depended on. Psychopaths are self-centered individuals who blame other people or circumstances for whatever difficulties they cause or encounter, and they feel fully justified in doing just as they please (see Meloy, 1988: Quay, 1987b; Schalling, 1978).

Asocial attitudes and a lack of concern for the welfare of others make psychopathic young people highly prone to characterologically delinquent behavior. Usually they are deterred from antisocial acts only by fears of being caught and punished, rarely by internal standards of decency and propriety. However, even though psychopaths are demonstrably more likely than most people to behave in ways that violate the law, there is no exclusive relationship between psychopathy and criminality. Law-breaking may occur for sociocultural or psychobiological reasons that do not involve characterological defects, as noted throughout this chapter. Even among the most frequently and seriously delinquent group of youngsters in Robins's (1966, p. 159) large sample, for example, only half could be diagnosed as psychopathic, and undersocialized youth constitute just one fourth of adolescents institutionalized for delinquent behavior (Quay, 1987b).

Conversely, not all psychopaths become law-breakers. Numerous stories could certainly be told about "psychopaths among us"—selfish and self-aggrandizing individuals who heartlessly exploit people and circumstances to their own ends but stop short of overt criminal acts. Clinicians should accordingly avoid being too restrictive in diagnosing psychopathic personality disorder. Like schizophrenia and depression, this condition occurs in degrees of severity. The fact that a person has made a friend or two, or has married, or has some appealing personal qualities does not rule out psychopathy. Psychopathy implies the presence of at least some of its defining characteristics, but it does not entail extreme, unrelieved manifestations of all of the personality distortions that may be associated with it. These observations are consistent with current trends in diagnostic classification away from categorical and toward dimensional ways of looking at psychological disorders (see Widiger, Frances, Spitzer, & Williams, 1988).

Currently, the clinical evaluation of psychopathy must also take into account some vagaries in the terminology used to designate this condition and some issues concerning whether personality characteristics or behavioral difficulties constitute its core characteristics.

Problems of Terminology

Although there is general agreement concerning the personality characteristics associated with psychopathy, efforts to understand this condition have been accompanied by indecision about what to call it. *Psychopathic personality* was originally named and distinguished from neurotic and psychotic disorders by Cleckley (1976) in *The Mask of Sanity*, which first appeared in 1941. Many subsequent writers have recommended calling the disorder "sociopathic personality," to identify it as a social problem and call attention to its implications for inadequate socialization (Wolman, 1987). The American Psychiatric Association, beginning with the *DSM-II* published in 1968 and continuing in *DSM-III* and *DSM-III-R*, has chosen to call it "antisocial personality."

This condition, as described in the last two DSMs, can be reliably diagnosed and validly distinguished from other personality disorders (Blashfield & Haymaker, 1988; Morey, 1988; Wulach, 1983). However, the DSM terminology has some drawbacks, both conceptually and practically. Conceptually, the essence of the condition is an *asocial*, not an *antisocial* orientation; antisocial perspectives are a defining feature of socialized delinquency, not characterological delinquency. Practically, the original term *psychopath* (and even *sociopath* to some extent) has retained considerable popularity over the years among both clinicians and researchers. Hence, for the same condition there is one term that is commonly used in the literature and in daily conversations among clinicians (*psychopathic personality*) and a different term that must be used for official diagnostic purposes (*antisocial personality*).

Choice of terms is complicated further by age distinctions in *DSM-III-R*. Although a diagnosis of *antisocial personality disorder* requires a history of certain characteristics prior to age 15 and others between ages 15 and 18, the condition cannot be diagnosed before age 18. For juveniles showing the features of this disorder, the diagnostic category was *undersocialized conduct disorder* in *DSM-III* and is *solitary aggressive type conduct disorder* in *DSM-III-R*. Although there is some merit in recognizing that personality disorders rarely become crystallized before late adolescence, it may be somewhat arbitrary to label the very same condition one way at age 17 years and 364 days and another way the following day when the person turns 18. *DSM-III-R* addresses this issue in part by acknowledging a specific correspondence between conduct disorder in children and adolescents and antisocial personality disorder in adults (p. 335). Mental health professionals may accordingly be likely to continue to think of young people with this disorder as budding psychopaths or antisocial personalities, even though in clinical settings, they will have to record a formal diagnosis of conduct disorder.

Personality Versus Behavioral Descriptions

Instead of regarding psychopathy as consisting of certain personality characteristics, *DSM-III* defined it strictly in behavioral terms. Viewed behaviorally, psychopaths are persons who rarely form enduring interpersonal relationships, do poorly in school and on the job, have difficulty supporting themselves and their dependents, are irritable and aggressive, and engage regularly in irresponsible and illegal activity. In response to criticism that this behavioral description omits the guiltlessness classically associated with psychopathology, a criterion for lack of remorse was added in *DSM-III-R*. Yet the *DSM-III-R* diagnosis remains largely behavioral, taking little notice of the values and attitudes with which people view their world, and the diagnosis can be made even if the criterion of remorselessness is not met.

On this basis, numerous writers regard the DSM criteria for antisocial personality as more useful for identifying inadequate individuals and criminals than for diagnosing what has usually been considered to constitute psychopathy (Doren, 1987; Frances, 1980; Hare, 1983; Millon, 1981, Chapter 7). There are some data to warrant concern that the *DSM-III* overdiagnoses criminals as psychopaths. Approximately 30% of criminal populations were diagnosed with antisocial personality using earlier nomenclatures, such as

DSM-II, that focused on personality traits; by contrast, diagnostic studies using *DSM-III*-type criteria label approximately 75-80% of prison inmates with this diagnosis (Wulach, 1983).

The choice between personality-focused and behaviorally focused descriptions of psychopathy is brought into particularly sharp focus with respect to aggressive behavior. From a behavioral perspective, aggression is among the cardinal symptoms of undersocialized or solitary-type delinquency, along with impaired interpersonal relationships and low popularity (Quay et al., 1987). Because this emphasis on aggression discounts the possibility of violence without psychopathy, it can lead to overly inclusive diagnosis of antisocial personality disorder. To avoid being overinclusive, clinicians working in this frame of reference need to rule out numerous other conditions that are sometimes manifest in violent behavior, including schizophrenia, paranoia, mania, attention deficit hyperacticity disorder, and socialized delinquency.

Such diagnosis by *exclusion* is usually regarded as less efficient and more prone to errors of oversight than diagnosis by *inclusion*. Diagnosis of psychopathy by exclusion involves ruling *out* other possible explanations of inadequate or illegal behavior and hoping that none have been overlooked. Diagnosis by inclusion involves identifying psychopathy by ruling *in* such distinctive personality attributes as guiltlessness and lovelessness, which may or may not be associated with overt aggression but are always manifest in a selfish, exploitative, and manipulative nature and a propensity to lie, cheat, and take advantage of others, without remorse.

For childhood conduct disorder, as well as adult antisocial personality, an emphasis on aggression appears to contribute to overdiagnosis. In one major study of psychiatric inpatients, for example, violence was found to be the main factor distinguishing adolescents diagnosed as conduct-disordered from those receiving other diagnoses (Lewis, Lewis, Unger, & Goldman, 1984). Significantly, however, these conduct-disorder patients were as likely as other diagnostic groups to have had psychotic symptoms noted in their records, and their most common discharge diagnosis was schizophrenia. These researchers concluded that the violent behavior criterion for conduct disorder results in overuse of this diagnosis, insufficient initial attention to signs and symptoms of other disorders, and delays in definitive diagnosis and treatment planning. Because violent behaviors accompany so many other disorders, they argue, violence should be eliminated altogether from the criteria for conduct disorder.

Documenting further the nonspecificity of aggression for undersocialized conduct disorder, as well as for impaired interpersonal relationships and popularity, are data indicating that aggressive young people are not uniformly isolated and unpopular—Some are, but others have good friends and enjoy group membership (Cairns, Cairns, Neckerman, & Gest, 1988). This research finding seems consistent with the distinction between undersocialized and socialized delinquents, the latter being a group known to behave violently at times without being psychopathic. Whereas the aggressive behavior of so-cialized delinquents typically is collaborative and elicits peer support and acceptance, however, violence in undersocialized conduct-disordered adolescents tends to be confrontational and to evoke alienation from peers.

Asocial Attitudes and Coping Capacities

DSM-III aside, most checklists for assessing psychopathic personality disorder, such as Hare's (1980) Psychopathy Checklist, comprise two kinds of items: (a) items referring to inconsiderate, uncaring actions toward others that reflect asocial attitudes of guiltlessness and lovelessness and (b) items referring to behavioral ineptness due to low frustration tolerance, limited impulse control, incapacity to plan ahead, inability to learn from experience, and other inadequate coping capacities. Hare and his colleagues have in fact formulated a two-factor conceptualization of psychopathy in which one factor consists of a chronically unstable and antisocial life-style and the other factor comprises selfish, remorseless, and exploitative uses of other persons (Harpur, Hakstian, & Hare, 1988; Harpur, Hare, & Hakstian, 1989).

Over the years, a substantial body of research appeared to confirm that both asocial attitudes and deficient coping capacities differentiate psychopathic delinquents from subcultural and neurotic delinquents. Much of this earlier research can be called into question, however, because it was conducted primarily in institutional settings. Studies of institutionalized delinquents are limited by virtue of sampling to only those psychopaths who have become overtly criminal, and to only those psychopathic criminals who have been caught and incarcerated.

By contrast, when noninstitutionalized psychopaths, as well as prisoners, have been included in research studies, the results have failed to document any consistent group deficits in frustration tolerance, flexibility, self-restraint, planning capacity, and abilities to abstract, learn, persist, and remember (Arbuthnot et al., 1987; Quay, 1986; Sutker & Allain, 1987). Similarly, although characterological delinquents as a group show less tolerance for inaction and more stimulus-seeking behavior than other types of delinquents, as individuals they are highly variable in this regard, with some psychopaths being quite capable of tolerating inactivity and low-stimulus situations (Johnson & Fennel, 1983; Spielberger, Kling, & O'Hagen, 1978; Widom, 1978).

Hence, the adequacy of a young person's cognitive and social skills have little bearing on whether he or she should be considered psychopathic. In those who have a psychopathic disorder, however, their level of such skills is likely to influence how they behave. Whereas all psychopaths will lack concern for any harmful impact of their actions on other people, some will be keener than others in anticipating what this impact will be and more capable, should it serve their purposes, of refraining from harmful actions.

This formulation runs contrary to a body of research that once appeared to identify undersocialized delinquents as characteristically immature in their capacity for moral reasoning, deficient in interpersonal sensitivity, and unable to grasp the nature of friendship ties and reciprocal social roles (Jurkovic & Prentice, 1977; Panella & Henggeler, 1986; Quay, 1986; Walsh & Kurdek, 1984). These findings of sociocognitive skill deficits in antisocial adolescents have not stood the test of consistent replication, however. Psychopathic young people are inclined to misconstrue social situations as being more hostile than they in fact are, but they have more recently been found not to differ from subcultural and neurotic delinquents in empathy or role-taking skills (Lee & Prentice, 1988; Slaby & Guerra, 1988). Maturity of moral judgment has also proved to be a variable dimension. Undersocialized delinquents show judgmental deficits as a group, but many function at higher levels of moral reasoning as well (Arbuthnot et al., 1987).

In light of these findings, psychopathy needs to be conceptualized as a disorder accompanied by highly variable patterns of life adjustment. Psychopaths regularly suffer the moral and interpersonal bankruptcy that mark this condition and engender asocial attitudes, but they differ widely in the quality of their coping capacities. Some are well-functioning individuals who plan carefully, manipulate others effectively, find ways of attaining academic and vocational success, and rarely become mental patients or prison inmates. Smith (1978, Chapter 2) captured this group well in a discussion of the "charm and winning ways" of the "superior psychopath." Others function less well and, hampered by limited skills and poor judgment, seldom succeed in life endeavors and frequently are found in clinics, hospitals, and penitentiaries.

Among the cognitive skills that mediate between the core personality characteristics of psychopaths and how they actually behave, particular note should be taken of intelligence. Working with psychopathic prison inmates, Heilbrun (1979) found that having an undersocialized personality was associated with violent and impulsive crime only for the less intelligent half of his subjects (average IQ 93.7). The more intelligent half of his sample (average IQ 114.9) were no more likely to have been violent or impulsive than a comparison group of nonpsychopathic prisoners. Subsequent data confirmed the particularly serious risk for violence against others that derives from a combination of asocial attitudes and low intelligence (Heilbrun, 1990). Similarly for adolescent delinquents, intellectually limited psychopaths have been found significantly more likely to engage in violence than either nonpsychopaths or psychopaths with higher levels of intellectual functioning (Walsh, Beyer, & Petee, 1987).

The reasons why intelligence moderates violent behavior have not yet been determined. One possibility is that having average or better intelligence buffers young people who are at risk for antisocial behavior against experiences of failure and frustration. Intellectually limited children and adolescents, on the other hand, are likely to encounter more than their share of difficulty in doing their schoolwork, in finding solutions to problem situations, and in sorting out their prospects for the future. Such difficulties increase the susceptibility of asocial youngsters to being drawn toward aggressive delinquent behavior (Kandel, Mednick, Kirkegaard-Sorensen, Hutchings, Knop, Rosenberg, & Schulsinger, 1988; Moffitt, Gabrielli, & Mednick, 1981; White, Moffitt, & Silva, 1989).

Origins of Psychopathic Personality Disorder

Like virtually all patterns of psychopathology, psychopathic personality disorder runs in families. In psychopathy, this familial incidence results mainly from the ways in which antisocial parents rear their children. Genetic factors appear to contribute to criminality and antisocial personality disorder, however, and constitutional as well as environmental determinants may accordingly influence the onset and severity of psychopathy in some young people.

Parental Influences

Psychopathic personality disorder originates in early childhood experiences of parental rejection and neglect. As infants and young children, future psychopaths fail to receive the kinds of attention and affection that promote bonds of attachment to other people and foster a sense of trust in the world. They consequently grow into middle childhood with little capacity for warmth or compassion and little expectation of being loved or nurtured by others. Instead, they see the world as a hostile and uncaring place in which quarter is neither asked not given, consideration is neither tendered nor received, and survival and success depend on looking out for yourself. This picture of the early life experiences of psychopathic individuals, many of whom are found to have been physically as well as psychologically abandoned or abused, is extensively documented in the clinical and research literature (Deutsch & Erickson, 1989; Rosenthal & Doherty, 1985; Sines, 1987; Walsh et al., 1987; Widom, 1984).

Pathological parenting of future psychopaths usually progresses from emotional deprivation in early childhood to inadequate discipline and insufficient supervision during middle childhood and adolescence. Having previously lacked supportive nurturance when they needed it, these young people now lack constructive guidance when they need it. Whether because of disinterest or poor judgment, parents of future psychopaths typically fail to set clear limits and expectations for their children, and they typically fail to reward and punish them in a consistent and logical relationship to how they behave. Instead, these parents vacillate. Sometimes they make few rules, and, at other times, they lay down a host of regulations ("Here's how we're going to do things around here from now on"). Sometimes they pay little attention when their rules are broken, and, at other times, they administer harsh punishment for minor infractions or even for none at all ("Now you're really going to get it").

Like neglect, ineffectual discipline has been widely observed in the childhood histories of psychopathic individuals (Barth, 1987; Loeber & Dishion, 1984; Quay et al., 1987; Snyder & Patterslon, 1987). When parents are lax, punitive, or inconsistent, they fail to help their children develop internalized standards of conduct and increase the likelihood of their becoming aggressive, inconsiderate, and irresponsible in their actions toward others.

As testimony to parental influences on emerging psychopathy, the most reliable known predictor of this personality disorder is growing up in a home in which one or both parents are prominently antisocial. Conduct-disordered young people seen in outpatient clinics are far more likely to have parents with antisocial personality disorder than youthful patients with other conditions (Lahey, Piacentini, McBurnett, Stone, Hartdagen, & Hynd, 1988; Robins, 1978). Parents who drink excessively or are only sporadically employed also significantly increase their children's risk for conduct disorder (Farnworth, 1984; West & Prinz, 1987).

Parental psychopathy, alcoholism, and unemployment foster antisocial personality formation by contributing to a chaotic and stressful family life. In these homes, sustenance is unpredictable from one day to the next, strife simmers constantly, and self-sacrifice plays second fiddle to self-protection. In addition, marriages involving psychopaths are particularly likely to be exposed to the strains of parental separation and divorce. In this regard, it is important to keep in mind that it is not the fact of divorce that contributes to developmental psychopathology, but rather the parental conflict that often attends family break-up. As for broken homes, a house can be broken under the roof, if parents who stay together are constantly at each other's throats. Such family living can be much more detrimental to the psychological well-being of children than a separation or divorce in which the parents amicably go their separate ways while remaining mutually devoted to the care of their children.

Although stresses associated with divorce are often included among factors contributing to developmental psychopathology, recent data confirm that any such contribution to antisocial personality development is secondary to parental psychopathology. Lahey and his colleagues found that clinic-referred boys with diagnosed conduct disorders were much more likely than clinic-referred boys with other diagnoses to have divorced parents, and they were also much more likely to have parents with antisocial personality disorder. However, parental personality disorder held the key to both divorce and childhood conduct disorder in this sample. Divorce was not directly related to conduct disorder and had no bearing on it, except insofar as it was associated with antisocial personality disorder (Lahey, Hartdagen, Frick, McBurnett, Connor, & Hynd, 1988).

To some observers, parent–child concordance for psychopathy has suggested a modeling effect in which the acorns simply fall close to the tree. Despite superficial appearances, however, identification with parents is rarely implicated in the familial incidence of this disorder. The disinclination of psychopaths to identify with anyone has already been noted. Parental psychopathy and antisocial personality formation co-occur not because of modeling, but as a consequence of the frequently pathogenic childrearing practices of antisocial parents. Psychopathic parents are particularly likely candidates to ignore their children and abdicate or abuse their responsibility for nurturing and disciplining them.

Constitutional Influences

As reported by Rutter, Macdonald, Le Couteur, Harrington, Bolton, and Bailey (1990), research findings have consistently demonstrated that having a criminal parent is a major risk factor for juvenile delinquency. Heredity very probably plays a role in this family pattern, but substantial evidence that genetic factors contribute to misconduct in young people has not yet appeared. Twin and adoption studies appropriately designed to separate genetic from experiential influences have been reported, but the subjects in most of these studies have been identified law-breakers, but not identified psychopaths.

Among twins, for example, six studies summarized by Gottesman, Carey, and Hanson (1983) showed an 87% concordance for juvenile delinquency among identical twins and a 72% concordance for nonidentical twins. The small difference between the two groups and the high concordance rate for nonidentical twins are consistent with substantial environmental influences and not with much in the way of a genetic contribution. On the other hand, some researchers have discounted these data by arguing that genetic dispositions do not become fully manifest until adulthood.

The twin concordance data for adult criminals are in fact more definitive, including a 69% concordance for identical twins and a 33% concordance for nonidentical twins reported by Wilson and Hernstein (1985) and concordance rates of 51% versus 21% for identical compared to nonidentical twins reported by McGuffin and Gottesman (1985). Rutter et al. (1990) suggest that this age difference may be due to the frequency, among adolescents, of delinquent behavior that is transient in nature and unlikely to be determined by the kinds of genetic influences that contribute to chronic personality disorder or persistent criminality. Further research with carefully defined psychopathic subjects, not just detected law-breakers, will be necessary to assess this possibility.

As for adoption studies, there is some positive genetic evidence that being born to a father with a criminal record increases the likelihood of criminality among offspring even if they are adopted away early in life and reared by noncriminal parents. In a long-term study following 657 adoptees into adulthood, Mednick and Hutchings (1978) found that adopted-away children born to fathers with a criminal history and reared subsequently by noncriminal fathers were twice as likely to become criminal themselves (21.4%) as children born to noncriminal fathers, whether reared by noncriminal (10.5%) or criminal (11.5%) adoptive fathers. At the same time, however, the frequency of criminality among adopted-away offspring both born to and reared by criminal fathers almost doubled again, to 36.2%, giving evidence of a substantial environmental contribution.

Taken together, the twin and adoption data are consistent with some slight genetic contribution to criminality, but they provide only indirect evidence at best for genetic dispositions to psychopathy (Mednick, Gabrielli, & Hutchings, 1984; Plomin, 1989; Quay, 1986). Moreover, whatever genetic risks for antisocial personality disorder may eventually be identified, they are unlikely to lead to criminal behavior in the absence of the experiential influences discussed previously (see Cloninger & Gottesman, 1987).

Issues of genetics aside, certain biological dispositions may in some cases contribute to conduct disorder and antisocial personality formation. Biochemical studies have found significantly lower dopamine activity in undersocialized delinquents than in socialized delinquent and nondelinquent comparison groups (Quay et al., 1987; Rogeness, Hernandez, Macedo, & Mitchell, 1982). Dopamine inactivity provides a physiological basis for a person's having an overactive reward system and an underactive inhibitory system. Quay (1986, 1987b) suggests on this basis that people may become psychopathic as a consequence of being overresponsive to reward (because they are biologically disposed to reward- and stimulus-seeking) and underresponsive to punishment (because they are biologically disposed to being impulsive and uninhibited). Studies of response perseveration under differential conditions of reward have yielded some preliminary evidence in support of this possibility (Newman, Patterson, & Kosson, 1987; Shapiro, Quay, Hogan, & Schwartz, 1988).

In formulating his theory, however, Quay emphasized that any such constitutional influences combine with parental influences to produce a complex biopsychological causative process. He also notes that the data demonstrating distinctive biological characteristics come almost entirely from incarcerated delinquent psychopaths. Whether psychopathic young people who refrain from law-breaking or manage to stay out of jail show these characteristics is not known. Consistent with the distinction drawn earlier between asocial attitudes and coping capacities, it may be that physiologically deviant reward and inhibitory systems constitute a dimension of adaptive capacity along which psychopaths vary, rather than a core characteristic of the disorder. Those who have this biological disposition may then be at increased risk for becoming delinquent and ending up in an institution.

Some further data on the measured IQ of delinquents is interesting to consider in this regard. The previously noted indications that intelligence can minimize the likelihood of psychopaths becoming criminals and of criminals getting caught and imprisoned do not preclude the possibility of intellectual disadvantage even among nondetected delinquents. Extensive research has in fact consistently identified an average IQ gap of about 8 points between groups of delinquent and nondelinquent adolescents, independently of their socioeconomic status (Binder, 1988; Moffitt et al., 1981; Quay, 1987a; Schonfeld, Shaffer, O'Conner, & Portnoy, 1988).

This intellectual disadvantage is found among self-reported (unofficial) as well as official delinquents, even when special care is taken to identify self-reported delinquents whose law-breaking has not been detected (Hirschi & Hindelang, 1977; Moffitt & Silva, 1988). Perhaps, then, intelligence should be considered a constitutional influence that plays some part in determining whether young people are prone to becoming delinquent when it is low or are insulated against antisocial personality developments when it is high. In light of the approximately 50% heritability of intelligence, such a role of intellectual abilities would lend weight at least to an indirect genetic contribution to delinquency.

The Course of Psychopathic Personality Disorder

Psychopathy is a chronic disorder that begins early in life, crystallizes in late adolescence, and usually persists throughout the adult years. The antisocial conduct that accompanies this condition accordingly shows considerable continuity from childhood into adolescence and beyond. Overly aggressive children tend to become assaultive adolescents and violent adults; children who steal tend to become adolescent thieves and adults who commit crimes against property (Barth, 1987; Loeber & Stouthamer-Loeber, 1987; Moskowitz, Schwartzman, & Ledingham, 1985; Stattin & Magnusson, 1989).

Future psychopaths begin in elementary school to lie, cheat, steal, and behave cruelly toward others. They bully children younger or smaller than themselves, they mistreat animals as well as people, and, early on, they display a demanding and self-centered style of life.

In adolescence, the persistence of these childhood characteristics brings budding psychopaths increasingly into conflict with their peers, parents, teachers, and community. They are more likely than other young people to lack friendships and to be argumentative and disobedient at home. In school, they are much more likely than their classmates to skip class and to be suspended or expelled for aggressive or disruptive conduct, especially fighting and insubordination. Unless they are sufficiently intelligent to succeed academically without conscientious effort, they often get held back one grade or more. They frequently come to the attention of the police, especially if their coping capacities are limited.

The predictability of such progressive adjustment difficulty varies in the individual case with several features of a young person's misconduct. The more frequently children misbehave and the more harmful their actions are to other people and their property, the more likely they will be to show persistent and serious antisocial behavior in adolescence. The earlier the onset of their misconduct, the more varied it is (e.g., both stealing and fighting), and the more settings in which it occurs (e.g., both at home and in school), the more likely it is to persist and the more serious it will become. Conversely, relatively late onset of minor, infrequent, and situation-specific antisocial conduct minimizes the likelihood of persistent and increasingly severe offenses (Kelso & Stewart, 1986; Loeber, 1990; Loeber & Stouthamer-Loeber, 1987).

These findings identify a stepping-stone effect that assists in the clinical identification of characterological delinquency. Misbehaving children are generally at risk for subsequent antisocial behavior, but not all childhood conduct problems eventuate in adolescent delinquency. On the other hand, adolescents rarely become conduct-disordered without previously having been misbehaving children. Characterological delinquency will, with few exceptions, have been preceded by childhood misconduct, and most chronic delinquents will have been recognizable in elementary school from such behavior (Loeber, 1988; Loeber & Stouthamer-Loeber, 1987). These findings are sufficiently reliable to contraindicate the diagnosis of psychopathy or antisocial personality disorder in the absence of such early developmental difficulties.

Among childhood patterns of misconduct, fire-setting appears particularly important in identifying the severity and probable persistence of antisocial behavior. Kolko and Kazdin (1988) report that about one fifth of the outpatients and one third of the inpatients they studied in a child psychiatric facility had a history of fire-setting. Fire-setting has been found to emerge following a sequence of increasingly serious antisocial acts, including other kinds of aggressive and destructive behavior (Jacobson, 1985; Kolko, Kazdin, & Meyer, 1985; Lowenstein, 1989). Hence, fire-setting appears to mark an especially serious form of conduct disorder that is highly predictive of persistent antisocial conduct.

The life course of psychopaths as adults depends on the extent to which their character defects in morality and interpersonal caring are balanced by other personality resources. As previously mentioned, those with good coping capacities may fashion successful lives for themselves as charmers and manipulators, although they are likely to be popular only among people who fail to see through them. More often than not, the way in which antisocial young people conduct themselves and treat others leads to their being disliked and rejected, which in turn augurs poorly for their prognosis (Asarnow, 1988). Those with low intelligence or limited skills will be at high risk as adults for criminal records, job failure, alcoholism, marital instability, and other chronic social problems.

CASE 13.   PSYCHOPATHIC PERSONALITY DEVELOPMENT IN EMERGING CHARACTEROLOGICAL DELINQUENCY

Martin D. was 13 when his school principal recommended professional help for him. The referral was precipitated by the latest episode in a long history of aggressive behavior, which included numerous unprovoked beatings of younger children. Martin has also been disruptive in class and had recently begun to yell out, "I hate everyone." According to the principal, Martin was "the worst boy we've ever seen at his age."

Martin's father did most of the talking during an initial interview with the parents, both of whom were high school teachers. Mr. D. said he was very upset by his son's aggressive and unruly behavior in school. He described Martin as a lazy, easily frustrated boy who wanted to achieve without working, who could not tolerate losing in anything, and who lied constantly. Mr. D. could offer no explanation for Martin's misconduct, except to say, "Maybe he was just born bad." He added, however, that because he was a stern disciplinarian, he had no trouble with Martin at home. Perhaps Martin's teachers, he suggested, by not being firm enough and by accusing him whenever there was a class disturbance, were at least partly responsible for his record of poor conduct.

A subsequent meeting with Martin's mother alone told a much different story. Saying she had been afraid to speak up in her husband's presence, Mrs. D. complained that Mr. D.'s description of their son was equally true of him. Although he was good at impressing other people with his competence and sincerity, Mrs. D. said, Mr. D. was a nasty, irresponsible, dishonest man who paid little attention to family affairs and frequently absented himself from the home for days at a time without explanation. Much of his self-description, she continued, especially his being a stern disciplinarian, was a lie: "He likes to think of himself as a big man, but he's never done anything constructive to discipline Martin; when he is home, which isn't often, he can't be bothered."

These interviews suggested that Martin was being reared by a self-centered father who failed to discipline him and a browbeaten mother who was too passive to compensate for the disinterested meanness of her husband. This nonnurturant family environment, together with Martin's long history of misconduct, suggested that his problem behavior was being orchestrated by emerging psychopathic personality disorder.

A conversation with Martin produced further evidence of a characterologically asocial orientation in the making. He was courteous and responsive, but dishonest and self-righteous. He scoffed at any suggestion that he had been behaving badly or might have some personal problem. He was particularly derisive when asked about the reports of his aggressiveness. He did not get into nearly as many fights as these reports claimed, he said, and he had never hit anyone "who didn't have it coming." He expressed little regret for ever having hurt anyone "who was asking for it." As far as he was concerned "They would of done the same to me if they could of."

NEUROTIC DELINQUENCY

In neurotic delinquency, young persons commit illegal acts neither as well-integrated members of a delinquent subculture nor as a reflection of personality disorder. Instead, they break laws as an individual and personally meaningful attempt to communicate unmet psychological needs. In common with many other neurotic behaviors, neurotic delinquency is thus symptomatic of underlying concerns that it serves indirectly to express.

Whereas socialized and characterological delinquency often involve recurrent antisocial conduct that becomes a way of life, neurotic delinquency typically consists of occasional, situationally determined episodes of law-breaking. These episodes usually begin following the emergence or exacerbation of some personal problem that generates feelings of tension, remorse, or discouragement, and they tend to stop soon after this problem has been resolved. Accordingly, other labels that have been used for this pattern of antisocial behavior include "acute," "accidental," "situationally provoked," and "anxious–withdrawn–dysphoric" (Genshaft, 1980; Hare & Cox, 1978; Quay, 1987b). Although adolescents who fall into this category do not fit usual stereotypes of being a "juvenile delinquent," anxious-withdrawn-dysphoric youths account for one fourth of institutionalized delinquents (Quay, 1986, 1987b).

Instead of demonstrating the long-standing antisocial attitudes seen in socialized delinquents or the childhood aggressiveness and selfishness associated with characterological delinquency, neurotic delinquents have typically been cordial and conforming youngsters. Their present misconduct stands in sharp contrast to a developmental history of propriety, and people who know them express surprise at their sudden loss of respect for law and order. As a general principle, the more a delinquent adolescent's behavior diverges from a past history of model conduct, the more reason there is to consider him or her a neurotic delinquent.

Similarly, the likelihood that delinquent behavior is neurotically determined increases when apparently precipitating events precede its onset. Neurotic delinquency tends to follow closely on the heels of some "last straw" in a series of rebuffs or disappointments that have been intensifying a young person's unmet needs. When such precipitating events are not readily apparent, delinquent behavior probably stems from subcultural deviance or characterological defects rather than from neurotic concerns. The following discussion elaborates the way in which neurotic delinquency communicates needs, the manner in which family interactions can provoke this pattern of delinquency, and some clinical guidelines for differentiating neurotic from characterological delinquents.

Communication of Needs in Neurotic Delinquency

Adolescents who commit delinquent acts are often attempting to get other people to respond to needs they feel are being overlooked or ignored. The specific needs that most commonly underlie such indirect, neurotic efforts to communicate are *needs to be recognized and respected* and *needs to receive help*.

Needs for Recognition and Respect

Needs for recognition and respect sometimes lead young persons who feel unnoticed and unappreciated to misbehave in some dramatic fashion. A detected delinquent act can command the attention of teachers, police, and other important adults; it can require otherwise unavailable parents to become engaged in court, school, or clinical deliberations; and it can promote visibility among otherwise disinterested peers.

Acts of daring and bravado, such as attempting to shoplift under a store clerk's nose, trying to outrace a police car, or climbing the school flagpole are well-suited for such purposes. These ends may also be served by behaviors that embarrass or disrupt established authorities or institutions, such as calling in a bomb threat that results in a school or movie theater being emptied and searched; the case of Wilma in Chapter 4 (pp. 123–124) illustrates such attention-seeking delinquency. The use of public antisocial behavior to gain recognition and peer status, especially in young persons suffering from low self-esteem, has been observed in numerous clinical and research studies (Berndt & Zinn, 1984; Bynner, O'Malley, & Bachman, 1981; Cary, 1979; Rosenberg & Rosenberg, 1978).

Because their actions can serve communicative purposes only if they are detected, neurotic delinquents almost always manage to get caught. A boy stealing something in school will commit the crime at a time when he is likely to be seen, or he will leave the stolen items someplace where they are certain to be noticed and traced to him. If, despite himself, he appears to be getting away with the theft, he will find some way to leak word of his guilt—such as confiding to a friend, as Wilma did. No matter what penalties follow, detected neurotic delinquents enjoy their temporary notoriety as "the one who did it." When no evidence can be found of apparent carelessness leading to being caught, delinquent acts are likely to have other than neurotic origins.

Neurotically determined delinquent acts can also be identified by their lack of any apparent purpose beyond attracting attention. Objects stolen are neither needed nor used. Demonstrations of bravado provide no pleasure beyond what comes from any ensuing notoriety. When delinquents need and use what they have stolen, and when they seem to have enjoyed their escapades, even without having been detected, clinicians should look to sociocultural or characterological rather than neurotic explanations of the misconduct.

Needs for Help

Troubled young persons who are afraid or embarrassed to confide their concerns to others, or whose efforts to confide have been falling on deaf or disinterested ears, may resort to visible acts of delinquency as an indirect way of communicating their need for some help. Their delinquent behavior compels recognition by others that they are having a problem and forces something to be done about it. As already noted, for example, inattentive parents who are called before a school principal or a juvenile court judge to discuss their child's misbehavior can no longer deny or overlook his or her psychological difficulties. Often, such confrontations result in a referral for needed professional help that the young person might otherwise not have received.

The problem most commonly associated with communication of psychological neediness through delinquent acts is an underlying depression. Uncharacteristic recalcitrance and the sudden onset of stealing can often be traced to events in a young person's life that have left him or her feeling lonely or discouraged. Frequently observed in this regard is the appearance of these neurotic problem behaviors soon after the loss of some important person in an adolescent's life, as when a parent dies or an unfriendly divorce is finalized (Chiles, Miller, & Cox, 1980). Sexual promiscuity can also occur as a reflection on underlying depression, especially in young women with unmet needs for affection. As mentioned in Chapter 4, depressed females may seek sexual intimacy not for erotic reasons, but as a means of feeling close to and receiving attention from another person, and persistent depression can motivate such youngsters to repetitive, indiscriminate sexual activity.

A 17-year-old brought for help by her parents because of declining school performance, for example, complained that she felt stupid and unattractive, that her friends were snubbing her, and that life seemed barely worth living. She then described her wish to find "some boy who would stick by me," and she confessed to one-night stands with a large number of young men to whom she offered herself sexually in her search for someone "who would accept me and give me a reason to be alive."

CASE 14.   NEEDS FOR ATTENTION AND HELP IN NEUROTIC DELINQUENCY

Jack was 15 and a high school sophomore when his mother died. She had been his major source of affection and support. An older brother with whom he had a good relationship was away at college, and his father, although caring about him, was a busy professional man who had depended on his wife to look after the children. In the absence of any replacement for the nurturance his mother had provided him, Jack slipped into a mild but persistent depression. He lost interest in school and other activities, grew listless and lethargic, and spent hours dwelling on the bleakness of his future.

For a few months, Jack suffered inwardly, however, and no one sensed that he was a boy in need of help. He had always been on the quiet side and not very active in school, and he was bright enough to continue earning good grades even though he was no longer working very hard. At home, he was reluctant to tell his father that he was troubled, primarily because he felt his father was himself struggling with more grief than he could handle.

Then Jack's outward behavior changed as well. He began writing hammer-and-sickle emblems on his papers and textbooks, carrying around the *Communist Manifesto*, and monopolizing class discussions with long-winded comments on the merits of socialism. Before long, he was being labeled and teased by his classmates as "the commie," which apparently met some of his needs to get attention but still brought him little in the way of nurturance.

One day, Jack managed to get a copy of the master key to his school, and he began using it to "borrow" tape recorders and other equipment, without permission. He would return these items after a few days, but his timing was consistently poor—there was always someone around when he attempted to replace the "borrowed" items, and he was caught every time. This stealing behavior, like his becoming the "commie," seemed clearly to reflect his underlying depression and his wish to get help in overcoming it. The school recommended treatment, and Jack's attention-seeking and delinquent behavior stopped abruptly after an initial interview in which arrangements were made for ongoing psychotherapy. In succeeding months, as Jack was helped to work through the loss of his mother and to develop new relationships, especially among his peers, he dropped his "commie" role and gradually regained his previous good spirits and levels of interest and energy.

Family Interaction in Neurotic Delinquency

In contrast to the family circumstances surrounding characterological delinquency, the families of neurotic delinquents typically display reasonable stability, mutual affection, and generally law-abiding and socially adaptive behavior. This is not to say that there are no family problems accompanying neurotic delinquency. Neurotic delinquents may use their deviant behavior in part as hostile acts toward their parents, whom they resent for not fully appreciating their needs, and their parents are usually more than a little displeased with them for their misbehavior. If delinquent patterns truly reflect neurotic rather than characterological difficulties, however, this current falling out between adolescents and their parents will overlay caring and concern for each other and a genuine wish to draw closer together. At the same time, family interaction often contributes to neurotic delinquency through inadvertent *parental fostering* and *reinforcement* of antisocial behavior.

Parental Fostering

Parents who are neither psychologically disturbed nor asocial may nevertheless model disrespect for the law in certain ways that foster illegal behavior in their children. For example, generally law-abiding parents who cheat on their income tax or drive over the speed limit communicate to their children that such illegal acts are acceptable. If they take obvious pleasure in their law-breaking ("I've figured out how to charge off our vacation as a business expense"), they teach their children that flouting law may be desirable as well as acceptable.

Such teaching makes an especially strong impression when parents are heard to lie about a problem ("Honest, officer, I had no idea I was going over 35"), or deny any intention of changing illegal behavior ("It was worth a try: I'll be more careful next time"), or propose a deception ("Scrunch down so you won't look so tall, and maybe we can get you in at half-fare"). The more that young people are exposed to parental modeling of this kind, the more they are likely to conclude that lying and cheating are appropriate ways to act, at least on some occasions in certain circumstances. Such selective defects in conscience were aptly described by Adelaide Johnson (1949) as "superego lacunae." Circumscribed gaps or lacunae in an otherwise well-socialized morality explain how adults who are for the most part ethical and most certainly not psychopathic may in some contexts behave illegally, immorally, or unethically and in so doing set an example with which their otherwise well-socialized children may identify.

Parental Reinforcement

Once a delinquent act has been committed, parents sometimes respond in ways that reinforce the antisocial behavior and encourage its repetition. Especially problematic are situations in which the parents see nothing particularly wrong with what their children have done and hence discipline them in an ambivalent or inconsistent manner that tacitly communicates approval of the delinquent behavior.

For example, delinquency-reinforcing parents sometimes deplore a delinquent act by their youngster but collaborate with him or her to prevent its being detected or punished. Should he or she be caught, they minimize the significance of the offense to the authorities. At other times, they accept flimsy excuses for misdeeds and describe them to others in a tone of bemused tolerance. They criticize the outcome of an offense but pay scant attention to the offense itself: "If you had to speed, why did you have to do it right in the center of town where you were sure to get caught," or "If you want to fight, you could at least pick a kid you can handle."

The evidence for such inadvertent parental fostering and reinforcement in neurotic delinquency comes largely from clinical reports. Nevertheless, this maladaptive family contribution to delinquent acts has long been noted and is supported by some research (Carek, Hendrickson, & Holmes, 1961; Gallenkamp & Rychlak, 1968). Clinically, this role of family interaction can prove helpful in understanding initially puzzling instances of delinquency in young persons who do not belong to any deviant subculture, who show neither psychopathic nor other serious psychopathological tendencies, who are deriving no obvious gratification from their misbehavior, and whose parents are apparently stable, conforming adults who cannot comprehend their youngster's conduct. Careful investigation in such cases may well identify subtle defects in the parents' codes of values and behavior and equally subtle ways in which they are fostering or reinforcing their youngster's illegal actions.

Differentiating Neurotic from Characterological Delinquency

Among delinquent adolescents who are psychologically disturbed and are not misbehaving as well-integrated members of an antisocial subculture, neurotic delinquency can usually be differentiated from characterological delinquency on the basis of the clinical history. Most reliable in this regard is the unexpected onset of neurotic delinquency in adolescence, manifest in behavior patterns that are atypical of the individual and at variance with his or her prior conduct. Such late-onset delinquency of neurotic origins contrasts with the typical early onset of characterological delinquency in the form of childhood conduct disorder that is continuous with and predictive of adolescent misbehavior.

Also reliable but sometimes more difficult to identify than the age of onset of these two conditions is the family context in which they emerge: neurotic delinquency in a close-knit family in which parents and children care for each other but are currently not communicating effectively, and characterological delinquency in a chaotic family in which the parents care primarily for themselves, and the children, at least those who are becoming psychopathic, have long been deprived of nurturance and supervision.

The differential diagnosis of delinquency is sometimes aided by the nature of an adolescent's misconduct. Virtually any kind of antisocial acts, including crimes against both people and their property, can reflect a characterologically asocial orientation. However, crimes against people, especially violent crimes, are rarely committed by neurotic delinquents. Adolescent who are trying to resolve underlying psychological conflicts express their needs primarily through crimes against property or by "victimless" crimes—that is, offenses in which no one but themselves suffers directly, such as running away or breaking a curfew. Aggressive acts in which other people have purposely been hurt will almost always signify characterological rather than neurotic delinquency in disturbed adolescents.

Finally, the distinction between neurotic and characterological delinquency can be reliably guided by attention to a young person's basic personality style as inferred from interview and psychological test data. The more the conversation of delinquent adolescents demonstrates lack of remorse and personal loyalties and the more clearly it points to shallow interpersonal relatedness and underdeveloped affectional needs, the more likely their misconduct is to be associated with psychopathic personality formation. Conversely, the less prominently they manifest such personality characteristics, especially when there are indicators of neurotic concerns and parental fostering that could account for their antisocial behavior, the more likely it is that their delinquency is symptomatic in nature.

In relating to a clinician, furthermore, neurotic delinquents tend to be embarrassed and hesitant but nevertheless eager to talk about currently troubling events in their lives. Psychopathic delinquents, on the other hand, regard the interview as an opportunity to make an impression and usually show less concern with what they are saying than with how they are presenting themselves. Some psychopaths transparently reveal the nature of their disorder by a surly show of insolence, negativism, and bravado rarely seen in neurotic delinquents. Others, like Martin (see p. 321), able to exercise better judgment and self-control, keep their "cool" and concentrate on how best to manage the interview to emerge admired and unscathed. Then, unlike neurotic delinquents, they may avoid talking about or admitting current difficulties, especially if these include delinquent acts that have not yet been detected or adjudicated. In these instances, an extended evaluation may be necessary to obtain a history confirming psychopathic tendencies. Kaplan (1988) for example, reports a study in which 60% of delinquent adolescents with a history of cruelty to animals and 40% who had set damaging fires—both of which point to psychopathy rather than neurosis—denied such activities in a first interview but admitted to them in subsequent sessions.

PSYCHOTIC AND NEUROPSYCHOLOGICAL DELINQUENCY

Psychopathic personality disorder and neurotic symptom formation account for most instances of delinquent behavior associated with psychological disturbance. However, clinicians must also be alert to occasions when antisocial behavior derives from psychotic or neuropsychological disorder. Studying 285 adolescents referred to a juvenile court clinic, Lewis and Balla (1976, Chapter 7) found that one third showed signs of psychosis, central nervous system impairment, or both. Although delinquents in general are not as likely to demonstrate such serious disorders as this sample of adjudicated law-breakers referred for mental health care, the Lewis and Balla findings indicate the advisability of considering their possible presence in the individual case.

Psychotic delinquency emerges primarily in schizophrenic adolescents whose faulty logic, impaired judgment, and shaky self-control lead them into antisocial behavior (see Chapter 3). Lewis et al. (1984) found, in their previously mentioned psychiatric hospital sample, that schizophrenia was the most common discharge diagnosis among adolescents with an admission diagnosis of conduct disorder. Evidence that antipsychotic medication reduces violence associated with schizophrenia demonstrates the importance of prompt and accurate differential diagnosis in planning treatment for aggressive, psychotic adolescents (Cavanaugh, Rogers, & Wasylow, 1981).

Neuropsychological delinquency occurs most often in connection with attention-deficit hyperactivity disorder (ADHD) and temporal lobe epilepsy (TLE). The susceptibility of ADHD children to problematic interpersonal relationships and antisocial conduct, as well as to school learning difficulties, is discussed in Chapter 7 (see pp. 270–273). Among adolescents, social and conduct problems are the most prominent manifestations of persisting ADHD (Brier, 1989; Brown & Borden, 1986; Lambert, 1988). In one prospective study, previously hyperactive boys at age 14, compared to boys without an ADHD history, were found seven times more likely to have been suspended from school on one or more occasions and six times more likely to have had trouble with the law (Lambert, Sassone, Hartsough, & Sandoval, 1987).

For preexisting ADHD, as in the case of psychotic disorder, accurate differential diagnosis in a delinquent adolescent has important implications for specialized treatment planning. Stimulant medication is a demonstrably effective means of achieving improved behavior in ADHD adolescents, especially those who remain hyperactive and distractible, and cognitive and perceptual–motor skill training can boost the low self-esteem that contributes to delinquency in neuropsychologically impaired young people (Henker & Whalen, 1989; Jacob, 1983; McDaniel, 1986; Quay, 1987b). Failure to employ medication and skill training when the origins of adolescent misconduct call for them may perpetuate behavior problems that will not respond to therapies designed for working with characterological or neurotic delinquents.

With respect to epileptic disorder, explosive outbursts of angry, assaultive, antisocial behavior that resemble manifestations of psychopathy sometimes constitute psychomotor seizures, also referred to as TLE because of the usual temporal focus of the abnormal brain activity associated with this condition (Bear, Freeman, & Greenberg, 1984; Blumer, 1982). Psychomotor seizures occurring independently or in combination with other types of epileptic attack are characterized by a sudden onset of strange body movements that serve no apparent purpose. These actions persist in an automatic, stereotyped fashion for anywhere from a minute to several hours, and efforts to stop the person or to change his or her behavior during the attack often provoke combative rage. Subsequently, the person usually has little or no memory for what he or she has done and, unlike psychopathic individuals following an aggressive outburst, sincerely regrets any damage or offense to others that may have occurred.

Aggressive outbursts occurring in temporal lobe epileptics are not part of a comfortable life-style, as they are in psychopaths. Instead, they are unwelcome and ego-alien losses of control into which these persons are precipitated by events over which they have no control. Along with their propensity to seizures during which they behave in ways they regret, however, many TLE individuals have a somewhat paranoid orientation. Even when they are not having an attack, they are likely to become angry or to get into altercations in response to imagined insults or threats (Devinsky & Bear, 1984; Lewis, 1976; Sherwin, 1982).

Among the court clinic-referral studies by Lewis and Balla, 6.3% were diagnosed, after careful evaluation, as having TLE. An even larger frequency of TLE was found by Lewis and her colleagues in an evaluation of 97 incarcerated delinquent boys, 18 of whom were concluded to be having psychomotor seizures (Lewis, Pincus, Shanok, & Glaser, 1982). Of further significance, almost 90% of the psychomotor epileptics in the clinic sample described paranoid concerns, and 50% of the crimes they had committed were offenses against people, compared to just a 2–3% incidence of violent offenses in the total juvenile court sample studies (Lewis & Balla, 1976, Chapter 5).

These findings confirm the role that TLE can play in delinquent behavior, especially in cases of sudden, violent, and seemingly unprovoked attacks on other people. Accordingly, episodic aggressive outbursts followed by amnesia and remorse should be investigated for their possible origin in TLE. When this explosive behavior disorder is positively identified, moreover, beneficial effects are likely to result from including anticonvulsant medication in the treatment plan (Kellner, 1981; O'Donnell, 1985; Stewart, Myers, Burket, & Lyles, 1990).

CASE 15.   AGGRESSIVE OUTBURSTS IN TEMPORAL LOBE EPILEPSY

Johnny was 14 when his parents sought help in connection with a 4-month history of temper tantrums and violent aggressive outbursts. They associated the onset of his disturbed behavior with the birth of their youngest child, whose arrival was unwelcome to Johnny. According to the parents, he had complained bitterly that the family was already too large (the newcomer was the fifth child) and required too much sharing of everything. In the 4 months since the birth, he had become increasingly intolerant of not getting his own way, and in response to the slightest frustration or provocation, he would now storm around the house, yelling, throwing things, and sometimes striking out physically at his siblings.

Further inquiry revealed that poorly controlled aggressive outbursts had been present for many years and had merely been intensified by the birth of the new baby. Johnny's parents reported that he had always had a quick temper and had been the most demanding of their children. He had never had much capacity for delay of gratification; he had characteristically been mean and cruel to his siblings; he had been consistently unruly, inattentive, and combative in school; and he had rarely shown consideration for others or remorse for his physical attacks on them.

Johnny arrived for his first interview angry, sullen, and suspicious, and he alternated throughout the session between smoldering resentment at having been forced to come and attempts to treat the situation as a lark. These initial findings suggested an emerging psychopathic personality disorder, expressed in an undersocialized aggressive behavior pattern. The fact that his father had impressed the interviewer as being himself a physically aggressive, short-tempered, self-centered person lent weight to this diagnostic impression. However, a detailed developmental history brought to light birth complications and some delay in Johnny's learning to sit up, stand, walk, and talk. Because of the implications of such findings for possible central nervous system impairment, neurological consultation was utilized. Johnny's EEG identified paroxysmal abnormalities, consistent with convulsive disorder, with a midtemporal focus.

In this complicated case, the clinical evaluation of Johnny's behavior problems revealed some clearly psychopathic features, such as his remorselessness, and also some intrafamilial conflicts, of which his misconduct seemed symptomatic, such as sibling rivalry for parental attention. The interviewer additionally sensed beneath Johnny's hard exterior some capacities for warmth and loyalty that could provide a basis for engaging him effectively in psychotherapy. Nevertheless, he was, at the same time, suffering from an epileptic disorder. Not only could some of his episodic dyscontrol be understood as seizure discharges, but also it seemed likely that he had derived some of his abrasive personality characteristics from being reacted to by others as an aggressive, unpredictable boy. Subsequent psychotherapy did in fact help Johnny to work through many problems in relating to his parents, siblings, teachers, and peers, while anticonvulsant medication prescribed and regulated by his pediatrician substantially reduced the extent and frequency of his temper tantrums and aggressive outbursts.

INTERVENTION

The diversity of juvenile delinquency calls for a diversified approach to treating it. When antisocial behavior is associated with schizophrenia, attention-deficit hyperactivity disorder, or temporal lobe epilepsy, effective treatment of these disorders is usually necessary to reduce or eliminate the misconduct. For other patterns of delinquency, there is a broad spectrum of potentially effective interventions, which includes social-action programs, outpatient individual and group counseling and psychotherapy, residential and day-care milieus, and home-based family and behavioral methods. These treatment approaches often work best when tailored in combinations to meet the special needs of *socialized, characterological*, and *neurotic delinquents.*

Socialized Delinquency

Because socialized delinquency stems from group endorsement of antisocial behavior in the relative absence of individual disturbance, efforts to curb it have traditionally focused more on prevention through social change than on treatment. Noteworthy in this regard are such community projects as home-study and job-upgrading programs, the organization of neighborhood citizens' committees, and the Police Athletic League. These projects seek to involve delinquent youths in ways of enjoying themselves and making money within the law rather than by breaking it (Coates, 1981; Gottschalk, Davidson, Gensheimer, & Mayer, 1987; Safer, 1982).

Unfortunately, the bonds of existing group membership among socialized delinquents frequently limit the impact of such prosocial programs, except when especially positive interactions with law-abiding adults and peers can influence these young people to shift their loyalties to a new, nondelinquent group. On the other hand, even though socialized delinquents are rarely motivated to participate in psychological treatment, counseling and psychotherapy holds some promise for producing change if it can be adequately directed toward educating them in different ways of viewing their lives. In addition, some community and family approaches have been designed to prevent delinquency before it even begins.

Educational Psychotherapy

Success in educationally oriented psychotherapy with socialized delinquents depends on getting these young people to recognize how their current behavior is wasting their talents and energies and could be replaced by more satisfying nondelinquent means of making progress in school and work situations. This kind of educational therapy with socialized delinquents can often draw support from maturational changes in group behavior and identity formation, especially in late adolescence. Older adolescents normatively begin to loosen their previous group ties in favor of forging a firm individual identity, and they gravitate toward fewer but more intimate personal relationships than before. Psychologically stable but subculturally delinquent adolescents who are in the process of this transition may conclude on their own that their law-breaking will interfere with their getting ahead in the world. Such spontaneous and self-determined decisions to stop breaking the law are sometimes referred to formally as the "natural cessation" of delinquency. In one study of natural cessation, Mulvey and LaRosa (1986) found in a group of untreated but reformed late-adolescent delinquents that their behavior change had been preceded in each case by their arriving at a changed perspective on their current behavior and future prospects and resolving to change the former in order to improve the latter. Therapists can frequently accelerate this natural recovery process by encouraging and helping young persons to think about what would be best for them in the future.

Particular success in prosocial intervention has been realized with an approach centered on vocationally oriented psychotherapy. Shore and Massimo (1973) were among the first to experiment with offering job training and placement to delinquent boys who had dropped out of school or been expelled. Those who were willing to participate also received preemployment counseling, guidance in such tasks as opening a bank account and getting a driver's license, and a supportive ear for discussing personal problems. A 10-year follow-up indicated that this combined psychotherapy, remedial education, and job-placement approach had helped these boys avoid trouble with the law and achieve academic and occupational goals that would probably otherwise have been beyond their grasp.

More recently, Friedman, Utada, and Glickman (1986) have described an activity treatment program in a vocational high school for court-referred delinquent boys. Within 2 years of entering the program, students in this high school, as a group, showed significantly improved behavior, adjustment, and social attitudes. Interestingly, this improvement was related more to the vocational training and job placement programs than to an off-campus supportive life skills program that was also provided.

Community-Based Prevention

Although not directed specifically at socialized delinquency, numerous community programs have sought to prevent delinquency from emerging or worsening by psychosocial intervention with young persons identified as "predelinquent." The first of these programs was the well-known Cambridge–Somerville Youth Study, which began in 1939. Several hundred 5- to 13-year-old boys, some considered "difficult" and some "average" were referred to the program in working-class urban areas of Massachusetts. Half of the boys were assigned to a control group and merely provided information about themselves. The other half constituted a treatment group who, for an average period of 5 years, received twice-monthly family visits from a counselor and some combination of academic tutoring, individual psychotherapy, summer camp placement, and involvement with the Boy Scouts, the YMCA, and other community programs (Powers & Witmer, 1951).

Thirty years later, official records and personal contacts with 253 men who had been in the treatment group and an equal number of control subjects revealed that the two groups were almost equally likely to have committed crimes as juveniles and were equally likely to have been convicted for some crime as adults (McCord, 1978). Despite these disappointing results and the failure of other multifaceted intervention programs through the 1960s to demonstrate success in preventing delinquency, a new wave of preventive intervention programs was stimulated in the 1970s by advances in behaviorally oriented treatment and the use of community-based, noninstitutional treatment facilities.

A leading example of this approach is the Achievement Place model, in which a small number of youngsters identified as predelinquent on the basis of aggressive or disruptive behavior are placed in a homestyle residence in their community with a pair of professionally trained houseparents. They continue to attend their regular school, but their home life is now managed to provide a regular routine, rewards for socially desirably behavior, and individual tutoring or counseling, as needed (Kirigan, Braukmann, Atwater, & Wolf, 1982; Phillips, Wolf, Fixsen, & Bailey, 1976). Another contemporary example is the St. Louis Experiment, reported by Feldman, Caplinger, and Wodarski (1983), in which several hundred 8- to 17-year-olds referred for antisocial behavior received group and behavioral therapy and participated in a broad range of activities in a community center over 1 year's time, while continuing to live at home and attend school.

Although such community-based behavioral interventions as Achievement Place and the St. Louis Experiment have clearly benefited some adolescents to some extent, research reviews to date indicate that their average effect may be slight in the short run and questionable in the long run. Whether this lack of more positive findings is due to faulty concepts or inadequate implementation remains to be seen (Binder, 1988; Gottschalk et al., 1987; Kazdin, 1987).

Home-Based Prevention

As an alternative to long-term community-based programs, attention in delinquency prevention has been shifting toward home-based interventions involving structured family therapy, parent management training, and social skills training. Structured family therapy seeks to modify the structure of the family unit's interaction patterns in ways that will lead to improved communication, increased positive reinforcement, and more effective joint problem-solving among family members. In one application of this approach, intended to avoid institutionalization of delinquent adolescents, 87% of adolescent delinquents considered at risk for out-of-home placement were still at home through 12 months of treatment (Tavantzis, Tavantzis, Brown, & Rohrbaugh, 1985).

Parent management training programs are designed to guide parents in interacting with their children in ways that encourage and reward prosocial behavior. The therapist works primarily with the parents in a didactic fashion, to increase their awareness of problematic behaviors and to instruct them in monitoring and managing their children's conduct. In the home, the parents carry out various carefully orchestrated and rehearsed techniques of (a) reward, such as praise and other reinforcements for prosocial behavior; (b) punishment, such as loss of privileges; and (c) *contingency contracting*, in which parents and their children prepare and sign a formal written agreement to behave toward each other in certain mutually agreeable ways (Goldstein, Glick, Irwin, Pask-McCartney, & Rubama, 1989; Gordon & Arbuthnot, 1987; Mann, 1987; Patterson, 1986).

Numerous outcome studies have documented the potential effectiveness of parent management training in leading to improved child behavior, and dramatic lasting changes are particularly evident when the therapy is not time limited and extends to 50 or more sessions (Kazdin, 1987). In practice, however, successful utilization of this approach requires a delinquent adolescent's parents to be available to attend sessions, to be capable of learning new childrearing techniques, and to be willing to persist in employing these techniques despite slow and painful progress. The best-laid plans for working with parents in a treatment program can founder on what may be called the "three Us" of nonproductive parental involvement—being unavailable, unable, and unwilling (3-U).

Unfortunately, in the treatment of socialized delinquency, the adolescent problem behavior has emerged at least in part because the parents were not able or sufficiently interested to function effectively in their childrearing roles. Ironically, because of parents' being unavailable, unable, or unwilling to participate, parent management training may be most difficult to implement in the very cases in which it is most needed. The more available parents are and the more able and willing they are to change their own behavior, the less likely their children are to have become socioculturally delinquent in the first place.

Social skills training for delinquents who are treated while remaining at home is a cognitive–behavioral approach that focuses on increasing the young person's repertoire of interpersonal skills and his or her capacities for judgment and self-control. The treatment consists of practical training exercises involving modeling, role-playing, rehearsal, and other structured tasks designed to enhance the person's effectiveness in solving social problems in daily living (Kendall & Braswell, 1985; Ladd, 1984; Ronan & Kendall, 1990). The rationale for this approach is that, like improved academic and work skills, enhanced social skills will help delinquent adolescents find a rewarding life along noncriminal paths.

Social skills training has proved effective in improving the interpersonal communication and relatedness of young persons and in reducing aggressive and impulsive behavior in nonclinical samples of schoolchildren (Kazdin, Esveldt-Dawson, French, & Unis, 1987; Milan & Kolko, 1985). Among clinically referred adolescent delinquents, however, the evidence indicates that enhancing their social skills does not necessarily reduce their antisocial behavior (Dishion, Loeber, Stouthamer-Loeber, & Patterson, 1984; Tisdelle & St. Lawrence, 1988). These negative findings reflect the fact that the skill deficiencies many delinquents show are a concomitant but not a direct cause of their misconduct. To prevent or reduce antisocial behavior, social skills training needs to be combined with efforts to address such primary causes of delinquency as deviant subcultural influence and ineffective parenting.

Some good results have, in fact, been reported in treating delinquent adolescents through skills training programs in which their parents also participated (Collingwood & Genthner, 1980; Serna, Schumaker, Hazel, & Sheldon, 1986). These programs combine features of parent management training with efforts to improve parent–child interactions through the teaching of reciprocal social skills. As in the case of parent management training, however, this type of intervention can succeed only in so far as the parents are able to participate in it meaningfully.

Characterological Delinquency

The relationship of characterological delinquency to psychopathic personality disorder makes it very difficult to treat. Because characterologically delinquent adolescents do not readily trust or identify with other persons and because they seldom see any need to change their ways, they have little interest in being treated. If they nevertheless are referred for individual or group psychotherapy, their self-centeredness, self-righteousness, and aversion to intimacy are likely to obstruct a productive treatment relationship. In addition, because the family detachment typically associated with this condition produces a high frequency of 3-U parents (unavailable, unable, or unwilling to participate in an intervention plan) prospects for being able to utilize parent management or social skills training effectively are limited.

Despite the difficulties of working with characterological delinquents, considerable effort has been devoted over the years to finding ways of modifying their asocial orientation. This work was pioneered by August Aichhorn, who established a residential treatment center for delinquent boys and girls in Austria in the 1920s. In *Wayward Youth*, Aichhorn (1925) provided the earliest description of applying psychological principles in the treatment of delinquent adolescents. For aggressive delinquents with a history of early emotional deprivation, he recommended a permissive approach to compensate for their lifelong experiences of rejection. No pressures or demands were to be articulated, no restrictions were to be imposed except as absolutely necessary to prevent physical injury, and they were to enjoy "a consistently friendly attitude, wholesome occupation, plenty of play to prevent aggression, and repeated talks with [staff]" (p. 172).

Although Aichhorn's formulation remains influential in some quarters, clinical and research studies indicate that permissive warmth seldom produces any genuine change in the attitudes or behavior of characterological delinquents. Developing psychopaths shun intimacy and distrust demonstrations of warmth and affection. Intimacy threatens them with rejection, and they ward off interpersonal closeness by being sufficiently offensive to keep others at a distance. They regard people who are consistently kind in the face of such unpleasantness as stupid or insincere, which means they cannot be trusted. They regard people who consistently tolerate their shenanigans as weak or indifferent, which means they cannot be expected to be helpful.

For similar reasons, permissiveness tends to make matters worse rather than better in the treatment of developing psychopaths. Lack of restrictions conveys inattention and ineptness, whereas firm but fair controls are necessary to convey competence and caring. Contrary to Aichhorn's prescriptions, the tactics of control have been found to work better than permissive approaches in reducing the delinquent behavior of psychopathic adolescents (Gardner, 1988, Chapter 13; Meeks & Cahill, 1988; Reid, 1983).

Recognizing the drawbacks of a permissively warm treatment approach to psychopathic delinquents can help therapists avoid the pitfall of deceptive collaboration. *Deceptive collaboration* consists of mutually comfortable conversations between patient and therapist, unaccompanied by any change in the young person's behavior. Therapists should suspect this possibility whenever they experience early in treatment an apparently positive working relationship and otherwise smooth sailing with a psychopathic adolescent. The charming "superior psychopath" described earlier is especially adroit at deceptive collaboration and can lead an unsuspecting therapist on a merry chase. He or she maintains a facade of openness and politeness, talks earnestly about problem behavior, and endorses a host of "insights," without any alteration of his or her attitudes or behavior outside of the therapist's office. Antagonism and intractability in the early stages of working with characterological delinquents, although painful to bear, provide therapists better assurance than smooth sailing that they are not being snookered.

Aside from taking care to avoid warmth and permissiveness, clinicians working with characterological delinquents can increase the prospects for positive behavior change by applying certain principles of *collusive* and *residential* treatment.

Collusive Treatment

Collusive treatment was formulated by Noshpitz (1957) as a means of circumventing the initial resistances of psychopathic adolescents to getting involved in an interpersonal relationship designed to change them. The essence of collusion is an appeal to the self-interests of the adolescents through a focus on how they can become more adept at getting what they want without having to become a different kind of person. The therapist encourages discussion of the details of their antisocial actions but, instead of commenting on the immorality of how they have manipulated or exploited others, suggest ways in which particular situations could have been turned even more favorably to their advantage.

This initial sharing of positive interest in a delinquent youngster's escapades avoids the adversarial stance that most antisocial adolescents have come to expect from adults, and it also lends itself to establishing a pattern of mutual communication. The therapist's sustained positive interest in learning about the young person's antisocial acts may also have the paradoxical effect of diminishing their frequency. Misconduct in psychopaths serves in part to ward off intimacy and to elicit responses that justify a feeling of standing alone against an unsympathetic world. A therapist's lively and engaged reactions to such behavior negates its intended effect and diminishes its utility.

Nevertheless, considerable caution is necessary in using the collusive approach to get treatment underway with characterological delinquents. Although suggesting better ways to manipulate other people, therapists cannot allow themselves to be manipulated. Being manipulable is being weak and permissive, to the detriment of building a workable treatment relationship. Therapists also need to guard against suggesting antisocial acts beyond those the young person has committed. Any such new proposals cast the therapist as a collaborator, rather than just a commentator, and violate ethical principles, as well the purposes of therapy.

Although collusive treatment for psychopathy was originally described by Noshpitz in psychodynamic terms, it has been endorsed from a cognitive-behavioral perspective as well. Various reports document positive behavioral change achieved (a) by training psychopaths in more effective (and less destructive) ways of manipulating the environment; (b) by *cognitive reframing* (which consists of verbal explanations that change the meanings people attach to a situation but that are compatible with their frame of reference); (c) by *paradoxical instruction* (which consists of the therapeutic prescription of problematic behavior); and by exercises in *perspective-taking* that help the person view other people as objects in their own right rather than merely as means or obstacles to his or her getting what he or she wants (Doren, 1987; Kolko & Milan, 1983; Templeman & Wollersheim, 1979). The central strategy in these collusive tactics is reduction of antisocial conduct not through personality change, but by convincing characterological delinquents that there are effective prosocial ways of satisfying their needs and helping them become skillful in behaving in these ways—such as acting in a considerate way toward others even while continuing not really to care about their feelings.

Therapists can facilitate the positive impact of a collusive approach by judicious demonstrations of power and giving on their patient's behalf. The supportive exercise of power can help convince psychopathic delinquents that their advantage lies on the therapist's good side, and their self-interest can then be relied on to strengthen the treatment relationship. Typically, the therapist's allegiance and power will be tested early in the treatment by requests that he or she intercede with parents, teacher, or other authorities about some issue. At this point, adolescents will be all too ready to perceive the therapist as having little influence or, when the chips are down, siding with the establishment against them. Either way, they can feel reinforced in their belief that they can rely only on themselves and that they can then justify to themselves no further engagement in the treatment. Thus, initially, it may be very important for the therapist to be able and willing to influence the adolescent's environment on his or her behalf, such as by prevailing on parents to restore some privilege or persuading a teacher to allow a make-up examination.

In exercising such power to build the relationship, the therapist must continue to guard against being manipulated. For the adolescent to ask the therapist to engage in antisocial behavior (e.g., participating in or helping to plan a criminal act) represents provocation rather than a meaningful test of the therapist's power and interest and must be responded to as such. The same can be said for requests that would get the young person into trouble rather than out of it (e.g., providing illegal drugs) or would call for doing the impossible (e.g., getting him or her a high school diploma without completion of the minimum requirements).

Repetitive demands for the exercise of the therapist's power without concomitant progress in the relationship similarly point to manipulation. Each demonstration by the therapist of power and willingness to intercede should be followed by noticeably more positive participation by the young person in the treatment. Furthermore, after a few such demonstrations, testing should give way altogether to infrequent, modest appeals for help that can be given without stretching the boundaries of propriety.

The collusive approach to forming a treatment relationship with psycho-pathic adolescents hinges on (a) adopting a firm, controlling stance without being overbearing, punitive, or rejecting; (b) showing interest and a willing-ness to listen while not appearing easy to impress or manipulate; (c) dem-onstrating determination to persist in trying to be helpful without seeming to offer or ask for much personal involvement; and (d) presenting oneself as someone who knows the ways of the world, has been successful in managing his or her own affairs and can be counted on to talk sense and offer some good advice. Clinicians experienced in working with characterological delinquents generally agree that successful implementation of this approach, as measured by at least a foothold of minimal trust and grudging respect, almost always requires residential care over an extended period of time (Condry, 1987; Lion, 1978; Marohn, 1981; McCord, 1982).

Residential Treatment

The necessity of extended residential care derives mainly from the interper-sonal alienation of these young persons, which makes it extremely difficult to establish an engaged relationship with them in short-term therapy or on the basis of office visits alone. In addition, by providing opportunities for around-the-clock observation, a milieu setting spares the therapist from having to rely entirely on the veracity of delinquents' self-reports to monitor how they are behaving. Finally, residential care offers the salutary impact of a controlled external environment, which promotes the building of better internal controls in these young people.

Residential treatment programs for characterological delinquents are most likely to be effective when they are provided in specialized units staffed by personnel specifically trained to work with antisocial adolescents. Whether such units are located in a primarily correctional or a primarily therapeutic institution has been found to have less to do with achieving good results than whether they offer a well-structured environment in which dedicated staff combine concern, firmness, discipline, and sound guidance (Reid, 1983; Rutter & Giller, 1984, Chapter 9). Residential programs should also include careful planning for transition back into the community following discharge. Recidivism can be reduced among institutionalized delinquents by adequate predischarge arrangements for where they will be going and what they will be doing. Short-term halfway-house placement and continuing outpatient therapy are particularly helpful in sustaining treatment benefits, especially when such aftercare is provided by professionals who were involved in the residential program (Jenson, Hawkins, & Catalano, 1986; Meeks & Cahill, 1988; Reid & Solomon, 1981).

If a collusive approach in a therapeutic milieu succeeds in engaging psychopathic delinquents in a treatment relationship, they may go beyond merely behaving better in their own self-interest and gradually begin to identify with their therapist's good judgment and concern for others. This expectation may appear inconsistent with the psychopathic individual's characteristic incapacity for identification, which sometimes leads clinicians to conclude that no meaningful psychotherapy will be possible with this group.

However, it must be kept in mind that the incapacity of psychopaths to identify with other people, like most pathological impairments, is a relative rather than absolute deficit. Deficient capacity to identify does not signify total inability to do so. Although the limited identificatory capacity of psychopathic delinquent will present special difficulties in the early stages of treatment, whatever limited capacity they have will offer opportunities for these difficulties to be surmounted by skilled and determined therapists who are able to implement collusive treatment in a structured setting.

Should psychopathic adolescents begin to incorporate some of their therapist's standards and behavior patterns, they may then develop some uncharacteristic conflicts and concerns, as well. Uncertainty about how to deal with other people can generate feelings of anxiety, and dawning awareness of having missed out on pleasurable developmental experiences or of being unprepared for a truly rewarding adult life can lead to moments of depression. Such affects in a previously unreflective and unflappable psychopath are a reliable sign of progress in the therapy and open up possibilities for achieving personality, as well as behavior, change. Even when these possibilities are present, however, a considerable expenditure of staff energy over many months in a milieu setting may be necessary to generate such neurotic symptoms in psychopathic adolescents.

Neurotic Delinquency

As an acute symptomatic reaction to current precipitating circumstances, neurotic delinquency typically has a good prognosis and is readily amenable to psychological intervention. The much more favorable outcome of neurotic delinquency than of antisocial conduct associated with characterological defects bears witness to the importance of seeking to understand why problematic behavior is occurring. Acts of delinquency that are likely to persist and call for long-term residential care in a psychopathic adolescent can, if occurring as a symptomatic expression of neurotic concerns, yield relatively easily to outpatient therapy, often on a short-term basis.

Therapy with neurotic delinquents should focus on the needs they are attempting to communicate through their problem behavior. Unmet needs for recognition and for admiration can be satisfied in part merely by having a relationship with a therapist who is providing a measure of interest and respect that the young person has not been getting elsewhere. Unlike psychopathic adolescents, neurotic delinquents yearn to receive and respond to such interest. Working within the context of a positive treatment relationship that quickly forms, the therapist should first help the young person recognize the attention- and status-seeking motives of his or her misbehavior and the self-defeating consequences to which it is leading. Attention should then shift to identifying and carrying out more constructive means by which symptomatic adolescents can gain the notice and respect of their parents, teachers, and peers. In the case of Wilma (see pp. 123–124), for example, discussion of the various punishments and embarrassing notoriety with which she paid for a brief moment of glory paved the way for exploring ways other than bomb scares to capture attention and win respect.

For delinquent adolescents with previously unnoticed needs for help, being brought or sent for professional attention can, by itself, be sufficient to lessen the motivation to misbehave. Although the therapist needs to work on resolving whatever kinds of difficulties the adolescent needs help to overcome, the specific delinquent acts that led to the referral in such cases often stop occurring once a treatment relationship has begun, as in the case of Jack (see pp. 325–326). Especially when depression related to object loss has precipitated the delinquent behavior, having a new regular relationship with an understanding and interested adult often stems the misconduct, whatever the specific content of the sessions.

Conversely, failure to recognize and address underlying depression in a delinquent adolescent can retard treatment progress. In a study of 91 behavior-problem adolescents who were treated with a management-oriented approach aimed at reducing their problem behavior, initial Rorschach assessment indicated substantial underlying depression in 24 of them, including marked sadness and low self-esteem. This depressed group showed less improvement in response to the behavior-management treatment approach than did the nondepressed behavior-problem adolescents (Exner & Weiner, 1982, pp.140–142). What the depressed misbehaving adolescents in this sample apparently needed and did not receive was intervention aimed at resolving their depressive concerns. In a contrasting study, disruptive students who were given opportunities to talk about previous loss experiences in school-based group counseling showed a reduction in angry outbursts and in improved school performance as well (Fleisher, Berkovitz, Briones, Lovetro, & Morhar, 1987).

To the extent that parental fostering is contributing to symptomatic delinquency, the therapist also needs to help misbehaving adolescents recognize the relationship of their misconduct to their interactions with their parents. If these young persons can be made aware that their delinquency relates more closely to the actions and reactions of their parents than to their own needs and goals, they may then be able to separate themselves from the interaction patterns that have fostered and reinforced their misbehavior. Thus the therapist may observe, "It sounds like you did it more because your father was making such a fuss about it than for anything it really meant to you"; or "I get the feeling that wanting to see the expression on your mother's face had more to do with it than anything you really got out of it."

Because of the role that parents may play in fostering or reinforcing neurotic delinquency, they usually should be involved directly in the treatment as well. Unlike the relatives of characterological delinquents, whose minimal family interest and serious adjustment problems of their own typically produce the previously noted 3-U problems of counterproductive family work, the parents of neurotic delinquents are usually available, able, and willing to participate actively in their children's therapy. A supportive relationship with delinquency-fostering parents may be utilized effectively both to identify the exact statements and actions by which these parents are inadvertently fostering their youngster's delinquency and to recommend changes in these aspects of their behavior.

As elaborated in Chapter 11, effective engagement of adolescents in psychotherapy generally requires considerable therapist activity to establish a positive relationship and to focus on central concerns. A relatively neutral and unfocused psychotherapeutic approach is likely to produce a silent, unproductive, and prematurely terminated relationship. However, the necessity for being active poses some unique difficulties in the treatment of neurotic delinquency. For the therapist to be warm, friendly, and engaging without referring to the antisocial behavior can be taken as permissive whitewashing and implicit sanction of the delinquency. On the other hand, concentrating on the antisocial behavior can cast the therapist as a hostile, disapproving inquisitor or as someone who is taking vicarious gratification in pressing for its details.

These companion risks call for the therapist to steer a delicate course between skirting the delinquency and meeting it head on. Without actively exploring the misconduct and its origins, therapists need to acknowledge explicitly its relevance to the adolescent's being in treatment. Concurrently, it is important for therapists to convey by their attitude that they have not prejudged the youngster and are open to being favorably impressed with his or her interests, desires, goals, talents, and virtues: "We both know that the reason you're here is this stealing you've been doing, and we need to talk about it; but I'd also like to hear generally how things are going for you and what you enjoy doing."

This therapeutic strategy will commonly be tested by the adolescent through apparent relapses of misbehavior once the therapy is underway. In the middle and later stages of long-term treatment with a symptomatic delinquent, any such recurrent acting-out should be explored in relation to persisting interpersonal issues or aspects of the treatment relationship. In the early stages of treatment or in brief therapy, however, the therapist's most helpful response will usually be a nonpunitive effort to clarify once more the ultimately self-defeating aspects of such antisocial behavior and to suggest nondelinquent responses to the situations that have provoked it.

By emphasizing nondelinquent solutions to problems, the therapist provides positive values and goals that can insulate adolescents against antisocial pressures stemming from unmet needs and concerns. The extent to which delinquent young persons incorporate such values and goals will depend both on their personality style and the therapist's skill in fostering identification with them. In successful psychotherapy, neurotic delinquents usually begin to identify with their therapist once an initial phase of fencing and testing has been concluded. As evidence of this identification, they report taking a big-sister or big-brother role in relationships to other young persons, or they talk about future careers for themselves in the helping professions, or they show interest in learning about the therapist's background, attitudes, and family life. In the absence of clear indications that such identification is occurring, therapists need to reconsider either the accuracy of their diagnosis or the adequacy of their treatment approach.

REFERENCES

Aichhorn, A., (1925). *Wayward youth*. New York: Viking.

American Psychiatric Association (1987). *Diagnostic and statistical manual of mental disorders* (3rd ed., rev.). Washington, DC: American Psychiatric Association.

Arbuthnot, J., Gordon, D. A., & Jurkovic, G. J. (1987). Personality. In H. C. Quay (Ed.), *Handbook of juvenile delinquency* (pp. 139–183). New York: Wiley.

Asarnow, J. R. (1988). Peer status and social competence in child psychiatric inpatients: A comparison of children with depressive, externalizing, and concurrent depressive and externalizing disorders. *Journal of Abnormal Child Psychology*, *16*, 151–162.

Barth, R. P. (1987). Assessment and treatment of stealing. In B. B. Lahey & A. E. Kazdin (Eds.), *Advances in clinical child psychology* (Vol. 10, pp. 137–170). New York: Plenum.

Bear, D., Freeman, R., & Greenberg, M., (1984). Behavioral alterations in patients with temporal lobe epilepsy. In D. Blumer (Ed.), *Psychiatric aspects of epilepsy* (pp. 197–225). Washington, DC: American Psychiatric Press.

Berndt, D. J., & Zinn, D. (1984). Prominent features of depression in affective- and conduct-disordered inpatients. In D. Offer, E. Ostrov, & K. I. Howard (Eds.), *Patterns of adolescent self-image* (pp. 45–56). San Francisco: Jossey-Bass.

Binder, A. (1988). Juvenile delinquency. *Annual Review of Psychology, 39,* 253–282.

Blashfield, R. K., & Haymaker, D. (1988). A prototype analysis of the diagnostic criteria for *DSM-III-R* personality disorders. *Journal of Personality Disorders, 2,* 272–280.

Blumer, D. (1982). Specific psychiatric complications in certain forms of epilepsy and their treatment. In H. Sands (Ed.), *Epilepsy* (pp. 97–110). New York: Brunner/Mazel.

Borduin, C. M., Pruitt, J. A., & Henggeler, S. W. (1986). Family interactions in black, lower-class families with delinquent and nondelinquent adolescent boys. *Journal of Genetic Psychology, 147,* 333–342.

Bowker, L. H., & Klein, M. W. (1983). The etiology of female juvenile delinquency and gang membership: A test of psychological and social structural explanations. *Adolescence, 18,* 739–751.

Brier, N. (1989). The relationship between learning disability and delinquency: A review and reappraisal. *Journal of Learning Disabilities, 22,* 546–553.

Brown, B., Clasen, D. R., & Eicher, S. A. (1986). Perceptions of peer pressure, peer conformity dispositions, and self-reported behavior among adolescents. *Developmental Psychology, 22,* 521–530.

Brown, R. T., & Borden, K. A. (1986). Hyperactivity at adolescence: Some misconceptions and new directions. *Journal of Clinical Child Psychology, 15,* 194–209.

Bynner, J. M., O'Malley, P. M., & Bachman, J. G. (1981). Self-esteem and delinquency revisited. *Journal of Youth and Adolescence, 10,* 407–441.

Cairns, R. B., Cairns, B. D., Neckerman, H. J., & Gest, S. D. (1988). Social networks and aggressive behavior: Peer support or peer rejection? *Developmental Psychology, 24,* 815–823.

Campbell, A. (1988). Intrapersonal and interpersonal discrepancy among delinquent and nondelinquent girls: A research note. *Journal of Child Psychology and Psychiatry, 29,* 73–78.

Carek, D. J., Hendrickson, W., & Holmes, D. J. (1961). Delinquency addiction in parents. *Archives of General Psychiatry, 4,* 357–362.

Cary, G. L. (1979). Acting out in adolescence. *American Journal of Psychotherapy, 33,* 378–390.

Cavanaugh, J. L., Rogers, R., & Wasylow, D. E. (1981). Mental illness and antisocial behavior. In W. H. Reid (Ed.), *The treatment of antisocial syndromes* (pp. 3–19). New York: Van Nostrand Reinhold.

Chiles, J. A., Miller, M. L., & Cox, G., B. (1980). Depression in an adolescent delinquent population. *Archives of General Psychiatry, 37,* 1179–1184.

Cleckley, H. (1976). *The mask of sanity* (5th ed.). St. Louis: Mosby.

Cloninger, C. R., & Gottesman, I. I. (1987). Genetic and environmental factors in antisocial behavior disorders. In S. A. Mednick, T. E. Moffitt, & S. A. Stack (Eds.), *Causes of crime* (pp. 92-109). Cambridge, England: Cambridge University Press.

Cloward, R., & Ohlin, L. E. (1960). *Delinquency and opportunity: A theory of delinquent gangs*. New York: Free Press of Glencoe.

Coates, R. B. (1981). Community-based services for juvenile delinquents. *Journal of Social Issues, 37*, 87-101.

Cohen, A. K. (1955). *Delinquent boys: The culture of the gang*. Glencoe, IL: Free Press.

Cohen, R., Parmelee, D. X., Irwin, L., Weisz, J. R., Howard, P., Purcell, P., & Best, A. M. (1990). Characteristics of children and adolescents in a psychiatric hospital and a corrections facility. *Journal of the American Academy of Child and Adolescent Psychiatry, 29*, 909-913.

Collingwood, T. R., & Genthner, R. W. (1980). Skills training as treatment for juvenile delinquents. *Professional Psychology, 11*, 591-598.

Condry, S. (1987). Therapy implementation problems in a residence for delinquents. *Journal of Applied Developmental Psychology, 8*, 259-272.

Deutsch, L. J., & Erickson, M. T. (1989). Early life events as discriminators of socialized and undersocialized delinquents. *Journal of Abnormal Child Psychology, 17*, 541-551.

Devinsky, O., & Bear, D. M. (1984). Varieties of aggressive behavior in temporal lobe epilepsy. *American Journal of Psychiatry, 141*, 651-656.

Dishion, T. J., Loeber, R., Stouthamer-Loeber, M., & Patterson, G. R. (1984). Skill deficits and male adolescent delinquency. *Journal of Abnormal Child Psychology, 12*, 37-54.

Doren, D. M. (1987). *Understanding and treating the psychopath*. New York: Wiley.

Elliott, D. S., & Huizinga, D. (1983). Social class and delinquent behavior in a national youth panel: 1976-1980. *Criminology, 21*, 149-177.

Elliott, D. S., Huizinga, D., & Ageton, S. S. (1985). *Explaining delinquency and drug use*. Beverly Hills, CA: Sage.

Eme, R. F. (1984). Sex-role stereotypes and the epidemiology of child psychopathology. In C. S. Widom (Ed.), *Sex roles and psychopathology* (pp. 279-316). New York: Plenum.

Empey, L. T. (1982). *American delinquency: Its meaning and construction* (rev. ed.). Homewood, IL: Dorsey.

Erickson, M. L., & Jensen, G. F. (1977). "Delinquency is still group behavior": Toward revitalizing the group premise in the sociology of deviance. *Journal of Criminal Law and Criminology, 86*, 262-273.

Exner, J. E., & Weiner, I. B. (1982). *The Rorschach: A comprehensive system*. Vol. 3. *Assessment of children and adolescents*. New York: Wiley.

Farnworth, M. (1984). Family structure, family attributes, and delinquency in a sample of low-income, minority males and females. *Journal of Youth and Adolescence, 13*, 349-364.

Farrington, D. P. (1983). Offending from 10 to 25 years of age. In K. T. Van Dusen

& S. A. Mednick (Eds.), *Prospective studies of crime and delinquency* (pp. 7-37). Boston: Kluwer-Nijhoff.

Farrington, D. P. (1987). Epidemiology. In H. C. Quay (Ed.), *Handbook of juvenile delinquency* (pp. 33-61). New York: Wiley.

Farrington, D. P. (1986) The sociocultural context of childhood disorders. In H.C. Quay & J. W. Werry (Eds.), *Psychopathological disorders of childhood* (pp. 391-422). New York: Wiley.

Feldman, R. A., Caplinger, T. E., & Wodarski, J. S. (1983). *The St. Louis conundrum: The effective treatment of antisocial youths.* Englewood Cliffs, NJ: Prentice-Hall.

Flanagan, T. J., Hindelang, M. J., & Gottfredson, M. R. (Eds.) (1980). *Sourcebook of criminal justice statistics—1979.* Washington, DC: U.S. Department of Justice.

Flanagan, T. J., & Jamieson, K. M. (Eds.) (1988). *Sourcebook of criminal justice statistics—1987.* Washington, DC: U.S. Department of Justice.

Flanagan, T. J., Van Altstyne, D. J., & Gottfredson, M. R. (Eds.) (1982). *Sourcebook of criminal justice statistics—1981.* Washington, DC: U.S. Department of Justice.

Fleisher, S. J., Berkovitz, I. H., Briones, L., Lovetro, K., & Morhar, N. (1987). Antisocial behavior, school performance, and reactions to loss: The value of group counseling and communication skills training. *Adolescent Psychiatry, 14,* 546-555.

Frances, A. (1980). The *DSM-III* personality disorders: A commentary. *American Journal of Psychiatry, 137,* 1050-1054.

Friedman, A. S., Utada, A., & Glickman, N. W. (1986). Outcome for court-referred drug-abusing male adolescents of an alternative activity treatment program in a vocational high school setting. *Journal of Nervous and Mental Disease, 174,* 680-688.

Gallenkamp, C. R., & Rychlak, J. F. (1968). Parental attitudes of sanction in middle-class adolescent male delinquents. *Journal of Social Psychology, 75,* 255-260.

Gardner, R. A. (1988). *Psychotherapy with adolescents.* Creeskill, NJ: Creative Therapeutics.

Genshaft, J. L. (1980). Personality correlates of delinquent subtypes. *Journal of Abnormal Child Psychology, 8,* 279-283.

Gibbons, D. C. (1980). Explaining juvenile delinquency: Changing theoretical perspectives. In D. Sichor & D. C. Kelly (Eds.), *Critical issues in juvenile delinquency* (pp. 9-26). Lexington, MA: D. C. Heath.

Glueck, S., & Glueck, E. T. (1950). *Unraveling juvenile delinquency.* New York: Commonwealth Fund.

Glueck, S., & Glueck, E. T. (1952). *Family environment and delinquency.* Boston: Houghton-Mifflin.

Gold, M. (1987). Social ecology. In H. C. Quay (Ed.), *Handbook of juvenile delinquency* (pp. 62-105). New York: Wiley.

Gold, M., & Petronio, R. (1980). Delinquent behavior in adolescence. In J. Adelson (Ed.), *Handbook of adolescent psychology* (pp. 495-535). New York: Wiley.

Goldstein, A. P., Glick, B., Irwin, M. J., Pask-McCartney, C., & Rubama, I. (1989). *Reducing delinquency.* New York: Pergamon.

Gora, J. G. (1982). *The new female criminal: Empirical reality or social myth?* New York: Praeger.

Gordon, D. A., & Arbuthnot, J. (1987). Individual, group, and family interventions. In H. C. Quay (Ed.), *Handbook of juvenile delinquency* (pp. 290–324). New York: Wiley.

Gottesman, I. I., Carey, G., & Hanson, D. R. (1983). Pearls and perils in epigenetic psychopathology. In S. B. Guze, E. J. Earls, & J. E. Barrett (Eds.), *Childhood psychopathology and development* (pp. 287–300). New York: Raven Press.

Gottschalk, R., Davidson, W. S., Gensheimer, L. K., & Mayer, J. P. (1987). Community-based interventions. In H. C. Quay (Ed.), *Handbook of juvenile delinquency* (pp. 266–298). New York: Wiley.

Hanson, C. L., Henggeler, S. W., Haefele, W. F., & Rodick, J. D. (1984). Demographic, individual, and family relationship correlates of serious and repeated crime among adolescents and their siblings. *Journal of Consulting and Clinical Psychology, 52,* 528–538.

Hare, R. D. (1980). A research scale for the assessment of psychopathy in criminal populations. *Personality and Individual Differences, 1,* 111–117.

Hare, R. D. (1983). Diagnosis of antisocial personality disorder in two prison populations. *American Journal of Psychiatry, 140,* 887–890.

Hare, R. D., & Cox, D. N. (1978). Clinical and empirical conceptions of psychopathy, and the selection of subjects for research. In R. D. Hare & D. Schalling (Eds.), *Psychopathic behaviour* (pp. 1–22). Chichester, England: Wiley.

Harpur, T. J., Hakstian, A. R., & Hare, R. D. (1988). Factor structure of the Psychopathy Checklist. *Journal of Consulting and Clinical Psychology, 56,* 741–747.

Harpur, T. J., Hare, R. D., & Hakstian, A. R. (1989). Two-factor conceptualization of psychopathy: Construct validity and assessment implications. *Psychological Assessment, 1,* 6–17.

Heilbrun, A. B. (1979). Psychopathy and violent crime. *Journal of Consulting and Clinical Psychology, 47,* 509–516.

Heilbrun, A. B., (1990). Differentiation of death-row murderers and life-sentence murderers by antisociality and intelligence measures. *Journal of Personality Assessment, 54,* 617–627.

Henker, B., & Whalen, C. K. (1989). Hyperactivity and attention deficits. *American Psychologist, 44,* 216–223.

Hindelang, M. J., Hirschi, T., & Weis, J. G. (1981). *Measuring delinquency.* Beverly Hills, CA: Sage.

Hirschi, T., & Hindelang, M. J. (1977). Intelligence and delinquency. *American Sociological Review, 42,* 571–587.

Huesmann, L. R., Eron, L. D., Lefkowitz, M. M., & Walder, L. O. (1984). Stability of aggression over time and generations. *Developmental Psychology, 20,* 1120–1134.

Jacob, D. H. (1983). Learning problems, self-esteem, and delinquency. In J. E. Mack & S. L. Ablon (Eds.), *The development and sustaining of self-esteem in childhood* (pp. 209–222). New York: International Universities Press.

Jacobson, R. R. (1985). Child firesetters: A clinical investigation. *Journal of Child Psychology and Psychiatry, 26,* 759–768.

Jenkins, R. L. (1955). Adaptive and maladaptive delinquency. *Nervous Child, 11,* 9–11.

Jenson, J. M., Hawkins, J. D., & Catalano, R. F. (1986). Social support in aftercare services for troubled youth. *Children and Youth Services Review, 8,* 323–347.

Johnson, A. M. (1949). Sanctions for superego lacunae of adolescents. In K. R. Eissler (Ed.), *Searchlights on delinquency* (pp. 225–245). New York: International Universities Press.

Johnson, A. M., & Szurek, S. A. (1952). The genesis of antisocial acting out in children and adults. *Psychoanalytic Quarterly, 21,* 323–343.

Johnson, J. H., & Fennell, E. B. (1983). Aggressive and delinquent behavior in childhood and adolescence. In C. E. Walker & M. C. Roberts (Eds.), *Handbook of clinical child psychology* (pp. 475–497). New York: Wiley.

Jurkovic, G., & Prentice, N. M. (1977). Relation of moral and cognitive development to dimensions of juvenile delinquency. *Journal of Abnormal Psychology, 86,* 414–420.

Kandel, E., Mednick, S. A., Kirkegaard-Sorensen, L., Hutchings, B., Knop, J., Rosenberg, R., & Schulsinger, F. (1988). IQ as a protective factor for subjects at high risk for antisocial behavior. *Journal of Consulting and Clinical Psychology, 56,* 224–226.

Kaplan, W. H. (1988). Conduct disorder. In C. J. Kestenbaum & D. T. Williams (Eds.), *Handbook of clinical assessment of children and adolescents* (pp. 562–582). New York: New York University Press.

Kazdin, A. E. (1987). Treatment of antisocial behavior in children: Current status and future directions. *Psychological Bulletin, 102,* 187–203.

Kazdin, A. E., Esveldt-Dawson, K., French, N. H., & Unis, A. S. (1987). Problem-solving skills training and relationship therapy in the treatment of antisocial child behavior. *Journal of Consulting and Clinical Psychology, 55,* 76–85.

Kellner, R. (1981). Drug treatment in personality disorders. In W. H. Reid (Ed.), *The treatment of antisocial syndromes* (pp. 20–29). New York: Van Nostrand Reinhold.

Kelso, J., & Stewart, M. A. (1986). Factors which predict the persistence of aggressive conduct disorder. *Journal of Child Psychology and Psychiatry, 27,* 77–86.

Kendall, P. C., & Braswell, L. (1985). *Cognitive-behavioral therapy for impulsive children.* New York: Guilford.

Kirigan, K. A., Braukmann, C. J., Atwater, J. D., & Wolf, M. M. (1982). An evaluation of teaching-family (Achievement-Place) group homes for juvenile offenders. *Journal of Applied Behavioral Analysis, 15,* 1–16.

Kolko, D. J., & Kazdin, A. E. (1988). Prevalence of firesetting and related behaviors among child psychiatric patients. *Journal of Consulting and Clinical Psychology, 56,* 628–630.

Kolko, D. J., Kazdin, A. E., & Meyer, E. C. (1985). Aggression and psychopathology in childhood firesetters: Parent and child reports. *Journal of Consulting and Clinical Psychology, 53,* 377–385.

Kolko, D. J., & Milan, M. A. (1983). Reframing and paradoxical instruction to overcome "resistance" in the treatment of delinquent youths: A multiple baseline analysis. *Journal of Consulting and Clinical Psychology, 51*, 655-660.

Kvaraceus, W. C., & Miller, W. B. (1962). *Delinquent behavior, culture, and the individual.* Washington, DC: National Educational Association

Ladd, G. W. (1984). Social skill training with children: Issues in research and practice. *Clinical Psychology Review, 4*, 307-337.

Lahey, B. B., Hartdagen, S. E., Frick, P. J., McBurnett, K., Connor, R., & Hynd, G. W. (1988). Conduct disorder: Parsing the confounded relation to parental divorce and antisocial personality. *Journal of Abnormal Psychology, 97*, 334-337.

Lahey, B. B., Piacentini, J. C., McBurnett, K., Stone, P. A., Hartdagen, S., & Hynd, G. W. (1988). Psychopathology and antisocial behavior in the parents of children with conduct disorder and hyperactivity. *Journal of the American Academy of Child Psychiatry, 27*, 163-170.

Lambert, N. M. (1988). Adolescent outcomes for hyperactive children. *American Psychologist, 43*, 786-799.

Lambert, N. M., Sassone, D., Hartsough, C. S., & Sandoval, J. (1987). Persistence of hyperactivity symptoms from childhood to adolescence and associated outcomes. *American Journal of Orthopsychiatry, 57*, 22-32.

Lee, M., & Prentice, N. M. (1988). Interrelations of empathy, cognitions, and moral reasoning with dimensions of juvenile delinquency. *Journal of Abnormal Child Psychology, 16*, 127-139.

Lempers, J. D., Clark-Lempers, D., & Simons, R. L. (1989). Economic hardship, parenting, and distress. *Child Development, 60*, 25-39.

Lewis, D. O. (1976). Delinquency, psychomotor epileptic symptoms, and paranoid ideation: A triad. *American Journal of Psychiatry, 133*, 1395-1398.

Lewis, D. O., & Balla, D. (1976). *Delinquency and psychopathology.* New York: Grune & Stratton.

Lewis, D. O., Lewis, M., Unger, L., & Goldman, C. (1984). Conduct disorder and its synonyms: Diagnoses of dubious validity and usefulness. *American Journal of Psychiatry, 141*, 514-519.

Lewis, D. O., Pincus, J. H., Shanok, S. S., & Glaser, G. H. (1982). Psychomotor epilepsy and violence in a group of incarcerated adolescent boys. *American Journal of Psychiatry, 139*, 882-887.

Lewis, D. O., Shanok, S. S., Cohen, R. J., Kligfeld, M., & Frisone, G. (1980). Race bias in the diagnosis and disposition of violent adolescents. *American Journal of Psychiatry, 137*, 1211-1216.

Lion, J. B. (1978). Outpatient treatment of psychopaths. In W. H. Reid (Ed.), *The psychopath* (pp. 286-300). New York: Brunner/Mazel.

Loeber, R. (1982). The stability of antisocial and delinquent behavior: A review. *Child Development, 53*, 1431-1446.

Loeber, R. (1988). Natural histories of conduct problems, delinquency, and associated substance use. In B. B. Lahey & A. E. Kazdin (Eds.), *Advances in clinical child psychology* (Vol. 11, pp. 73-124). New York: Plenum.

Loeber, R. (1990). Development and risk factors of juvenile antisocial behavior and delinquency. *Clinical Psychology Review, 10,* 1-41.

Loeber, R., & Dishion, T. (1983). Early predictors of male delinquency: A review. *Psychological Bulletin, 94,* 68-94.

Loeber, R., & Dishion, T. J. (1984). Boys who fight at home and school: Family conditions influencing cross-setting consistency. *Journal of Consulting and Clinical Psychology, 52,* 759-768.

Loeber, R., & Schmaling, K. B. (1985a). Empirical evidence for overt and covert patterns of antisocial conduct problems: A metaanalysis. *Journal of Abnormal Child Psychology, 13,* 337-352.

Loeber, R., & Schmaling, K. B. (1985b). The utility of differentiating between mixed and pure forms of antisocial child behavior. *Journal of Abnormal Child Psychology, 13,* 315-336.

Loeber, R., & Stouthamer-Loeber, M. (1987). Prediction. In H. C. Quay (Ed.), *Handbook of juvenile delinquency* (pp. 325-382). New York: Wiley.

Lowenstein, L. F. (1989). The etiology, diagnosis and treatment of fire-setting behavior of children. *Child Psychiatry and Human Development, 19,* 186-194.

Lowney, J. (1984). The Wall Gang: A study of interpersonal process and deviance among twenty-three middle-class youths. *Adolescence, 19,* 527-538.

Mann, R. A. (1987). Conduct disorders. In M. Hersen & V. B. Van Hasselt (Eds.), *Behavior therapy with children and adolescents* (pp. 419-439). New York: Wiley.

Marohn, R. C. (1981). Hospital treatment of the behaviorally disordered adolescent. In W. H. Reid (Ed.), *The treatment of antisocial disorders* (pp. 146-161). New York: Van Nostrand Reinhold.

Masten, A. S., & Garmezy, N. (1985). Risk, vulnerability, and protective factors in developmental psychopathology. *Advances in Clinical Child Psychology, 8,* 1-52.

McCord, J. (1978). A thirty-year follow-up of treatment effects. *American Psychologist, 33,* 284-289.

McCord, J. A. (1980). Patterns of deviance. In S. B. Sells, R. Crandall, M. Roff, J. S. Strauss, & W. Pollin (Eds.), *Human functioning in longitudinal perspective* (pp. 157-165). Baltimore: Williams & Wilkins.

McCord, W. (1982). *The psychopath and milieu therapy.* New York: Academic Press.

McDaniel, K. D. (1986). Pharmacologic treatment of psychiatric and neurodevelopmental disorders in children and adolescents. *Clinical Pediatrics, 25,* 65-71.

McGuffin, P., & Gottesman, I. I. (1985). Genetic influences in normal and abnormal development. In M. Rutter & L. Hersov (Eds.), *Child and adolescent psychiatry* (2nd ed., pp. 17-33). Oxford, England: Blackwell.

Mednick, S. A., Gabrielli, W. F., & Hutchings, B. (1984). Genetic influences in criminal convictions: Evidence from an adoption cohort. *Science, 224,* 891-894.

Mednick, S. A., & Hutchings, B. (1978). Genetic and psychophysiological factors in antisocial behaviour. In R. D. Hare & D. Schalling (Eds.), *Psychopathic behaviour* (pp. 239-254). Chichester, England: Wiley.

Meeks, J. E., & Cahill, A. J. (1988). Therapy of adolescents with severe behavior problems. In S. C. Feinstein (Ed.), *Adolescent psychiatry* (Vol. 15, pp. 475–486). Chicago: University of Chicago Press.

Meloy, J. R. (1988). *The psychopathic mind.* Northvale, NJ: Aronson.

Milan, M. A., & Kolko, D. J. (1985). Social skills training and complementary strategies in anger control and the treatment of aggressive behavior. In L. L'Abate & M. A. Milan (Eds.), *Handbook of social skills training and research* (pp. 101–135). New York: Wiley.

Miller, W. B. (1958). Lower-class culture as a generating milieu of gang delinquency. *Journal of Social Issues, 14,* 5–19.

Millon, T. (1981). *Disorders of personality.* New York: Wiley.

Moffitt, T. E., Gabrielli, W. F., & Mednick, S. A. (1981). Socioeconomic status, IQ, and delinquency. *Journal of Abnormal Psychology, 90,* 152–156.

Moffitt, T. E., & Silva, P. A. (1988). IQ and delinquency: A direct test of the differential detection hypotheses. *Journal of Abnormal Psychology, 97,* 330–333.

Morey, L. C. (1988). A psychometric analysis of the *DSM-III-R* personality disorder criteria. *Journal of Personality Disorders, 2,* 109–124.

Moskowitz, D. S., Schwartzman, A. E., & Ledingham, J. E. (1985). Stability and change in aggression and withdrawal in middle childhood and early adolescence. *Journal of Abnormal Psychology, 94,* 30–41.

Mulvey, E. P., & LaRosa, J. F. (1986). Delinquency cessation and adolescent development: Preliminary data. *American Journal of Orthopsychiatry, 56,* 212–224.

Murray, J. P. (1983). *Status offenders.* Boys Town, NE: Boys Town Center.

Newman, J. P., Patterson, C. M., & Kosson, D. S. (1987). Response perseveration in psychopaths. *Journal of Abnormal Psychology, 96,* 145–148.

Noshpitz, J. D. (1957). Opening phase in the psychotherapy of adolescents with character disorders. *Bulletin of the Menninger Clinic, 21,* 153–164.

O'Donnell, D. J. (1985). Conduct disorders. In J. M. Weiner (Ed.), *Diagnosis and psychopharmacology of childhood and adolescent disorders* (pp. 251–287). New York: Wiley.

Olweus, D. (1979). Stability of aggressive reaction patterns in males: A review. *Psychological Bulletin, 86,* 852–875.

Panella, D., & Hengeller, S. W. (1986). Peer interactions of conduct-disordered, anxious-withdrawn, and well-adjusted black adolescents. *Journal of Abnormal Child Psychology, 14,* 1–11.

Patterson, G. R. (1986). Performance models for antisocial boys. *American Psychologist, 41,* 432–444.

Patterson, G. R., DeBaryshe, B. D., & Ramsey, E. (1989). A developmental perspective on antisocial behavior. *American Psychologist, 44,* 329–335.

Phillips, E. L., Wolf, M. M., Fixsen, D. L., & Bailey, J. S. (1976). The Achievement Place model: A community-based, family-style behavior modification program for predelinquents. In E. Ribes-Inesta & A. Bandura (Eds.), *Analysis of delinquency and aggression* (pp. 171–202). New York: Erlbaum.

Plomin, R. (1989). Environment and genes. *American Psychologist, 44,* 105–111.

Powers, E., & Witmer, H. (1951). *An experiment in the prevention of delinquency: The Cambridge–Somerville Youth Study.* New York: Columbia University Press.

Quay, H. C. (1986). Conduct disorders. In H. C. Quay & J. S. Werry (Eds.), *Psychopathological disorders of childhood* (3rd ed., pp. 35–72). New York: Wiley.

Quay, H. C. (1987a). Intelligence. In H. C. Quay (Ed.), *Handbook of juvenile delinquency* (pp. 106–117). New York: Wiley.

Quay, H. C. (1987b). Patterns of delinquent behavior. In H. C. Quay (Ed.), *Handbook of juvenile delinquency* (pp. 118–138). New York: Wiley.

Quay, H. C., Routh, D. K., & Shapiro, S. K. (1987). Psychopathology of childhood. *Annual Review of Psychology, 38,* 491–532.

Quinton, D. (1988). Urbanism and child mental health. *Journal of Child Psychology and Psychiatry, 29,* 11–20.

Reid, W. H. (1983). *Treatment of the DSM-III psychiatric disorders.* New York: Brunner/Mazel.

Reid, W. H., & Solomon, G. F. (1981). Community-based offender programs. In W. H. Reid (Ed.), *The treatment of antisocial syndromes* (pp. 76–94). New York: Van Nostrand Reinhold.

Richards, P., Berk, R. A., & Forster, B. (1979). *Crime as play: Delinquency in a middle class suburb.* Cambridge, MA: Balinger.

Robins, L. N. (1966). *Deviant children grown up.* Baltimore: Williams & Wilkins.

Robins, L. N. (1978). Aetiological implications in studies of childhood histories relating to antisocial personality. In R. D. Hare & D. Schalling (Eds.), *Psychopathic behaviour* (pp. 239–254). Chichester, England: Wiley.

Roff, J. D., & Wirt, R. D. (1984). Childhood aggression and social adjustment as antecedents of delinquency. *Journal of Abnormal Child Psychology, 12,* 111–126.

Rogeness, G. A., Hernandez, J. M., Macedo, C. A., & Mitchell, E. L. (1982). Biochemical differences in children with conduct disorder socialized and undersocialized. *American Journal of Psychiatry, 139,* 307–311.

Ronan, K. R., & Kendall, P. C. (1990). Non-self-controlled adolescents: Applications of cognitive-behavioral therapy. In S. C. Feinstein (Ed.), *Adolescent psychiatry* (Vol. 17, pp. 478–505). Chicago: University of Chicago Press.

Rosenberg, F. R., & Rosenberg, M. (1978). Self-esteem and delinquency. *Journal of Youth and Adolescence, 7,* 279–291.

Rosenthal, P. A., & Doherty, M. B. (1985). Psychodynamics of delinquent girls' rage and violence directed toward mother. In S. C. Feinstein (Ed.), *Adolescent psychiatry* (Vol. 12, pp. 281–289). Chicago: University of Chicago Press.

Rutter, M., & Giller, H. (1984). *Juvenile delinquency.* New York: Guilford.

Rutter, M., Macdonald, H., Le Couteur, A., Harrington, R., Bolton, R., & Bailey, A. (1990). Genetic factors in child psychiatric disorders: II. Empirical findings. *Journal of Child Psychology and Psychiatry, 31,* 39–83.

Safer, D. J. (Ed.) (1982). *School programs for disruptive adolescents.* Baltimore: University Park Press.

Schalling, D. (1978). Psychopathy-related personality variables and the psychophysiology of socialization. In R. D. Hare & D. Schalling (Eds.), *Psychopathic behaviour* (pp. 85–106). Chichester, England: Wiley.

Schonfeld, I. S., Shaffer, D., O'Connor, P. & Portnoy, S. (1988). Conduct disorder and cognitive functioning: Testing three causal hypotheses. *Child Development*, *59*, 993–1007.

Serna, L. A., Schumaker, J. B., Hazel, J. S., & Sheldon, J. B. (1986). Teaching reciprocal social skills to parents and their delinquent adolescents. *Journal of Clinical Child Psychology*, *15*, 64–77.

Shapiro, S. K., Quay, H. C., Hogan, A. E., & Schwartz, K. P. (1988). Response perseveration and delayed responding in undersocialized aggressive conduct disorder. *Journal of Abnormal Psychology*, *97*, 371–373.

Shaw, C. R., & McKay, H. D. (1942). *Juvenile delinquency and urban areas*. Chicago: University of Chicago Press.

Shaw, W. (1983). Delinquency and criminal behavior. In C. E. Walker & M. C. Roberts (Eds.), *Handbook of clinical child psychology* (pp. 880–902). New York: Wiley.

Sherwin, I. (1982). Neurobiological basis of psychopathology associated with epilepsy. In H. Sand (Ed.), *Epilepsy* (pp. 77–96). New York: Brunner/Mazel.

Shoemaker, D. J. (1984). *Theories of delinquency*. New York: Oxford University Press.

Shore, M. F., & Massimo, J. L. (1973). After ten years: A follow-up study of comprehensive vocationally-oriented psychotherapy. *American Journal of Psychotherapy*, *43*, 128–132.

Sines, J. O. (1987). Influence of the home and family environment on childhood dysfunction. In B. B. Lahey & A. E. Kazdin (Eds.), *Advances in clinical child psychology* (Vol. 10, pp. 1–54). New York: Plenum.

Slaby, R. G., & Guerra, N. G. (1988). Cognitive mediators of aggression in adolescent offenders: I. Assessment. *Developmental Psychology*, *24*, 580–588.

Smith, R. J. (1978). *The psychopath in society*. New York: Academic Press.

Snyder, J., & Patterson, G. (1987). Family interaction and delinquent behavior. In H. C. Quay (Ed.), *Handbook of juvenile delinquency* (pp. 216–243). New York: Wiley.

Soloff, P. H. (1985). Personality disorders. In M. Hersen & S. M. Turner (Eds.), *Diagnostic interviewing* (pp. 131–159). New York: Plenum.

Spielberger, C. D., Kling, J. L., & O'Hagan, S. E. J. (1978). Dimensions of psychopathic personality: Antisocial behaviour and anxiety. In R. D. Hare & D. Schalling (Eds.), *Psychopathic behaviour* (pp. 23–46). Chichester, England: Wiley.

Stattin, H., & Magnusson, D. (1989). The role of early aggressive behavior in the frequency, seriousness, and types of later crime. *Journal of Consulting and Clinical Psychology*, *57*, 710–718.

Steinberg, L. (1986). Latchkey children and susceptibility to peer pressure: An ecological analysis. *Development Psychology*, *22*, 433–439.

Steinberg, L. (1987). Single parents, stepparents, and the susceptibility of adolescents to peer pressure. *Child Development*, *58*, 269–275.

Stewart, J. T., Myers, W. C., Burket, R. C., & Lyles, W. B. (1990). A review of the psychopharmocotherapy of aggression in children and adolescents. *Journal of the American Academy of Child and Adolescent Psychiatry*, *29*, 269–277.

Sutker, P. B., & Allain, A. N. (1987). Cognitive abstraction, shifting, and control:

Clinical sample comparisons of psychopaths and nonpsychopaths. *Journal of Abnormal Psychology, 96,* 73–75.

Tavantzis, T. N., Tavantzis, M., Brown, L. G., & Rohrbaugh, M. (1985). Home-based structured family therapy for delinquents at risk for placement. In M. P. Mirkin & S. L. Korman (Eds.), *Handbook of adolescents and family therapy* (pp. 69–88). New York: Gardner Press.

Templeman, T. L., & Wollersheim, J. P. (1979). A cognitive–behavioral approach to treatment in psychopathy. *Psychotherapy, 16,* 132–139.

Thompson, R. J., & Lozes, J. (1976). Female gang delinquency. *Corrective and Social Psychiatry, 22,* 1–5.

Thornberry, T. P., & Farnworth, M. (1982). Social correlates of criminal involvement: Further evidence on the relationship between social status and criminal behavior. *American Sociological Review, 47,* 505–518.

Tisdelle, D. A., & St. Lawrence, J. S. (1988). Adolescent interpersonal problem-solving skill training: Social validation and generalization. *Behavior Therapy, 19,* 171–182.

Tolan, P. H. (1987). Implications of age of onset for delinquency risk. *Journal of Abnormal Child Psychology, 15,* 47–66.

Tolan, P., Ryan, K., & Jaffe, C. (1988). Adolescents' mental health service use and provider, process, and recipient characteristics. *Journal of Clinical Child Psychology, 17,* 229–236.

Walsh, A., Beyer, J. A., & Petee, T. A. (1987). Violent delinquency: An examination of psychopathic typologies. *Journal of Genetic Psychology, 148,* 385–392.

Walsh, L. M., & Kurdek, L. A. (1984). Developmental trends and gender differences in the relation between understanding of friendship and asociality. *Journal of Youth and Adolescence, 13,* 65–71.

West, M. O., & Prinz, R. J. (1987). Parental alcoholism and childhood psychopathology. *Psychological Bulletin, 102,* 204–218.

Westendorp, F., Brink, K. L., Roberson, M. K., & Ortiz, I. E. (1986). Variables which differentiate placement of adolescents into juvenile justice or mental health systems. *Adolescence, 21,* 23–37.

White, J. L., Moffitt, T. E., & Silva, P. A. (1989). A prospective replication of the protective effects of IQ in subjects at high risk for juvenile delinquency. *Journal of Consulting and Clinical Psychology, 57,* 719–724.

Widiger, T. A., Frances, A., Spitzer, R. L., & Williams, J. B. (1988). The *DSM-III-R* personality disorders: An overview. *American Journal of Psychiatry, 145,* 786–795.

Widom, C. S. (1978). A methodology for studying noninstitutionalized psychopaths. In R. D. Hare & D. Schalling (Eds.), *Psychopathic behaviour* (pp. 71–84). Chichester, England: Wiley.

Widom, C. S. (1984). Sex roles, criminality, and psychopathology. In C. S. Widom (Ed.), *Sex roles and psychopathology* (pp. 183–217). New York: Plenum.

Williams, J. R., & Gold, M. (1972). From delinquent behavior to official delinquency. *Social Problems, 20,* 209–229.

Wilson, J. Q., & Herrnstein, R. J. (1985). *Crime and human nature*. New York: Simon & Schuster.

Wolfgang, M. E., Figlio, R. M., & Sellin, T. (1972). *Delinquency in a birth cohort*. Chicago: University of Chicago Press.

Wolman, B. B. (1987). *The sociopathic personality*. New York: Brunner/Mazel.

Wulach, J. S. (1983). Diagnosing the *DSM-III* antisocial personality disorder. *Professional Psychology, 14*, 330–340.

CHAPTER 9

Suicidal Behavior

Adolescents struggling with psychological problems often think fleetingly about harming themselves. Although such fleeting thoughts do not necessarily signify psychopathology, overt suicidal acts always reflect pathological concerns, and young people who survive suicide attempts should always receive professional attention. The present chapter reviews the demography of youthful suicidal behavior and discusses its origins, assessment, and treatment.

Before proceeding, it should be recognized that suicidologists are not of one mind concerning whether people who kill themselves and people who make nonfatal suicide attempts are basically similar to or basically different from each other psychologically. Evidence reviewed by Pfeffer (1989) in this regard does not point conclusively one way or the other, at least with respect to adolescents. What seems most likely is that youthful suicide completers and suicide attempters both resemble and differ from each other in certain ways.

For the purposes of this chapter, suicidal behavior is conceptualized as a continuum comprising suicidal ideation, suicide attempts, and completed suicide. Suicidal ideation does not necessarily lead to suicidal actions, and suicide attempts are not inevitably followed by actual suicide. Nonetheless, people rarely make suicide attempts without having previously harbored suicidal ideation, and they seldom kill themselves without having previously attempted or at least threatened suicide. Completed and attempted suicide are accordingly considered jointly in the discussion that follows, with particular attention to the increased risk of a fatal outcome that accompanies any progression along the suicidal continuum.

DEMOGRAPHY OF ADOLESCENT SUICIDAL BEHAVIOR

Young persons seldom take their own lives. Of 30,905 known deaths by suicide in the United States in 1986, only 5 involved children less than 10 years old, 250 were ages 10-14, and 2151 were 15 to 19 years old. These young persons committed 7.0% of the suicides reported nationwide that year, whereas young adults (ages 20 to 29) accounted for 21.5% and persons over 60 for 26.3% of the known suicides (National Center for Health Statistics (NCHS), 1988).

As these data indicate, however, the suicide rate increases sharply during the adolescent years. From 1.5 per 100,000 among 10- to 14-year-olds, it grows almost sevenfold by ages 15–19, to 10.2 per 100,000 persons. Suicidal frequency continues to climb in adulthood, reaching 15.8 per 100,000 among 20- to 24-year-olds, increasing gradually to 17.0 by the middle 50s, and becoming well over 20 per 100,000 in persons over age 70 (NCHS, 1988). Although these frequency data might appear to suggest that suicide is a more pertinent topic for adult than for adult psychopathology, three additional facts leave little doubt that suicidal behavior must be a central concern in the evaluation and treatment of troubled adolescents.

First, youthful suicide has increased at an alarming rate during the past quarter century. Between 1960 and 1986, the rate of suicide in the total United States population grew by 20.1% from 10.6 to 12.8 per 100,000. Over the same period, the suicide rate for 15- to 19-year-olds tripled, from 3.6 per 100,000 in 1960 to 10.2 in 1986. As recently as 1980, it was 8.5 per 100,000, which indicates a 20% increase during the 1980s alone (Lewis, Johnson, Cohen, Garcia, & Velez, 1988; NCHS, 1988).

These data and other published reports concerning the frequency of adolescent suicide need to be interpreted carefully with respect to the age groups being considered. The National Center for Health Statistics (NCHS) reports mortality rates both by 5-year and 10-year age groups. Not infrequently, statements about youthful suicide, as well as other events recorded in *Vital Statistics of the United States* (NCHS, 1988), are based on information provided for the 10-year group of 15- to 24-year-olds. On the basis of suicide data for 15- to 24-year-olds, for example, some authors have concluded that the suicide rate for young people is leveling off or declining (e.g., Blumenthal & Kupfer, 1988; Pfeffer, 1989).

Although it may be appropriate to regard 15- to 24-year-olds as "youth," 20- to 24-year-olds are largely an adult population of young men and women who are no longer dealing with primarily adolescent developmental tasks. Neither researchers studying the developmental psychology of adolescence nor clinicians specializing in the assessment and treatment of adolescent problems are particularly concerned with young adults in their 20s. They do, however, tend to be interested in postpubescent youngsters who have not yet turned 15. Accordingly, the nature of suicidal behavior in adolescence will be indicated more accurately by data on 5-year groups of 10- to 14-year-olds and 15- to 19-year-olds than by information on 10-year groups of 5- to 15-year olds and 15- to 24-year-olds.

Close inspection of the suicide data does, in fact, reveal temporal differences between adolescents and "youth." From 1978 to 1986, the suicide rate among 20- to 24-year-olds declined from 16.9 to 15.8 per 100,000 persons. Among 10- to 14-year-olds, by contrast, the suicide rate almost doubled during this same period, from 0.8 to 1.5, and among 15- to 19-year-olds, it increased by over 25%, from 8.0 to 10.2. Among adolescents, then, an end to climbing suicide rates does not yet appear to have arrived.

The reasons for a generation of increasing adolescent suicide are uncertain. One popular hypothesis attributes this mounting problem to the stresses of modern times and the rigors of growing up in an increasingly complex and insecure world. Hollinger and Offer (1982) have suggested specifically in this regard that the increasing percentage of adolescents among the population at large has generated a corresponding increase in competition among them (e.g., for jobs and college admission) and thereby increased the amount of suicide-provoking stress they may experience. Although making sense, this hypothesis is challenged by the fact that the aging of the United States population during the 1980s and a decreasing proportion of adolescents in it was not accompanied by any decrease in the teenage suicide rate. As for modern society in general, Hawton and Osborn (1984) point out that this is not the first time in our history that suicide rates have climbed. The suicide rate among 15- to 24-year-olds in 1974 was very similar to the rate that existed in 1908–1912, for example.

A second reason for paying special attention to suicidal behavior in adolescence is the fact that self-inflicted harm is a more frequent cause of death among 15- to 19-year-olds than among any other age group. Because they no longer contract various childhood diseases and are not yet susceptible to many of the chronic illnesses that plague older people, adolescents enjoy relatively good physical health. The three leading causes of death among 15- to 19 year-olds are not diseases or illnesses of any kind, but preventable mishaps—in order, accidents, suicide, and homicide, with rates respectively of 48.3, 10.2, and 10.0 per 100,000 persons per year. Death by suicide is four times more common in 15- to 19-year-olds than fatal heart disease, which is the leading cause of death in the total population, and it is twice as common as dying from cancer, the second most frequent cause of death overall. As for preventable mishaps in the total population, accidents rank fourth, suicide eighth, and homicide twelfth in frequency among causes of death (NCHS, 1988).

As dramatic as these findings are, they probably underestimate the number of adolescent lives that end in suicide. Uncounted are instances in which youthful death by suicide is recorded otherwise to ease the pain of a grieving family or to limit the liability of an agency or institution that might be held responsible. In one study of 229 young people under age 19 who apparently died by their own hand, 15% had been recorded by the medical examiner as accidental deaths (Hoberman & Garfinkel, 1988). Of special significance with respect to undetected suicidal intent in apparent accidents are automotive fatalities. Automobile accidents account for over three quarters of the deaths by accident recorded each year for 15- to 19-year-olds. Although intentionality is often difficult to determine in fatal accidents, at least some of these, especially vehicular accidents involving just one car in which a teenager was driving alone, are very likely to be suicides.

In addition to being underreported, in all likelihood, adolescent suicides are often inadequately anticipated. In one retrospective study of 27 teenage suicide victims, for example, only one third were found to have had any contact with a mental health professional, and only 2 were in treatment at the time of their death (Brent, Perper, Goldstein, Kolko, Allan, Allman, & Zelenak, 1988).

Third, along with dying from suicide in disproportionate numbers, adolescents are as likely as adults to think about suicide and to make suicide attempts. Over the years, clinicians have estimated that for every actual suicide among 15- to 19-year-olds there are 50 to 150 attempts (McAnarney, 1975; McIntire, Angle, & Schlicht, 1977). Recent research suggests an even higher ratio than this. Among 380 economically advantaged high school students surveyed by Friedman, Asnis, Boeck, and DiFiore (1987), 52.9% reported that they had thought about killing themselves at some time, and 8.7% had made at least one attempt to do so. Dubow and his colleagues found a 36% incidence of suicidal thoughts in the past year among 1,384 junior and senior high school students in a semirural community and a 7% incidence of their reporting a suicide attempt (Dubow, Kausch, Blum, Reed, & Bush, 1989). Studying 962 students in three different colleges, Westefeld and Furr (1987) learned that 32% had considered committing suicide, and 4.5% had made an attempt. Stiffman, Earls, Robins, and Jung (1988) interviewed 2787 inner-city 13- to 18-year-olds coming to health clinics in several communities, of whom 24.3% had had suicidal ideation and 4.4% had made a suicide attempt in the previous year.

Taken together, these data from diverse groups suggest that, in contrast to an actual suicide rate of 1 per 10,000 per year among 15- to 19-year-olds, as many as 1 in every 3 or 4 may think about committing suicide and 4–7% may make some kind of suicide attempt each year. At the same, like suicide completers, these suicide attempters and threateners often do not get the help they need. Fewer than one half of the suicide attempters in the Friedman et al. survey and fewer than one third of those with suicidal ideation in the Stiffman et al. study had sought or received professional attention addressed to this problem.

Sex and Race Differences

Among adolescents who engage in suicidal behavior, boys are far more likely to kill themselves than girls, by a ratio of more than four to one (NCHS, 1988). Girls, on the other hand, account for 80–90% of suicide attempts in this age group (Hawton, 1986, Chapter 5). This same difference characterizes adults, among whom men are three to four times more likely to commit suicide and women three to four times more likely to attempt it.

The reasons for this sex difference remain unknown, although it has commonly been ascribed to differences in sex-role attitudes and preferences. Lester (1979), for example, has suggested that actual suicide tends to be seen as more "masculine" than attempted suicide, and that males are accordingly more likely than females to consider suicide only when they intend to complete the act. If this hypothesis were correct, the general trend in our society toward less-distinct sex roles than in the past should have been reducing sex differences in suicide behavior. To the contrary, however, the ratio of male to female suicides among 15- to 19-year-olds has increased from 3.4:1 in 1965 to 4.1:1 in 1978, and 4.3:1 in 1989.

Also, for as-yet-unknown reasons, white and black adolescents and adults differ markedly in their inclination to suicidal behavior. The suicide rate for the total population is twice as high for whites as for blacks, and among 15- to 19-year-olds, white young people are 2.5 times more likely to kill themselves than black youth. These black–white differences are found for both males and females at all ages (NCHS, 1988).

Whatever their eventual explanation, these sex and race differences have implications for clinical assessment. While considerable caution should be exercised in ruling out suicidal risk among adolescents because the patient happens to be female or black, the epidemiological data indicate that being white and male increases the likelihood of a patient's committing suicide.

Methods Used

Among 15- to 19-year-old males who commit suicide, almost two thirds (64.2%) end their lives with handguns or other firearms. Death by hanging or strangulation accounts for another one fifth (20.9%) of these youthful suicides, and the next two most frequent methods are taking gas (9.4%) or poison (3.2%). Adolescent females who kill themselves are also most likely to use handguns or firearms, just under half of the time (45.1%). Unlike suicidal boys, however, suicidal girls are almost as likely to use either gas (16.0%) or poison (19.5%) as they are to shoot themselves. Hanging, the second most common suicidal method among males, ranks fourth (12.8%) among adolescent females (NCHS, 1988).

This tendency of males to use more violent and immediately lethal methods of suicide characterized the adult as well as the adolescent population of people who kill themselves. This might appear to suggest that the greater frequency of actual suicide among males than females is a consequence of their opting for more dangerous ways of being self-harmful. However, clinical observations argue for regarding choice of suicidal method as deriving from rather than leading to sex differences (Rich, Ricketts, Fowler, & Young, 1988). That is, sex-linked psychosocial factors may influence how people go about killing themselves, but males and females can be equally successful in taking their lives through highly lethal methods if such is their intent.

An entirely different pattern of preferred method characterizes adolescents who attempt but do not complete suicide. For both males and females, ingestion of some toxic substance has been observed in various studies to account for 80–90% of youthful suicide attempts (Garfinkel, Froese, & Hood, 1982; Hawton, 1986, Chapter 5; Withers & Kaplan, 1987). This difference between preferred methods in actual and attempted suicide corresponds to differences in their lethality. Putting a gun to one's head and pulling the trigger has a high probability of resulting in death and rarely leaves any time to reconsider one's intent. Ingesting some substance, on the other hand, allows for a wide range of nonlethal doses and also typically provides some opportunity between swallowing and dying for one to be rescued or to call for help. People who are determined to die select highly lethal methods of harming themselves, whereas those who wish to make a suicide attempt but not perish in the process choose a method that does not endanger their lives.

On occasion, however, suicide attempters may misjudge the lethality of the means by which they inflict harm on themselves or the certainty of being rescued. Then an unintended tragedy can result, as when the belief that "a few of these can't hurt me" leads to a fatal overdose of some toxic substance, or the person who always gets home at five o'clock and will turn off the gas is unexpectedly delayed. It can only be surmised how many fatal "accidents" or apparently intended suicides were in fact suicide attempts that went awry in such ways.

The accuracy with which suicidal people judge lethality complicates the distinction between actual and attempted suicide. Suicide attempts are customarily defined as apparently suicidal acts committed by persons who have no conscious wish to die and who survive any self-inflicted damage. As just noted, however, there are instances in which miscalculation, such as an unintended fatal dose of poison, results in would-be attempters killing themselves. Hence, any identified group of suicide completers, while comprising mostly persons who were intent on killing themselves, may also include some whose death was in fact accidental. Likewise, individuals determined to die by their own hand may survive, thanks to an unanticipated rescue or some other fortuitous circumstance, and become designated as suicide attempters.

Clinicians need also to recognize that unconscious wishes to die may have led a supposedly accidental suicide victim to underestimate the toxicity of what he or she ingested. Conversely, a deep determination to live may lie behind an apparently intended suicide completer having left open possibilities to be rescued in time to survive. These complexities of suicidal behavior suggest that the distinction between attempted and completed suicide might better be based on what people intend than on the outcome of their actions. As matters stand, however, statistical reports and research studies have for the most part defined suicide attempters and completers according to outcome, and these reports and studies may consequently describe groups that are not entirely homogeneous with respect to intent. As is elaborated later in this chapter, these subtleties regarding intent should be examined closely in the clinical assessment of future suicidal risk among adolescents who have made a suicide attempt.

ORIGINS OF ADOLESCENT SUICIDAL BEHAVIOR

Suicidal behavior in adolescents is typically preceded by some frustrating or disappointing event, such as failing a test, losing a friend, or coming up short in an argument with parents. In the immediate wake of a suicide attempt, adolescents commonly describe such distressing experiences as their reason for having harmed themselves, and first impressions frequently suggest that their self-destructiveness occurred as a sudden and impulsive act. However, clinical and research findings demonstrate to the contrary that suicidal acts are multiply determined, deliberately chosen coping efforts that almost always emerge as the end result of a gradually unfolding process of adaptive decompensation. The unfolding process that leads young persons to harm themselves is typically characterized by (a) long-standing family instability, (b) mounting distress, (c) dissolving social relationships, and (d) repeated failures to find nonsuicidal solutions to persistent problems.

Family Instability

Suicidal adolescents and young adults are much more likely than their peers to have grown up in a disrupted and disorganized family environment. Sometimes due to parental absence or abusiveness, sometimes because of chronic physical illness or incapacity in the family, sometimes as a result of parental psychopathology or substance abuse, and sometimes in response to marital discord, these young persons are frequently found to have passed through their childhood with little expectation of being able to rely on their parents for support or on their home as a place of sanctuary (Brent et al., 1988; Friedman, Corn, Hurt, Fibel, Schulick, & Swirsky, 1984; Kosky, Silburn, & Zubrick, 1990; Pfeffer, 1986, Chapter 8; Shafii, Carrigan, Whittinghill, & Derrick, 1985).

For example, Withers and Kaplan (1987) found in a study of 173 patients ages 10–20 years admitted to a pediatric hospital following a suicide attempt that only 10% were experiencing harmonious family relationships at the time of their attempt. Wright (1985), examining suicidal ideation among several hundred high school seniors and college freshmen, found that those who had considered suicide attempts were troubled by numerous family problems. Significantly more often than their nonsuicidal classmates, they described their parents as having a conflictual marriage, saw at least one of their parents as being angry or depressed much of the time, and complained of not getting along well with their father. By contrast, and with important implications for clinical assessment and intervention, a secure and cohesive family environment has been found to act as a protective factor that reduces the likelihood of suicidal behavior in otherwise risky circumstances (King, Raskin, Gdowski, Butkus, & Opipari, 1990; Rubenstein, Heeren, Housman, Rubin, & Stechler, 1989).

As in the case of unraveling the disposition to depression, the role of long-standing family instability in setting the stage for suicidal behavior should not be equated with growing up in a home broken by death, divorce, or separation. There is no evidence to implicate a one-parent home in suicidal risk, independently of marital disharmony, generational strife, or parental inadequacy. Data reported by Spirito, Stark, Fristad, Hart, and Owens-Stively (1987) indicate that broken homes are neither commonly nor distinctively associated with youthful suicidal behavior. They compared 71 adolescents admitted to a general pediatrics unit after attempting suicide with a matched sample of adolescents referred for psychiatric consultation while hospitalized for a variety of medical conditions unrelated to suicidal behavior. Approximately three quarters of the patients in both groups were from currently intact families.

Even when young people have experienced parental breakup, no assumptions should be made concerning increased disposition to suicide or to any other behavior problem. Inordinate family conflict, not unusual family constellation, is the harbinger of developmental psychopathology; what matters is not who is in the family, but how they get along with each other. Clinicians have long recognized that the breakup of an antagonistic or violently discordant marriage may even produce a calmer and more stable home that, although now "broken," improves an adolescent's sense of psychological well-being (Hodges, 1986, Chapter 3; Kelly, 1988).

Whether living together or apart, troubled parents can influence their children toward suicidal behavior not only by failing to provide a stable family environment, but also by providing suicidal models themselves. In two of the earliest influential studies of youthful suicidal behavior, Shaffer (1974) found that 13% of a group of adolescents who killed themselves had experienced suicidal behavior by a parent or sibling, and Teicher and Jacobs (1966) found among a group of adolescent attempters that 25% of their mothers or fathers had previously attempted suicide. Subsequent research has consistently confirmed that young persons who consider harming themselves are significantly more likely than nonsuicidal adolescents to have experienced the suicide or attempted suicide of one of their parents (Brent, Kolko, Allan, & Brown, 1990; Harkavy & Asnis, 1985; Spirito, Brown, Overholser, & Fritz, 1989).

Although these findings speak to the role of familial modeling in fostering suicidal behavior, the vast majority of suicidal adolescents have no family history of suicidal behavior. Hence, familial incidence, while a risk factor, is by no means a necessary condition for such behavior. Adolescents can become self-destructive without any history of such behavior in their families, and a negative family history should never be used as a basis for ruling out suicidal risk in a troubled young person. On the other hand, previous suicidal behavior in an adolescent's family should always be considered to increase the risk that he or she might also select self-inflicted harm as a way of attempting to cope with life problems.

Aside from the probable influence of modeling, the familial incidence of suicidal behavior raises the possibility of genetic factors. In this regard, available data do demonstrate a much higher incidence of suicide among the biological relatives of adopted individuals with affective disorder than among their adoptive relatives (Wender, Kety, Rosenthal, Schulsinger, Ortmann, & Lunde, 1986). However, there is no conclusive evidence for any direct genetic transmission of suicidal tendencies. What seems most likely is that genetic factors contribute to suicidal behavior, but only indirectly through dispositions to affective disorder. A shared disposition to depression in particular, which is genetically transmitted in part, can account for a disposition to suicidal behavior that is shared by parents and their biological children (Rainer, 1984).

Escalating Distress

Diagnosable psychopathology is neither a necessary nor a sufficient condition for actual or attempted suicide to occur. Nevertheless, suicidal behavior rarely appears in adolescents who are not feeling overwhelmed by more stress than they can handle. Young persons who harm or kill themselves are typically suffering from frustrations and disappointments that have left them feeling sad, angry, and hopeless. In most suicidal adolescents, distressing thoughts and feelings are sufficiently pronounced to warrant a diagnosis of depressive disorder. In one study of 100 consecutively admitted patients, ages 13–18 years, who were hospitalized following a suicide attempt, for example, 91 were judged to meet *DSM-III-R* criteria for depressive disorder (Chabrol & Moron, 1988).

As for young persons with depressive disorder, a study of 92 adolescents with diagnosable depression being seen in an outpatient clinic revealed a 58% frequency of suicidal ideation and a 28% frequency of having made a suicide attempt (Ryan, 1989). Although further research is necessary to establish the precise frequency with which suicidal behaviors and depression are likely to co-occur, they are widely recognized to go hand-in-hand (Asarnow & Guthrie, 1989; Cole, 1989; Kovacs, 1989).

In addition to experiencing substantial distress and having suffered through more negative life events than their peers, suicidal young persons are frequently found to be responding unhappily to conflicts with significant persons in their lives, especially their parents (Brent et al., 1988, 1990; Harkavy & Asnis, 1985; Rubenstein et al., 1989; Schotte & Clum, 1987). In the Withers and Kaplan (1987) sample of adolescent suicide attempters, unresolved disputes with parents were a precipitating factor in one half of the cases.

Family problems contributing to suicidal behavior have typically been escalating in the months preceding an adolescent's attempting or committing suicide. Especially common is a sharp increase in parent–child conflict during this presuicidal period. Often, the parents have become highly critical of their youngster and have begun to impose rigid, restrictive limits on his or her behavior. In turn, the adolescent has usually complained bitterly about the parents' attitudes and impositions, and angry confrontation has become the order of the day. Almost always, the adolescent has come away the loser in these confrontations and has grown to feel powerless to influence his or her own destiny.

The unresolved conflicts and seemingly unrelenting frustrations that typically precede youthful suicidal behavior are commonly manifest in feelings of sadness, anger, and hopelessness. The majority of adolescent suicide attempters report having felt intensely angry or painfully lonely just prior to harming themselves, and the presence of such depressive affects has been widely demonstrated to increase suicidal risk in young persons (Khan, 1987; Pfeffer, Lipkins, Plutchik, & Mizruchi, 1988; Robbins & Alessi, 1985; Spirito, Brown, Overholser, & Fritz, 1989).

Among the feelings from which suicidal inclinations emerge, special attention must be paid to hopelessness. For both adolescents and adults who contemplate suicide, coming to the conclusion that there is no light at the end of the tunnel frequently constitutes the driving force in their deciding to take drastic self-destructive action. There is considerable evidence that suicidal risk increases directly in relation to how hopeless a person is feeling (Beck, Brown, & Steer, 1989; Fawcett, Scheftner, Clark, Hedeker, Gibbons, & Coryell, 1987; Kazdin, French, Unis, Esveldt-Dawson, & Sherick, 1983; Pfeffer, 1986, Chapter 5; Westefeld & Furr, 1987). With respect to the origins of suicide, then, the disposition to self-harmful behavior that emerges from family instability is joined in the months preceding a suicidal act by escalating distress that includes a precipitating onslaught of hopelessness.

Dissolving Social Relationships

Feeling alienated from uncaring and overcontrolling parents and powerless to curb their escalating distress by themselves, suicidal adolescents have typically sought support in a close relationship with some other relative, with a teacher or other respected adult, or with a boyfriend or girlfriend. Because of their desperate need for such a relationship, however, presuicidal adolescents tend to have little tolerance for its being disrupted for any reason. What is often found in the recent history of suicidal adolescents is either a failure to establish compensatory contacts with other persons or the dissolution of such desperately needed relationships, as by a relative dying, a teacher moving away, or a boyfriend or girlfriend no longer wanting a close or exclusive relationship.

Research findings confirm not only that suicidal adolescents lack social support networks enjoyed by their nonsuicidal peers, but also that close ties to family and friends, like a secure family environment, can counteract suicidal tendencies that may be provoked by stressful experiences (King et al., 1990; Rubenstein et al., 1989; Spirito, Overholser, & Stark, 1989; Zayas, 1987). Thus, interpersonal circumstances often make a crucial difference between whether distressed young persons merely think about suicide or actually attempt it. In an illustrative study by Cantor (1976), female college students who had thought about suicide often and those who had made one or more attempts both showed strong needs to be close to people and to be nurtured by them, combined with little ability to tolerate frustrations of these needs. However, those who had just thought about suicide had been successful in satisfying these needs in their interpersonal relationships, whereas those who had attempted suicide had been unable to reach out and establish supportive relationships with others.

Especially important among interpersonal aspects of the unfolding process that leads to suicidal behavior are needs to communicate certain feelings and concerns and to bring about a change in how one is being viewed and responded to, particularly by parents. Suicidal adolescents are often angry about being mistreated or neglected, and their self-destructive acts may then be intended in part to lay a retaliatory burden of distress, humiliation, and regret on those who are perceived as ignoring or depriving them ("They'll be sorry now").

With respect to bringing about change, suicide attempts have long been recognized as constituting a "cry for help" (Farberow & Shneidman, 1961). This kind of request for things to be different is typically addressed to a suicidal person's immediate circle of friends and relatives and most commonly to his or her parents. The need of suicidal adolescents to make some impact on their parents is reflected in the findings of numerous research studies. These young persons typically feel that their parents are unaware of or indifferent to their problems; their attempts are usually made at home, often while their parents are in the house; and their parents commonly do in fact have little understanding of what has been bothering them or has precipitated their suicide attempts (Garfinkel et al., 1982; Jacobs, 1971; Mehr, Zeltzer, & Robinson, 1981).

On occasion, considerable attention is drawn by coverage in the news media to instances in which two or more adolescents kill themselves or make suicide attempts in a group. Suicidal pacts make good stories, and Romeo and Juliet, the star-crossed teenage lovers who kill themselves rather than face the prospect of living without each other, have, through Shakespeare's talent, implanted themselves firmly in the public mind. Such couple or group suicidal behavior may appear to suggest that close interpersonal relationships can sometimes contribute to rather than help to avert self-harmful acts. However, considerable caution should be exercised in inferring that multiple suicidal behavior signifies a supportive social network. Among young persons who act suicidally together, and who are at that moment in a sense supporting each other, each individual is very likely to be feeling estranged from his or her parents, from other persons in whom to confide and who can act powerfully on his or her behalf, and from rewarding and nurturant group memberships.

On the other hand, the typical alienation of suicidal adolescents does not mean that they are immune to the influence of suicidal models among their peers. Adolescents who attempt or complete suicide are more likely than other young persons to have been exposed to suicidal behavior among friends as well as family members, and clinicians and communities must be concerned about what has become known as suicidal "clustering" or "contagion." When suicidal behavior clusters or becomes contagious, the self-destructive actions of one young person are shortly followed by a rash of similar acts among his or her classmates, and the local newspaper carries expressions of concern about an epidemic of suicide.

The professional literature confirms that, as a consequence of social influence and imitation, suicide clustering is a real phenomenon. Suicidal behavior by an adolescent increases the risk of such behavior among other adolescents with whom he or she has been interacting on a regular basis (Allen, 1987; Robbins & Conroy, 1983; Shaffer, 1984). Significantly, however, such imitation has not been demonstrated to occur in the absence of personal familiarity. Concern is raised from time to time that newspaper stories and television programs about youthful suicide may actually foster suicidal behavior. Thus far, research findings have not demonstrated any relationship between newscasts and television films about suicide and an increase in rates of youthful suicide behavior following the airing of these programs (Berman, 1988; Kessler, Downey, Milavsky, & Stipp, 1988; Kessler, Downey, Stipp, & Milavsky, 1989). Only when suicide victims or attempters are well-known to a young person does news of their behavior influence him or her to act in the same way.

Unsuccessful Problem-Solving Efforts

On top of lacking or losing supportive relationships, suicidal adolescents have usually progressed through a series of increasingly desperate efforts to resolve their escalating problems. Often, they have begun with reasonable attempts to iron out differences with their parents or to find support and stability outside of their families. Proving unsuccessful, these efforts have then given way to more provocative attempts to convey their distress and to influence a change in their circumstances, such as by rebelling, running away, or ignoring their schoolwork. With neither reason nor provocation solving their problems, these young people have next surrendered to overt symptoms of anxiety and depression and finally decided that suicide was the only remaining way of escaping their difficulties or at least impressing them on the important persons in their lives.

Suicidal behavior is thus rarely the initial response of a young person to undesirable or unpleasant life circumstances. Any situation in which suicidal tendencies have seemingly emerged "out of the blue" should be examined carefully for previously unrecognized problem-solving failures that have ushered in the suicidal behavior. Clinical and research studies have confirmed that suicidal individuals are more likely than other persons to be grappling with problems they cannot solve (Orbach, 1986; Schotte & Clum, 1987; Spirito, Brown, Overholser, & Fritz, 1989). The months preceding an actual suicide are in fact characterized not only by an elevated frequency of rebellious and antisocial behavior, but also by an increased likelihood of drug abuse and suicide attempts (Rich, Young, & Fowler 1986; Shaffer, 1974; Withers & Kaplan, 1987). Shafii et al. (1985) found in their psychological autopsy of adolescent suicide victims that 40% of these young persons had previously attempted suicide, 55% had made suicide threats, 70% had been involved in antisocial behavior, and 70% had been abusing alcohol or drugs.

To summarize this formulation of the unfolding process that lead to self-destructive acts, it is lonely and alienated young people from disrupted or disorganized homes who have been failing in numerous efforts to resolve mounting problems who constitute a high-risk group for suicidal behavior.

ASSESSMENT

Clinicians who work with young persons need to be constantly alert to circumstances that increase the likelihood of their engaging in suicidal behavior. Few would disagree with Pfeffer's (1988a) urging in this regard that every child or adolescent seen by a mental health professional should be thoroughly assessed for self-destructive potential. Suicide attempts must be anticipated before they occur, if at all possible, and attempts that have already occurred must be evaluated with respect to their implications for life-threatening behavior in the future.

Anticipating Suicidal Behavior

Although suicidal behavior is difficult to predict in adolescents who have not previously made a suicide attempt, its risk can be estimated from certain features of a young person's psychological status, support networks, and adjustment history. With respect to *psychological status*, suicidal behavior emerges most commonly in the context of a depressive constellation of feelings, of deprivation, anger, inadequacy, and hopelessness. Adolescents who harm or kill themselves typically feel lonely and abandoned; they are mad at the world for not meeting their needs and upset with themselves for not being able to manage their lives more effectively; and they very much doubt that future events will bring them any relief from their distress.

The onset of depressive symptoms of any kind is the psychological event most likely to precede adolescent suicidal behavior and hence to warn of its risk. The possibility of suicide should always be considered when a young person begins to exhibit dysphoric moods, pessimistic and self-depreciatory attitudes, depleted energy, eating and sleeping disturbances, or the manifestations of these core features of depressive disorder in withdrawn or rebellious behavior (see Chapter 4). This does not mean that every adolescent who becomes despondent, discouraged, lethargic, anorexic, insomniac, isolated, or cantankerous is on the verge of suicidal behavior. However, very few adolescents become suicidal without having displayed such depressive characteristics, and adequate attention to these warning signs can help clinicians cast a sufficiently broad diagnostic net to minimize instances in which suicidal risk goes undetected.

At the same time, excessive overestimation of suicide risk can be avoided by examining some personality characteristics that bear on whether angry, dispirited, and self-critical young people will harm themselves. Generally speaking, the risk of suicide is greater in individuals (a) who are action-oriented rather than contemplative in their approach to problem-solving; (b) who tend to express themselves freely rather than with restraint; and (c) whose judgments and preferences tend to be idiosyncratic and unrealistic rather than conventional and commonplace. Accordingly, suicidal potential in depressed young persons is reduced by evidence that they are relatively introspective and unemotional individuals who typically exercise good judgment and subscribe to conventional modes of conduct.

Turning to *support networks*, depressive concerns contribute most to suicidal behavior when they cannot be adequately communicated to other people. The more extensively and directly depressed adolescents can share their concerns with friends and relatives who care about then, the less likely they are to harm themselves. Conversely, the less opportunity young persons have for mutually supportive conversations with significant figures in their lives, the more likely they are to resort to suicidal behavior as a channel of communication.

The risk of suicidal behavior becomes particularly grave among depressed and psychologically needy individuals following some breakdown in support networks they have previously enjoyed. Adolescents who have people to confide in and to receive succor from rarely harm themselves, and losing this kind of support can quickly turn mild into serious suicidal risk. Hence, there are few questions more important to ask in the evaluation of a potentially suicidal adolescent than, "Who is there you can talk to about what's bothering you?" The sparser the response to this question, and the more bereft the young person seems of support from people who matter to him or her, the grimmer the specter of suicide and the more closely he or she needs to be followed clinically.

Regarding *adjustment history*, suicidal risk in troubled adolescents increases in proportion to the duration of their depressive complaints and the extent of their previously unsuccessful problem-solving efforts. Adolescents who have recently developed mild depressive symptoms and are only beginning to pursue ways of ameliorating their difficulties are unlikely to consider suicidal alternatives. Those who have a long history of increasingly incapacitating symptom formation, on the other hand, and who have already worked their way unsuccessfully through a series of increasingly maladaptive efforts to cope, may well be on the verge of harming themselves. Particularly when such distressed and discouraged young persons seem no longer able to maintain a realistic appraisal of their situation or of possibilities for improving it, suicidal behavior may emerge as the only solution or mode of communication that seems left to them.

Among depressed adolescents with inadequate support networks, then, suicide risk mounts with the degree of depression and its manifestation in problem behaviors. This risk is especially great when the young person (a) has lost interest in or has become unable to carry on with his or her usual daily activities; (b) has become preoccupied with thoughts of death; or (c) has already resorted to school failure, running away, delinquency, sexual promiscuity, or substance abuse in failed efforts to bring about improved circumstances or feelings of relief. Above all, adolescents who have previously talked about or threatened harming themselves should always be considered as having serious potential for doing just that unless they can find other ways of changing how others are treating them.

The suicidal implications of increasingly maladaptive efforts at problem-solving become most serious when they include previous suicide attempts. The fact of a troubled adolescent having previously attempted suicide increases enormously the likelihood that suicidal behavior will occur in the future. Hawton and Osborn (1984) report that 10% of adolescents who make a suicide attempt do so again within a year. Clinicians are thus well-advised always to consider adolescents who have made suicide attempts as being at risk for future suicidal behavior, even when they are not currently being evaluated for this reason, and always to include suicide prevention measures in their treatment plan, even when other types of difficulty will be the major focus of the intervention.

Because of the predictive significance of previous suicidal behavior and the irreversible consequences of actual suicide, this aspect of a young person's history must be pursued carefully in clinical evaluations. Troubled young persons are usually reliable reporters of prior suicide attempts, especially if they remain concerned about finding ways of communicating their distress to others, but parents should also be asked whether their youngster has ever behaved in a physically self-harmful fashion.

Two other questions should regularly be asked of parents with a child who shows suicide potential. First, is there a family history of suicidal behavior or any recent instance of attempted or completed suicide among the adolescent's daily companions? Other things being equal, suicide risk is considerably increased by the presence of either circumstance. Second, to what extent are firearms accessible to the adolescent? Because of the frequency with which adolescent suicide victims shoot themselves, having rifles and handguns in the home must be considered a risk factor for self-destructive behavior, in suicidally prone young persons (Berman, 1987; Brent et al., 1988; Shaffer, Garland, Gould, Fisher, & Trautman, 1988).

Evaluating the Implications of Suicide Attempts

As would be expected from the communicative purposes of suicidal behavior, many suicidal adolescents come to professional attention not before but after they have made a suicide attempt; only in the wake of the attempt have the young person's concerns become sufficiently appreciated for help to be sought. In evaluating the seriousness of attempts that have been made and the likelihood of their being repeated, clinicians can be guided by some known implications of the onset, method, intent, and consequences of adolescent suicidal actions.

With respect to *onset*, the prospects for reducing future suicidal risk through appropriate intervention are best when suicidal behavior has developed relatively recently and rapidly. Almost every suicide attempt will have been preceded by some period of gradually worsening circumstances and mounting concerns. Nevertheless, important questions to pursue in the individual case are how long this period has been, how bad the circumstances have become, how high the concerns have mounted, and how numerous the adolescent's previous problem-solving failures have been. The worse the situation, the longer the history of apparently self-destructive behaviors, and the more numerous and self-harmful any previous suicide attempts have been, the greater the risk of further attempts and the more extensive the need for treatment and surveillance.

Concerning the *method* by which a young person has attempted suicide, consideration should be given to the lethality of the means that were employed and the possibilities that were left open for rescue. Adolescents who have survived shooting or hanging themselves are at much greater risk for further suicidal behavior than those who have swallowed a few aspirin or made superficial scratches on their wrists. As already noted, however, the person's own appraisal of lethality must be taken into account. An adolescent who has taken a dozen aspiring tablets expecting them to cause death is probably a greater suicide risk than a boy or girl who has become seriously ill after swallowing a highly toxic substance that was thought to be relatively harmless.

In the course of eliciting this kind of information, the clinician should also find out how the attempt was planned. Young persons who have thoughtfully selected a particular time, place, and method for attempting suicide in order to maximize lethality and minimize possibilities of rescue are at relatively grave risk for eventually killing themselves. On the other hand, to the extent that they have acted without much forethought and with whatever means happened to be available, or chosen a time and place at which other responsible persons were either present or certain to come on the scene, the possibilities for averting repetitive or life-threatening suicidal behavior are relatively good.

As for a suicidal adolescent's *intent*, it should be determined as clearly as possible whether the young person wanted mainly to die or mainly to achieve some communicative or manipulative purposes. In many cases, intent can be inferred from how and where an attempt has been made. Highly lethal attempts made in isolation, as when a boy walks deep into the woods and hangs himself from a tree, only to be rescued by a chance passerby, are much more likely to indicate a wish to die than slight injuries self-inflicted at home with others present, as when a girl scratches the back of her wrist with a knife right in front of her parents.

The absence of any such interpersonal context, especially when a suicidal adolescent cannot suggest or refuses even to consider social motives for his or her self-destructive behavior, increases the risk of further life-threatening behavior. The risk of suicidal young persons eventually taking their own lives is greatest of all when their previous attempts have been accompanied by a conscious wish to die. The clinician should accordingly never hesitate to ask a suicide attempter, "Did you want to die?"

Despite how badly they may have felt at the time of making a suicide attempt, most adolescents subsequently report that their intent was not to die, but rather to have some effect on their environment. Generally speaking, the more clearly and consciously a suicide attempt was intended to influence the actions or attitudes of others, the fewer are the implications for further, more serious self-destructive acts. However, the predictive significance of communicative intent will always be a function of how successful the young person was in getting his or her point across and how much his or her circumstances changed as a result of the suicide attempt.

The *consequences* of suicidal behavior will in fact speak volumes about the likelihood of its persisting. Was an adolescent's suicide attempt greeted with sympathetic concern, or with indifference, or with anger, scorn, and ridicule? Did the attempt result in a young person's family and friends changing how they think about and treat him or her, or did matters remain about as they were or become even more distressing than before?

When the important persons in a suicidal adolescent's life rally to his or her cause, they create possibilities for some favorable resolution of the young person's difficulties. In the absence of positive parental concern and desirable changes in family or friendship patterns following a suicide attempt, on the other hand, suicidal risk continues unabated. It is the adolescent whose message remains unheard or unheeded who is at greatest risk for further, more serious self-destructive behavior and who most requires careful clinical surveillance. The next two cases illustrate many of these clinical considerations, first in a relatively mild and second in a relatively serious instance of attempted suicide.

CASE 16.   A MILD SUICIDE ATTEMPT

Noreen, age 13, had swallowed 8 ounces of straight whiskey and had been brought to the hospital unconscious. She had drunk the alcohol in the bathroom at home following an argument with her parents. The sound of her falling to the floor had alerted her parents, who rushed to her assistance. Significantly, they found the bathroom door unlocked and standing ajar.

When Noreen was seen in consultation the following day, she was alert and responsive to questions and seemed eager to discuss what had happened. She could not offer any explanation for her suicide attempt, however, other than to say that it was a silly thing to have done and that she had absolutely no wish to kill herself. It seemed clear that she had not anticipated the physical consequences of the ingestion and had been very frightened by losing consciousness.

Although Noreen could not immediately account for her conduct, other readily available information helped to identify her motives. The argument she had been having with her parents just prior to her suicide attempt concerned her relationship with a particular girlfriend of whom they did not approve. Their main objection to this girlfriend was her somewhat nonconforming, intellectually oriented life-style, which did not fit well with their conservative, business-oriented approach to the world. Over many months, Noreen's parents had become increasingly insistent that she find other companionship. Then, on the day of the suicide attempt, they learned that Noreen had gone with her girlfriend to a shopping mall that they had declared off-limits because of their concern about the type of young persons who tended to gather there. For them, this was the last straw, and during the argument just preceding the suicide attempt, they had forbidden any further association with this girlfriend.

These data revealed both Noreen's concern about having to give up a valued friendship and her needs to impress on her parents the extent of her distress, in the hope that they might change their minds. When these communicative and manipulative aspects of her suicidal behavior were suggested to her, she quickly recognized and acknowledged their accuracy. She added that her parents generally did not understand her and that getting through to them when something was troubling her had often proven difficult.

The acute nature and obvious communicative intent of Noreen's suicidal behavior pointed to mild rather than serious suicidal risk, and several additional findings helped to indicate that only brief intervention would be necessary. Noreen appeared free from any pervasive personality disturbance or decompensation. There were no suggestions in the history or on interview of any significant depressive features or conduct problems, and she had been doing consistently good work in school.

Moreover, despite the evident problems of communication within the family and some apparent history of marital disharmony, Noreen's parents were genuinely worried about and eager to do something for her. They requested and effectively utilized counseling concerning why Noreen had attempted suicide, how they might have contributed to her distress, and what they might do to diminish the danger of any further such behavior. The positive treatment response of all family members gave promise that the communication gap between them could be closed sufficiently to prevent further suicidal behavior, and there were in fact no recurrences during an 18-month follow-up period.

CASE 17.   A SERIOUS SUICIDE ATTEMPT

Sara, age 16, had been in constant conflict with her mother since the mother had remarried 6 years earlier. Sara's father had died when she was 4, and she and her mother had lived alone together from that time until the arrival on the scene of her stepfather, whom she disliked intensely. Sara and her mother fought about anything and everything—dress, friends, table manners, dating privileges, proper attitude toward stepfather, and the like. When Sara was 15, her mother had sought professional help to improve their relationship.

In the course of a brief treatment relationship at that time, Sara and her mother impressed the therapist as two strong-willed, stubborn, and argumentative individuals who magnified minor disagreements and exaggerated their differences. During some joint sessions, they were helped to examine the various sources of tension between them and to agree to a truce, with compromises on both sides.

Matters improved steadily for almost a year following these sessions. Rules of conduct were discussed and negotiated, and family bickering diminished in both frequency and intensity. Then on New Year's Eve, as Sara was dressing for a date that had been arranged weeks in advance, her mother suddenly decided that she was not old enough for a New Year's date and could not go. Instead, she was to remain at home with the family. Sara stayed at home, crushed by this arbitrary decree, only to have her mother and stepfather subsequently decide to go out, leaving her alone in the house. At this point, feeling abandoned and hopeless and convinced that her parents had little regard for her needs, she swallowed some barbiturates. She was careful, however, to limit herself to a small dose that only made her groggy. She went to bed and the next morning told her parents what she had done.

Her mother became so distraught at this news that she called her sister to come over to their house to help her deal with the situation. The aunt's approach was to berate Sara, calling her an actor and a fake and accusing her of trying to drive her mother crazy. At the height of these accusations Sara went upstairs and slashed deeply into both of her wrists with a razor blade. She then came downstairs, dripping blood, to ask, "Am I faking now?" The failure of her initial, mild suicide attempt to focus constructive attention on the family issues had thus precipitated a second, much more serious self-destructive act. This family was unfortunately lost to follow-up after Sara received medical treatment for her injuries. The history in this case would point to continued risk of increasingly life-threatening behavior in the absence of improved family relationships.

TREATMENT

Although suicide attempts vary in lethality and in their implications for subsequent suicidal behavior, even the mildest attempt is typically intended to communicate problems for which no solution seems available. Hence, the overriding consideration in working with suicidal young people is that every *suicide attempt must be taken seriously.* As illustrated in the case of Sara, unconcerned or unsympathetic responses to a suicide attempt often set the stage for further and more serious attempts.

Whatever the circumstances that bring a suicidal youngster to professional attention, persistent unappreciated distress and disrupted interpersonal relations are almost certain to have contributed to his or her actions. The treating clinician should accordingly focus first on opening lines of communication between suicidal youngsters and the important persons in their lives, in order for their distress to be adequately recognized. Then, in the context of a warm and supportive treatment relationship, the therapist needs to work with these adolescents to identify the motives underlying their self-destructive behavior.

Opening Lines of Communication

Suicidal adolescents have frequently become convinced that they are cut off from the affection, nurturance, and support of others. From the first moment of contact with these young persons, the therapist should strive to alter this conviction by being at least one person who is concerned about their welfare and committed to hearing them out and helping them with their difficulties.

The therapist also needs to make an explicit commitment to becoming the suicidal adolescent's lifeline. This commitment involves saying words to the effect of, "Hurting yourself is not going to solve any of your problems, and we're going to do everything we can to make sure that you don't do it again"; it includes being reachable around the clock to talk about troubling concerns, especially thoughts of another suicide attempt; and it should also include eliciting a specific promise from the adolescent to contact the therapist immediately upon experiencing any onset of self-harmful inclinations. By restoring hope that drastic action may not be necessary to get someone to pay attention and by creating opportunities to talk before acting on any further suicidal impulses, this mode of intervention can sharply reduce the present danger of recurrent attempts.

Although the depression and hopelessness of suicidal adolescents may limit their initial willingness to talk with the therapist, their needs for help and the therapist's warm receptivity make a potent combination that ordinarily gets significant communications flowing in short order. Once such lines of communication are formed with a suicidal adolescent, the next and eventually much more important step involves extending them to his or her family and friends. Clinicians knowledgeable about youthful suicidal behavior are uniformly agreed that the best way to prevent young people from killing themselves or making suicide attempts is to get them and keep them enmeshed in a supportive network of friends and relatives (Allen, 1987; Pfeffer, 1988b, 1989; Walker & Mehr, 1983).

Regarding the family, working with the parents collaterally and meeting in family sessions are essential if the therapy is to have any sustained effect. The parents must be helped to recognize that they have not been sufficiently cognizant of or concerned about their children's problems, and the young persons must be helped to find ways of communicating with their parents through words rather than actions. Family discussions in the therapist's presence often reveal just how and when communication breaks down and must provide a setting for encouraging more positive patterns of family interaction.

With this in mind, some clinicians suggest that family therapy is the treatment of choice for adolescents who have attempted suicide (Berman, 1987; Richman, 1984). However, clinical findings indicate that a variety of treatment modalities can effectively reduce suicidal intent, including individual and group as well as family sessions, and involving dynamic, nondirective, cognitive restructuring, and problem-solving approaches (Patsiokas & Clum, 1985; Pfeffer, 1986, Chapters 13–16). What is crucial to a successful outcome in treating suicidal adolescents is not the modality or combination of modalities chosen, but whether the therapist's approach promotes interpersonal communication and support networks.

With respect to friends, the therapist should pursue every possible avenue for helping suicidal adolescents expand or enrich their peer relationships. The friendship losses that often precede suicide attempts have usually fostered feelings of isolation and hopelessness. Encouragement to seek new friends and guidance in more effective ways of handling friendship and dating relationships can contribute to a more optimistic view of the future and more gratifying interactions with others.

Some therapists report success in mobilizing supportive peer networks for suicidal adolescents through various outreach methods. These include conducting group discussions with friends of the persons being treated and enlisting friends to take turns spending time with them on a rotating basis, to ensure that a "suicide sitter" or confidante is always by the person's side (Allen, 1987; Saffer, 1986). Whether with family or friends, the more people with whom adolescents can communicate, the less likely they are to contemplate suicide. Hence, the need for continuing professional care following a suicide attempt can be measured by how much progress has been made in establishing lines of communication outside the therapist's office.

Identifying Underlying Motives

Adolescents who have attempted suicide often describe their actions as having occurred for no good reason, as being completely out of character for them, and as unlikely ever to happen again. In those instances, when adolescent suicide attempters do volunteer some explanation for what they have done, they often place the blame entirely on some final argument or disappointment that preceded their attempt. Moreover, when they are feeling encouraged by prompt supportive responses to a suicide attempt, young persons may want to brush it off as having been "just one of those things," and their preference may be to get on with their lives without discussing their suicidal behavior further.

While not neglecting to endorse an optimistic, forward-looking stance, the therapist must nevertheless resist a suicidal adolescent's wish to gloss over the origins of his or her behavior. As long as a young person fails to acknowledge and understand the motives underlying a suicide attempt, suicidal risk will persist. Hence, in the context of a supportive emotional relationship, the therapist must seek with the adolescent to identify what these motives were.

Once open communication has been established in the therapy, identifying the underlying motives of suicidal behavior involves reviewing the entire sequence of mounting distress, dissolving social relationships, and unsuccessful problem-solving efforts that will have preceded a suicide attempt. The young person needs to express the feelings associated with these events and to appreciate how they led to a decision to take physically self-harmful action. The specific communicative or manipulative purposes the suicide attempt was intended to serve also must be discussed. What was the young person trying to communicate, and to whom? What changes was he or she hoping to bring about in whose behavior? Answers to these questions provide a basis not only for eliminating suicidal behavior as a problem-solving strategy, but also for resolving the problems that brought matters to such a pass in the first place. Until patient and therapist succeed in identifying and discussing directly whatever communicative or manipulative features were involved in the suicide attempt, further suicidal behavior will remain an acute and present danger.

The suicidal adolescent's parents also must be helped to understand why their child has acted in such an extreme fashion. Once family members begin to communicate more openly, they can make good use of knowing what bones of contention led to the suicidal behavior. This allows them to work constructively on the problems that ought to be addressed and to make informed decisions about how best to change their ways of thinking and acting.

In summary, then, treatment of suicidal young people should be governed by the expectation that the more they encounter warm concern, attempts to understand their behavior, and desired changes in family patterns, the less likely they are to consider suicide attempts in the future. From the perspective of reinforcement theory, this formulation may appear to raise the possibility of suicidal tendencies that succeed in mobilizing family, friend, and mental health professionals on a young person's behalf becoming strengthened rather than extinguished. However, an adequate treatment approach reinforces the communication, not the suicide attempt. The therapist needs to emphasize that increased communication is the main key to resolving whatever difficulties the adolescent has experienced. Concurrently, every effort should be made to foster ways of communicating that are neither as painful nor as dangerous as attempting suicide. Then the rewarding experience of feeling better will become associated in the adolescent's mind not with having made a suicide attempt, but also with becoming more openly involved with a support network.

Finally, in treating suicidal adolescents, clinicians must give careful consideration to indications for hospitalization. Depressed and alienated young persons who are at risk for suicide but have not yet physically harmed themselves can usually be treated adequately on an outpatient basis. However, the more intensely depressed an adolescent becomes, especially when attitudes of hopelessness and self-loathing are prominent, and the less support there appears to be from his or her social networks, the more advisable it may be to arrange hospitalization for preventive purposes.

With few exceptions, adolescents who have already made a suicide attempt should be hospitalized at least for an initial period of observation and any necessary medical treatment. Among patients under age 18 years seen in psychiatric emergency rooms, in fact, the group most likely to be admitted to the hospital are those with suicidal tendencies, followed second by victims of physical abuse and third by those showing signs of schizophrenia (Hilliard, Slomowitz, & Deddens, 1988). If adolescent suicide attempters are sent home or kept only overnight after receiving emergency room evaluation, the risk of future attempts may not be reduced at all. Clinical reports indicate that brief evaluations often fail to follow through with suicide prevention recommendations (Litt, Cuskey, & Rudd, 1983). As in other crisis interventions, some sustained follow-up is necessary to guarantee that suicidal adolescents and their families take the steps that will minimize the likelihood of recurrent self-injurious acts.

REFERENCES

Allen, B. P. (1987). Youth suicide. *Adolescence, 22,* 271-290.

Asarnow, J. R., & Guthrie, D. (1989). Suicidal behavior, depression, and hopelessness in child psychiatric inpatients: A replication and extension. *Journal of Clinical Child Psychology, 18,* 129-136.

Beck, A. T., Brown, G., & Steer, R. A. (1989). Prediction of eventual suicide in psychiatric inpatients by clinical ratings of hopelessness. *Journal of Consulting and Clinical Psychology, 57,* 309-310.

Berman, A. L. (1987). Adolescent suicide: Clinical consultation. *Clinical Psychologist, 40,* 87-90.

Berman, A. L. (1988). Fictional depiction of suicide in television films and imitation effects. *American Journal of Psychiatry, 145,* 982-986.

Blumenthal, S., & Kupfer, D. J. (1988). Overview of early detection and treatment stategies for suicidal behavior in young people. *Journal of Youth and Adolescence, 17,* 1-24.

Brent, D. A., Kolko, D. J., Allan, M. J., & Brown, R. V. (1990). Suicidality in affectively disordered adolescent inpatients. *Journal of the American Academy of Child and Adolescent Psychiatry, 29,* 586-593.

Brent, D. A., Perper, J. A., Goldstein, C. E., Kolko, D. J., Allan, M. J., Allman, C. J., & Zelenak, J. P. (1988). Risk factors for adolescent suicide. *Archives of General Psychiatry, 45,* 581-586.

Cantor, P. (1976). Personality characteristics found among youthful suicide attempters. *Journal of Abnormal Psychology, 85,* 324-329.

Chabrol, H., & Moron, P. (1988). Depressive disorders in 100 adolescents who attempted suicide. *American Journal of Psychiatry, 145,* 379.

Cole, D. A. (1989). Psychopathology of adolescent suicide: Hopelessness, coping beliefs, and depression. *Journal of Abnormal Psychology*, *98*, 248–255.

Dubow, E. F., Kausch, D. F., Blum, M. C., Reed, J., & Bush, E. (1989). Correlates of suicidal ideation and attempts in a community sample of junior high and senior high school students. *Journal of Clinical Child Psychology*, *18*, 158–166.

Farberow, N. L., & Shneidman, E. S. (Eds.). (1961). *The cry for help*. New York: McGraw-Hill.

Fawcett, J., Scheftner, W., Clark, D., Hedeker, D., Gibbons, R., & Coryell, W. (1987). Clinical predictors of suicide in patients with major affective disorders: A controlled prospective study. *American Journal of Psychiatry*, *144*, 35–40.

Friedman, J. M. H., Asnis, G. M., Boeck, M., & DiFiore, J. (1987). Prevalence of specific suicidal behaviors in a high school sample. *American Journal of Psychiatry*, *144*, 1203–1206.

Friedman, R. C., Corn R., Hurt, S. W., Fibel, B., Schulick, J., & Swirsky, S. (1984). Family history of illness in the seriously suicidal adolescent: A life-cycle approach. *American Journal of Orthopsychiatry*, *54*, 390–397.

Garfinkel, B. D., Froese, A., & Hood, J. (1982). Suicide attempts in children and adolescents. *American Journal of Psychiatry*, *139*, 1252–1261.

Harkavy, J. M., & Asnis, G. (1985). Suicide attempts in adolescence: Prevalence and implications. *New England Journal of Medicine*, *313*, 1290–1291.

Hawton, K. (1986). *Suicide and attempted suicide among children and adolescents*. Beverly Hills, CA: Sage.

Hawton, K., & Osborn, M. (1984). Suicide and attempted suicide in children and adolescents. In B. B. Lahey & A. E. Kazdin (Eds.), *Advances in clinical child psychology* (Vol. 7, pp. 57–107). New York: Plenum.

Hillard, J. R., Slomowitz, M., & Deddens, J. (1988). Determinants of emergency psychiatric admissions for adolescents and adults. *American Journal of Psychiatry*, *145*, 1416–1419.

Hoberman, H. M., & Garfinkel, B. D. (1988). Completed suicide in children and adolescents. *Journal of the American Academy of Child and Adolescent Psychiatry*, *27*, 689–695.

Hodges, W. F. (1986). *Interventions for children of divorce*. New York: Wiley.

Hollinger, P. C., & Offer, D. (1982). Prediction of adolescent suicide: A population model. *American Journal of Psychiatry*, *139*, 302–307.

Jacobs, J. (1971). *Adolescent suicide*. New York: Wiley.

Kazdin, A. E., French, N. H., Unis, A. S., Esveldt-Dawson, K., & Sherick, R. B. (1983). Hopelessness, depression and suicidal intent among psychiatrically disturbed inpatient children. *Journal of Consulting and Clinical Psychology*, *51*, 504–510.

Kelly, J. B. (1988). Longer-term adjustment in children of divorce: Converging findings and implications for practice. *Journal of Family Psychology*, *2*, 119–140.

Kessler, R. C., Downey, G., Milavsky, J. R., & Stipp, H. (1988). Clustering of teenage suicides after television news stories about suicides: A reconsideration. *American Journal of Psychiatry*, *145*, 1379–1383.

Kessler, R. C., Downey, G., Stipp, H., & Milavsky, J. R. (1989). Network television news stories about suicide and short-term changes in total U.S. suicides. *Journal of Nervous and Mental Disease, 177*, 551-555.

Khan, A. U. (1987). Heterogeneity of suicidal adolescents. *Journal of the American Academy of Child and Adolescent Psychiatry, 26*, 92-96.

King, C. A., Raskin, A., Gdowski, C. L., Butkus, M., & Opipari, L. (1990). Psychosocial factors associated with urban adolescent female suicide attempts. *Journal of the American Academy of Child and Adolescent Psychiatry, 29*, 289-294.

Kosky, R., Silburn, S., & Zubrick, S. R. (1990). Are children and adolescents who have suicidal thoughts different from those who attempt suicide? *Journal of Nervous and Mental Disease, 178*, 38-43.

Kovacs, M. (1989). Affective disorders in children and adolescents. *American Psychologist, 44*, 209-215.

Lester, D. (1979). Sex differences in suicidal behavior. In E. S. Gomberg & V. Franks (Eds.), *Gender and disordered behavior* (pp. 287-300). New York: Brunner/Mazel.

Lewis, S. A., Johnson, J., Cohen, P., Garcia, M., & Velez, C. N. (1988). Attempted suicide in youth: Its relationship to school achievement, educational goals, and socioeconomic status. *Journal of Abnormal Child Psychology, 16*, 459-471.

Litt, I. F., Cuskey, W. R., & Rudd, S. (1983). Emergency room evaluation of the adolescent who attempts suicide: Compliance with follow-up. *Journal of Adolescent Health Care, 4*, 106-108.

McAnarney, E. R. (1975). Suicidal behavior of children and youth. *Pediatric Clinics of North America, 22*, 595-604.

McIntire, M. S., Angle, C. R., & Schlicht, M. L. (1977). Suicide and self-poisoning in pediatrics. *Advances in Pediatrics, 24*, 291-309.

Mehr, M., Zeltzer, L. K., & Robinson, R. (1981). Continued self-destructive behaviors in adolescent suicide attempters: Part I. *Journal of Adolescent Health Care, 1*, 269-274.

National Center for Health Statistics. (1988). *Vital statistics of the United States, 1986: Vol. 2. Mortality.* Hyattsville, MD: Author.

Orbach, I. (1986). The "insolvable problem" as a determinant in the dynamics of suicidal behavior in children. *American Journal of Psychotherapy, 40*, 511-520.

Patsiokas, A. T., & Clum, G. A. (1985). Effects of psychotherapeutic strategies in the treatment of suicide attempters. *Psychotherapy, 22*, 281-290.

Pfeffer, C. R. (1986). *The suicidal child.* New York: Guilford.

Pfeffer, C. H. (1988a). Child and adolescent suicide risk. In C. J. Kestenbaum & D. T. Williams (Eds.), *Handbook of clinical assessment of children and adolescents* (pp. 672-688). New York: New York University Press.

Pfeffer, C. H. (1988b). Clinical dilemmas in the prevention of adolescent suicidal behavior. In S. C. Feinstein (Ed.), *Adolescent psychiatry* (Vol. 15, pp. 407-421). Chicago: University of Chicago Press.

Pfeffer, C. R. (1989). Suicide. In L. K. G. Hsu & M. Hersen (Eds.), *Recent developments in adolescent psychiatry* (pp. 116-134). New York: Wiley.

Pfeffer C. R., Lipkins, R., Plutchik, R., & Mizruchi, M. (1988). Normal children at risk for suicidal behavior: A two-year follow-up study. *Journal of the American Academy of Child and Adolescent Psychiatry, 27,* 34–41.

Rainer, J. D. (1984). Genetic factors in depression and suicide. *American Journal of Psychotherapy, 38,* 329–340.

Richman, J. (1984). The family therapy of suicidal adolescents. In H. S. Sudak, A. B. Ford, & N. B. Rushforth (Eds.), *Suicide in the young* (pp. 393–406). Boston: Wright.

Rich, C. L., Ricketts, J. E., Fowler, R. C., & Young, D. (1988). Some differences between men and women who commit suicide. *American Journal of Psychiatry, 145,* 718–722.

Rich, C. L., Young, D., & Fowler, R. C. (1986). San Diego suicide study: I. Young vs. old subjects. *Archives of General Psychiatry, 43,* 577–582.

Robbins, D. R., & Alessi, N. E. (1985). Depressive symptoms and suicidal behavior in adolescents. *American Journal of Psychiatry, 142,* 588–592.

Robbins, D., & Conroy, R. C. (1983). A cluster of adolescent suicide attempts: Is suicide contagious? *Journal of Adolescent Health Care, 3,* 253–255.

Rubenstein, J. L., Heeren, T., Housman, D., Rubin, C., & Stechler, G. (1989). Suicidal behavior in "normal" adolescents: Risk and protective factors. *American Journal of Orthopsychiatry, 59,* 59–71.

Ryan, N. D. (1989). Major depression. In C. G. Last & M. Hersen (Eds.), *Handbook of child psychiatric diagnosis* (pp. 317–329). New York: Wiley.

Saffer, J. B. (1986). Group therapy with friends of an adolescent suicide. *Adolescence, 21,* 743–745.

Schotte, D. E., & Clum, G. A. (1987). Problem-solving skills in suicidal psychiatric patients. *Journal of Consulting and Clinical Psychology, 55,* 49–54.

Shaffer, D., Garland, A., Gould, M., Fisher, P., & Trautman, P. (1988). Preventing teenage suicide: A critical review. *Journal of the American Academy of Child and Adolescent Psychiatry, 27,* 675–687.

Shaffer, D. (1974). Suicide in childhood and early adolescence. *Journal of Child Psychology and Psychiatry, 15,* 275–291.

Shaffer, D. (1984). Developmental factors in child and adolescent suicide. In M. Rutter, C. E. Izard, & P. B. Read (Eds.), *Depression in young people* (pp. 383–396). New York: Guilford.

Shafii, M., Carrigan, S., Whittinghill, J. R., & Derrick, A. (1985). Psychological autopsy of completed suicide in children and adolescents. *American Journal of Psychiatry, 142,* 1061–1064.

Spirito, A., Brown, L., Overholser, J., & Fritz, G. (1989). Attempted suicide in adolescence: A review and critique of the literature. *Clinical Psychology Review, 9,* 335–363.

Spirito, A., Overholser, J., & Stark, L. J. (1989). Common problems and coping stategies: II. Findings with adolescent suicide attempters. *Journal of Abnormal Child Psychology, 17,* 213–221.

Spirito, A., Stark, L., Fristad, M., Hart, K., & Owens-Stively, J. (1987). Adolescent suicide attempters hospitalized on a pediatric unit. *Journal of Pediatric Psychology, 12,* 171–190.

Stiffman, A. R., Earls, F., Robins, L. N., & Jung, K. G. (1988). Problems and help seeking in high-risk adolescent patients of health clinics. *Journal of Adolescent Health Care, 9*, 305–309.

Teicher, J. D., & Jacobs, J. (1966). Adolescents who attempt suicide: Preliminary findings. *American Journal of Psychiatry, 122*, 1248–1257.

Walker, B. A., & Mehr, M. (1983). Adolescent suicide—A family crisis: A model for effective intervention by family therapists. *Adolescence, 18*, 285–292.

Wender, P. H., Kety, S. S., Rosenthal, D., Schulsinger, F., Ortmann, J., & Lunde, I. (1986). Psychiatric disorders in the biological and adoptive families of adopted individuals with affective disorders. *Archives of General Psychiatry, 43*, 923–929.

Westefeld, J. S., & Furr, S. R. (1987). Suicide and depression among college students. *Professional Psychology, 18*, 119–123.

Withers, L. E., & Kaplan, D. W. (1987). Adolescents who attempt suicide: A retrospective clinical chart review of hospitalized patients. *Professional Psychology, 18*, 391–393.

Wright, L. S. (1985). Suicidal thoughts and their relationship to family stress and personal problems among high school seniors and college undergraduates. *Adolescence, 20*, 575–580.

Zayas, L. H. (1987). Toward an understanding of suicide risks in young Hispanic females. *Journal of Adolescent Research, 2*, 1–11.

CHAPTER 10

Substance Abuse

During the past generation, substance abuse has emerged as a prominent topic in the psychopathology of adolescence. The first edition of this book, published in 1970, did not discuss drug use and was not at the time considered deficient in this regard. Currently, however, a large percentage of young persons who come to the attention of mental health professionals are having problems controlling their use of alcohol and drugs, and, not infrequently, substance abuse is their primary presenting problem. Moreover, among adults with substance abuse disorders, one half are found to have become drug dependent by age 21 in the case of alcohol and by age 18 in the case of other addictive substances (Burke, Burke, Regier, & Rae, 1990).

Assessment and treatment planning with adolescents who use alcohol and drugs needs to be informed by normative data on the use and implications of intoxicating and potentially addictive substances. Because mythology of the kind described in Chapter 1 abounds with respect to substance use, such normative guidelines often prove elusive. As an example, published statements about youthful alcohol and drug use frequently refer in broad terms to some "percentage of adolescents" who "use drugs." Such statements lack precision and rarely merit serious consideration. Adolescents of different ages differ in whether and how frequently they use drugs; adolescents of all ages differ in their reasons for using drugs; and various concomitants and consequences of using drugs differ for different substances.

To provide adequate information on which to base clinical judgments, statements about youthful substance use should specify which age groups are using what drugs with what frequency and for what purpose. The present chapter elaborates the importance of these distinctions in reference to the frequency of substance use, stages and categories of substance use, factors associated with substance use, and considerations in the treatment and prevention of substance abuse.

FREQUENCY OF SUBSTANCE USE

Dozens of surveys of youthful substance use have been reported in the literature, and newspapers and magazines add regularly to what has become a confusing overload of misleading information. Many of these surveys involve narrow or unrepresentative samples, and most are difficult to compare with each other because of such variations in methodology as the difference between asking, "Have you *ever used* marijuana?" as opposed to asking, "Do you *use* marijuana?"

The most reliable source of epidemiological data on drug use is the National Institute on Drug Abuse (NIDA), which periodically publishes the results of two national surveys: the *National Household Survey on Drug Abuse* (NIDA, 1989), which samples households representative of 98% of the U.S. population and includes data on 12- to 17-year-olds, and *National Trends in Drug Use and Related Factors Among American High School Students and Young Adults* (Johnston, O'Malley, & Bachman, 1987a, 1987b), which annually collects information from approximately 17,000 high school seniors in some 135 public and private high schools across the country. When examined both cross-sectionally and longitudinally, the findings of these surveys identify some substantial differences in frequency of substance use associated with different drugs, with prevalence as opposed to incidence of use, with age, and with trends over time.

Differences among Drugs

Alcohol is by far the most commonly used drug among young persons, with approximately 50% of 12- to 17-year-olds reporting that some time in their lives they have consumed an alcoholic beverage. Second in frequency is marijuana, which 17.4% of 12- to 17-year-olds report having used, followed at much smaller frequencies by cocaine (3.4%), stimulants (4.2%), sedatives (2.4%), hallucinogens (3.5%), and heroin (less than 1%). These widely ranging percentages indicate why the frequency of adolescent drug use cannot be described accurately without reference to specific drugs. Most noteworthy in this regard is the fact that alcohol is the only drug that has been used by as many as half of all adolescents surveyed. Except for alcohol, the prevailing pattern among 12- to 17-year-olds is nonuse of drugs, from almost 83% who have never tried marijuana to over 99% who have never used heroin.

Incidence versus Prevalence

The percentage of persons who report ever having used a drug constitutes its *incidence*. Incidence data identify the extent of drug familiarity in a given population at a particular time, and they can be useful for making cross-sectional comparisons between groups and across different moments in time. However, the "ever used" statistic provides no information concerning the *prevalence* of use of a drug, that is, how many persons are currently using the drug and how often they are using it. Incidence data have the further limitations of giving the same weight to occasional use as to regular use of a drug and continuing to count previous users of a drug even if they have stopped using it. Hence, incidence data are of little use in longitudinal studies. Over time, in the same group of people, the measured incidence of drug use can only go up, as additional members of the target sample try a drug and former users remain counted regardless of their current practices.

Because the cumulative and unweighted nature of incidence figures inflate their size, "ever used" data are often chosen in efforts to dramatize drug-related problems. At times, unfortunately, an "ever used" figure is presented or interpreted as an indication of how many persons are currently using drugs. Only prevalence data suffice for this purpose, and only detailed information concerning how frequently particular drugs are being used can help to identify the current frequency of problematic substance abuse that requires clinical intervention.

Prevalence data in the NIDA surveys indicate that the majority of young persons who report ever having used a drug do not become regular users. In contrast to the 50% of 12- to 17-year-olds who have drunk alcohol at some time in their lives, only 25% report having done so within the past month. The 30-day prevalence for marijuana use is 6.4%, compared to the lifetime incidence of 17.4%, and fewer than 30% of those reporting any use ever of cocaine, stimulants, sedatives, and hallucinogens report having used these drugs within the previous month.

Age Differences

Just as it is misleading to speak of adolescent drug use without specifying which drugs are meant or to cite incidence (ever used) data as if they were prevalence (current use) data, it is misleading to speak of "adolescents" as if they were all the same age. Available data indicate that the frequency of drug use among adolescents increases as they grow older. For all drugs, senior high school students are more likely to report past or current use than junior high school students, and high school seniors are more likely to report drug experience than high school freshmen.

Specifically, the NIDA survey of high school seniors reveals the following higher prevalences of use of a drug within the past month than is found for 12- to 17-year-olds as a whole: for alcohol, 65% use in the previous 30 days compared with 25% in 12- to 17-year-olds; for marijuana, 23.4% compared to 6.4%; for cocaine, 6.2% compared to 1.1%; for stimulants, 5.5% compared to 1.2%; for sedatives, 2.2% compared to 0.6%; for hallucinogens, 2.5% compared to 0.8%; and for heroin, less than 1% in both groups. It should be noted that the NIDA data on seniors come from currently enrolled high school students. Hence, they represent the approximately 85% of teenagers nationwide who stay in high school, but not those who drop out. There is some reason to believe that high school dropouts as a group are more likely to be involved with drugs than stay-ins, in which case the NIDA data may underestimate drug use prevalence somewhat for young persons of high school senior age.

Turning to the late adolescent years, the NIDA data indicate that drug use, except for alcohol, levels off in college students relative to the high school years. Approximately 80% of college students report having used alcohol in the previous 30 days, compared to 65% of high school seniors. Otherwise, high school senior and college student use in the past month are essentially the same: for marijuana, 22.3% in college students; for cocaine, 7.0%; for stimulants, 3.7%; for sedatives, less than 1%; for hallucinogens, 1.4%; and for heroin, less than 1%. One likely explanation for these findings is that the increasing maturity and goal-directedness of college students tends generally to abrogate any further increases beyond the high school years in involvement with intoxicating substances.

Data on the general population of 18- to 25-year-olds also point to abatement of regular drug use with maturity. The 30-day prevalence figures for drug use in this age group are somewhat lower than for high school seniors and college students: 65% for alcohol, 15.5% for marijuana, 4.5% for cocaine, 2.4% for stimulants, 0.9% for sedatives, 1.9% for hallucinogens, and less than 1% for heroin. Among late adolescents and young adults generally in the United States, 35% have not used alcohol in the past month, almost 85% have not used marijuana in the past month, and over 93% have not used cocaine in the past month.

These cross-sectional suggestions of declining drug use from adolescence to young adulthood are confirmed in longitudinal data reported by Kandel and Raveis (1989). These investigators collected follow-up information on drug use at ages 24 to 25 years and again at ages 28 to 29 on 1222 men and women who had initially been interviewed as high school students at ages 15 to 16. Illicit drug use was strongly related to age in this group, whose drug-taking peaked in their late teens and early 20s and declined thereafter. Taken together, the available cross-sectional and longitudinal data point to a maturational process in which use of illicit drugs typically decreases sharply by or soon after age 25. Kandel and Raveis concur with the hypothesis that this maturation process involves the assumption of adult roles and responsibilities and a corresponding disengagement from adolescent activities and behaviors.

Trends Over Time

For substance use, as for other potentially problematic behaviors, an accurate perspective on trends over time helps to limit the influence of mythology on impressions of what constitutes normative behavior. A ready illustration of such mythical history is a widespread belief that drinking on college campuses has reached proportions nowadays that were never approached in previous generations. To the contrary, factual data indicate that neither the percentage of college students who drink nor the proportion having problems associated with heavy drinking changed appreciably from the 1950s to the 1980s (Engs, 1977; Engs & Hanson, 1983; Hanson, 1977). As for the late 1980s, recent NIDA data show a 1989 prevalence of 82% of college students having used alcohol in the past month and 6.5% drinking daily for the past 30 days; the 1986 figures were 80% for drinking at all in the past month and 4.6% for drinking every day (Johnston et al., 1987a). Hence, some drinking by college students is common now but no more so than in previous years, while it is no more warranted now than in the past to regard daily drinking as an unremarkable feature of college life. Daily drinking by students is unusual behavior and should be taken as an alerting signal to psychological disorder.

With respect to substance use among junior and senior high school students, the data indicate that drug-taking increased sharply in the United States during the 1960s and 1970s but in the 1980s began to level off and decline. In the NIDA nationwide household surveys, for example, the 25% prevalence in 1988 of 12- to 17-year-olds who had drunk alcohol in the past month represented a decrease from 37% in 1979 and 32% in 1985. Similarly for marijuana, use by adolescents in the past month peaked at 16.7% in 1979 and fell to 12.3% in 1985 on the way to its 6.4% 30-day prevalence in 1988. Cocaine and stimulant use by young people increased somewhat from 1979 to 1985, when the reported 30-day prevalence was 1.8% for both, but both then decreased to their respective 1988 rates of 1.1% and 1.2%.

Comparing present with previous NIDA information on high school seniors also confirms a slow but steady decline in drug use during the 1980s. With respect to alcohol use, in 1983, 41% of this group reported having taken five or more drinks in a row during the past 2 weeks; in 1988, the prevalence of this drinking pattern had decreased to 35%. In 1978, 1 in 9 (10.7%) high school seniors reported smoking marijuana every day; in 1988, daily use of marijuana had dropped to 1 in 37 (2.7%) seniors. During this same 10-year period, any use of marijuana in the past year by high school seniors decreased by one third, from 50% to 34%.

Since 1985, cocaine use among high school seniors has declined as well. In 1987, 15% of seniors reported having tried cocaine at least once in their lives, and 4.5% reported using it within the past month. In 1988, these rates had dropped to a 12% lifetime incidence and a 3.4% 30-day prevalence of cocaine use. During this same 1-year period, the percentage of high school seniors who expressed disapproval of even experimenting with cocaine increased from 80% to 83%.

These epidemiological data demonstrate that the use of intoxicating substances other than alcohol is not widespread among adolescents in the United States, and furthermore that regular current use of drugs including alcohol is infrequent. These findings run contrary to what many persons believe and to widely publicized societal concerns about curbing youthful drug abuse. This discrepancy between fact and impression, like the mythology of adolescent turmoil discussed in Chapter 1, appears to have derived from inappropriate generalizations from unrepresentative samples, particularly disadvantaged and patient populations of young people.

Substance abuse problems are especially prevalent in deteriorated neighborhoods with high crime rates, and problematic drug use usually runs high among adolescents seen in mental health settings. However, neither disadvantaged nor patient populations are representative of young persons in general, and assuming that they are is likely to generate erroneous inferences about adolescent drug use nationwide. By contrast, the NIDA surveys drawn on in the present discussion were carefully designed to be broadly representative, and there are no compelling grounds for challenging their reliability.

On the other hand, the generally low prevalence of adolescent substance use does not in any way signify that drug-taking is not a mental health or social problem. Very few adolescents become schizophrenic (Chapter 3), and most adolescents are not seriously delinquent (Chapter 8), but these facts do not make schizophrenia and delinquency unimportant to clinicians. As in the case of other conditions calling for professional intervention, the fact that heavy drug use is normatively infrequent means instead that when it does occur, it cannot and should not be written off as "just one of those things a lot of adolescents do these days." Substance use is not an everyday phenomenon among young people, and it should be carefully evaluated for the presence of or the future risk of a drug-abusing pattern that constitutes psychopathology and requires treatment.

STAGES AND CATEGORIES OF SUBSTANCE USE

As first delineated by Kandel (1975), substance use ordinarily proceeds through a sequence of four stages: drinking beer and wine, drinking hard liquor, smoking marijuana (commonly referred to as "soft" drug use), and using such other substances as cocaine, stimulants, sedatives, hallucinogens, and heroin (known as "hard" drugs). Kandel's findings and those of other investigators indicate that, with very few exceptions, only young persons who have used substances at one stage become users at the next stage. Thus, almost all adolescents who drink hard liquor have previously drunk beer or wine; almost all who smoke marijuana have previously drunk hard liquor; and almost all who become involved with hard drugs have had prior experience with marijuana. Previous nonusers of drugs rarely try marijuana without having progressed through the stage of alcohol use, and drinkers rarely experiment with other illegal drugs without first having tried marijuana (Mills & Noyes, 1984; Yamaguchi & Kandel, 1984).

The fact that hard drug use evolves from soft drug use—which has become known as the "stepping-stone hypothesis"—does not mean that one drug necessarily leads to another. Adolescents who drink are not inevitably drawn to smoking marijuana, nor are those who use marijuana destined to become hard drug users. To the contrary, as is apparent from the frequency data on use of alcohol, marijuana, and other substances, most adolescent drinkers do not progress to marijuana, and most marijuana users do not progress to hard drugs.

On the other hand, the sequential stage findings do indicate that the likelihood of using a substance at a particular stage will be higher among young persons who have used a substance at a previous stage than among those who have not. In the original work by Kandel and Faust (1975), for example, a 6-month follow-up study of high school students found that 27% of those who smoked cigarettes or drank subsequently used marijuana, whereas only 2% of those who neither smoked cigarettes nor drank subsequently used marijuana. Similarly, 26% of the marijuana users had gone on to try hallucinogens, stimulants, or heroin, but only 1% of those who had never used marijuana did so.

The reasons why some young persons progress from alcohol to marijuana to hard drugs while others do not are not fully understood. It is known, however, that the extent of use within a particular stage correlates with progression to the next stage.

Heavy drinkers are more likely than occasional drinkers to move on to marijuana, and regular users of marijuana are more likely than infrequent users to try hard drugs. Some personal, social, and family factors associated with drug use, discussed in the next section, also appear to influence the progression from one stage of drug use to the next. In addition, much can be learned about the likely future implications of substance use by distinguishing among various categories as well as stages of use.

Particularly helpful in this regard is differentiating among categories of experimental, social, medicinal, and addictive use. *Experimental users* try drugs once or perhaps a few times out of curiosity or to have a new experience and then stop using them. *Social users* take drugs as a way of participating in a mutually interactive group activity with their peers. Although adolescents may in some instances get together primarily to share a drug experience, social drug use is largely limited to parties, dances, and other special occasions. Like experimental drug use, then, social use tends to involve only occasional and infrequent drug involvement.

Medicinal drug use consists of taking drugs to relieve anxiety or tension or to enjoy a drug experience for its own sake. Because of the purposes it serves, medicinal drug use is primarily an individual experience. Two or more medicinal users may take drugs in each others' company, but they are likely in doing so to be concerned more with their own mental state than with facilitating any personal interaction. In fact, medicinal drug use tends to breed attachment more to drugs than to people. Medicinal users take more drugs more often than experimental and social users, and their drug experiences come to give them more pleasure and solace than their interpersonal relationships. Friendships among medicinal drugs users, despite any appearances to the contrary, are accordingly likely to be shallow and distant affairs of convenience in which the participants use rather than care about each other.

Addictive drug use is also an individual, largely asocial affair, but it involves not merely enjoying a drug experience but also becoming habituated to one or more drugs to the point of depending on their effects to feel good physically and mentally. Such drug dependence is marked by withdrawal symptoms, in the form of real physical or psychological distress that ensues when drugs are not available. Because of their drug dependence, addictive users are the most likely of these four types to take drugs regularly and frequently. They are also more likely than other users to demonstrate what Henly and Winters (1988) have called "transituational" drug taking, which consists of taking drugs at times and in places that are inappropriate and serves as a reliable index of the severity of a drug use problem. Transituational drug use is illustrated by the difference between taking a drink at a party and, because of an alcohol dependence, carrying a flask to school, in order to drink between classes.

The categories of experimental, social, medicinal, and addictive drug-taking provide a basis for distinguishing between substance *use* and substance *abuse*. From a psychological point of view, using a drug is not necessarily a self-abusive behavior. People can take modest amounts of alcohol or marijuana occasionally without doing themselves any harm, as far as is known (Marlatt, Baer, Donovan, & Kivlahan, 1988; Newcomb & Bentler, 1989). Legal and moral issues aside, it is the heavy use of any drugs and the taking of hard drugs that are most likely to abuse a person's physical and psychosocial functioning. Experimental and social drug use seldom result in such abuse, whereas medicinal use may have this result, and addiction to a drug always constitutes drug abuse.

The previously noted differences between lifetime incidence and 30-day prevalence of drug use among adolescents suggest that youthful drug *abuse* is relatively infrequent. The vast majority of adolescents who have tried drugs appear to be experimental or social users, inasmuch as only a small minority of them show the pattern of current, regular drug-taking that characterizes medicinal or addictive use. As further evidence in this regard, among high school seniors, the reported prevalence of daily use of a drug is 4.8% for alcohol, 4.0% for marijuana, 0.4% for cocaine, 0.3% for stimulants, 0.1% for sedatives, 0.3% for hallucinogens, and 0.0% for heroin (Johnston et al., 1987a).

This distinction has important implications for current psychopathology and future adjustment difficulties. With respect to current functioning, medicinal and addictive drug users are typically found to suffer from significant psychopathology, whereas experimental and social drug users are generally no more likely than their non-drug-using peers to exhibit psychological disorder. By and large, the heavier the use of alcohol and other drugs by young persons, the more likely they are (a) to dislike school and do poorly in the classroom, (b) to withdraw from peer-group activities and have strained relationships with their parents, (c) to engage in delinquent behavior and become sexually promiscuous, and (d) to feel personally disaffected (Barnes & Welte, 1986; Brook, Gordon, Brook, & Brook, 1989; Donovan, Jessor & Costa, 1988; Kovach & Glickman, 1986; Shedler & Block, 1990). Accordingly, evidence in drug-taking adolescents of declining achievement, deteriorating interpersonal relationships, and behavior that is bringing harm to other people and their property indicates progression from substance use to substance abuse and a corresponding need for intervention.

Determining whether psychosocial difficulties have resulted from or contributed to drug use becoming problematic may sometimes be difficult. There is little doubt, however, that drug abuse and problems in living go hand in hand. There is also considerable evidence that youthful drug abuse has substantial negative implications for the future, in two respects.

First, longitudinal studies indicate that adult drug use is largely continuous with and predictable from adolescent drug use, with 60% of the variance in adult use patterns accounted for by high school use (Bachman, O'Malley, & Johnston, 1984; Newcomb & Bentler, 1987). The earlier the age at which adolescents begin using drugs and the more heavily they become involved with them, furthermore, the more likely they are to use or abuse drugs as adults (Kandel, Davies, Karus, & Yamaguchi, 1988; Schuckit & Russell, 1983).

Second, adults in their middle and late 20s who have continued heavy drug use from their adolescent years tend to have an elevated frequency of adjustment problems in many aspects of their lives. Compared to non-drug-using adults, they are more likely to suffer from physical health problems and emotional distress, to have unstable marriages and troubled family relationships, to perform poorly in their work, and to get into difficulties with the law (Buydens-Branchey, Branchey, & Noumair, 1989; Kandel, 1984; Newcomb & Bentler, 1988).

FACTORS ASSOCIATED WITH SUBSTANCE USE

Certain personal, social, and family factors are associated with how frequently adolescents use drugs and with their beginning to use them in the first place. These experiential factors exert different kinds of influences at different stages of drug use, and addictive drug use appears to be influenced by genetic factors as well. Among adolescents who have progressed from drug use to drug abuse, moreover, there is more likely than not to be some coexisting psychological disorder, calling in *DSM-III-R* terms for a dual diagnosis.

Personal, Social, and Family Factors

Numerous studies have identified some consistent personal correlates of adolescent initiation into drug use. These include a high degree of openness to experience, tolerance of deviance, sensation seeking, unconventionality, impulsivity, and rebelliousness, on the one hand, and a low degree of social inhibition, self-acceptance, interest in achievement, and involvement with religion, on the other hand. The more marked their unconventionality, impulsivity, and sensation seeking, the more heavily adolescents are likely to use drugs and the more likely they are to progress to higher stages of drug use. By contrast, cautious, dependent, conforming, socially inhibited, self-satisfied, achievement-oriented, and religious adolescents are relatively unlikely to try drugs or to use them with any frequency (Andrucci, Archer, Pancoast, & Gordon, 1989; Bentler, 1987; Brook, Gordon, & Whiteman, 1986; Brook, Whiteman, Gordon, & Cohen, 1986).

Some interesting data reported by Block, Block, and Keyes (1988) suggest that some of these personal characteristics associated with adolescent drug use are continuous with and predictable from personality orientations that are apparent many years earlier. In a sample of 105 adolescents age 14 years, Block et al. found not only that marijuana use was associated with current nontraditional values, inability to delay gratification, and deemphasis on achievement, but also that these adolescents' current drug-use patterns were significantly related to observational evidence recorded in their nursery schools, when they were ages 3 to 4, of overreactivity, emotional lability, and inability to delay gratification.

Research with young people has also pointed to some identity formation and expectancy corollaries of drug use. With respect to their stage of identity formation, junior and senior high school students who show identity diffusion are significantly more likely to begin using drugs and to use them heavily than are their peers whose identity formation has been achieved or is in a state of foreclosure or moratorium. On the other hand, young people with foreclosed identities are significantly less likely to try or become involved with drugs than those in a diffused, moratorium, or achieved identity status (Christopherson, Jones, & Sales, 1988; Jones & Hartman, 1988). With respect to their expectations, adolescents who anticipate that alcohol and drugs will facilitate their social functioning and enhance their cognitive and motor capacities are at relatively high risk for progressive drug involvement, whereas those who regard drugs as dangerous to their health are relatively unlikely to try or to continue using them (Christiansen, Smith, Roehling, & Goldman, 1989; Marlatt et al., 1988; Sarvella & McClendon, 1988).

Socially, the disposition to use drugs is influenced by the behavior of an adolescents' peers. Drug-using peers can influence initial and continuing drug use by modeling it, by encouraging it, and by helping to make drugs available. The more closely young persons interact with friends who use drugs, the more likely they are to become involved with drugs themselves. The more drugs these friends use and the more important these friends are to them, the stronger this influence tends to be. Consistently with general trends in peer conformity among young people, however, adolescents are most susceptible to the influence of drug-taking peers during the junior high school and early high school years. In middle adolescence, especially after ages 15 or 16, the extent to which adolescents are influenced by their peers' actions to become or remain involved with drugs begins to diminish (Brook, Lukoff, & Whiteman, 1980; Huba & Bentler, 1980; Morgan & Grube, 1989).

As for family factors, research findings indicate that parents are likely to influence the drug-taking behavior of their children by the example they set with their own behavior and by the climate they create in their home. With respect to modeling, drug-taking among young people has been found to be directly related to whether and how frequently their parents take drugs. Parents who do not use drugs seldom have children who do, whereas the more heavily parents use any particular drug, the more likely their children are to use or abuse the same drug. Interestingly, however, parental drinking is less likely than parental use of marijuana to be associated with progressive drug use in their adolescent children. The likelihood that adolescents whose parents use marijuana will progress from marijuana to hard drugs is greater than the likelihood that adolescents whose parents drink will progress from alcohol to marijuana use (Chassin, McLaughlin, & Sher, 1988; Johnson, Shontz, & Locke, 1984; Rees & Wilborn, 1983; West & Prinz, 1987).

Regarding climate in the home, psychologically unstable and unconventional parents who are preoccupied with their own affairs, disinterested in their children, and given to permissive or authoritarian forms of discipline are relatively likely to have adolescent youngsters who become involved with drugs. Conversely, well-adjusted parents who maintain a well-organized household, nurture and communicate with their children, and set and enforce limits in a democratic fashion are relatively unlikely to have offspring who become regular or continuing users of drugs (Barnes, 1984; Brook et al., 1986; Jurich, Polson, Jurich, & Bates, 1985; McDermott, 1984; Shedler & Block, 1990). As would be expected, these features of negative climate in the homes of adolescents who become involved with drugs are similar to family relationship difficulties observed among young persons with a wide range of behavior problems discussed in several previous chapters.

In the course of their extensive investigations of adolescent substance use, Brook and her colleagues have found further that associated personality, peer, and parental factors can exert their influence independently of each other (Brook, Nomura, & Cohen, 1989a; Brook, Whiteman, & Gordon, 1983). As is the case whenever several different factors interact to shape some outcome, this finding has three important implications. First, the maximum likelihood of trying drugs or using them heavily arises when all three kinds of influence—personal, social, and family—coexist to a substantial extent. Second, a particularly strong influence of one kind or another may be sufficient to foster drug use even when the other influences are minimal. For example, heavy parental drug-taking and a very negative climate in the home can lead to drug use in adolescents who would otherwise not be personally oriented toward drugs and who are not experiencing much social influence in this direction. Similarly, a personal attraction to drugs and strong peer pressure can result in drug use even when parents are neither modeling drug use nor neglecting their parental responsibilities.

Third, especially positive influences of one kind or another can protect an otherwise high-risk adolescent from becoming involved with drugs. In some studies, for example, close and supportive parent–child relationships have appeared to inoculate young persons against being attracted to drugs even when they are immersed in a heavily drug-using peer culture. In other cases, protective factors in a positive school environment have been found to dissuade young persons from substance use even when drug-taking is common and accepted practice in their homes (Brook, Brook, Gordon, & Whiteman, 1990; Brook, Nomura, & Cohen, 1989a, 1989b; Marston, Jacobs, Singer, & Widaman, 1988).

Stage-Related Influences on Substance Use

Although most authorities concur that personal, social, and family factors each play a role in adolescents' beginning and continuing to use drugs, there are different opinions concerning the relative importance of these factors. Some researchers place particular emphasis on peer influences (Sarvella & McClendon, 1988; Swaim, Oetting, Edwards, & Beauvais, 1989), others are particularly attentive to parental influences (Johnson et al., 1984), and others stress the role that personal and psychopathological factors may play in promoting progressive drug involvement (Block et al., 1988). With respect to sorting out these alternatives, Kandel and her colleagues noted early in their work that personality, peer, parental influences on drug behavior differ in their impact at the three stages of hard liquor, marijuana, and hard drug use (Adler & Kandel, 1981; Kandel, Kessler, & Margulies, 1978).

Specifically, the cumulative data indicate that starting to use hard liquor is determined primarily by parental and peer influences and not very much by personality characteristics. Parental and peer influences for this stage of drug use carry about equal weight and are exerted in a similar way, through modeling effects. More than anything else, then, adolescents who start to drink hard liquor are imitating the behavior of important persons in their lives. Neither the quality of the parent–child relationship nor the parents' attitudes and values seem to have much influence at this stage.

Starting to use marijuana is more likely than the initiation into drinking to involve some of the personal factors associated with drug use. These include relatively liberal, nonconforming attitudes as well as believing that marijuana is a nonharmful substance that should be legalized. Young persons who begin using marijuana are also likely to have been frequent drinkers and to show some of the problems associated with drug use, such as minor delinquencies and relatively poor school performance. They are not especially likely to have serious psychological problems, however.

Beginning to use hard drugs is the stage most likely to involve serious personality problems. Hard-drug users will typically have a history of heavy or at least regular marijuana use, and they are especially likely to feel depressed and alienated and to be dealing unsuccessfully with a variety of situations in their lives. Often, the best friends of hard-drug users will also be heavily involved with drugs. As previously noted, however, by this stage of drug use, peers taking drugs together is much more a matter of convenience than influence. Adolescents who start to use hard drugs tend to be withdrawn or cut off from peer-group activities and well beyond the use of drugs for social purposes. Hence, peer-group influence in the general sense does not play a particularly important role in a young person's progressing to hard-drug use.

Parental influences, on the other hand, assume a major role at this last stage. Although the attitudes that parents hold toward hard drugs do not make much difference in whether their offspring use them, both the models they set and the quality of family life they provide do matter. Parental use of marijuana, cocaine, stimulants, and sedatives is an important predictor of adolescent initiation into drug use other than marijuana, as already noted. In addition, parental neglect and lack of close family relationships exert a strong influence on movement to this stage of drug-taking.

These stage-related differences confirm further how misleading it can be to make broad generalizations about aspects of youthful substance use. They also help to predict whether an adolescent who has begun to drink hard liquor will progress to other stages of drug use. In addition to the predictive significance of heavy drug use at a particular stage for progression to the following stage, movement from hard liquor to marijuana will be influenced primarily by peer involvements, and movement from marijuana to harder drugs will be influenced primarily by personal psychological problems and disturbed parent–child relationships.

Genetic Factors in Addiction

Along with the influence of personal, social, and family experiences on beginning and continuing to use drugs, accumulating evidence suggests that genetic factors contribute to the disposition to progress to problematic and addictive drug use. Alcoholism in particular has been found to run strongly in families, with children of alcoholics being about four times as likely to develop drinking problems as children of nonalcoholics (Marlatt et al., 1988). As in the case of demonstrable genetic influences on conditions discussed in previous chapters, studies of twins and adoptees indicate that this familial concordance cannot be attributed solely to shared experience or parental modeling.

In particular, among adults who have been placed for adoption at or soon after birth, alcoholism occurs significantly more frequently in those whose biological parents were problem drinkers than in those who have no history of heavy drinking in their biological relatives, independently of the drinking behavior of their adoptive parents. Because heavy drinking increases the likelihood that alcohol users will progress to stages of marijuana and hard drug use, any genetic influences on becoming addicted to alcohol can be expected to play a role in how frequently or heavily young persons become involved with these other drugs as well (Bohman, Sigvardsson, & Cloninger, 1981; Cadoret, Troughton, O'Gorman, & Heywood, 1986; Cloninger, Bohman, & Sigvardsson, 1981).

On the other hand, genetic studies of substance abuse have so far focused primarily on adults, and there are very few data concerning the heritability of addiction in young people (Rutter, Macdonald, Le Couteur, Harrington, Bolton, & Bailey, 1990). Moreover, the genetic disposition to alcoholism in some cases does not mean that drug addiction is primarily an inherited condition. To the contrary, there is as yet no consistent evidence of premorbid biological differences between people who become drug-dependent and those who do not, and approximately one half of adults who are hospitalized for alcoholism do not have any family drinking history (Alford, 1989; Goodwin, 1985; Searles, 1988). On the other hand, those alcoholics who do have problem drinkers among their biological relatives, compared to those without a family history, tend to have begun heavy drinking at an earlier age and then both to become more seriously impaired by their addiction and to respond less favorably to drug treatment programs (Frances, Timm, & Bucky, 1980; Goodwin, 1985; Marlatt et al., 1988). Hence, a genetic component may lead to a more serious form of alcoholism than results from personal or social difficulties alone, even though inherited characteristics are neither necessary nor sufficient for this condition to occur.

Coexisting Psychological Disorder in Substance Abuse

Medicinal and addictive drug-using adolescents can be expected, with few exceptions, to have a coexisting psychological disorder that requires evaluation and treatment in its own right. In clinical practice, this means that a diagnosis of substance use disorder by DSM-III-R criteria in a young person will ordinarily be accompanied by a dual diagnosis of some other distressing or problematic condition. Only rarely will an adolescent become a heavy drug user in the absence of psychological pain or coping inadequacies that have made adaptation without drugs unappealing or impossible.

Although virtually any kind of cognitive, affective, or behavioral disorder may be found in conjunction with substance-use disorder, two conditions in particular are likely to coexist with youthful drug abuse. One of these is depression, often involving suicidal ideation or tendencies and sometimes reflecting bipolar or borderline disorder (see Chapters 4 and 5). The other is delinquent behavior, often involving diagnosable conduct disorder with emerging antisocial personality formation (see Chapter 8). In clinical work with drug-abusing adolescents, depression and misconduct are as likely as the young person's drug history to have resulted in referral for professional help, and the chronicity and severity of these coexisting problems have considerable bearing on the prognosis for bringing the drug abuse under control. The following two cases illustrate these two common dual diagnoses in drug abuse.

CASE 18.   DRUG ABUSE WITH DEPRESSION

Ever since her parents divorced when she was age 8, Paula had been troubled by anxieties and nightmares that her father, who had moved to another city, would return to kidnap her and take her to live with him. Her father had been emotionally and physically abusive to her mother, her 7-years-older sister, and her 4-years-older brother prior to the divorce. His abuse had not been sexual and had not involved Paula, as far as was known, but her fears of his coming for her nevertheless included specific concerns that he would physically and sexually abuse her. Whether some wish fulfillment of being an object of her departed father's attention played a role in her apparently unjustified fears was an interesting aspect of this case that was never resolved.

At any rate, when she was 15 years old, Paula completed the ninth grade at a middle school and began tenth grade at a high school located in a different neighborhood. She had difficulty making friends in her new surrounds and felt lonely and alienated. Her mother was "tired and irritable most of the time," according to Paula, and "couldn't pay attention to my problems." Her brother was living at home but "never understood me," and her sister was now married and "into problems of her own." Paula's loneliness on top of her previous anxieties gradually mounted, her grades plummeted from a B average she had proudly maintained in the past, and her self-esteem went likewise into a tailspin. To ease her psychological pain she began to drink whenever she had the opportunity. A road to substance abuse had been well-paved in this family. Paula's father was a recovered alcoholic, her sister had had drug-related problems while in high school, and her brother was currently having difficulty controlling alcohol and drug use.

As Paula's problems worsened, she began to isolate herself in her room for long periods of time, to have fits of crying, to sleep poorly, to overeat and gain weight, and to think about killing herself. It took almost a year for her mother finally to appreciate the severity of Paula's difficulties and to seek help for her.

When first seen, Paula, now 16 and in the eleventh grade, reported that she had been drinking daily for several months "because I need it to hide behind when I feel bad." Yet the drinking made her feel even worse, she said, because it was a bad thing to do and she was a weak person for not being able to stop herself from doing it. Because of her suicidal ideation and self-depreciation ("I don't like myself very much," she said, "nothing about myself"), she was admitted to a short-term adolescent inpatient unit for evaluation and treatment planning.

During a brief hospitalization, Paula's depression lifted markedly in response to medication, psychotherapy, and family counseling. She took an active role in planning for continued therapy after discharge and for a reinvigorated social life that would free her from any further need to drown her sorrows. Paula's case illustrates the onset of medicinal drug abuse as an unwelcome necessity secondary to anxiety and depression, with a good prognosis for recovery if she could be helped to gain some perspective on her fears about her father and to draw strength from a supportive family and peer network.

CASE 19. DRUG ABUSE WITH CONDUCT DISORDER

Steven was 14 years old when his mother arranged against his wishes for him to be admitted to a psychiatric hospital. She gave the following reasons for taking this action: (a) Steven was becoming increasingly defiant and rebellious, beyond her capacity to control; (b) he was drinking alcohol and smoking marijuana regularly; (c) he was skipping school frequently and, despite having demonstrated superior intelligence on school evaluations, had received two Fs on a recent report card; and (d) as the last straw, he had been apprehended by the police for driving without a license and had been arrested for having drug paraphernalia in his possession.

Steven's mother initially reported that these conduct problems had emerged subsequent to two distressing events in the past 2 years. He had been involved in an automobile accident in which his best friend, sitting next to him in the car, had been killed, and his father, described by the mother as "a wonderful man who had a good relationship with his children," had died suddenly of a heart attack. As reported, these events might suggest underlying depression, perhaps with unresolved grief, as the source of Steven's problem behaviors. Additional information obtained from his mother as his hospitalization proceeded suggested otherwise, however.

First of all, it was learned from Steven's mother that he had always been a difficult child to manage. From early in life, he had shown little emotion, been unresponsive to punishment, and seemed determined to do things his own way even if he got into trouble as a result. When he was age 6, in fact, she had had him evaluated for his "poor attitude and behavior," and while he was still in elementary school, she had had problems with his stealing money from her purse. With regard to school, it turned out that he had always done marginal work, usually just enough to get promoted from one grade to the next but no more.

As for his ties to the friend killed in the accident, Steven's mother reported that he had always seemed to be popular, talking about many acquaintances and receiving frequent telephone calls, but that he had never had any really close friends. Even the possible impact of his father's dying was lessened by his mother's commenting that the father had not been nearly as close to Steven as to their other two children (an older sister and an older brother) and that Steven had not seemed to miss him as much as the other members of the family. Finally of note, the mother stated that she and her husband both "loved" marijuana and had used it regularly. Only within the past few months had she stopped using marijuana, when "It occurred to me that I might be setting a bad example."

As for Steven himself, he was a physically mature boy who looked several years older than his 14 years. Sullenness, resentment, and talking tough were his trademarks as a hospital patient, although he was usually willing to talk about himself as long as no one took exception to what he was saying. He freely admitted getting high almost every weekend on beer or marijuana and occasionally using hallucinogens as well. Why did he do this? "I like to get high," he said, "and I like to fight, too, because it's cool to get into fights." Steven stated his opinions concerning his habitual drug with similar clarity: There was nothing wrong with taking drugs, he said, using drugs was not causing him any problems, he had no desire to get off drugs, and he would start drinking beer and smoking pot as soon as possible after leaving the hospital.

Regarding the hospital, Steven viewed his admission much as a prison sentence and saw his unit as a place of detention. Like an unrepentant felon doing time, he seemed intent on proving he could endure incarceration. If he kept out of trouble, his term would end, he would be released, and he would be free without further interference to return to his preferred way of life.

Steven's long history of misconduct and apparently distant interpersonal relatedness suggested that his current problems, including his drug abuse, were associated with an emerging antisocial personality disorder rather than any acute or ego-alien reaction to disturbing events of the recent past. His total acceptance of his drug involvement and his disinterest in modifying his drug use were consistent with this impression of characterological difficulties, as was his negative attitude toward participating in a treatment program. These circumstances indicated that only long-term residential care in a drug treatment unit would offer prospects for altering his perspectives on using drugs and relating to people, and an appropriate placement was made.

TREATMENT AND PREVENTION

As is generally the case in considering intervention for possibly problematic behavior, treatment planning for adolescents who use drugs should begin with a careful differential diagnosis among the four categories of substance use identified earlier. Adolescents who are experimental or social drug users rarely require treatment. Typically, they either stop using drugs of their own accord or use them infrequently in ways that do not interfere with their psychosocial functioning and do not constitute psychopathology.

Medicinal and addictive use of drugs by young persons, on the other hand, are very likely to compromise normal development and call for professional intervention. When people reach the point of valuing a drug experience as a way of escaping or altering their thoughts and feelings, they have become drug abusers and have developed a psychological disorder. Likewise, when people have become habituated to an intoxicating substance and become dependent on it to sustain their mental and physical well-being, they have developed a psychologically debilitating condition from which recovery is usually a long and painful process requiring sensitive and sophisticated help from others.

Among adolescents considered to be abusing drugs, the demonstrated role of personal, social, and family factors in leading to heavy drug use provides some general guidelines in formulating treatment strategies. In particular, it is reasonable to assume that some psychological concerns or dissatisfactions, some strained or untowardly influential peer relationships, and some incohesiveness or drug-modeling behavior in the family have contributed to a young person's having begun to use drugs and progressing to a stage of self-medication or drug dependence. Accordingly, successful intervention for drug abuse requires a multifaceted treatment approach that relieves psychological distress, promotes positive and supportive peer networks, and fosters a nurturant climate in the home. Should there be obstacles to change that prevent these three treatment aims from being realized, they will more often than not prevent a drug-abusing adolescent from achieving or sustaining a drug-free existence. More specific strategies that are likely to prove effective in treating substance abuse differ with respect to whether the drug-abusing pattern is medicinal or addictive.

Treating Medicinal Drug Abuse

Because medicinal drug abusers are typically struggling to enliven pallid life experiences or to avoid painful ones, they often respond well to individual or group psychotherapy aimed at easing their disappointments and tensions and helping them to find more effective ways of coping with situations that are causing them to feel depressed or anxious. As in the case of other behavior problems that are secondary to psychological concerns, such as passive-aggressive underachievement (see Chapter 7) and neurotic delinquency (see Chapter 8), some resolution of the underlying concerns offers good prospects for reducing the problem behavior by reducing its basic source.

Nevertheless, whatever the intensity of a medicinal drug abuser's underlying concerns, the clinician should not expect him or her to come into therapy any more eagerly than the typical passive–aggressive underachiever or neurotic delinquent. Adolescents who are self-medicating with drugs will usually be seen by a mental health professional only after having been cajoled or coerced into an office visit or hospital admission. As involuntary patients, they often deny having any problems, explain that they "are just doing what all the other kids are doing," and assure the therapist that they could stop using drugs any time they wanted to. As noted in this regard by Sbriglio, Hartman, Millman, and Khuri (1988), there is no little risk that adolescent substance abusers will bring off such a charade, because often they are more knowledgeable than their would-be therapists about drugs, drug subcultures, and drug-related behaviors.

In the face of such assurances from medicinal drug abusers, clinicians should keep firmly in mind that self-medication is always associated with psychological distress and adjustment difficulties, that substance abuse is most definitely not what all young people are doing, and that use of drugs to ease persistent pain is much more likely to be out of control than under it. Confronting self-medicating adolescents with these facts to overcome initial resistance to treatment should be employed only after gentler and more supportive strategies have proven unsuccessful, however. An initial interview will typically have been preceded by some period of time during which these reluctant patients have received criticism from many different quarters. Meeting with a stranger who represents authority and the mental health profession will be stressful enough, without the therapist becoming still one more disapproving adversary.

Hence, a supportive approach, in which the therapist accepts the adolescent as he or she is and proposes only that they talk a bit about what is going on in the young person's life is a preferable way to begin. Once such a supportive, accepting, and nonjudgmental beginning is made, self-medicating adolescents often can proceed fairly quickly to touch on matters of concern with which they need and want help, and the seeds of a workable treatment relationship are thus sown.

Successful engagement in psychotherapy and progress toward resolving psychological concerns rarely proves sufficient by itself to curtail medicinal drug abuse, however. Although self-medication can be conceptualized and treated largely as an instance of individual psychopathology, the treatment plan should also take into account the likelihood that a drug-abusing adolescent's parents have contributed to the problem by setting a drug-using example, failing to provide proper discipline, or having difficulty maintaining a cohesive and supportive family environment. As much as seems indicated and feasible, then, therapy for youthful drug abusers should include counseling for their parents, to encourage them to control their own substance use, take a strong and explicit stand against drug-taking, and modify any inclinations they may have to be too lax or too strict in their childrearing practices. In addition, family sessions should be used, along with individual therapy, to prevent drug abusers' parents from minimizing the seriousness of their child's problem and to foster improved parent–child communication and a more congenial home life.

Together with recognizing the necessity of parental involvement, therapists need to keep in mind that families are often found to share with their adolescent members some resistance to becoming engaged in a drug treatment program (Kaufman, 1985; Szapocznik, Perez-Vidal, Brickman, Foote, Santisteban, Hervis, & Kurtines, 1988). Some families, in establishing patterns of relating to a substance abuser in their midst, will have created a homeostasis that resists change. In these instances, giving up familiar even though often unpleasant patterns of family interaction without knowing in advance what their new patterns of interaction will be like may seem not to be worth the risk. At other times, a drug-abusing adolescent, like offspring with other kinds of behavior problems, will have become a scapegoat to whom family difficulties can be attributed and whose improvement or recovery would deprive other family members of ready rationalizations for their own contributions to family problems. Hence therapists intent on addressing family difficulties that have fostered or are sustaining an adolescent's drug abuse must be prepared first to address family patterns that are likely to discourage change and to limit effective engagement in treatment.

Research examining the effectiveness of various approaches to treating medicinal drug abuse is very limited. What few studies there are tend to confirm that involving families enhances the impact of treatment programs. Prognosis for a successful outcome is also more favorable for adolescent drug abusers when they are able to continue in therapy longer, have remained in school, were older when they first began to abuse drugs, and have avoided becoming multiple drug abusers (Davidge & Forman, 1988; Lewis, Piercy, Sprenkle, & Trepper, 1990; Newcomb & Bentler, 1989). There is also some evidence that the more that adolescents are more consciously aware of their problems and the more concerned they are about the psychological pain for which they are medicating themselves, the more self-revealing, trusting, and motivated they will be on entering therapy and the more benefit they will derive from it (Friedman & Glickman, 1987).

A final interesting question to consider is whether self-medicating adolescents need to be treated in an inpatient setting. In most cases, medicinal drug users can participate effectively in outpatient psychotherapy, especially if they are prepared to be forthcoming about the disappointments and anxieties they are experiencing and if their parents can be meaningfully engaged in the treatment program. On the other hand, the more close-mouthed a drug-abusing adolescent is and the more serious his or her comorbid condition appears to be, the more necessary it may be to consider hospital admission. Inpatient care is especially likely to be well-advised for medicinal drug users who are depressed to the point of contemplating suicide, who are angry or impulsive to the point of constituting a threat to the physical safety of others, or who lack a strong family commitment to their well-being.

Treating Addictive Drug Abuse

Unlike medicinal drug use, which emerges secondarily to other psychological concerns, addiction to drugs has typically become a primary disorder in its own right. As a habitual pattern, coalesced into a way of life and no longer a reaction specific to currently distressing circumstances, drug addiction poses many of the same obstacles to effective intervention as do other characterological disorders. Even more so than self-medicating young persons, drug-addicted adolescents tend to deny needing any psychological help and to resist a close relationship with a therapist. Office visits rarely prove sufficient to influence changes in what has become a customary life-style for the drug-dependent adolescent. For this reason, successful treatment of addictive drug use is widely believed to require a residential setting in which a therapeutic environment can be provided over an extended period of time (Alford, 1989; de Leon, 1988; Friedman, Glickman, & Morrissey, 1986; Meeks, 1988).

Clinical and research reports also help to identify some guiding principles for conducting inpatient treatment with drug-dependent adolescents (Barrett, Simpson, & Lehman, 1988; Cox & Klinger, 1988; Horan & Straus, 1987; King & Meeks, 1988). First, behavior shaping should take precedence over promoting understanding, at least initially. There is little reason to expect that learning more about themselves or why they came to be drug dependent will influence adolescents to change their life-style. Instead, the best prospects for modifying drug dependence are to be found in reinforcement strategies that make the positive consequences of getting off drugs more rewarding than any positive effects of continuing to use them.

This particular emphasis draws on the frequent finding that positive reinforcement of desirable behaviors carries more weight than negative reinforcement of undesirable behaviors. Often from the media, and sometimes from professionals as well, youthful drug abusers are subjected to scare messages concerning the terrible things that drugs do to you, such as destroying your mind. Experience indicates that adolescents who have become dependent on drugs are less likely to heed such avoidance messages than they are to listen to approach messages that emphasize opportunities for satisfaction and success that will be available to them if they can become drug-free. Adolescents who are encouraged to consider the good things that can happen to them if they stop abusing drugs will show a more favorable response to intervention than those that are chastened with the bad things that will happen to them if they continue to abuse drugs.

A second principle in working with drug-dependent adolescents is that abstinence is not enough. An addicted adolescent's decision to get off drugs and his or her initial success in doing so is a step in the right direction, but this first step provides little protection against relapse. For abstinence to persist, it must be accompanied by immersion in a satisfying drug-free life-style that includes adequate academic and social functioning. Stopping drug use does not automatically produce or restore age-appropriate intellectual, cognitive, social, and emotional functioning. To achieve this end, a variety of treatment approaches may need to be utilized to supplement the original drug-focused strategies, including academic remediation, social skills training, psychotherapy addressed to a broad range of personal concerns and adjustment difficulties, and engagement in such self-help groups as Alcoholics Anonymous and Narcotics Anonymous. To help a drug-addicted adolescent opt for a different life-style, in other words, a treatment program must help him or her to build one.

Third, to help sustain adolescents in a drug-free life-style, supportive family and peer networks must be cultivated. Like psychotherapy, family counseling and peer planning do not have the same initially significant role in treating addictive drug use as they do in alleviating medicinal drug use. However, once an addicted adolescent has made a commitment to attempt abstinence, adequate support from family and friends is almost always essential to his or her remaining off drugs. Accordingly, as treatment progresses, parents should be counseled to reward in every reasonable and possible way both curtailed drug use and efforts to establish a successful life-style. Similarly, everything possible should be done to increase the adolescent's degree of involvement with academically and socially successful non-drug-using peers, while decreasing their contact with friends who have drug-related problems.

Preventing Substance Abuse

Successful treatment of substance abuse is a fragile fabric, difficult to knit together from its diverse personal, family, and social origins and then difficult to keep from coming unraveled. Especially for abusers who have become drug dependent, prospects for recovery without relapse, even after appropriate treatment, are uncertain at best. As is so often the case with chronic disorders, then, the best way to treat substance abuse is to prevent it from occurring in the first place.

With this in mind, enormous resources have been poured into drug-prevention programs over the past 20 years or so. Only recently, however, have lessons learned from the frequent failure of these programs begun to shape preventive methods that offer some promise of being effective.

Drug-prevention efforts began with the expectation that adolescents who are informed about the hazards of using drugs will keep away from them. Despite the sensibility of this rationale, no consistent evidence has ever emerged that participating in a drug education program deters adolescents from using drugs. To the contrary, some investigators have found that providing young people with information about drugs may contribute to their becoming more rather than less involved with them (Bangert-Drowns, 1988; Fialkov, 1989; Goodstadt, 1980).

However, it would be unwarranted to conclude that drug education does more harm than good. Hindsight suggests instead that drug-education programs for adolescents may frequently have failed because they were too little and too late. Giving high school students facts about drugs, at an age when drug use is already well underway for most of those who will subsequently have drug-related problems, cannot be expected to pack much preventive wallop. Similarly, moralistic preaching or scare tactics aimed at teenagers, when their value systems have already been largely shaped by family and peer influences, cannot be expected to find receptive ears. On this basis, drug education in the schools has gradually been shifted to the lower grades, and more attention has been paid to the previously noted advantage of emphasizing the benefits of avoiding drugs rather than the hazards of using them.

Whether such modifications will improve the effectiveness of drug-education programs remains to be seen.

In the meantime, the initial failure of drug-education programs led clinicians and counselors to try supplementing or replacing these programs with exercises in social development and community participation. The rationale for this approach was the belief that because social alienation and personal incompetence are high risk factors for drug abuse, training in social skills and problem-solving strategies, combined with involvement in community recreation activities, would reduce drug involvement. Like the initial efforts at drug education, however, these personal enhancement programs have not shown evidence of being sufficiently powerful to curtail drug abuse (Beaulieu & Jason, 1988; Fialkov, 1989; Tobler, 1986).

On the other hand, recent efforts to increase the potency of these psychosocial approaches to drug-abuse prevention are beginning to show some promise. Instead of addressing social skills in general, these approaches focus specifically on training young people to cope effectively with the determinants of drug abuse. Most important in this regard is helping adolescents become sufficiently assertive and decisive to resist social influences to become drug-abusive and to be able to say "No" to drugs (Fialkov, 1989; Horan & Straus, 1987; Killen, 1985).

In addition, contemporary approaches emphasize that helping adolescents to build specific cognitive and behavioral abilities for avoiding substance involvement, such as being able to resist social pressure, addresses only one component of societal drug problems, the "host." In addition, just as in efforts to treat drug abuse, attempts to prevent it need to address the two other components of "environment" and "agent" (Newcomb & Bentler, 1989; Schinke & Gilchrist, 1985). Regarding the environment, steps must be taken to promote a climate in a young person's home and community that fosters, supports, and rewards nonabusive behavior. As for the agent of abuse, the fact remains, finally, that psychosocial efforts to prevent substance abuse will be more or less successful in relation to the effectiveness of civil efforts to keep drugs out of the hands of young people.

REFERENCES

Adler, I., & Kandel, D. B. (1981). Cross-cultural perspectives on developmental stages in adolescent drug use. *Journal of Studies on Alcohol, 42*, 701–715.

Alford, G. S. (1989). Psychoactive substance use disorders. In L. K. G. Hsu & M. Hersen (Eds.), *Recent developments in adolescent psychiatry* (pp. 310–331). New York: Wiley.

Andrucci, G. L., Archer, R. P., Pancoast, D. L., & Gordon, R. A. (1989). The relationship of MMPI and sensation seeking scales to adolescent drug use. *Journal of Personality Assessment, 53*, 253–266.

Bachman, J. G., O'Malley, P. M., & Johnston, L. D. (1984). Drug use among young adults: The impacts of role status and social environment. *Journal of Personality and Social Psychology, 47,* 629-645.

Bangert-Drowns, R. L. (1988). The effects of school-based substance abuse education: A meta-analysis. *Journal of Drug Education, 18,* 243-264.

Barnes, G. M. (1984). Adolescent alcohol abuse and other problem behaviors: Their relationships and common parental influences. *Journal of Youth and Adolescence, 13,* 329-348.

Barnes, G. M., & Welte, J. W. (1986). Adolescent alcohol abuse: Subgroup differences and relationships to other problem behaviors. *Journal of Adolescent Research, 1,* 79-94.

Barrett, M. E., Simpson, D. D., & Lehman, W. E. (1988). Behavioral changes of adolescents in drug abuse intervention programs. *Journal of Clinical Psychology, 44,* 461-473.

Beaulieu, M. A., & Jason, L. A. (1988). A drug abuse prevention program aimed at teaching seventh grade students problem-solving strategies. *Children and Youth Services Review, 10,* 131-149.

Bentler, P. M. (1987). Drug use and personality in adolescence and young adulthood: Structural models with nonnormal variables. *Child Development, 58,* 65-79.

Block, J., Block, J. H., & Keyes, S. (1988). Longitudinally foretelling drug usage in adolescence: Early childhood personality and environmental precursors. *Child Development, 59,* 336-355.

Bohman, M., Sigvardsson, S., & Cloninger, R. C. (1981). Maternal inheritance of alcohol abuse: Cross-fostering analysis of adopted women. *Archives of General Psychiatry, 38,* 965-969.

Brook, J. S., Brook, D. W., Gordon, A. S., & Whiteman, M. (1990). The psychosocial etiology of adolescent drug use: A family interactional approach. *Genetic, Social, and General Psychology Monographs, 116,* 111-267.

Brook, J. S., Gordon, A. S., Brook, A., & Brook, D. W. (1989). The consequences of marijuana use on intrapersonal and interpersonal functioning in black and white adolescents. *Genetic, Social, & General Psychology Monographs, 115,* 349-369.

Brook, J. S., Gordon, A. S., & Whiteman, M. (1986). Stability of personality during adolescence and its relationship to stage of drug use. *Genetic, Social, & General Psychology Monographs, 111,* 317-330.

Brook, J. S., Lukoff, I. F., & Whiteman, M. (1980). Initiation into adolescent marijuana use. *Journal of Genetic Psychology, 137,* 133-142.

Brook, J. S., Nomura, C., & Cohen, P. (1989a). A network of influences on adolescent drug involvement: Neighborhood, school, peer, and family. *Genetic, Social, & General Psychology Monographs, 115,* 125-145.

Brook, J. S., Nomura, C., & Cohen P. (1989b). Prenatal, perinatal, and early childhood risk factors and drug involvement in adolescence. *Genetic, Social, & General Psychology Monographs, 115,* 221-241.

Brook, J. S., Whiteman, M., & Gordon, A. S. (1983). Stages of drug use in adolescence: Personality, peer, and family correlates. *Developmental Psychology, 19,* 269-277.

Brook, J. S., Whiteman, M., Gordon, A. S., & Cohen, P. (1986). Some models and mechanisms for explaining the impact of maternal and adolescent characteristics on adolescent stage of drug use. *Developmental Psychology, 22,* 460–467.

Burke, K. C., Burke, J. D., Regier, D. A., & Rae, D. S. (1990). Age at onset of selected mental disorders in five community populations. *Archives of General Psychiatry, 47,* 511–518.

Buydens-Branchey, L., Branchey, M. H., & Noumair, D. (1989). Age of alcoholism onset: I. Relationship to psychopathology. *Archives of General Psychiatry, 46,* 225–230.

Cadoret, R. J., Troughton, T. W., O'Gorman, T. W., & Heywood, E. (1986). An adoption study of genetic and environmental factors in drug abuse. *Archives of General Psychiatry, 43,* 1131–1136.

Chassin, L., McLaughlin, L. M., & Sher, K. J. (1988). Self-awareness theory, family history of alcoholism, and adolescent alcohol involvement. *Journal of Abnormal Psychology, 97,* 206–217.

Christiansen, B. A., Smith, G. T., Roehling, P. V., & Goldman, M. S. (1989). Using alcohol expectancies to predict adolescent drinking behavior after one year. *Journal of Consulting and Clinical Psychology, 57,* 93–99.

Christopherson, B. B., Jones, R. M., & Sales, A. P. (1988). Diversity in reported motivations for substance use as a function of ego-identity development. *Journal of Adolescent Research, 3,* 141–152.

Cloninger, R. C., Bohman, M., & Sigvardsson, S. (1981). Inheritance of alcohol abuse: Cross-fostering analysis of adult men. *Archives of General Psychiatry, 38,* 861–868.

Cox, W. M., & Klinger, E. (1988). A motivational model of alcohol use. *Journal of Abnormal Psychology, 97,* 168–180.

Davidge, A. M., & Forman, S. G. (1988). Psychological treatment of adolescent substance abusers: A review. *Child and Youth Services Review, 10,* 43–53.

de Leon, G. (1988). The therapeutic community perspective and approach for adolescent substance abusers. In S. C. Feinstein (Ed.), *Adolescent psychiatry* (Vol. 15, pp. 535–556). Chicago: University of Chicago Press.

Donovan, J. E., Jessor, R., & Costa, F. M. (1988). Syndrome of problem behavior in adolescence: A replication. *Journal of Consulting and Clinical Psychology, 56,* 762–765.

Engs, R. C. (1977). Drinking patterns and drinking problems of college students. *Journal of Studies on Alcohol, 38,* 2144–2156.

Engs, R. C., & Hanson, D. J. (1983, January 19), Drinking patterns and drinking problems of college students: 1983. *Chronicle of Higher Education,* p. 9.

Fialkov, M. J. (1989). Substance use disorders. In C. G. Last & M. Hersen (Eds.), *Child psychiatric diagnosis* (pp. 356–387). New York: Wiley.

Frances, R. J., Timme, S., & Bucky, S. (1980). Studies of familial and nonfamilial alcoholism. *Archives of General Psychiatry, 37,* 564–566.

Friedman, A. S., & Glickman, N. W. (1987). Effects of psychiatric symptomatology on treatment outcome for adolescent male drug abusers. *Journal of Nervous & Mental Disease, 175,* 425–430.

Friedman, A. S., Glickman, N. W., & Morrissey, M. R. (1986). Prediction of successful treatment outcome by client characteristics and retention in treatment in adolescent drug treatment programs: A large-scale cross-validation. *Journal of Drug Education, 16*, 149–165.

Goodstadt, M. S. (1980). Drug education—A turn on or a turn off? *Journal of Drug Education, 10*, 89–99.

Goodwin, D. W. (1985). Alcoholism and genetics. *Archives of General Psychiatry, 42*, 171–174.

Hanson, D. J. (1977). Trends in drinking attitudes and behaviors among college students. *Journal of Alcohol and Drug Education, 22*, 17–22.

Henly, G. A., & Winters, K. C. (1988). Development of problem severity scales for the assessment of adolescent alcohol and drug abuse. *International Journal of the Addictions, 23*, 65–85.

Horan, J. J., & Straus, L. K. (1987). Substance abuse. In M. Hersen & V. B. Van Hasselt (Eds.), *Behavior therapy with children and adolescents* (pp. 440–464). New York: Wiley.

Huba, G. J., & Bentler, P. M. (1980). The role of peer and adult models for drug taking at different stages in adolescence. *Journal of Youth and Adolescence, 9*, 449–465.

Johnson, G. M., Shontz, F. C., & Locke, T. P. (1984). Relationships between adolescent drug use and parental drug behaviors. *Adolescence, 19*, 295–299.

Johnston, L. D., O'Malley, P. M., & Bachman, J. G. (1987a). *National trends in drug use and related factors among American high school students and young adults, 1975–1986.* Washington, DC: National Institute on Drug Abuse.

Johnston, L. D., O'Malley, P. M., & Bachman, J. G. (1987b). Psychotherapeutic, licit, and illicit use of drugs among adolescents. *Journal of Adolescent Health Care, 8*, 36–51.

Jones, R. M., & Hartmann, B. R. (1988). Ego identity: Developmental differences and experimental substance abuse among adolescents. *Journal of Adolescence, 11*, 347–360.

Jurich, A. P., Polson, C. J., Jurich, J. A., & Bates, R. A. (1985). Family factors in the lives of drug users and abusers. *Adolescence, 20*, 143–159.

Kandel, D. B. (1975). Stages in adolescent involvement in drug use. *Science, 190*, 912–914.

Kandel, D. B. (1984). Marijuana users in young adulthood. *Archives of General Psychiatry, 41*, 200–209.

Kandel, D. B., Davies, M., Karus, D., & Yamaguchi, K. (1986). The consequences in young adulthood of adolescent drug involvement. *Archives of General Psychiatry, 43*, 746–754.

Kandel, D., & Faust, R. (1975). Sequence and stages in patterns of adolescent drug use. *Archives of General Psychiatry, 32*, 923–932.

Kandel, D. B., Kessler, R. C., & Margulies, R. Z. (1978). Antecedents of adolescent initiation into stages of drug use: A developmental analysis. *Journal of Youth and Adolescence, 7*, 13–40.

Kandel, D. B., & Raveis, V. H. (1989). Cessation of illicit drug use in young adulthood. *Archives of General Psychiatry, 46*, 109–116.

Kaufman, E. (1985). Adolescent substance abusers and family therapy. In M. P.

Mirkin & S. L. Koman (Eds.), *Handbook of adolescents and family therapy* (pp. 245–254). New York: Gardner Press.

Killen, J. D. (1985). Prevention of adolescent tobacco smoking: The social pressure resistance training approach. *Journal of Child Psychology and Psychiatry, 26,* 7–15.

King, J. W., & Meeks, J. E. (1988). Hospital programs for psychiatrically disturbed, drug-abusing adolescents. In S. C. Feinstein (Ed.), *Adolescent psychiatry* (Vol. 15, pp. 522–534). Chicago: University of Chicago Press.

Kovach, J. A., & Glickman, N. W. (1986). Levels and psychosocial correlates of adolescent drug use. *Journal of Youth and Adolescence, 15,* 61–77.

Lewis, R. A., Piercy, F. P., Sprenkle, D. H., & Trepper, T. S. (1990). Family-based interventions for helping drug-abusing adolescents. *Journal of Adolescent Research, 5,* 82–95.

Marlatt, G. A., Baer, J. S., Donovan, D. M., & Kivlahan, D. R. (1988). Addictive behavior: Etiology and treatment. *Annual Review of Psychology, 39,* 223–252.

Marston, A. R., Jacobs, D. F., Singer, R. D., & Widaman, K. F. (1988). Adolescents who apparently are invulnerable to drug, alcohol, and nicotine use. *Adolescence, 23,* 593–598.

McDermott, D. (1984). The relationship of parental drug use and parents' attitude concerning adolescent drug use to adolescent drug use. *Adolescence, 19,* 89–97.

Meeks, J. E. (1988). Adolescent chemical dependency. In S. C. Feinstein (Ed.), *Adolescent psychiatry* (Vol. 15, pp. 509–521). Chicago: University of Chicago Press.

Mills, C. J., & Noyes, H. L. (1984). Patterns and correlates of initial and subsequent drug use among adolescents. *Journal of Consulting and Clinical Psychology, 52,* 231–243.

Morgan, M., & Grube, J. W. (1989). Adolescent cigarette smoking: A developmental analysis of influences. *British Journal of Developmental Psychology, 7,* 179–189.

National Institute on Drug Abuse (1989). *National household survey on drug abuse: Population estimates, 1988.* Rockville, MD: Author.

Newcomb, M. D., & Bentler, P. M. (1987). Changes in drug use from high school to young adulthood: Effects of living arrangements and current life pursuit. *Journal of Applied Developmental Psychology, 8,* 221–246.

Newcomb, M. D., & Bentler, P. M. (1988). Impact of adolescent drug use and social support on problems of young adults: A longitudinal study. *Journal of Abnormal Psychology, 97,* 64–75.

Newcomb, M. D., & Bentler, P. M. (1989). Substance use and abuse among children and teenagers. *American Psychologist, 44,* 242–248.

Rees, C. D., & Wilborn, B. L. (1983). Correlates of drug abuse in adolescents: A comparison of families of drug abusers with families of nondrug abusers. *Journal of Youth and Adolescence, 12,* 55–64.

Rutter, M., Macdonald, H., Le Couteur, A., Harrington, R., Bolton, P., & Bailey, A. (1990). Genetic factors in child psychiatric disorders: II. Empirical findings. *Journal of Child Psychology and Psychiatry, 31,* 39–83.

Sarvella, P. D., & McClendon, E. J. (1988). Indicators of rural youth drug use. *Journal of Youth and Adolescence, 17,* 335-348.

Sbriglio, R., Hartman, N., Millman, R. B., & Khuri, E. T. (1988). Drug and alcohol abuse in children and adolescents. In C. J. Kestenbaum & D. T. Williams (Eds.), *Handbook of clinical assessment of children and adolescents* (Vol. II, pp. 915-937). New York: New York University Press.

Schinke, S. P., & Gilchrist, L. D. (1985). Preventing substance abuse with children and adolescents. *Journal of Consulting and Clinical Psychology, 53,* 596-602.

Schuckit, M. A., & Russell, J. W. (1983). Clinical importance of age at first drink in a group of young men. *American Journal of Psychiatry, 140,* 1221-1223.

Searles, J. S. (1988). The role of genetics in the pathogenesis of alcoholism. *Journal of Abnormal Psychology, 97,* 153-167.

Shedler, J., & Block, J. (1990). Adolescent drug use and psychological health. *American Psychologist, 45,* 612-630.

Swaim, R. C., Oetting, E. R., Edwards, R. W., & Beauvais, F. (1989). Links from emotional distress to adolescent drug use: A path model. *Journal of Consulting and Clinical Psychology, 57,* 227-231.

Szapocznik, J., Perez-Vidal, A., Brickman, A. L., Foote, F. H., Santisteban, D., Hervis, O., & Kurtines, W. M. (1988). Engaging adolescent drug abusers and their families in treatment: A strategic structural systems approach. *Journal of Consulting and Clinical Psychology 56,* 552-557.

Tobler, N. S. (1986). Meta-analysis of 143 adolescent drug prevention programs: Quantitative outcome results of program participants compared to a control or comparison group. *Journal of Drug Issues, 16,* 537-568.

West, M. O., & Prinz, R. J. (1987). Parental alcoholism and childhood psychopathology. *Psychological Bulletin, 102,* 204-218.

Yamaguchi, K., & Kandel, D. B. (1984). Patterns of drug use from adolescence to young adulthood: III. Prediction of progression. *American Journal of Public Health, 74,* 673-681.

CHAPTER 11

Psychotherapy

Psychotherapy with disturbed adolescents is a demanding task that is sought by some clinicians, approached with trepidation by many, and avoided by most. The reluctance of otherwise skilled therapists to grapple with adolescent problems is well-known to practitioners in the field, as is the limited number of professionals in most communities who work competently with this age group.

The difficulty of treating troubled teenagers has been noted over the years even by clinicians distinguished for their contributions to adolescent psychotherapy. Anna Freud (1958, p. 261) described the analytic treatment of adolescents as "a hazardous venture from beginning to end." Josselyn (1971, p. 172) regarded therapy with adolescents as "the most challenging of all therapies." According to Meeks (1980, p. 4), "Adolescent patients can be very frustrating . . . At times it even appears that the young patient is more intent on making the therapist miserable than on using his help." Laufer and Laufer (1984, p. xi) comment as follows:

> A large part of the professional community remains hesitant to treat [psychologically disturbed] adolescents. To some extent, this reluctance . . . can be understood as part of the historical caution or uncertainty in applying psychoanalytic and psychiatric views to a period of psychological development that is characterized by changes of body and mind of such a magnitude that they might make our work unpredictable at best and dangerous at worst.

As counterpoint to caution and uncertainty in treating teenagers, the developmental characteristics of adolescence make young people rather uniquely accessible to psychological interventions. Compared to children, adolescents are more likely to possess sophisticated capacities to think about themselves, express their feelings, understand other people, and take responsibility for their actions. Compared to adults, they are less likely to suffer from crystallized psychopathology or chronic personality warps, and they are also freer from current obligations that restrict them from taking their lives in new directions.

Hence, despite whatever challenges and hazards it may entail, working with adolescents to help them overcome psychological disturbances and achieve positive behavior change can be a fruitful and rewarding endeavor. Professionals who understand adolescents and are adept at engaging these young persons in a psychotherapeutic relationship can often make a big difference in their lives.

In turn, adolescents who need professional help are generally able to derive considerable benefit from it. Research studies indicate that about 75% of adolescents who participate in individual, group, or family therapy show a positive outcome (Tramontana, 1980). Outcome research with children and adolescents combined has demonstrated similarly that the average young person who receives some form of dynamic, client-centered, behavioral, or cognitive-behavioral therapy is better off at the end of treatment than 76–79% of young people from similar populations who do not receive treatment (Casey & Berman, 1985; Weisz, Weiss, Alicke, & Klotz, 1987). Taken together, the available data confirm not only that psychotherapy is more effective than no treatment in alleviating the psychological difficulties of young people but also that children and adolescents are just about as likely as adults to profit from psychotherapy (Kazdin, 1990).

However, the treatment of adolescents usually requires frames of reference different from those that guide work with either children or adults. Most child patients are brought to psychotherapy by their parents, without having participated in the decision to seek help, and most have little sense of the professional identity and role of the therapist. Child therapists may offer their young patients such explanations as, "This is a place where we try to help children who are having problems in school," or "Your parents wanted me to see you because they're worried that you aren't getting along with your friends very well." Even so, child patients are more typically engaged through games, storytelling, and other indirect or metaphorical activities than through direct discussion of the referral problem. They rarely comprehend the purpose of coming for regular visits, and they usually relate to the therapist much as to a benign and understanding parent.

Adult patients, by contrast, ordinarily come voluntarily for help with matters of concern to them and participate in psychotherapy through talking about themselves and their problems. Even so-called involuntary patients whose treatment is being mandated by someone else have made their own decision to appear for sessions rather than suffer some sanction with which they are being threatened, such as dissolution of a marriage or revocation of a suspended sentence. In further contrast to children, most adults understand that the treatment situation is a cooperative endeavor intended to discuss and resolve their personal difficulties. Additionally, no matter how little they know about the procedures of psychotherapy, they recognize that being in treatment identifies them in the minds of others as a person with mental or emotional problems who is receiving professional help.

Adolescents are in a transitional point in the life cycle in which they "are no longer a child; not yet an adult" (Kimmel & Weiner, 1985, Chapter 1). Most adolescents are too old to accept the therapist as a substitute parent and too mature to put up with indirect techniques that have no obvious purpose. Most have become too worldly to be oblivious to the implications of being taken to see a "shrink," about which they typically feel anxious, angry, and embarrassed. Hence, the time is past when a therapist can engage them effectively with activities or by conducting sessions as if there were any reason for the sessions other than dealing with the adolescent's psychological problems. Few things offend or humiliate adolescents more than being treated as if they were children.

Treating adolescent patients as if they were adults rarely solves this problem, however. Most troubled teenagers are still too young to have made an independent decision about whether to seek psychological help and too immature to recognize the extent of their problems. Not having sought help voluntarily and often not feeling any need for it, adolescents rarely come any more prepared than children to talk about themselves with a total stranger, professionally qualified or not. Hence, efforts to engage them in the verbally spontaneous and cooperatively exploratory conversations that characterize psychotherapy with adults are unlikely to have much success.

In addition to recognizing these ways in which adolescents differ from children and adults, therapists need to gear their approach to the particular developmental level of each individual patient. The younger and less mature adolescents are, the more frequently their treatment can be enhanced by incorporating features of child therapy; the older and the more mature they are, they more likely they are to respond positively to therapy resembling treatment of an adult with similar problems.

With the developmental status of young people as backdrop, this chapter addresses several key aspects of conducting psychotherapy with disturbed adolescents. These include determining the depth and goals of the treatment, initiating the patient–therapist interaction, building the treatment relationship, arranging for termination, and working with parents. The strategies elaborated in the discussion do not transcend any of the specific guidelines for treating schizophrenic, depressed, borderline, anxious, underachieving, delinquent, suicidal, or substance-abusing young people presented in Chapters 3 through 10. Rather, they supplement these previous treatment recommendations by indicating ways of conducting psychotherapy whenever it is part of a treatment plan.

Whereas the treatment recommendations in Chapters 3–10 touch on many different modalities, this last chapter on psychotherapy is written from the perspective of individual, dynamically oriented outpatient treatment. This perspective was chosen for three reasons. First, it is the approach with which the author is most familiar. Second, principles of dynamic psychotherapy are helpful in designing and understanding the impact of a wide range of treatment methods. Third, dynamically oriented psychotherapy appears presently to be the most common form of treatment being given to troubled adolescents (Blos, 1983; Kovacs & Paulauskas, 1986; Swift & Wunderlich, 1990).

Some interesting data in this later regard have been published by Kazdin, Siegel, and Bass (1990), who surveyed the clinical practices and beliefs of 898 psychologists and 264 psychiatrists actively engaged in treating adolescents. Asked to rate the effectiveness of specific treatment methods with young patients, both groups of practitioners selected individual psychotherapy as their first choice. Of the total sample, 79% considered individual psychotherapy to be effective most or all of the time, compared to approximately 60% expressing similar confidence in the next two most frequently chosen methods, behavior modification and family therapy. With respect to the general usefulness of various approaches in treating young people, 73% of these practitioners rated an eclectic approach as useful most or all of the time, following which they also strongly endorsed psychodynamic approaches (59%), family approaches (57%), and behavioral approaches (55%).

For in-depth discussion of other perspectives in treating disturbed adolescents, the reader is referred to contributions on behavioral therapy (Devany & Nelson, 1986; Feindler & Kalfus, 1990; Hersen & Van Hasselt, 1987), cognitive–behavioral therapy (Barth, 1986; Bernard & Joyce, 1984; Schrodt & Fitzgerald, 1987), family therapy (Fishman, 1988; Mirkin & Koman, 1985; Schaefer, Briesmeister, & Fitton, 1984), group therapy (Azima & Richmond, 1989; Berkovitz, 1972; Rose & Edelson, 1987; Sugar, 1975), residential care (Quay, 1986; Schaefer & Swanson, 1988; Steinberg, 1986), school-based and social skills training (Hansen, Watson-Perczel, & Smith, 1989; L'Abate & Milan, 1985; Macmillan & Kavale, 1986; Safer, 1982), and psychopharmacology (Gittelman & Kanner, 1986; Wiener, 1985).

DETERMINING DEPTH AND GOALS

Psychotherapy should always be planned in terms of the treatment depth and goals that are most appropriate to the psychological needs and personality resources of the individual being treated. As traditionally defined, *depth* of treatment is measured by the extent to which a patient's psychological defenses against anxiety are either to be explored for the unconscious conflicts and previous painful experiences that have generated them ("uncovering" psychotherapy), or to be strengthened in reference to conscious concerns and current problem solving ("supportive" psychotherapy) (Weiner, 1975, Chapter 4). The *goals* of treatment correspondingly involve the degree to which therapist and patient aim at increased self-understanding and personality reorganization or rather at stabilization and improved functioning without major personality change.

For most adolescents, excepting those whose cognitive and emotional maturity is approaching adult levels, psychotherapy cannot be usefully directed toward stripping away defenses, reworking previous experience, achieving deep insights, or reorganizing personality structure. Personality structure is usually still in a formative stage during the adolescent years, and most troubled teenagers have no firm personality organization that needs undoing before more adaptive developments can be fostered. Instead, adolescents are in the process of integrating a great many new biological, social, sexual, and academic experiences, and adolescent personality development is largely defined by an ongoing thrust toward the establishment and consolidation of a consistent style of coping with life events. Hence, in most adolescents, defensive styles are forming, rather than already formed, and only in instances of early crystallizing characterological disorder does a young person's behavior reflect a well-defined and highly stabilized coping style. For this reason, efforts in psychotherapy to penetrate an adolescent's defensive style tend to be unproductive, and interpretations designed to strip away whatever defenses can be found often have the counterproductive effect of mobilizing an adolescent's anxiety and attenuating his or her engagement in the treatment.

All interpretations are implicitly critical, and every interpretation implies that the person is thinking, feeling, or doing something that is foolish or unwarranted. Consequently, repetitive interpretations of the coping behaviors of adolescent patients are likely to induce a self-consciousness that constrains them from the normal adolescent business of experimenting and also leads them to regard the therapist as a picky, hostile, disapproving person who is pessimistic about their future. A therapist who focuses extensively on irrational and unconscious motives for an adolescent's behavior risk communicating to the young patient, "I don't think much of you" or "I don't see much hope for you," either of which can undermine the adolescent's expectations that something good might come out of the treatment relationship.

As for achieving deep insights and reworking previous experiences, adolescents typically have little patience with rehashing the vicissitudes of their earlier years. They are far too absorbed with the complexities and uncertainties of the present to spare much concern with matters they consider over and done with. Furthermore, their needs to view themselves as maturing, almost adult, almost self-sufficient individuals makes it distasteful and embarrassing for them to review their childish foibles of only a few years earlier.

Because a depth approach seems accordingly ill-advised in psychotherapy with adolescents, contemporary practice favors for the most part a relatively supportive framework that focuses on growth and development, features a here-and-now perspective, and emphasizes problem solving over insight. Such views are expressed by psychoanalytic as well as psychodynamically oriented clinicians. Sarnoff (1987) states that therapy with adolescents should aim at insight and change through interpretation, just as therapy with adults, but that "One should avoid intervention that would interpret and undo defenses in such a global fashion that the development of the mature personality will be impaired" (p. 198). Ekstein (1983, p. 145) is even more specific in this regard: "In work with adults, we restore somewhat normal functioning. In work with adolescents, we clear the way for further development." Meeks (1980) goes one step further by observing that, although confrontations may commonly be used in the psychotherapy of the adolescent, interpretations of unconscious content are rarely indicated:

> Most, if not all, psychoanalysts would agree that the adolescent patient is not a candidate for a thoroughgoing and complete psychoanalysis. It would be even more foolish to attempt total resolution of the adolescent's conflicts through psychotherapy. The goal, instead, should be to assist the adolescent to achieve

an ego synthesis which would permit him a moderate degree of gratification within the limits of social reality. (p. 131)

This emphasis on personality development and consolidation in adolescent psychotherapy has been endorsed by many other therapists, past and present, as a way of promoting ego adequacy and synthesis in young people (Berman, 1957; Esman, 1985; Gitelson, 1948; Lamb, 1978; Masterson, 1958; Mishne, 1986; Swift & Wunderlich, 1990). From this point of view, the goal of psychotherapeutic work with adolescent youngsters is to provide them with a new emotional experience that will strengthen the functions of their ego, thereby increasing their mastery over situations in their lives, and permit them to achieve an adaptive character synthesis. Adaptive character synthesis is achieved when young people can manage their biological tensions and other impulses comfortably, when they can relate realistically to their parents and other adults, and when they can channel their creative and productive energies into rewarding social and educational accomplishments.

Despite its emphasis on immediacy, the ego-synthesis approach to psychotherapy with adolescents does not preclude efforts to enhance a young person's self-understanding. To consolidate rewarding patterns of managing needs and impulses, relating to others, and channeling creative and productive energies, disturbed adolescents need to understand to the limit of their capacity the manner in which their current attitudes, feelings, and behavior may be impeding such consolidation.

With these considerations in mind, psychotherapy with adolescents will typically not involve an ontogenetic reconstruction of their personality style, but it will encourage them to look critically at their current behavior patterns and will help them to recognize unrealistic and self-defeating aspects of how they are confronting life events. Interpretation of present rather than past experiences will be the most common aspect of this limited-insight approach, as illustrated in the following types of therapist observation: "It sounds like you're afraid to speak up to your father but get back at him by managing to get poor grades"; "I don't think it's just starting in at the high school building that's bothering you, I think you're generally not too happy with the whole idea of growing up"; "It seems to me that you're turning people off by acting more grouchy than you really feel—maybe you don't like the idea of having people get close to you, even though you feel you'd like to have more friends." Given adequate personality resources and the building of a positive treatment relationship, adolescents will usually be able to utilize such interpretations as a first step in learning new and more adequate ways of coping with their experience.

INITIATING THE INTERACTION

A swift, incisive launching of the patient–therapist interaction is vital to successful psychotherapy with adolescents, often more so than with other age groups. As already noted, most children are oblivious to broader implications of being in therapy and approach initial sessions without much worry or resentment, prepared to spend some time in pleasant conversations or activities. Adults, whatever their knowledge or prior opinion of psychotherapy, typically come prepared to see what talking with a professional person will be like and to decide whether continuing to do so might be worthwhile.

Adolescents lack the naïvete of children and the options of adults. Although they may have incorrect notions about the nature of psychotherapy and the role of the psychotherapist, they know full well that they have been brought to a mental health professional by others who are empowered to continue bringing them for sessions. Even if they have become aware of and concerned about personal problems in their lives, they are likely to be troubled by being considered a "head case" and distressed by the prospect of having to talk about their problems with someone they have never met before. Accordingly, adolescent patients can be expected to be on the lookout during their initial visits for reasons to conclude that therapy is irrelevant to their needs or the therapist insensitive to their problems.

Given the apprehension and antipathy with which adolescents customarily enter the office, the therapist's most important task in a first session is to conduct it in such a way that a psychologically needy young person returns for a second session. In the absence of crisis situations requiring immediate diagnostic determinations and emergency interventions, such as evaluating suicidal risk or arranging hospitalization, conversation with an adolescent patient should concentrate initially on fostering his or her willingness to participate in a treatment relationship. To generate such willingness, early interviews must be designed to allow the young person to be comfortable, to engage him or her beyond what is superficial and obvious, and to get the adolescent to acknowledge and respect his or her own role in determining the course of the treatment.

Allowing Comfort

Adolescents usually begin the first interview with a clinician uncertain of what to expect and hard put to suppress their apprehension. Children can be helped to relax with unthreatening activities, and adults can occupy themselves with presenting their complaints, symptoms, and social history while they are appraising the situation. Adolescents, however, cannot be deflected from their initial anxieties by activities that have no apparent purpose; nor, for the most part, do they have any verbal content with which to begin. The complaints and symptoms that have brought them are largely the concerns of their parents, school, or family physician, and they see little reason to review their background with a total stranger whose role is unclear to them.

Hence, if initially undirected, tested with unstructured questions, requested to expose deep personal feelings, or challenged to account for problem situations, most adolescents will become extremely uncomfortable. They may squirm in painful silence and even burst into tears, or they may angrily refuse to respond and even stalk out of the office. To avoid such an impasse, the therapist needs to minimize initial discomfort by actively focusing the interview on factual information and not asking for explanations of behavior or elaborations of emotions.

Attention to comfort in initial interviews with adolescents should start with the therapist's opening remark. Even an apparently innocuous invitation to discuss the presenting problem ("What brings you here?") may be upsetting to young people. They may not know for sure why they have been brought, in which case they may be embarrassed at having no answer to the therapist's question; or they may know the reason—which is almost always some inadequacy, failure, or misbehavior on their part—and hence feel badly at having been asked to put their worst foot forward first. To make matters worse, therapists who begin by asking, "What brings you here?" may convey either that they have not bothered to find out in advance what prompted the referral, in which case they appear disinterested or inert; or that they are asking a question to which they already know the answer, in which case they come across as devious and untrustworthy.

Such initial obstacles to comfort can be avoided by beginning with a statement that is both unequivocal and open-ended, such as, "I understand you've been having some problems in school—what's it like?" While concrete and straightforward, this kind of opener also leaves room for alternative ways of responding. A boy asked this question can plunge right in and talk about his poor grades or unruly behavior, if these are the problem, or he can temporize with superficial, impersonal comments about what the school is objectively like—its building, classes, students, teachers, and so forth. Mention of any such subjects provides a basis for further specific inquiries ("How many are there in your class?" "Do you have men or women teachers or both?") that will yield potentially useful information while facilitating an active, relatively painless verbal interchange.

With respect to explaining behavior and elaborating feelings, such questions as "Why do you think you've been taking things from stores?" or "How do you feel about your mother?" will seldom stimulate a productive exchange early in the treatment relationship. Whether because of embarrassment, concern about being criticized, or uncertainty about how far the therapist can be trusted, adolescents will initially be reluctant to dredge up and share strong feelings with him or her. On the other hand, a differently phrased question, such as asking a girl, "What is your mother like?" allows her the option of expressing affect, if she is ready to do so, or of communicating comfortably by describing some of the mother's objective physical characteristics ("Oh, she's okay, a little taller than I am, and she spends a lot of time keeping the house clean").

Generally speaking, then, therapists can help adolescents feel comfortable by guiding treatment sessions with easily answered questions. Especially easy to answer are open-ended inquiries that allow optional ways of responding and thereby give patients an opportunity to proceed at their own pace without feeling threatened. If nondemanding, open-ended questions still prove too difficult for a frightened or resistive adolescent to handle, the therapist should follow them up with more specific but still nonthreatening inquiries. For example, if "What is your mother like?" is answered with a fearful "What do you mean?" or a grumpy "I don't know," then the situation calls for "How would you describe her to someone else" or even "Tell me something about how she looks and what she likes to do."

Conversely, therapists will do well initially to avoid questions that require self-disclosure or speculation. Although the clinical significance of responses to such inquiries as "What do you think led you to do that?" makes them very tempting to employ, probes of this kind often convince already apprehensive adolescents that they are indeed under an unfriendly gun. By limiting themselves instead to uncomplicated, unchallenging requests for seemingly mundane information, clinicians can turn a quick therapeutic profit. The responses to simple questions are often surprisingly revealing (e.g., the patient's mother is described as a fastidious housekeeper) and provide background information the therapist will eventually want to have anyway (e.g., the mother is physically larger than the patient). Even more important, a directive, nonchallenging approach in the initial interviews gives adolescents the experience of having been engaged in a relaxed mutual conversation, albeit with a "shrink," and not in any type of awkward, embarrassing, or painful interaction.

Although some period of painless communication is almost always necessary to initiate effective psychotherapy with adolescents, a persistently comfortable treatment relationship can be as detrimental to beneficial results as an initial failure to help the young person feel comfortable. For the treatment to make a difference, attention must sooner or later turn to problems that are distressing to think about and feelings that are difficult to express, even at the expense of confrontations that scatter comfort to the winds. In response to such a shift of focus, adolescent patients can be expected periodically to become unwilling to talk, to question the purpose of their coming for sessions, and to express dissatisfaction with the therapist's efforts. Continuing pleasant conversations, undisturbed by confrontations imposed by the therapist and resistances displayed by the adolescent, constitute a deceptive collaboration in which engagement, the second crucial element in initiating psychotherapy, has not been achieved.

Achieving Engagement

Engagement with adolescent patients is achieved by demonstrating that the treatment relationship will differ from relationships they have had with other people, including well-meaning professionals who may have attempted to help them with their difficulties. In particular, therapists need to give evidence that their special knowledge and training allow them to perceive thoughts and feelings that are not put into words and that they use this sensitivity to help their patients understand themselves better and cope more effectively with life situations.

To display their ability and willingness to go beyond the face value of things, therapists should begin as soon as they sense adolescent patients can tolerate it to challenge or interpret superficial aspects of what they are saying: "I find it hard to believe that *all* of your teachers have it in for you," or "You say you couldn't care less, but from the look on your face I'd say you were pretty upset about it." In the absence of such therapist efforts at engagement, adolescents are likely to perceive treatment as little more than a pleasant interlude in which they can discuss bland topics of their choice, however they please, with an accepting, unthreatening adult. They are equally likely to doubt whether the relationship or the therapist can offer them anything more than they could get from other kindly, attentive adults. For some emotionally deprived adolescents, pleasant interpersonal interludes may in themselves be significantly therapeutic. Most adolescents, however, will soon tire or despair of a comfortable but nonengaging treatment relationship because it gives them no reason to believe that the therapist has any particular capacity to understand or to help them.

For the typical adolescent who enters therapy anxious and apprehensive, efforts to achieve engagement ordinarily follow the establishment of comfort. Different priorities obtain, however, when young persons have steeled themselves beforehand to remain uninvolved in the proceedings. Without appearing nervous or embarrassed, some such teenagers will sit steeped in petulance—arms crossed, feet firmly planted, and eyes averted—and respond with little more than an occasional grunt or uninformative monosyllable. Some will fix the therapist with a hostile stare and announce that they were forced to come, that they have nothing wrong with them, and that they have no intention of getting involved in any mind games. Some will answer questions politely but with a derisive, patronizing smirk on their face that conveys the impression of laughing up their sleeve. Some may take a buddy-buddy, it's-all-a-big-mistake approach, in which they affect a friendly nonchalance, comment affably about how well they are getting along, and offer some advice: "It's got nothing at all to do with you, Doc, you seem like a nice enough person, but you should work on kids that really have troubles and need you, of which I know a lot but I'm not one of them."

Although initial behaviors of these kinds are likely to derive from underlying discomfort, they insulate the adolescents from situational anxiety so well that efforts to help them feel comfortable do little good. In such instances, a well-intended supporting hand, extended through such words as, "I guess you're a little anxious coming here to talk with me," is likely to elicit only a rebuff: "Not me—I just want out of here." In the face of this extent of initial resistance from adolescents who are in need of help, therapists may have to bypass comfort and search instead for ways to penetrate a facade of scorn or bravado and shake adolescents free from an aloof stance long enough to engage them in interactive conversation.

What ways will work are likely to vary considerably from1 one case to the next and may not always be readily apparent. However, Schimel (1986, p. 185) is probably correct when he notes in this regard that "For the alert therapist, the material is always there." The following two exchanges with initially resistive adolescents illustrate efforts to latch on to what little material was available in order to achieve engagement:

PATIENT: I don't mind being here, but I want you to know there's no reason for it.
THERAPIST: So why did you come?
PATIENT: My mother told me I had to.
THERAPIST: Do you always do what your mother tells you to?

This last question obliged the boy in this case to admit one of three things: Either he was totally subservient to his mother, or some type of bribe had been attached to his coming, or, if he was neither subservient to nor bribed by his mother, something more than just her request must be involved in his having kept the appointment. Although provocative, each of these alternatives had some potential for getting engaged conversation underway. Such provocation, given in a matter-of-fact way that conveys interest without disparagement, may often prove more effective than supportive techniques in making a connection with a sullen or detached patient.

THERAPIST: You seem awfully mad that I'm asking you a few questions. What's bothering you?
PATIENT: I've already made up my mind I'm not going to talk to you.
THERAPIST: Why not?
PATIENT: There's nothing wrong with me, I don't have any problems, and it's none of your business anyway.
THERAPIST: Maybe there is nothing wrong with you and maybe it is none of my business. But don't tell me you don't have any problems. Your parents are fed up with you and your principal is thinking about expelling you from school. That adds up to trouble no matter how you look at it. Maybe it's not your fault, but I'd at least like to hear your side of the story.

For the girl in this case, as for most young persons who feel put upon, the opportunity to defend herself was hard to resist, and her self-justifications provided openings for engaged communication. Often, such direct identification of trouble and an accompanying offer to help with it, without any assumption or implication that the adolescent is responsible for the trouble, can help to melt an initial resolve to remain silent.

Therapists need to balance comfort and engagement techniques in their approach to adolescent patients, according to each young person's needs. From observing new patients in the waiting room, exchanging greetings with them, and getting them seated in the office, the therapist should already have a fairly good idea of whether a particular adolescent is anxious and frightened and needs first to be made comfortable, or is hostile and resistive and needs first to be engaged. The challenge for the therapist, as elaborated by Katz (1990), is to anticipate and be prepared for whatever affects and concerns adolescents bring to a first interview. Then, as the initial phase of treatment proceeds, therapists will need to be prepared to shift their emphasis as the occasion demands, pressing engagement when the adolescent appears comfortable enough to tolerate it and providing comfort in response to exacerbations of anxiety.

Establishing Motivation

Beginning with the initial contact with adolescent patients, therapists must work to establish their motivation to return for further sessions, if such are indicated. The motivation necessary for adolescents to participate profitably in psychotherapy differs from what usually is required in treating adults, however. Whereas adult patients need consciously to endorse a course of psychotherapy addressed to their difficulties, overtly expressed motivation rarely occurs in adolescents and plays little role in their successful treatment. Just as adolescents seldom seek treatment voluntarily, they cannot be expected to embrace it warmly when it is offered to them. Typically they are either too intent on denying their psychological difficulties or too embarrassed, frightened, or counterdependent to ask directly for help with them.

Hence, adolescents will not initially be saying that they appreciate the chance to discuss their problems with someone and believe that further talks would prove helpful, nor are they likely to report that they have been thinking about entering psychotherapy and would like to arrange for regular visits. At best, given a reasonably well-handled first interview in which the therapist has been able to achieve a good blend of patient comfort and engagement, the adolescent will respond to the idea of returning with such comments as "I don't mind," "Today wasn't so bad—I suppose I could come another time," "Sure, if you think it will do any good," or "I don't see much purpose in it, but if you can put up with me, I guess I can take you."

Each of these seemingly noncommittal, lukewarm comments represents for an adolescent a substantial endorsement of the therapist as a potentially helping person and of talking as a potentially helpful means of resolving difficulty. To expect any more than this from most adolescent patients is unrealistic, and to view such remarks as reflecting insufficient motivation for psychotherapy is to misunderstand the adolescent's style of approaching treatment, even when he or she feels a strong need for it. By and large, the only expression of motivation necessary to initiate the treatment is the adolescent's stated willingness to come back for additional appointments.

Comments expressing willingness to return should be elicited from the adolescent patient during the first interview. As the session draws to a close, preferably after some channels of communication have been established, the therapist needs to ask the young person something on the order of, "What thoughts did you have about coming in to talk with me today?" Such a question gives patients a chance to air their preconceptions, apprehensions, or hopes in coming for the session, if these have not already come up for discussion, and to contrast what the experience has been like with what they thought, feared, or wished it would be. From this information, the therapist can identify and correct, as necessary, any misconceptions the adolescent may have had (e.g., "You thought I was going to lay you out on a couch and let you do all the talking, but as you see we've just been sitting here in these chairs talking back and forth"; "You expected me to lecture you about doing what your parents and teachers tell you to do, but I think you realize now that I'm interested in hearing your side of the story and seeing what could help to make things better for you").

The therapist can then proceed with a question such as, "How would you feel about coming in again and talking further as we have today?" This inquiry into the adolescent's feelings about returning is essential for establishing the necessary spirit of mutual participation in the therapeutic venture. To tell the young person, "I'm going to give you an appointment for next week" or, worse yet, merely to instruct waiting parents to bring their youngster for a return visit, seriously frays the adolescent's dignity as a blossoming adult. Even for early adolescents, to be treated with such disregard for the self-sufficiency and independence they are proudly nourishing often convinces them that neither therapy nor the therapist has much likelihood of meeting their needs.

While recognizing the crucial importance of having adolescents participate responsibly in planning and implementing their treatment, therapists must make allowances for their usual difficulty in acknowledging responsibility for their problems or admitting any need for help. Should they defer to the therapist's judgment about a return visit ("If you think I should"), the therapist will often do well to spare them from having to present a specific request for therapy: "Yes, I think we should talk again; we've already seen today that there are some things going on that you haven't quite understood, and I think it would be helpful to look at the situation some more"; or "I realize you haven't felt anything was wrong with you, but things certainly haven't been going as well for you as you would like; maybe by talking further we could get some ideas about how to improve the situation"; or "You don't have to think it's a great idea or that you really need it; if you're willing to go along with the idea of coming in again, I think we could talk about some more things that might be helpful to you."

Even while they are directly and emphatically encouraging a return visit, however, therapists must be sure to involve the young person in the eventual decision to continue. To become an engaged participant who will eventually assume his or her share of responsibility in the treatment, the adolescent needs to be able to say words to the effect of "I guess you've got a point, so *I* wouldn't mind coming back" or "If you think there's some reason for it, *I'm* willing to come again." The therapist should not be satisfied with responses that refer the decision entirely to someone else. To the adolescent who says, "I'll come back if *you* say so," the therapist's reply must communicate, "Not because I say so; I'm saying it would be a good idea and that I want to see you again, but whether you do or not is up to *you*."

The therapist should likewise challenge any decision about return visits that is referred to the parents. Near the end of a comfortable but not yet engaged first interview with a 14-year-old boy, the following interchange took place when he was asked how he felt about a return visit:

PATIENT: It's up to you and my folks.

THERAPIST: You've left yourself out.

PATIENT: That's the way it is. If you think I should come, my folks will send me.

THERAPIST: What if you don't want to come but I think you should?

PATIENT: I'll come; my folks would make me.

THERAPIST: They'd make you?

PATIENT: Yes.

THERAPIST: You wouldn't have any choice?

PATIENT: No.

THERAPIST: You wouldn't have any control over the situation?

PATIENT: No.

THERAPIST: I wonder if there aren't times you get angry when you don't have any control or say in things.

The therapist in this instance elected to digress from establishing motivation to take advantage of this suggestive information concerning issues of autonomy. The last statement in this dialogue was followed by the patient's first significant affective engagement in the interview, as he let off considerable steam about his parents always treating him like a child. This was followed a bit later by the therapist's being able to say, "It may be true that your folks would send you if I say so, but what I want to find out is how *you* feel about it, because that will be important in *you* and *I* deciding what *we* should do."

Therapists should resist any temptation to sidestep discussions of motivation in this kind of situation. The easy road taken, which would involve going along with the likelihood that the adolescent will be brought for sessions and bypassing any struggle to get him or her to construe therapy as voluntary, usually turns out to be a road to nowhere. Adolescents who are allowed to regard themselves as involuntary patients will regard the therapist as someone else's agent, and not much will happen in the treatment.

Research findings confirm that the more adolescents perceive themselves as having chosen voluntarily to enter and remain in psychotherapy, the more benefit they are likely to derive from it (Bastien & Adelman, 1984). Similarly, the more strongly young people feel committed to their therapy, the more effectively they become engaged in it and the more rapidly they make progress (Adelman, Kaser-Boyd, & Taylor, 1984). Furthermore, in this regard, the prospects for an effective therapeutic alliance are enhanced initially when the therapist, in addition to inviting discussion of how the adolescent feels about discussing personal matters in a professional context, conveys sincerely that the adolescent's feelings will play an important role in determining whether and how the treatment will proceed.

Motivational readiness for treatment can be facilitated in particular by indicating to adolescents what they can expect with respect to confidentiality (Barker, 1990, Chapter 5; Gustafson & McNamara, 1987; Taylor & Adelman, 1989). Whether asked by young people or not, the question of who will find out what they say to the therapist will be very much on their minds as they weigh whether to say anything at all. As in discussing other considerations in getting therapy underway, moreover, raising the issue of confidentiality contributes to adolescents' feeling that they are being actively involved in planning their treatment.

For this reason, therapists need to include in their initial explanations of how matters will proceed some explicit statements about the boundaries of the adolescent's rights to privacy. These statements should touch on the following three generally accepted clinical guidelines for balanced safeguarding of patient confidentiality and public welfare: (a) generally speaking, whatever the adolescent says to the therapist will be private between them and not shared with anyone else; (b) exceptions to this rule will be made only if what the adolescent is saying raises the possibility of harm coming to him or her or to other people; (c) should the therapist decide that the parents or anyone else should be informed about a matter discussed in the therapy, he or she will first inform the adolescent of this decision and will encourage his or her participation in implementing it.

No matter how carefully these guidelines are presented, most adolescent patients will occasionally test just how dependable their therapist is, usually by dropping some juicy tidbit of information unknown to their parents and waiting to see if it gets back to them. Because actions speak louder than words, it is only when therapists pass such tests that they convince adolescent patients of their commitment to respecting confidence. Even so, much is to be gained by providing an explicit statement about confidentiality up front rather than merely allowing the therapist's trustworthiness to become inferred, implicitly, during the course of the therapy. Also, for many other features of how the treatment will be conducted, these clear and accurate expectations formed during the initial phase of therapy facilitate engagement and progress. Research findings confirm that ambiguous and incorrect expectations concerning the nature and purposes of the treatment can undermine an adolescent's motivation for therapy and contribute to early dropout (Blotcky & Friedman, 1984; Day & Reznikoff, 1980).

To summarize this section, efforts to allow comfort, achieve engagement, and establish motivation are critical treatment strategies in initiating psychotherapy with adolescent patients. Although these strategies may continue to foster progress later on as well, it is becoming involved during the initial phase of treatment in a trusting relationship with their therapist that makes it possible for adolescents to tolerate the discomfort of working meaningfully on difficult issues as their therapy proceeds.

BUILDING THE TREATMENT RELATIONSHIP

Therapists who initiate treatment with adequate attention to an adolescent patient's comfort, engagement, and motivation will have laid the foundation for an effective working relationship. From this point, the further building of the relationship rarely proceeds in terms of well-defined, sequential therapeutic tasks. Despite the underlying stability and continuity that characterize normal adolescent development (see Chapter 1), most teenagers, still dealing with new developmental tasks and sorting out their sense of identity, are likely to be changeable if not unpredictable in their attitudes and concerns from one treatment session to the next. As a result, flexibility and facile short-term adjustments are more likely to characterize effective psychotherapy with adolescents than any regularized employment of specific tactics. With respect to overall strategies, however, the salutary impact of the treatment relationship therapists build with their adolescent patients will customarily depend on how well they are able to (a) maintain a steady flow of communication during sessions, (b) foster the patient's positive identification with them, and (c) regulate the concerns adolescents inevitably have about the implications of the treatment relationship for their psychological independence.

Maintaining the Flow of Communication

Even after having committed themselves to a course of psychotherapy during some initial sessions, adolescents are still not as prepared as most adults to be spontaneous and forthcoming, especially in talking with a relative stranger. Moreover, young people are more likely than adults to worry about sessions that seem to go awkwardly ("If I weren't such a nerd there would be more to talk about") or that involve long silences ("I wonder what will happen next"; "What is he thinking about me?" "Why can't I think of anything to say?"). As the treatment proceeds, the therapist needs to minimize awkwardness and silences by taking responsibility for maintaining the flow of communication during sessions. Two useful ways of implementing this strategy involve *activity* and *directness*.

Activity

Therapists can help adolescent patients communicate by continuing to guide them during treatment sessions and responding promptly to what they have to say. This calls for therapists to be more active than is usually necessary in working with adults and to avoid the common practice of waiting for the patient to take the initiative in beginning sessions and choosing topics for discussion. The silent therapist or one who favors an unstructured approach, such as leading off with "Where would you like to begin" or "What would you like to talk about today?" often creates unproductive uncertainty in an adolescent's mind. A preferable approach is to start the session with some guidance, as in "What's been happening since last week?" As a session proceeds, the therapist should similarly be prepared to bring up topics for discussion, as in "How did that party you were talking about turn out?" or "I think we should spend a little time today talking about what's been going on in school."

As for responding promptly, the pregnant pauses that often stimulate significant verbalizations in adult patients are perplexing to adolescents, who more often than not will take them to mean that the therapist is inattentive, disinterested, or at a loss for words. Communicating effectively in psychotherapy with adolescents usually requires a rapid-cadence technique that does not allow therapists much time to contemplate what their patient is saying or to formulate precisely phrased replies. Indeed, therapist whose preferred treatment style involves reflecting leisurely on what is transpiring during a session and couching their observations in carefully chosen words often do not work as effectively with adolescent as with adult patients. Adolescents will communicate best in response to a forthcoming, up-front, nonmysterious style that gives them little occasion to wonder what is going through their therapist's mind.

Although most adolescents require a considerable level of therapist activity to remain productively engaged, for some, having the therapist initiate sessions and keep up a running commentary may not be necessary and may even be experienced as patronizing or intrusive. Therapists need to recognize when an adolescent has a story to tell or some feelings to express and would prefer not to be interrupted or told what to talk about. In addition, some low-keyed young people who feel particularly put upon by adults may communicate more easily if the therapist, as a rule, gives them some breathing space.

Sally, a 16-year-old contemplative and somewhat laconic girl, seemed to become increasingly anxious and disorganized during an initial interview in which the therapist utilized a rapid-cadence approach. Concerned about imminent personality breakdown or possibly an underlying schizophrenic disorder, he decided to conduct the second interview in a less structured way, to determine whether disordered thinking or bizarre fantasies would emerge if he did not suppress them by talking so much himself. In the relatively unstructured interview that ensued, Sally was surprisingly relaxed, reflective, and able, with little encouragement, to present an orderly review of her major concerns. The therapist's earlier active style had apparently been too dissonant with her preferred way of having a conversation and had put too much pressure on her for her to be able to respond comfortably.

For adolescents such as Sally, who do not need or are even disconcerted by a high level of therapist activity, treatment sessions may proceed very similarly to those with adults. There also may be times when therapists need to inject some nonverbal activity into a treatment session in order to repair a break in communication. Youngsters who are otherwise responsive may periodically become reluctant to go further into matters they have been discussing and may fall silent. Numerous standard verbal strategies are available for dealing with silences that appear to reflect some resistance to talking about painful or embarrassing events (Graafsma & Anbeek, 1984; McHolland, 1985; Weiner, 1975, Chapter 9).

However, therapists working with adolescents will often move matters along better not by employing interpretive or probing strategies but by commenting on the order of, "You don't seem to feel much like talking today, so what would you like to do?" If the adolescent should respond with "I've been learning to play chess—you wouldn't happen to have a chess set here would you?" or "My favorite hobby is drawing, that's what I really like to do most," then therapists may be able to utilize the interaction around a chessboard or their patient's artwork to reopen channels of communication. Although such activities have something in common with play therapy techniques, their effectiveness is by no means limited to work with children. Successful utilization of selected activities in psychotherapy with adolescents is well-described in the literature (Corder, 1986; Serok, 1986).

Directness

To be direct, as well as active, therapists need to state their thoughts explicitly, phrase their questions concretely, and respond fully to requests that they explain the basis of their impressions and inquiries. Such directness and willingness to explain themselves promote a steady flow of communication with adolescent patients. By contrast, the partial interpretations, veiled allusions, and nondirective probes ("What ideas do you have about why I asked you that?" "It's as if something is making you afraid") that often help adults increase their self-awareness are frequently perceived by adolescents as subterfuge or mystification. Once more from a developmental perspective, adolescents already have more than enough questions to which they are trying to find the answers, without their therapist adding to this burden. The more ambiguous therapists are, the more difficult it is for their adolescent patients to understand what they mean or intend by a particular comment, and the more difficult they will find it to continue responding.

For this reason, the best way for therapists to phrase their observations on what an adolescent is saying is with as little ambiguity or conjecture as possible. Hence "I think you're afraid of something" is better than "It's as if something is making you afraid," because it is more explicit; it places the matter directly on the table as something to be discussed, without asking the adolescent to meditate on its possible existence and without leaving the therapist's impression uncertain. Even better would be, "I think you get a little frightened whenever you get in a situation where you might fail," because in addition to being explicit, it identifies in concrete terms the nature of the apparent problem.

Even in response to such explicit, concrete comments, adolescents may feel unsure about whether to disclose themselves or exactly what the therapist has in mind. Then they are likely to ask in turn, "Where did you get that idea?" or "What do you mean by that?" or "Why did you bring that up?" With adolescents, such questions do not call for the therapist to remain silent or noncommittal or to turn them back on the patient ("What do you think I had in mind?"). This again illustrates a tactic that can work effectively with a reflective, voluntary adult patient who has made a commitment to work in exploratory psychotherapy, but that will be viewed by adolescents as an insincere, ungenuine way of playing games. Instead, therapists working with adolescents need to be prepared to explain themselves. Questions about what the therapist means or why he or she has asked about something should be answered, promptly and directly ("The reason I asked is that, as best I recall, each time you've gone to a school party before, you've sort of hung around without talking to anyone, and this last time you've just described sounds like it was a little different").

There are limits to how far the therapist should go in providing such explanations, however, and directness should not be allowed to spare a young person his or her share of responsibility in the treatment work. On some occasions, what the therapist has meant will be perfectly obvious, or the circumstances to which a statement refers will already have been discussed several times—and yet the adolescent asks "What do you mean?" or "What are you talking about?" At points of such obvious superficial resistance, the types of partial interpretation and nondirection that the therapist would otherwise avoid often prove more incisive than complete and unambiguous statements. When adolescents seem not perplexed, but only stalling or perhaps "playing dumb," the strategy of directness calls for the therapist to say, "I mean just what I said" or "You know what I'm talking about." Such seemingly testy confrontations of resistance, used at the proper time and expressed without rancor, serve the useful purpose of conveying to the adolescent that the therapist, in return for his or her being direct, does not expect the adolescent to play games either.

At the same time, therapists seeking to build an effective working relationship must be able to recognize when it may be important not to break up a flow of conversation by focusing on elements of resistance, including those that touch on the therapist's commitment to the treatment:

Andy, a surly and guarded high school sophomore, was describing with enthusiasm and in some detail his plans to organize a rock band with Rick, a friend he had mentioned some weeks earlier. He suddenly broke off this therapeutically significant and for him rare sharing of personal experience to ask, somewhat querulously, "Do you know who Rick is?" His question seemed a transparent test of whether the therapist had been sufficiently attentive and interested to remember Rick. The therapist elected not to interpret the challenge implicit in his question or to point out the underlying need for reassurance it suggested. Instead, he directly and in as much detail as had been reported to him reviewed who Rick was. Andy nodded with satisfaction and returned to his story. The therapist had prevented any intrusion on the relationship-building import of Andy's continuing with his story, and at the same time, he had concretely demonstrated his interest and attention. Although questions about whether the therapist or people in general could care enough about him to listen to and remember what he had to say seemed to be a topic that would eventually take center stage in Andy's therapy, the time for dealing effectively with such issues comes after and not before a solid working relationship has been built.

Fostering Positive Identification

Psychotherapy with adolescents proceeds most effectively when young people identify positively with their therapist. Positive identification helps motivate teenage patients to become mature, successful adults, which able therapists are perceived to be. In addition, wanting to resemble their therapists helps adolescents come to trust and respect them, and this trust and respect, in turn, help adolescent patients accept their therapists' efforts to modify their attitudes and behavior. In order to foster the positive identification that treatment will require, therapists have to demonstrate *genuineness* as a person, an *understanding* of their adolescent patients, and their *liking for and interest in* helping them.

Genuineness

To present themselves to their adolescent patients as a genuine person, therapists need to address them with the same candor, conversational tone, and emotional spontaneity they would use in talking with a casual friend. With respect to being candid, some self-disclosure concerning who they are and what they believe in is necessary for therapists to come across as a real person and to give adolescents a clearly defined object with whom to identify. This does not mean revealing intimate details of their private lives that would ordinarily be shared only with close friends and relatives, but it does mean forgoing the evasive, interpretive manner in which they might choose to respond to personal questions from an adult patient. Asked about a vacation trip, for example, therapists will not achieve genuineness by remaining silent or saying, "I wonder why you're asking me that," or "You have some feelings about my having been away." Being a real person in this situation calls instead for telling the young person matter-of-factly where they went, what they did, how the weather was, and so on, just as they would in conversation with a casual acquaintance.

In addition to providing objective information about themselves, therapists should be candid in letting their attitudes and preferences enter into discussions of events not directly related to the treatment. If their adolescent patients want to know whether they are a Democrat or Republican, what kind of music they like, or whether they have any favorite hobbies, they should tell them. If there are underlying motives for such questions that need to be explored, the time for doing so is after and not before the therapist has demonstrated genuineness with a forthright response.

Even when they are not asked, therapists should inject their views into the conversation from time to time to help define themselves clearly and facilitate an adolescent patient's identifying with them. If a young person describes enjoying a recent movie or television program, for example, the therapist may honestly be able to say, "I saw it too, and I also thought it was pretty good," or "I guess I didn't like it as much as you did." Disagreements can work just as well as a consensus to promote the therapist's identifiability. Thus, an adolescent's tirade against restrictive drinking laws may give the therapist an opportunity to present an equally vigorous defense of the current legal drinking age. The adolescent does not have to be persuaded for such agreements to serve the purposes of the therapy; he or she needs only to recognize that the therapist has a definite point of view that he or she has been willing to articulate.

Along with clarifying the therapist's attitudes and thereby increasing his or her availability as an object of identification, overt disagreement in the context of the treatment relationship can help young people realize, perhaps for the first time, that sensible and compatible people may hold opposing points of view. Many adolescents who become psychologically disturbed have had long years of negative experience with anger. In their home and among their peers, disagreement has too often been the prelude to anger, and anger the prelude to rejection or abuse. To sit with the therapist and argue with gusto about the redeeming features of hard rock music or the practical benefits of a good education, without either party getting upset, breaking off the conversation, vacating the premises, calling names, or threatening violence, can be a new and salutary experience. Like a mature and self-composed adult, and not a childish individual lacking self-control, the young person begins to learn that people can take issue with each other and express their opinions openly without anything bad happening as a result.

Turning to the importance of a conversational tone and emotional spontaneity in demonstrating genuineness, therapists need to avoid as best they can any hint of artificiality or restraint in how they talk to adolescent patients. Neither the soft, supportive tone often assumed in talking with children nor the impersonal, businesslike stance often assumed with adults—both of whom expect to be talked to in these ways—is likely to pass muster with adolescent patients. Instead, a relaxed, natural, informal, unpretentious, noncritical, and nonpatronizing tone—in other words, the way one would ordinarily talk with a casual acquaintance in the absence of any hidden agenda—is necessary for adolescents to feel that the therapist is being genuine with them.

Likewise, most adolescents will quickly spot the efforts of reserved therapists to be more open and spontaneous than is comfortable for them. Therapists who tend naturally to be open and spontaneous in their interpersonal relationships will foster positive identification just by being themselves. Clinicians who, on the other hand, are by nature reticent or circumspect and not easy for other people to read may find that psychotherapy with adolescents is not the specialty in which they are most effective. Therapists need to be able to let their feelings as well as their attitudes come spontaneously into play in order to build an effective treatment relationship through fostering identification with them. If something an adolescent patient says strikes them as funny, they should laugh. If it was meant to be funny, they and their patient will have shared a genuine personal interaction. Should adolescents not see the humor in remarks that have drawn a laugh, the therapist's spontaneous reaction can be used to expand their awareness of how they are perceived by others: "I can see that you meant what you said to be serious, but something about the way you said it made me laugh; the same thing must happen to you with other people, and maybe we can learn something from this about how you strike people funny without meaning to."

Likewise, should adolescents be trying to make a joke of a serious situation, the therapist's spontaneous impatience or disapproval can be the first step in helping them to consider the extent to which their behavior in the situation was inappropriate or self-defeating. To a boy who laughingly describes how his disruptive behavior led to his being ejected from a classroom, for example, the therapist might respond, "I don't see anything funny in that, and I don't think you really do either; all you got from it is your teacher mad at you, and if any of the other students in the class were laughing, they were laughing at you and not with you, and that's not what you want."

Therapists have to judge carefully just how spontaneous they should be, however. When they sense a degree of distress that calls more for comfort than for challenge, they need to refrain from laughing at a serious remark or scowling at a jocular one. They must also be sufficiently in tune with their patient to recognize occasions when motives underlying a remark call for interpretation rather than affect. For example, a boy who tells a dirty joke probably has something on his mind other than being amusing, and the therapist needs to respond not with laughter but with curiosity about why something lewd or perverse has been brought into the conversation. Is the boy testing the therapist's knowledge of pornograhic vernacular, or seeing what it takes to shock the therapist, or gauging the extent of the therapist's willingness to continue working with him? Alternatively, does he perhaps have some disturbing sexual thoughts on his mind that he is looking for indirect ways to approach?

Similarly, in listening to a girl tearfully describe tragic events and serious setbacks in her peer-group and family relationships, therapists will need to conceal the affective responses they are likely to have. They will not help the patient by expressing their concern about her and their real sadness for her misfortunes, let alone concern that therapy may not be sufficient to reverse them. Rather, they need to acknowledge her distress and to attempt as best they can to support her: "I know things are difficult for you, but let's keep trying to see what we can do to help."

Finally, with respect to being a genuine person and an object of identification, therapists working with adolescents should conduct themselves as adults. Experienced clinicians are agreed that adolescents need and want their therapist to look and act like a grown-up, not a teenager, and to enter their lives as a sympathetic and understanding adult, not as a peer (Esman, 1985; Lamb, 1978; McHolland, 1985; Meeks, 1980). Beginning therapists taking on teenage patients may be tempted to affect adolescent ways of dressing and talking, in the expectation that doing so will help overcome adolescent resistances to interacting with an adult. Such affectations only serve to stamp the therapist as a phony in the adolescent's eyes, and the inauthenticity of an adult pretending to be one of the guys or gals rarely achieves any useful end. To the contrary, therapists who pretend to be something they are not usually succeed only in convincing their young patients that they probably cannot be trusted.

Understanding

Therapists demonstrate their understanding of adolescent patients by being able to appreciate their thoughts and feelings and to recognize their underlying concerns. To achieve such empathy with young people, therapists must first of all be thoroughly familiar with the psychology of adolescence. This involves being knowledgeable about and sensitive to adolescent vicissitudes of maturing physically, making and losing friends, reaching out for heterosocial relationships, wresting self-determination from parents, and struggling for academic, social, athletic, artistic, and other successes.

To help them build a good treatment relationship by demonstrating understanding, therapists should also be conversant with whatever transient values, heroes, fads, and figures of speech are currently dominating the adolescent scene. To draw a blank when their patient refers to a popular musical group or uses various slang expressions of the day marks the therapist as being out of tune with the adolescent's experience. Therapists cannot be expected to know everything and may, in fact, achieve therapeutic gain by expressing interest in learning from their adolescent patient: "That expression is a new one on me—can you fill me in?" On the other hand, constant unfamiliarity with what adolescents are talking about and repeated requests that they translate their parlance into dictionary language is likely to raise doubts in patients' minds about whether their therapist is capable of understanding and helping them. In keeping with the previously noted importance of genuineness, however, the desirability of knowing adolescent language is widely recognized as referring to understanding it, not speaking it (Barker, 1990; Shapiro, 1985).

In conveying their ability to understand their adolescent patients, therapists will also find it helpful to be familiar with the environments in which they live. This includes not only their home and family setting, but also their school and neighborhood. Being informed about the ambience or the disadvantage that characterizes these environments, the values that define what is most important in them, and the spirit of camaraderie or competition with other schools and neighborhoods that prevails in them all provide a useful backdrop for understanding what adolescents say about their daily experiences.

Aside from their knowledge of adolescent psychology and teenage life, the ability of therapists to communicate understanding to their adolescent patients will ultimately depend on how empathic they are. *Empathy*, the sensitivity of one person to the inner life of another, cannot be learned from didactic instruction or supervised experience. Therapists will bring empathy to their professional work to the extent that their personality style and developmental experiences have made them empathic people.

To be sure, personal psychotherapy, an openness to reflecting on their own adolescence, and what they have learned from their education and training about personality dynamics may enhance therapists' sensitivity to the experiences of their adolescent patients. Yet as a function of their own basic personality, most therapists remain empathic to differing degrees with different kinds of patients. Some find themselves more fully empathic with children and others with adults, some more with women and others with men, and some more with ideationally oriented patients than with those who prefer affective modes of expression, and the effectiveness of their therapeutic work will reflect these differences.

Even among clinicians who are devoted to and talented in working with adolescents in general, most recognize that they are more successful in treating some kinds of young people than in treating others. Clinicians who work together in adolescent treatment programs can usually identify who among their group is particularly effective at drawing out depressed and inhibited youngsters, who is particularly good at getting through to defiant and rebellious young people, and who seems to have a special knack for communicating with confused and disorganized patients. Accordingly, in deciding whether to take on adolescent patients, as well as how to work with them, and in selecting types of disturbed adolescents on whom to concentrate their treatment efforts, therapists need to know themselves.

Liking and Interest

To become truly involved in therapy and benefit from it, adolescents need to perceive their therapist as respecting and valuing them as persons and caring about what happens to them. This perception is particularly important at those points in the treatment when it is necessary to confront adolescents with unpleasant facts or to express disapproval of their behavior. Therapists should demonstrate their liking for their adolescent patients and their interest in their welfare primarily by being sincerely and unstintingly dedicated to helping them worry less, feel better, and deal more effectively with people and events in their lives. Positive regard for teenage patients can rarely be communicated more directly than this without seeming ungenuine. It is no more natural for therapists to say, "I like you" to an adolescent patient than to a casual friend, and most young people will quickly recognize the artificiality of such comments.

Should specific questions arise concerning the therapist's attitudes ("Do you really like me?"), they can seldom be taken at face value without risking ungenuineness. Adolescents who ask such questions usually have some purpose in mind other than eliciting a testimonial to the therapist's affection. Accordingly, this creates one of those situations in which therapists, instead of being candid and direct, need to respond by exploration ("Why do you ask me that?") or, if they already have some understanding of the young person's behavior, by affirming the indirect evidence of their positive regard: "If I didn't want to talk to you, I'd say so; you've had these problems that are making life difficult for you, and I want to help you get on top of them, and I'm ready to keep working at it as long as you are."

Holmes (1964) elaborates in some detail the relationship-damaging inauthenticity of direct responses to questions about liking and the extent to which just being there is sufficient to convey the therapist's interest. The therapist who feels compelled to tell an adolescent patient "I like you," says Holmes, "will have to work a long time to get the hook out of his mouth" (p. 16). Holmes points out further that adolescent patients are fully aware that it would be much easier for the therapist not to have to bother with them at all and that troubled adolescents will accordingly infer affectionate concern primarily from the therapist's determined efforts to persist in trying to help them (pp. 21, 207).

Consistently with Holmes's point, a simple but nevertheless effective response to a question such as "Do you really care?" might be "I'm here, aren't I?" A more insistent demand for therapists to explain just what it is they care about, if anything ("You could care less—you're just doing this for the money"), may still need only a simple response to demonstrate caring: "Yes, I do this for a living, but I'm concerned about helping you overcome your problems and feel better about yourself."

Like simple words, simple actions may add considerably to a young person's feeling of being cared about by his or her therapist. The therapist may suggest some reference sources to a boy who is having difficulty collecting material for a report he has to write, or the therapist may call a girl who has missed a session because of illness to ask how she is feeling and whether there is anything she would like to discuss over the telephone. Such concrete expressions of therapist interest, especially if they go beyond what the young person may have expected, usually help contribute to building a solid relationship.

As a caution, however, communicating liking and interest to adolescent patients should not lean too heavily on first person pronouns. Therapists being told about some obvious success or improvement in a young person's life may be tempted to say, "I'm pleased to hear that," but there are definite disadvantages to adolescents' perceiving their therapist as being pleased or displeased by what they do. One of these disadvantages is an adolescent's concluding that the therapist can be made to feel better or worse by what he or she does or talks about doing. Such impressions open the door to adolescents engaging in adaptive or self-defeating actions not in response to intrinsic motivations, but as a way of making an impact on the therapist. The more this occurs, the more likely it is that relationship issues in the therapy will interfere with adolescents using good judgment, acting with awareness of why they are behaving as they are, and progressing toward psychological independence.

When therapists regularly report how they feel about events in an adolescent's life, they also intrude on and demean the importance of how young people themselves are responding to these events. Although the therapist cares, how he or she feels about good or bad news should take a back seat to how the adolescent feels. Hence, to avoid a sticky treatment relationship and to foster independence, therapists should replace such statements as "I'm pleased to hear that" with such statements as "You must feel good about that"; instead of "I'm sorry to hear that," a preferable statement is "I guess that made you feel pretty bad." While conveying that the therapist cares, responding in these latter ways keeps attention focused on the adolescent's needs and perspective.

Regulating Independence

To build and sustain an effective treatment relationship with adolescent patients, therapists need to regulate carefully their normative developmental concerns about becoming independent persons in their own right. Most teenagers are looking forward eagerly to the autonomy and privileges of being an adult, while they are also looking back longingly to the dependent gratification and freedom from responsibility that came with being a child. Some early adolescents may not yet be addressing issues of independence, and same late adolescents may already have left these issues behind. Most adolescents, however, across a broad age range, seek in their relationships with adults both to be treated as self-sufficient equals and to be advised, guided, and protected when they run into difficulties they are not yet equipped to handle. In light of these conflicting needs, therapists need to guard against causing their adolescent patients to feel either that they are being babied or that they are being left to their own devices.

Because psychotherapy is a helping relationship, patients cannot undertake it without surrendering some of their independence to their therapist. Although excessive dependence ("I can't get along without you") impedes the work of the therapy and is a problem to be overcome, total independence ("I don't need you at all") also deters progress in patients who are not ready for termination of treatment. Participation and improvement in therapy require a belief that the therapist has something useful to offer beyond what patients can provide for themselves. Yet typical adolescent determination to be self-reliant and qualify for adult autonomy can make it difficult to admit needing or benefiting from what the therapist has to offer. Youthful aversion to being put in a dependent position means that therapists must not be too heavy-handed in saying or demonstrating how much their adolescent patients need their help and how much they are going to do for them. At the same time, because troubled adolescents do in fact need help and must be willing to accept some guidance and direction, therapists need to find ways of being tolerant without seeming detached, interested without seeming intrusive, critical without seeming derogatory, and advisory without seeming domineering.

A judicious blend of requiring dependence and fostering independence should govern all phases of an adolescent's treatment. In the beginning, as already noted, adolescent's dignity and capacity for self-sufficiency are acknowledged by including them in the decision to embark on psychotherapy. Concurrently, therapists present themselves as trained professionals who work with young people to help them deal with problems more effectively than they have been able to do on their own. With treatment underway, therapists must display respect for their adolescent patients' points of view, even as they begin to suggest more constructive and realistic points of view. They need similarly to refrain from depreciating adolescents' capacities to think things through and decide how to act, even as they begin to encourage clearer ways of thinking and more effective ways of planning what to do. Therapists need especially to be restrained in their manner of handing out advice or making pronouncements, either of which can have an unintended patronizing effect and can imply that adolescents seem incapable of managing their own affairs.

In time, as adolescent patients come to appreciate their therapist's regard for their prerogatives and capabilities, guidance and direction will no longer threaten their autonomy and will instead meet unspoken needs to rely on an interested, understanding adult who is more experienced than they are in the ways of the world. To the extent that a therapist can give the impression of being a knowledgeable, clear-thinking, successful person, adolescents will be able to learn from and be influenced by the therapist without having to think less of themselves for doing so.

ARRANGING FOR TERMINATION

Termination of psychotherapy with adolescent patients becomes appropriate when they have achieved the limited insights and adaptive character synthesis that define the previously noted goals of clinical work with troubled teenagers. When disturbed adolescents do not require extended inpatient care, their relative freedom from crystallized psychopathology and usual capacity for rapid behavior change often make it possible to reach this termination point with brief or short-term psychotherapy. Effective psychotherapy of adolescents does not necessarily require intensive working through of insights or a thorough exploration of transference feelings. Successful treatment is instead likely to have occurred when young people achieve sufficient relief from their symptoms and concerns to settle comfortably into an adaptive daily routine. To prolong psychotherapy beyond such a point tends to promote excessive dependence on the therapist and to cause patients and their families unnecessary concern about the severity of the problem. Meeks (1980, pp. 192, 194) comments succinctly on these considerations in planning termination:

Individuation, the goal of adolescent development, is best served by assisting the adolescent toward a workable character synthesis and then quickly moving aside so that the adolescent's new strengths propel him toward real and available objects outside of the sheltered therapy office . . . One does not try to accompany the adolescent on his entire developmental journey, only to guide him off sidetracks and back to his age-appropriate station on the main trunk of the developmental line.

The brief or short-term psychotherapy that most adolescents require has no specific length of time or number of sessions. The treatment of adolescents should last for as long as is necessary to achieve the circumscribed goals of limited insight and character synthesis. In making decisions about terminating, then, therapists need not only to avoid prolonging the treatment unnecessarily, but also to be wary of ending it too quickly in response to initial improvements.

With respect to ending treatment too quickly, therapists considering termination need to be reasonably confident that whatever gains have been realized are sufficiently well established to persist. Premature termination, prior to some consolidation of behavior change, can undo much of what has been accomplished and can precipitate recurrence of the difficulties that led to therapy being undertaken. Treatment that has been too brief or superficial to buffer an adolescent patient against reemerging psychological disturbance needs to be continued, not ended. Although adolescent patients generally become ready for termination when their anxieties diminish and they feel in control of themselves and their lives, therapists should not be satisfied with symptomatic improvement when they can still see distinct possibilities for future adjustment difficulties.

In addition to gauging the likely persistence of positive behavior change in an adolescent patient, therapists considering termination need to examine the status of the treatment relationship, particularly with respect to dependency issues. The more that behaviorally improved adolescents appear no longer to need their therapist's regular presence in their lives and the more they appear to resent continued treatment as an affront to their capacity for self-reliance, the more ready they are for termination. Conversely, the more an adolescent appears still to need a treatment relationship, the more caution the therapist should exercise in broaching termination, no matter how impressive the young person's symptomatic improvement has been.

Adolescents whose increased self-awareness and enhanced coping capacity would warrant termination will usually reveal in various ways how they feel about ending the treatment relationship. The behaviorally improved adolescent who says, "I feel like I've been doing pretty well, and I wonder if I couldn't stop coming in or at least have these appointments less often," is displaying considerable readiness to begin the terminal phase of his or her treatment. To let such remarks pass without inviting consideration of whether to taper off the treatment may detract from patients' confidence in the improvements they have made and may foster resurgent, unwelcome dependency. By contrast, responding to displays of self-sufficiency and social comfort by interpreting them as evidence of a behaviorally improved person's decreased need for therapeutic contact often speeds progress toward timely termination.

On the other hand, behaviorally improved adolescents who still make full and uncomplaining use of the opportunity to review their ideas and activities with the therapist are probably still in the process of replacing the treatment relationship with adequate interpersonal investments elsewhere. Thus, the patient who asks during the session, "How much longer do I have to come here?" but at the end of the interview comments eagerly, "See you next week, right?" usually is not yet prepared to contemplate terminating.

Suggesting termination or less-frequent sessions to adolescents who are sending such messages is likely to be perceived by them as abandonment or rejection. It is as if the therapist was looking for an excuse to end the relationship and jumped at the first opportunity to be rid of them. When termination is broached prematurely in response to offhand comments, the result is often some reversal in the patient's progress. Adolescents who are made to feel on the brink of losing a therapist they still need are at risk for reexperiencing previously conquered symptoms and slipping back into former maladaptive behavior patterns. Such setbacks typically persist for as long as it takes overzealous therapists to recognize their mistaken leap for termination and to offer reassurances that the treatment commitment will be continued for as long as necessary.

Being cautious in suggesting termination does not mean being passive about doing so, however, especially with adolescents who have made substantial treatment progress. Circumstances that interfere with the regular schedule of appointments will usually provide opportunities from time to time to test the status of the treatment relationship. For example, a therapist who must miss a session, due to a business trip, may say to a patient being seen once weekly, "I have to be away next Wednesday, so I won't be able to meet with you." The adolescent who responds to this announcement with, "We'll meet again in two weeks then, huh?" is closer to termination than the one who states, "Could I come in on Tuesday or Thursday then?" Patients who do not respond to the therapist's telling them of a forthcoming absence should be asked directly, "What would you like to do?" to allow their feelings to emerge. If this direct question is still too open-ended for the young person to answer, the therapist needs then to specify some alternative possibilities for the next visit (e.g., in 2 weeks on the regular day or next week on some other day) and invite the patient to express a preference.

Other events may similarly lend themselves to the therapist's not merely waiting for a behaviorally improved adolescent to indicate interest in termination, but instead pointing out evidence of readiness to terminate that the patient may otherwise not have recognized. When an adolescent's treatment has been interrupted by illness or a family vacation, for example, the therapist may be able to remark, "You seem to have gotten along pretty well since we met last; maybe we don't have to have our sessions as frequently as we have been." At other times, the therapist may be able directly to stimulate a young person's thinking about such spacing of visits: "Your school vacation is coming up in a few weeks; have you thought at all about how you'd like to work out our meetings during the summer?"

Should an adolescent respond to such overtures with obvious concern or disappointment, the therapist needs promptly to reendorse the current treatment arrangement. Questions about scheduling that have proven distressing should be countered by efforts to prevent them from conveying imminent therapist desertion. The message implicit in the therapist's approach to termination needs to be, "I'm willing to stick with you as long as it's necessary and helpful, but it's starting to appear that you can just about handle things for yourself." Termination proceeds best when it connotes praise and reward, not criticism or rejection.

As indicated in the preceding examples, psychotherapy with adolescents should not be ended abruptly. Instead, a schedule for gradually decreasing the frequency of interviews typically strikes a good balance in behaviorally improved adolescents between their strengthening desires to put the therapy behind them and their weakening but still very real desires to hold on to it. As one specific approach, sequentially halving the frequency of sessions often works well in allowing patients to test their capacity for independent functioning without feeling that bridges to the therapist are being burned behind them. While making clear their readiness to revert to the original frequency of visits if necessary, therapists can utilize continued good functioning at one interval (e.g., every 2 weeks, a reduction from once weekly) to suggest still longer ones (e.g., once a month) and eventually no further appointments at all. Even at the point of arranging not to schedule a return visit, therapists should indicate that they are no further away than a telephone call should the adolescent need them or even just want to let them know how things are going.

WORKING WITH PARENTS

Psychological care of disturbed adolescents rarely proceeds effectively in the absence of a working relationship with their parents. For psychotherapy with young people to achieve its goals, key family members need to be involved in the evaluation, planning, and continuation phases of the treatment.

Conducting the Evaluation

The evaluation of disturbed adolescents almost always requires one or more interviews with their parents. Especially in the case of adolescents who are initially unwilling or unable to relate the difficulties that have led to their being seen, information obtained from the parents may be essential for an adequate assessment. Without sufficient information to support reasonably thorough diagnostic formulations, therapists are vulnerable to oversights and errors of procedure, some of which may have grave consequences. Particularly serious in this regard is remaining unaware of previous suicide gestures or episodes of dyscontrol and failing to include appropriate precautionary measures in the treatment approach. Steinberg (1989) discusses at length the importance of including adolescents' families in information-gathering sessions in order to be able to assess these and other harbingers of potential emergency situations. In addition, to begin with only limited knowledge of the history of an adolescent's presenting problems, of the orientation and circumstances of the family, and of the events leading to the referral for help may complicate the therapist's task of finding ways to allow comfort, achieve engagement, and establish motivation in initial treatment sessions.

Even when adolescents are forthcoming about themselves from the very first session, information that can come only from their parents may be indispensable to gaining a good grasp of the presenting problems. Interviews with an adolescent's parents help to identify how they view their youngster's difficulties, what kind of person they think he or she is, and what part their perspectives and personality styles may be playing in the problem. Background data unknown to the patient but available from parents, such as details of the young person's early development and of any family history of disturbance, can, in addition, help to resolve issues of differential diagnosis.

If at all possible, the initial diagnostic session with parents should include both mother and father and usually should precede the first meeting with the adolescent. Despite mounting evidence of the crucial role that fathers play in the development of their children (Bronstein & Cowan, 1988; Lamb, 1981), therapists still may be inclined to underestimate the contribution of fathers to developmental psychopathology and too easily dissuaded from requiring fathers to participate in the evaluation and treatment process. In one not uncommon scenario, the mother reports over the telephone that the father is only peripherally engaged with the family, the father protests the inconvenience of having to come for an appointment, and both parents concur that the mother by herself can provide all of the necessary information. To the contrary, however, the mother by herself can seldom provide all of the necessary information, let alone a sample of the father's personality style. By excusing the father from the evaluation, moreover, the therapist may inadvertently sanction his distance from family affairs and from the young person who is having psychological difficulty.

Many fathers who agree only reluctantly to attend an initial interview later come to regard the therapist's insistence on their being present as an endorsement of their importance in the family's affairs. Not uncommonly, a father is flattered to have had his views solicited and cooperates much more fully with the diagnostic process than his original resistance or his wife's statements would have led the therapist to expect (e.g., "Don't bother to call him; I'm sure he wouldn't be interested in talking with you"). As testimony to the significance of paternal participation, La Barbera (1980), who studied 128 adolescents brought to an outpatient clinic intake session, found that 72% of those whose fathers came with them continued with further appointments, whereas only 44% of those whose fathers did not come with them returned to the clinic for a second visit.

As for seeing parents before meeting with the adolescent, experienced therapists are not of the same mind. Many who strongly urge active parental participation in the evaluation process nevertheless concur with Barker (1990, Chapter 5) and Gardner (1988, Chapter 3), who prefer to begin with the adolescent and bring the parents in later, into either joint or a separate interviews. However, proceeding in this way sacrifices some distinct advantages of meeting with parents first. One such advantage is getting some clear idea of the problem that has precipitated the referral. Having this information in advance can minimize awkwardness and oversights during the first session with an adolescent patient and can guide the therapist both in probing for crucial diagnostic data and in forming a good working relationship.

As an even more important advantage of meeting with parents first, therapists can use an initial discussion with parents to anticipate problems they may have in presenting their youngster with the idea of seeing a mental health professional. Even parents who are consciously committed to seeking help may be too anxious, embarrassed, or misinformed about psychotherapy to discuss arrangements for it in a constructive fashion. Left without guidance, some may pick up their youngster after school and, without previous explanation, suggest "stopping by to talk with someone" on the way home. Others may tell their youngster that they have scheduled "a doctor's appointment" for him or her, without indicating the nature of the "doctor" or the reason for the appointment. Others may begin weeks in advance to "prepare" their teenager to see the psychotherapist and, by repetitively emphasizing the painlessness of the process, fill him or her with apprehensions and misgivings. Adolescents who have been deceived or misled in such ways frequently arrive for a first visit harboring preconceived notions, resentments, or anxieties that interfere with their being able to relate comfortably to the therapist.

Therapists can minimize the likelihood of such destructive preparation by suggesting to parents some simple and straightforward ways of discussing an appointment with their youngster. Often, it will suffice for the parents merely to state the concerns they have about how their child's life is going and to suggest that it might be helpful for him or her to talk with a trained person who is familiar with the problems of young people. Although resistive parents may erect obstacles to their youngster's agreeing to be seen, despite the therapist's efforts to minimize or skirt such obstacles, preparatory guidance will help many highly motivated but anxious and psychologically unsophisticated parents to smooth their youngster's path to the therapist's door.

Like other aspects of therapeutic work with adolescents, on the other hand, parental participation in the diagnostic process must be handled flexibly. Generally speaking, the younger or less mature adolescents are and the more serious their disturbance, the more extensively their parents will need to be involved in the evaluation. Conversely, the necessity of parental involvement tends to diminish in relation to how mature adolescents are and how free they are from disabling disorder. Esman (1985) describes a common practice in this regard of regularly seeing the parents of early adolescents first in beginning an evaluation, but starting with middle adolescents, to shift to a strategy of seeing the teenage patient first.

Particularly for middle and especially late adolescents who call for their own appointments, there is therapeutic benefit in respecting and rewarding their independent behavior by seeing them first. The therapist can then discuss with the adolescent his or her feelings about the manner in which the parents should be contacted to involve them, as appropriate, in planning and continuing the treatment.

Planning the Treatment

In planning treatment for adolescent patients, therapists need to make every possible effort to obtain the cooperation and support of their parents. Even parents who have been sufficiently concerned and psychologically oriented to bring their youngsters for diagnostic evaluation may have difficulty accepting a recommendation for psychotherapy. Treatment recommendations are especially unwelcome to parents who have sought consultation reluctantly, in response to pressures from their family doctor, school officials, or the juvenile justice system. For many parents, whether self-referred or mandated to see a mental health professional, the need for therapy connotes their failure to have reared their child properly; in others, it generates grave concern about their child's future; and for others, it constitutes humiliation and inconvenience imposed on them by the therapist. The anxiety, guilt, and resentment that are often evoked by a recommendation for therapy can motivate parents to deny or resist needed help for their adolescent youngster unless the therapist can discuss their feelings with them and can help them to understand and endorse the treatment that is being proposed.

For this reason, clinicians are generally agreed that adequate treatment planning requires therapists to forge a working alliance with parents, as well as with the adolescent who is to be the patient. Forging such an alliance involves not only obtaining parental endorsement of beginning treatment, but also making sure that the parents understand the conditions under which the therapy will proceed, including the boundaries of confidentiality (Gustafson & McNamara, 1987; Schimel, 1974). Various negative consequences of overlooking sufficient parental involvement in arranging to conduct psychotherapy with adolescents have been confirmed in research studies. Inclusion of parents in treatment planning has been found to be a critical variable in predicting how long adolescents will remain in therapy and how much progress they will make, and unresolved disagreements between adolescents' parents and the therapist concerning their perception of what the young person's problems are and how they will be addressed is a reliable predictor of premature termination (Blotcky & Friedman, 1984; Tolan, Ryan, & Jaffe, 1988).

In the process of providing information to parents and of soliciting the parents' endorsement of a treatment plan, therapists should be especially alert to two specific patterns of parental resistance that can undermine efforts to help a troubled adolescent. The first is a readily observable refractoriness in which the parents either express overt skepticism about psychological methods and their youngster's needs for professional help or, having agreed to a treatment plan, manage in numerous ways to prevent their child from keeping to it. Parents who are resisting therapy in the latter way repeatedly find themselves unable to bring their youngster for appointments, readily reinforce his or her slightest expression of reluctance to come, and regularly report how beautifully he or she is getting along. Such parental ploys are usually attempts to deny the young person's difficulties by proving that their adolescent can adapt perfectly well without professional assistance. Therapists must be able to help parents resolve the anger, anxiety, or guilt that motivates such obvious resistances if they are to have much success in initiating effective psychotherapy with an adolescent.

The second and more subtle pattern of parental resistance is the "dumping syndrome." Parents who "dump" their child defend against the implications of a recommendation for treatment by surrendering him or her to the ministrations of the therapist with no questions asked and retreating in graceless haste to the bleachers. As far as they are concerned, they have been good and dutiful parents, their youngster's problems are of his or her own making, and they will support whatever treatment is needed as long as they are not called on to be a part of it. Such parents pose few apparent problems for therapists. They endorse the treatment recommendations, guarantee their child's regular and prompt attendance at sessions, pay their bills, and seldom intrude on the therapy with inquiries about method or progress.

The dumping syndrome may seem to give adolescents' therapists a free hand, and it may therefore be tempting to allow. Parents who dump can offer welcome relief from therapists' more common diet of hassles with dissatisfied parents who want to know why improvement is taking so long and with intrusive parents who want to know what is being discussed in sessions. The price of such relief is steep, however, because disengaged parents frequently cancel the treatment equation in two insidious respects. First, therapists who allow youthful patients to be dumped condone a situation that confirms the adolescents' impressions of their parents' disinterest in them and increases their feelings of being alienated from their family. Second, parents who wash their hands of their child's treatment may nevertheless remain furious with him or her for the inconvenience, embarrassment, and expense the psychotherapy is causing them and, unbeknownst to the therapist, may find subtle ways of forcing its premature end.

Continuing the Psychotherapy

Continuing the psychotherapy with adolescents usually requires sufficient contact with their parents to gather information about ongoing events in the family's life, to monitor parental attitudes toward the treatment and its goals, and to anticipate parental actions that might undermine the therapy. Among the practitioners surveyed by Kazdin et al. (1990), 85% concurred that parental involvement is strongly related to prospects for progress in the treatment of young people. Particularly at points where changes in an adolescent's behavior alter a family's equilibrium or tax the parents' understanding of how to cope with their youngster, preparation and guidance from the therapist can minimize parental anxiety and reduce the likelihood of reactions that would impede the progress of the treatment.

There are several alternative modes of engaging parents in continuing psychotherapy for their adolescent daughter or son. Which mode works best depends primarily on the parents' needs and interests in receiving psychological help for themselves. Some parents utilize the occasion of their youngster's referral to report personal or marital problems for which they would like to receive professional assistance. In these instances, a course of individual or couples therapy may be indicated, conducted independently of their child's treatment and by a different therapist. For the same therapist concurrently to take on the treatment of parents and their child is likely to cause confusion concerning his or her primary commitment and to create obstacles to maintaining appropriate boundaries of confidentiality. When therapists do recommend independent sessions for the parents of an adolescent patient, they then need to make other arrangements for sufficient channels of communication to ensure the necessary information gathering, monitoring, and anticipatory purposes of parental contact noted previously.

In some cases, parents who would otherwise not require psychological help have become so perplexed and distressed by their child's difficulties that they would benefit from discussions of the nature of the problem and how they should be responding to it. Here too a recommendation for independent treatment may be in order. These may be parents who have unwittingly complicated their youngster's development by their unfamiliarity or unease with the needs and concerns of adolescents.

Such parents may appreciate an opportunity to air their apprehensions and uncertainties and be counseled regarding them. Informative and supportive counseling for parents of disturbed adolescents can be provided provided either in individual sessions or in discussion groups with parents of other adolescents in therapy. Individual and group counseling that is sensitive to parents' needs and concerns can increase their understanding and tolerance of adolescent behavior, help them perform their parental functions more comfortably and effectively, and reduce family tensions that would otherwise perpetuate problem behavior in their children.

By contrast with these two types of situations, some parents who seem in need of psychotherapy or counseling may nevertheless show little interest in treatment for themselves and little wish to explore the implications of being a parent to a troubled teenager. Although the therapist may, in such instances, still choose to recommend independent treatment or childrearing discussions for them, he or she should usually refrain from insisting on either as a part of the treatment plan for their child. Parents who present no psychological concerns of their own and who doubt any relationship between family circumstances and their child's difficulties rarely take kindly to suggestions, let alone requirements, that they receive therapy or counseling for themselves. The implications of parental blame and the burden of time and expense that attend such recommendations may anger or disturb them sufficiently to foster resistance to a treatment plan for their child, and they may counter by questioning the competence of the therapist and whether seeing him or her is likely to do their child any good.

For parents who present in this more overtly resistive way, as well as for those who do not appear to need any independent treatment, psychotherapy with their adolescent is best served by forming a working relationship with them in which the therapist focuses on the problems of the patient and on information-gathering, monitoring, and anticipatory functions without probing their personal problems or perspectives. This kind of relationship with parents can usually be managed best by the adolescent's therapist, without calling on a collateral professional. Although concerns about commitment and confidentiality may be raised when a therapist confers with an adolescent patient's parents, proceeding in this way can offer distinct advantages and can build in safeguards as well.

With respect to its advantages over involving collateral personnel, parents who do not consider themselves as being in psychotherapy, and indeed are not, may find it awkward and artificial to be told that they must speak with someone other than their youngster's therapist to discuss his or her progress. A conjoint approach seems natural and avoids the inefficiencies of collateral arrangements that occur when parents ask questions about their child that their interviewer cannot answer because his or her communication with the therapist is imperfect, or when therapists lack information from parents that would help them conduct a session because the parents' interviewer failed to obtain or pass on the information.

As for safeguarding commitment and confidentiality, meetings with parents do not need to exclude an adolescent patient. Instead, it is helpful periodically to ask the parents to join their youngster for a family session. Proceeding in this way allows the necessary parent–therapist interaction to occur without implying that the adolescent is not mature enough to sit with the grown-ups, or that they cannot or should not be party to whatever is said about them, or that the therapist's allegiance to them is secondary to a responsibility to the parents. Such joint sessions have also been recognized as good ways for therapists to keep abreast of patterns of family interaction and to utilize techniques of family treatment that may prove helpful (Feldman, 1988; Madanes, 1983, Chapter 6).

As in the diagnostic and planning phases of psychotherapy, the extent of parental involvement in the ongoing treatment will vary with how disturbed and immature a young person is. The less serious their difficulties and the more closely they are approaching adulthood, the less frequently adolescents' parents will be seen and the more responsible they will be for their own treatment, and conversely. During the course of psychotherapy, furthermore, behavioral improvement will call for reduced contact with the parents in the same way that it warrants decreasing the frequency of sessions. In all of these procedural judgments, therapists should be guided by whatever means they feel will stimulate, nourish, reward, and maximize an adolescent's progress toward maturity.

REFERENCES

Adelman, H. S., Kaser-Boyd, N., & Taylor, L. (1984). Children's participation in consent for psychotherapy and their subsequent response to treatment. *Journal of Clinical Child Psychology, 13*, 170–178.

Azima, F. J., & Richmond, L. H. (Eds.). (1989). *Adolescent group psychotherapy.* New York: International Universities Press.

Barker, P. (1990). *Clinical interviews with children and adolescents.* New York: W. W. Norton.

Barth, R. P. (1986). *Social and cognitive treatment of children and adolescents.* San Francisco: Jossey-Bass.

Bastien, R. T., & Adelman, H. S. (1984). Noncompulsory versus legally mandated placement, perceived choice, and response to treatment among adolescents. *Journal of Consulting and Clinical Psychology, 52*, 171–179.

Berkovitz, I. H. (Ed.). (1972). *Adolescents grow in groups.* New York: Brunner/Mazel.

Berman, S. (1957). Psychotherapy of adolescents at clinic level. In B. H. Balser (Ed.), *Psychotherapy of the adolescent* (pp. 86–112). New York: International Universities Press.

Bernard, M. E., & Joyce, M. R. (1984). *Rational–emotive therapy with children and adolescents.* New York: Wiley.

Blos, P. (1983). The contribution of psychoanalysis to the psychotherapy of adolescents. In M. Sugar (Ed.), *Adolescent psychiatry* (Vol. 11, pp. 104–124). Chicago: University of Chicago Press.

Blotcky, A. D., & Friedman, S. (1984). Premature termination from psychotherapy by adolescents. *Journal of Clinical Child Psychology, 13*, 304–309.

Bronstein, P., & Cowan, C. P. (Eds.). (1988). *Fatherhood today.* New York: Wiley.

Casey, R. J., & Berman, J. S. (1985). The outcome of psychotherapy with children. *Psychological Bulletin, 98*, 388–400.

Corder, B. F. (1986). Therapeutic games in group therapy with adolescents. In C. E. Schaefer & S. E. Reid (Eds.), *Game play* (pp. 279–290). New York: Wiley.

Day, L., & Reznikoff, M. (1980). Social class, the treatment process, and parents' and childrens' expectations about child psychotherapy. *Journal of Clinical Child Psychology, 9*, 195–198.

Devany, J., & Nelson, R. O. (1986). Behavioral approaches to treatment. In H. C. Quay & J. S. Werry (Eds.), *Psychopathological disorders of childhood* (3rd ed., pp. 523–557). New York: Wiley.

Ekstein, R. (1983). The adolescent self during the process of termination of treatment: Termination, interruption, or intermission? In M. Sugar (Ed.), *Adolescent psychiatry* (Vol. 13, pp. 125–146). Chicago: University of Chicago Press.

Esman, A. H. (1985). A developmental approach to the psychotherapy of adolescents. In S. C. Feinstein (Ed.), *Adolescent psychiatry* (Vol. 12, pp. 119–133). Chicago: University of Chicago Press.

Feindler, E., & Kalfus, G. (Eds.). (1990). *Handbook of behavior therapy with adolescents*. New York: Springer.

Feldman, L. B. (1988). Integrating individual and family therapy in the treatment of symptomatic children and adolescents. *American Journal of Psychotherapy, 42,* 272–280.

Fishman, H. C. (1988). *Treating troubled adolescents: A family therapy approach.* New York: Basic Books.

Freud, A. (1958). Adolescence. *Psychoanalytic Study of the Child, 13,* 255–278.

Gardner, R. A. (1988). *Psychotherapy with adolescents.* Creeskill, NJ: Creative Therapeutics.

Gitelson, M. (1948). Character synthesis: The psychotherapeutic problems of adolescence. *American Journal of Orthopsychiatry, 18,* 422–431.

Gittelman, R., & Kanner, A. (1986). Psychopharmacotherapy. In H. C. Quay & J. S. Werry (Eds.), *Psychopathological disorders of childhood* (3rd ed., pp. 455–495). New York: Wiley.

Graafsma, T., & Anbeek, M. (1984). Resistance in psychotherapy with adolescents. *Journal of Adolescence, 7,* 1–16.

Gustafson, K. E., & McNamara, J. R. (1987). Confidentiality with minor clients: Issues and guidelines for therapists. *Professional Psychology, 18,* 503–508.

Hansen, D. J., Watson-Perczel, M., & Smith, J.M. (1989). Clinical issues in social-skills training with adolescents. *Clinical Psychology Review, 9,* 365–392.

Hersen, M., & Van Hasselt, V. B. (Eds.). (1987). *Behavior therapy with children and adolescents.* New York: Wiley.

Holmes, D. J. (1964). *The adolescent in psychotherapy.* Boston: Little, Brown.

Josselyn, I. (1971). *Adolescence.* New York: Harper & Row.

Katz, P. (1990). The first few minutes: The engagement of the difficult adolescent. In S. C. Feinstein (Ed.), *Adolescent psychiatry* (Vol. 17, pp. 69–81). Chicago: University of Chicago Press.

Kazdin, A. E. (1990). Psychotherapy for children and adolescents. *Annual Review of Psychology, 41,* 21–54.

Kazdin, A. E., Siegel, T. C., & Bass, D. (1990). Drawing on clinical practice to inform research on child and adolescent psychotherapy: Survey of practitioners. *Professional Psychology, 21,* 189–198.

Kimmel, D. C., & Weiner, I. B. (1985). *Adolescence: A developmental transition.* Hillsdale, NJ: Erlbaum.

Kovacs, M., & Paulauskas, S. (1986). The traditional psychotherapies. In H. C. Quay & J. S. Werry (Eds.), *Psychopathological disorders of childhood* (3rd ed., pp. 496–522).

LaBarbera, J. D. (1980). Fathers who undermine children's treatment: A challenge for the clinician. *Journal of Clinical Child Psychology, 9,* 204–206.

L'Abate, L., & Milan, M. A. (Eds.). (1985). *Handbook of social skills training and research.* New York: Wiley.

Lamb, D. (1978). *Psychotherapy with adolescent girls*. San Francisco: Jossey-Bass.

Lamb, M. E. (Ed.). (1981). *The role of the father in child development* (2nd ed.). New York: Wiley.

Laufer, M., & Laufer, M. E. (1984). *Adolescence and developmental breakdown: A psychoanalytic view*. New Haven, CT: Yale University Press.

Macmillan, D. L., & Kavale, K. A. (1986). Educational intervention. In H. C. Quay & J. S. Werry (Eds.), *Psychopathological disorders of childhood* (3rd ed., pp. 583–621).

Madanes, C. (1983). *Strategic family therapy*. San Francisco: Jossey-Bass.

Masterson, J. F. (1958). Psychotherapy of the adolescent: A comparison with psychotherapy of the adult. *Journal of Nervous and Mental Disease, 127*, 511–517.

McHolland, J. D. (1985). Strategies for dealing with resistant adolescents. *Adolescence, 20*, 349–368.

Meeks, J. E. (1980). *The fragile alliance: An orientation to the outpatient psychotherapy of the adolescent* (2nd ed.). Malabar, FL: Krieger.

Mirkin, M. P., & Koman, S. L. (Eds.). (1985). *Handbook of adolescents and family therapy*. New York: Gardner Press.

Mishne, J. M. (1986). *Clinical work with adolescents*. New York: Free Press.

Quay, H. C. (1986). Residential treatment. In H. C. Quay & J. S. Werry (Eds.), *Psychopathological disorders of childhood* (3rd ed., pp. 558–582). New York: Wiley.

Rose, S. D., & Edelson, J. L. (1987). *Working with children and adolescents in groups*. San Francisco: Jossey-Bass.

Safer, D. J. (Ed.). (1982). *School programs for disruptive adolescents*. Baltimore, MD: University Park Press.

Sarnoff, C. A. (1987). *Psychotherapeutic strategies in late latency through early adolescence*. Northvale, NJ: Aronson.

Schaefer, C. E., Briesmeister, J. M., & Fitton, M. E. (Eds.). (1984). *Family therapy techniques for problem behaviors of children and teenagers*. San Francisco: Jossey-Bass.

Schaefer, C. E., & Swanson, A. J. (Eds.). (1988). *Children in residential care*. New York: Van Nostrand Reinhold.

Schimel, J. L. (1974). Two alliances in the treatment of adolescents: Toward a working alliance with parents and a therapeutic alliance with the adolescent. *Journal of the American Academy of Psychoanalysis, 2*, 243–253.

Schimel, J. L. (1986). Psychotherapy with adolescents: The art of interpretation. In S. C. Feinstein (Ed.), *Adolescent psychiatry* (Vol. 13, pp. 178–187). Chicago: University of Chicago Press.

Schrodt, G. R., & Fizgerald, B. A. (1987). Cognitive therapy with adolescents. *American Journal of Psychotherapy, 41*, 402–408.

Serok, S. (1986). Therapeutic implications of games with juvenile delinquents. In C. E. Schaefer & S. E. Reid (Eds.), *Game play* (pp. 311–330). New York: Wiley.

Shapiro, T. (1985). Adolescent language and its use for diagnosis, group identity, values, and treatment. In S. C. Feinstein (Ed.), *Adolescent psychiatry* (Vol. 12, pp. 297–311). Chicago: University of Chicago Press.

Steinberg, D. (Ed.). (1986). *The adolescent unit*. Chichester, England: Wiley.

Steinberg, D. (1989). Management of crises and emergencies. In L. K. G. Hsu & M. Hersen (Eds.), *Recent developments in adolescent psychiatry* (pp. 87-114). New York: Wiley.

Sugar, M. (Ed.). (1975). *The adolescent in group and family therapy*. New York: Brunner/Mazel.

Swift, W. J., & Wunderlich, S. A. (1990). Interpretation of transference in the psychotherapy of adolescents and young adults. *Journal of the American Academy of Child and Adolescent Psychiatry, 29*, 929-935.

Taylor, L., & Adelman, H. S. (1989). Reframing the confidentiality dilemma to work in children's best interests. *Professional Psychology, 20*, 79-83.

Tolan, P., Ryan, K., & Jaffe, C. (1988). Adolescents' mental health service use and provider, process, and recipient characteristics. *Journal of Clinical Child Psychology, 17*, 229-236.

Tramontana, M. G. (1980). Critical review of research on psychotherapy outcome with adolescents: 1967-1977. *Psychological Bulletin, 88*, 429-450.

Weiner, I. B. (1975). *Principles of psychotherapy*. New York: Wiley.

Weisz, J. R., Weiss, B., Alicke, M. D., & Klotz, M. L. (1987). Effectiveness of psychotherapy with children and adolescents: A meta-analysis for clinicians. *Journal of Consulting and Clinical Psychology, 55*, 542-549.

Wiener, J. M. (1985). *Diagnosis and psychopharmacology of childhood and adolescent disorders*. New York: Wiley.

Author Index

Wasson, E. J., 198
Wasylow, D. E., 329
Waterman, A. S., 15
Watson-Perczel, M., 416
Watt, N. F., 74
Wehr, T. A., 152
Weigel, R. M., 68
Weilburg, J. B., 228
Weinberger, G., 246
Weiner, I. B., 6, 14, 16-17, 46, 56-57, 58, 60, 62, 75, 87, 113, 137, 143, 200, 227, 282-283, 342, 414, 430
Weingartner, H., 119
Weinhold, C., 115
Weinstein, R. S., 266
Weintraub, S., 131
Weis, J. G., 303
Weiss, B., 414
Weiss, G., 271-272
Weissman, M. M., 14, 117, 130, 131, 147
Weisz, J. R., 301, 414
Wellborn, J. G., 260
Welner, A., 19
Welner, Z., 19
Welte, J. W., 392
Wender, P. H., 130, 173, 364
Wenning, K., 177
Werry, J. S., 38, 152
West, K. L., 72
West, M. O., 317, 395
Westefeld, J. S., 360, 366
Westen, D., 44, 173, 177, 186, 190
Westermeyer, J. F., 76
Westerndorp, F., 301
Wethington, D., 67
Wetzel, J. R., 259, 262, 263
Wetzel, R. D., 151
Whalen, C. K., 271, 330
Whitaker, A., 115, 116, 212
Whitaker, L. C., 58

White, J. L., 316
White, K. R., 229, 263
Whiteford, H. A., 138
Whiteman, M., 394-396
Whitmore, K., 234
Whittinghill, J. R., 363
Widaman, K. F., 396
Widiger, T. A., 37, 173, 177, 179, 189, 311
Widom, C. S., 301, 314, 316
Wiener, J. M., 416
Wiens, A. N., 37
Wierzbicki, M., 129
Wilborn, B. L., 395
Wild, K. V., 151
Willer, J., 94
Williams, D. T., 151
Williams, J., 37
Williams, J. B., 173, 311
Williams, J. R., 303
Williams, R. A., 30
Wilson, D. R., 97
Wilson, J. Q., 318
Wilson, P. T., 33
Wilson, W. H., 195
Winnicott, D. W., 8
Winokur, G., 117, 130, 136
Winsberg, B. G., 97
Winters, K. C., 131, 136, 392
Wirt, R. D., 305
Wirtz, P. W., 267
Wiss, C. A., 173, 177
Wissler, T., 77
Withers, L. E., 361, 363, 365, 368
Witmer, H. L., 334
Wixom, J., 173
Wodarski, J. S., 303, 334
Woerner, W., 14
Wolf, M. M., 226, 334
Wolfgang, M. E., 303
Wolkowitz, O. M., 134
Wollersheim, J. P., 338
Wolman, B. B., 311
Wolpe, J., 224-225

Wood, J., 261
Woods, M. G., 118
Woolson, R. F., 145
Wortman, C. B., 118
Wright, L. S., 363
Wulach, J. S., 312-313
Wunderlich, S. A., 415, 418
Wunsch-Hitzig, R., 14
Wurtele, S. K., 97
Wynne, L. C., 72

Yamaguchi, K., 390, 393
Yates, B. T. 61
Yates, W. R., 217
Ye, W., 131
Young, D., 361-368
Young, J. E., 123, 151
Young, M. A., 117
Young, R. D., 32, 232
Youngren, M. A., 118
Youniss, J., 262
Ysseldyke, J. E., 270
Yule, W., 12, 114, 234, 248
Yurgelun-Todd, D., 67-68

Zanarini, M. C., 182, 183, 186, 189
Zanna, M. P., 260
Zarb, J. M., 260, 262
Zax, M., 72
Zayas, L. H., 366
Zeiss, A. M., 118, 144, 147
Zelenak, J. P., 360
Zeltzer, L. K., 367
Zigler, E., 55, 69, 76
Zigmond, N., 287
Zimmerman, M., 133, 138
Zinn, D., 324
Zins, J. E., 286
Zohar, J., 229
Zohar-Kadouch, R., 229
Zubin, J., 33, 66, 73
Zubrick, S. R., 363

Subject Index

communication of needs in, 323–
326
differentiated from
characterological delinquency,
327–329
family interaction in, 326–327
family therapy in, 342
nature of, 322–329
needs for help in, 324–326
needs for recognition and respect
in, 323–324
parental fostering in, 326–327
parental reinforcement in, 327
treatment of, 341–343

Object splitting, *see* Splitting
Obsessions, *see* Obsessive-compulsive
disorder
nature of, 213–214
Obsessive-compulsive disorder, *see*
Compulsive personality style
age of onset in, 212
behavioral therapy in, 224–228
case illustrations of, 223–224,
227–228
characteristics of, 212–220
compulsions in, 214–215
drug therapy in, 228–229
experiential factors in, 221–223
frequency of, 212
genetic factors in, 220–221
obsessions in, 213–214
origins of, 220–223
outcome of, 229
personality style in, 217–218
psychotherapy in, 230–231
sex differences in, 212
symptoms of, 213–215
Obsessive-compulsive personality
style, 217–218. *See also*
Obsessive-compulsive disorder
affects in, 218–219
behavior in, 219–220
ideation in, 218
social relationships in, 219–220

Paranoid status, 68–69
Parental fostering, in neurotic
delinquency, 326–327

Passive-aggressive behavioral style:
in academic underachievement,
282–283
psychotherapy in, 288–290
Passive-aggressive underachievement,
274–284
Peer-group relationships, in
schizophrenia, 79–80
Physical status, in affective disorder,
120
Problem behavior, in depression, 123
Psychological test performance:
in academic underachievement,
283–284
in borderline disorders, 171, 174–
175, 177
in schizophrenia, 86–87
Psychopathic personality disorder,
310–322; *See also* Antisocial
personality disorder
antisocial attitudes in, 314–316
behavioral therapy in, 338
case illustration of, 321–322
cognitive functioning in, 314–316
collusion in, 337–339
constitutional influences in, 319–
320
coping capacities in, 314–316
course of, 320–321
nature of, 310–316
origins of, 316–320
parental influences in, 316–318
personality vs. behavioral
descriptions of, 312–314
terminology problems in, 311–
312
treatment of, 336–341
Psychotherapy:
in academic underachievement,
286–290
activity in, 428–430
in affective disorder, 146–147
allowing comfort in, 419–421
in borderline disorders, 193–195
in characterological delinquency,
327–339
communication in, 428–432
depth and goals in, 416–418
directness in, 430–432